Praise for *Integrated Inventory Management*

"With organizations exploring ways to remain competitive in the world market-place, integrated inventory management is one critical component of an organization's long-term success. This book provides ideas and a framework for such an integrated inventory strategy."

Dr. Paul Pittman, CPIM, Indiana University Southeast,
Division of Business and Economics

"Integrated Inventory Management will become a definitive reference for all who attempt to understand and control inventory."

Blair Williams, Director, Materials Management,
Tyco Submarine Systems, and author, *Manufacturing for Survival*

"Everyone engaged in inventory management or control should read Paul Bernard's *Integrated Inventory Management.* The book's power comes from the author's technique of shifting from principles to down-to-earth, practical advice."

Merle Thomas, Jr., CFPIM,
West Virginia College of Engineering and Mineral Resources

"Inventory management has traditionally been inward focused and tries to reach optimal decisions in an environment that is full of uncertainty and rapidly changing. This book reverses that focus and presents inventory management as a tool for consistently supporting the strategies of the organization."

Roly White, CFPIM

INTEGRATED INVENTORY MANAGEMENT

Oliver Wight
Manufacturing Series

INTEGRATED INVENTORY MANAGEMENT

Paul Bernard

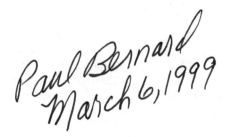

JOHN WILEY & SONS, INC.

New York • Chichester • Weinheim • Brisbane • Singapore • Toronto

This book is printed on acid-free paper. ∞

Copyright © 1999 by Paul Bernard. All rights reserved.

Published by John Wiley & Sons, Inc.

Published simultaneously in Canada.

This publication is designed to provide accurate and authoritative information in regard to the subject matter covered. It is sold with the understanding that the publisher is not engaged in rendering legal, accounting, or other professional services. If legal advice or other expert assistance is required, the services of a competent professional person should be sought.

Library of Congress Cataloging-in-Publication Data
Bernard, Paul, 1953–
    Integrated inventory management / Paul Bernard.
        p.   cm.
    Includes index.
    ISBN 0-471-32513-9 (cloth : alk. paper)
    1. Inventory control.   I. Title.
TS160.B47 1998
658.7′87—dc21   98-35369
                                                                             CIP

Printed in the United States of America.

10 9 8 7 6 5 4 3 2 1

Carl Stein has been actively involved in APICS since before there was any such thing as an "APICS Body of Knowledge." He truly represents the professionalism which is the very foundation of the society. This book is dedicated to Carl and all of the other professionals without whom APICS would not exist.

Contents

INTEGRATED INVENTORY MANAGEMENT

—Choices—

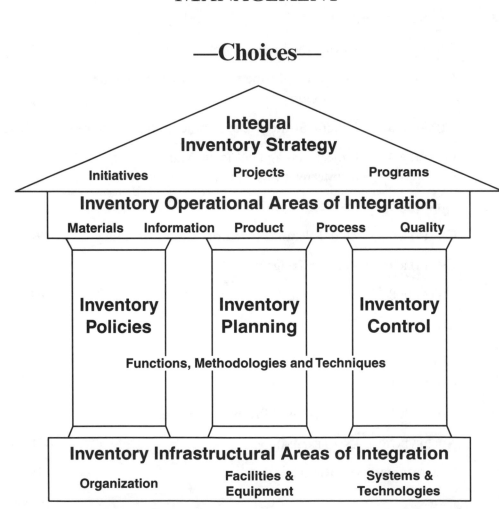

Integral Inventory Strategy

Initiatives   Projects   Programs

Inventory Operational Areas of Integration

Materials   Information   Product   Process   Quality

Inventory Policies   **Inventory Planning**   **Inventory Control**

Functions, Methodologies and Techniques

Inventory Infrastructural Areas of Integration

Organization   Facilities & Equipment   Systems & Technologies

Preface

THE CHALLENGE

Suppose your company has reached the point where senior management recognizes that "business as usual" cannot ensure a competitive advantage or is not meeting customer expectations. Suppose further that they ask you to lead or join a team to develop and implement a new (to the company) strategy to achieve and sustain a competitive advantage. How quickly can you become an individual contributor to your team's development of a business case for changing the status quo, convincing the organization of the advantages of following a strategy which encompasses aspects of operational, organizational, and technological change and creating an environment where significant improvement is the norm?

The fact is, this is the type of challenge faced every day by inventory practitioners. The more competitive one company becomes, the more competitive it becomes for everyone else. One approach for developing an inventory strategy in a highly competitive environment is to structure the strategy based on integration principles. Integration strengthens the natural synergism between the infrastructural and operational areas of the business.

This book is a continuation of other production and inventory management references. As such, it is not so much about the *subject* of inventory management as it is about the *practice* of managing inventory in a variety of business environments. Its uniqueness is in the application of an integration methodology as a unifying theme and in its scope from strategy development through implementation of projects and programs. The basic structure is shown in Figure P.1.

Key Integration Concepts Developed and Used Throughout This Book

Strategies are the means by which a company focuses and aligns their and their suppliers' resources and capabilities to create a competitive advantage and provide value to their customers. Following a defined strategy demonstrates commitment within the organization and establishes clear roles, responsibilities, and performance measures.

There are two basic types of strategies referred to in this book. *Traditional* strategies focus inwardly on one or more functional areas within the business.

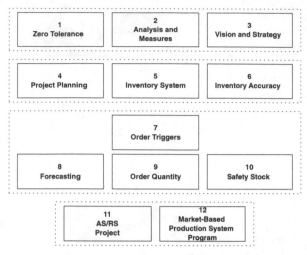

1 Zero Tolerance	2 Analysis and Measures	3 Vision and Strategy

Establish a Solid Business Case for a Zero-Tolerance Vision and Integral Strategy

4 Project Planning	5 Inventory System	6 Inventory Accuracy

Begin with the Basics: Develop Measures and Tools, and Demonstrate an Intolerance for Inventory Inaccuracy

7 Order Triggers

8 Forecasting	9 Order Quantity	10 Safety Stock

Prove to the Organization that the Improvements Can Be Achieved by Driving Inventory Balances DOWN while simultaneously *INCREASING* Customer Service Levels

11 AS/RS Project	12 Market-Based Production System Program

Make the Strategy *INTEGRAL* to the Business

Figure P.1   Chapter Outline

They target incremental improvements or maintenance of the status quo. *Integral* strategies remove artificial barriers to improvement in order to focus on the mission-critical areas of the business related to customer value and company profitability. They target significant improvements in cost, quality, and overall responsiveness.

When operating philosophies are considered individually, they support visions for traditional strategies. Computer Integrated Manufacturing focuses on computerization, Short Cycle Manufacturing focuses on time, Concurrent Engineering focuses on design cooperation, and so on. When any single philosophy fails to meet all of a company's needs for vision and focus (which invariably happens), the tendency is sometimes to become less focused by adopting an even less tangible World Class or Best in Class philosophy. What companies really need to do is take the best concepts and principles from a variety of functional area operating philosophies and develop their own company-specific philosophy. This *integral philosophy* then forms the basis of the *integral strategy*.

The integration matrix in Figure P.2 illustrates the general structure of an integral inventory strategy. The overlap of inventory management with the various areas of integration defines the boundaries which are shared with the other functional areas of the business. These areas include manufacturing, design engineering, manufacturing and industrial engineering, facilities engineering, purchasing, production planning and control, marketing, sales, customer service, MIS, and accounting. Inventory management can be defined in terms of its policy, planning, and control categories.

Inventory is perhaps the most important of the common integrating factors within an integral strategy. Much of a company's focus is either totally or significantly involved in the procurement and transformation of inventory into products. Because of the breadth and depth of this transformation process, no

	INVENTORY ZERO-TOLERANCE VISION			
Areas of Integration	Inventory Policies	Inventory Planning	Inventory Control	Inventory Strategy
Operational - Materials - Information - Product - Process - Quality	Operational Policies - Inventory Turns-related - Customer Service-related - Storage-related - Handling-related - Inventory Accuracy-related	Planning Methodologies - Order Planning - Safety Stock Planning - Forecast Planning	Control Techniques - Cycle Counting - Cyclical Counting - Economic Order Quantity - Fixed Order Quantity - Fixed Safety Stock - Lot-for-Lot Order Quantity - Statistical Safety Stock - Time Period Order Point - Time Period Safety Stock	Analyses and Models Measures and Indicators Initiatives and Programs
Infrastructural - Organizational - Facilities and Equipment - Systems and Technologies	Infrastructural Policies - Education - Training - Layout - Automation - Integration - Computerization	Program Planning - Organizational Development - Facilities Re-layout - Equipment Refurbishment - System Evaluations - Technology Assessments	Project Control - Material Handling - Material Storage - ERP / MRPII - Bar Code - Radio Frequecny	Simulation Capabilities Initiatives and Projects

Figure P.2   Integration Matrix

traditional inventory strategy can ever be completely successful. They tend to focus on areas over which inventory management has control, and therefore, fail to completely address the factors which are external to the inventory department. To be successful, an inventory strategy must incorporate elements which ensure *external integration* consistency with the strategies of the other company areas, suppliers and customers. At the same time, the inventory strategy must ensure *internal integration* consistency within the core inventory management areas related to policies, planning, and control. This is the focus of an integral strategy.

The following key integration concepts are used throughout this book:

- *Traditional vs. Integral:* A traditional strategy is concerned with maintaining the status quo and with obtaining incremental improvements as compared to past history. An integral strategy focuses on fundamental changes within the business. The intent is to achieve significantly improved performance levels as compared to demonstrated levels.

- *Necessary vs. Unnecessary Inventory:* Within an integral environment, average inventory investment is an indicator of the success of the enterprise and related strategies. That level of inventory which matches the target established within the integral strategy is necessary to the cost effective operation of the business while that which exceeds the target is waste. At the point where inventory becomes waste, it is the organization's cumulative responsibility to address the causes. It is not the inventory department's sole responsibility to reactively address the reality.

- *Proactive vs. Reactive:* Strategies encompass both proactive and reactive elements. Proactive elements address the company's vision of the future. Reactive elements address the present day reality. The effect of existing barriers and constraints to improvement must be addressed in a reactive fashion.

Preventing these same barriers and constraints from existing in the future requires a proactive effort.

- *Policies, Planning, and Control:* Inventory management consists of the three areas encompassed by policies, planning, and control. Management sets overall direction via policies which apply to part categories. The planner sets specific part-level targets through order, forecasting, and safety stock planning. Physical and logical control of inventory is maintained via the company's handling, storage, and inventory system infrastructure.

- *Operational vs. Infrastructural Areas of Integration:* Operational areas of integration encompass the day-to-day managerial areas of materials management, information management, product management, process management, and quality management. Infrastructural areas of integration encompass the supporting areas of organizational, facilities and equipment, and systems and technologies. All of the different functional areas of the company can be defined in terms of their relationships within each of these areas of integration.

- *Internal vs. External Integration:* Internal integration with respect to inventory management refers to being internally consistent within the policies, plans, and controls for materials, parts, categories, subassemblies, assemblies, and products. External integration refers to being consistent and supportive of the strategies of the other functional areas of the business in terms of the eight areas of integration.

- *Methodologies vs. Techniques:* Methodologies are processes by which two individuals may not arrive at the same conclusion given the same input. Their experience and background cause them to process data and information differently. Facility layout design and order planning are methodologies. Techniques are processes by which two individuals should arrive at the same conclusion, regardless of their experience. Calculating a time period order quantity for a part is a technique. Therefore, methodologies tend to be supported by procedures and practices which may be computer-supported. Techniques tend to be performed largely by computers, as modified by constraints, qualifiers, and variables supplied by company personnel.

- *Measures, Indicators, and Capabilities:* Performance "measures" measure something which has been performed against an established target. Confirming that a part has 100 units in stock when the computer says there are 100 provides a 100 percent Inventory Accuracy measure of the receiving, storage, and issuing processes for the particular part. Indicators "indicate" that performance may change, but do not themselves have a direct relationship to the degree of change. Counting the stock for 100 different parts and confirming that they are 100 percent accurate based on count provides an indication that other similar parts may be 100 percent accurate as well, but *there is no guarantee.* Capabilities are something which the company has to a greater or lesser extent. Having them improves performance but likely has no direct measurable relationship. For example, flexibility in terms of volume or mix has a value to the company. However, it does not make sense to say that the company is 50 percent flexible or that increasing flexibility by 10 percent will reduce cycle times by 24 percent. Capabilities must be defined in ranges, minimums, maximums, and so on.

- *Initiatives, Projects, and Programs:* Change within a company occurs via initiatives, projects, and programs. Initiatives are short-term in nature and address the removal of barriers or constraints to improvement. Projects have defined beginning and ending points and generally address improvements in the three infrastructural areas of integration. Programs have no defined ending point and generally become the day-to-day operation of the business within the five operational areas of integration.

- *Analysis, Model, and Simulation:* Analyses, models, and simulations are tools. *Analyses* provide specific answers to specific questions. How many storage locations are required to store a 5-day's supply? *Models* provide insight into inventory interrelationships. How many storage locations of what type are required in order to provide a two-day order turnaround time if the manufacturing cycle time is three days and the 4-wall day's supply target is reduced by 25 percent per year over the next three years? *Simulations* provide an understanding of the dynamic interrelationships within the facility of a given production rate and mix. How many Automated Guided Vehicles (AGVs) are required to tow trains of material from the warehouse to the production lines to support a production rate of 100 units per hour, given a distribution of load/unload times, move distances, and aisle blocking factors?

- *Targets:* The vision set for an integral strategy is to achieve a zero-tolerance deviation from target. The targets associated with each philosophy and area of integration define the focus of the organization efforts. The associated measures of performance determine how closely the targets are being met. Performance is not measured as 110 percent or 90 percent of target, but as +/−10 percent from target, respectively. This constantly reinforces the target and the current level of required improvement.

Effectiveness of the integral strategy is measured in terms of deviation from target. Targets will change over time as the company is able to reach and sustain successively higher levels of performance. Setting a zero-tolerance from deviation performance target sends a message of commitment to the organization. Achieving and then sustaining a zero-tolerance from deviation performance level sends a message of responsiveness to the customers.

Acknowledgments

This book is a blending of both theory and practice. The following individuals performed reviews of some or all of the sections and contributed many insightful comments. Thank you.

Dave Back

Mike Blough

John Collins

Eileen Game

Louis Giust

Craig Gustin

Daniel Marrone

Jim Rice

Brian Sanford

Ron Stratton

Blair Williams

The references list at the back of the book might have been longer, but I have loaned or given away many of the books and articles which helped me to form the basis of my thinking over the years. Perhaps the best compliment I can give these authors is that I have internalized the information and have made it my own over time.

I would like to acknowledge the companies, suppliers, and customers I have worked with and for over the years. It is this experience which I used to help bridge the theory to practice in this book.

Chapter 1

Having the Integral Strategy Choice

Company CEOs would like to be confident that just the right mix and level of inventory is consistently available to meet the needs of the business and their customers. Few feel that confident. In fact, this lack of confidence is mirrored at each level in the organization. What typically happens is that daily, weekly, and monthly snapshots of the business are used to determine the exact quantity and type of inventory to order based on information available at that point in time. However, the validity of decisions to acquire or build inventory based on these snapshots may not be known for days, weeks, or even months. The longer the forecast period relative to the firm plan horizon, the lower the confidence level.

It is this lack of confidence in inventory availability that should signal the necessity for a change in inventory strategy. Even so, companies all too often recognize that a strategy change is necessary only when forced to do so by their competitors and customers. Whether this recognition is internally or externally initiated, the rest of the process is basically one of making choices.

Two common choices related to strategies are to do little or nothing. This means sticking with the company's existing traditional strategy. These are safe choices, since the company is already aware of the consequences. However, this may not be a responsible business choice if the company is losing market share or otherwise failing to support their customers. In this case, the more comprehensive improvements achievable with an integral strategy may be the better or only viable choice. These alternatives are outlined in Figure 1.1.

The strategy choices reviewed in this chapter build on the following set of premises:

1. Companies must understand where they are and how they got there. This involves taking a critical look at the current strategy and identifying where it is facilitating, constraining, or obstructing the improvement process.

1

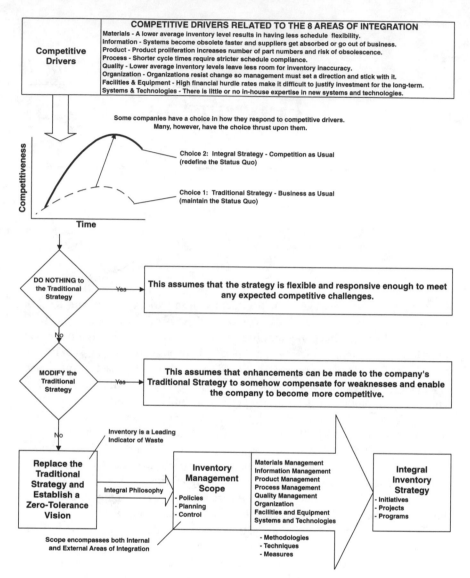

Figure 1.1   Traditional vs. Integral Strategy Choice

Companies need to develop the mindset that there are no rules other than what they themselves define.

2. Companies need to develop their own operating philosophy by taking the best elements of those already proven to work in other businesses. The "Your Company Name Here" operating philosophy must be designed into, rather than edicted into, the business. This means that the strategy must be-

come integral to the business itself, not simply management's concept of how the business should operate.

3. Integration is an engineering methodology which addresses the types of initiatives, projects, and programs required of an integral strategy. Using such a methodology to develop an inventory strategy ensures that both the *external* and *internal* elements of integration are properly understood and addressed.

4. The primary premise of an integral strategy is that the necessary level of inventory is *not* waste. Therefore, every policy, planning, and control decision within inventory management must be made with this target level of inventory in mind.

Inventory practitioners are on the firing line every day to plan future material availability while supporting daily shortages. This role has not changed much in recent decades, though the advent of widespread computerization has certainly changed their tools. In spite of the technology changes, however, many companies still treat inventory management as a clerical function to be managed by one or a few knowledgeable individuals. Planners are expected to spend most of their time sitting in front of computer terminals making decisions using computer system tools which are fine for data management but marginal for decision support. As a consequence, many of today's planners are not provided the opportunity to obtain the hands-on knowledge of the parts, products, and processes their predecessors had. Therefore, today's companies have a greater need for inventory professionals who understand when to follow, bend, break, or ignore the rules since computers only follow programmed logic.

INVENTORY MANAGEMENT'S MISSION (NO CHOICE HERE)

Inventory levels are driven by the company's sales and marketing strategy for its product lines, an understanding of customer buying patterns, and the competitive and economic environment. These factors are all external to the inventory management department. How they are translated into inventory levels and availability is the function of the inventory strategy as translated into internal planning and control processes and procedures. This is the responsibility of the inventory manager and planners.

The goal of a traditional strategy is to have the right inventory—at the right place—at the right time. Companies often informally translate this into "having extra material on-hand in plenty of time to support changes to order quantities and priorities." Note that this interpretation satisfies the literal translation of the goal, which says nothing about having too much, too early. Management may rationalize this interpretation in their own minds by claiming that it improves flexibility and responsiveness. In fact, it does, but at a cost of not really having a formal strategy.

As companies reduce cycle times and inventory levels, the traditional goal of inventory management has been redefined to recognize the existence of other dimensions. An integral inventory strategy, therefore, addresses a vision of having the *Target inventory*—at the target *time*—at the target *place*—in the target *quantity*—of the target *quality*—in the target *orientation*—*with Zero deviation from target*.

From an absolutely practical perspective, zero-deviation performance for all parts across all dimensions all the time is impossible to achieve. This does not invalidate the vision, but simply reinforces its necessity. Without it, the result is mediocrity.

A zero-tolerance vision differs significantly from a vision which views all inventory as waste. An "all inventory is waste" vision encourages a certain amount of misdirection since no amount of effort will result in the elimination of all of a company's production inventory. Suppliers do not want a company's inventory forced onto them without adequate compensation. The fact is that any inventory which is necessary to operate the business profitably is not waste. The focus of any effective inventory strategy must, therefore, be directed not at eliminating all inventory, but at ensuring that the target level of inventory is available.

An integral strategy is based on the recognition that a given level of inventory is *necessary* to the effective operation of the business. This level is a function of business conditions which existed at the time the inventory was ordered and which are forecasted to exist through the duration of the stocking horizon. Ensuring that the target level of inventory is available to support the needs of the business is the mission of inventory management.

COMPANIES NEED TO MAKE THE RIGHT BENCHMARKING CHOICE

Change is inevitable. Even so, companies use every tactic in the book to delay it. For companies which are slow at improving on their own, external factors often provide the catalyst. This may be losing a major customer, introducing a new technology, merging with another company, hiring a new senior manager, or moving to a new facility. Whatever the event, the natural tendency when faced with an unfamiliar change is to search the literature or use personal contacts to identify companies with a history of demonstrated business success to emulate. World class or best in the industry objectives can then be established based on performance levels achieved by these exemplar companies.

With the objectives set, management then begins the process of determining how to quickly achieve this level of performance based on their own environment and with their own products. For an inventory strategy, world class inventory turns may exceed 100 per year as demonstrated in automotive and other repetitive industries. However, this level is irrelevant in an industry characterized by lengthy job shop operations which barely achieve six turns per year. Setting some type of "best in the industry" objective is necessary in this case. Companies need to be realistic in the establishment of aggressive targets.

Setting aggressive targets is easy. Developing a strategy to achieve them is not.

One technique for shortcutting the development process is to visit the exemplar companies. This enables the company team to see first-hand what these companies are doing. Teams consisting of management, engineering, and hourly personnel demonstrate a real commitment to the improvement process.

Exemplar companies are justifiably proud of their achievements and are often eager to discuss their approach. They can be a tremendous source of information and inspiration. However, what visiting companies often fail to understand is that an approach which has proven effective in a different industry with different customers and under different business conditions may not apply to them. While the experienced exemplar company may understand this, they have no way of knowing the needs or situation of the visiting company. There is also no way to possibly convey the full magnitude of commitment or problems which the company has addressed over years of improvement efforts. In fact, they may be unwilling to honestly discuss some of the organizational or managerial problems they faced.

The improvement-minded company leaves justifiably impressed by the accomplishments of the exemplar company. What they do not leave with is a complete understanding of the magnitude of the effort ahead. The team returns to their own company and attempts to mimic what they observed. They obtain some initial successes but are surprised when the improvement program stalls. The problem is that what they observed at the exemplar companies has taken years to develop. When the company bypasses the necessary infrastructural development (organization, facilities, equipment, systems, and technologies) in order to skip right to the end result, the result is a failure. Management then gets blamed for a lack of commitment, when the problem is really one of a lack of an effective strategy.

The fact is, companies cannot find answers to their problems by looking to other companies. What they can identify in this process are choices others have made which have lead to varying levels of success. Management needs to recognize that the answer to competitiveness lies within the company itself. Benchmarking against companies in other industries provides the knowledge that at least someone is actually achieving a given level of performance under a given set of conditions. Benchmarking the company's capabilities against their customer's needs provides a more valuable insight into what the company really needs to do to fulfill its mission. Companies need to resist the temptation to base their strategy on achieving performance levels which seem impressive but are not necessarily relevant to their business.

TRADITIONAL STRATEGIES ARE A CHOICE TO MANAGE BY PERFECT HINDSIGHT

The need for a new strategy does not become apparent overnight. Instead, it sneaks up on an unwary company. People get so used to living with problems that they no longer recognize them as such. In fact, some individuals become convinced that fire-fighting skills are a measure of their true worth to the company.

They view any change to the status quo as a personal threat to their perception of their value to the company.

Perfect hindsight is always an effective technique for determining the need for a new strategy. With hindsight, anyone can see that part lead times have not kept pace with marketing lead times, that partial loads are increasing material handling efforts, that storage utilization is becoming increasingly inefficient, that materials are taking longer to deliver to the production line, that schedule change decisions are increasingly being made by gut feel, that inventory turns and customer service levels rarely reach their target, that when key personnel are absent no decisions are made, and so on. Perfect hindsight takes time, however, a commodity which is not in plentiful supply in a competitive environment.

The problem with the management-by-perfect-hindsight style is that choice flexibility becomes a function of the time remaining to develop and implement a new strategy. The less time there is to respond to a competitive challenge, the fewer the choices a company has with respect to the strategy. An integral strategy requires at least six months to formulate. Implementation takes years. Every month counts.

Consider the following choices which are essentially removed from the company's control when management delays too long in formulating and implementing a strategy:

Team Choice—Strategy development and implementation requires experienced strategic planners. Such individuals may be unavailable or overworked in companies which have saved money over the years by not investing in Production and Inventory Management (P&IM) training and education. Team membership is arguably the most important decision company management makes when initiating a strategy development process. Companies should definitely consider third-party team members or facilitators who have a proven track record to jump-start the process. This introduces a noncompany point of view, while supplementing and complementing in-house resources. Having the right team is crucial to the success of the strategy.

Schedule Choice—There is always a sense of urgency with perfect hindsight since the company is reacting to the strategies of its competitors. Like most things done in a hurry, shortcuts are used. Analyses are skipped or done poorly, resulting in an inadequate justification or requirements definition. Equipment, system, technology, supplier, and other assessments are cursory or delegated to third-party consultants. Organizational issues may be ignored on the assumption that support and acceptance will be forthcoming. Initiatives that can provide a quick payback end up absorbing resources needed by long-term projects and programs. Companies need to recognize the simple fact that they did not get where they are overnight. They need time to develop and implement a strategy properly.

Philosophy Choice—Being forced to establish a new operating philosophy because of outside pressures may result in adopting the three-letter-acronym

(TLA) of the day for expediency purposes. A trendy new (to the company) operating philosophy is easier and quicker to propose and accept if everyone can be convinced that the company is embarking on a leading edge strategy, while not being the pioneer. Identifying what the pioneers have done lends credibility. This can be especially compelling if the pioneers are in the same industry or have name recognition. To be most effective and relevant, however, philosophies should be apparent based on the needs of the company, not "chosen."

Companies maximize the choices related to their inventory strategy when they develop it in anticipation of their customers' needs and their competition's response. This enables the inventory manager to establish a dedicated team, provide sufficient time and direction, and translate the strategy into company-specific terms which support ownership and commitment. An integral strategy then becomes a choice.

LEADERS FOLLOW "RULES" OF THEIR OWN CHOOSING

Companies that introduce new products or lines on regular intervals based on new product and process technologies recognize the danger of becoming complacent. Such companies are constantly pushing one horizon or another. They thrive on change. As leaders, they do not play by the same rules as everyone else. The fact is most people say that "rules are made to be broken," and then they take special pains to make sure they never break any. Leaders treat rules more like guidelines. They obey, bend, or break the rules as necessary to complete their mission. Rules are for the followers.

When developing a new inventory strategy, the core team must first identify the past decisions which are now the determinants of current inventory levels and performance. These are typically the decisions which have somehow achieved an unquestioning legitimacy. They are either accepted without question or are not permitted by management to be questioned in an open forum. They are the company's inventory-related paradigms.

There is no problem obtaining the decision history if the individual(s) who made these earlier decisions are on the team. However, one of the biggest problems a company faces is that these same individuals may be the most blind to the effect of their own past decisions. In this situation, third-party team members are invaluable in countering feelings of ownership and a lack of objectivity on the part of company team members.

Leaders make choices which support their mission, while followers tend to choose the more traditional path. Choices companies make to support a traditional strategy are identified in the following points. The choices leaders make are provided as a contrast and are then covered in more detail in the rest of the book. Consider the following inventory paradigms (commonly accepted beliefs).

Companies need an all-encompassing "name-brand" operating philosophy to provide overall direction and focus. Leaders understand that there is no such thing as the single "canned" operating philosophy. Leaders take the principles from as many operating philosophies as are applicable to their business and blend them into an integral philosophy. The result is the "Their Company Name Here" philosophy. This involves establishing a zero-tolerance to deviation vision and selecting relevant functional area operating philosophies and related principles based on the eight areas of integration.

Inventory is waste. Leaders understand that having the right level of inventory is a necessary element of any competitive strategy. They, therefore, view inventory investment compared to target as an indicator of the company's overall performance. The right level of inventory is not waste. The real waste is when a company focuses all of its resources on a target and then misses it because the company's infrastructure and day-to-day operational tactics are misaligned.

The company's strategy must be formalized; informality leads to failure. Leaders understand that any successful strategy must be integral to the business. They also understand that formality without flexibility leads to a reduction in responsiveness. Therefore, leaders use formality to define boundaries. Strategies remain informal in areas where individual initiative and creativity leading to a competitive advantage improves responsiveness and flexibility.

System and technology suppliers are no different than any other type of vendor—using detailed bid specs ensures the company of the lowest price and best system. Leaders understand that integrated system projects and ongoing programs are most successful when the company partners with suppliers using a design/build approach. Leaders know that bid specs have the effect of assigning full project risks to the company, whereas a design/build approach minimizes risks before the final design is established. Bid specs restrict the company's involvement to development or approval of a stack of paper (i.e., the bid spec). Design/build actively involves company personnel in the actual design and implementation of the system.

Inventory systems should be implemented and used "as is" without any customization—this will force the company to (finally) conform to industry standards and simplifies MIS's job with regard to upgrades. Leaders understand that no competitive advantage is achieved if they have the same tools as their competitors in terms of systems. They look beyond a system's standard features and functions to determine the degree of decision support provided. Decision support is the critical system differentiator among inventory management systems, especially where thousands of decisions are made daily to support production and service part demand. Systems which constrain the planner's ability to manage the basic inventory planning and control processes will certainly constrain the company's ability to achieve inventory targets and vice versa.

A-item minimum dollar accuracy should be 100 percent, B-items 98 percent, and C-items 95 percent. Leaders understand that any count accuracy target less than 100 percent causes problems with order promising and scheduling decisions. They also understand that permitting any level of inaccuracy sends a message to the organization that inventory accuracy is unimportant. This is in basic conflict to the message that customer on-time shipments are of critical importance. The key to inventory accuracy is not to cycle count more often, but to design all of the company's processes in a manner which eliminates the need to cycle count at all.

Planners must manually review and release all orders in order to maintain control. Leaders understand that repetitive orders (depending on the business) can be released without any planner action once the proper edit checks are systemized. This leaves more time to address the critical few which will most benefit from planner/buyer review. Planners make the choices; computers execute the processes related to these choices.

Forecasts will never be 100 percent accurate, so there is little to be gained by trying to make them better. Leaders understand the mathematics associated with forecasting since they take special effort to educate and train their personnel. They realize that the focus of forecasting is to minimize the deviation of forecasted from actual usage. They also understand that statistical calculations based solely on history need to be manually adjusted to reflect future conditions. Planners use the computer to crunch forecasting-related numbers; they do not totally relegate the forecasting function to the computer and blindly accept the results.

All materials should be received just in time. Leaders understand that receiving all materials just in time may be infeasible due to freight costs or logistics. Ordering and carrying costs are only two of the cost elements which must be accounted for when determining replenishment quantities. Planners take the total cost perspective.

Statistical safety stock equations indicate that it is mathematically impossible to achieve a 100 percent safety stock coverage—customers will have to be satisfied with something less. Leaders understand that there is a difference between statistical and "business" math. There *is* a finite level of safety stock for every part and product which will provide a 100 percent customer service level under normal business conditions. The real issue is how much investment the company is willing to make to ensure a given level of customer service.

Large complex integration projects can be implemented by the same personnel and in the same way as small focused system projects. Leaders understand that integral systems require a professional project approach unlike that used for small internally-managed projects. They also understand that mismanagement can result in hundreds of thousands of dollars of unnecessary costs. Developing and managing an integral strategy cannot be delegated to functional managers who will focus on short-term gains at the expense of long-term improvements.

Comprehensive ongoing integration programs can be successfully implemented in short phases over an extended time frame and still enable the company to achieve all of the benefits. Leaders understand that programs encompassing operational, organizational, and technological change cannot be implemented in little bits and pieces. *It is impossible to get "a little bit pregnant."* Significant improvement requires a company-wide commitment and aggressive schedules.

Leaders differentiate themselves by setting more aggressive strategies than those of the next competitor and then achieving them. They know that it only takes a little effort to be better than most and a sincere commitment to be the best.

It is like the old story of the two men hiking in the mountains who get chased by a hungry bear. After a short distance, the first man stops to put on his sneakers. The second asks him why, since it is obvious that even with sneakers, neither one of them can outrun the bear. The response from the first man to the second is that he does not have to outrun the bear, just him. Leaders understand that progress is made one competitor at a time.

THE OLD TRADITIONAL STRATEGY MAY NO LONGER BE A CHOICE

Traditional inventory strategies *reactively* focus on inventory reduction as the primary and often only performance measure. The emphasis is on the mechanics of inventory planning and control via ordering methodologies and order quantity, safety stock, and forecasting techniques. Even improvements to traditional strategies where principles of Just in Time and other philosophies are implemented often fail to fully address the factors which cause unplanned levels of inventory to exist. Strategies which focus on maintaining the status quo do not support the forward planning required to position the company for growth and change. They simply react to the current situation.

Companies have too many differences to attempt to pigeonhole something as complex as a strategy. However, there are indicators of strategies developed via traditional means which act as warning signals that the company may need a new strategy. These indicators can be used as discussion points with management when considering development of an integral strategy, since many of them are often taken for granted.

Indicators that a company with a traditional inventory strategy may need a major overhaul include the following:

- The strategy is not documented.

- There is a documented strategy which is not followed.

- Company personnel cannot describe the strategy in their own words.

- Goals are stated in terms of percent of inventory reduction per year rather than in terms of inventory levels required to support target customer service levels.

- Goals and objectives are known by management but are not communicated to the organization.

- Goals and objectives are based on annual schedules and, if not met by the end of the year, drastic actions are taken to achieve the numbers.

- Performance measures consist only of financial measures (e.g., inventory accuracy in terms of dollar, not count accuracy; inventory levels in terms of total dollars rather than quantity as compared to target, and so on).

- Less than 100 percent inventory accuracy targets send a message to the organization that it is okay for part counts to be inaccurate.

- Inventory levels react to, rather than anticipate, business changes.

- Inventory count accuracy is 60 percent while inventory dollar accuracy is ≥98 percent.

- Obsolete inventory is left in storage rather than allowing a scrap charge to reduce profits.

- The storage cube is inefficiently utilized.

- Production is not confident that materials will be available when required.

- Production orders regularly experience unexpected stock outs.

- Personnel are not properly educated, trained, and APICS-certified in the use of inventory planning and control methodologies and techniques.

- Computer systems are designed for data entry rather than decision support.

- Material cannot be found when the computer indicates it is available.

- Service to production must be halted to perform cycle counting.

- Problems leading to inventory inaccuracy cannot be identified and eliminated.

- There is insufficient storage for the amount of material required to operate the business.

- No one knows the relationship of storage space to business level.

- Material has one or more physical inventory tags when the next physical inventory occurs.

- The company performs an annual physical inventory.

- Different revision material is mixed and then issued to the wrong orders causing rejects and/or scrap.

- Disposable dunnage is used for parts where returnable dunnage is more cost effective.

- No one knows whether returnable or disposable dunnage is more cost effective.

- Packaging does not adequately protect materials during transport, storage, and handling.

- Orders with insufficient lead times are consistently released to suppliers.

- Order quantity variations do not mirror production variations.

- The dust on the carton weighs more than the material inside.

It would be unfair to say that an integral strategy does not have some or many of these same problems. After all, integration must begin where the company is *now*. Problem resolution takes time. However, an integral strategy does not permit the above conditions to continue to exist. There are two key areas which differentiate integral from traditional strategies with respect to inventory. The first is the magnitude and scope of change envisioned. The second is in how improvements are achieved.

Traditional strategies are designed to be effective in achieving incremental improvements from year to year or at least in providing the appearance of improvements. They are not really intended to initiate, facilitate, and integrate major organizational, operational, and technological changes. Rather, they support the status quo through the process of continuous (but incremental) improvement. Re-focusing the inventory-related mission-critical business processes of the company via a highly engineered integration approach is not considered within the realm of a traditional strategy. These two different focuses are contrasted in Figure 1.2.

Traditional inventory strategy goals and objectives are typically based on a percentage improvement over last year's ending inventory value. Percentages are often in the 5–10 percent range or are set unrealistically high in order to "moti-

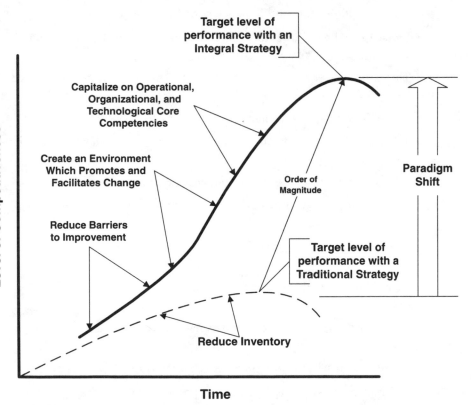

Figure 1.2   Integral vs. Traditional Strategy Focus

vate" the organization. If not met, the strategy fails. Even if achieved, however, the strategy may or may not have been executed as planned. Some companies are very adept at implementing extraordinary last-ditch efforts to achieve a particular financial inventory target. When these efforts result in achieving the desired results without actually following a strategy (or worse, by subverting the strategy), the strategy itself is ineffective.

This leads to the second differentiation (how improvements are achieved). An integral strategy sets targets as a means to an end, not as an end in and of themselves. These targets are based on the level of performance the organization is capable of achieving, given the infrastructure and operational capabilities in place to support these efforts. While it is very important to achieve target performance levels, achievement must come by working within the guidelines set for the strategy. The strategy does not fail if a particular target is not achieved on a certain date. Rather, the company fails if the strategy is circumvented to create the illusion of success. Traditional strategies set annual goals which become an ending each year. The next year requires a new beginning. Integration is ongoing since it encompasses the fundamental business processes themselves.

Traditional strategies are a reaction against existing performance levels. When the performance is not high enough, the company manipulates and adjusts single factors of performance in order to force an increase. Once this process begins, it must be continued in order to sustain the artificial gain. This creates a high-maintenance situation where the inventory manager and planners must constantly fiddle with order quantities and safety stocks in order to sustain the gains.

Integral strategies rely on operational and infrastructural improvements to achieve higher levels of performance. Integration orchestrates, as opposed to manipulates, performance.

PROBLEMS ASSOCIATED WITH THE TRADITIONAL STRATEGY CHOICE

Traditional inventory strategies are typically administered internally by the inventory department. This limits their effectiveness since most causes of unnecessary inventory are the result of external factors. Engineering supersedes parts, creating excess, surplus, and obsolete inventory. Service part demands can be very erratic. Customers change their buying patterns. Procuring stock to support optimistic forecasts increases average inventory levels. Any and all of these things can undo the best of plans.

Even a seemingly clear "98 percent" customer service level objective leaves loopholes. Does it mean that 98 percent of all order line items must be satisfied on time with 100 percent of the required material? Does it mean that 100 percent of the line items must be satisfied on time 98 percent of the time? Does it mean that 98 percent of the line items must be satisfied on time 98 percent of the time? Does it mean that 98 percent of the quantity ordered must be satisfied on time 100 percent of the time? Does it mean that 98 percent by dollar value of an order must be satisfied on time? Company personnel are experts at finding loopholes. The more arbitrary the objective, the less likely there is a clear approach for achieving it. This is typically the point where formal strategies are unmasked for the unstructured informal strategies they really are.

There is a common reason why companies fail to achieve significant improvements in inventory-related performance. It is simply that many companies lack the managerial ability to create a practical path between where they are and where they need to be. This is not so difficult to understand. Strategy development and implementation requires primarily program management (application of methodologies, techniques, education, training, and experience) and project management (planning, scheduling, and control) skills. These are long-term and multidisciplinary in nature. By comparison, daily production operations require quick response and problem-solving skills. Companies which apply quick response skills to strategies end up focusing on short-term gains. This actually creates barriers to long-term improvement.

A second reason for lack of significant improvement is management's unwillingness or inability to first reinforce the company's infrastructure. This must be done before attempting to change *how* the company operates. From an inventory perspective, infrastructure refers to organization, facility and equipment, and systems and technologies. These areas encompass the necessary foundation required to launch and then sustain permanent improvement. Without a strong foundation, incremental improvements can be achieved in given areas. However, they will only be sustained as long as the company specifically focuses on them. Incremental improvements without the proper infrastructure cannot sustain themselves because they are changes to the status quo. Cycle counting is a perfect example of something that will not go away no matter how many times a part is counted. Inventory accuracy improves momentarily and then cannot be sustained because the root causes of inaccuracy are not addressed. Improvements must become the status quo as a result of permanent change.

The third reason for lack of significant improvement with a traditional strategy is failure to implement the strategy as a series of parallel activities. Improvement is not a serial process. A certain amount of progress must be made in each area of integration before benefits begin to accrue. Each successive iteration then improves upon this foundation. A serial approach results in the implementation of some portion of the necessary strategy, with the expectation that it will provide immediate benefits. What companies find is that partial efforts are often not sufficient in and of themselves to create an environment of permanent change. Even an effort such as implementation of bar codes which seems complete in and of itself is only an element of an overall inventory strategy. An unreasonable expectation of immediate improvement leads to a perception of failure in these instances. This perception then hampers improvements in other areas, creating a cascading effect which can lead to failure.

A fourth reason for lack of results when using a traditional strategy is based on a lack of focus and commitment. Companies which pursue the ever-elusive "latest acronym" philosophy fail to understand that the fundamentals for business success never really change. It is valuable to use acronyms such as Computer

Integrated Manufacturing (CIM), Total Quality Management (TQM), and Just-in-Time (JIT) since they provide an abbreviated way to portray a wide variety of concepts, principles, methodologies, techniques, and tactics. What must be guarded against is the tendency to hear about a *new* acronym and believe that it is a totally new and unique way of doing business.

Companies should use well-recognized acronyms to associate concepts and principles with programs and projects within the company. This is why they were developed and refined in the first place. The key is not to confuse the organization with frequent changes or to create unnecessary nervousness with talk of drastic changes. There are few real inconsistencies among the current business philosophies found in the literature. The basics required for business success remain essentially unchanged. Understand what the customers need, want, and are willing to pay for—then provide it.

INTEGRATION IS A RESPONSE TO THE "DEATH SPIRAL" CHOICE

Integration is an engineering methodology used to develop, design, implement, and operate integrated systems. It is based on managing or controlling cause and effect relationships. The ability to know with a good degree of certainty that a desired result will occur once a variety of conditions exist or actions are taken is a good indication that the particular process is integrated. If implementing returnable dunnage for a part guarantees that every unit load contains exactly 100 parts and eliminates the possibility of inventory inaccuracy, it is fair to say that the containerization process for that part is integrated from an inventory accuracy perspective.

However, it is not fair to say that since the use of returnable dunnage has enabled the company to go from 99.5 percent to 99.99 percent inventory accuracy, the company is somehow *more* integrated than it was before the use of returnable dunnage. As a methodology, there is no integration measure per se. It does not make sense to imply that a process is not integrated at 94.9 percent of something but somehow becomes integrated at 95 percent. Methodologies do not have performance measures.

Therefore, simply achieving some degree of improvement in results is no clear indication that the inventory management function is integrated. How many times has senior management set an arbitrary percentage inventory reduction target for a year and then had it achieved through tactics that were detrimental to the business? Delaying supplier receipts scheduled for this month into the next to artificially increase inventory turns by reducing average inventory level hurts on-time shipping performance. Not paying suppliers on time to improve cash flow harms supplier relationships. Reducing safety stock levels and order quantities to increase turns without increasing the responsiveness of suppliers and manufacturing hurts customer service. These are all tactics used to achieve incremental inventory cost reductions in response to arbitrary objectives. Such tactics are collectively referred to as the "death spiral" syndrome. Once begun, they must be continued or the artificial gain is lost.

All three of these tactics were used by an electronics manufacturer. Service to their two largest customers (two other divisions of their corporation) got so bad and products were of such poor quality that their own sister divisions threatened to buy from a competitor. This action would have put the electronics division out of business. The sad thing was that the death spiral tactics never resulted in any significant inventory savings. There were so many shortages that orders could not be completed by manufacturing. The partially completed orders piled up in the factory, further extending the order cycle times. Tactics which reduced raw material inventory simply increased more expensive work in process inventory. Plant personnel made good overtime pay, but even that was becoming less of a motivator as overtime became mandatory. This particular company finally did make the changes required to transition from a job shop to a repetitive manufacturer. However, it was a difficult two-year process involving moving to a new facility and three senior division manager changes.

With death spiral tactics, manufacturing, suppliers, and customers end up paying the immediate costs of inventory shortages and expediting. Those who are supposed to be helped the most by the strategy end up being hurt the most. The company pays in the long term when suppliers become less responsive and dissatisfied customers buy elsewhere. Manufacturing of course remains a captive, but unsatisfied, customer.

Integration is neither the first nor the final step in the process; it *is* the process. It is a fallacy to believe that no matter how a process begins, a company can somehow become integrated in the end. The goal is not to become integrated but rather to become more competitive and profitable. Integration is simply the means to an end.

INTEGRATION-RELATED CHOICES EXTERNAL TO THE INVENTORY STRATEGY

When a company decides to make a strategy change, going "back to the basics" of production and inventory management is no longer a choice. These basics have their foundation in the 1960s and 1970s. During those periods, technology was not the driver it is today. In fact, the increased power and decreased cost of computer systems are driving the development of ERP (Enterprise Resource Planning), MES (Manufacturing Execution), WMS (Warehouse Management), and other computer-based systems. This is just the reverse with early MRPII systems which were constantly pushing the limits of computing technology. Companies are using other inventory-related technologies as well, including Radio Frequency (RF) terminals, bar coding, automated storage and handling systems, and simulation.

Because of ever increasing labor costs and the need to collapse lead times, inventory planning, storage, handling, and control systems are gradually becoming integral to the day-to-day operation of many businesses. This differs from the past where such technology applications were more focused and companies could work around them if necessary. When integral systems are inoperative in a company, production stops. Such systems, therefore, typically incorporate redundant equipment or vehicles and support a manual backup capability in order to improve system availability.

When a company elects to implement an integral strategy, there are a number of choices to make with regard to the strategy itself. The following choices are representative of those for an integral strategy.

Zero-Tolerance Integral Vision Choice

An integral inventory strategy begins with development of a 5–10 year vision. Five years is typically considered as the long-term horizon for traditional strategies. This duration is based on the time to build a new facility, implement sophisticated technologies, and develop, market, and produce a new product design. What is much more difficult to accomplish and fine-tune in five years is acceptance by the organization of new philosophies, development of superior customer and supplier relationships, and permanent change in interdepartmental, intercompany, and interpersonal relationships.

The vision established for inventory management must be the corporate vision restated in inventory terms. Table 1.1 translates a zero-deviation vision into inventory terms as they relate to the eight areas of integration. As with any vision, the translation is based on an operation where everything goes "right." Strategies then deal with the reality.

With respect to the operational areas of integration, for example, the vision is that the exact required quantity of each part will be available as required. "As re-

Table 1.1   Zero-Deviation Vision in Inventory Terms

	AREAS OF INTEGRATION	ZERO-DEVIATION INVENTORY VISION (INVENTORY AREAS OF APPLICATION)
OPERATIONAL	Materials	Right Quantity (Order Quantity and Safety Stock)
	Information	Right Time (Forecasting and Scheduling)
	Product	Right Material (MPS and MRP Planning)
	Process	Right Sequence and Orientation (Process Planning)
	Quality	Right Quality and Accuracy (of Parts and Information)
INFRASTRUCTURE	Organization	Right Knowledge, Skills, and Measures (Education and Training)
	Facilities and Equipment	Right Capacities and Throughput (Layout, Storage, and Handling)
	Systems and Technologies	Right Tools (Decision Support, Material Identification, and Tracking)

quired" means per the established Master Schedule (MS) and Material Requirements Plan (MRP) and in the right mix to support the product-related customer service target. Materials will be delivered in the required sequence and orientation to production. Any part counts and related storage, handling, and identification data will be maintained accurately and in a timely manner. All of this will be done with zero-deviation from the resource and requirements plans and established processes, procedures, and work instructions.

Integral Target Choices

Within inventory management, a zero-tolerance vision is translated as zero-tolerance from the target investment (inventory turns), zero-tolerance from the target required date (customer service level), and zero-tolerance from the inventory accuracy target. Other targets may be set as well for storage utilization, cycle time, cross training, and so on. Targets may apply to inventory in total, inventory by category, and inventory by part. A part will have targets related to investment level, safety stock level, forecast accuracy, storage density, ease of handling, type of identification, and so on.

Targets are determined as the result of progressively translating the company's high level cost, quality, and responsiveness goals into inventory terms. Targets must be quantifiable. Whereas a goal addresses 100 percent inventory accuracy by count or a 100 percent customer service level, targets (also referred to as objectives) may be intermediates. At the beginning of an improvement process, the target may be to achieve a 100 percent customer service level for preferred customers in six months and a 98 percent customer service level by a specific date for all others. This may be what the company feels is achievable given the resources available and current business environment.

Any cause of deviation from target identifies a need for some type of action. This is easier to address for causes under the company's control and more difficult for causes associated with suppliers, customers, or the environment. The amount of deviation identifies the magnitude of improvement required. Once a target is achieved and can be sustained over time with normal effort (i.e., it becomes the status quo), a more aggressive target is set.

The primary value to a company of a zero-tolerance vision with respect to inventory targets is really twofold. It (1) requires the company to quantify the targets for all inventory-related areas. Once they have been quantified, they can be checked for consistency. The associated measures then (2) inherently identify the magnitude of improvement required as the deviation from target.

With a traditional measure such as inventory accuracy, for example, no one ever really knows what the real accuracy level is. In the first place, dollar accuracy is not equivalent to count accuracy. Secondly, certain parts are permitted to be accurate to a plus or minus tolerance. The less expensive a part, the greater the likelihood that the count is inaccurate. When a zero-tolerance inventory accuracy of 98.6 percent for a part is reported against a target of 100 percent, inventory accuracy by count deviates from target by −1.4 percent. There is no need to wonder whether the part is a B or C item and is permitted to be inaccurate by a certain percent. The count is inaccurate. The deviation is −1.4 percent.

Integral Operating Philosophy Choices

Operating philosophies dictate the basic principles by which the company will operate. A simple number, for example, is a principle which dictates that all order quantities will be an integer multiplier or divisor of a given shift quantity. For example, a simple number of 100 and a shift production quantity of 1,000 may result in 1,000, 500, 100, or 50 unit (pallet, cart, or tote) quantities of all materials.

The operating philosophy for an integral strategy is a composite developed specifically for the company. Given the company's corporate vision and related enterprise strategy, the "Company Name Here" operating philosophy can be established. Table 1.2 identifies representative area operating philosophies associated with the eight areas of integration. Principles from each, when taken together, form a composite integral philosophy.

Inventory management is a fourth-level strategy as shown in Figure 1.3. Therefore, the enterprise, manufacturing, and materials management strategies should ideally be developed first or concurrently. Plans, schedules, controls, methodologies, techniques, processes, procedures, and measures for bottom-up execution are then developed as appropriate at each level in the hierarchy.

There is no reason to restrict an entire company to a focused philosophy such as Computer Integrated Manufacturing or Just in Time. Each functional area has their own unique needs. A general philosophy such as world class is too general. It falls into the category of "buy low—sell high." No one can argue with it, but it has no relevancy until it is broken down into its constituent elements. This is in essence what an integral strategy does. The principles are taken from a number of

Table 1.2   Integral Operating Philosophy

	AREAS OF INTEGRATION	AREA OPERATING PHILOSOPHIES	INTEGRAL PHILOSOPHY FOCUS
OPERATIONAL	Materials	JIT–Just in Time	Planning
	Information	CIM–Computer Integrated Manufacturing	Scheduling
	Product	CE–Concurrent Engineering	Designs
	Process	SCM–Short Cycle Manufacturing	Processes
	Quality	TQM–Total Quality Management	Requirements
INFRASTRUCTURE	Organization	IO–Integral Organization	Responsibility
	Facilities and Equipment	IF–Integral Facility	Reliability
	Systems and Technologies	IS–Integral Systems	Flexibility

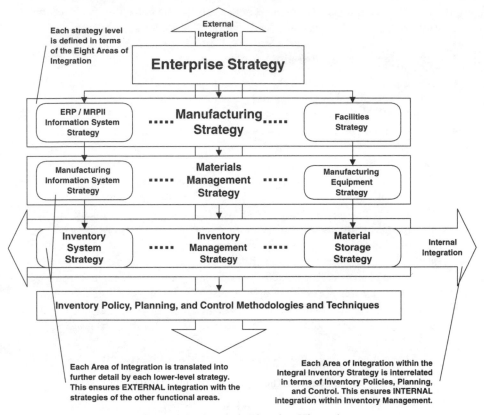

Figure 1.3   Strategic Planning Hierarchy

focused philosophies and applied within the company in a manner which makes business sense.

Just in Time is certainly a relevant philosophy for inventory management in a repetitive manufacturing environment. JIT principles are applicable to other manufacturing environments as well. In fact, with its focus on eliminating the actions or inactions which cause waste, it has relevance for every area of the company. It may not make much sense to design engineering, though, to claim to have a Just in Time operating philosophy when it takes three months to engineer a product. In their case, a concurrent engineering philosophy and related methodologies and techniques have more relevance as a core philosophy.

From an integration perspective, therefore, the need is not for the perfect (off-the-shelf) operating philosophy. The need is for the perfect set of integrated operating concepts and principles. These then form the basis of an integral philosophy which binds the missions and strategies of the various functional areas and departments together.

The integral philosophy-related concepts and targets guide the development of the integral strategy. The principles guide the execution. Principles establish guidelines for policies, which in turn govern the company's actions with respect to inventory days supply, level of automation, level of integration, layout, equipment dedication or flexibility, ordering, safety stock, forecasting, inventory accuracy, ergonomics, and so on.

Traditional inventory strategies which attempt to pigeonhole an entire inventory strategy into a non-integral philosophy end up focusing only on things over which the inventory department has control. They fail to address actions by other departments which cause excess inventory because these departments do not see the relevancy of someone else's operating philosophy to their area. Blending the key principles across operating philosophies results in a true company-wide philosophy.

Integral Strategy Choice

When considered within an overall strategic planning and implementation hierarchy, an integral strategy is the bridge between philosophies and methodologies as shown in Figure 1.4. Inventory management specifically focuses on policy, planning, and control methodologies and techniques as they relate to materials.

An integral inventory strategy has three primary directives:

1. *Be clear and understandable.* The strategy provides a common vision and direction. The strategy plan must clearly define how the vision will be implemented in terms of policies, planning, and controls with respect to inventory management and in terms of initiatives, projects, and programs as a course of action. People in the organization must clearly understand their role, responsibilities, and level of authority. This understanding is one of the focuses of ISO 9000.

2. *Be internally integrated.* The strategy identifies how the various inventory policy, planning, and control elements will be integrated. Internal integration ensures consistency of approach and execution between and among

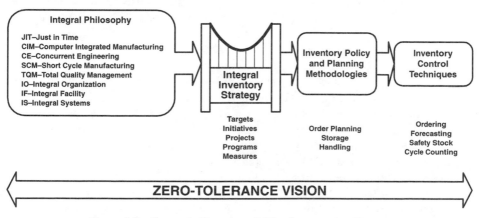

Figure 1.4   Strategic Planning and Implementation Process

parts, and within each inventory category. From a practical perspective, this means that order quantities, forecasting, and safety stocks are consistent within each part based on investment and customer service targets. Infrastructural elements such as storage and handling systems must support planned volumes and rates. Internal integration is, therefore, a highly engineered and strictly controlled process.

3. *Be externally integrated.* The inventory management function cannot be allowed to constrain the ability of the company to meet cost, quality, and responsiveness goals. This means that inventory management must support planning and scheduling activities by ensuring accurate part counts, by accurate and timely transaction processing, and so on. The more effectively each lower level strategy supports the higher level ones as shown in Figure 1.3, the higher the degree of external integration and ability to achieve and sustain improvements. External integration is, therefore, a managed process since many materials, information, product, process, and quality variables are outside of inventory management's direct span of control.

The key to a successful inventory strategy then, is to engineer and execute it as a formal and measurable business process. There is a lot of truth in the statement that anything which cannot be measured cannot be controlled. Management's task is to define the *right* measures and implement the *right* controls. An integration approach formalizes and then facilitates this process.

INTEGRATION-RELATED CHOICES INTERNAL TO THE INVENTORY STRATEGY

Within a manufacturing and distribution environment, the right level and mix of inventory improves flexibility and competitiveness. In fact, for those businesses with peak cyclical demands and limited capacity, finished goods inventory may form the foundation of the sales and marketing strategies. It is not uncommon, for example, for large distribution centers to vary by as much as 30–50 percent in total dollar volume and capacity from low to peak seasons. That range may be substantially greater than manufacturing can accommodate, requiring a build-ahead manufacturing strategy to support peak sales.

Inventory can be categorized for inventory turns purposes as operational, business, and financial. Accounting categories include Raw, Work in Process (WIP), and Finished Goods (FG), and active, excess, surplus, inactive, and obsolete. Other categories include floor stock, automated, conventional, and bulk storage. Still others are stratified by dollar value as A, B, or C items. No matter how a company slices up the inventory, the level of inventory required to profitably and cost effectively operate the business is the focus of the integral strategy.

The previous section addressed making the integral strategy choice itself. This is an *external* aspect of the strategy process from an inventory management perspective. Once done, all of the functional areas within the business should relate to each other in a consistent manner. Each functional area then develops their own internal integration structure based on the eight areas of integration and related operating philosophy concepts and principles. With inventory, choices in the following areas must be made.

Inventory as an Indicator of Waste

Rather than viewing inventory as waste in and of itself, companies must think of it as a leading or lagging indicator of waste. As a *leading indicator,* inventory in excess of that required to support current operations and other customer service or R&D requirements is considered waste. This is a forward-looking perspective which supports Just in Time, Short Cycle/Agile Manufacturing, and other time-based philosophies. Current operations may be measured in hours, shifts, days, or weeks, depending on the environment or part. As a *lagging indicator,* surplus inventory or that in excess of reasonable need which exists due to all of those conditions which can be identified through perfect hindsight is considered waste. Reasonable need is based on the environment or part and is situation dependent. Inventory may become waste, but is rarely waste to begin with.

Eliminating waste in the form of unnecessary inventory is a sound business objective. Using a qualifier such as "unnecessary" also takes an unfocused vision and targets the specific area of improvement, once "unnecessary" is defined. Since inventory levels are generally the result of actions or inactions in engineering, manufacturing, marketing, service, and other departments, or due to business conditions, the inventory strategy must be given broad latitude within a company. Departmental silos cannot be used as excuses for barriers to improvement. Integral (proactive) strategies address these areas of waste in other parts of the business by addressing the source of the problems in the departments before they adversely affect inventory levels. Traditional (reactive) strategies address unnecessary inventory after the fact, once the inventory becomes waste and is under inventory management's control.

Inventory Strategy Fundamentals—Methodologies and Techniques

Methodologies are processes for arriving at solutions. They require knowledge and experience and, therefore, allow some latitude in determining the solution. Two individuals or teams using the same methodology may or may not develop the same solution or reach the same conclusion. Strategies are developed using methodologies, as are inventory targets and material plans. Methodologies use processes.

Techniques are procedures for deriving a specific answer to a set of conditions. They require skill and understanding of when to use one technique versus another. Little if any latitude in how an answer is arrived at is permitted. Two individuals or teams using the same technique should develop essentially the same solution or reach the same conclusions. Double-smoothed forecasting is a technique for projecting a future period's forecast based on historical demand. Techniques use equations or definitive work instructions.

Methodologies are used to develop layouts, determine when to release a replenishment order, establish customer service level targets, perform analyses, and develop project plans and schedules. Techniques are used to calculate order quantities and safety stock levels to support a specific safety stock customer service percent. Methodologies relate more to inventory policy and planning areas, whereas techniques relate more to control areas. Methodologies are used to set zero-tolerance inventory targets. Techniques are used to implement the integral strategy and measure deviation from targets. People use methodologies and techniques. Computers systemize techniques and provide data in a decision support format to support people's use of methodologies.

Table 1.3 provides a general comparison of the inventory methodologies and techniques companies commonly use to establish and maintain inventory levels. A representative mapping to the five operational areas of integration is shown in the table as well. The methodologies and techniques are fundamental to the day-to-day operation of the business from an inventory management perspective. The areas of integration provide the relationship to the other areas of the business which affect and are affected by inventory levels.

Inventory policies set the direction for planning and control actions. Each of the operational areas of integration have policies which relate specifically to their associated performance measures. Planning methodologies enable planners to implement the strategic direction established by the inventory manager. Control techniques provide consistency of action.

Integral Measure Choices

The value of establishing an integral company infrastructure is that the organization is able to focus less on dealing with the constant irritations of internal con-

Table 1.3   Inventory Integration Scope—Operational Elements

OPERATIONAL AREAS OF INTEGRATION	POLICIES (RELATED TO PERFORMANCE)	PLANNING (METHODOLOGIES)	CONTROL (TECHNIQUES)
Materials	Inventory Turns	Order Quantity	Time Period Fixed Economic
Information	Customer Service	Safety Stock	Statistical Fixed Time Period
Product	Storage Utilization	Forecasting	Single or Double-Smoothing Weighted Average
Process	Dock-to-Dock Cycle Time	Order Review	Material Requirements Planning (MRP) Reorder Point (ROP)
Quality	Inventory Accuracy	Cycle Counting	Part Count $ Accuracy

Note: The Areas of Integration apply equally well to manufacturing, engineering, MIS, and so on.

straints and more on achieving the inventory strategy targets shown outside the web in Figure 1.5. When the As-Is web in the polar/snowflake diagram collapses to a dot, it indicates that the target inventory is available—at the target place, at the target time, in the target quantity, of the target quality, in the target orientation,—with zero deviation. The web can be constructed for individual parts, part categories, and total inventory. Each target has its own measure(s).

The intent is for the web to collapse. This indicates that progress is being made toward the targets. Permanent improvements have been made when the web remains collapsed over time with normal effort as part of day-to-day operations. New targets can be established at this point for the next stage of the improvement process. Note that this decision is not dependent on all factors reaching their target levels, but should occur any time a single factor of performance is consistently achieving the target. For example, the definition of the "target time" for a given part may originally be defined as one week prior to need. Over time, the definition may be tightened to one day and then two hours to reflect a dedicated milk run to a point-of-use dock as is becoming more common with In-Line Vehicle Sequencing (ILVS) in automotive assembly plants.

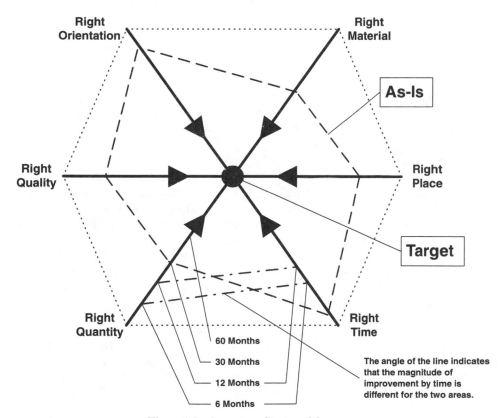

Figure 1.5   Inventory Strategy Measures

Managing Conflict Choices

The difficulty of using traditional approaches in an environment requiring integration is due in large part to each functional area having somewhat conflicting, yet interrelated operating philosophies, missions, and performance measures. A key element of any strategy based on integration principles, therefore, is its ability to reduce the risk of failure from both external and internal factors while facilitating the chances of success within an overall atmosphere of conflict.

A typical example is a purchasing strategy of buying in large lots to obtain the lowest piece price versus an inventory strategy of stocking in small quantities to minimize inventory investment, carrying cost, and the risk of obsolescence. The difference between these strategies is one of balancing purchase cost and customer service level with inventory investment, carrying cost, and inventory turns. These decisions address costs from direct and indirect material costs, respectively. Both strategies have the same goal of reducing costs, yet both approach it from different and potentially conflicting directions. Buyer-planners run into this difficulty frequently since they are really measured differently on both parts of their job.

If it were simply a matter of balancing price with carrying cost, the Economic Order Quantity (EOQ) equation provides a precise answer for an independent demand part. The problem is that other factors not included in the EOQ equation have a significant bearing on the decision of how much to buy (or make) and stock. Product cost and customer service level as previously mentioned are just two, while freight cost can be a significant factor in a Just in Time environment. Traditional inventory equations do not adequately account for cases where a variety of cost, quality, and responsiveness issues must be considered.

Integral strategies address these types of problems where the easy surface appeal solution does not in fact address the real issues. These are the cases where equations produce the illusion of precise answers for situations which may be imprecise at best. The integration process identifies, quantifies, correlates, and incorporates these and other key interrelationships into the decision process. This enables management to establish a complete closed loop strategy of policies and targets, the tactics required to achieve them, and the measures necessary to monitor performance. From an inventory management perspective, this involves establishing specific part-related strategies which can be managed and controlled within the inventory, material requirements planning, master scheduling, purchasing, and production activity control systems.

Choice of the Basic Integral Inventory Strategy Premise

Any inventory strategy which focuses on the elimination of inventory as an end in and of itself under the guise of Just in Time or any philosophy sets unreasonable expectations. When the inventory is not eliminated, the strategy fails. The plain and simple fact is that manufacturing companies need inventory. Integration strategies focus on the cause and effect relationships which result in unnecessary inventory. Improvement expectations are set based on the difficulty of controlling and/or managing these relationships. The focus is on multiple target measures, with reduction in inventory investment being just one measure of overall inventory performance.

The basic premise upon which an integral inventory strategy is based is that *inventory level is an indicator of company performance.* Company performance is the result of the formal and informal aspects of the business strategy. Therefore, inventory which supports the business strategy and which enables target performance to be achieved is an asset, while that which does not is waste. This is not a clear-cut issue (no integration issue ever is) and cannot be treated as such. In fact, the definition of *waste* in a company will change over time as more of the strategy is implemented and as business conditions change.

Table 1.4 illustrates the general inventory integration structure which is followed when developing an integral inventory strategy. The areas of integration are

Table 1.4 Inventory Areas of Integration

	AREAS OF INTEGRATION	REPRESENTATIVE INVENTORY INTEGRATION STRATEGY SCOPE *
OPERATIONAL AREAS	Materials	Inventory Management Policies (Inventory Level and Investment) Inventory Planning Policies (Stocking, Issuing) Inventory Control Policies (Adjustments, Count Cycle)
	Information	Inventory (Part, Balance, Orders, Requirements) Inventory Analysis (Operational, Business, and Financial) Decision Support (History and Forecasted Usage Rate)
	Product	Forecasting Methodologies and Techniques Order Quantity Methodologies and Techniques Safety Stock Methodologies and Techniques
	Process	Raw Material-related Processes Work in Process Material-related Processes Finished Goods Material-related Processes
	Quality	Inventory Accuracy (Customer and Production Support) Data Accuracy (Inventory Manager and Planner Support) Forecast Accuracy (Supplier and Production Support)
INFRASTRUCTURE AREAS	Organization	Education (Methodologies and Techniques Knowledge) Training (Equipment and Systems Skills Development) Personal and Professional Development (Certification)
	Facilities and Equipment	Storage Systems, Equipment, and Related Facilities Handling Systems, Equipment, and Related Facilities Receiving, Staging, Disposition, and Shipping Facilities
	Systems and Technologies	Computer (ERP, MRPII, WMS, EDI, Decision Support) Automation (AS/RS, AGVS, AEMS, Conveyor, Robotics, Palletizing) Identification and Dispatching (Bar Code, RF)

*Note that scope is not restricted to a single area of integration; each supports the other.

segregated into operational and infrastructure areas. Infrastructure areas provide the strong foundation required to build an integration capability. They make it possible to obtain maximum benefit from the operational areas. Operational areas encompass the key management functions which jointly enable the resources of the company to be focused upon improvement actions. At each level of the strategy development process (enterprise, manufacturing, materials management, and inventory), the areas of integration and the area operating philosophies remain the same. This ensures consistency of purpose throughout the organization.

SUMMARY

An integral strategy aligns and then focuses the resources of the business. Development of the integral strategy provides management with the opportunity to set targets, schedules, and budgets in a manner consistent with the commitment and capabilities of the organization. Engineered improvements to the infrastructure ensure that the organization, facilities, equipment, systems, and technologies will not act as a constraint to improvements. This then enables the integral strategy to be implemented in the operational areas of integration related to materials, information, product, process, and quality management.

Companies intending to implement an integral strategy must understand the following:

- *Incremental* improvements can be achieved via traditional methods, with or without a formal strategy. *Significant* levels of improvement can best be achieved and sustained via the regimentation of an integral strategy based on an integration methodology.

- Inventory certification tests have correct answers. Inventory management has correct methodologies and techniques. An effective approach for one company in a given situation may not be as effective for a different type of company in a similar situation or a similar type of company in a different competitive environment. Every company and competitive environment has some degree of uniqueness. In International Standards Organization (ISO) terminology, "a process is a process except for uniqueness."

- Complete strategies encompass both proactive and reactive elements. Proactive elements address the vision, while reactive elements address the reality.

- It is not enough to blindly use computerized ordering, forecasting, and safety stock techniques. Planners must understand the principles and mathematics upon which they are based. Only then can they be sure they are applying the right equations, variables, techniques, and methodologies. This requires a formal education and training program.

- While inventory can literally become waste overnight, the conditions which cause waste take time to develop. The strategy development, infrastructure improvement, and operational, organizational, and technological change processes take time as well.

- Knowledgeable and skilled personnel with the right systems and technologies are required to manage, plan, and control inventories. Businesses must make a continuing investment in their personnel and tools to maintain the appropriate knowledge and skill levels.

- Good suppliers can cover many company deficiencies related to planning and scheduling. However, even the best cannot compensate for all of a company's problems all of the time. Companies need to get their own house in order and be realistic in their expectations of their suppliers.

Managers too often adopt a caretaker role rather than risk the possibility of failure associated with a change to the status quo. Leaders do not view themselves as caretakers. They certainly do not view the status quo as something to be maintained. Leaders recognize that change is required, that change is within their control, and that there is no compelling business reasons to delay. Then they go out and do what needs to be done. Management needs to identify and develop leaders within their own company. Developing and implementing an integral strategy is one way to do this.

Chapter 2

Establish a Business Case for Changing the Status Quo

Companies do not need a reason to develop a new strategy. What they need is a compelling reason to change their existing strategy. Companies resist changing anything, strategies included, unless some external or internal condition acts as a catalyst.

Whatever the catalyst, change begins by establishing a business case which is more compelling than the company's natural resistance to change. The business case establishes the types and magnitudes of required improvements, along with a financial justification. Companies are in business to make a profit, and strategies need to reflect that. Once the required improvement levels cannot be met by the current strategy, an integral strategy is indicated. This may mean that required levels of cost improvement are in the range of 30 to 50 percent as compared to current operations, and that other performance areas such as lead time reduction and inventory accuracy require doubling, tripling or order of magnitude improvements.

The entire subject of performance measurement is often confusing to company personnel. This is not surprising since companies often confuse actual quantifiable performance measures with aggregate indicators and more general operational capabilities. The axiom which states that "if you can't measure it, you can't control it" really defines the key element of performance—it must be measurable.

This chapter addresses many of the issues faced by companies when establishing strategy-related targets and measures:

- Types of *measures, indicators, and capabilities* commonly used in inventory management are discussed, along with the differences among analyses, models, and simulations.

- A *10-step analysis methodology* is provided, along with analysis development considerations which can be used for consistency purposes.

- Representative types of analyses useful in developing an overall business case for significant improvement are discussed for each of the key aggregate inventory performance indicators, one per each of the operational areas of integration.

Performance measures relate to processes. Processes are repeatable. The value in knowing performance levels is in being able to calculate deviations from target. Integral inventory strategies, therefore, focus on performance as it relates to processes and required magnitudes of improvement.

COMPELLING NEEDS MUST BE BALANCED BY REASONABLE EXPECTATIONS

Anyone can recognize that a company has a compelling need to change its inventory strategy once performance levels consistently fall short of business targets. It is much more difficult to project when this may occur in the future based on trends which are only in the development stage. The key to such insight is to fully understand current capabilities and how they map to projected needs. The magnitude of the change is then measured from a baseline consisting of current performance levels within the five operational areas of materials, information, product, process, and quality management. Basic questions the company addresses via the analysis process include the following:

- What processes are being measured and how?
- Are measures internally (within inventory management) and externally consistent?
- Are measures meaningful in and of themselves?
- What is the current performance level?
- Which factors are constraining performance?
- Which improvements can be made in each area of integration to improve performance?
- What is preventing improvement actions from being taken now?
- Are the current measures being manipulated in order to falsify performance?
- Are measurements being taken frequently enough to be of operational value?
- What will the improvement efforts cost?
- How will changes affect current operations?
- What will be gained by changing the company's performance metrics?

- How much will performance improve if constraints to performance are eliminated?

The most important reason for performing analyses at the beginning of any change process is to establish reasonable expectations. While there may be no limits to what a company can imagine, there are limits to what it can reasonably expect to do.

Analyses, models, and simulations evaluate the actual performance measurement and strategy development process by closing the loop between requirements and performance. Just as capacity requirements planning checks the material requirements plan for validity, analyses, models, and simulations check the integral strategy plan. The result is a practical strategy based on a balance between the company's targets and capabilities.

Within an integral strategy, performance is measured as a function of deviation from target. This is a key difference as compared to traditional performance measures which relate performance to zero rather than the target. The intent is to hit as closely to the established targets as possible with zero deviation. The magnitude of deviation indicates the magnitude of required improvement. For example, performance is not 96 percent as measured from zero but -4% based on the target of 100 percent. Always focus on the target.

It is very important that companies understand the difference among performance measures, indicators of performance, and capabilities which support improved performance. Each has its own area of application and use within the business. As a result, each is determined and evaluated differently. Figure 2.1 provides a general comparison. Capabilities are evaluated via simulation, indicators via models, and performance measures via analyses. Inventory policies, planning, and control relate to the eight areas of integration. Policies relate more to the operational areas of integration, while control relates to the infrastructural areas of integration. Planning bridges both areas.

PERFORMANCE MEASURES *MEASURE* BUSINESS PROCESSES

The subject of performance measurement is not treated in a consistent manner by companies or in the literature. People tend to categorize any and all types of measures, indicators, and capabilities as "performance" measures. This leads to confusion at best and misdirection at worst. Performance measures directly measure a process.

Indicators aggregate performance measure results over time or project the performance related to a small sample over the entire population. Inventory turns is an aggregate indicator of the level of inventory investment required to support a given business level based on cost of goods sold. As an indicator, it can be monitored from period to period to detect trends. Inventory accuracy of all parts in inventory is a projection based on the small sample actually counted each period. Neither of these indicators directly measures a process. Capabilities encompass the " . . . ilities" words such as flexibility, reliability, maintainability, repeatability,

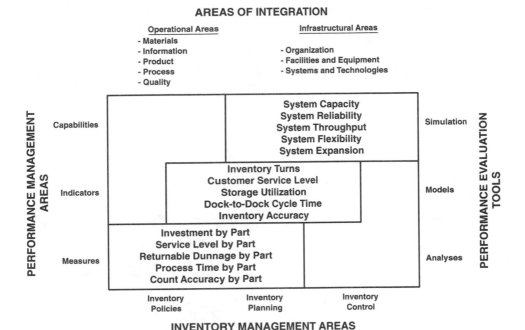

Figure 2.1   Performance "Measures" and Evaluation

and related terms such as ergonomics and responsiveness. While indicators and capabilities are performance related, they are not performance measures per se since they do not directly measure a process.

Simply stated, something must have been "performed, achieved, or provided" in order for it to have a performance measure. A process meeting at least the following three basic criteria is involved:

1. The process must have a target. Improving inventory accuracy of a particular part by eliminating causes of inaccuracy involves a process which is performed. The measure of performance improvement is determined directly by counting the part quantity. It is not really a part accuracy process which is being measured by counting the part quantity but the inaccuracy elimination process.

2. The target must be quantifiable and meaningful. Performance must relate to a numeric measure such as days, quantity, percentage, and so on. If performance has improved by 10 percent, for example, the company must be 10 percent closer to the ideal of either 100 percent, zero, the intermediate target, and so on. With respect to a percentage, therefore, the measure is from the target. If current count accuracy is 80 percent based on traditional measures, a 10 percent target improvement is measured from 100 percent, not 80 percent. Therefore, the next intermediate target is 90 percent, not 88

percent. Performance is not measured from what has already been determined to be an unacceptable performance level (80 percent in this case).

3. The measure itself must lend itself to daily operations and improvement processes. Measures must be independent of artificial manipulation (refer to Table 2.1).

Example: A company using Acceptable Quality Level (AQL) criteria to establish sample quantities received a shipment from one of their suppliers on the required date. Incoming inspection rejected the sample quantity of one, and the lot was returned to the supplier for replacement. The only de-

Table 2.1   Performance Measures "Measure" the Effectiveness of Processes

OPERATIONAL AREAS OF INTEGRATION	PROCESS BEING MEASURED	HOW MEASURES CAN BE MANIPULATED (TO THE COMPANY'S OR CUSTOMERS' DETRIMENT)
Materials (Inventory Turns)	Manufacturing process by which materials are converted into finished goods (rate of InventoryTurnover)	-Delay required receipts at month-end (causes next month's orders to have inventory shortages) -Reduce safety stock (reduces Customer Service) -Delay labor reporting (artificially reduces WIP value)
Information (Customer Service)	Customer service process by which materials are made available to support dependent and independent demand (Customer Service Level %)	-Take credit for on-time shipment of partial order -Take credit for shipment no more than 1-week late compared to the required ship date -Measure service based on line items shipped on time rather than orders shipped on time
Product (Storage Utilization)	Storage, staging, and buffering process by which storage space is allocated for materials (Storage Utilization %)	-Report high utilization by including materials which should not be in storage (obsolete, and so on) -Report high utilization of inefficiently used space (1 small carton on a pallet)
Process (Dock-to-Dock Cycle Time)	Manufacturing and handling process rate at which materials are converted into finished goods (Cycle Time Days)	-Report IE times (which may not be achievable in actual practice) -Report averages (without the high and low values)
Quality (Inventory Accuracy)	Storage, handling, planning, and control processes by which material quality is maintained while in the facility and by which information and data is provided in an accurate and timely manner (Inventory Count Accuracy %)	-Report dollar accuracy (net of overages and shortages) -Report accuracy based on a tolerance (+/– 10% for a C item) -Infer cycle count accuracy in one inventory category across dissimilar categories

fective part in the lot was the one which had been sampled. It was replaced, and the material was returned to the customer one week later. The supplier received his On-time Performance Evaluation the next month indicating that the order had been one week late. He objected to this since the initial shipment was on time. He did not feel that on-time performance had anything to do with the quality of the material. His customer did not agree. This is one example where performance targets are interrelated. The supplier's below-target quality performance also adversely impacted his on-time performance.

Performance targets must be absolutes in terms of improving something or meeting a target. Targets are set at levels which can be achieved, with ideal targets (goals) typically being 100 percent. The measure must be meaningful in and of itself. For example, 99.5 percent inventory count accuracy means that in an inventory consisting of 10,000 part numbers, 9,950 parts are known with confidence to be 100 percent accurate. Also, a change in the measure must conform to a mathematical relationship. If returnable dunnage is used for 250 of the parts which were not 100 percent accurate, inventory accuracy should now be 99.75 percent. This leaves another 250 parts where the company is not totally confident that 100 percent count accuracy will be maintained over time without some type of cycle counting. Performance measures are applicable to the five operational areas of integration. Measures relate to processes which can be evaluated and monitored with respect to individual parts, operation cycle times, costs, dates, products, orders, workstations, and so on.

Performance indicators suggest that performance should increase, decrease, or remain the same. They do not necessarily have a direct mathematical relationship to the area of performance. A reduction in part lead time, for example, is an indicator that forecasts should be more accurate since the forecast time frame is shorter. There is no guarantee, however, that forecasts will be more accurate. Also, a 50 percent reduction in lead time does not infer that forecast accuracy will improve by the same 50 percent. Performance indicators are applicable to the three areas of internal inventory integration (inventory policies, planning, and control).

Companies affect inventory-related performance indicators through ordering, safety stock, and forecasting processes. Aggregate measures across all parts in inventory or a specific category provide an indication of improvement or change from one period to the next. Once the aggregation process has occurred, however, it may not be possible to directly relate specific actions to specific levels of improvement. If inventory turns improves from one period to the next, it is not readily apparent from the improvement itself what caused the change since so many different factors are involved.

Capabilities refer to flexibility, maintainability, producibility, reliability, expandability, effectiveness, responsiveness, and so on. It makes no sense to say that a company is performing at a 50 percent flexibility level. Installing a new machine will not make the company 60 percent flexible (though it may improve part routing flexibility or volume flexibility). Capabilities are applicable to the three inventory infrastructural areas (organization, facilities and equipment, and systems and technologies).

Companies have capabilities to a greater or lesser extent. These capabilities can be enhanced to improve a company's overall performance but are not themselves measured in terms of performance. They do, however, ultimately support performance measures and indicators. Capabilities relate to efficiency, productivity, uptime, utilization, availability, capacity, and throughput. Capabilities exist and can be reinforced or improved, but they are not performed per se.

SINGLE FACTOR MEASURES VS. AGGREGATE INDICATORS

Measures relate to specific elements of improvement, while indicators relate to categories. Elements addressed by single factor measures include individual parts, products, machines, operators, workstations, cycle times, costs, and dates. These elements have targets which are based on the company's cost, quality, or responsiveness goals. They can be measured at a point in time. Aggregate indicators are the result of combining the results of all elements within a category into a single measure. Rather than attempting to visualize the performance of 20,000 individual part numbers, aggregating by part category reduces the process to a handful of indicators. Measures and indicators can be compared to targets and to themselves over time to see if performance is improving or deteriorating.

Count accuracy of a particular part number is a single factor measure. The absolute target is to achieve 100 percent count accuracy 100 percent of the time. Therefore, if a cycle count indicates that there are 98 pieces when the computer indicates there should be 100, part count accuracy is –2 percent of target (–2 in absolute terms). The focus of any improvement effort is to achieve a zero deviation from target. With respect to target, therefore, the count accuracy of this part has somehow become 2 percent out of tolerance on the low side.

Combining the results of single factor measures creates an aggregate measure (refer to Table 2.2). Inventory accuracy is an aggregate measure calculated from individual cycle counts. Employing a consistent cycle counting methodology over time permits the effectiveness of accuracy improvement actions to be monitored and assessed. Inventory turns is an aggregate indicator which provides insight into the level of inventory investment available (though not necessarily required) to support current business levels. It is most useful as a comparison from period to period.

Inventory goal targets are derived from the company's cost, quality, and responsiveness goals. The manufacturing, materials management, and the inventory strategies then successively translate these three goal areas into their components. Figure 2.2 illustrates the basic process and a few of the elements. The further from the enterprise strategy, the less direct the relationship between the enterprise goals and the functional area goals, objectives, and targets. Once the objectives are as consistent as they can be made (i.e., are externally integrated) among the strategy levels, the strategies themselves can be developed in terms of

Table 2.2   Inventory-Related Performance Measures and Indicators

AREAS OF INTEGRATION	SINGLE FACTOR MEASURES (AS COMPARED TO TARGET)	AGGREGATE PERFORMANCE "MEASURES"	PERFORMANCE INDICATORS
Materials (Right Materials)	- Inventory investment = target - Part balances = target - Part costs = target	Inventory Turns	- Operational inventory reducing - Business inventory reducing - Financial inventory reducing
Information (Right Time)	- Parts issued on required date - Unplanned demand within target satisfied - Customer orders = forecast	Customer Service Level	- On-time shipments increasing - Backorders reducing - Expediting reducing
Product (Right Place)	- Operating inventory locations = target - Business inventory locations = target - Financial inventory locations = target	Storage Utilization	- Increased container standardization - Increased point of use storage - Overall storage area reducing
Process (Right Orientation)	- Time from receipt to store = target - Time from store to production = target - Time from order start to complete = target	Dock-to-dock Cycle Time	- Material wait/queue time reducing - Floors remain clear - Double handling reducing
Quality (Right Quantity and Quality)	- Part count accuracy = target - Bin location accuracy = target - Causes of errors are assignable	Inventory Accuracy	- Count frequency reducing - Error frequency reducing - Time to resolve errors reducing

initiatives, projects, programs, suitable measures, and appropriate methodologies and techniques.

With quality, for example, the customer's view of quality relates to tangibles such as conformance to requirements, durability, functionality, and so on. This must be the same view taken by the business at the enterprise level. Manufacturing's view of quality may focus on the 1st-time quality level of the various production processes. Materials management may focus on supplier incoming part quality, which supports 1st-time manufacturing quality. Inventory management is responsible for maintaining part quality while the part is in storage or being transported. This supports maintaining the supplier's incoming part quality levels. All of these actions directly support the physical quality of the product.

At each strategy level, the "information" product which supports the physical product is equally as important. This refers to having accurate plans, schedules, bills of material, routings, process instructions, and so on. All of the elements which support them are included as well, such as accurate part counts, accurate part records, and having reliable equipment and processes. All of these support elements are an integral part of each lower level strategy and directly relate to their mission.

The value of inventory analyses with respect to establishing quantified targets and relevant performance measures cannot be overemphasized. A structured approach replaces someone's good intentions with an understanding of the relevant policy, planning and control interrelationships. Analyses are essential to an integral inventory strategy because they provide the foundation for agreement

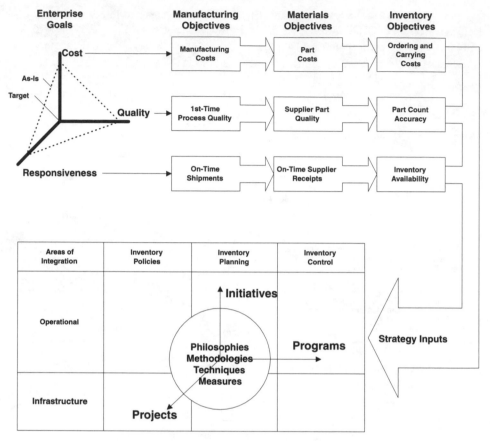

Figure 2.2   Goal Setting is a Top-Down Process

among the various departments responsible for quantifying and achieving the company's inventory-related targets.

QUANTIFYING PERFORMANCE VIA ANALYSES, MODELS, AND SIMULATIONS

Performance management encompasses elements of time and quantifiable improvement within each area of integration. Requirements set by the integral strategy establish the quantifiable relationships. The strategy schedule defines the time element, subject to the rate at which the company can support change. Requirements, time, and capabilities can all be evaluated by the three computer-based tools available to any company: analysis, modeling, and simulation. The ability to quickly create and evaluate alternate scenarios is the key to strategy development.

The term "analysis paralysis" refers to overanalyzing to the point where no action actually occurs. It also refers to analyzing beyond the point where the added accuracy provides an equivalent added value. There is often no way short of perfect hindsight to pinpoint when an analysis turns into "paralysis." With any analysis, therefore, the most effective control is to ensure that the proper tool and methodology is used. The real paralysis occurs when companies fail to commit to a course of action when they know they should.

Inventory management encompasses a variety of financial, volume, rate, and physical characteristics associated with parts, products, and company processes. As a substrategy (4th level) to Materials Management (3rd level) as illustrated in Figure 2.3, there are more quantitative and fewer qualitative elements. This pattern reverses the further up the strategy hierarchy one looks. For example, the Enterprise Strategy is concerned with broad aspects such as competitive cost, product families, programs, and product life cycles. The Inventory Strategy encompasses part-specific costs, methodologies, techniques, and scheduling time frames. This reduces the subjectiveness of any inventory-related analyses.

Inventory Performance-Related Analyses and Models

The enterprise strategy cost goal is probably the easiest one to analyze. However, all three of the enterprise goals have cost attributes. This means that any cost-related analysis effort must consider the quality and responsiveness elements of cost as well. This also means that the quality goal has responsiveness elements and that the responsiveness goal has quality elements. Figure 2.4 illustrates part of the

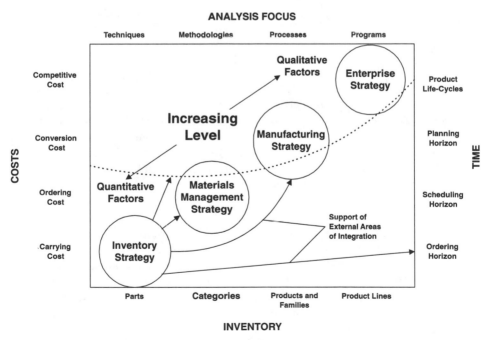

Figure 2.3   Relationship of Strategic Level to Structured Analysis

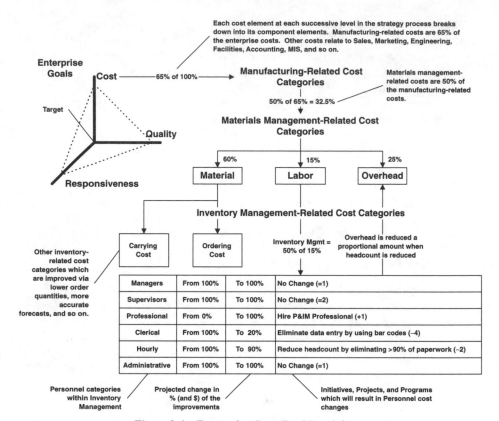

Figure 2.4   Enterprise Cost Goal Breakdown

path used by inventory management to identify cost savings related to personnel. Note that some of the personnel savings in Figure 2.4 come from bar coding (minus four clerical personnel) and reduced paperwork through the use of systems (minus two hourly personnel), which is one of the quality of information elements.

Inventory accuracy is the primary inventory management quality measure (i.e., quality of information). Inventory availability in terms of customer service is the primary responsiveness measure. Inventory investment is the primary cost measure. These primary measures are supported by others in each area of integration.

Maintaining part quality once a part is in storage is not the key inventory quality measure, for example, because it has few benefits beyond supporting manufacturing's 1st-time quality goal. Achieving and sustaining 100 percent part count accuracy levels has a much broader impact on the organization because it supports development of valid plans and schedules. Ensuring 100 percent inventory availability on the required date has the same type of global impact on the organization. Inventory goal areas must, therefore, be far-reaching in terms of their benefits to the organization. They should lead to improvements in capabilities not simply resolve problems.

Once the interrelationships between the various enterprise strategy levels are defined, the objectives are further stratified into the five operational and three infrastructural areas of inventory integration. The result is a balance of proactive and reactive strategy elements which, when fleshed out with supporting initiatives, methodologies, techniques, and processes, provides a performance structure for the inventory function.

Decision Support: Analyses vs. Models vs. Simulations

There is a certain degree of similarity among analyses, models, and simulations. Each relies on a structured methodology as described in the following subsections. However, each has its own use and area of application as compared in Table 2.3. Each also applies a different set of tools and methodologies to determine a result.

Table 2.3 Comparison of Decision Support Alternatives

COMPARISON AREAS	ANALYSIS (Measures)	MODEL (Indicators)	SIMULATION (Capabilities)
Tools	Spreadsheets	Spreadsheets or Databases	Simulation Software
Inputs	- Operating Parameters - Controllable Variables - Constraints	- Policies - Cycle Time - Variability	- Volumes and Rates - Shift Profiles - Layout and Physical Constraints
Interrelationships	Equations	Functions	Distributions
Typical Application	Well-defined Issue	Generally-defined situation with snapshots of changes over a long period of time	Vehicle, operator, container, and material movement in a constrained environment over a shift or day
Example Application	AS/RS Sizing for 7 Days Supply at a given number of unit loads per production rate	Effect on Inventory Turns of reducing inventory levels over time by changing policies, reducing cycle times, and controlling variability	Material flow from AS/RS to AGV to production line work stations and return of empty dunnage under varying rates and constraint conditions
Development	Hours–Days	Days–Weeks	Weeks–Months
Deliverables(s)	Annotated Printout	Documentation, Graphs, Charts, and Tables sufficiently detailed so the Model can be rerun at a later time	Graphical simulation, video, and report

Analyses

Analyses are the simplest of the decision support tools. They provide specific answers to specific questions. By varying one or more variables within a range, the effect of inaccuracy or uncertainty can be assessed. For example, the capacity of an Automated Storage and Retrieval System (AS/RS) can be calculated and then varied by changing the aisle length, height of bin openings, overall height, and number of aisles. Given the number of unit loads per end item, a spreadsheet can be used to assess the effect on number of aisles, height of aisles, and floor space requirements given different days supply and production rates. Actual system configuration then depends upon required throughput in terms of number of dual cycles (stores and retrieves) per hour, Storage and Retrieval Machine (SRM) and conveyor system operating rates, load sizes and weights, floor space availability, and height restrictions.

Models

Models are developed in situations where companies must assess the effect (in terms of a series of snapshots) of changes over time against a baseline. They evaluate relationships which are too complex for simple analysis. Switching to rate-based from production order-based scheduling and replacing static with dynamic queue times should improve forecast accuracy since the forecast horizon shortens. More accurate forecasts reduce required safety stock levels and enable lower average inventory levels to be maintained. Dynamic scheduling reduces work in process, which in turn reduces dock-to-dock cycle times and increases inventory turns. Concurrently evaluating the effect of all of these factors on average inventory level requires the use of mathematical functions to determine interrelationships rather than simple equation-type relationships.

Modeling in terms of functions is useful for quantifying relationships which require judgement. Implementing a new ERP/MRPII/MES/WMS/WCS integrated system, for example, requires the team to relate system capabilities to the company's cost, quality, and responsiveness goals. Functions must be established which relate the system's improved decision support capabilities and timeliness of information to reductions in inventory investment, improvement in customer service level, and reduction in manpower levels. Modeling these functional relationships then enables a new system to be compared to current operations with respect to a variety of areas of improvement.

Multivariate models permit the effect of a variety of changes to be evaluated across a number of categories. The changes are varied gradually to represent how they will occur in actual operation (refer to Figure 2.5). The sequence of modeled scenarios begins by first varying parameters which are under control of inventory management. Remaining scenarios then analyze the effect of parameters under material management's, manufacturing management's, the company's, supplier's, and then customer's control. This follows the general methodology of internal followed by external integration.

Policy decisions are analyzed first since they are totally under control of each

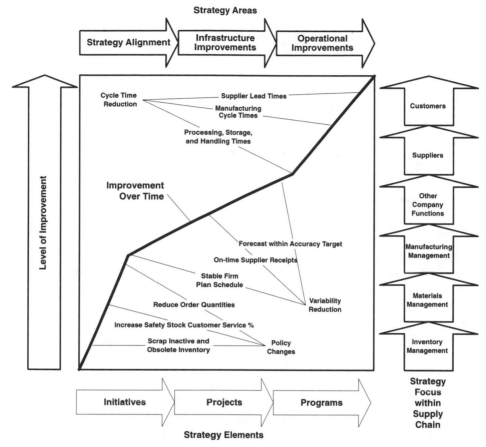

Figure 2.5 Multivariate Analyses

functional area or company. Policies apply to every area of inventory management, including stocking, order quantity, safety stock, service level percent, forecasting, and storage to name a few. Ordering material in smaller lots in containers suited for point-of-use staging rather than in bulk quantities which require centralized storage is an example of a set of interrelated policies. The ordering and stocking policies can be considered separately but will not have the desired effect unless implemented together. Note that while the intent is to establish order of magnitude improvement projections, use common sense when changing policies. If there is no possible way to economically receive every part every day, do not recommend that it be done. However, it may be of value to know what the potential for improvement would be if it were possible. Understanding potential is consistent with a 5 to 10 year vision. Understanding reality is consistent with a 1- to 2-year tactical implementation plan.

Policy improvements are followed by actions which reduce variability and the associated adverse effects on inventory. More accurate forecasts, for example, reduce the risk of stock-outs and having to carry extra safety stock. Smoothing the flow of incoming materials and leveling production rates permits more point-of-use staging and reduces the need for centralized storage. This in turn reduces handling and replenishment cycle times.

Finally, the effect of shorter lead and cycle times can be evaluated within the company's broader supply chain perspective. This is the final step since the inventory, materials, and manufacturing infrastructures must be substantially in place to support the company's, suppliers', and customers' elements of the overall cycle time. However, in actual practice, policy, variability reduction, and cycle time reduction may be implemented in any order or mix that makes business sense.

Simulations

Whereas models provide snapshots over time, simulations provide a dynamic operational view of the company's material handling and storage processes. Plant-wide simulations begin with a CAD layout of the facility. Including elevations of storage systems, conveyors, and equipment enables a 3-D effect to be produced. Actual vehicle accelerations, operating speeds, decelerations, blocking effect of traffic in aisles, work station delivery and pickup distributions, and operator or automated load/unload times can all be simulated. Changing the operating variables, altering flow paths, volumes, and rates within the facility, and changing the number or assignments of operators can be evaluated in order to fine-tune layouts, equipment, and personnel levels.

Simulations are developed in situations where the number and type of equipment may be in question, especially with regard to future upgrades and modifications. Production lines, buffer staging and storage systems, and material handling systems operating in constrained environments and subject to variation due to operator or other factors are likely candidates for simulation. A common application is to determine the number of automated guided vehicles required to deliver unit loads to work stations located throughout the facility. Each station may consume or produce loads at varying rates based on changes in the production profile among products or lines. Some loads may require the return of dunnage to the shipping department while others result in an empty vehicle at one place which may be dynamically assigned to new work elsewhere. To further complicate matters, station operations vary based on line rates, operator rates, lunch breaks, rail car changes which block certain aisles due to bridges being raised, and so on.

Example: Selection of the simulation software (i.e., the correct tool) can be a critical decision. One company simulated a high-volume manufacturing facility in tremendous detail. The intent was to assess changes involving synchronous delivery of materials from a central storage area directly to the various assembly lines and production markets via automated and manual means. The simulation software and hardware used were underpowered. As a result, the simulation ran four times slower than real time, making it difficult to use it as a decision tool. The value of simulation along with its ability to adequately model a future environment is in its speed. The company certainly did not gain that advantage in this application.

10-STEP ANALYSIS/MODELING METHODOLOGY

Companies commit millions of dollars in facility layout modifications, new construction, and capital equipment investment on the basis of analyses, models, and simulations. Management commits this level of investment only when convinced that the conclusions and recommendations are based on a valid representation of current and/or future conditions. While the decision-makers may not take the time to completely understand the actual mathematics and software logic, they do need to be confident that a structured methodology has been followed. They must trust the modeler.

Confidence in the modeler is complicated by the fact that no two people will ever perform an analysis or develop a model in exactly the same way. This can lead to different results based on the same requirements. Following a structured methodology is not so much to guarantee that the same results will be achieved with the same requirements, but that a valid result will be developed. Anyone who ever developed a bid spec and solicited proposals for an integrated system will attest to the fact that there is no such thing as the *single right solution*.

Even with differences, there should be a range of outputs where modelers agree. They should certainly agree on any aspect of the model which can be verified against current operations. If there are widely divergent conclusions and recommendations based on the same requirements, something is probably wrong. Having and using a structured methodology enables results to be understood, repeated, and evaluated.

The importance of graphing relationships pictorially via figures, tables, charts, and graphs cannot be overemphasized. Decision-makers trust a modeler's conclusions and recommendations more when the mathematics are translated into a visual format. This is one of the reasons why graphics-based simulations are such powerful tools.

Another commonly used technique when developing System Requirements Documents (SRDs) and bid specs is to represent flow rates via block diagrams as shown in the Functional Flow in Figure 2.6. This is a rather sterile treatment of flows and does a disservice to those readers who are not intimately familiar with the facility and analysis. To make matters worse, separate pages are often used to segregate full from empty moves and carton, tote, pallet, and rack moves. Overlaying the same flows on a facility layout as shown in the Facility Flow version makes a lot more sense. In fact, providing a feel for move distances and from/to points highlights the long moves and any reverse flows.

Developing and evaluating inventory analyses and models[1] can generally be accomplished using the following 10-step methodology:

---

1. Note that analysis and modeling use essentially the same approach. Simulation uses a similar approach but makes substantially greater use of actual layouts and distances and specific equipment and vehicle operating speeds or rates.

Functional Flow

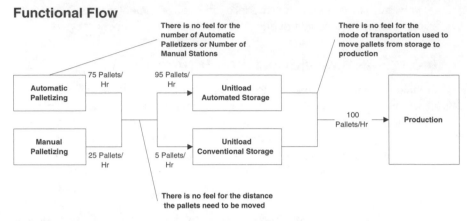

Facility Flow

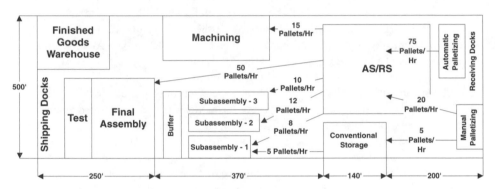

Figure 2.6   Flow Rate Representations

1. *Develop Plan*—Specify the intent of the analysis. Identify the issues and related performance or other targets to be evaluated. Document the methodology to be followed. Specify the deliverable(s). The plan should additionally identify who will provide information or evaluate results, list assumptions and their likely effect on any conclusions and recommendations, and provide a schedule and budget, as applicable.

2. *Quantify Interrelationships*—Document the order quantity, safety stock, forecasting, storage, handling, cost, rates, volumes, facility layout parameters, and other factors in the form of equations, ratios, or if/then relationships in a system requirements document. This is an approval document and must be signed off prior to actual model development if the effort involves any significant monetary outlay or third-party involvement.

3. *Obtain Source and Reference Data*—Identify the minimum amount of data which will provide the results and insight required of the analysis.

Verify its accuracy and timeliness. Source data refers to load size and weight data, as well as lead times, bill of material quantities by product, number of unit loads per production order or end item, and so on. Source data is acted upon by variables. Reference data refers to available storage cube or parameters such as aisle width minimums, ergonomic weight maximums for manual lifting, and so on. Reference data typically acts as constraints or qualifiers.

4. *Develop the Baseline Analysis/Model*—Program the analysis/model in the form of a spreadsheet or database. Incorporate as-is information as a point of reference from which to compare changes. Either add notes directly into the analysis/model, add annotations via graphics enhancements to the spreadsheet or database printout, or add handwritten notes on the print-out directly. *Do not* assume that other company personnel will understand the nuances of the results. *Tell them* what they need to understand.

5. *Validate the Analysis/Model*—Test the model using reference values. It should react in a known or anticipated way to the test data. Ideally, the results should match demonstrated results in the actual environment. Since models are based on categories, averages, minimums, maximums, and ranges, they may not be exactly correct with regard to every category, part, and every part attribute. Validation should convince the company that the analysis/model is accurately representing the situation being evaluated. Once it is, any conclusions and recommendations should be valid and reasonable as well, given the assumptions or simplifications used.

6. *Evaluate Alternative Scenarios*—Make a series of runs, varying one or more variables each time. Continue the process until the desired results have been achieved or the required magnitude of change or impact has been determined. Each run should mirror the type of changes or conditions the company is actually capable of implementing. Otherwise, the analysis/model is more of a theoretical exercise than a tool for performance improvement.

7. *Document the Results*—Append a copy of each scenario to a summary of the condition(s) being evaluated and conclusions reached. Document the sequence of improvements and changes across runs via graphs, tables, or figures. The individual runs provide detailed backup information but may not be as important as the trends over time. Mark up the printouts as required to highlight key points.

8. *Document Any Conclusions*—Assess the ability of the organization to implement the magnitude and type of changes required to achieve the inventory targets. Timing must be reasonable given the organization's resources, capabilities, and commitment. If not, incorporate timing constraints into the analysis.

9. *Specify Improvement Actions*—Identify the sequence and type of actions required to achieve the inventory-related improvements identified by the analysis process. Part of this process may involve additional data gathering or analysis, depending on the original level of detail or accuracy used. At this point, the intent is to generally establish a sequence of actions and evaluate expected results, not get into the details. That is the function of the integral strategy plan.

10. *Document the Analysis Tool*—Document the key aspects of the analysis to enable reuse or reverification at a later point in time. This includes the assumptions made, business conditions used as the basis, manufacturing rates, cycle times, product mix and volumes, and equations used. If these change over time, new data can be used if the analysis is rerun at a later point in time.

Failure of an analysis to adequately model a particular situation may not be known until after the fact. Such failures can usually be attributed to either not performing some of the preceding steps or using invalid assumptions. The most common steps either skipped or performed inadequately include Step 1 (Plan), Step 2 (Quantify), and Step 5 (Validate). Without a Plan (1), the analyst has no clear direction in terms of deliverables and approach. This translates into false starts, missed schedules, or shortcuts. Without properly understanding and quantifying relationships (2), the analyst will create an invalid model. If the model is not validated (5), the problems associated with Step 2 will not be caught. Finally, there may simply be no good way to determine if an assumption is invalid. In this case, a range of possible values must be applied in an attempt to bracket success and failure ranges.

INVENTORY ANALYSIS PARAMETERS

As a 4th-level strategy, most of the inventory management goals and objectives are derived from the higher level materials management strategy. The inventory goal areas fall within the three enterprise areas of cost, quality, and responsiveness. *Inventory cost* refers to capital investment and related operating costs, as well as actual inventory investment. *Inventory quality* refers to maintaining part quality once materials are received and quality of information data such as count accuracy, part status, and location. *Inventory responsiveness* refers to customer service level as supported by order planning, forecasting, and safety stock. Meeting inventory goals and objective targets in these areas directly supports the higher level materials management, manufacturing, and enterprise goals and objectives.

Table 2.4 identifies many of the categories and fields related to an inventory turns analysis. These are the fields requiring some type of defined parameters and relationships. Examples of the process are included in the following sections.

It is extremely important to get out into the factory before performing an analysis. One electronics company was having problems wave soldering their

Table 2.4 Inventory Targets

ENTERPRISE GOAL AREAS	INVENTORY AGGREGATE INDICATOR	TARGET AREAS	REPRESENTATIVE ANALYSIS PARAMETERS
Cost	Inventory Turns as a Function of Target Inventory Investment	Correct operating investment for customer or forecast orders and customer service target, given an acceptable measure of risk: - Operating Inventory (Orders) 　− Raw 　− WIP 　− FG - Business Inventory (Service) 　− Forecasted Inventory 　− Safety Stock 　− R&D 　− Service Parts - Financial Inventory (Risk) 　− Excess 　− Surplus 　− Inactive 　− Obsolete - MRO	Part Cost Labor Cost Overhead Rate Days Supply Order Cost Carrying Cost Setup Cost Order Quantity Safety Stock Quantity Forecast Quantity Minimum Quantity Maximum Quantity Rounding Quantity Minimum Days Supply Maximum Days Supply Price Break Quantities Price Break Prices Lead Time Storage Capacity
Quality	Inventory Accuracy as a Function of Target Count Accuracy	Count Accuracy Dollar Accuracy Location Accuracy	Risk of Inaccuracy Cost of Inaccuracy Accuracy Tolerance Count Frequency Count Duration (Hours) Control Group Causes of Inaccuracy Number of Parts by Category Number of Categories Category Characteristics Hours to Identify Problems
Responsiveness	Customer Service Level as a Function of Target Customer Service Level	Cycle Time: - Receiving - Incoming Inspection - Storage - Kitting - Production - Test - Warehousing	Customer Service Target Dock-to-Dock Cycle Times Acceptable Stock-out % Acceptable Late Dates Acceptable Line Item Shortages Acceptable Kitting Shortages Acceptable In-Process Scrap Operation Cycle Times Normal Backlog Normal Variability

Note: Refer to chapters 6–10 for details which can be used to determine parameter values.

printed circuit boards. Wave soldering is a process where the component leads are soldered to the board by running the board over a cylinder which solders the leads to the bottom of the board. Management authorized an analysis to determine the number of additional boards and component sets needed to be ordered to offset the scrap percentage. The assigned engineer inspected the stockroom to see how the boards were being stored, since the incoming inspection records indicated that the boards were acceptable upon receipt. The boxes of boards were stacked on top of each other. The stacks straddled the gap between two pallets since there was insufficient storage space. This caused the boxes to sag in the middle under their own weight, warping the printed circuit boards. As a result of that quick inspection, the operators received new instructions, and the boxes were stored properly. No safety stock required—no analysis required—end of problem.

ORDER QUANTITY (INVENTORY TURNS) ANALYSIS CONSIDERATIONS

The multimillion dollar question regarding inventory is always "how much should the company carry?" All "how much and how many" questions are candidates for analysis, modeling, or simulation. This particular question is the number one inventory issue facing any manufacturing company.

Inventory turns is universally recognized as an inventory performance-related "measure." If 100 percent of a company's inventory can be converted into products and sold, the inventory turns value indicates the number of times during the year the inventory will have to be replaced. For example, if inventory turns 12 times over the course of the year, the company will purchase or manufacture and then consume its inventory 12 times. This is strictly a dollar measure, since some parts will *turn* on an hourly, daily, weekly, monthly, quarterly, or longer basis. Inactive and obsolete inventory does not turn at all.

Inventory turns is more appropriately an indicator of performance, as opposed to a measure. An increase in turns may indicate an improvement in performance if it is the result of requiring a lower average inventory level to support a given level of sales. However, there is no guarantee that an increase in inventory turns means that overall operations and competitiveness are improving. It is possible for an appearance of improvement to be achieved through nonperformance-related actions.

For example, a 2 percent increase in inventory turns does not necessarily mean that 2 percent worth of operational improvements has occurred. The 2 percent may be lost as fast as it was gained if it is due to normal variability within the business. Also, what often happens is that the increase in turns comes at the expense of operational effectiveness. For example, any increase achieved by arbitrarily reducing operational inventory below the necessary level while maintaining excess, surplus, inactive, and obsolete levels provides a misleading indication of improvement. Continuing the same death-spiral tactics will only worsen the company's customer service level.

Conversely, increasing turns by scrapping obsolete inventory has no real impact on operational effectiveness. Therefore, an improvement in inventory turns in the short term is only an indicator of performance. The improvement must first be sustained and then continue to improve over time due to initiatives, projects, and programs within the integral strategy. Once the improvement is maintained through normal sustaining efforts, inventory turns is a good indicator of performance.

Inventory Turns Calculation

As an indicator, inventory turns identifies a trend over time in the level of inventory on-hand to support the business. An increasing trend indicates that less inventory is required per dollar of cost of goods sold. On-hand inventory is not necessarily a measure of "required" inventory, however. Inventory turns should not be considered separately from other measures and indicators. The calculation is as follows:

$$\frac{\text{Inventory}}{\text{Turns}} = \frac{\text{Cost of Goods Sold}}{\text{Average Inventory}}$$

The Cost of Goods Sold (CGS) numerator is sometimes erroneously represented as cost of sales in the literature. This is inappropriate since companies calculate cost of sales in a variety of ways. In many companies, cost of sales is simply sales-related costs. The material, labor, and overhead used by accounting to determine product cost is, therefore, the more consistent and correct numerator.

Theoretically, average inventory is calculated as the "average" level during the time period being evaluated. What typically happens is that companies use fiscal or actual month-ending inventory level. Since this is not actually an average level, it has the effect of artificially increasing inventory turns. For example, engineer-to-order and batch-build environments may have a large inventory balance during the month to support month-end product shipments. In these environments, average inventory level during the month may be substantially higher than the month-end level (refer to Figure 2.7). Still other companies add ending inventory from the previous to the current period and then divide by two. In any event, the selected number may not represent a true daily average at all. The selection of when to determine average inventory is the primary way inventory turns is manipulated.

Within an integral environment, inventory turns must be based on the company's true average inventory level. This could be determined by adding the inventory level remaining at the end of each day and dividing by the number of days per month. Not using an accurate average can adversely affect business decisions made on the basis of inventory turns. For example, storage requirements may be based on inventory turns. If an artificially low month-end number is used, the company may end up with insufficient storage capacity. Handling and storage costs will increase because of the related inefficiencies. A month-end number

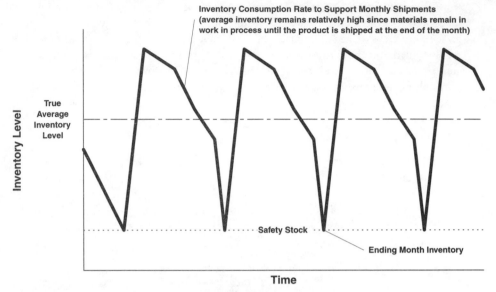

Figure 2.7   Average Inventory Timing Affects the Inventory Turns Calculation

may need to be factored or not used at all if it is too low for certain facility-planning decisions.

Note that Maintenance, Repair, and Operating Supplies (MRO) are excluded from the inventory turns calculation. These materials are usually considered as expense items. This means that they are purchased against a departmental budget and are not charged against specific orders as they are used. Even though inventory records may be maintained, MRO materials are not considered raw material. Only inventory included on the product's bill of material should be considered part of cost of goods sold.

Inventory Turns Deviation from Target

Inventory turns provides an indication of change over time. What it does not provide is an indication of how close current performance is to target performance. There is no indication of the magnitude of improvement required. An integral strategy uses a slightly different inventory turns indicator in order to identify the deviation from target.

The magnitude of improvement is established by comparing target CGS and target average inventory with actual CGS and actual average inventory. This results in an inventory turns deviation from target percent calculation as follows:

$$\text{Inventory Turns Deviation from Target} = \frac{(\text{Actual Turns} - \text{Target Turns})}{(\text{Target Turns})} \times 100\%$$

When target inventory turns equals actual inventory turns, the inventory turns deviation from target is 0 percent. This is the objective. The value to a company of using a "deviation from target" indicator is that it is consistent. Target inventory turns changes over time. The deviation percent remains consistent—0 percent is always the target.

A negative deviation percent identifies the magnitude by which the company has missed the target. A company achieving 4 turns with a target of 20 is below target by 80 percent, calculated as $(4 - 20)/20 \times 100\% = -80\%$. A positive value indicates the degree by which actual turns exceeds the target (e.g., $(21 - 20)/20 \times 100\% = +5\%$). A positive measure may indicate that performance is ahead of schedule. It may also indicate that inventory levels are too low. If so, there is a risk of not achieving target customer service levels. Therefore, a positive deviation from target is not necessarily a good thing. If performance is really ahead of schedule, a new target should be established.

Setting the Inventory Turns Target

There is no quick way to establish the "right" inventory investment target. Inventory investment is one of the cost elements of the enterprise strategy. The level itself is based on the level of business, customer buying patterns, marketing lead times, manufacturing cycle times, customer service target, and so on. Essentially, the level is set in relationship to other investment categories. Senior management is responsible for setting these levels.

Setting the target level does not happen in a vacuum, though. The company knows the current level. Management can probably also approximate their competitor's level knowing their market share and cost structure. The cost structure can be estimated via reverse-engineering techniques knowing parts, approximate material costs, lead times, and sell price.

With this as an introduction, companies still struggle with setting the investment and turns target. There is no such thing as the "right" amount. Should it be double or triple the current value? Should it be an order of magnitude improvement? Suppose current turns are five turns per year. Doubling provides a 10 turns target. Is this number any better than a 9.9 or a 10.1 target if none of them has any real basis for selection? Probably not. Therefore, setting arbitrary targets is more likely to be found with traditional strategies.

With integral strategies, targets are set within the modeling process itself. They are not an arbitrary selection. The process is closed loop and iterative. The focus is on achieving stepwise improvements. This consists of defining a series of actions the company is actually capable of performing and a target which indicates when the improvement has been achieved. The targets are aggressive. Anything less does not force the company to consider radical approaches to improvement (radical for the company, perhaps, not necessarily for the competition).

Inventory Turns Model

An inventory turns model essentially evaluates the effect of changes over time. The analyst begins by establishing inventory categories based on a similarity of reaction to business conditions. A variety of changes is then evaluated with regard to how they affect these inventory categories. The key to believing the results is to know that the company is capable of implementing the changes being modeled.

The inventory turns analysis must, therefore, integrate the level of required improvement with the company's ability to achieve the improvement. Improvement is accomplished by actions in three areas. The first is order quantity, safety stock, and forecasting policy changes. These are under the company's control. The second is in variability reduction due to forecast inaccuracy or processes and procedures which result in excess inventory levels. These areas are partially under the company's control. The third is in lead or cycle time reductions related to supplier lead times and dock-to-dock processing, handling, and storage activities. These are areas which require cooperation between the company and their suppliers and customers. Any changes in these three areas must be something that can be realistically expected given the company's operational, organizational, and technology infrastructure. Any discrepancy between target and achievable performance must be quantified as part of the analysis process. The result provides tactical direction for the inventory strategy in terms of areas and magnitude of improvement.

Table 2.5 identifies accounting-related subcategories for the inventory turns analysis. These Raw, WIP, and FG categories lend themselves to further breakdown by operating, business, and financial inventory considerations. These categories represent a similarity of response with respect to policy, time, and variability actions and reactions. The current level of inventory represents the "baseline."

Table 2.5 Integral Inventory Strategy Subcategories

INVENTORY CATEGORY	OPERATING INVENTORY	BUSINESS INVENTORY	FINANCIAL INVENTORY

RAW	Allocated Parts
	Kitted Parts
	MS Planned
		Planned Safety Stock
		Service Parts and
		  Materials
		R&D Parts and Materials
		Price Break Quantities
			Excess
			Surplus
			Inactive
			Obsolete
			Inspection Pending Acceptance
			Reject Pending Disposition
			Partial Kits Held Due to
			  Shortages

WIP	Released Kits Parts in Queue Parts in Process Parts Being Moved Products in Inspect/Test	Emergency Float Repair Materials	Parts Held for Repair Subassemblies Held for Repair

FG	Stock Waiting
	Shipment
		In-Plant Finished Goods
		Warehouse Finished
		  Goods
			Returned Goods Waiting
			  Disposition
			Lifetime Build (for phased-out
			  parts)

Operating Inventory includes any on-hand balances required to support current production. This may be based on days supply, materials purchased or manufactured for actual customer orders, and so on. The definition of "current" varies by product and part. Operating inventory represents allocated inventory or inventory where there is a high confidence level of being used in the near future. Policy changes and cycle time reductions specifically focus on the operational inventory portion of total inventory.

Business Inventory includes discretionary balances kept on-hand to maintain target customer service levels, to support R&D activities, or to optimize the costs associated with procuring and carrying inventory. Inventory procured on the basis of a forecast, dependent-, or independent-demand safety stock, and service parts stocked to support the existing customer base are the primary components of business inventory. The inventory level is largely a function of the difference between manufacturing and marketing lead times. Cycle time and variability reduction specifically focus on the business inventory portion of total inventory.

Financial Inventory is considered a company asset for financial accounting purposes, but not by manufacturing, materials management, inventory management, or the customers. It generally includes all excess, surplus, inactive, and obsolete inventory. Companies establish these inventory categories as shown in Figure 2.8 based on their own environment. The following definitions and time frames are representative, with each category representing a range in time based

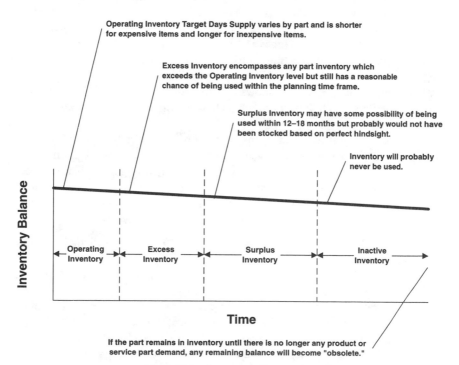

Figure 2.8   Inventory Categories

on days supply including on-hand and on-order inventory. The ranges are policy variables set by accounting, with input from engineering based on product life-cycles and sales and marketing, customer service, and inventory management based on forecasted usage. While it is easiest to use the same time frames for all parts, it is more correct to use time frames appropriate to the part. Time frames should be set shorter for products with short lifetimes and longer for stable products with requirements for service parts support. For example:

- *Excess Inventory* is defined as any inventory balance greater than the operating and business level which is expected to be used within 12 months. The actual time frame may be set based on the planning horizon.

- *Surplus Inventory* is defined as any inventory balance which is expected to be used within the 12–18 month time frame.

- *Inactive Inventory* is defined as any inventory balance which has no real expectation of being used.

- *Obsolete Inventory* is defined as any inventory which is no longer used by the company. Inventory becomes obsolete when product lines are phased out, when one part supersedes another, or when a part is eliminated from the product design.

With subcategory turns calculations, the effect of small operational changes in a particular area can be evaluated. These include changes which might be inconsequential in magnitude when compared to total inventory value. Having separate indicators prevents changes in one area from having the appearance of positively or negatively affecting another. For example, scrapping obsolete inventory reduces average inventory value and increases turns. Using a separate financial turns category clearly shows that the improvement was a one-time occurrence and not due to any operational changes which may be in process at the same time.

With an integral strategy, the focus is on improving operating inventory turns. This constitutes the bulk of the inventory investment. The emphasis is on reducing the days supply. As improvements are made in operating inventory, business inventory (primarily safety stock) improves as well. What is left over is financial inventory, which the company needs to scrap or sell. Operating, business, and financial turns are calculated using their portion of total inventory.

Example: Consider a Cost of Goods Sold of $40,000,000 and the inventory categories shown following.

The $4,000,000 in Operating Inventory is allocated to current orders. The Business Inventory covers materials required to service the existing customer base, forecasted orders, and new product development. Mathematically, this equates to a 7.8 weeks supply ([$6,000,000/$40,000,000] × 52 weeks). Adding business to operating inventory reduces turns from 10.0 to 6.7. Financial Inventory carries a significant percentage of the total inventory and reduces inventory turns from 6.7 to 4.4.

TURNS SUBCATEGORY	INVENTORY CATEGORY	AVERAGE INVESTMENT	CATEGORY TURNS	CUMULATIVE TURNS
Operating Inventory	Production Raw Kit WIP FG for Customer Orders	2,000,000 400,000 1,400,000 200,000	@ $4,000,000 = 10	10.0
Business Inventory	Production Safety Stock WIP Repair Stock Service Parts New Product Development FG for Forecast Orders	60,000 10,000 30,000 100,000 1,800,000	@ $2,000,000 = 20	6.7
Financial Inventory	Excess Surplus Inactive Obsolete	1,500,000 1,000,000 0 500,000	@ 3,000,000 = 13.3	4.4
Average Inventory		$9,000,000		4.4

If $38,000,000 of the $40,000,000 Cost of Goods Sold is due to operating inventory and $2,000,000 to Business Inventory (for example), a more definitive weeks supply can be determined as:

- Operating Inventory of 5.5 Weeks Supply = $4,000,000 / $38,000,000 × 52 weeks

- Business Inventory of 52.0 Weeks Supply = $2,000,000 / $2,000,000 × 52 weeks

- Financial Inventory has an infinite Weeks Supply

A common strategy for increasing inventory turns is to receive the "production raw" A items more frequently. With the preceding example, if the A item order quantities are reduced by half, the value of the production raw A item inventory will be reduced to:

$$800,000 = $2,000,000 × 80\% \text{ A Items} × 0.5$$

This translates into an average Production Raw Material investment of $1,200,000. The operating turns rate is, therefore, 12.5 (25 percent improvement), the business turns rate is 7.7 (15 percent improvement), and the financial turns rate is 4.9 (a 10 percent cumulative improvement compared to 4.4). Increasing receipt frequency has a positive effect on inventory turns. However, *all* categories of inventory must be systematically reduced if the intent is to *significantly* increase turns.

The inventory system should provide a tool for viewing inventory turns and the inventory turns deviation from target at any time. The system should additionally enable the planner to view details, to perform "what if" calculations (sometimes erroneously referred to in the literature as simulations), and to view progress over time and targets into the future. Refer to Figure 2.9. If inventory turns is a performance indicator, it should be available to the organization's decision-makers every day.

SAFETY STOCK (CUSTOMER SERVICE) ANALYSIS CONSIDERATIONS

There is a real value in having safety stock in companies which experience demand variability. It tends to be an invisible asset, however. Very few individuals

08:00 am 07/01/YY		MGT—Inventory Turns		
Turns Category:	OPERATING	BUSINESS	FINANCIAL	TOTAL
Current Turns:	10.0	20.0	13.3	4.4
Turns Targets:	48.0	25.0	0.0	24.0
Deviation from Target:	−79%	−20%	-----	−82%
Date Target Set:	04/19/YYYY	04/19/YYYY	04/19/YYYY	04/19/YYYY
Cost of Goods Sold:	$40,000,000		Date Set:	04/19/YYYY
Formula:	(Actual Turns − Target Turns)/Target Turns × 100%			
Number of Parts:	10,000	8,900	4500	10,248
Average Inventory:	$4,000,000	$2,000,000	$3,000,000	$9,000,000
	V	V	V	V
Production Raw:	$2,000,000			
Kit:	$ 400,000			
Work In Process (WIP):	$1,400,000			
FG for Customer Orders:	$ 200,000			$4,000,000
Production Safety Stock:		$ 60,000		
WIP Repair Stock:		$ 10,000		
Service Parts:		$ 30,000		
New Product Development:		$ 100,000		
FG for Forecast Orders:		$1,800,000		$2,000,000
Excess Inventory:			$1,500,000	
Surplus Inventory:			$1,000,000	
Obsolete Inventory:			$ 500,000	$3,000,000
DETAILS	HISTORY	FUTURE	WHAT-IF	MODIFY

Note that the total Number of Parts is not the sum of the operating, business, and financial parts since some parts appear in multiple categories.

Figure 2.9   Inventory Turns Deviation from Target Screen

even know when safety stock is used or to what extent. The only indication that safety stock has been used is when an actual stock-out affects what they are scheduled to work on. The design of the inventory system should track not only the safety stock quantity, but also the value of having safety stock with regard to planning and scheduling flexibility and accuracy.

Safety stock supports the company's customer service target. Service in an integral environment consists of the elements shown in Table 2.6 in the Customer Perspective column. Note that a representative Company Perspective column is included for comparison. These are the perspectives which the company may be taking as part of their traditional approach and which are, therefore, candidates for change as part of the integral strategy.

The odds of having sufficient lead time to order all required materials and manufacture the product after receipt of order are higher for project and engineer-to-order companies than for assemble-to-order or make-to-stock companies. The company must forecast demand for some or all of the parts in environments where quoted marketing delivery lead times are less than the cumulative lead time. Cumulative lead time refers to the manufacturing time plus

Table 2.6   Representative Customer Service Elements

SERVICE ELEMENT	INVENTORY MANAGEMENT AND CUSTOMER PERSPECTIVE (INTEGRAL STRATEGY)	COMPANY PERSPECTIVE (TRADITIONAL STRATEGY)
On-Time Shipment or Delivery	Requested Ship/Required Date	Acknowledged Ship Date
Correct Part	Required Part	Ordered or Alternate (Equivalent or Better) Part
Correct Quantity	Exact Required Quantity	Required Quantity (+/– a Tolerance for Some Parts, Rounding Quantity, Minimum Quantity)
Correct Method of Shipment	As Specified or Required	As Specified or Required to Ensure Delivery Date
Correct Material Identification	Required Part Identification (by Customer or Industry Standard Identification)	Required Identification for Revision Control and Reordering
Correct Paperwork	Packing Slips and Required Certifications	Same
Correct Container	Requested Container Type (as applicable for Returnable Dunnage and/or Ergonomic Handling Requirements)	Suitable Container for Quantity and Part Protection
Correct Quality	100% Conformance to Incoming Inspection or Usage Requirements	Acceptable Quality Level (Varies by Part)
Correct Delivery Location	Specific Dock Location or Door	Same
Response Time for Information	Immediately Upon Request	Within Same Day of Request

longest lead time part as back-scheduled from its required date. In Figure 2.10, this includes any parts with lead times longer than six weeks. The choice of how much safety stock to carry then becomes a management policy decision based on forecast accuracy and customer service level.

Increased safety stock or safety lead time is intended to improve customer service levels by limiting the number of stock-outs within a given number of opportunities for stock-out. Chapter 10 Safety Stock covers the mathematical relationships used to balance the risk of stock-outs with the order quantity, forecast error, and safety stock service level percent. A safety stock (customer service) analysis balances the amount of required investment against the value the company places on providing a given level of service.

The planner has a choice among three basic alternatives when performing a safety stock analysis. The first alternative is to establish individual part safety stock quantities based on statistical, fixed, or time-period techniques (refer to Chapter 10, Safety Stock, for additional details). This requires setting a safety stock level for each part independent of any product relationships and is most appropriate for independent-demand parts. The second alternative involves establishing the value of having safety stock by product or product line and then allocating the cost among the various parts in order to provide a consistent level of protection. This is referred to as overplanning at the MS level and is most appropriate for dependent-demand parts. Both of these alternatives establish a customer service level and then calculate the quantity of safety stock required. The third alternative is to set an arbitrary dollar level for safety stock investment. This value is then allocated among parts via one of the two methods described previously. Allocation is used in situations where the amount of money available to in-

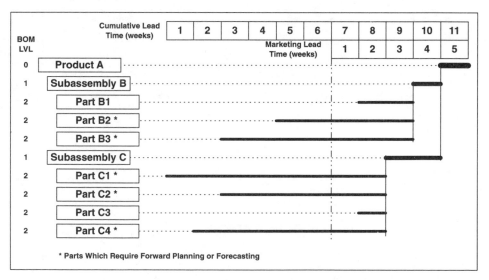

Figure 2.10   Forecasting is a Function of Cumulative vs. Marketing Lead Time

vest in safety stock is limited. Customer service level then becomes the *result* in this case, rather than the target.

CYCLE COUNTING (INVENTORY ACCURACY) ANALYSIS CONSIDERATIONS

Manufacturing cannot substitute one part's excess dollars for another part's shortage dollars and build a product. Dollar accuracy does not mean count accuracy. However, count accuracy does ensure dollar accuracy. Therefore, assuring inventory accuracy means assuring count accuracy.

If inventory by count is not 100 percent accurate, it is inaccurate. The goal of any inventory accuracy program, project, or initiative, therefore, is to achieve 100 percent inventory accuracy of 100 percent of the parts 100 percent of the time. Dollar accuracy based on the net of overages and shortages gives the appearance of accuracy without the benefits of actually having the quantities the computer specifies. This view of inventory accuracy is one of the significant differences between integral and traditional strategies.

The purpose of a cycle counting analysis is twofold. The first is to identify the cost to the company of implementing a cycle counting program designed to achieve and sustain a 100 percent accuracy level by count. The second is to identify the savings or cost avoidance of not having to count in the first place once count accuracy is sustained at a 100 percent level. Whereas the counting process is a reaction to inaccuracy, the cost of implementing a returnable dunnage program, using bar codes, and standardizing on order and container quantities are all proactive efforts targeted at eliminating the possibility of having an inaccurate count in the first place.

The characteristics assessed via a cycle counting analysis include the following cost and cost tradeoff elements:

Operating Cost—What is the cost of the program, considering time to count, number of counts per day, and time to resolve discrepancies? Stockroom personnel time is calculated as Number of Counts × Time to Count. The duration allotted per day determines the number of stockroom personnel required. For example, 60 counts/day × 8 minutes/count to be performed in a 1-hour time frame each day requires eight stockroom operators. Time for planners to resolve discrepancies is a less tangible calculation and should be based on the company's actual experience.

Cost Avoidance—What is a representative cost of an unplanned stock-out due to a count discrepancy which creates the need to expedite materials or reschedule production? How many times do such situations occur? Time to expedite unplanned stock-outs should be based on actual experience. The cost to reschedule production is a less tangible factor and lends itself to a range of values for analysis purposes.

Infrastructure Investment—Can the operating cost and cost avoidance savings be applied to standard containers or improved processes and procedures in order to reduce or eliminate the need to cycle count? At some point, the cost of one or more full-time individuals strictly involved with countering the effects of inventory inaccuracy can be better applied elsewhere according to a traditional strategy. An integral strategy says any such cost can be applied better elsewhere.

The cycle counting analysis identifies the costs to meet the objective of 100 percent count accuracy via reactive methods as a comparison to meeting the objectives through proactive initiatives. Reactive methods include cycle counting every day in order to correct mistakes after the fact. Proactive initiatives eliminate the need to count by eliminating the possibility of a count error in the first place. This topic is covered in more detail in Chapter 6, Zero-Tolerance Inventory Count Accuracy.

CYCLE TIME (FLOW RATE) ANALYSIS CONSIDERATIONS

A significant portion of dock-to-dock cycle time is the result of inventory-related processing, handling, and storage. To the extent that reductions in inventory cycle times can be translated into reduced dock-to-dock cycle time, overall customer responsiveness improves. The analysis needs to balance the ability to reduce inventory-related cycle times with the ability of manufacturing to reduce overall production times.

The inventory portion of dock-to-dock cycle time generally encompasses receiving, incoming inspection (as applicable), and storage, handling, and processing times.

Receiving time includes actual truck or rail unloading, receipt processing, and discrepancy resolution. Discrepancies are typically related to either the shipping manifest (manifest does not match the number of containers delivered) or the packing slip (packing slip information identifying what is included in the carton does not match the actual material and/or quantity received). Either type of discrepancy will cause a mismatch when accounting processes the supplier's invoice. For automotive, distribution centers, and other high-volume operations, the time material sits in trailers or shipping containers waiting to be unloaded may also need to be considered. The first thing to check is whether the company's ERP or MRPII system has a fixed length of time in the lead time program for receiving. One day is commonly used, but less time is typically experienced.

Incoming Inspection time typically includes the actual inspection time as well as queue time. Some companies inspect materials the same day they are received while others seem to run a perpetual backlog. After the purchase order receipt is processed, those materials requiring inspection or test are moved to the inspection staging area or visually identified (e.g., via a colored tag) to ensure that they are not moved to storage. At this point, the materials have been received but are not part of raw material inventory since they may fail incoming inspection or test. MRP considers the material as being "in-plant but unavailable."

Storage may or may not be performed the same day the inventory is received. Raw material inventory is not typically updated until the material is actually stored and the storeroom receipt is processed. Since storage duration usually represents the longest portion of inventory-related cycle time, reducing storage duration has the highest return on any cycle time reduction efforts. Many companies have a mix of parts which bypass storage and are issued directly to Work in Process or Finished Goods inventory.

Techniques for shortening cycle times include using bar codes and radio frequency terminals to shorten identification and transaction processes, bypassing centralized storage and routing materials directly to the point-of-use, purchasing materials from certified suppliers and eliminating incoming inspection, and reducing order quantities. Other techniques can be applied once material is issued to Work in Process such as rate-based scheduling and in-line layouts to reduce the time from order release to order completion.

Performing a forecasting lead and cycle time analysis is fairly straightforward. It varies somewhat based on whether the parts being evaluated are product-related or truly independent. A product-related analysis takes the cumulative lead times of all of the parts by bill of material level and compares the longest duration against the target (or marketing) lead time for the product. For example, marketing may quote a 5-week lead time to customers for a product which has an 11-week cumulative lead time. Any parts which cannot be procured, fabricated, or assembled within five weeks must be forecasted and stocked against the expectation of orders. The longer the forecast duration, the greater the risk that the forecast will be inaccurate. This topic is represented in Figure 2.10. The intent of a cycle time analysis is to shorten these long lead times and reduce the need to forecast. A part-related analysis is similar, only without the contribution of other parts to lead time.

The planner begins the cycle time analysis process by documenting the As-Is baseline in terms of the various elements of lead time as illustrated in Figure 2.11. A lead time reduction assessment is then performed to identify ways to shorten each element and to set targets for improvement. Achieving these targets may involve policy, procedural, equipment, technology, facility, supplier, or other changes. For example, the company may have established lead time parameters in ERP/MRPII based on one week for supplier shipping, three days for receiving and inspection, and two days for storage and handling. Streamlining logistics in order to recognize an actual 2-day shipping duration and a 1-day receipt-to-storage target duration reduces the forecasting time by seven days. The first place to look for lead time reductions is in the parameters used by the ordering and scheduling software.

The greatest opportunity for cycle time reduction is typically through shorter manufacturing cycle times. The extent of the opportunity can be generally determined by subtracting the industrial engineering product manufacturing time from the demonstrated or planning production elapsed time. Determining the actual duration which can be reduced then requires an in-depth understanding of the manufacturing process. Areas to consider include production/work order

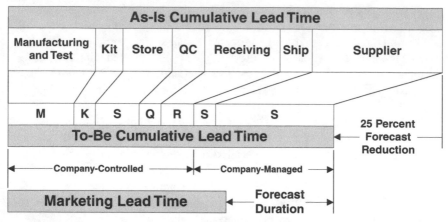

Figure 2.11   Cycle Time Analysis

quantity reductions (which reduce queue times), replacement of "canned" queue, wait, and move times (by using projected or calculated times based on the actual work load), separation of internal and external setup times, and reduced run times through use of higher throughput equipment or splitting lots among multiple machines.

STORAGE (STORAGE UTILIZATION) ANALYSIS CONSIDERATIONS

Increased storage utilization makes more effective use of space. Having the right type of storage system also improves handling and storage processes. Increasing storage density may also make additional space available for production or enable materials to be stored closer to the point of use where space is at a premium. The analysis needs to balance the space required for various storage and staging alternatives with the cost of facilities, equipment, systems, and labor. The deciding factor is the ability of each type of system to support production. The basic issues are use of centralized versus distributed storage or staging and the technologies used.

The storage utilization analysis considers the following:

Eliminate storage which is not required. Excess storage capacity attracts excess material. One company installed a separate storeroom to separate surplus and inactive from production materials. This made available a considerable number of storage locations in the other storerooms for a while. With the extra storage space, it became unnecessary to regularly dispose of materials no longer needed by the company. The other storerooms were full again in less than a year with no increase in business.

Standardize load quantities and container types. Storage locations are fixed in size. It costs the same whether the company stores air or material. Standardizing quantities and container types enables the company to size and locate storage as most appropriate for each part. Standardization also makes it easier to implement automatic ID, storage, and handling processes.

Implement "market" buffer areas (see Chapter 12) for materials which will benefit from visual storage techniques. This ensures that an exact amount of storage is provided based on days supply, container size, and capacity.

Automate storage to make effective use of floor space and available storage height. With maximum flexibility systems designed to enable any load to be stored in any location, a partial pallet with one small box takes up as much space as a full pallet. The alternative is to stratify inventory by location height to improve utilization.

In general, storage capacity for a part must account for the maximum receipt quantity plus the on-hand quantity at the time of receipt (generally the safety stock quantity). A safety factor then accommodates early receipts or lower production rates. Additional storage is then required for Work in Process (as applicable) and Finished Goods. Storage space must also account for aisles, runout distance for the storage and retrieval machine at the end of the aisle with an AS/RS, conveyors, laydown area, work stations, control cabinets, charger locations, and projected expansion requirements.

For example, an automotive assembly plant uses an average of 2.5 unit loads (pallets) from the AS/RS per job/order. With an additional but similar production line being installed, an assumption of a similar relationship may be made. The storage baseline is then calculated as Days Supply × Jobs per Day × Unit Loads/Job, with a safety factor divisor of 0.85 for peak demands. A 7-Days Supply × 1,000 Jobs/Day × 2.5 Loads/Job/0.85 = 20,589 storage locations required. This calculation was validated by knowing the number of storage locations currently required to support production. Such an analysis needed to incorporate factors to reflect a planned reduction in Days Supply through Just in Time (In-line Vehicle Sequence—ILVS) receipts of certain parts (resulting in the need for fewer centralized storage locations) and increased parts standardization among product lines (resulting in fewer than 2.5 Unit Loads/Job for the new operation).

SUMMARY

People do that on which they get measured. That is a fact of life. In the absence of published measures, they either do what they believe they are measured on, what they believe is right, or simply what they want to do. An integral strategy removes individual initiative and creativity from the performance measuring process. A top-down process progressively translates goals at the enterprise level to objectives and targets at the inventory management level. A bottom-up process then ensures that achieving the targets will support the higher level materials management, manufacturing, and enterprise goals. The company needs measures which directly relate to the areas of performance and which are resistant to manipulation. Personnel need to understand how their performance contributes toward the achievement of improved performance and how it will be measured.

Analyses, models, and simulations tools permit the company to relate performance measures to performance requirements. They enable company personnel to progressively assess the effect of changes over time on storage and handling requirements and organizational, facilities and equipment, and systems and technology-related areas.

Analyses, models, and simulations are as good as the information upon which they are based. The analyst is responsible for accurately modeling the appropriate relationships in a manner which enables conclusions to be reached and recommendations to be made. Management is responsible for ensuring that the analyst is provided with complete and valid information. Both are responsible for understanding where to draw the line based on the level of detail and how much time and effort to expend.

Each tool has its area of application. Analyses provide specific answers to specific questions. They are useful for defining measures and targets at part, workstation, product, and other specific levels of detail. Models provide snapshots of interrelationships over time against a baseline. They establish the broader relationships across inventory categories, the five Operational Areas of Integration, and the three Inventory Management Policy, Planning, and Control areas. Models are used in situations requiring aggregate measures and indicators. Simulations provide a dynamic view of handling, storage, and manufacturing processes over a shift or day. They enable the company to test various scenarios in order to identify bottlenecks and evaluate alternative equipment, vehicles, and layouts on overall performance.

In an integral environment, performance is calculated as the deviation of performance from target. This focuses attention on the target itself and the degree of deviation. Instead of figuring out how to get from 90 to 91 percent of a 100 percent target, the company focuses on how to minimize the 10 percent deviation from target. Focusing on the deviation from target as opposed to incremental improvements as measured from current performance is one of the areas which differentiates integral from more traditional strategies.

Every company has an appropriate level of inventory. The problem is not in figuring out what it is. There are analyses, models, and simulations which can do this. The problem is in determining how to change those things the company is either doing or not doing which is preventing the target inventory level from being achieved and sustained, with zero-deviation from target. This is where the business case gets established.

Chapter 3

Integral Strategy Development Methodology

The complexity of the integral inventory strategy mirrors manufacturing complexity. The greater the degree of change and variability in the environment, the more complex the strategy. Company CEOs faced with such environments can choose to implement strategies which thrive on such conflict (and in turn create further conflict) or attempt to maintain the status quo.

Maintaining the status quo is accomplished via traditional strategies structured to minimize conflict. The focus is on performing order, safety stock, and forecasting planning incrementally more effectively each year. Incremental improvements focus on the policies, planning, and control inventory areas of integration since these fall within the scope of the inventory department. Traditional strategies have a 1-year time span with respect to performance improvements. This limits the vision which guides initiatives, projects, and programs to at most a 1- to 2-year time frame.

A traditional strategy is essentially a rut. The company is admitting that they cannot do much better and so must maintain their current level of performance. Once this rut becomes so ingrained in the company's operating mentality, even the possibility of achieving significant improvements is no longer seriously considered. Companies only get out of the rut when some compelling need forces management to question their basic beliefs and approaches. The most likely time when this occurs is when someone asks the question "Why . . ." and everyone realizes that the answer "because . . . " ends with all of the reasons "why not."

At some point in a company's capital investment, a point is reached where the resulting infrastructure becomes integral to the business. This means that the combination of technologies, philosophies, methodologies, techniques, and attitudes becomes greater than the sum of their parts and inseparable as a result. In other words, failure of the integral system as a result of a failure of any of its integral elements results in loss of productivity, production, and profits. This type of infrastructure does not happen by accident. It takes a formal strategy to provide the vision. Both formal and informal elements within initiatives, projects, and programs then provide the execution.

A traditional inventory strategy is based on a *reaction* to the previous year's performance. This year's targets are based on a percentage improvement over those from the previous year. This differs from an integral inventory strategy which is actually a reaction to the company's historical approach to the competitive environment. An integral strategy addresses the company's need to change, not simply the magnitude of change. What happened last year is not as relevant as what needs to happen this year and in future years.

This chapter addresses the methodology used to develop an integral inventory strategy. Key points include:

- *The "Voice" of the Customer* and how the environment affects the inventory strategy.

- *10-Step Methodology* for developing an integral inventory strategy, with emphasis on the need for a structured approach employing internal and external checks and balances.

- *Strategy Plan* format, with brief discussions of each section. The plan provides a link between the strategy itself and the project management methodologies and techniques (refer to Chapter 4, Project Management is the Management of Interrelationships) required for effective implementation.

Strategy development is a methodology. As such, no two individuals will ever develop a strategy plan the same way. This chapter provides an approach based on an integration methodology. Do not confuse the plan with the strategy. The plan is developed and documented. The strategy is implemented.

COMMON MANAGEMENT-CREATED PROBLEMS TO AVOID

An integral strategy creates internal conflict because choices must be made. No company has all of the resources necessary to do everything that needs to be done. This creates a risk of failure if the conflict cannot be resolved, if the wrong priorities are established, or if the wrong decisions are made. An integral strategy process, therefore, recognizes that at least the following management problem areas must be addressed. These are the types of misdirection which can occur if the strategy development process is treated in a traditional instead of an integral manner.

Management often overestimates the accuracy and relevancy of available data and documentation. As a consequence, the schedule does not include sufficient time to perform a comprehensive requirements definition and analysis process. Data tends to be a great predictor of the past and is in plentiful supply in the host system history files. Historical data, however, is more relevant to the development of a traditional strategy since targets are based on incremental improvements compared to the past. Development of an integral strategy requires up-to-date and forecasted business information of the type not commonly available in history files. Developing and verifying this information takes time. Having historical data is not as important as having business, customer, competitor, equipment, system, and technology-related assessments. Management must recognize that a consolidation and translation process is inevitably required in order to establish a knowledge base for strategy-related decision-making.

Management often bases schedules on time frames more applicable to traditional strategies since they are most familiar with this. Traditional strategy development processes are short. They need to be since each year requires a new beginning. The focus is internally oriented and restricted in scope to primarily the inventory department. Integral strategies as a comparison require six months or longer to develop. This development time frame consumes half of the duration required to implement a traditional strategy. From an integration perspective, therefore, strategy development is not considered an annual process. Once the strategy is set, only the updates are performed on an annual or as-required basis. Assessing each new technology takes months by the time suppliers and products are identified and evaluated, applications are defined, and justifications are developed. Management must set the expectations for an integral strategy time frame accordingly.

Management often fails to dedicate the required team members for the duration of the development period. Development of an integral strategy requires visionary and experienced company personnel. As such, they are also the ones who are already the most overworked. Companies need to release these individuals from their daily responsibilities. Daily firefighting and strategic planning do not mix well. Supplementing these individuals with experienced outside personnel is often a necessity. Outsiders will question things that company personnel take for granted. There is no substitute for experience. Company personnels' experience is often limited to the company itself. Often, that is too narrow a viewpoint.

Developing an integral strategy is *not,* therefore, a trivial effort. It is always complicated by the necessity to evaluate multiple solutions due to cost, schedule, product, process, geographic, governmental, technology, competitive, and other factors. There is never[1] only one alternative or approach. In short, there are always choices.

The Inventory Strategy Must Reflect the "Voice of the Customer"

Traditional strategies do the company a disservice when they focus on the *golden rule.* The company treats their customers as they wish their suppliers would treat them. While being an admirable sentiment, this may not be what their customers want. An integral strategy focuses on the "platinum rule." The company performs as their customers wish them to perform. This means that the integral

---

1. APICS certification questions shy away from *always/never* statements on the theory that there is *always* an exception. Because strategies deal with so many issues, companies must make a number of trade-off choices. Integration is, by its very nature, a series of trade-offs.

inventory strategy must be based on the "Voice of the Customer." This is not restricted to the external customers either. It includes all of the various internal customers and suppliers that support and are supported by the inventory management function.

The difficult task for any company with respect to the "Voice of the Customer" is to recognize it when they hear it. Companies do not have to listen very hard when their customers tell them what they want in the form of a purchase order, RFQ, or specification. It becomes much more difficult to hear the customer when they talk with their actions, such as buying from a competitor. Internal customers may be no easier to hear either. Some people will not speak up unless asked. Others feel so frustrated that they may not volunteer anything constructive even when asked. Inventory management needs to learn how to listen to all of the customers.

All of the areas in Table 3.1 are addressed by the enterprise, manufacturing management, and materials management strategies. Elements of each must also be addressed in inventory-related terms in order to properly support the higher level strategies and those of the other functional areas. These are discussed in a general fashion in the following subsections.

Strategic Drivers

Strategic market drivers generally define what customers are willing to buy and at what price. Drivers commonly consist of product design, price/performance, product availability, service responsiveness, delivery time, and system or product reliability. These and other factors vary based on type and size of customer within the market, as well as business relationship with the company. Producers serving the market respond to these drivers based on their market share or niche, product life cycle, manufacturing capabilities, financial stability, geographic area, customer base, and name recognition. Certain drivers may at times seem to override the others in terms of importance with certain customers. However, *all* must be addressed concurrently by the enterprise and functional area strategies with an appropriate level of emphasis.

Market drivers are generally categorized as order winners, order losers, order qualifiers, or order disqualifiers. Order winners are those which convince the customer to purchase a particular product, service, or system from the company, perhaps without seriously considering a competitor.[2] Order losers convince the customer to purchase from a competitor, perhaps without seriously considering the company. Price and availability, especially for consumer goods, are often the order winner or loser criteria.

In those cases where the customer makes a conscious evaluation among suppliers, order qualifiers are the factors which provide a positive impression of the product, service, or system. Order disqualifiers provide a negative impression.

---

2. This definition of order winners and qualifiers does not exactly match usage found in other literature (which in turn does not discuss order disqualifiers or losers).

Table 3.1   Competitive Characteristics of the Inventory Vision

AREAS OF INTEGRATION	STRATEGIC AREAS	STRATEGIC FACTORS	LINKAGE TO VALUE
Materials Management	Strategic Drivers	Order Winners Order Qualifiers Order Disqualifiers Order Losers	Profitability
Information Management	Manufacturing Environment	Engineer-to-Order Make or Assemble-to-Order Make or Assemble-to-Stock	Service
Product Management	Product Life Cycle	Design and Development Launch and Refinement (Introduction) Market Penetration and Acceptance (Rapid Growth) Market Stabilization and Saturation (Maturity) Phase-Out and Balance-Out (Decline)	Voice of the Customer
Process Management	Manufacturer Type	Project Job Shop Batch Line Continuous Process	Cycle Time
Quality Management	Manufacturing Focus	Product Focus Process Focus	Voice of the Company
Organizational	Structure	Hierarchical Matrix Team	Capability
Facilities and Equipment	Plant Focus	Multi- vs. Single-Plant Centralized vs. Distributed Warehousing Functional vs. Focused Factory Layout High vs. Low Volume Equipment Dedicated vs. Nondedicated Equipment	Reliability
Systems and Technologies	Enablers	Integral Systems Integrated Systems Focused Systems	Flexibility

Note that strategic areas and factors cross Areas of Integration.

Order qualifiers must, therefore, outweigh the disqualifiers among suppliers or products for one to be selected over another. Some composite of order qualifiers ultimately becomes the order winner as illustrated in Figure 3.1, while some composite of order disqualifiers becomes the order loser. Since each customer develops their own weighting criteria, it is that much more difficult for the company to "hear the Voice of the Customer" on an individual basis.

This whole area is complicated somewhat since order winners, losers, qualifiers, and disqualifiers for one customer do not necessarily carry the same weight for another. Therefore, a company strategy of focusing on one or two of the total possible order winners or qualifiers is not likely to be effective for all potential customers.

Inventory's primary role in supporting the company's order winners and

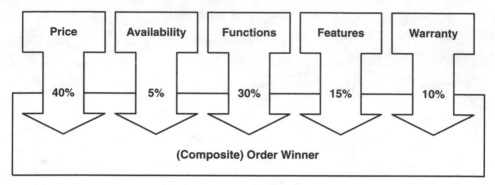

Figure 3.1   Order Qualifiers and Order Winners

qualifiers is to ensure that the company can meet its commitments with regard to customer service. From a proactive perspective, this means having the target inventory level available in the time frames specified by dependent-demand requirements and independent-demand forecasts. This is a shared responsibility with purchasing and manufacturing. The reactive aspect means not promising more in terms of quantity or delivery timing to manufacturing or customers than the company can deliver.

Manufacturing Environment

Once material has been received, inventory control procedures and practices are fairly independent of the manufacturing environment. Engineer-to-order, make or assemble-to-order, or make or assemble-to-stock manufacturing environments all have a requirement to know how much of what material is where. Nuances within a company may involve lot control, serial number traceability, special incoming inspection or Quality Assurance (QA) release requirements, quarantine, customer order control, segregation of materials based on value or due to environmental or flammability reasons, and so on. These aspects of inventory control may apply to any manufacturing environment. However, the degree of control differs significantly based on the company's manufacturing processes, volumes, rates, and ability to eliminate handling and storage steps through point-of-use staging, automation, and Kanban techniques.

Manufacturing environments do, however, have a significant effect on overall inventory policy and planning functions. Engineered vs. standard products, few large vs. many small lot sizes, high vs. low mix, few vs. many parts, and long vs. short manufacturing cycle times all affect how a company manages and plans inventory levels, investment, timing, and availability. The integration of all of these aspects within the business must be accommodated and facilitated by the inventory, material requirements planning, master (production) schedule, and/or final assembly schedule systems. This type of complexity manifests itself via different ERP/MRPII system designs.

Companies in engineer-to-order environments typically stock a certain number of parts or raw materials. The balance of the assemblies and parts are designed and/or manufactured only when an order is received. Storage racks in a rack-supported AS/RS are not so common or standard a purchase that it makes sense for rack suppliers to stock much inventory, for example.

Companies in make-to-order environments may stock raw materials such as steel and electrical or electronic components which can be used to fabricate parts and assemblies upon customer order. Forklift manufacturers fall into this classification.

Companies in assemble-to-order environments use stocked parts and assemblies, in addition to assemblies which are ordered upon very short notice from suppliers. These environments typically have too many possible combinations of assemblies to make it feasible to stock final assemblies. Automotive assembly plants configure and assemble cars and trucks after customer order, with some vehicles being made to forecast to level production schedules and provide dealer inventory.

Companies in assemble or make-to-stock environments typically respond to customer orders in less than the cumulative lead time for the finished goods. Parts are either stocked or ordered specifically for batch production runs. Finished goods inventory becomes a significant percentage of the company's inventory. Computers and peripherals are examples of make or assemble-to-stock items, though companies are increasingly configuring such products to order as well.

Note that some companies incorporate multiple manufacturing environments within a single plant and across vertically integrated plants. This may be due to serving both commercial and industrial customers, to having products in various phases of the product life cycle, and to having both high and low volume product lines in order to be a full-service supplier. The more complex the environment, the more complex the inventory infrastructure and managerial aspects. Representative differences or special considerations with respect to the major areas of an inventory system are identified in Table 3.2.

Manufacturing environment is really a combination of manufacturer type and manufacturing focus. These business aspects are covered in later subsections. The general relationship among these areas is illustrated in Figure 3.2. Many companies actually encompass multiple aspects from an inventory management perspective, making the planning aspects more complex.

Product Life Cycle

Market drivers tend to change emphasis over time based on the product life cycle. This change is less a replacement of previous drivers and more a redefinition of focus as previous drivers reach a level where they are largely satisfied. For example, purchase price, product quality in terms of durability and reliability, and responsiveness in terms of product lead times, availability, and service are nearly always important to customers (refer to Figure 3.1). These elements vary by product and emphasis at any given time for any given customer and represent the company's three goal areas.

Table 3.2   Representative Manufacturing Environment Effect on the Inventory System

AREA OF COMPARISON	ENGINEER-TO-ORDER	MAKE OR ASSEMBLE-TO-ORDER	MAKE OR ASSEMBLE-TO-STOCK
Usage History	Useful for Stocking Decisions	Useful for Safety Stock	Useful for Forecasting
Inventory Order Quantity Logic	Use for Stock Items (use MS and FAS for Others)	Use for Floor Stock Items (use MS and MRP for Others)	Use for Floor Stock Items (use MS and MRP for Others)
Safety Stock Quantity Logic	Any Technique (fixed) for Independent-Demand Items (none required for Dependent-Demand Items)	Any Technique (statistical) for Independent-Demand Items (either none required or over plan at MS level for Dependent-Demand Items)	Any Technique (time period) for Independent-Demand Items (MS over planning for Dependent-Demand Items)
Planning and Scheduling Module	Final Assembly Schedule	Master Schedule	Master Schedule
Order Status	Customer Order Number, Item Number, and Related Open Purchase or Work/Production/Shop Orders	Open Purchase or Work/Production/Shop Orders and Allocations	Open Purchase or Work/Production/Shop Orders Time-Phased with Requirements
Stock Balance/Location	Customer Order and Item by Location	Quantity and Revision by Location	Quantity by Location
Transaction Processing	All Types	All Types	All Types (Backflush Likely)
Backflush	Least Likely	Likely	Most Likely

It is safe to assume that one or some combination of at least these factors constitutes the order winner criteria at any time. Other factors then combine to establish the base of order qualifiers, such as product functions, features, ease of use, and availability of spare parts, documentation, and training. Producers serving a limited customer base in a market niche may be able to focus on one or two individual order winners and qualifiers at a time. However, those competing in large, very competitive markets must address a broad mix of order winners and qualifiers concurrently. An integral strategy then focuses on ensuring an engineered infrastructure as required to support the winners and qualifiers, while minimizing the effect of disqualifiers and losers.

For example, the primary drivers are often product quality and availability during the introduction phase of a new product (refer to Figure 3.3). Poor quality can slow the launch and refinement process (introduction phase). This drives costs up at best or causes a loss of long-term customers at worst due to dissatisfaction with early purchases. Lack of availability prohibits the company from establishing an early market leadership position and achieving the signifi-

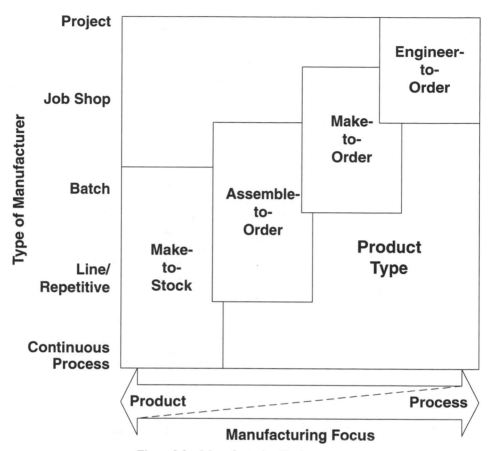

Figure 3.2   Manufacturing Environment

cant economies of scale required for competitive positioning on the experience curve.

During the market penetration and acceptance process (growth phase), the primary drivers are often quality, reliability of delivery from suppliers (including internal suppliers), and cost reduction. This enables the company to maintain a leadership or parity position while addressing the need to be cost competitive with new producers.

During the market stabilization and saturation process (maturity phase), companies introduce product variations to appeal to a broader market. Manufacturing process and material supersedures continue to reduce production costs and improve quality. This enables the company to build on company and product strengths while preventing competitors from (seriously) eroding profits.

Companies phase out some of the low margin features and functions in the phase-out (decline phase) and balance-out (lifetime build) period. This frees up resources which can be more effectively or profitably applied elsewhere.

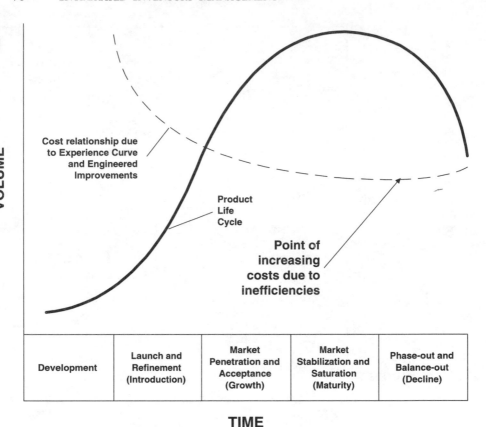

VOLUME

Cost relationship due
to Experience Curve
and Engineered
Improvements

Product
Life
Cycle

Point of
increasing
costs due to
inefficiencies

Development	Launch and Refinement (Introduction)	Market Penetration and Acceptance (Growth)	Market Stabilization and Saturation (Maturity)	Phase-out and Balance-out (Decline)

TIME

Figure 3.3   General Relationship: Life Cycle vs. Economies of Scale

The focus of an inventory strategy changes over time based on the product's life cycle as shown in Table 3.3. During each phase, the inventory strategy must adapt to actual market conditions. The proactive elements address the company's established strategic direction, while the reactive elements address reality. Over time, the intent is to minimize the need to react to changing business conditions after the fact by using more effective forward planning methodologies and techniques.

As production volume increases, experience and cost reduction initiatives should drive costs down as shown by the cost curve in Figure 3.3. Note that there may be points in time where the curve actually increases due to adding options or changing suppliers, materials, or manufacturing processes. At some point, though, the cost of production begins to increase due to the cumulative effect of increases in material, labor, and overhead, all things being equal.

Manufacturer Type

From an inventory perspective, manufacturer type has a broad impact on all aspects of inventory policies, planning, and control. There may be a significant dif-

Table 3.3 Representative Product Life Cycle Effect on Inventory

PRODUCT PHASE	PROACTIVE ELEMENTS OF THE INVENTORY INTEGRATION STRATEGY	REACTIVE ELEMENTS OF THE INVENTORY INTEGRATION STRATEGY
Design and Development	Setup for and stock new materials and parts Modify existing infrastructure as required: - Organization (education, training, assignment) - Facility layout and equipment improvements - System and technology improvements	Supersede parts being replaced Use up existing stocks of superseded parts Scrap unnecessary parts or assemblies
Launch and Refinement	Develop and implement management policies Develop and implement planning methodologies Develop and implement control techniques	Overforecast to prevent stock-outs Carry high levels of safety stock Cycle count to identify inaccuracy problems
Market Penetration and Acceptance	Improve supplier relationships Improve customer relationships Improve logistics pipeline	Refine management policies Refine planning methodologies Refine control techniques
Market Stabilization and Saturation	Reduce days supply Reduce cycle time Stabilize material flows	Forecast unplanned usage Carry minimal levels of safety stock
Phase-Out and Balance-Out	Reduce risk of excess inventory Reduce risk of surplus inventory Complete lifetime build of service parts	Reapply excess and surplus inventory Scrap obsolete inventory

ference among types with regard to dock-to-dock cycle time (which affects inventory turns), inventory delivery speed due to collapsed or multilevel bills of material (which affects customer service level), and quantity, cost, and variety of parts (which affects handling, storage, and inventory accuracy level). Inventory management is least complicated for continuous and line manufacturers which tend to have fewer parts and consistent run or batch sizes. It is most complicated for job shops and project companies which tend to have many low volume or one-time parts, low production volumes, and numerous engineering changes.

A *Project Manufacturer* typically requires anywhere from months to years to engineer, manufacture, and implement a complete system. Some raw materials and parts may be stocked for service parts or because there is a repetitive nature to the projects. The majority, at least on a dollar basis, are fabricated and assembled per the project schedule. Parts are typically purchased or manufactured on an order-for-order basis (lot-for-lot order quantity technique), without needing any special safety stock or forecasting logic. Once received, parts are allocated directly to the order and either stored or used. For all practical purposes, these parts are not transferable among orders. Cycle counting is typically not performed on customer order parts because there is no ongoing issue or receipt activity to cause inventory inaccuracies. Examples of project manufacturers include shipbuilding, environmental control systems for new construction, automated material handling and storage systems, and assembly or machining line manufacturers.

A *Job Shop Manufacturer* typically requires anywhere from weeks to months to engineer and manufacture an order. There may be a periodic nature to orders, thus eliminating or at least reducing the engineering element of lead time on repeat orders. From an inventory perspective, job shops are more similar to project manufacturers than to batch manufacturers. If there is some confidence in repeat orders, job shops will stock certain long lead time components or basic raw materials and component parts. They may purchase in larger lot sizes than are required for booked orders to obtain price breaks. Where this is done, these items are not allocated to orders when they are stocked but are added to raw material inventory. Examples of job shops include welding fabricators and large motor manufacturers.

A *Batch Manufacturer* typically requires anywhere from days to weeks to produce an order. Marketing lead time is usually a function of backlog. This means that production cycle times may be considerably less than elapsed time from order receipt to order shipment. This is the portion of lead time which Just in Time and Short Cycle/Agile Manufacturing philosophies specifically target for the greatest reduction. The decision to produce in batches is usually the result of setup times which inhibit mixed model scheduling or having processes which are not balanced in terms of cycle times from one to the next.

Orders must typically be produced in less than cumulative lead time (i.e., longest lead time purchased part plus manufacturing cycle time). This means that end-items must be forecasted at the master schedule level so the component parts can be stocked. The order quantity technique set by inventory is then executed through Material Requirements Planning (MRP) explosions. Independent demand is additionally forecasted and added to the MRP order quantity to establish a stocking quantity. Examples of batch manufacturers include computer terminals, pharmaceutical, and medium motor manufacturing.

A *Line/Repetitive Manufacturer* typically requires anywhere from minutes to days to produce an order. Machining and assembly lines are used in repetitive manufacturing where process times are balanced from one operation to the next or can be balanced by redistributing workload among team members on the line. From an inventory perspective, line manufacturers are similar to batch manufacturers at the product line and product family levels. The differences become more pronounced as lines become dedicated to products. An example is a transfer line which may be dedicated to one part (e.g., a camshaft) with one or a few minor variations related to cam profile.

A *Continuous Process Manufacturer* typically requires from minutes to hours to produce an order, depending on backlog and order size. Lines may be dedicated to a single product or configured for changeover within a product family or line. Setup speed for a new product may require equipment cleaning and process parameter resetting and test prior to production. There may be a logical production sequence to minimize the effect of changes, such as a progressive color, formula, or dimension change. This affects scheduling and inventory tim-

Table 3.4 Representative Inventory Techniques as a Function of Type
of Manufacturer

TYPE OF MANUFACTURER	ORDER QUANTITY TECHNIQUE	SAFETY STOCK TECHNIQUE	FORECAST TECHNIQUE
Continuous Process	Time Period	Scrap %	At Master Schedule Level
Line	Time Period	Overplan at Master Schedule	At Master Schedule Level
Batch	Adjusted Lot-for-Lot	Time Period	At Master Schedule Level
Job Shop	Lot-for-Lot	Double-Smoothed for Independent-Demand Parts	Double-Smoothed for Independent-Demand Parts
Project	Lot-for-Lot	N/A	N/A

Note: These techniques are covered in more detail in later chapters.

ing. The number of finished goods may well exceed the number of component materials, especially where packaging creates the primary complexity differences. This lends increased importance to packaging materials and finished goods warehousing than may be encountered with project and job shop manufacturers. Examples of process manufacturers include paper products, plastics, textiles, glass, and steel.

A company may migrate from one manufacturing type to another over time as products mature, as new product lines are added while others phase out, as volumes increase or decrease, and as expansions or downsizing occurs. As long as "transition" points are not crossed, the inventory strategy may not require major revision. However, at major transition points of job shop to batch and batch to line/repetitive, the use of different inventory policy, planning, and control methodologies and techniques must be considered. Representative inventory planning techniques are illustrated in Table 3.4.

Manufacturing (Product vs. Process) Focus

Manufacturing focus refers to whether the company is "facilitated" (has the infrastructure) to produce a product, family of products, or product lines or whether the company can produce any product within a given process capability and product profile. Companies with a product focus[3] employ manufacturing processes which are configured to produce the company's products. Even though these companies may incorporate product nonspecific processes such as heat

---

3. Note that some references refer to manufacturing having a product or process orientation (Hill or Hayes, Wheelwright, and Clark), but disagree on the definition. The convention stated by Hill follows common practice and is used in this book.

treating, grinding, and drilling, the end-items are products for which the company is a recognized supplier.

For example, a division of an automotive company producing transmissions has equipment capable of producing any type of gear within a given profile. However, the equipment is configured to produce only those specific gears required for the four complexities (versions) of transmissions sold by the company. The company has, therefore, dedicated their process capabilities to support a transmission product focus. They are not in the business of producing and selling gears, except as needed for their transmissions. Continuous, line, and batch manufacturers typically have a product focus with regard to both their manufacturing and engineering functions.

A process focus refers to the manufacturing processes being configured to produce any part or product within a given profile which requires those particular processes. Product profile restrictions refer to size, weight, type of materials, manufacturing process, and quality tolerance levels. A machine (job) shop capable of producing parts for other companies has a process focus. The machine shop is selling a "process capability" rather than a particular product. A gear manufacturer producing the same gears as in the preceding example and selling them to the automotive division has a process focus. These gears are only some of the many products produced by the company. Job shop and project manufacturers will typically have a process focus within manufacturing and engineering. Many will additionally have a product focus within engineering when specialization occurs within certain types of product such as custom machine tools.

Therefore, if the company produces a defined range of products, product families, and product lines, it is product focused regardless of its processes. If it produces a range of products based simply on having an ability to produce products which require a given set of process capabilities, it is process focused. The gear producer is a perfect example of a company with both a process and product focus. Companies may not have a single focus, and this increases the complexity within inventory management.

Manufacturing focus has relevance for inventory management since companies tend to be more flexible than is defined by what they happen to be producing at a point in time. This flexibility cannot be taken advantage of if inventory has been structured based on a limited set of functions as defined by the current mix of products. Therefore, the inventory operational and infrastructural elements of integration may need to be more flexible for process manufacturers than for product manufacturers. However, the dynamics of the business blur this difference as product mix increases and as product life cycles shorten.

Organizational Structure

Organizational structure is one area which should have little if any effect on inventory levels. Inventory decisions reflect business targets which are independent of the organizational structure. Structure is more likely to have an effect on responsiveness of the inventory department to production changes or anomaly conditions such as late shipments, unexpected rejections in incoming inspection, and slow disposition processes. The more removed the decision-makers are from the problem area, the longer the problem resolution process takes.

However, the single most important factor in determining whether the company can achieve significant improvements and meet their target objectives is its people. They must clearly understand how their actions support the achievement of the company's goals and objectives. Only then can a commitment have any meaning. Just as a company must get its own house in order before expecting suppliers to do the same, so must each individual personally accept and facilitate organizational change before operational and technological improvements will be most effective. *Anyone who is not working in support of the strategy is working against it.*

The organizational structures in Table 3.5 all have advantages and disadvantages with respect to inventory. Advantages provide proactive support of the inventory integral strategy. Disadvantages must typically be dealt with in a reactive fashion when they create roadblocks to improvement. Hierarchical organizations

Table 3.5   Organizational Structure Impact on Inventory Management

ORGANIZATIONAL STRUCTURE	ADVANTAGES WITH RESPECT TO INVENTORY MANAGEMENT	DISADVANTAGES WITH RESPECT TO INVENTORY MANAGEMENT
Hierarchical	A hierarchical organization lends itself to the Inventory Policies, Planning, and Control hierarchy of functions. Responsibilities and breadth of authority are well defined.	Inventory-related investment and other decisions tend to be made by one or a few individuals and may reflect performance measures upon which that individual is evaluated rather than operational or customer-oriented measures.
Matrix	A matrix organization enables individuals to bypass traditional organizational barriers between departments and so address issues more directly and faster. There is less tendency to take actions which adversely affect another department, such as reducing safety stock or reducing stocking levels below target in order to artificially increase Turns.	Since a matrix organization is often more of an informal arrangement within a hierarchical organization (often for purposes of a project), actions may still be taken by one department which cause excess, surplus, or obsolete inventory without the knowledge or approval of the other organization areas.
Team	There is a much greater likelihood that decisions will consider all of the ramifications of an Integral Strategy if the team is represented by Materials, Information, Product, Process, Quality, Human Resources, Facilities and Equipment, and Systems and Technologies personnel who can team to produce a balanced viewpoint.	The consensus process slows the decision-making process and may or may not result in desisions which are any better than what an experienced and knowledgeable individual would make.

have a well-defined manager/subordinate series of relationships. Organizational boundaries are well-defined as well, which tends to be very restrictive when improvements must cross the boundaries (as is typical with an integral strategy). Matrix organizations provide a formal means of teaming to evaluate alternatives and make decisions which cross organizational boundaries. However, each functional area typically remains autonomous for execution purposes. Team organizations take this one step further by combining the various knowledge and skills required to engineer, produce, and possibly market a product into a single core team. Support is provided by other company personnel on an as-required basis. Sharing support team personnel ensures a certain amount of information transfer and consistency within the various company teams.

Example: In one company where the buyer/planners determine the order quantity, the standard practice is to overorder based on the requirements. They also delay notifying the suppliers of schedule changes when MRP regenerates the *weekly* material plan.[4] Overordering provides an excess inventory level so the buyer/planner can lengthen the period between orders and reduce the frequency of stock-outs. Delaying notifying suppliers of schedule changes is based on a recognition that rescheduling occurs frequently. The feeling is that delaying notification gives the schedule time to settle down and indicate "true" requirements.

The inventory manager wonders why the company has excess inventory. Accounting is taking a favorable variance based on the difference between the standard cost and lower cost paid to obtain price breaks. Production planning sees that the suppliers have not changed their delivery dates and so is in a constant replanning mode to address the lack of on-time deliveries. *This is an organizational problem! Everyone is doing their job as they perceive it, just not together.*

Plant Focus

One of the most important factors with respect to managing a company's inventory relates to the plant environment. If a single focused factory is considered one end of the spectrum, the other end is one consisting of the elements in the right-hand column shown in Table 3.6. The more variability inherent in the environment, product mix, market, and overall logistics, the more complex the inventory management function.

With multiple plants under centralized inventory management and planning, the inventory system must accommodate a multiplant capability. The system segregates data by site using a site code but allows data to be viewed and transferred among sites. Since the company owns any inventory being transferred among locations, transfer time must be directly incorporated in scheduling and routing logic.

---

4. While some companies have evolved beyond the early 1980s, more than we think are still struggling with the basics.

Table 3.6   Plant Focus Factors

PLANT CHARACTERISTICS	LESS COMPLEX INVENTORY MANAGEMENT	MORE COMPLEX INVENTORY MANAGEMENT
PLANT	Single Plant	Multiple Plants
VERTICAL INTEGRATION	Independent Plants	Interplant Relationships
FINISHED GOODS WAREHOUSING	At Plant	Multiple Distribution Centers
FACTORY LAYOUT	Focused	Functional Groupings
EQUIPMENT CAPABILITY	High Volume	Low Volume
EQUIPMENT FLEXIBILITY	Dedicated	Nondedicated

Factory layout may have an effect on days supply, handling and storage, and the inventory system. A focused factory or in-line layout streamlines material flows within machining, subassembly, and final assembly operations. A more traditional layout groups equipment or assembly stations by function. In this case, for example, drill presses are located in one area, inspection equipment is located in another, assembly stations are located in a third, and so on. Material must be routed to and through these areas. With a line layout, material starts at the first station and flows through the rest with a minimum of work-in-process buildup.

Figure 3.4 compares functional and in-line layouts. Machines which are grouped in a functional layout (e.g., metal removal, grinding, drilling, washing) are distributed by line in an in-line layout. This reduces and possibly simplifies set-ups, thus providing more production capacity and reducing quality problems related to setup frequency. With respect to inventory management, line layouts enable dedicated material handling to be designed for each station. A technique such as backflushing then reduces the number of manually performed inventory transactions.

Equipment capability is a function of the company's manufacturing strategy. If the product mix is low and the sales rate is high, the company may use high volume equipment. From an inventory perspective, this requires some type of rate-based scheduling and demand-flow techniques. If the product mix is high and volume is low, equipment must support frequent setup and mixed-model production.

Equipment flexibility is a function of dedication vs. nondedication. A piece of equipment in a functional flow layout may be capable of processing parts within every product the company has. The same piece of equipment in a dedicated line becomes restricted to only those parts required for the particular product or family. Other considerations include the production tolerance levels which the equipment is capable of holding and required setup or changeover time. Flexibility typically has little effect on inventory, since equipment simply represents a required capability. It may affect safety stock levels if scrap occurs.

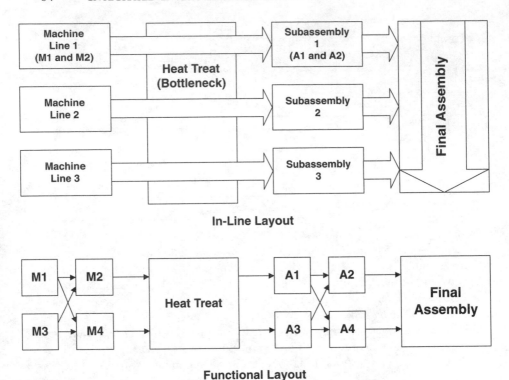

Figure 3.4 Functional vs. In-Line Layout

Systems and Technology Enablers

The availability of systems and related technologies enable a small group of inventory personnel to effectively manage, plan, and control millions of dollars worth of inventory. From an inventory perspective, this encompasses communications between and among suppliers, customers, and company personnel via EDI, Internet, and internal network communications. Material identification and tracking control is provided via bar codes and radio frequency. Storage and handling is provided via conventional and automated storage and retrieval systems, and manual, conveyor, automated guided vehicle, and automated electrified monorail systems. Stock balance and location processing is automated via issues, receipts, adjustments, and transfers performed by inventory and decision support systems.

Systems fall into the three basic categories shown in Figure 3.5 in the upper three circles. Each category may also include stand-alone equipment (the lower left circle) in addition to equipment, vehicles, controls, and software which are integrated to some degree.

1. The lowest system category consists of focused systems designed for a specific function. A single-aisle point-of-use buffer storage system with a

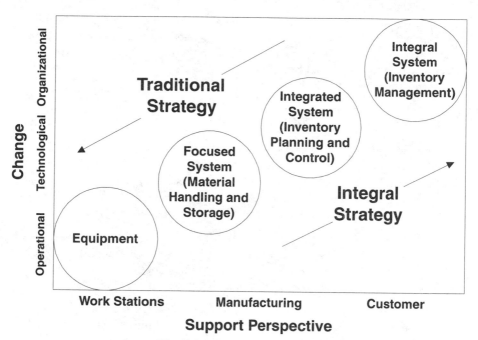

Figure 3.5   System Categories

PC controlling equipment operation and providing basic inventory control (part quantity per location) is a focused system. If a focused system breaks down, the company will suffer some inconvenience, but production will not be seriously impacted.

2. Integrated systems are essentially multiple focused systems which have been physically integrated via handling systems and logically integrated via Warehouse Management (WMS) and Control (WCS) Systems (refer to Chapter 5). A multiaisle AS/RS with inbound and outbound conveyors, bar code identification, forklift load and unload stations, and pick tunnels under WMS/WCS computer control and supporting a host system interface for inventory and order management is an integrated system. A breakdown of an integrated system may impact production for the duration of the breakdown or until a work-around solution is implemented.

3. Integral systems are those which integrate operational processes with infrastructural capabilities to improve the company's overall ability to provide goods and services. They break down barriers between functional areas, streamline processes, facilitate cooperation throughout the logistics pipeline, and progressively eliminate or minimize barriers to improvement. Failure of an integral system will seriously impact production.

Focused systems support specific manufacturing operations. From an inventory perspective, the focus is on physical handling and storage processes. Integrated systems support manufacturing functions and production lines. Planning and scheduling is added to the physical handling and storage processes. An integral system integrates infrastructural storage, buffering, and manufacturing systems with operational policies, methodologies, and techniques to support an integral philosophy.

10-STEP STRATEGY METHODOLOGY

While the level of effort to develop an integral inventory strategy varies based on the company, development via the 10-step process shown in Figure 3.6 fits most situations. There is no single right way to develop a strategy, just right results. Using a systems engineering methodology provides some consistency regardless of the type of company, industry, or competitive environment.

1. *Establish a Zero-Tolerance Vision*—The vision sets the long-term direction and strategy emphasis. It addresses zero-tolerance to deviation against measures of perfection. The integral strategy then addresses zero-tolerance to deviation against target based on phased objectives.

2. *Quantify Targets*—Inventory is a 4th-level strategy. Inventory targets in terms of goals and objectives are the result of refining the enterprise goals (level 1) via the manufacturing (level 2) and materials management (level 3) strategies into inventory-related elements. Target areas encompass cost, quality, and responsiveness, as translated into inventory turns, inventory accuracy, and customer service level respectively.

3. *Define the Inventory Strategy Scope*—Inventory encompasses policies (inventory level and investment), planning (service level and timing), and control (accuracy, storage, and handling) areas. Within these areas, the scope consists of both internal (within inventory) and external (to inventory) integration elements within the eight areas of integration.

4. *Develop the As-Is Baseline*—A baseline provides the starting point against which to measure the effect of engineered improvements. An inventory baseline generally consists of current inventory levels by part, category, and product. These are retranslated into investment, service, and accuracy levels to determine effectiveness. Physical elements include layout, equipment, and floor space requirements. Product and process profiles relate inventory to manufacturing requirements. Management policies, formal procedures, and informal practices identify how the organization manages the day-to-day aspects of inventory management. Ordering, safety stock, and forecasting methodologies and techniques identify the current focus with respect to inventory turns and customer service levels. Data and information availability and timeliness and containerization, handling, storage, and identification characteristics establish current standards regarding part-level controls.

Input		Output
Competitive and Market Assessment	**1** Establish a Zero-Tolerance Vision	Integral Set of Operating Philosophies and Guiding Principles
Enterprise, Manufacturing, and Materials Management Goals and Objectives	**2** Quantify Goals and Objectives	Inventory Turns, Inventory Accuracy, and Customer Service Level
Inventory Policies, Planning, and Control	**3** Define Inventory Strategy Scope	Materials, Information, Product, Process, Quality, Organizational, Facilities and Equipment, and Systems and Technologies
Profiles, Processes, Procedures, Practices, Performance, Constraints, Assumptions, Relationships	**4** Develop As-Is Baseline	Comprehensive Knowledge and Understanding of the Business
Time-Phased Financial, Operational, and Organizational Targets	**5** Define Time-Phased To-Be Environments	Comprehensive Description of the To-Be Environments over time
Magnitude of Required Improvement	**6** Identify Improvement Actions	Proactive and Reactive Initiatives, Projects and Programs
Requirements for Change Internal to the Inventory Function	**7** Perform an Internal Integration Assessment	Inventory Management Commitment and Realistic Expectations
Requirements for Change External to the Inventory Function	**8** Perform an External Integration Assessment	Company Management Commitment and Realistic Expectations
Strategic Direction, Assumptions, Constraints, and Qualifiers	**9** Document the Strategy	Vision, Plan, Targets, Scope, Schedule, Budget, and Issues
Project Planning, Budgeting, and Scheduling	**10** Adopt Measures and Controls	Performance Measures, Indicators, and Capabilities

Figure 3.6   Inventory Integral Strategy Development Process

5. *Define the Time-Phased To-Be Environments*—Targets are the stepwise improvements which bridge the As-Is and To-Be environments. They are performance measure-related (single factor), performance indicator-related (multifactor or aggregates), and capability-related (infrastructural). For each new improvement stage, layouts, descriptions of operation, flow charts, functional flows, and so on help the organization to understand the changes being planned for the company.

6. *Identify Improvement Actions*—Compare the As-Is baseline and time-phased To-Be scenarios and identify the issues to be resolved and actions to be taken to achieve the To-Be targets. Actions encompass a balance of both proactive and reactive elements in terms of infrastructural improvements (organizational, facilities, equipment, systems and technologies). Policy, variability reduction, and cycle time initiatives within the materials, information, product, process, and quality management areas of integration address operational improvements.

7. *Perform an Internal Integration Assessment*—The company must be capable of and willing to address the issues and implement the actions in Step 6. This means that requirements must be realistic with respect to level of improvements as a function of time. Investment funding must be available for infrastructural improvements. Inventory personnel must individually commit to the change and the engineered improvement/conflict process. If not, Step 6 must be repeated using different types or combinations of actions until a satisfactory balance is achieved.

8. *Perform an External Integration Assessment*—Inventory levels are the result of actions and inactions in each area of the business or the marketplace. The impact of these decisions has a more significant impact on inventory levels than any decisions made within the inventory department. The same realistic requirements, funding, and commitment required to address the internal areas of integration are required for the external areas. These are additionally complicated by having to extend improvement efforts into the supplier and customer base. Constraints to improvements encountered in these areas may require a reassessment of Steps 5 to 7.

9. *Document the Strategy*—Once management has committed to the course of actions identified in the previous steps, a comprehensive integral strategy is developed. This includes a strategy plan describing the vision and time-phased targets, integrated schedule of initiatives, projects, and programs, Work Breakdown Structure (WBS), Organization Breakdown Structure (OBS), Work Authorization Plans (WAPs), budget, schedule, and open issues.

10. *Adopt Measures and Controls*—A comprehensive, long-term set of tactical initiatives and more strategic projects and programs requires a struc-

tured set of measures and controls against which to monitor progress. These become inventory management's regular financial, operational, and organizational zero-tolerance performance measures and indicators.

Once the strategy is developed, remember that the key to gaining targeted improvements is to actually implement the strategy. Engineered improvements then result in increased responsiveness as initiatives are completed, projects are implemented, and programs are launched.

The Enterprise Strategy Dictates Inventory's Vision

Strategic direction is often defined as achievement of "World Class" levels of performance at the company level. This involves establishing benchmarks which are generally accepted as obtainable by only the best companies in the world. World Class performance requires a total company commitment to an engineered improvement process. When using World Class performance targets, companies are striving for demonstrated performance levels which are industry nonspecific.

World Class targets are not for everyone. Companies which feel that competitive factors should directly relate to those of their competitors are likely to establish "Best in Industry" targets. Best in Industry targets tend to be more specific as compared to World Class targets. The risk in this type of strategy is that the market leader is not likely to wait for their competition to overtake them. Strategies must be formulated accordingly.

The Enterprise Strategy Dictates Inventory's Goals

Achieving a given level of performance is a means to an end, not the end. World Class or Best in Industry performance is meaningless in and of itself if not an integral aspect of the company's cost, quality, and responsiveness goals. The "end" is to increase the company's profitability while providing increased performance and value to its customers. Figure 3.7 contrasts a traditional strategy with an integral strategy. Without an effective strategy, goal areas compete for company resources and force tradeoffs to be made. This has the effect of negating some of the performance improvements in given areas, or making them less effective, or delaying them, or missing targets entirely. With an integral strategy, tradeoffs are still made but in a planned fashion in accordance with business decisions.

> *Example:* Consider a 100 percent customer service goal in an environment which involves variability in demand and service parts requirements. This may require a large investment in safety stock to cover the demand peaks. If the cost of the safety stock is greater than the *value* to the company of 100 percent customer service (a difficult thing to quantify), the service goal is inappropriate. Investment in safety stock *must support* the value to the company of increased service. If it does not, the money may be better invested in shortening manufacturing-related cycle times. This in turn reduces the required safety stock investment and improves customer serv-

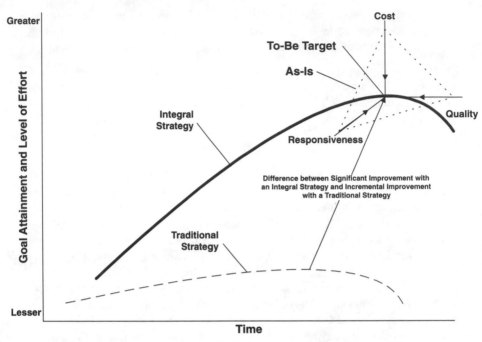

Figure 3.7   Company Goals Establish Direction and Consistency of Purpose

ice. Within inventory management, there is often more than one way to achieve a particular target.

Note that this issue of goal *tradeoffs* is controversial when discussing philosophies and strategies. Traditional thinking says that tradeoffs are inevitable, for example, costs must increase if quality is to increase. The company must incur additional costs of inspection, quality assurance, training, education, and higher tolerance equipment in order to increase quality levels. The real issue, however, is not whether costs must increase in order to obtain an increase in quality. The issue is whether the *value* of such an increase in quality offsets the increase in cost. This is the focus of engineered improvement initiatives, projects, and programs, none of which are "no cost" for a company.

Current theory when taken literally implies that synergism among areas should totally eliminate any need for tradeoffs. Therefore, having 100 percent quality levels eliminates any need to expend costs associated with increasing quality. The problem with accepting this theory at face value is that companies do not instantly arrive at a condition where there is no need for tradeoffs. Tradeoffs are inevitable because perfection is never achieved and no company has infinite resources. From a practical perspective, therefore, there are *always* tradeoffs. Integration strategies which balance goals and objectives with constraints and capabilities recognize and make the most of the tradeoff process. This is not to say that the long-term vision cannot be one where tradeoffs do not exist; only that shorter-term strategies must be based on what is practical and achievable.

The purpose of an integral strategy, therefore, is to create a competitive advantage where each goal area mutually supports the others. This removes (or at least minimizes) any constraints to overall performance. This is accomplished by translating the higher level enterprise goals into the goals and objectives of the various lower level strategies until each is solidly ingrained into each operational and infrastructural area of the business. Ingraining inventory accuracy principles into the operational processes and procedures of the company, for example, eliminates the need to cycle count. Having accurate inventory in turn eliminates the planning and scheduling problems related to count inaccuracies.

The three key elements of the enterprise strategy which ultimately translate directly into inventory strategy targets include the following:

1. *Cost (reduce to and contain at target levels)*—The inventory management function is considered a non value-adding process. This means that inventory-related labor and overhead do not enhance the value of the material component of the company's product. Rather, it increases product cost by the amount of inventory-related overhead allocated to the product. Therefore, the primary emphasis of inventory management is to minimize the costs associated with planning, ordering, handling, and storing inventory through the use of appropriate policies, plans, controls, methodologies, and techniques. This requires automating the planning and ordering processes to the extent possible and reducing the number of times personnel "touch" material once it is received. Inventory policies focus on the enterprise cost goal.

2. *Quality (protect material quality and ensure inventory accuracy)*—The inventory management function may adversely affect material quality due to poor handling or storage practices. Material availability may be compromised due to inaccurately processing or maintaining information. Therefore, from a reactive quality perspective, the inventory function must ensure that materials and products are processed, handled, and stored in a manner which maintains their quality and ensures related information accuracy and timeliness. From a proactive perspective, every effort must be made to reduce the variability inherent in planning and control functions. This means preventing the possibility of inaccuracies or damage in the first place. Inventory control focuses on the enterprise quality goal.

3. *Responsiveness (reduce lead and cycle times and ensure material availability)*—The inventory management function is a key contributor to the company's delivery speed, reliability, and flexibility capabilities. This is accomplished primarily through making the target inventory (parts and quantities) available at the target place (point of use, staging, or storage) at the target time (per schedule or request, neither too early nor too late) of the target quality (undamaged and properly identified) and in the target orientation (as required for the particular type of handling, storage,

or process). Inventory planning focuses on the enterprise responsiveness goal.

How effectively these three areas support the goals and objectives of the business is a function of the degree of integration of the inventory strategy itself. This is not enough in and of itself though. The other functional areas of the business must also be in a position to take advantage of the provided capabilities. The inventory strategy ensures that the inventory function is both internally and externally integrated. Internal integration (between and among the inventory policy, planning, and control functions) ensures that the capabilities exist to support the goals and objectives of the inventory strategy at part and product levels of detail. It ensures that these capabilities are being managed in the company's best interests. External integration ensures that the inventory function facilitates, while not constraining, the strategies of the other functional areas.

The Inventory Goals Dictate the Inventory Strategy Scope

Inventory management encompasses a hierarchical set of policy, planning, and control elements as shown in Figure 3.8. Each of these elements supports the translation of the enterprise goals as mentioned in the previous section into in-

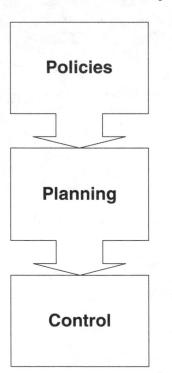

Inventory Policies:
- Stocking Level and Inventory Turns
- Order Frequency and Quantity
- Safety Stock and Customer Service
- Surplus and Excess Definition
- Storage and Handling
- Inventory Accuracy and Adjustments
- Organizational Development, Education, and Training

Inventory Methodologies and Techniques:
- Dependent vs. Independent Demand
- Inventory Allocation
- Order Quantity
- Safety Stock
- Forecast

Physical and Logical Control:
- Issues
- Receipts
- Adjustments
- Transfers
- Bin Lock
- Cycle Counting
- Containerization
- Identification

Figure 3.8   Inventory Scope Hierarchy

ventory-specific targets. Constraints, qualifiers, processes, and procedures established at the policy level provide overall direction and boundaries. These must be consistent with the direction established by the materials management (level 3) and manufacturing (level 2) strategies. Planning includes the various ordering, safety stock, and forecasting methodologies and techniques used to ensure that the right level and mix of materials are available. Control encompasses physical control of inventory via storage and handling processes and logical control via techniques which ensure count and data accuracy.

Within any integral strategy, the various areas of integration are assigned to either the Operational or Infrastructure category as shown in Table 3.7. The operational category encompasses the various managerial areas where the capabilities of the inventory function are applied to the policy, planning, and control inventory functions. These capabilities are then facilitated and supported via the

Table 3.7   Representative Inventory Management Areas of Integration

	INVENTORY MANAGEMENT AREAS OF INTERNAL INTEGRATION	AREA OPERATING PHILOSOPHIES TO ENSURE EXTERNAL INTEGRATION	INVENTORY STRATEGY SCOPE
OPERATIONAL CATEGORY	Materials Management	JIT Just in Time	Stocking Level (Investment) Inventory Replenishment (Turns) Order Quantity
	Information Management	CIM Computer Integrated Manufacturing	Customer Service Level Safety Stock Forecasting
	Product Management	CE Concurrent Engineering	Storage Staging Handling
	Process Management	SCM Short Cycle Manufacturing	Issues Receipts Adjustments
	Quality Management	TQM Total Quality Management	Part Accuracy Containerization Identification
INFRASTRUCTURE CATEGORY	Organization	IO Integral Organization	Education Training Professional Development
	Facilities and Equipment	IF Integral Facility	Facility Layout Automation (AS/RS, AGV, AEM, and so on) Vehicles and Equipment
	Systems and Technologies	IS Integral System	Computer (ERP, MRPII, WMS, WCS) Identification (Bar Code) Communication (RF, EDI, Internet)

infrastructure category where the resources of the business are aligned with the established strategic direction of the inventory strategy.

For example, *when* to apply a particular order quantity technique is a function of the educational component of the organizational infrastructure. It is based on a knowledge of the business and the various order quantity techniques. *How* to apply each particular technique is a combined function of the educational and training components. The operational areas must, therefore, be learned before they can be applied. This differs from the infrastructural elements of the inventory strategy which must be (substantially) implemented before the operational elements can be used most effectively.

The following eight areas of integration must at least be considered in relation to strategy decisions. Each area is associated with a guiding philosophy. Philosophies make it easier to extend a vision into functional areas, since philosophies tend to be functional area dependent. For example, engineering is concerned with product performance and design, as well as cost, maintainability, and serviceability. A Concurrent Engineering philosophy is relevant for engineering and ensures that functionality, performance, reliability, safety, manufacturing, material handling, storage, and other factors will be considered in the overall design process. The integral inventory strategy is concerned with the product storage, staging, and handling aspects of the Concurrent Engineering philosophy.

Materials Management—JIT (Just in Time): Just in Time can be defined as a logistics philosophy targeting a smooth material flow through the entire logistics pipeline. Each stage of the process can be viewed as a supplier/customer relationship. Actions which impede this flow or which create greater than target levels of inventory create waste. These actions are candidates for elimination or engineered improvement. The inventory scope areas which address waste encompass all of those listed in Table 3.7. Specifically, the materials management area establishes the strategic direction for the inventory function and JIT philosophy. This encompasses determining required stocking levels (which defines required investment), setting inventory replenishment targets (which translates into inventory turns), and setting inventory order quantities within minimum and maximum constraints.

> *Example:* Consider an integration view of a Kanban-type demand-pull system. The Kanban may be a card, electronic "Kanban," or an empty container or cart. Each area of integration contributes toward the overall system. Materials management sets policy, product management sets quantity per Kanban based on consumption and replenishment rates, and so on as shown in Table 3.8. The various operational and infrastructure areas distribute the design, implementation, and support effort into logical organizational areas where roles and responsibilities can be defined.

Information Management—CIM (Computer Integrated Manufacturing): Computer Integrated Manufacturing can be defined as a computerization philosophy targeting a paperless information flow between the various users of the information. Any processing which involves double entry of data, paperwork as

Table 3.8   Representative Kanban Areas of Integration

	INTERNAL INTEGRATION	INTEGRATION	KANBAN SCOPE
OPERATIONAL AREAS	Materials Management	Policy	Number of Kanbans in System Replenishment Priority
	Information Management	Timing	Rate-based Production Schedule Backflush Inventory
	Product Management	Quantity	Quantity per Kanban Marked and Sized Staging Locations
	Process Management	Operation	Demand-Pull Replenishment Signals Emergency Float Quantity
	Quality Management	Containers	Dedicated Containers Permanent IDs or Slots for Kanbans
INFRASTRUCTURE AREAS	Organization	Technique	Education on JIT Operating Philosophy Training on Kanban Technique
	Facilities and Equipment	Support	Kanban WIP Staging Areas Staging and Handling Equipment
	Systems and Technologies	Kanbans	Electronic Kanbans Bar Coding

the means of information transfer which can be replaced with automated data collection, or processing delays which can otherwise be eliminated are targets for engineered improvement. The inventory scope areas which address computerization encompass most of those listed in Table 3.7. Specifically, the information management area provides the data, translated into information and decision support, which enables materials to be scheduled, managed, planned, ordered, stocked, issued, and otherwise controlled. This encompasses all of the policy, inventory balance, inventory category, historical usage, future requirements, and other data required to calculate order quantities and safety stocks and perform forecasting.

Process Management—SCM (Short Cycle [Agile and Lean] Manufacturing): Short Cycle Manufacturing can be defined as a time-based philosophy targeting minimum information or product throughput or delivery time in support of customer need. Anything which limits the ability to produce two dissimilar parts or products as quickly and economically as two similar ones, regardless of lot size, or to provide requested information or services in the minimum absolute time are targets for engineered improvement. The inventory scope areas which address those processes related to policy, planning, or control functions encompass most of those listed in the Operational category of Table 3.7. Specifically, the process management area establishes the processes and procedures which "pull" inventory through production.

Product Management—CE (Concurrent Engineering): Concurrent (simultaneous) Engineering can be defined as a design philosophy targeting inter- and intracompany cooperation in the design of products and services. This includes related manufacturing, materials, information, and quality management processes. Lack of cooperation or involvement which results in adding time, effort, and expense to the design process and subsequent manufacturing and distribution processes or which results in reliability, maintainability, ergonomics, safety, or other problems are targets for engineered improvement. The inventory scope areas which address design aspects encompass all of those listed in the Infrastructure category of Table 3.7. Specifically, the product management area encompasses the storage, staging, and handling of materials, parts, and products.

Quality Management—TQM (Total Quality Management): Total Quality Management can be defined as an accountability philosophy targeting the delivery of 100 percent first-time defect-free goods and services by the supplier. Goods or services include materials, parts, products, training, education, information, and so on. Operations in the factory or office which introduce, cause, or otherwise contribute to defects are targets for engineered improvement. The inventory scope areas which address such areas of waste encompass all of those listed in Table 3.7. Specifically, the quality management area encompasses the safe and accurate storage of materials and the availability of all information required to make informed business decisions. For example, designing a pallet of returnable dunnage specifically formed to hold and protect 50 pieces of a particular part helps to ensure that no damage will occur during shipping, storage, staging, and handling. It also simplifies planning and control since all transactions are in multiples of 50, including orders, receipts, issues, and cycle counts.

Organization—IO (Integral Organization): The Integral Organization supports a capabilities philosophy targeting the ability and willingness of people to be both individual and team contributors. Failure of the company to educate, train, and develop individuals or of the individual to contribute at full potential when the opportunity exists are targets for engineered improvement. The inventory scope areas which address organizational capabilities encompass all of those listed in Table 3.7. Specifically, the organization area encompasses all aspects related to inventory policies, planning, and control. Education addresses the knowledge (when and why) aspects; training addresses the skill (what and how) aspects. Professional development addresses general business and team-building skills such as technical and business writing, public speaking, presentation development, brainstorming, planning, spreadsheet and database analysis, and word processing.

Facilities and Equipment—IF (Integral Factory): The Integral Factory supports a reliability philosophy targeting the ability to significantly improve and sustain cycle times, throughput, and quality levels. This applies to the full range of design volumes via integrated process, test, and inspection equipment, material storage and handling systems, and controls and support functions. Operations which exceed desirable ergonomic limits, which are less reliable than required, which cannot hold required tolerances, and which cannot meet cycle times are targets for engineered improvement. The inventory scope areas related to reliable factory operation encompass all of the infrastructure areas listed in Table 3.7. Specifically, the facilities and equipment area encompasses the facility layout related to storage, staging and handling, integrated system specification, implementation and operation, and vehicle and equipment selection and operation.

Systems and Technologies—IS (Integral System): The Integral System supports a flexibility philosophy targeting the use of integrated systems and technologies to achieve and sustain a competitive advantage. Manual or non-integrated operations which are not flexible and reliable across the company's range of products or volumes are targets for engineered improvement. The inventory scope areas which address systems and technology applications encompass all of the infrastructure areas listed in Table 3.7, in support of all of the operational areas. Specifically, the systems and technologies area includes computer, identification, and communication technologies.

The As-Is Baseline Defines the Company's Starting Point

A knowledge of the current *baseline* is a prerequisite to establishing any strategy. A baseline is a factual accounting of current operational and infrastructural requirements, capabilities, and performance levels. It provides an internal benchmark against which to measure progress toward objectives and goals and performance against targets. An inventory baseline can be thought of in terms of the five Ps:

- *Profiles* provide a comprehensive overview of a particular area of integration. These make it easier to understand scope, issues, priorities, pressure points, operational and infrastructural characteristics, and relationship to other functions. Product profiles, for example, identify storage and handling characteristics, volumes, production rates, and demand rates.

- *Policies* provide guidelines within which the organization establishes stocking, customer service, and inventory accuracy levels. Policies also need to be defined as they relate to order quantities, safety stocks, independent demand forecasts, and system, storage, staging, handling, and facility layout parameters. Order quantity policies, for example, identify target days supply for each inventory category as well as specific minimum and maximum conditions within which the policies can be modified.

- *Procedures* identify the formalized steps by which the various policy, planning, and control functions are implemented and executed. Documentation takes the form of written step-by-step procedures and information, process, and functional flows. Storage procedures, for example, identify where certain materials can be stored in systems having zoning requirements. ISO 9000 provides an excellent procedural framework.

- *Practices* identify the undocumented procedures, initiatives, and tactics related to policy, planning, and control functions. Plant practices also define layout, safety, ergonomic, and other design and operating parameters which must be satisfied within the strategy development process. Layout practices, for example, define forklift operating aisle widths and vehicle speeds in certain areas.

- *Performance* levels relate to cost, quality, and responsiveness areas. As these measures may be subject to some degree of manipulation, the team also needs to determine the source and reference information upon which they are based. The key to baseline performance measures is not so much to understand what they are but why they are not better.

On the surface, it would seem that establishing an As-Is baseline is the easiest part of the strategy development process. After all, companies should certainly know how they are currently operating and performing. However, there are at least three problems with this view. The first is that operational performance is somewhat subjective. It should not be surprising that companies often interpret performance in their own favor. This makes it difficult to be objective. The second is that it is difficult at times to get three different people in the company to agree on how a certain process is performed or why certain policies, practices, or procedures are followed. It is imperative that a consensus is achieved among those who perform a function, those who manage the function, and those who are the customers. The third is that companies rarely seem to have their policies, processes, and procedures documented in a formal manner. Those who do may not follow them because changes tend to make them out-of-date. It always seems to take longer than anticipated to determine whether company documentation is accurate, complete, and to the level of detail required as the basis for strategy development. Consider the following examples as they illustrate the preceding three problem areas:

Problem Area 1—Inventory accuracy performance is commonly interpreted by companies in their own favor. The problem is that manufacturing does not view inventory accuracy the same way as the departments responsible for determining the measure. This creates distrust within the organization. Manufacturing considers count accuracy while accounting considers dollar accuracy. Count accuracy is an absolute measure, since it is impossible to net overages of one part against shortages of another. Dollar accuracy permits the dollar value of overages to be netted against the dollar value of shortages. This has the effect of increasing reported inventory accuracy but provides a false indication of inventory accuracy for promising and scheduling purposes.

A company in the electronics industry was proud of their 98+ percent cycle count inventory accuracy level based on dollars. At the same time, they often missed the production schedule due to part shortages. A physical inventory identified that their count accuracy was approximately 60 percent. Any measure where 100 percent dollar accuracy can be achieved with 0 percent count accuracy is not a valid integration performance measure.

Problem Area 2—Agreement on a process or procedure does not necessarily guarantee understanding. It is often easier to obtain consensus regarding what is done, rather than why. A highly profitable company producing precision machined parts for military usage used an algorithm of 2,000 hours for each work order release. This 2,000 hours consisted of a mix of run vs. setup hours which varied by part. Setup hours averaged from 20 to 30 percent of the total. Everyone knew that the 2,000 hour production run was the standard. When asked what the justification was, the answer ranged anywhere from "I don't know" to "It is some type of economic order quantity." When the production planning manager was asked, he stated that his predecessor used 2,000 hours and that was how he was trained. This algorithm had been in use without question for nearly 30 years.

Common practice gains a certain momentum. In this situation, the wall-to-wall WIP appeared normal to company personnel. No one questioned the planning algorithm. It is very important when establishing a baseline to understand what is being done. However, it is often more instructive to understand why. It is much easier to get people to change what is being done if the why is also changed.

Problem Area 3—Formal documentation is no problem to obtain. It is on the shelf in somebody's office. Companies can bury someone in computer reports alone. The question is not one of volume but of accuracy, relevancy, and usefulness. With ISO 9000, companies are getting better at documenting their procedures and work instructions.

During an initial tour of a manufacturing plant, a request was made for copies of the shop floor paperwork. This consisted of preprinted multipart forms stored in a wall unit. MIS heard about the request and interpreted it as a request for copies of all of the company's computer reports. Eighteen boxes of computer reports were received one week later. The majority fell into the category of never used or used once (probably to see what they looked like). The intent of the original request had been to cross-reference the actual shop floor paperwork against the flow of material. Be specific when requesting information; some people will be helpful to a fault.

Table 3.9 provides an overview of the areas included in the inventory As-Is baseline. The matrix format cross-references the eight areas of integration to the three inventory areas of policies, planning, and control. For example, stocking policies must be defined for the three inventory categories of operating (required) inventory, business (safety stock, service parts, and R&D) inventory, and financial (surplus and excess) inventory. Each of these three areas may then in turn be further defined in terms of Raw, Work in Process, and Finished Goods inventory. This same hierarchical breakdown process applies to each of the other areas as well.

The baseline is critical in any strategy development process. It provides the comparison against which all justifications are based for changing the status quo. The level of detail is subjective. To the extent that certain processes and proce-

Table 3.9   As-Is Baseline Areas of Definition

AREAS OF INTEGRATION (Performance)	POLICIES (Policies)	PLANNING (Profiles and Procedures)	CONTROL (Practices)
Materials Management (Inventory Turns)	Stocking Replenishment Ordering	Operating Inventory Financial Inventory Business Inventory	Raw Material Work In Process Finished Goods
Information Management (Customer Service)	Customer Service Safety Stock Forecasting	Data Entry Data Correction Information Flows	Data Elements Forms Reports
Product Management (Storage Density)	Storage Staging Handling	Storage Profiles Handling Profiles Material (Product) Flows	Sizes Weights Orientation
Process Management (Flow Rate)	Issuing Receipt Adjustment	Dependent Demand Independent Demand Process (Functional) Flows	Transaction Types Transaction Volume Transaction Timing
Quality Management (Inventory Accuracy)	Containerization Identification Inventory Accuracy	Part Characteristics Product Characteristics Decision Characteristics	Part/Product Protection Part/Product Identification Count/Dollar/Data Accuracy
Organization (Capability)	Education Training Personal Development	Knowledge Skills Abilities	Tasks Priorities Durations
Facilities and Equipment (Reliability)	Facility Layout Automation Vehicles/Equipment	Mix Throughput Capacity	Volumes Rates Uptime
Systems and Technologies (Flexibility)	ERP/MRPII/Inventory Material ID (Bar Code) Communication (RF,EDI)	Hardware and Software Functions and Features Capabilities and Expansion	Response Times Error Rates Recovery Time

dures will change, it can be argued that little emphasis should be placed on the As-Is definition. On the other hand, it may take a well-defined As-Is baseline to convince management to make changes. The team needs to work closely with the steering committee to ensure that the level of detail meets the decision-making needs of management and the team. The following process is used to document the As-Is inventory baseline:

1. *Scope*—Develop a scope of work. The example shown in Table 3.8 using an integration methodology is representative. From an understanding of the effort required, develop a work plan, schedule, and budget for the effort. Assign team members and establish roles and responsibilities. Let people in the company know who is involved and what the purpose is. Set up a master filing system.

Deliverable(s): Statement of work for each work breakdown structure area, Gantt schedule, assignments (organization breakdown structure and work authorization plans), budget (in terms of hours per team member, contractual costs for purchased services, and expenses), and description or definition of deliverables.

Use: This information is used to manage and control the strategy definition and development processes.

2. *Interviews*—Interview key inventory personnel and their customers. Document daily/weekly/monthly activities in terms of who, what, when, where, why, and how. Start with the most experienced personnel and compare what they do with what the least experienced individuals do. Focus on both time-critical and time-consuming activities, priorities, methodologies, techniques, and reasons. Define the interrelationships among policies, procedures, and practices. How can activities be eliminated? For those which cannot be eliminated, how can they be streamlined or facilitated? Publish the notes and get feedback from the interviewees and others in the organization.

Deliverable(s): Interview notes, activity profiles per time period, observations, insights, and recommendations for improvement.

Use: This information is used to obtain undocumented operational and organizational information and to verify consistency across functional areas.

3. *Documentation*—Obtain copies of relevant labels, forms, paperwork, and report pages. Develop a cover sheet identifying purpose, frequency, users, fields, usefulness, accuracy, and so on. How can they be eliminated? How can they be improved? Reports and forms represent the *paper* infrastructure of the inventory function.

Deliverable(s): Reference library which can be cross-referenced to flows.

Use: Documentation examples (blanks and fully completed forms) support definition of the information, data, material, vehicle, and container flows. Many individuals will not fully understand these processes so matching logical with physical flows acts as an information transfer. Documentation and related processes are always targets for possible elimination or improvement since they are opportunities to misidentify data.

4. *Flows*—Obtain or develop material, product, vehicle, container, paperwork, process, information and decision flows, rates, and timing profiles. For each step, document supporting information in the form of a cross-referenced matrix. Include personnel involved, time, equipment, systems, floor space, and alternatives. What is the relationship between and among the various flows? What are the key precedence/successor relationships? What percentage of flow takes one path vs. another (e.g., centralized storage or floor stock, inspection or no inspection, and so on)? How many

times is material handled? What are the rates as they relate to full containers, empty containers, disposable dunnage, and scrap? What must occur for steps to be eliminated, shortened, or simplified? Use CAD or a flow charting program. Color-coding the various paths or activities helps to segregate normal from exception (infrequent) from anomaly (error) flows.

Deliverable(s): Material flows, information flows, product flows, process flows, exception flows, and decision flows as required to document operations such as receiving, storage, kitting, issuing, cycle counting, ordering, forecasting, and safety stock planning.

Use: This information is used to better understand operations and to identify time and labor intensive operations which are targets for elimination or improvement. One company in the defense industry required in excess of 100 separate steps to get a resistor received, inspected, and stored. They never realized it until after the actual flow was documented as part of a new product line introduction.

5. *Personnel*—Develop an organizational profile. What are the internal (within inventory) and external (between inventory and the rest of the organization) reporting relationships? What are everyone's roles and responsibilities? What priority is assigned to each task, who defines priorities, and how and when are priorities changed? How much time is involved? What cost in terms of labor hours and dollars is attributable to tasks or activity areas? How can activities be eliminated? How can they be simplified? What are the opportunities for improvement? Inventory is primarily a cost-adding function. Are the costs being offset by greater value to the company in other areas? If so, by how much?

Deliverable(s): Organization chart, roles and responsibilities, and assessment of tasks vs. times vs. priorities.

Use: This information is used to assess how much effort is required to perform operations, to assess existing skills and capabilities, and to formulate personnel reduction, retraining, reassignment, and related plans.

6. *Facility*—Develop a facility profile. What is the current layout? Which areas have adequate space for materials and vehicle access, and which have problems? How much space is allocated to storage, staging, and handling? How effectively is the space utilized? Are there expansion plans? Is storage centralized or distributed? What distance do parts travel? What routes through the facility are used? What are site building height or other restrictions? What are the floor to bottom-of-truss clear height(s)? Are there floor loading restrictions? Are there aspects of the facility which cannot be changed or relocated such as rest rooms, heat treat facilities, power substations, and so on? What are standard aisle widths, equipment access requirements (for safety and maintenance), ergonomic standards, available

floor space, layout restrictions (equipment which must remain in a certain sequence), and so on? If possible, locate parts or part categories on the CAD layout where they are used.

Deliverable(s): CAD layout, layout guidelines and constraints, current space utilization, material flows, and point-of-use locations and empty container/rack/carrier flows overlaid on the facility layout.

Use: This information will be used to compare layout alternatives and, therefore, the magnitude of effort required to make changes.

7. *Equipment*—Develop an equipment profile. What equipment is currently in use? How much storage of what type (pallet, bulk, bin, and so on) is available? What weights and sizes can be supported? Are there special environmental, safety, ergonomic, maintenance/access, or security requirements? How closely coupled are material handling and storage systems with manufacturing processes and equipment? What capabilities such as height or weight capacity do vehicles or other special equipment possess? Assess equipment capabilities against requirements. Define access requirements in terms of aisle widths, turning radius, travel restrictions (such as move distance which a forklift can perform before it is more economical to use a tugger), and capacities.

Deliverable(s): Equipment located on CAD layout, equipment capabilities and restrictions, and opportunities for relocation.

Use: This information is used to compare layout and production alternatives, especially with respect to reducing handling distances and improving work station layouts.

8. *Systems*—Develop an inventory system profile. What hardware and software is currently in use, and how does it fit within the company's overall architecture? Is it integrated with other company systems (ERP, MRPII, MES, WMS, WCS, storage, handling, bar code, radio frequency, and so on)? What screens, reports, and data fields are available? How accurate and timely is the information? How is it used? Is the data formulated in decision support format? Can data be downloaded to spreadsheets or database programs for analysis? Systems typically handle the mechanics related to processing inventory transactions fairly well. They vary widely in their ability to support the planning and decision support process. Homegrown or heavily customized systems (sometimes referred to as "legacy" systems if the company is unwilling to consider upgrades or replacement) entail a great deal of ownership. Maintaining objectivity regarding their value is difficult.

Deliverable(s): System assessment in terms of its ability to support current and future operations and performance objectives of inventory turns, cycle time reduction, and inventory accuracy. Screens and flows which may require change, elimination, or replacement should be documented.

Use: This information is used to assess how well the system supports the organization and whether it is constraining further improvements.

9. *Inventory*—Develop a Raw, Work in Process, and Finished Goods inventory profile. What are the company's product lines and products? What types and classifications of inventory are stored and handled? What are the relevant order quantity, safety stock, forecasting, handling, storage, and identification characteristics? Which factors result in surplus, excess, inactive, and obsolete inventory? What rates must be supported (usage and replenishment)? What timing considerations or shelf lives apply? How is inventory stratified in terms of categories for planning, control, and accounting purposes? Planning information related to "logical" control (i.e., ordering, safety stock, and forecasting) is typically readily available. Information related to "physical" control such as part, container, and unit load weights and dimensions for storage and handling purposes must often be produced from scratch.

Deliverable(s): Stratify inventory in terms of operating (required to support current operations), business (safety stock, service, and R&D), and financial (surplus and excess) inventory. Create a database of storage, handling, and identification characteristics.

Use: This information, along with an understanding of the manufacturing focus and environment, product life cycles, and so on enables changes consistent with the To-Be environment to be evaluated.

10. *Performance*—Assess the current and historical performance of the inventory function. What measures and indicators are used to monitor daily, monthly, and annual performance? How much control does inventory have over these measures? How are they calculated? What actions are taken if targets are missed? What tolerances are allowed? How is performance trending? What factors (business volume, new product introduction, and so on) cause the measures to vary or to experience spikes or dips? Are the measures being manipulated by delaying receipts, changing policies, and so on? Document information at an agreed point in time to act as a baseline for inventory turns, customer service, storage utilization, cycle time, and inventory accuracy.

Deliverable(s): Current measures and indicators, supporting analyses, and identification of pressure points.

Use: This information is used to assess the relevancy of current measures with respect to the integral strategy and to define a fixed inventory baseline in time against which to compare targets.

The To-Be Targets Quantify Each Level of Improvement Over Time

An arbitrary target is one which has intuitive appeal without having any real correlation to required performance or company strategies. "Reduce inventory investment by 10 percent" is an arbitrary target. This type of target sounds impressive to management. It gives the appearance of having set a strategic direction without having to actually spend any time or effort to develop a strategy.

The problem with arbitrary performance directives is that there is no integrated set of tactics, initiatives, projects, and programs for achieving them. Arbitrary targets invite arbitrary tactics. These are likely to be detrimental to other areas of the company. Reducing inventory balances by reducing order quantities and safety stock levels increases inventory turns. Who can say that a related increase in expediting, airfreight, and shop overtime costs are the result of this particular tactic? These types of cost increases are *external* to the inventory function and will, therefore, not adversely affect any *internal* inventory performance measures. This explains why these tactics are used so often.

To-Be targets need to be internally consistent within the inventory management area and externally consistent with the strategies of the other functional areas. Once companies have a cohesive rationale for the way they operate, targets become obvious.

Improvement Actions Dictate the Level of Required Commitment

One significant difference with integration as compared to traditional improvement approaches is the focus on infrastructural improvements as enablers of operational improvements. Companies can only go just so far without changing the capabilities with which the next level of improvement is gained. It is the infrastructural changes themselves which enable the company to sustain the improvement by making it impossible to backslide to previous methods of operation. As a consequence, infrastructural changes cannot be left incomplete once begun. If they are, the company ends up with partially integrated systems which do not satisfy the justification requirements related to the original investment.

The "improvement actions" step begins by setting the As-Is baseline performance at one end of a scale and the To-Be performance at the other. The effect of a series of actions is then assessed via analysis, modeling, and simulation techniques and methodologies in a stepwise fashion until the To-Be performance is achieved. Initial actions are those which are completely under the control of the inventory function. These include changing inventory-related policies, procedures, and practices.

As each improvement level is reached, it becomes successively more difficult to achieve the next level as shown in Figure 3.9. This is where external integration factors must be accounted for in terms of interdepartmental cooperation. The highest levels of performance then require even further cooperation among the company, suppliers, and customers.

The strategy development process begins by evaluating initiatives first, followed by projects and programs. The process itself is essentially one of asking and answering a series of questions. The key is not to stop once a perceived barrier to improvement is reached. Continue to identify what is actually required to obtain the required levels of performance. The intent is to identify what it takes to achieve the results, not to provide a value judgment. Management must

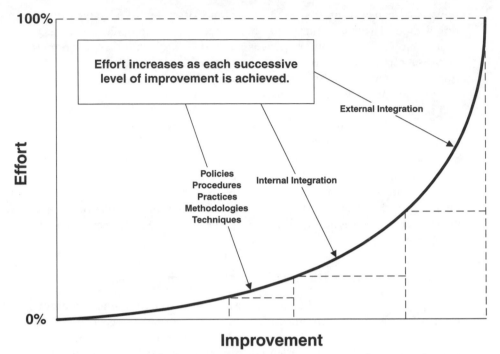

Figure 3.9   Improvement vs. Effort

make any judgments. Types of questions relate to the actual performance measure. What is it? What does it need to be? What must be done to achieve the target? What is stopping the company from achieving the increased performance now?

Inventory Policies, Plans, and Controls Ensure Internal Integration

The inventory internal areas of integration include policies, planning, and control. If the integral strategy describes these areas consistently with what the company is currently doing, then the strategy has probably not been developed properly. Business as usual means results as usual. However, if it appears that a logical migration path exists from the As-Is operations to the To-Be performance levels, then the strategy objectives may have been satisfied. This is not to imply that the strategy will be successful, just that the proper business methodology has been used.

- *Materials*—Has an integrated set of policies been established for the Raw, WIP, and FG categories? This applies to each of the operating, business, and financial categories as discussed in Chapter 2. Can the policies be implemented effectively at part levels of detail to achieve the inventory turns target?

- *Information*—Is the necessary customer or forecast demand, capacity, part, and historical data and information available to support the planning processes? Can the statistical or other relationships among planning techniques be used to achieve the customer service level target?

- *Product*—Are the physical storage, staging, and handling characteristics of the parts identified to the level of detail required to establish equipment requirements? Can the data be used to establish containerization and identification standards which meet ergonomic and automation requirements?

- *Process*—Are the inventory processes documented? Is each process consistent with the integral environment, without carrying any excess baggage associated with the old way of doing business?

- *Quality*—Is the company willing to replace dollar with count accuracy measures? Will the dunnage and related handling, storage, and identification practices protect the parts from damage and misapplication?

- *Organization*—Has the organizational assessment established a clear direction for education, training, personnel development, and assignments? Will company personnel support the required changes?

- *Facilities and Equipment*—Do the layout and equipment represent a sound strategic move to an integral environment? Is the company being realistic regarding timing and justification?

- *Systems and Technologies*—Do the inventory-related systems and technologies enable the organization to achieve the personnel reductions, cycle time reductions, data integrity, timeliness and accuracy of information improvements, flexibility, and so on required to support the integral environment? Will existing systems constrain the ability of other areas of the organization from achieving the significant improvement levels required to meet the company's goals?

The internal integration assessment is intended to force the company to be realistic about their ability and willingness to change existing processes as required to support the initiatives, projects, and programs. All of this must be done while sustaining projected business levels during the transition and implementation time frame. The most important consideration at this point is to clearly understand the commitment and actions involved. Good intentions are for traditional strategies; a sound business plan and approach are required for integration.

Initiatives, Projects, and Programs Ensure External Integration

Perhaps the most difficult aspect of developing any strategy is confirming the company's real intentions and level of commitment. This can be aggravated if key individuals are unwilling to state their concerns when they perceive that top management is pushing hard for acceptance. With traditional strategies, one functional area may not have much say regarding strategies within the other areas.

Integral strategies require *consensus* because they require a tearing down of departmental and functional area boundaries. Issues involve the philosophy itself, as well as costs and schedule.

> *Example:* The first external integration issue is always one of the enterprise operating philosophy choice. Few companies starting out on a path of significant change will target anything less than being World Class. One manager of an electronics company was adamant that all efforts to develop a manufacturing strategy for a new manufacturing plant were to be targeted at World Class levels of performance. This manager felt that setting such a goal would force the organization to overcome their inadequacies. These included having no documented production/work order routings, few documented manufacturing procedures, low quality levels, and a dismal on-time performance record.
>
> At the same time, the manager constrained the team by directing them to use existing component insertion equipment in order to save money. This same equipment had already been targeted for replacement due to an inability to hold tolerances and inability to be integrated into the new production lines. The system integrator hired to manage the transition process advised the manager that World Class performance targets were too aggressive for the company at the time. This was reiterated by the corporate project manager assigned to the project.
>
> This manager had a marketing background and understood the value of World Class competitiveness. However, he lacked any manufacturing management experience. He would not be dissuaded until all of the effort had been expended to develop a World Class strategy and define the related costs in terms of time and effort. Since there was no way the company had the money or capabilities at the current time to pursue a World Class strategy, Best in Class performance was set as the new target. This was much more realistic but required undertaking a significant redefinition effort. The loss of time caused the project to incur a cost and schedule overrun. The final result for the company was a strategy which was much more realistic. However, the cost overrun caused the company to settle for less automation than originally planned. Years later the company is still paying the price in terms of longer cycle times and higher inventory levels. The manager was "encouraged" to find other employment and did.

Once the issue of strategic direction is resolved, the second external strategy issue is always one of cost. Management must establish a capital investment and cost savings direction before the strategy is developed. This enables the team to establish "design to cost" targets for the strategy development effort. The issue of cost is what differentiates realistic from unrealistic companies. Strategic initiatives always seem to cost more than the original budget. Delays are one reason, since costs escalate over time. Scope changes are another. As each milestone is achieved, everyone is more aware of the capabilities being provided and are, therefore, in a better position to focus future efforts into areas of benefit to the company. While this is a mark of flexibility and responsiveness, such changes come with a price tag.

The unrealistic company will fail to recognize such costs or their magnitude. They will overly rely on internally or consultant-developed specifications for systems and equipment. These may overspecify elements which add costs without comparable value. A company's bid specs overspecify systems and equipment when they start designing the supplier's equipment. The more detailed the requirements, the more responsibility the company is taking for system performance. This includes responsibility for the cost increases over the supplier's standard system as well. Warning signals of potentially overspecified and over cost requirements include the following:

- Specifying the number of gear teeth on sprockets when what is important is the conveyor speed.

- Specifying paint thickness when what is important is that the supplier use a painting process that is adequate for the application.

- Specifying the number of threads above a fully tightened nut when what is important is that the nut not loosen up.

- Specifying minor variations in dimensions of standard products when what is important is that the equipment properly handle loads within a range of sizes and weights.

- Specifying accelerations, speeds, and decelerations when what is important is total cycle time.

- Specifying stopping distance of a load when what is important is stopping precision.

Once the issues of commitment and cost are satisfactorily resolved, the decision rests on the business merits of the strategy. If the development process was conducted properly, this should not be an issue. The most visible areas of external integration include facility layout changes to accommodate different material and vehicle flows, computer system changes to graphical user interfaces and decision support formats, use of in-plant or returnable dunnage, and use of RF terminals and bar codes for transaction processing, material identification, and tracking.

The Strategic Plan Formalizes the Integral Inventory Strategy

There are as many ways to document a strategy as there are people developing them. Strategy development is a methodology. The format is not as important as the content. Given that the purpose is to communicate a common direction and purpose, the key is to ensure that the strategic plan becomes a living document. Purpose will typically not change, barring some significant change to the business. However, direction in the form of progress toward objectives and relative priorities will vary over time. A regular process to measure progress is required. This is the function of project management and is discussed in more detail in Chapter 4. A representative format is discussed later in this chapter.

Measures and Controls Translate the Strategy into "People" Terms

A comprehensive, long-term set of tactical initiatives, projects, and programs require a structured set of measures and controls for monitoring progress. Performance measures only apply to areas where something has been performed. Indicators of performance imply an increase or decrease in performance but are not directly related from a mathematical perspective. Capabilities relate to the infrastructural areas and include measures such as reliability, flexibility, maintainability, timeliness, and so on.

Update the Strategy As Required

The strategy development, refinement, and implementation process is a continuous effort. It represents the dedication of a significant amount of time and effort on the part of the company. As such, there needs to be a defined review and update process. Monthly reviews with senior management provide a regular forum for updates, discussions of open issues, and notification of upcoming activities. The meeting should be planned in advance, an agenda published, and a schedule followed. Minutes should be published and distributed. The plan itself is updated as required.

The "11th" Step

It may seem redundant to say this, but so many companies do not finish what they start. The final or "11th" step is really the beginning. *Implement the strategy.*

Integral Inventory Strategy Plan

It is the strategy manager's responsibility to identify and then manage the various pressure points which ensure strategy success. This must occur while controlling those issues which can adversely affect strategy results. Where this does not occur, strategies tend to gain a life of their own or die a slow painful death. The strategy plan identifies the scope elements required for a successful implementation. In addition, a plan establishes the common ground rules which enable different individuals, departments, and organizations to perform as a team.

The strategy plan is developed concurrently with the strategy development phase. It defines how the strategy itself will be developed and then implemented. The business reasons for developing the strategy need to be identified, as well as any constraints, qualifiers, and assumptions. Each new phase then adds to, updates, or replaces the original plan. There will be more detail for short-term efforts and summary level detail for later phases. The purpose of the plan is to establish guidelines for implementing the strategy development scope of work. The plan acts as a consistent means of information transfer, since members added to the team over time may not be familiar with the project scope and ground rules.

The strategy plan generally consists of at least the following sections (refer to Figure 3.10):

- *Preface*—contains the table of contents and general information regarding the plan document.

- *Plan Overview*—establishes the business case for developing the integral inventory strategy. This section provides an overview of what the team will ac-

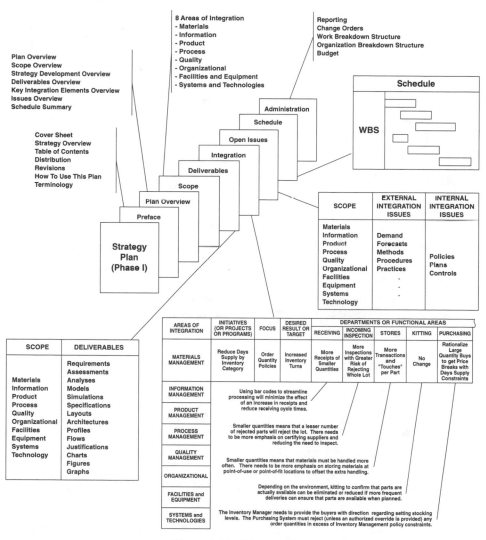

Figure 3.10   Strategy Plan

complish during each phase and establishes expectations of results or improved competitiveness.

- *Strategy Scope*—provides a comprehensive outline of the definition, analysis, flow charting, layout, specification, simulation, assessments, profiles, initiatives, projects, programs, and other work to be performed or developed in order to define and implement the strategy. These efforts span each of the areas of integration (materials, information, products, processes, quality, organization, facilities and equipment, and systems and technologies).

- *Deliverables*—identifies the output of team members, key suppliers, or subcontractors. Deliverables require review and/or approval and are associated with schedule milestones. For an integral strategy, this includes a variety of analyses, plans, specifications, graphical visualizations, procedures, facility layouts, systems and equipment assessments and implementation, and budgets and schedules.

- *Key Integration Elements*—identifies the key operational, organizational, and technological elements which either impact or are impacted by inventory. These are the pressure points which require special emphasis during the strategy development and implementation process.

- *Open Issues*—identifies those issues which must be resolved as part of the next phase of the strategy development process. They are often identified by the necessity to use assumptions in the absence of having a resolved issue.

- *Project Schedule*—uses a Gantt chart to provide an indication of duration, as well as key precedence and successor relationships. Schedule-related details provide explanations which team personnel need in order to fully understand the various interrelationships. Highlight the critical path in red.

- *Project Administration*—specifies the various controls required to ensure that the strategy development and implementation effort is executed in accordance with company management practices and guidelines.

The following subsections provide details.

Preface (Section 0.0)

The strategy plan is going to introduce a number of change concepts to the organization, as well as undergo change itself over time. The Preface section establishes a structure for introducing the plan to the organization and maintaining a degree of revision control over time.

- The *Cover Sheet* identifies the internal company name given to the integral strategy. The date, revision number, and a statement indicating whether copies are "controlled" or not should be included.

- The *Strategy Overview* is a two to three page high level overview of the inventory integral strategy. It describes the inventory vision, states the business benefit to be achieved, and provides key milestones.

- The *Table of Contents* lists each section and subsection. Keep the plan sections short and readable. Include analysis details and source and reference information in the Appendix.

- The *Distribution* page identifies those individuals having authorized copies of the plan. These individuals will receive updates as they are published. Details in alphabetic sequence by name include title, company, address or mail code, phone, fax and e-mail numbers, revision, date, and number of copies, as applicable.

- The *Revisions* page identifies the current revision level and briefly describes the change(s) associated with each revision. Major revisions due to scope or content changes are identified by integer. Minor updates for cosmetic or correction purposes are identified by decimal (e.g., 1.2 is the second update of the first major revision). An overview of each revision is included for quick reference on the Revisions page. Strikeouts and redlines are used to highlight actual changes within the plan itself. Details in tabular format include revision number, revision date, individual making the revision, and revision description.

- *How to Use This Plan* identifies any special conventions used within the documentation which may be unfamiliar to some of the plan users. These are the things which are known to the plan author but which may not be intuitively obvious to the reader. Discussions may be segregated by section and provide equations used for budgeting, hours per week used for production planning, work days and shift hours used in scheduling, and so on.

- *Abbreviations, Jargon, and Terminology* provides a glossary of company-specific or inventory-related terminology. This may go beyond mere definitions with respect to company terms and include number of storage locations, number of parts by category, conveyor rates, percent of storage spaces to number of parts, and so on. The intent is to ensure that everyone has a complete and consistent understanding of terminology used in the documentation. This information may be located at the end of the document if it is longer than one to two pages.

When developing other strategy documentation such as specifications and manuals, these same categories of information may also be included in the prefaces of these documents. The revision information is especially important when the documentation is part of a contractual obligation.

Plan Overview (Section 1.0)

This section acts as a stand-alone overview for individuals interested in understanding the scope and approach, but who do not need all of the details. The intent is to describe each aspect of the plan in a 1-page summary level of detail. The Overview section provides a basic understanding of the scope and how the strategy will be developed. A 1-page summary schedule provides the time frame. Each following section then provides the details. The plan describes the process to be followed to develop the integral strategy. It follows the 10-step process described earlier.

- The *Plan Overview* identifies the business aspects of the plan. This includes clearly stating the business reasons for undertaking the development and implementation effort and performance improvements to be gained. This is the most difficult section of the entire plan to write for its size.

- The *Scope Overview* identifies the inventory-related policy, planning, and control scope encompassed by the plan. Scope includes quantifying goals and objectives and establishing targets, initiatives, project and program definition, and project planning, scheduling, and budgeting. Summarize using the eight areas of integration.

- The *Strategy Development Methodology* identifies the steps involved in the process. This begins with establishment of the inventory vision and then proceeds through definition, analysis, concept, development, and implementation steps. The reader should generally understand the structured methodology which will be used to translate the qualitative vision into a quantitative strategy.

- The *Deliverables Overview* identifies the documentation, analyses, models, simulations, layouts, implementations, and so on to be provided. These include the tangible things that company personnel will see as support or actual changes to current operations. Phase I deliverables, for example, include As-is and To-be facility layouts, graphical visualizations of new processes, requirements definition, flow charts, and related plans, schedules, and budgets for the following phases.

- The *Key Integration Elements Overview* identifies how the key internal and external integration elements will be addressed by the strategy. These elements typically include how goals and objectives will be quantified where they are affected by other than inventory department factors. Procedures for addressing organizational, facilities and equipment, and systems and technologies choices will also be addressed.

- The *Issues Overview* identifies the known areas where restrictions, constraints, qualifiers, and unknowns exist with regard to the integral strategy. These are areas which must be resolved as part of the strategy process or which must be assigned a risk factor and addressed at a later time.

Strategy Development Phase I Scope (Section 2.0)

The Strategy Scope section establishes the boundaries of the development effort. Inventory scope typically includes definition and analysis of inventory objectives and establishment of targets, specification of management policies and inventory-related procedures, selection of inventory methodologies and techniques by product (line) or inventory category, facility layout, specification of systems and equipment related to material handling and storage, and definition of decision support system(s) required to support strategic planning and engineered improvement. Scope limits or constraints are identified in order to focus efforts into acceptable areas. "Sacred cows" in the form of organizational restrictions, "legacy" information systems which management will not allow to be changed, and facility and equipment restrictions are also identified.

Table 3.10 identifies the general areas encompassed by the scope. At the Phase I strategy level, the Scope encompasses all inventory policy, planning, and control elements, as well as all integration aspects of the operational and infrastructural areas of integration.

- The *Focus* column identifies the special emphasis of each area of integration. This must be consistent with the vision, which provides the common focus. The focus identifies the type of information to be obtained and the use which will be made of the information.

- The *Type of Information* column identifies the balance of As-Is and To-Be information required to support the strategy development effort. In general, this will additionally require various types of analyses in order to translate As-Is data into decision support information. Each deliverable will have a specific set of source and reference information required to support the development effort.

- The *Deliverables* column is essentially a compilation of the plans, layouts, specifications, analyses, and so on, required to complete the strategy and plan. In general, the deliverables encompass all of the elements required to initiate the strategy implementation process.

Keep in mind that scope, constraints, or restrictions established at the beginning of the strategy development process may not survive a strong business case to change them. Any strategy development and implementation effort will uncover areas which either were not considered when the process was initiated or became apparent after other improvements were identified. If this happens, it may profit the company to revise the initial project ground rules.

Each follow-on phase then has its own initiative, project, and program definitions. Section 2.0, therefore, encompasses all four strategy development and implementation phases, to an appropriate level of detail.

Strategy Deliverables (Section 3.0)

The primary strategy plan deliverable in Phase I is the plan itself. Elements of the plan vary based on the needs of the company and the scope but include at least the following:

- *Layouts*—A To-Be layout identifies the facility and equipment arrangement targeted to support the integral strategy. There may be multiple layouts to reflect the need to time phase changes. Each layout should use a color

Table 3.10   Representative Phase I Inventory Integral Strategy Development Scope

AREA OF INTEGRATION	FOCUS	TYPE OF INFORMATION	DELIVERABLE
Materials Management	establish inventory investment levels to target by category, product line, product family, product, and part	- as-is and historical turns/investment - industry turns for benchmarking - justifiable inventory level - inventory stratification - inventory drivers - barriers to improvement	time-phased inventory investment assessment and targets, with policies and plans by category (Raw, WIP, and FG) and/or product, product family, or product line

Information Management	define information requirements to achieve customer service level targets	- as-is and historical service levels
		- industry levels for benchmarking
		effectiveness in supporting:
		  - managerial decisions
		  - planning decisions
		  - control decisions
		- information and paperwork flows
			time-phased customer service assessment and targets, with product profiles in marketing lead time and quality terms sufficient for establishing safety stocks and forecast requirements. Inventory computer system assessment, with recommendations for upgrades, replacement, further integration, and so on, as required to support the daily planning and control operations of the company

Product Management	establish storage utilization levels consistent with inventory and customer service targets	- product profiles - part profiles - containerization profiles - identification profiles - barriers to improvement	- storage requirements - staging requirements - point-of-use requirements - point-of-fit requirements - containerization standards - identification requirements
Process Management	define managerial, planning and control processes required to reduce cycle times	- formal processes - informal processes - process effectiveness - barriers to improvement	processes defined in terms of charts, visual aids, descriptive procedures, and so on, as required to ensure consistency and understanding of operations
Quality Management	identify inventory accuracy and part protection requirements	- current levels of count accuracy - effect of accuracy vs. inaccuracy - containerization and identification - causes of inaccuracy or damage	time-phased count accuracy assessment and targets, with part protection and containerization profiles
Organization	organizational assessment	- as-is and to-be personnel profile - training profile - education profile - development profile	to-be organization and assignments, with a migration path outlined in terms of training, education, transfers, and new hires

Table 3.10 *Continued*

AREA OF INTEGRATION	FOCUS	TYPE OF INFORMATION	DELIVERABLE
Facilities and Equipment	existing vs. new equipment, layout, and facilities	- as-is and to-be layout(s) - equipment specifications - material and vehicle flows - facility and layout parameters	to-be layout and alternatives showing new or relocated equipment as a comparison to existing operations
Systems and Technology	existing vs. new systems and technologies	- as-is and to-be system profiles - system specifications - software and hardware parameters	to-be system architecture and definition of a migration path, as a comparison to existing operations

scheme to differentiate changed areas. Annotations (brief text descriptions) identify the nature of the changes. Detail layouts may include work stations, elevation views of storage systems, and cross-sectional views of equipment and facility interfaces as required to understand the nature of the changes.

- *Subplans*—Each initiative, project, and program requires a subplan as part of the strategy plan. Each includes scope, deliverables, budget, and schedule.

- *Specifications*—System elements which cannot be purchased off-the-shelf require some type of purchase or design specification. This may encompass mechanical, electrical, controls, computer, dimension, installation, facility, safety, maintenance, ergonomics, and operational elements.

- *Analyses*—Analysis tools developed to define targets in the strategy phase can be used in the following phases to further detail actions and monitor improvements over time. As such, they require a level of documentation and definition that may not be provided for a tool only intended to be used once. Representative analyses for things which will change over time include inventory turns as a function of business and inventory levels, customer service as a function of safety stock investment, and storage sizing as a function of days supply.

- *Architecture*—Computer architectures encompassing business systems and network connections through PC controls for SRMs, Conveyors Systems, and so on provide a comparison between As-Is and To-Be systems.

- *Assessments*—Organizational, technical, and financial assessments provide the decision support information required to choose among business alternatives.

- *Profiles*—A variety of operational, organizational, and technological decisions must be based on an understanding of the company's business and competitive environment. Product, process, storage, handling, containerization, information, cycle counting, and inventory category profiles describe the relevant aspects of each business area or element related to the integral strategy. This sets standards by which strategy-related decisions can be made with some degree of consistency.

Key Integration Elements (Section 4.0)

The Key Integration Elements section identifies the external areas of integration with the rest of the organization and the internal areas of integration within the inventory management function. These are the areas which may be handled in an inconsistent manner if no overriding policies are preestablished. A representative example includes purchasing buying in large quantities to achieve lowest unit costs at the same time inventory management is attempting to lower quantities to increase inventory turns.

What appears like a good move from an inventory management perspective must be evaluated with respect to its effect on the other departments and functional areas. Depending on the complexity, one or more matrices may be developed in order to time-phase impacts, to focus on cost vs. quality vs. responsiveness areas, and so on. Each basic format should be consistent so personnel can find the things that affect them in the same place in each matrix.

The representative Integration Matrix shown in Figure 3.11 has the eight areas of integration as the vertical axis and the departments or functional areas as the horizontal axis. With the initiatives, projects, and programs listed as part of the vertical axis in each area of integration, the effects (as applicable) on the other areas can be identified. Once the summary level of detail is defined, individual matrices by department can be developed to more fully develop the requirements of the strategy development and implementation process.

Open Issues (Section 5.0)

The Open Issues section identifies those issues in each phase which must be resolved as part of the strategy development and implementation process. These are either unknowns which involve assumptions and which, therefore, have risk or are actual barriers to improvement. Table 3.11 provides a representative listing of relevant issues which must be addressed within each of the areas of integration.

Project-related issues can also be expected. These include time and budget constraints, justification levels which are based primarily on individual projects rather than comprehensive integration programs, and inability to commit full-time personnel for the complete duration. The strategy plan must accommodate all of the issues in a manner which best balances constrained resources with the strategy targets.

The core team is responsible for bringing such issues to the steering committee. The steering committee is responsible for establishing the proper balance and tradeoffs.

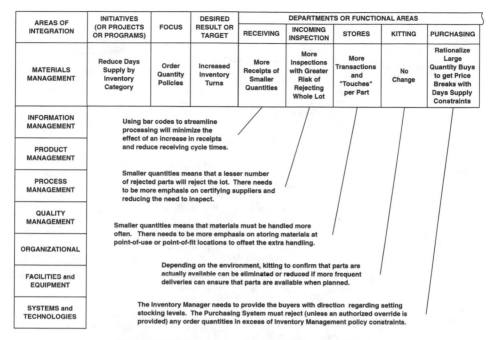

AREAS OF INTEGRATION	INITIATIVES (OR PROJECTS OR PROGRAMS)	FOCUS	DESIRED RESULT OR TARGET	DEPARTMENTS OR FUNCTIONAL AREAS				
				RECEIVING	INCOMING INSPECTION	STORES	KITTING	PURCHASING
MATERIALS MANAGEMENT	Reduce Days Supply by Inventory Category	Order Quantity Policies	Increased Inventory Turns	More Receipts of Smaller Quantities	More Inspections with Greater Risk of Rejecting Whole Lot	More Transactions and "Touches" per Part	No Change	Rationalize Large Quantity Buys to get Price Breaks with Days Supply Constraints
INFORMATION MANAGEMENT								
PRODUCT MANAGEMENT	Using bar codes to streamline processing will minimize the effect of an increase in receipts and reduce receiving cycle times.							
PROCESS MANAGEMENT	Smaller quantities means that a lesser number of rejected parts will reject the lot. There needs to be more emphasis on certifying suppliers and reducing the need to inspect.							
QUALITY MANAGEMENT								
ORGANIZATIONAL	Smaller quantities means that materials must be handled more often. There needs to be more emphasis on storing materials at point-of-use or point-of-fit locations to offset the extra handling.							
FACILITIES and EQUIPMENT	Depending on the environment, kitting to confirm that parts are actually available can be eliminated or reduced if more frequent deliveries can ensure that parts are available when planned.							
SYSTEMS and TECHNOLOGIES	The Inventory Manager needs to provide the buyers with direction regarding setting stocking levels. The Purchasing System must reject (unless an authorized override is provided) any order quantities in excess of Inventory Management policy constraints.							

Figure 3.11 Integration Matrix (Effect of Reducing Normal Purchasing Order Quantities)

Project Management (Section 6.0)

The Project Management section of the strategy plan includes the type of information required to obtain at least a basic understanding of the overall schedule and risk areas. The schedule itself includes a 1-page summary, with details as applicable. Both should highlight the critical path (in color), with the detail schedule additionally identifying key precedence-successor interrelationships.

A separate listing of key milestones enables the strategy manager to add descriptive information regarding decisions to be made and alternative courses of action based on the decisions. This is the type of information which cannot be obtained from the Gantt schedule. Any opportunities for schedule improvement are also identified, with the criteria necessary for such reduction.

Perhaps the most important, and most often neglected, schedule information is an assessment of the effect of a schedule delay at each milestone. "Time is money" is not just a statement. Delays really do cost a company money in terms of extra costs of delaying suppliers and delays in obtaining the cost reductions associated with the strategy. It sometimes seems an anomaly of project work that a company will go to a great extent in order to financially justify a project and then largely ignore the need to maintain the schedule upon which the financial justification is based.

Table 3.11   Integral Strategy Issues

AREAS OF INTEGRATION	EXTERNAL INTEGRATION	INTERNAL INTEGRATION
Materials (Inventory Turns)	- Dependent demand is controlled by Inventory Management - WIP level is not controlled by Inventory Management - FG level is not controlled by Inventory Management	- Inaccurate forecasts for independent-demand items - Material is not stored in a timely manner - Surplus and obsolete materials remain in stock
Information (Customer Service)	- Product forecasts are inaccurate - Customers demand shorter lead times than quoted - Schedule changes disrupt operations	- Part service levels may not be set high enough - Inventory system does not provide decision support - Not really sure what service level is being provided
Product (Storage Utilization)	- Production needs space used for storage - Storage methods not state-of-the-art - Poor use of the available storage cube	- Centralized storage has an inefficient layout - Need to stage more material at point-of-use - Need to stage more material at point-of-fit
Process (Cycle Time)	- Supplier lead times too long - Manufacturing cycle times too long - Marketing lead times too short	- Receipt processing is too slow - Incoming inspection processing is too slow - Storage and handling processing is too slow
Quality (Inventory Accuracy)	- Perception that financial accuracy is sufficient - Lack of follow-on to identify causes of inaccuracy - Lack of mistake-proof methods to ensure accuracy	- Accuracy tolerances permit count inaccuracy - Control groups are not used - There are no containerization standards
Organizational (Responsibility)	- Company has no formal education program - Company has no formal training program - Company has no personal development program	- Contractual restrictions - Resistance to change - Personnel turnover problems
Facilities and Equipment (Reliability)	- Layout restrictions - Aisle width restrictions - Ceiling height restrictions	- Forklifts cannot reach past 4th storage level - All storage is designed for the maximum size load - Location identification is inconsistent
Systems and Technologies (Flexibility)	- Legacy systems cannot be replaced - Batch processing - Lack of bar code identification standards	- Company cannot use supplier bar codes - Bar code positioning not consistent for automation - All transactions are via pick lists or paperwork

Appendixes (A-Z)

Any detail which is not of general interest to a large number of individuals should be in the Appendixes. This permits the strategy plan itself to be kept to a manageable number of pages since the Appendixes will grow over time. All of the source and reference information used as a basis for the balance of the strategy belongs in the Appendix.

SUMMARY

The only purpose an integral strategy has is to significantly improve the competitiveness of the company. This requires a long-term zero-tolerance vision which sets a very specific direction for the organization and a documented strategy which as clearly as possible defines how to achieve the various targets established in each area of integration.

Establishing an As-Is baseline is required to identify the barriers to improvement which have impeded past efforts. Just as the inventory infrastructure provides a strong foundation for the materials, information, product, process, and quality operational areas, the As-Is baseline provides the informed basis required to launch initiatives, projects, and programs with a high confidence of success.

The To-Be targets represent management's conviction of the level of performance which must be achieved in order to be competitive. This does not necessarily mean being the market leader, but it does mean being competitive regardless of competitive ranking.

The final element of the strategy is to confirm that the targets are achievable and that the required levels of commitment exist. Internal commitment within the inventory department is easy to obtain. External commitment to the company's inventory strategy is much more difficult since so many more variables exist once the strategy is broadened to include external inventory factors. This is an area where the company must make a series of business decisions based on choices and assumptions.

The strategy plan is the first formal deliverable of the core team. It sets the direction to be followed for all team personnel. As the strategy development and then implementation process continues, the plan should be kept current to act as a source of consistent information transfer as new team members become involved. Maintaining a time line as part of the Revision information in the Preface helps to keep track of direction changes and decisions over time.

Chapter 4

Project Management Is the Management of Interrelationships

Project management is essentially the management of interrelationships. These include intercompany, interdepartmental, interpersonal, task precedence and task successor interrelationships, budget and schedule tradeoffs, design and performance tradeoffs, documentation and specification precedence, and so on. The more effectively these are managed, the more successful the project. Each interrelationship involves choices.

An integral inventory strategy is essentially a complex series of initiatives, projects, and programs. The complexity comes from the fact that all aspects of how the company competes are being addressed concurrently. The projects relate to the infrastructural areas of facilities, equipment, systems, and technologies, with an emphasis on organizational issues. The organizational aspect then supports the longer term programs in the operational areas of integration. The same standard methodologies and techniques used to professionally plan, schedule, and control smaller projects apply to strategies.

Planning establishes a managerial infrastructure within which the integral strategy is developed and then implemented. The strategy development plan contains the guidelines for developing the strategy. These in turn embody the guidelines for achieving the company's inventory vision. Planning includes defining project scope and interrelationships, setting priorities, quantifying objectives, specifying constraints (limits), qualifiers (if/then), and assumptions, and assigning roles and responsibilities. The key element of any plan for developing an integral strategy, however, is an identification of the issues to be resolved which are preventing the company from achieving the vision. This permits profiles of the risk areas to be developed and managed. Once the strategy is implemented, individual detailed plans are required for each initiative, project, and program.

Scheduling time-phases work elements, determines the critical path based on resource loading and lead times, and identifies key milestones and task interrelationships. This involves developing a project schedule in terms of a Gantt chart and defining precedence and successor relationships. Personnel resource requirements in terms of hours and duration can then be defined. The schedule for the strategy development phase is less detailed than follow-on implementation phases since there are more unknowns.

Control establishes a project infrastructure within which to manage risk, track progress against targets, and accommodate changes. The first area of risk in a strategy development effort is that the strategy will not be developed properly. This type of risk requires experience and cannot be addressed by project control techniques. The second area of risk is that the budget costs or schedule will be exceeded. This is a situation that may well occur if the company begins with unrealistic expectations. Administrative elements of control include time card reporting and estimates to completion, cost monitoring, and status reporting.

Standard project methodologies and techniques support the scheduling and control processes. However, there is no substitute for experience with respect to project planning and managing team activities. The same, of course, may be said of inventory management. The key to effective planning is to use a structured integration methodology which is straightforward to understand and adaptable to change.

This chapter covers the following aspects of managing the implementation of the integral strategy:

- An overview of the four *Integral Strategy Phases* is provided, including a discussion of how initiatives, projects, and programs relate to the strategy development and implementation effort.

- A discussion of *project management-related issues* focuses on the question of strategy boundaries and approaches for teaming and developing the strategy.

- A review of key *project management methodologies and techniques* is used as a means of demonstrating how to translate the integral strategy effort into its project planning, scheduling, and control elements.

Strategies have an infrastructure in much the same way as the company does. The stronger and more well-defined the infrastructure, the more control the company has over the strategy implementation process. Project management fundamentals provide the control.

PROJECT MANAGEMENT INTERRELATIONSHIPS

The Windows-based project management and scheduling packages available on the market are fairly easy to use. Their primary use in actual practice is to produce Gantt charts. Advanced practitioners also use them to develop resource loaded schedules with time-phase personnel requirements and costs. Current schedules and status can be directly compared against a baseline to track deviations over time. Color Gantt charts enable the critical path to be displayed in red. A two-day training class in fundamentals and advanced principles is an excellent investment when getting started.

Each package has its own drawbacks. It is usually necessary to find them out in actual practice since suppliers do not publicize them. For example, an integrated master schedule consisting of multiple subschedules by program, project, or subproject area may have common milestones linking the various projects. Construction of a warehouse facility and installation of high-rise storage racks for an Automated Storage and Retrieval System (AS/RS) may be set up as two separate projects due to having different suppliers. Some of the milestones will be common. It may not be possible to link milestones automatically via the software package using a "master project" feature, which may only synchronize project beginning and ending dates. In this situation, it is possible for a subproject to get out of sync with related projects if the milestones do not remain fixed. This can be worsened if different subcontractors are updating their own schedules. A master scheduler should be assigned to an integral strategy so there is one *official* schedule.

Other issues packaged project management software cannot deal with relate to the choices of significance to integral strategies. These are the relationships which add to the complexity of the project management process, while not being directly under control of the process itself. These issues are where experience pays many times the cost of a project manager's salary:

Company specifications	vs.	Supplier standard products
Company expectations	vs.	Supplier commitments
Company goals	vs.	Company commitment
Project profit or savings	vs.	Project risk
Project budget	vs.	Actual cost
Schedule requirements	vs.	Supplier and subcontractor lead times
Proposed scope	vs.	Actual scope
Personnel requirements	vs.	Personnel availability and capabilities
Resource requirements	vs.	Resource availability
System performance	vs.	System design
Project changes	vs.	Ability to incorporate changes
Shared risk	vs.	Shared responsibility
Short-term solutions	vs.	Long-term costs and problems
Program size/complexity	vs.	Degree of control

These relationships change based on the effect of the following (and other) issues:

Integration targets	vs.	The time to achieve them
Company's expectations	vs.	What they will accept
Safety stock cost	vs.	Value of having safety stock
Order quantity level	vs.	Transportation cost
Standard	vs.	Nonstandard containers

Lead time reduction	vs.	Marketing lead time
Facility layout	vs.	Equipment and accessibility requirements
Centralized	vs.	Point-of-use storage
Cost	vs.	Value of education, training, and development
Capital investment	vs.	Justification
Time to achieve results	vs.	Level of available resources
Internal	vs.	External teaming
Bid specifications	vs.	Performance specifications
Technology applications	vs.	Technology costs and payback
Product proliferation	vs.	Product standardization
Process flexibility	vs.	Process reliability
Volume flexibility	vs.	Level of automation

As can be seen from these choices, strategy development and management is not a "typical" project. An experienced strategy manager and core team is required. The strategy will only be as good as the team and the ability of the company to accept reality and the compelling need to change. A variety of choices must be made and each will affect the development and implementation process.

INTEGRAL INVENTORY STRATEGY PHASES

Integral inventory strategy development and implementation progresses through four distinct phases. Each succeeding phase further solidifies and builds on the gains made in the previous phase(s). The focus is on strengthening the inventory management core competency areas. The four phases are shown in Figure 4.1 as a sequential process, though they overlap to a greater or lesser extent in actual implementation. Each new phase can be initiated once the necessary foundation elements are in place. Other considerations include whether the company has available resources and whether the timing is consistent with other ongoing initiatives, projects, and programs.

Phase I *Strategy Development* provides an opportunity for management to step back from the day-to-day operating problems and establish a strategic direction for the company. The need at this point is to develop a vision consistent with their customers' expectations and the company's capabilities. The process involves establishing a series of progressively more demanding targets, using the

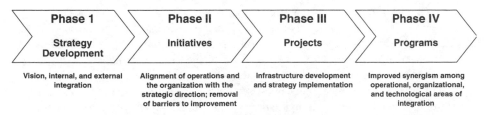

Figure 4.1 Integral Strategy Phases

current environment as the baseline. This was discussed in Chapter 2. The Strategy Plan (Chapter 3) then documents the process required to achieve them. The intent is to force a paradigm shift in the company's thinking and open up new opportunities for the company. This is the purpose of Just in Time, Short Cycle/Lean/Agile Manufacturing and other operating philosophies relevant to inventory management.

Phase II *Initiatives Phase* forces the company to get its own house in order. Initiatives are primarily preparatory in nature. They are designed to remove impediments to improvement or align business processes with the strategy. The intent is to break from practices which have acted as barriers to progress in the past. Examples include improving inventory accuracy and streamlining storage and handling flows and processes.

Phase III *Projects Phase* requires the company to invest in its organizational, facilities, equipment, systems, and technology infrastructure. This is the period during which the company burns its bridges behind itself. Layouts are changed, out-of-date systems and equipment are replaced or refurbished, and practices and procedures are redefined. The emphasis is on solidly reinforcing core competencies having to do with inventory policies, planning, and control. The intent is to ensure that the inventory management area will support the mission critical functions of the company while facilitating improvements in cost, quality, and responsiveness areas.

Phase IV *Programs Phase* finally enables company personnel to perform their jobs and achieve the level of performance consistent with the vision established in Phase I. Programs which began as engineered improvement processes become integral to the company's day-to-day operations because they become the day-to-day operations. The intent is to create an environment where company personnel can proactively refine the value-adding and cost reduction processes. This in turn increases the company's flexibility and responsiveness in a changing business environment.

From a project management perspective, each phase has a different focus as shown in Table 4.1. As such, the project planning, scheduling, and control elements vary as well. These are discussed in more detail in the following sections.

Phase I—Strategy Development

Strategic planning involves consensus and team building as well as establishing the integral strategy itself. Any and all current practices and procedures are subject to a critical in-depth review, analysis, and assessment. Since every aspect of current operations has probably been developed by existing personnel, the issue of ownership may become a problem with certain individuals. This is a crucial issue when creating the strategy team, especially if the strategy manager is likely to be one of those individuals with a great deal of ownership.

The organization must believe that senior management is firmly behind the strategy. Otherwise, some individuals provide lip service to the development

Table 4.1   Representative Project Management Focus Over Time

	PHASE I STRATEGY DEVELOPMENT	PHASE II INITIATIVES	PHASE III PROJECTS	PHASE IV PROGRAMS
FOCUS	INTEGRATION - Internal (to Inventory Area) - External (to Other Functional Areas, Suppliers, - and Customers)	PREPARATION - Minimize or eliminate barriers to improvement - Align operations and organization with strategic direction	INFRASTRUCTURE - Organization - Facilities - Equipment - Systems - Technologies	IMPROVEMENT - Materials Management - Information Management - Product Management - Process Management - Quality Management
Planning	Strategic	Tactical	Implementation	Operations
Scheduling	Vision (5–10 Years)	Short-term (1–12 Months)	Mid-term (6–36 Months)	Long-term (2–10 Years)
Control	Budgetary Costs	Minimal Expenses	Fixed Price	Target Operating Cost
Measures	Benchmarks	Progress	Completion	Target Performance

effort and related recommendations. This has the appearance of consensus without the commitment. Later efforts will be hampered by misdirection, misunderstanding, and schedule delays. These are all techniques used by individuals to prove their point that the strategy was no good in the beginning. Those with the power to make a strategy successful have the same power to make it fail.

Note that commitment is often referred to as "organizational commitment" or "managerial commitment." The fact is, only individuals can make commitments. People do not commit to the strategy, they commit to the success of the company. The two are not separable in an integral environment. Management's task is to make this point clear.

Strategic planning based on the eight areas of integration includes goals and objectives (targets) definition and time-phasing, information and material flow charting, material, part, subassembly, product, and process profiling, organizational assessments, facility layout, equipment and systems application and assessment, technology application and assessment, and so on. The focus at this point in the process is to establish an understanding of the business based on a maximum of factual data and a minimum of opinion, perspectives, or conjecture. The intent is to provide the company's decision-makers with the information required for assessing pressure points. Assumptions, forecasts, and projections are then made to compensate for unknowns. The result forms the basis for a common understanding between company management and team members.

Phase II—Short-Term Initiatives

Developing an integral strategy is easily a 6-month or longer effort. A large part of this is due to the number of iterations required to evaluate different alternatives and scenarios. Once this is done, implementation of some of the major projects and programs may still be a year or more away. With this being the reality, the company needs to begin certain initiatives before the strategy is fully defined and launched. These include activities which reduce or eliminate barriers to improvement and which align the organization or operations with the long-term inventory vision.

For example, an effort to identify those factors which contribute to inaccurate inventory balances can begin at any time. Doing so also helps to prioritize the various improvement actions which are included in the strategy plan. Removing impediments to material flow involves facility rearrangements and equipment refurbishment. Removing impediments to organizational improvements involves training and education in inventory-related philosophies, methodologies, and techniques such as provided by APICS. Aligning business processes with the strategy involves establishing more stringent disposition policies and scrapping excess and surplus inventory. Upgrading computer hardware and software provides access to a wider variety of decision support capabilities.

Refer to Table 4.2 for types of actions which reduce barriers to improvement within each area of integration. Barriers consume company resources which can be better applied elsewhere or reduce the efficiency or effectiveness of existing company resources. Resources include money, personnel, time, equipment, floor space, and so on. Initiatives are considered "reactive" if their intent is to resolve the effects of current problems. They are "proactive" if their intent is to ensure that problems, once solved, do not reappear. Initiatives are selected based on the following criteria and encompass each of the eight areas of integration:

- There should be some immediate value to the company.

- There should not be any significant cash outflow expenses.

- There should be some time flexibility to enable personnel to work them into their schedule.

- There should be a well-defined scope and measure of completion.

Materials—Surplus and obsolete inventory categories can be addressed immediately. These categories have an accounting book value but no customer value. This inventory consumes storage space, requires inventory and location tracking within the inventory system, is reported on a periodic/monthly basis, and requires engineering and materials management time to determine the proper disposition. The required *reactive* effort is to dispose of this type of inventory. Scrapping or otherwise disposing of it increases the inventory turns measure. Companies often delay this decision since it reduces profits in the period in which the inventory write-off occurs. The *proactive* effort is to determine which

Table 4.2   Phase II Initiatives for Reducing Barriers to Improvement

AREA OF INTEGRATION	ACTIONS TO REDUCE BARRIERS TO IMPROVEMENT	REASONING
Materials	Scrap excess and surplus materials	Dispose of material which has no business value; increase inventory turns
Information	Improve data and information accuracy	Ensure that decisions are based on accurate information; streamline information flows
Product	Reduce number of suppliers	Increase leverage with suppliers; standardize containers and material IDs across suppliers
Process	Remove materials, containers, scrap, equipment, and so on from places where it does not belong	Clean up areas; make additional floor space available
Quality	Improve count accuracy and control methods	Increase count accuracy; reduce damage due to handling or storage
Organization	Publicize strategy direction and status	Publicize the scope and type of changes being implemented; solicit suggestions
Facilities and Equipment	Refurbish equipment; implement a maintenance program	Assess the capability of existing equipment; improve the reliability of existing equipment
Systems and Technologies	Upgrade personal computer hardware and memory	Standardize computers; ensure that personnel have equal access to information

factors are contributing to the generation of excess and surplus inventory and initiate corrective actions.

Information—A number of strategic decisions will be based on the data contained in the inventory and other subsystem databases. Records which are no longer required for superseded or obsolete parts should be deleted. The remaining records should be reviewed for accuracy and completeness. Any written documentation regarding processes and procedures should also be reviewed and updated. The *reactive* effort involves correcting erroneous or missing data or information and eliminating unused records. The *proactive* effort involves documenting processes and updating fields to reflect current operations.

Product—The number of suppliers may or may not be relevant from a traditional inventory perspective since supplier selection is a purchasing/engineering responsibility. However, reducing the number of suppliers is a step toward container standardization, implementing simple number and ergonomic principles, and bar code identification. Establishing primary suppliers may also help to eliminate certain problems related to purchasing parts from multiple suppliers. For example, parts which have the same electrical or mechanical properties may not have the same dimensions or mounting characteristics. The *reactive* effort involves eliminating suppliers which do not contribute to the company's overall competitive advantage. The *proactive* effort involves establishing simple number, ergonomic, containerization, and identification standards and evaluating prototypes.

Process—Housekeeping is a visible indicator of the level of control within manufacturing and inventory areas. Manufacturing should only have the level and type of inventory targeted for production at any given time. This includes materials for actual released orders, floor stock materials such as hardware, wire, or tubing, and materials specifically staged at point-of-use (production line) or point-of-fit (work station) locations. The *reactive* effort is to remove excess materials, scrap, unused equipment and tooling, and unnecessary containers from the areas where they do not belong. The *proactive* effort is then to initiate housekeeping actions which ensure that the areas remain clear, that work station layouts are redesigned in accordance with ergonomic and dedicated location principles, and that the process of moving waste to as early in the process as possible is begun. Waste encompasses double-handling cardboard cartons which must be disposed of before they introduce contaminants into the production process, and so on. Early in the process means keeping waste from moving from suppliers to receiving, from receiving to storage, from storage to staging, and from staging to production.

Quality (of information)—Inventory location and stock balances are typically not 100 percent accurate. Anything less indicates the magnitude of required improvement. Companies usually implement cycle counting programs for the purpose of improving current count accuracy. They then neglect the most important aspect which is to locate and eliminate causes of inaccuracy. The *reactive* element of cycle counting which is to correct stock balances should be continued. The *proactive* element of error detection and elimination should be started or accelerated. Storage and handling practices should also be evaluated to ensure that materials are protected from damage and that there is no chance of mixing or misidentifying parts.

Organization—One of the most important organizational issues in the Initiatives Phase is to ensure that company personnel know and understand the purpose of the strategy development and implementation effort. Their interest is in how the strategy process is being implemented and in how it will affect them. Education, training, and professional development can begin as a *proactive* effort, while *reactive* efforts include possible reassignment or realignment of responsibilities. Refer to Table 4.3 for representative initiatives related to aligning the organization with the long-term vision within each of the areas of integration.

Facilities and Equipment—Companies which do not have a formal equipment maintenance and refurbishment program experience increasing levels of downtime and an inability to hold manufacturing tolerances. For any equipment required by the integral strategy, an assessment should be made of uptime, reliability, throughput, and remaining useful life. *Reactive* efforts then involve maintaining, repairing, or refurbishing equipment and systems. *Proactive* efforts include training maintenance personnel, establishing computerized maintenance records, stocking service parts, implementing an ongoing preventive maintenance program, and relocating equipment.

Table 4.3 Phase II Initiatives for Aligning the
Organization with the Inventory Vision

AREA OF INTEGRATION	EDUCATION AND TRAINING AREAS TO ALIGN THE ORGANIZATION WITH THE LONG-TERM VISION	SCOPE
Materials	Just in Time	Just in Time philosophy and related simplification principles education
Information	Computer Integrated Manufacturing	Computer Integrated Manufacturing philosophy and related paperless principles education
Product	Concurrent Engineering	Concurrent Engineering philosophy and related engineering principles education
Process	Short Cycle/Lean/Agile Manufacturing	Short Cycle or Lean Manufacturing philosophy and related time-based principles education
Quality	Total Quality Management	Total Quality Management philosophy and related conformance-based principles education
Organization	Employee Involvement	Professional Development in areas related to team building, problem solving, analysis, and so on
Facilities and Equipment	Storage and Handling Systems and Equipment	Safety, maintenance, and troubleshooting training
Systems and Technologies	Bar Code and RF Technologies	System and technology education and operator training

Systems and Technologies—Companies often have much of the data necessary for decision-making. The computer system infrastructure, however, may not be in place to provide equal or adequate access by company personnel needing the data. Upgrading network and computer capabilities to required integration standards is a *reactive* step designed to make existing information more readily available. Standardizing word processing, database, spreadsheet, flow charting, e-mail, CAD, and other types of software supports *proactive* efforts to improve the ability to transfer data and information among personnel and departments in a paperless office environment.

Refer to Table 4.4 for initiatives which align operations with the long-term vision within each of the areas of integration. The focus of Phase II is to get started.

Phase III—Infrastructure-Related Projects

The ability to achieve permanent and significant improvements begins by strengthening the company's infrastructure. This encompasses relayout of the facility (or new facility construction or purchase), equipment procurement and in-

Table 4.4   Phase II Initiatives for Aligning Operations with the Inventory Vision

AREA OF INTEGRATION	INITIATIVES TO ALIGN OPERATIONS WITH THE LONG-TERM VISION	REASONING
Materials	Establish performance measures	Accustom organization to new measures
Information	Simplify information flows and processing	Reduce paperwork
Product	Standardize container quantities	Synchronize container quantities to production quantities
Process	Simplify planning, ordering, forecasting, safety stock, storage, handling, and control processes	Reduce process steps
Quality	Evaluate returnable vs. nonreturnable dunnage alternatives	Standardize container types
Organization	Identify capabilities and education and training requirements for individuals	Develop a personnel profile
Facilities and Equipment	Determine floor space requirements and opportunities for consolidation	Identify the "ideal" layout
Systems and Technologies	Perform assessments of relevant systems and technologies	Determine current capabilities and fit of bar code, RF, and other systems and technologies

stallation, and system and technology implementation and integration. The outcome of this phase enables the resources of the company to be most effectively aligned in support of the mission critical functions of the business. The intent is to ensure that the company's inventory infrastructure supports achievement of the cost, quality, and responsiveness targets without creating any unnecessary barriers to improvements in other areas of the business.

Specific projects vary according to the specific needs of the company. A high volume operation with many parts may need an Automated Storage and Retrieval System (AS/RS) to act as a buffer, integrated with an automated delivery system. An engineer-to-order company may be able to store their raw material inventory in a conventional (nonautomated) storeroom and as Work in Process on the shop floor. This comparison is a specific difference between two companies, but both may rely on bar code labels and paperless processing to track inventory and reduce dock-to-dock cycle times. The integral strategy reinforces a company's strengths and provides for a company's needs while taking advantage of standard methodologies, techniques, products, processes, procedures, equipment, systems, and technologies.

Refer to Table 4.5 for programs and projects representative of those encompassed by an integral inventory strategy. Note that some may argue that Just in Time is a philosophy and not a program. It is definitely a philosophy. However, a

Table 4.5 Representative Phase III Projects as They Relate to Phase IV Programs

AREA OF INTEGRATION	PROGRAMS	PROJECT AND PROGRAM AREAS
Materials	Just in Time	- Reorder Point Definition - Order Quantity Definition - Inventory Turns Analysis - Inventory-Related Decision Support System
Information	Computer Integrated Manufacturing	- Inventory Planning System - Inventory Control System - Service Level Analysis - Forecasting Definition - Safety Stock Definition
Product	Concurrent Engineering	- Centralized Storage - Point-of-Use Staging - Point-of-Use Buffering - Supplier Consolidation
Process	Short Cycle/ Lean/Agile Manufacturing	- Material Handling - Receipt Processing - Storage Processing - Kitting
Quality	Total Quality Management	- Cycle Counting - Returnable Dunnage - Part Protection
Organization	Integral Organization	- Education - Training - Professional Development
Facilities and Equipment	Integral Facility	- AS/RS System - Automated Guided Vehicle system - Automated Electrified Monorail system - Conventional Storage System - Conveyor System - Forklifts, Tuggers, Pallet Jacks, and Battery Chargers
Systems and Technologies	Integral System	- Bar Code Labels - Radio Frequency (RF) Technology - ERP/MRPII/MES/WMS/WCS System - Voice Recognition System

Note that projects cross areas of integration.

philosophy without a vehicle for implementing it is of little value to an organization. It is easiest to define a waste reduction or a simplification program by the name of the related philosophy. The name conveys both the philosophical aspects as well as the related concepts and principles.

Phase IV—Operational-Related Programs

Programs in the materials, information, product, process, and quality areas of integration can be initiated once the infrastructure provides a solid foundation. Programs differ from projects in that they are long-term and continuous in nature. The emphasis is on philosophies and the qualitative aspects of the business such as flexibility, reliability, responsiveness, and so on. Programs have no defined endpoint since they are integral to the ongoing operation of the business. Programs have the primary purpose of aligning and integrating the company's three infrastructural areas of integration with the five operational areas of integration to achieve the objectives of the strategy.

The Projects Phase (Phase III) focuses on inventory tools, processes, and procedures as they relate to managing and controlling inventory in total or inventory by category. The Programs Phase (Phase IV) takes this level of management and control to a detailed level. The focus is on fine-tuning the relationships among individual parts, products, containers, work stations, vehicles, reports, forms, suppliers, employees, and customers. This is accomplished through the application of specific planning and control methodologies and forecasting, order quantity, and safety stock techniques.

Programs are the culmination of the company's integral strategy. They address business areas which require the integration of operational and technological elements with organizational changes. The focus is to proactively refine the day-to-day value-adding process, while continuing to reduce the necessity to react to the adverse effects of nonvalue-adding factors. The company builds on the flexibility inherent in the integrated infrastructure implemented in Phase III. This allows a continual improvement in its responsiveness to the changing demands of the marketplace, while countering the strategies of its competitors.

The engineered improvements targeted by the Programs Phase are methodical but not necessarily *continuous*. Each improvement requires an infrastructural plateau to be reached at some point in order to support the launch of the next level of improvement. The process only appears continuous when observed from a distance over time or by personnel who are not intimately involved with the improvement process. Refer to Figure 4.2. It is important to understand that an improvement effort is not a failure if improvement does not occur in some visible fashion each day or week or month. Both the level and timing of improvements must be planned. As a practical consideration, therefore, the focus of an engineered integral strategy is on permanent improvement against targets, rather than on continuous but undefined improvement as compared to current performance.

PROJECT MANAGEMENT-RELATED ISSUES

Where to draw the boundaries is the most significant issue related to developing an integral strategy from a project management perspective. This is also referred to as the "scope." The important element of the strategy is not how much (or how little) inventory to have or eliminate but how to integrate the integral inventory strategy with those of the rest of the organization to achieve the company's inventory-related goals and objectives. When this is accomplished, the answer of how much or how little inventory becomes a result, not an issue. By necessity, therefore, there can be no boundaries in terms of organizational or departmental silos with respect

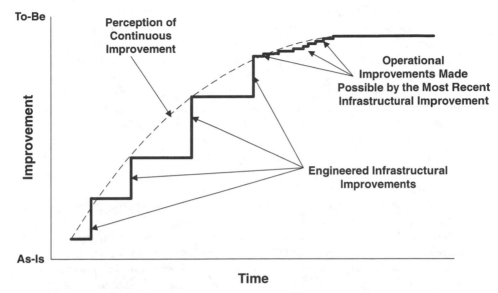

Figure 4.2 Engineered Improvements Associated with Projects and Programs

to the basic Areas of Integration, including materials, information, product, process, quality, organization, facilities, equipment, systems, and technologies.

There may, however, be constraints or qualifiers which limit the team in certain areas. For example, considering the construction of a new warehouse facility in a different geographic location may be specifically prohibited due to cost, timing, market uncertainty, or other factors. However, a new facility addition may well be appropriate from the long-term perspective of the inventory vision considering what the company *may do* or *should do*. The inventory strategy must be based on what the company *will do* in the near to midterm.

Internal vs. Integrator Team Leadership

Integration strategies encompassing significant organizational and operational change are by necessity long in duration and complex in scope. Companies do not reach their current level of opportunity for improvement overnight. There is also a certain business momentum or inertia to overcome. While order of magnitude improvements may be possible, they cannot be achieved overnight either. The first issue a company faces is whether to be its own integrator and manage the strategy development and follow-on phases internally or hire an integrator.

Integration responsibility is a critical issue for a strategy development process. Often, how the process gets started determines how successfully the organization is able to contribute to the development and implementation of the strategy. Creating a 100 percent internal team saves on cash outflow as compared to hiring an integrator. On one hand, if the integrator would have been successful in achieving higher levels of performance, greater long-term savings, and faster payback, saving money with an internal team is false economy. On the other hand, spending money on an integrator is no guarantee of better results. Team leadership is, therefore, a business risk issue.

A related issue when hiring an integrator is whether to contract for the services of an individual or an organization capable of providing its own support group. If the company can provide CAD, analysis, documentation, presentation, and other support services, a team leader may be all that is required. However, the larger and more complex the scope, the greater the need for the team leader to be able to provide core and support team personnel to complement and supplement company team members. This does not simply refer to additional bodies but to individuals having specific areas of materials management, engineering, or other expertise.

An integral strategy differs from more traditional inventory strategies with respect to team members. With integration, there is significantly more emphasis on systems, technologies, and equipment assessments as part of the strategy development process. Depending on the experience the company has with such areas, it may be advantageous to partner with one or more individuals or companies who specialize in providing the knowledge and experience required to supplement the internal team. Very few, if any, companies possess all of the capabilities, experience, and knowledge required of a major integral strategy development and implementation effort.

A number of companies today are partnering with 1st-tier suppliers in the development and implementation of automation and integration strategies. In these cases, the strategy process begins with an evaluation of the potential partners themselves, rather than ends with their selection after the strategy is fully defined. Evaluation criteria include how the supplier conducts business (i.e., availability of different types of contractual relationships), their systems, equipment and technology expertise and products, their project management and contracts administration expertise, and their willingness to provide third-party equipment, systems, and services as part of an integral solution. This has the benefit of reducing the number of suppliers the company must deal with, while increasing the supplier's knowledge and experience with the customer's personnel, facilities, processes, products, and specifications. The primary benefit is obtaining the supplier's skills and willingness to develop the right solution, often independently of their own products and services, as a contributing member of the customer's strategy development/concurrent engineering team.

Both the short- and long-term views are important when hiring an integrator. An integrator who can contribute to the strategy development process may or may not have a value-adding role for some of the follow-on implementation initiatives, projects, and programs. A supplier of systems, equipment, and services may not have a value-adding role with regard to strategy development. The largest system integrators will be capable of contributing in all areas of strategy development and implementation.

Partnership Approach

The company should consider a partnership approach to address this issue of project management and risk assignment when hiring an integrator. First, define the types of resources, knowledge, and experience required of the integrator to complement and supplement the internal project team. This enables one or more partners to be evaluated and selected. Assigning overall project management and risk to a third-party must be compensated for by the company as a part of the business contract.

Finding such partners is not a simple task. A starting point is with companies where there are already established business and working relationships. Trade magazine advertising is also a source, as are industry shows. A common mistake is to limit the search to the surrounding geographic area in order to reduce expenses. This can lead to false economy if an unqualified partner is hired. Representative types of partners which may be involved in developing aspects of an integral strategy include:

- *Consultant* providing development, design, and organizational and operational support services. Such individuals or companies may also specialize in areas such as management consulting, Just in time, ERP, MRPII, MES, WMS, WCS, and other types of automated or conventional implementations.

- *Construction Company* providing construction and installation services. Such companies may take overall responsibility for developing a new site, along with all of the related contractual management responsibilities. Services are more related to the site infrastructure than to operational or organizational aspects once the site is in operation.

- *Engineering Company* providing design and technical services. Such companies may specialize in overall engineering management or product, equipment, or process design. As a partner with a construction company, engineering companies may provide system integration services related to computer systems and equipment, while the construction company maintains responsibility for the site work and facilities.

- *Material Handling Company* providing integrated systems, equipment, and related services. The larger of such companies will manage certain types of integration projects which require the development of multicompany alliances, including construction.

- *Computer or Software Systems Company* providing hardware and/or software. Such companies offer technology and systems expertise in their and related companys' products and services and may also support a company's operational redefinition efforts related to the new systems.

Regardless of the partners selected, the company must provide expertise in their own products and processes. The company is always responsible for the overall success of the initiatives, projects, and programs and for the operational aspects of the final system. Responsibility for strategic competitiveness cannot be delegated to third-parties.

Risk Areas Requiring Some Type of Contingency

Once the preliminary strategy design is solidified in terms of initiatives, projects, and programs, all team members submit their portion of the schedule to the master scheduler. This master project schedule then identifies the critical path along with key precedence/successor relationships to be established. Risk areas require some type of contingency in terms of schedule, additional resources or budget, or all three.

- *Schedule Risk* is greatest for elements on the critical path. Some elements are more critical than others, however. The team must determine how much in lost savings it costs the company to miss a milestone so an assessment can be made as to how much additional cost can be incurred to remain on schedule. Some allowance for schedule flexibility must also be allowed for since the schedule and related critical path are developed well in advance of many aspects of a particular project or program. The company must be prepared to compensate suppliers for delays caused by the company which cause the supplier to incur additional costs. Suppliers must be prepared to exert extra effort in order to maintain schedule commitments.

- *Budget Risk* is greatest for strategy elements performed by the company and implementation areas where one company can delay another. Elements performed by the company typically entail more risk than hiring a supplier in areas where the supplier is more experienced. Suppliers will quote a firm fixed price, while companies typically accept internal delays as a normal occurrence. Delays which cause a supplier to incur extra costs in terms of expenses for extra trips, demobilization (leaving the site) and remobilization, extra hours, and so on, must be reimbursed from the contingency budget. Common areas where one company delays another is in construction and installation phases. Close cooperation and frequent communication helps to minimize delays associated with misunderstandings and omissions.

- *Organizational Risk* is greatest for elements where personnel must change how they perform their job functions. This involves changes to processes, methodologies, techniques, and procedures brought about by the adoption of new philosophies and implementation of new equipment, systems, and technologies. Organizational risk requires primarily a schedule contingency due to delays in developing and presenting the organizational-related impact of a new strategy.

- *Operational Risk* is greatest for elements of the integral strategy which rely on suppliers to reduce lead times and change containerization or customers to improve their forecasting accuracy in order to improve the company's cost, quality, and responsiveness performance measures. To a lesser extent, risk also exists for elements which rely on other company departments to modify their operations to support new inventory goals and objectives. Operational risk requires both a schedule and budget contingency. The greater the number of customers, suppliers, departments, and individuals involved in this area during the Strategy Development Phase, the longer the schedule must be to account for the logistics of coordinating meetings and review cycles.

- *Technological Risk* is greatest for equipment and systems which are unfamiliar to the company. The risk is in setting unrealistic expectations and being disappointed with the reality. Low price is not always "best" price. Companies need to do their homework. An assessment of this risk must be made during the Strategy Development Phase since it will affect schedule and budget considerations, as well as team configuration in follow-on phases.

Companies electing to develop their own integral strategy should consider having a third-party evaluation. Company personnel who are best at managing daily operations requiring primarily tactical skills may not be as effective developing a long-term integral strategy. Internal personnel do not look at the company the same way outsiders will and may not see the same opportunities or problems.

To be most effective, this third-party evaluation must involve regularly scheduled reviews. This enables the reviewer to remain current with progress to date and to understand why certain decisions or recommendations are being made. Otherwise, review meetings run the risk of becoming status meetings where the consultant is expected to rubber-stamp the team's recommendations.

Bid Spec vs. Design-Build Approach

Internal projects tend to gravitate naturally toward a "design/build" approach. Specific definition of the project scope, schedule, and budget is delayed until after a preliminary strategy definition is engineered. This reduces the risk to the company of establishing a direction and budget at a time when insufficient details are known. This is the approach used with concurrent engineering. Given that this is the natural tendency with an internal project, it is inconsistent when the same companies adopt a strict Bid Spec approach when dealing with integrated systems requiring significant levels of supplier involvement.

For externally-managed projects, companies often employ either a formal or informal "proposal" approach. With a more formal approach, the company first develops a Bid Specification or Request for Proposal (RFP). Otherwise, supplier contact may be as informal as a phone call or bid meeting. Typically two or more companies develop a proposal at their expense and submit it for evaluation and acceptance. The degree of specificity depends on the type of project and RFP requirements. Customers commonly require that a specific baseline be quoted and then allow options which enable a supplier to differentiate themselves from their competitors. The theory is that quoting in conformance with the baseline places everyone on an even pricing basis for comparison purposes. The fallacy with this is that companies often do not actually purchase the baseline system due to cost exceeding budget or due to better-priced alternatives offered by the suppliers.

Example: One consultant developed a controls solution requiring three PLCs to control a conveyor subsystem. The application was an air cargo facility where loads must be transferred between the truck docks (landside) and the aircraft (airside). Bidirectional operation is required in parts of the system as shown in Figure 4.3. There was no issue with automatic mode of operation. Loads could be moved from airside to landside and landside to airside completely under PLC and higher level computer control.

The configuration became a problem in manual mode. With the system divided into thirds, pallets could not be moved from the inbound to the outbound conveyors or back. The failure of any one of the three PLCs made flow of loads between airside and landside impossible. The supplier's proposed configuration reduced the number of PLCs by one, saving money while not impacting automatic operations at all. Segregating the system into halves ensured that loads could be moved from airside to landside in manual mode by the left half of the system. Loads could be moved from

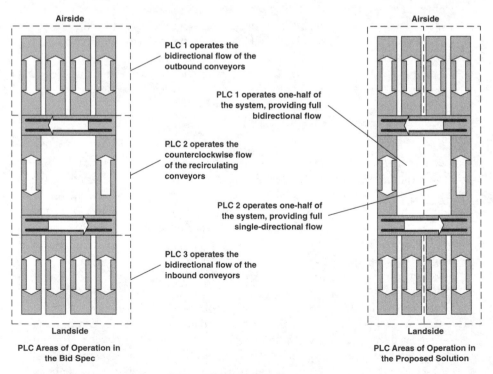

Airside

PLC 1 operates the bidirectional flow of the outbound conveyors

PLC 1 operates one-half of the system, providing full bidirectional flow

PLC 2 operates the counterclockwise flow of the recirculating conveyors

PLC 2 operates one-half of the system, providing full single-directional flow

PLC 3 operates the bidirectional flow of the inbound conveyors

Landside

Airside

Landside

PLC Areas of Operation in the Bid Spec

PLC Areas of Operation in the Proposed Solution

Figure 4.3   Bid Spec Example

landside to airside via either half of the system. A failure of either PLC would not shut down operations.

This is a common example of a Bid Spec requirement which does not consider all aspects of a company's operation. The original design was based on fully automatic operation with no consideration for manual backup. The consultant still required the supplier to quote to the baseline system containing three PLCs, even after being informed of the benefits of the two-PLC solution compared to the specified solution. The end result was that the supplier was able to provide a lower cost and more flexible solution based on their experience. All they needed to know was how the company intended to operate. They did not need the controls scheme predefined.

Companies hire consultants to develop a solution in terms of a Bid Spec and solicit pricing. When dealing with equipment suppliers, this is often the right approach. When dealing with the major system integrators, a Bid Spec approach is as likely to end up costing the company more and extending the schedule for no improvement in system performance or functionality. Providing a Performance Specification is often a much more cost-effective solution if it enables the suppliers to offer better designs. This is often the direction a consultant should pursue rather than a Bid Spec which attempts to design a supplier's equipment. Consultants are not equipment designers. They should not place themselves into a position where they specify changes to a supplier's equipment which are outside of the consultant's realm of expertise. If they do, they should be prepared to accept full responsibility for system uptime, reliability, maintainability, and throughput.

The Bid Spec process is commonly misused in that companies identify errors or omissions in their original thinking. This slows the process down while they revise their Bid Spec and then require the suppliers to submit a second new or revised proposal. This should be stated up front if it is the original intent or even a possibility. This enables the suppliers to establish their selling strategy appropriately. The preliminary proposal can then be followed up with a best and final offer after the suppliers have assisted the company to finalize requirements. In fact, if the company thinks their Bid Spec is not complete, they are much better off soliciting information directly from the suppliers regarding system or equipment operating characteristics, dimensions, throughput, and so on. This permits a better Bid Spec to be developed in the first place.

The RFP approach places much of the burden for project definition and ultimate success on the company's ability to specify systems, equipment, or services which they have not purchased recently (if ever). In this case, some companies hire a third-party to develop the Bid Specification. The theory is that the third-party will protect the company's interests by specifying the appropriate system(s) for the application. While this may have the desired result in certain applications, it typically also increases overall project costs and extends the schedule. Also, third-party companies may have no more experience in some areas than the company.

Pick the Desired Results, Then Develop the Approach

The most effective business approach with respect to developing and implementing an integral strategy is to combine the best of the preceding alternatives. This may mean developing specifications for portions of the project but only after the issues are resolved. Strategies and their related initiatives, projects, and programs are not some off-the-shelf commodity purchase which lend themselves to a price comparison from a number of suppliers. Bid Specs based on an assumption that the purchase can somehow be reduced to a dollars and cents decision are inappropriate in such situations.

- Deal with qualified suppliers. Low cost does not automatically mean best value. One company is replacing a 2-vehicle AGV system after one year. The vehicles cannot navigate the complete path without operator assistance. No spare parts are available so one vehicle had to be cannibalized to keep the other going.

- Educate yourself in the equipment, vehicles, software, controls, and technologies. Suppliers are likely to offer different solutions which may or may not be equally applicable in a particular environment. Learn to separate sales hype from sales support. Stay away from companies who rely on negative selling tactics against their competitors. Each supplier's equipment and systems should stand on their own merits.

- Involve the suppliers early in the design process. Time available is directly proportional to the quality of the solution. A red flag should go up any time the company provides their suppliers less than four weeks to quote a fairly standard system. A minimum of four to six weeks should be provided for complex integrated systems (longer where major construction is involved).

- Allow the suppliers to develop solutions around their strength. Overall system performance and functionality is more important than specifying roller wall thickness for conveyors carrying standard load weights. Tell suppliers what you really need. Let them tell you how they propose to do it.

- Give a supplier credit for coming up with a better solution than the next guy. Do not shop their ideas to the other suppliers as if they are your own. The whole idea is for the best supplier to be awarded the business. The supplier who failed to develop a winning solution and then lowballs the cost to get the contract has already demonstrated their capabilities. They will make up the cost difference through change orders. There are cases where companies have paid $3 to 4 million more after contracting with the low cost supplier. Low cost does not necessarily mean "final cost."

PROJECT MANAGEMENT FUNDAMENTALS

The three foundation elements of any project include planning, scheduling, and control. All activities must be managed, regardless of how responsibilities are assigned. This is especially true of activities performed by suppliers where direct control is not possible. The company has complete control (theoretically anyway) of those activities performed internally. It is the company's responsibility to treat internal scope, budget, and schedule with the same importance as their partners, suppliers, and subcontractors. This may be an area of difficulty, since company personnel may not be experienced in project management methodologies, techniques, and related software tools.

The methodologies and techniques in Table 4.6 provide the basis for effective project planning, scheduling, and control.

The various project interrelationships are shown in Figure 4.4. The Work Breakdown Structure (WBS) is similar to an exploded bill of material. Each element is a defined scope of work. The Organization Breakdown Structure (OBS) cross-references the people, departments, and organizations performing the work to the WBS. Each individual scope of work can then be defined in terms of a Work Authorization Plan (WAP). The Budget Work Breakdown Structure (BWBS) is a logical relationship which allows the cost of the organization performing each scope of work in terms of hours and expenses to be added to the material and other costs. A cost rollup then results in an accurate cost for the entire Work Breakdown Structure.

Work Breakdown Structure (WBS)

Strategy-related work scope consists of definition, profile development, analysis, evaluation, assessment, layout, specification, planning, scheduling, budgeting, and other elements. These are the Level 1 and lower elements shown in Figure 4.5. The highest (zero) level is the strategy itself in Phase I. Level 1 elements in Phases II to IV then include the various initiatives, projects, and programs which the strategy encompasses. To establish an effective project planning and control

Table 4.6   Project Management Methodologies and Techniques

	PROJECT PLANNING	PROJECT SCHEDULING	PROJECT CONTROL
Strategy Scope	Work Breakdown Structure (WBS)	Critical Path Methodology (CPM)	CPM vs. Baseline
Organizational Resources	Organization Breakdown Structure (OBS)	Resource Scheduling	Resource Availability vs. Plan
Financial Resources	Budget Work Breakdown Structure (BWBS)	Milestones	Actual $ vs. Budget $
Personnel Resources	Work Authorization Plan (WAP)	Task Scheduling	Actual Hours vs. Plan

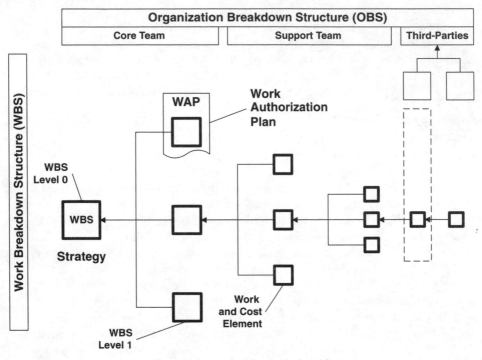

Figure 4.4 Project Interrelationships

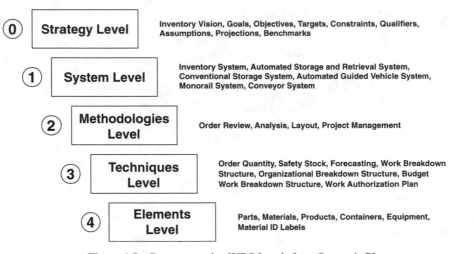

Figure 4.5 Representative WBS Levels for a Strategic Plan

structure, the interrelationships between and among each work element must be defined in terms of precedence/successor relationships. Developing a WBS, therefore, provides a comprehensive list of the tasks required to complete the strategy development process in Phase I. Each successively lower level then details the strategy in terms of methodologies, techniques, and elements.

The Work Breakdown Structure (WBS) defines the basic building blocks by which the strategy is planned, managed, and controlled. Every (significant) work element required to develop and implement the inventory integral strategy is included. Once developed, the WBS becomes the primary vehicle for translating the strategy scope into organizational, cost, and schedule elements. Each WBS element is a task in the Gantt chart. Therefore, the WBS defines "what will be done," without regard to:

- *Who* will do it—provided by the Organizational Breakdown Structure (OBS)

- *How* it will be done—provided by the Work Authorization Plans (WAPs)

- *When* it will be done—provided by the schedule (Critical Path Methodology)

- *How much* it will cost—provided by the budget plan (Budget Work Breakdown Structure)

- *Where* it will be done—provided by sourcing and subcontracting decisions

Developing a WBS for an integral strategy is a top-down iterative process similar to that used to develop a structured bill of material. The source is the strategy plan consisting of a definition of the vision, goals, objectives, targets, initiatives, projects, and programs as discussed in Chapter 3. Each successively lower level further defines various elements of the strategy in operational, organizational, facilities, equipment, systems, and technologies elements. Supporting information includes the various methodologies, techniques, and elements required to define, develop, and implement the strategy. Once each level is defined, a project plan, schedule, priorities, milestones, and budget for the entire strategy can then be developed.

Organizational Breakdown Structure (OBS)

Integral strategies require a teaming between individuals and departments, possibly extending to suppliers or subcontractors. The OBS identifies roles and responsibilities and is cross-referenced to the Work Breakdown Structure. This confirms that all project work elements are assigned at organizational, departmental, or individual levels.

Any strategy is only as good as the development team. After establishing the vision, management's most important decision concerns assignment of team members. This involves making three organizational-related choices. The first is the establishment and makeup of the management steering committee. The second is core and support team staffing. The third is whether to supplement the core team with outside personnel. These decisions, more than any other, will determine the quality of the strategy and ultimate acceptance by the organization.

The Organization Breakdown Structure begins with an organization chart as shown in Figure 4.6. When cross-referenced to the Work Breakdown Structure to ensure that every element of work is assigned, the result is the general OBS relationship illustrated in Figure 4.4. This cross-reference is established and maintained using Windows-based project software packages which enable companies, departments, functions, or individuals to be directly associated with each work element. The strategy manager is responsible for establishing strategy development roles and responsibilities. Hours or contractual relationships directly relate the departments or individuals assigned to the work to the program budget. Cost rollups within departments or organizations and expenses or other defined costs determine the overall budget.

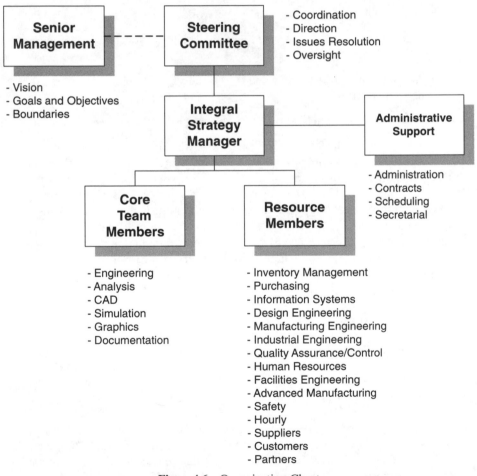

Figure 4.6   Organization Chart

The steering committee's primary function is to provide strategic direction to the core team. The committee represents the business interests of company management and at least the perceived business interests of the company's customers. Therefore, the committee's focus is to properly identify customer order winner and order qualifier criteria, establish business constraints and qualifiers, and set priorities. The committee acts as a sounding board for the team and ensures that team members or other resources are made available as required.

With corporations, the makeup of the steering committee may be a combination of corporate staff and company management personnel. With smaller companies, the committee consists of members of the management staff. The size of the committee should be small so members can meet on a scheduled and as-required basis. Members should be selected based on their direct association with the inventory processes within the company or their relevant experience or background in strategy development and implementation, finance or managerial accounting, facilities, equipment, systems, and technologies. In the case of an inventory strategy, a three-member steering committee consisting of the materials manager, manufacturing manager, and engineering manager may be appropriate.

The second organizational-related decision involves the makeup of the core team. These individuals are responsible for developing the strategy and then managing its implementation. This encompasses a variety of systems, industrial, and manufacturing engineering activities. Core team members must be very knowledgeable regarding company operations, products, and processes. Other company personnel then supplement the core team's knowledge. Team members should also be proficient in either developing or coordinating operational, organizational, and financial analyses, simulations and CAD layouts, and have breadth and depth of experience in the types of systems and equipment to be encompassed by the strategy.

The team leader should be well grounded and experienced in systems integration, inventory management planning and control methodologies and techniques, and project management fundamentals. In addition to all this, the team leader must be capable of dealing with personnel at all levels of the organization. A certain amount of expertise will be required to sell reluctant individuals on a strategy which will certainly result in change and the uncertainties and problems it can cause. The leader must also be able to deal effectively and professionally with suppliers and subcontractors. This requires a knowledge of contracts, specifications, and a willingness to develop win-win business relationships. Core team assignments should be full-time.

Having discussed the requirements and importance of the core team, the third decision becomes obvious. Not every company has all of the right personnel for an integral strategy development effort. Even those they have may be difficult to free up from their current work assignments and responsibilities. Hiring outside personnel may be the answer. They can supplement the team in areas where there are weaknesses or complement the team in areas where there is a need for additional resources. Outside personnel also provide an independent viewpoint.

One of the key advantages third-parties potentially bring to a strategy development process is experience in a variety of companies and industries. This falls into the category of "not invented here (NIH)," which may be just what the company needs. The whole reason for developing an integral strategy is to facilitate the type of change and improvement which has not been achievable by current methods. The fact that other companies are making significant improvements indicates that there are available tactics which the company is not using.

The strategy manager is responsible for ensuring that an integral strategy is developed and implemented which meets the company's business requirements. At the same time, the strategy must recognize project management constraints of time, budget, and available resources, while also accounting for infrastructural limitations related to the organization, facilities, equipment, systems, and technologies. Areas of responsibility during the strategy development phase which may be performed directly or delegated depending on the size and complexity of the effort include:

- *Project Management*—Develop a plan to execute the development effort within the schedule and resources available. Ensure that all team members understand their responsibilities and that they have specific action plans to complete their scopes of work.

- *Program Administration*—Establish a time-phased tracking system which can be used to monitor performance to plan and identify deviations in sufficient time to take corrective action. Maintain the system with up-to-date information and revise as required to incorporate company and supplier changes.

- *Subcontractor Management*—Develop contracts which incorporate all development requirements, evaluate, select, and manage partners, suppliers, and subcontractors, and manage payments and change orders. Coordinate site visits, progress reviews, submittals, runoffs, and inspections.

- *Design Management*—Develop an integral specification which identifies the functional (operational and organizational), physical (equipment and facility), and logical (systems and technologies) aspects of the integral system. Translate the specification into design guidelines and requirements for strategy elements within each of the areas of integration. These will be used for follow-on phases.

- *System Performance Evaluation*—Establish strategy performance criteria and measures. Manage simulation development or analyses to evaluate alternatives, designs, and layouts.

- *Documentation*—Establish documentation standards, publish requirements, and review work for accuracy and consistency prior to submittal to the company, partners, suppliers, or subcontractors. Manage the entire documentation development process.

- *Budget*—Allocate the budget into the various work breakdown structure categories and tasks and establish task numbers. Incorporate tasks and hours per the WBS and OBS into the time reporting system. Monitor budget vs. actual for identification of deviations.

- *Schedule*—Incorporate detail schedule elements from the Work Authorization Plans into the master schedule. Monitor time sheets and accounting documentation for performance to plan and estimates to completion (ETCs). Proactively track upcoming milestones so progress can be verified.

- *Document Control*—Maintain all source and reference files and documentation needed to support requirements, deliverables, invoices, change orders, and payments.

Budget Work Breakdown Structure (BWBS)

The Budget Work Breakdown Structure (BWBS) is developed once a schedule and related cost projections are established, calculated, or otherwise determined for all work elements. The schedule enables the costs to be time-phased, while the WBS enables them to be allocated to the various work elements. The intersection of the WBS with the OBS additionally enables target costs to be identified by individual, department, and organization.

Strategy development-related costs typically include time and expenses, but may include prototype or other costs as well. Cost breakdown within the BWBS can be accomplished by either:

1. Assigning a *percentage* breakdown to each successive lower level.

2. Calculating a *target* projected budget for each successive lower level.

The intent of the BWBS is to establish a baseline, representing what it will cost to develop and ultimately implement the strategy. Some reallocation of costs may occur once the detail cost categories and cost accounts are developed or over time as changes occur. These changes should then be imploded back up through the BWBS to reflect how the process will actually be managed.

Cost development generally encompasses factors for time, frequency of occurrences, scope of work, and risk. The Strategy Development Phase encompasses primarily hours-related costs while follow-on phases entail organizational development, facility, equipment, systems, and technologies related costs.

- *Time* is accommodated by extending labor hours over the schedule duration. Establishing a level-of-effort for certain aspects related to project management, administration, and meetings is easier than attempting to identify specific hours per period. For example, administration effort could be calculated as 5 percent for a 6-month duration at $50/hr. Level-of-effort calculations are solely for the purpose of budget planning.

- *Frequency* factors account for repetitive costs which can be estimated but which are subject to factors which cannot be known in advance with certainty. Expenses related to trips are typically estimated based on frequency. Trips encompass airfare or cost/mile for using a personal car, rental cars, hotel costs, meal expenses or per diem (a set dollar amount/day for meals and expenses), and miscellaneous costs associated with laundry, tolls, phone calls, ar.d so on. These costs vary by destination and trip duration.

- *Scope* costs relate to specific work breakdown (WBS) elements. These are easiest to calculate for standard strategy elements such as equipment systems or packaged software assessments. The elements of scope costs related to organizational or operational change are more complicated. In general, scope costs encompass hours for specification development, analysis, simulation and design completion, manufacturing, inspection and testing, shipping, permits, erection or installation, commissioning, spare parts, training, and warranty.

- *Risk* is a function of time, level of definition, potential for failure requiring extra time or effort to rectify, possibility of part damage needing repair or replacement, and so on. Contingency is usually accounted for as a percentage of those portions of the project which entail risk (not necessarily the entire project). Project risk is synonymous with safety stock which compensates for forecast risk.

Work Authorization Plan (WAP)

Experience has shown that there are at least as many ways to execute a project as there are individuals assigned to it. Unfortunately, all of these ways are not equally effective. The strategy manager exercises control over how a project is executed via the Work Authorization Planning process. This involves having the individual who is assigned to the work element define how the work will be performed, describe the deliverable(s) to be provided or results to be achieved, and specify how completion of the effort will be measured. Once a team consensus is reached regarding each WAP, the strategy manager authorizes the budget and approval necessary to complete the work for internal efforts or the paperwork necessary to complete the work for external efforts. This confirms the specific level of effort in terms of hours and schedule required to complete the given scope of work.

The department manager is responsible for making work assignments for departmental personnel. Project performance is then evaluated against the WAP. Companies differ on the issue of charging hours. In general, once the allocated hours are consumed, no additional hours should be charged to the project unless an authorized internal (IPCN) or project change notice (PCN) has been processed. In the event that modifications are required, the strategy manager may:

1. Assign additional hours (and add them to the accounting system once the change is approved), or

2. Instruct the individual to continue charging to the project (without additional hours assigned), thus incurring an overage, or

3. Instruct the individual to charge to the department general and administrative budget managed by the department manager.

The general WAP format is illustrated in Figure 4.7. The documentation effort lends itself to a personal computer database application. Once the general format is established, a preliminary copy is created for each area of the work breakdown structure. This simplifies the task of having a number of individuals complete the WAPs and ensures consistency of information transfer from the strategy manager to the team members.

- *Project Information* includes standard data such as project name, company, WBS number, parent WBS number, and relevant descriptions.

- *Initiator Information* includes the name of the individual who developed the WAP, date of initial development, revision, and revision comments. Changes over time must be identified for tracking purposes.

- *Roles and Responsibilities* identify generally how the work will be distributed. Individuals may cross departmental and even company boundaries. Equipment design, for example, may include mechanical and controls system engineering, as well as CAD effort. A brief description of roles and areas of responsibility ensures that all work areas are assigned.

- *Scope and Schedule* encompass the design, specification, analysis, documentation, implementation, manufacturing, and other steps required to complete the WBS element. Each step is briefly described, along with identifying the individual responsible, hours, required date, planned date, actual date completed, status, and measure of completion or deliverable.

- *Ground Rules* provide the requirements, specifications, constraints, qualifiers, and assumptions within which the effort must be completed. This ensures consistency among different areas of the project.

- *Risk* areas need to be accounted for in the planning and execution of each WBS element. The integral strategy manager will identify any known risk areas prior to beginning the work. The team member performing the work should identify any areas identified as the work continues. Risk is an important issue to bring before the entire team since there is often more than one way to solve a problem. This is a common issue between Level 2 Controls and Levels 3 and 4 Software, for example. A problem may be able to be solved at either level, but one solution will be more expensive than the other. Acknowledging the issue provides for the most cost effective solution. Otherwise, whoever identifies the problem invariably tries to solve it from their perspective, whether this is the best approach or not.

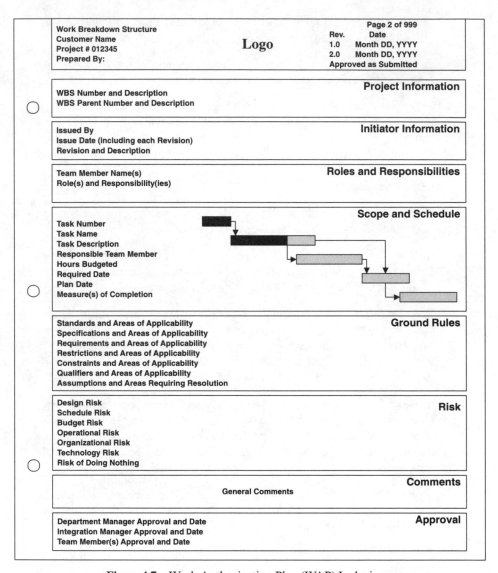

Figure 4.7   Work Authorization Plan (WAP) Inclusions

- *Comments* provide a free-format method to document discussions or instructions related to the WAP. Meeting minutes can be maintained directly against the WAP if a database is used for development and tracking purposes.

- *Approval* signifies agreement to budget and schedule and commitment of the necessary resources. Department manager approval indicates commitment to completing the scope per requirements, and integral strategy manager approval indicates that the scope of work is properly specified.

As a general statement, no work should be performed to develop or implement any part of the integral strategy without prior definition and approval. This is consistent with ISO 9000 requirements. Do not do it for that reason though. Do it because it is a good business practice.

SUMMARY

Managing an integral strategy development and implementation process which actively causes operational and infrastructural changes within a company requires a professional project management approach. Project management methodologies and techniques including Work Breakdown Structures (WBS), Organizational Breakdown Structures (OBS), Budget Work Breakdown Structures (BWBS), and Work Authorization Plans (WAPs) are all useful in setting scope, interrelationships, and targets.

Schedules and budgets lend themselves to zero-tolerance from deviation performance measures in the same way as the integral strategy. In fact, the same people who cause inventory levels to be what they are cause strategy development budgets and schedules to be what they are. After all, the strategy is a reaction to the external and internal environment which is preventing the company from achieving the significant levels of improvement desired.

Project management software simplifies establishing precedence/successor relationships. The master scheduler is still responsible for establishing reasonable task durations. Gantt charts showing both the planned duration and current level of completion are the most commonly used technique for keeping the team members and steering committee updated regarding progress.

Having and following Work Authorization Plans is the single most common area where project controls are neglected. Companies spend a great deal of time on cost and schedule areas and then ignore the closed-loop controls provided by the WAPs. Plan the work and work the plan. When this is done, the costs and schedule will take care of themselves.

Chapter 5

Inventory System

Companies typically select an ERP/MRPII system and by default end up with an inventory system. At that point, a conscious choice is made to either use the system as is or modify it for the specific needs of the company. Modification may be as simple as configuring fields to be consistent with company terminology or more extensive for companies with unique needs. Integration with existing accounting systems or lower level Warehouse Management (WMS) or Warehouse Control (WCS) systems will typically require some type of host interface modification as well.

The greatest portion of time with any system evaluation and selection process is spent on an evaluation of features and functions. With an inventory system being just one of many subsystems in an integrated ERP/MRPII System, it is extremely difficult to separate out the cost/benefit factors attributable to the inventory system alone. Companies attempt to solve this problem by weighting and summing values assigned to each inventory feature and function. This calculates a precise numerical score for the subsystem. Weights across all of the subsystems are then summed to determine the winner. If the team's preferred winner does not get the highest score, the weights are changed and/or additional soft factors are included in order to determine the final winner. Having a mathematical basis for the selection removes any doubt that a decision was made based on anything other than an objective and structured process which fairly evaluated every system.

Once a company must resort to a weighted checklist as the basis for selecting a system, a red flag should go up. If it was this easy and straightforward, only the system with the most features and functions would be for sale. Everyone else would be out of business. Having system features and functions is not as important as how they support the company's ability to manage and control its inventory. "How" is not determined via a checklist. "How" is defined by mapping the company's operations against the systems under consideration. In this way, one system can be profiled against another from an operational perspective. How does the system help to improve inventory turns? How does the system improve customer service levels? How does the system prevent inventory inaccuracies? Answering these types of questions identifies whether the system has any real value to the organization. None of them lend themselves to a features and functions comparison.

Profiling is a process where functions are actually defined in terms of the screens, reports, and decision support capabilities available within the system. Profiling the inventory functions on paper is significantly more revealing than having a committee fill out a subjective weighted checklist comparing features and functions. Companies have a choice in how they evaluate, compare, and select their systems.

This chapter covers the following aspects of inventory systems and related issues:

- A discussion of information system-related issues focuses on some of the design, operating, and organizational issues companies face.

- Three basic types of system designs are briefly compared, with emphasis on the value of decision support systems.

- Some of the common interfaces with external subsystems are discussed to provide an understanding of the role the inventory system plays within an integrated system environment.

- A variety of inventory system screen formats and commonly used fields are reviewed to promote an understanding of the various policy-making, planning, and control capabilities available to company personnel. The formats[1] are representative and do not reflect any specific system.

SYSTEM HIERARCHIES (LEVELS 1–5)

Inventory systems relieve the planner of the responsibility of performing the thousands of calculations required to plan and control inventory levels. The system maintains stock balances, on-order balances, requirements, forecast rates, part information, and history without much planner involvement. Systems also automatically apply policies and parameters set by the inventory manager and planners to part categories and individual parts. These are the features and functions on which evaluation checklists overly concentrate. What really tends to differentiate one system from another is in how this data is translated into policy,

---

1. The screen format used is intended for illustration purposes. The convention used is one of positioning a cursor on any line item and activating a "button" at the bottom of the screen via left/right arrows. The ENTER key provides access to the screen(s) associated with that button. This is synonymous with pull-down menus in a Windows environment. Older systems may associate function keys to other screens. The mechanism is not important for example purposes. Also, the screens presented in this chapter do not represent a complete inventory system, though they do cover the basics.

planning, and control information. Systems which provide graphic and decision support capabilities are much more useful from an inventory manager and planner perspective than one which simply performs data management.

The Master Schedule (MS) and Material Requirements Planning (MRP) subsystems initiate the company's investment in inventory, but they do not manage or control it. Both systems operate on the supposition of "all things being equal." That is, the MS and MRP plans are valid if lead times are *as stated*, if inventory balances are *as stated*, if orders can be expedited *as stated*, if forecasts become customer orders *as stated*, and if manufacturing can produce the quantities in the time frames *as stated*. MS and MRP subsystems establish top-down scenarios, but do not verify whether plans are achievable. This bottom-up validation is the function of the various other support subsystems, inventory being one. In fact, the inventory system plays a large part in making "all things equal." This is done by ensuring accurate inventory balances and available safety stock levels and by providing accurate forecasts of independent demand parts.

Systems vary significantly in terms of degree of integration. Over the years, variations have developed to address markets having unique requirements such as repetitive manufacturing and aerospace and defense. The basic resource and requirements planning architecture is shown in Figure 5.1.

Sales and related business plans are established at an infrastructure level in terms of dollars and resources. They are then successively translated into product line, product family, products, assemblies, subassemblies, part and material levels of detail, and associated labor hours via the Master Schedule, material planning, and production subsystems. Capacity verifications at each level close the loop between the plan and the company's ability to achieve the plan. This involves confirming that the plan can be executed in terms of available labor by category and machine hours by grouping, given the hours lost due to setups, holidays, planned downtime, and planned sequence of production. Purchasing, production, and inventory subsystems are tasked with ensuring that inventory will be available on schedule.

From a computer hierarchy perspective, enterprise and manufacturing resource planning systems are considered "host level" systems. Accounting, distribution resource planning, and other business level systems are also host level systems. In this book, host level is synonymous with Level 5. Inventory systems as part of ERP or MRPII are, therefore, also Level 5. Refer to Figure 5.2.

A typical characteristic of Level 5 systems is that data entry and reporting is not necessarily time critical. This means that information required for planning decisions does not need to reflect up-to-the-second data. Also, system operation can be independent of lower level equipment operation. Older Level 5 systems may be batch transaction-oriented systems which require nightly downtime in order to perform backups or other processing. Newer systems are more on-line and real time oriented.

A Level 4 facility manager provides an interface between the host and real time automation equipment such as found within Automated Storage and Re-

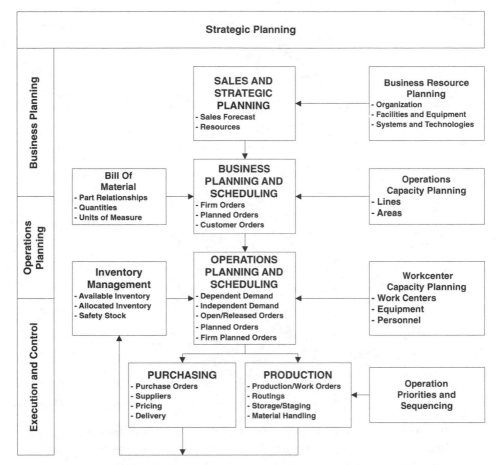

Figure 5.1   Manufacturing Resource Planning (MRPII)

trieval Systems and Automated Guided Vehicle Systems. Manufacturing execution and Warehouse Management Systems are at Level 4 and will likely have interfaces with Level 3 Warehouse Control and other systems. Where a Level 4 system exists, Level 5 inventory may consist primarily of total inventory by part without the actual inventory locations. Inventory control by location is then performed at Level 4 or Level 3.

Level 4 systems may be provided by a third-party or by the Level 3 automation supplier. Where automation is involved, there will typically be some duplication of functionality when a Warehouse Management System is provided by a third-party other than the automation supplier. This is due to some Level 4 functionality being provided by the automation supplier as part of their baseline system. Automation companies must be capable of interfacing with both Level 4 systems for companies which have them and Level 5 systems for companies which do not.

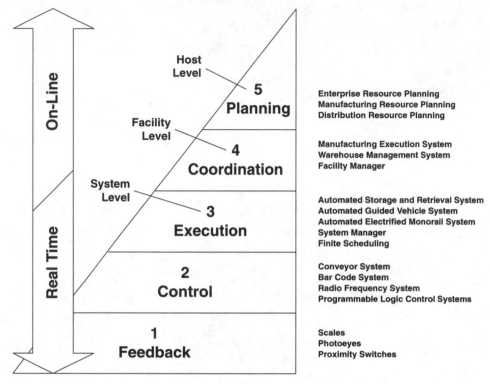

Figure 5.2   Computer Hierarchy Levels

System managers (Level 3) provide a real time interface to the automation equipment. Each automated system either has its own system manager or has it subsumed within that of a system at the next higher level. Automated Storage and Retrieval Systems (AS/RS), Automated Guided Vehicle Systems (AGVS), and Automated Electrified Monorail Systems (AEMS) will typically have their own system managers. This enables them to function under operator control in a stand-alone manner or as an integrated subsystem within an integrated system. Conveyor systems are an example of automation which may or may not have their own system manager. For systems where conveyors provide only inbound/outbound transfer to/from the AS/RS, there is no need for a separate system manager. However, in systems where conveyors are an integral part of the handling and distribution system such as in a distribution center, a separate system manager is warranted.

Level 2 refers to Programmable Logic Control (PLC) or equivalent PC control of machines or vehicles. This includes conveyor sections, Storage and Retrieval Machines (SRMs), and track switches in AEM systems. PC-based systems also include bar code or RF systems which are used for transaction processing and material control.

Level 1 encompasses the variety of bar code scanners, sensors, scales, photoeyes, limit switches, and other devices controlled by the PLC or PC. These provide real time or point-in-time feedback to the higher level systems.

INVENTORY SYSTEM INTEGRATION ISSUES

Integration issues associated with basic inventory system design and operation encompass functions and features, user needs and areas of responsibility, requirements for paperless operation, operating vs. maintenance transactions, and decision support vs. data management. These issues are most relevant when considering implementing a new Level 5 system, when adding automated systems at Levels 4 and 3, or when making organizational changes associated with an integral environment where past practices are changing. The preceding issues are typically resolved via the integral specification process or developed prior to purchase or development.

The following issues are typical of inventory system operation.

Negative Stock Balances

Inventory systems should never allow a negative stock balance. There is no such thing from a business math perspective. At worst, the stock balance should be set to zero and the planner should receive an action message via the system integration screen that some type of follow-up *may* be required. The fact that a transaction has the effect of a negative balance is an indication that an inventory inaccuracy condition has occurred. This usually means that the computer stock balance was lower than the actual inventory balance, though a data entry error may also be the cause.

The transaction itself (on the history file) should identify the magnitude of the negative balance. The following transaction has a -40 computer balance in theory. The reality had to have been that 100 pcs were actually in stock when the 100 pcs issue occurred. Providing all of the relevant data aids the planner in tracking the cause of the inaccuracy.

TRANSACTION TYPE	ISSUE QUANTITY	BEGIN BALANCE	END BALANCE	COUNTED QUANTITY	ERROR TYPE	CORECTIVE ACTION
Unplanned Issue	100 pcs	60 pcs	–40 pcs	0 pcs	NEGATIVE BALANCE	CODE–xxx

With Radio Frequency terminals mounted on forklifts, any negative balance can be identified when the operator processes the transaction. In this case, the operator can be instructed to confirm that the stock balance is zero. This confirmation can be added to the transaction (refer to the "Counted Quantity" field preceding) and also be processed as a cycle count. If the stock balance is not zero, the operator must identify the remaining balance. Negative balances can be caused by the following:

- Scale or hand counting may result in a small variation from one issue to another.

- The wrong part may be issued by mistake. This creates an error against both the correct and incorrect parts.

- The unit of measure may be incorrect. Fuses may be issued by the box (10/box). If there is one box in stock and the operator issues 10 (fuses), a 9-box negative stock balance will occur.

In actual fact, more material cannot be issued to Work in Process than is actually in inventory. When this appears to have occurred, accounting must process an offsetting transaction. This removes the equivalent dollars from Work in Process if they believe that the inventory has actually been issued to Work in Process over time. The transaction may simply write off the material as being lost and not accounted for. The inventory planner must initiate a corrective action against the part to correct the stock balance and determine and eliminate the cause of inaccuracy.

Authority to Make Inventory Adjustments

Inventory management requires a hierarchy of authority levels (consistent with ISO 9000) for making inventory adjustments. This ranges from automatic adjustments, if the change is minor, to planner, inventory manager, materials manager, or higher levels of management as the adjustment quantity increases.

Authorization is based on the lower of quantity or dollar value. Setting a quantity limit recognizes the importance of hours or days supply. This usually applies to rate-based parts. A part with a 1-day supply has a much lower tolerance to inaccuracy than one with a 30-days supply. Setting a dollar limit applies to parts which have a variable days supply. This is more applicable to a project, engineer-to-order, or make-to-order environment. Refer to Table 5.1. In either case, a quantity is established beyond which the authorization hierarchy takes effect. The inventory system should allow this to be set on a part-by-part and/or category basis. A $25.00 limit for a particular category (C-items, for example) has the effect of allowing large discrepancies for low dollar items and small discrepancies for higher dollar items.

Table 5.1   Representative (Initiatives Phase)
Inventory Adjustment Authorization Levels

INVENTORY CATEGORY	AUTOMATIC		PLANNER		MANAGER	
	COUNT	$	COUNT	$	COUNT	$
Daily Receipts	0	$0	0	$0	0	$0
Weekly Receipts	1-Hour	$25	1–2 Hours	$25–100	> 2-Hours	> $100
Biweekly Receipts	2-Hours	$25	2–4 Hours	$25–100	> 4-Hours	> $100
Monthly Receipts	4-Hours	$25	4–8 Hours	$25–100	> 8 Hours	> $100

Note: Hours refer to hours of supply, which is a variable by part.

Over time, automatic correction levels should be driven to zero as part of a zero-tolerance inventory accuracy program. This forces a planner to address every individual inaccuracy. This is the only way to initiate and verify the effectiveness of correction actions.

ABC Code by Dollar or Other Category

ABC codes have traditionally enabled global inventory planning and control parameters to be applied to a wide range of parts based on part cost. These codes are based on Pareto's 80/20 Rule. "A" parts typically constitute the top 80 percent of total inventory value, "B" parts the next 15 percent, and "C" parts the remaining 5 percent. This may translate into A parts being 5 percent of total inventory in terms of number of parts, B parts 15 percent, and C parts 80 percent. Percentages vary, as do the number of categories. Value is usually based on an annualized part value. This means that a lower value but higher volume part may be an A-item. Individual part cost may also be a factor for very expensive but low demand parts.

One of the problems with ABC codes is that boundaries between categories are absolute, no matter how similar parts are on either side of the boundary. A part with an annual value of $2,345.00 can fall into the B category while one with a value of $2,350.00 may fall into the A category, if that is where the split occurs. Since the split is somewhat arbitrary, one or the other part should be reassigned. The inventory system should provide an override ABC code in the part master file to enable the planner to reassign a part from one category to another.

It is easy to misuse ABC codes. They provide a mistaken impression that all parts in a category can actually be managed in a like manner. The ABC code can be used to establish maximum days supply for ordering logic by setting days supply to 10 from 20 (i.e., 2-weeks from 4-weeks), for example. This seems to be a simple way to force an increase in inventory turns. However, such an action does not account for the supplier's ability to ship every two weeks or the freight costs associated with twice as many deliveries. More deliveries doubles handling costs associated with twice as many receipts. Subjecting the part to twice as many exposures to stock-out also increases safety stock levels. Planners need to understand the ramifications of their actions.

"Official" Stock Balances

There are two levels of inventory control available with an Automated Storage and Retrieval System. The first is where the AS/RS computer maintains stock balances by location. The host identifies the part number and quantity required, and the AS/RS computer selects inventory storage and retrieval locations based on first-in first-out (FIFO), zoning, or other logic. The inventory or Warehouse Management System treats the AS/RS as a single "location" and maintains only the total and available stock balances for the part. All storage and retrieval functions can be performed in automatic mode (host control) and semiautomatic mode (operator control) since both Level 5 and Level 4 can identify the inventory by location. The second level of control is where the host inventory system maintains all of the individual storage locations and stock balances. The host directs the Storage and Retrieval Machine (S/RM) when and where to store and retrieve loads. All of the recovery logic which accounts for manual storage and retrieval, full bin errors, and so on, must be incorporated into the host inventory system. Semiautomatic mode is not available if the host is not communicating since the only inventory record exists in the host computer.

In either case, the official inventory is always maintained at the highest level within the system. This is usually the ERP/MRPII inventory system, but some companies maintain all of their inventory at Level 4. The less real time the Levels 4 and 5 interface becomes, the more difficult it is to maintain the two systems in sync. Inventory adjustments or cycle counts at the AS/RS level, for example, may occur hours or shifts in advance of an update to the host level. An inventory discrepancy may not even be known until the next day. With a real time interface, errors are identified, and corrections take effect, immediately. The material can be held in an Error Correction Station (ECS) until the discrepancy is resolved.

System designs should take advantage of their strengths while minimizing the effect of any weaknesses due to their interfaces. Host level ERP/MRPII inventory system strengths lie in managerial and planning areas. AS/RS system strengths lie in their ability to control stock balances and locations based on FIFO and other control algorithms.

"Vanilla" or Modified Inventory System

Everyone has opinions about a new inventory system. The trick is to have the same opinion after the system is implemented. The basic issue related to satisfaction in a system choice is whether the system or the company's operations need to be modified. Some company personnel assume that a new system will enable them to do the same things they are doing now, only somehow more efficiently. Finding out that the system does not support existing operations can be a serious problem. Others view a new system as an opportunity to adopt proven processes, methodologies, and techniques. Many companies do not realize the roadblocks they have created for themselves over time by relying on internally-developed systems until they implement a new fully-integrated system.

Contrary to what the people believe who promote the "vanilla" system approach of making no changes after a system is implemented, many companies are not totally served by off-the-shelf software packages. If off-the-shelf packages were so perfect, there would not be so many of them. The reality is that the market is not the same as it was fifteen years ago. There are as many different types of needs as there are companies, but only as many systems as there are system suppliers. The relatively small number of systems on the market cannot possibly satisfy the exact needs of the hundreds of thousands of companies in the world. In spite of this, companies leave no stone unturned convincing themselves how closely they match the "preferred" supplier's system. The most common tool is to create a weighted matrix to verify with mathematical precision just how closely their operations match one system vs. another.

MIS staffs promote the "vanilla" concept (no software changes). They do not have to integrate the company's changes into new revisions of the software since the company will somehow change all of their operations to conform to the software. This permits a smaller software staff to be maintained. Since the staff becomes smaller, the company's software tools become more inflexible since there are fewer programmers to take advantage of its capabilities. This is the death-spiral syndrome again. What the company really needs to do is select software which is configurable. Interfacing company-specific modules to the core modules then allows the core software to be upgraded over time by the supplier with little or no effect on the company add-ons. Do not be afraid of changing software to make it support the needs of the company. No one became more competitive by being afraid of change.

DECISION SUPPORT VS. DATA VS. INFORMATION MANAGEMENT SYSTEMS

System designs have changed substantially over the years due to the availability of lower cost and higher performance computer systems. Early data management systems primarily filed, sorted, and otherwise controlled data. If the data was in the computer, it could be selected, sorted, and listed. Later information management systems integrated data among departments. The ability to combine purchasing, inventory management, and production planning and control data enabled more effective planning and scheduling to be performed. Newer Decision Support Systems (DSS) are beginning to incorporate the logic necessary to generate scenarios from which the user can evaluate alternatives and make choices. The more responsive and flexible a company must be, the more the system needs to provide the ability to translate inventory management policies into effective decisions.

Example: Consider a simple case where an operator needs 20 units for a production requirement but finds only 18 in the location. A quick check verifies that this is the only location. The operator issues the 18 units to the requirement and processes an inventory adjustment of –2 to correct the inventory balance. Since a current requirement remains unfilled and the inventory balance is zero, MRP generates an *expedite* action message in the nightly run for the first open order for the part. The order required date becomes the current date.

This message is one day too late. The production planner will already have contacted the buyer to determine if the next order can be expedited when the operator identified the shortage. If the order cannot be expedited, the materials already issued to production can produce 18 of the 20 units scheduled. The balance will remain in Work in Process. An alternative is to hold all issued material until the order can be completed in total.

With a Decision Support System in an integral environment, the 2-unit shortage will cause the following to occur (on-line) when the adjustment transaction is entered:

1. The inventory system checks the part master file to determine if there is a substitute part (if not, go to Step 2). The available balance is checked to see if there are two unallocated units. If so, the units are issued to the order. If not, the planner is presented with a *scenario* based on the effect on other orders of applying two units to the requirement. If the planner elects to reapply the units, two units are issued to the requirement. *In this example, there is no substitute.*

2. If substitution is not an option, the MRP subsystem performs an *on-line* implosion to determine the source of the requirement. The intent is to determine if the two units are actually for a customer order, a forecast order, or for safety stock. If the two units are not for a customer order, the planner is presented with an option to reduce the order quantity to 18 from 20. MRP logic will then resynchronize demand with available and on-order inventory. *This is a possibility in this example.*

   If the two units are for a customer order, the MRP logic determines when the next order for the missing parts will be received. The receipt date is compared with the customer's requested ship date, since the production order may have been scheduled earlier than required to level load the schedule. If the company normally quotes a delivery range (i.e., 4 to 6 weeks ARO—After Receipt of Order), the latest time frame will be evaluated. This check identifies the actual schedule impact to the planner. *This is a possibility in this example.*

3. If delaying the order is not an option, an open order must be expedited. The inventory system will compare the earliest order due date between the part and the part's substitute (if there is one). It may be easier to expedite an open order for the substitute. In either case, the shortage of two units will be transmitted to the buyer via an on-line action message. This message includes the relevant requirement and open order information. Supplier information such as supplier contact name, phone number, price, and lead time is also included. It may be possible to procure the units from other than the primary supplier by paying a premium. If the buyer can obtain two units immediately from any supplier, the problem is resolved. If not, the best date which the buyer can achieve is entered into the purchase order record as the current promise (acknowledged) ship date. *This is a possibility in this example.*

4. If all of the preceding fails, the production order must be delayed or split.

5. However, a phone call to the customer may reveal that the later completion date is acceptable or that a split shipment is acceptable. If that
is the case, the order can be delayed. Customers may have some
flexibility based on how their system aggregates requirements and orders. Their MRP subsystem may have pulled requirements forward
in order to create a larger order quantity in just the same way as the
company's MRP system does. *This is a possibility in this example.*

Decision Support Systems view data as a means to an end. The focus is not so
much on calculating dates or quantities but on enabling inventory personnel to
fully understand a situation and the ramifications of any actions. This includes
the immediate effects as well as future impacts of "borrowing" material from one
order to satisfy another. Data has value only when it supports the decision-
making process.

Decision Support Systems use engines which do the work of translating volumes of data from the company's various databases into scenarios. The design of
the engine (refer to Figure 5.3) is structured to answer questions. Each area of
questions has its own engine which shares common application software which
checks stock balances, evaluates changes to schedules, and so on. The process is
similar to that of a flow chart, where different answers at different points cause
the engine to take a different path. The engine may stop once an acceptable answer is obtained or provide answers to all of the questions as shown in the callout
in Figure 5.3.

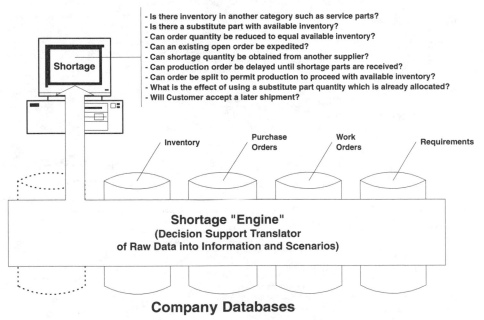

Company Databases

Figure 5.3   Decision Support "Engines"

EXTERNAL SUBSYSTEM INTEGRATION

Inventory management's most important interfaces are with the operations planning and scheduling, material planning and scheduling, purchasing, and production subsystems. These subsystems all affect requirements or orders. Refer to Figure 5.1.

Sales and Business Planning—At a high level, sales and business planning balances company resources and capabilities with a projection of customer demand. Inventory is considered from an overall inventory investment level as shown in Figure 5.4. Targets established at the SOP level by product line must be translated into inventory investment levels at part category and part levels of detail by the MPS, MRP, and inventory subsystems.

Master Schedule (MS)—The Master Schedule translates product line sales projections into product and option projections. Summaries may be provided in monthly, weekly, and daily time buckets. Available finished goods inventory is allocated to the oldest requirements, as applicable, or specific customer orders, leaving any remaining inventory in an available-to-promise category as shown in Figure 5.5.

Bill of Material (BOM)—Products are defined in terms of a bill of material. Single-level bills of material describe a particular assembly or subassembly. Multilevel bills of material identify a hierarchy of parent-child relationships. Level 0 is the end-item (finished goods) level. When engineering adds a new part to a bill of material, a part master record is created in the inventory subsystem as shown in Figure 5.6. When a bill of material revision is changed, the part master identifies the new revision and date. Inventory in turn identifies standard parts

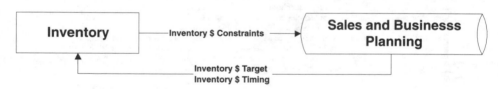

Figure 5.4   Sales and Business Planning Interface

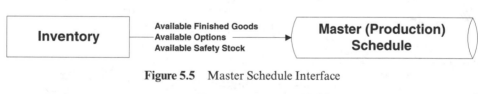

Figure 5.5   Master Schedule Interface

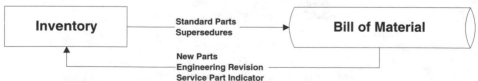

Figure 5.6   Bill of Material Interface

and supersedure timing to engineering. Adding a spare parts indicator flag to parts enables the service department to plan spare parts inventory.

Material Requirements Planning (MRP)—The MRP subsystem time-phases on-hand and on-order stock balances against demand. MRP makes substantial use of inventory-related data. Open orders released to suppliers, but not yet received and/or closed out appear in the "Scheduled Receipts" row in the MRP display. Available inventory balances, inventory allocated to firm-planned and released orders, and unavailable inventory due to being on hold or quarantine are all provided to MRP as part of the stock balance information. Safety stock quantity and technique, order quantity and technique, forecast quantity and technique, and supplier/manufacturing lead time provide the planning information needed to calculate a materials plan. This plan is then fed back to inventory as orders and requirements as shown in Figure 5.7.

Purchasing—The purchasing subsystem provides the information required to establish contracts with suppliers. The supplier master (names, addresses, contacts, and ordering data) and supplier pricing files (price breaks by quantity and order quantity conditions) are essentially extensions of the inventory part master file. The MRP subsystem generates order actions to purchasing to place purchase orders, revise order quantities or required dates, or cancel orders. Purchasing in turn provides supplier data to inventory, the most important of which is the preferred supplier lead time as shown in Figure 5.8. Inventory then adds order processing (MRP or inventory), order release (purchasing), order transmission (mailing or EDI), order shipment (transportation), order receiving (receipt processing), order inspection (inspection processing), and order handling (handling and storage) time, as applicable, to establish a cumulative lead time.

Production Planning and Control—The production planning and activity con-

Figure 5.7 Material Requirements Planning Interface

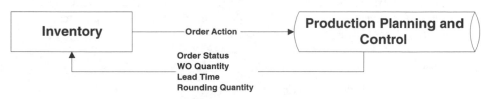

Figure 5.8 Purchasing Interface

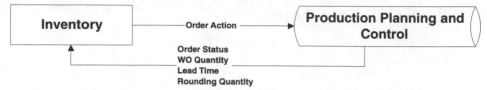

Figure 5.9   Production Activity Control Interface

trol (manufacturing execution system) subsystem provides the information needed to release orders for manufactured parts, assemblies, and products. The material planning system generates order actions, including placing a production/work order, revising an order quantity or required date, or cancelling an order. The production system in turn provides manufacturing data to inventory, the most important of which is the manufacturing lead time as shown in Figure 5.9. Inventory then adds order processing and order release production planning time to establish a total lead time.

There are few if any software modules in an integral system which do not add, modify, or use data in the inventory subsystem. Having features and functions which do this is *not* what differentiates one system from another. How effectively this is done is where the differentiation occurs. Features and functions are the order qualifiers when purchasing a new inventory system. The system's ability to support the company's integral strategy is the order winner.

INVENTORY SYSTEM DESIGN

From an operator perspective, inventory systems vary significantly in appearance from one supplier to another. This is a function of development era of the system, system design standards, preferences and experience, company development strategy, operating system and hardware platform, industry, and so on. However, there is a fair degree of similarity in fields, terminology, and logic, once the issue of appearance is settled. Refer to Figure 5.10 for a general system overview.

An integral inventory system supports a wide range of inventory policy, planning, and control functions. It is the key tool used by the inventory manager and planners to implement the company's integral strategy. The representative screen formats, fields, and related logic contained in the following pages provide an overview of this tool. System areas include inventory policies, the inventory master file, inventory planning, inventory stock balances, inventory operating and maintenance transactions, inventory activity, inventory accuracy, inventory replenishment, inventory storage and handling, inventory reports, and system integration. Access to all of these areas begins with the menu.

Menu

The Inventory System Menu (Figure 5.11) is accessed via the ERP/MRPII system menu. Selecting any item causes that screen to be displayed. In systems where

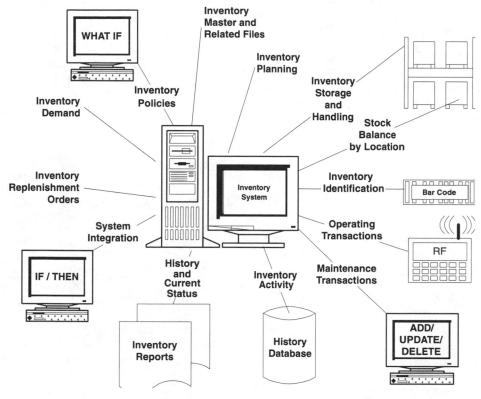

Figure 5.10   Inventory System

individuals must be authorized to access certain functions, only those commands or dialogues are displayed or accessible. This is defined via the operator profile where screens allow operators to be added or deleted, access to be modified, and a password to be assigned.

Inventory Policies

The inventory manager establishes policies based on broad management targets. They typically apply to a category of parts. Once established, the policies apply to every part in the category until overridden by the planner on a part-by-part basis. This override capability provides the ability to fine-tune planning and control elements to meet the specific needs of a part. Figure 5.12 identifies ordering policies based on days and dollars supply using the ABC code for sorting purposes.

Where it is possible to have an override, the part master file contains both the policy field and the override field. System logic uses the override field for calculations and sorting if it is nonblank. Otherwise, the policy or "default" field is used. If the policy field is modified, any part number where the override field does not match the new policy value is identified to the planner via an action message (re-

08:00am 07/01/YY				INV—INVENTORY MENU	
ADD	MODIFY	DELETE			
				INVENTORY PLANNER	
				PART INFORMATION	
Y	Y	Y	SKU	Part Master	
Y	N	N	ACT	Part Activity	
Y	Y	N	LOC	Part Location	
Y	Y	N	PCF	Planning and Control Fields	
Y	Y	N	REF	Part References and Notes	
				CYCLE COUNTING	
Y	Y	Y	CCR	Request for Cycle Count	
N	N	N	CCS	Cycle Count Summary	
N	N	N	CCE	Cycle Count Errors	
N	N	N	CCA	Cycle Count Accuracy	
				TRANSACTIONS	
N	N	Y	ERR	Error Transactions	
N	N	N	HST	Operating Transactions History	
Y	N	N	NON	Nonoperating Transactions	
				ORDERS	
N	Y	Y	ORD	Suggested Orders	
N	N	N	OPN	Open Purchase and Work Orders	
				ACTION MESSAGES	
Y	Y	Y	SYS	System Integration	
				INVENTORY MANAGER	
Y	Y	N	CTN	Containerization and Storage Profile	
N	N	N	MGT	Inventory Turns	
Y	Y	Y	POL	Management Policies	
N	Y	N	RPT	Report Menu	
N	N	N	SAE	Surplus and Excess	
				STOREROOM OPERATORS	
Y	N	N	TRN	Inventory Operating Transactions	

PURCHASING	MRP	PAC	BOM	MPS	MORE...

Note: Screens are typically listed in alphabetic or other generic sequence. Listing by user category shows which dialogues are available to support which types of functions. Menus may also be customized by individual based on authorization levels.

Figure 5.11   Representative Inventory System Menu

08:00am 07/01/YY		POL— Inventory Management Policies		
CATEGORY	**ELEMENT**		**POLICY**	**COMMENT(S)**
A—Daily	Minimum Days Supply		1	JIT parts from local suppliers
	Maximum Days Supply		1	
	Minimum $ Supply	$	0	
	Maximum $ Supply		$50,000	
B—Alternate Days	Minimum Days Supply		5	JIT parts from milk runs
	Maximum Days Supply		5	
	Minimum $ Supply	$	0	
	Maximum $ Supply		$20,000	
C—Weekly	Minimum Days Supply		10	Tote-size returnable dunnage parts
	Maximum Days Supply		10	
	Minimum $ Supply	$	100	
	Maximum $ Supply		$ 10,000	
D—Biweekly	Minimum Days Supply		20	Overseas parts in container quantities
	Maximum Days Supply		20	
	Minimum $ Supply	$	25	
	Maximum $ Supply	$	500	
E—Monthly	Minimum Days Supply		60	Bulk unit-load container parts
	Maximum Days Supply		120	
	Minimum $ Supply	$	100	
	Maximum $ Supply	$	250	
F—Quarterly	Minimum Days Supply		60	Hardware and inexpensive parts
	Maximum Days Supply		120	
	Minimum $ Supply	$	50	
	Maximum $ Supply	$	250	
POLICIES	MODIFY	GRAPH	DETAILS	WHAT IF

Figure 5.12   Inventory Management Policies Screen

fer to the system integration screen later in this chapter). The planner may accept the modification by deleting the override value or ignore the modification and leave the override field as is. Details on file for both fields should indicate when the policy was established, why it was established, and why the override field is different.

Inventory categories include ABC, accounting classification, commodity, make or buy, and so on. Policies within each category relate to cycle counting, order quantity constraints, inventory investment levels, service levels, and so on. A policy may define whether parts within the category can be released automatically as a purchase or work order without planner review if all of the ordering edits are passed. For inventory adjustments, a policy will identify the level of adjustment which will be accepted without planner override, the level that requires a planner override, and the level that requires the inventory manager's override. Table 5.2 provides some of the policies within the three internal integration areas of inventory management.

Once a category is selected, the inventory manager can modify any or all of the values established for the category. A "what if" capability identifies the effect of the change before it is actually initiated. For example, the inventory manager may be considering a policy change which defines surplus inventory as inventory which exceeds a 12-month supply (changed from an 18-month supply). Activating the "what if" function lists the parts which fall into this category and the value difference between 12- and 18-month supplies. Refer to Figure 5.13. In this case, inventory which had been previously classified as excess (in the range of 12 to 18 months) is being changed to surplus. The effect is to increase the surplus category by $77,000. The financial balance remains at $500,000, since both surplus and excess stock fall within the *Financial* category.

Policies relate to the five operational areas of integration. The system should support policies for the performance measures discussed in Chapter 2. How the support is provided is a function of the system design, as discussed following for customer service.

Information Management: Customer Service Levels—The system should enable the inventory manager to establish customer service targets by part, product, and customer (refer to Figure 5.14). Historical information enables actual performance to be tracked over time against target. This is based on number of op-

Table 5.2   Representative Categories and Policies

CATEGORY	POLICIES
Inventory Policies	- ABC category (percent by category) - Accounting-related (RAW, WIP, and FG; various classifications) - Turns-related (operating, business, and financial) - Inventory-related (operating, excess, surplus, inactive, obsolete) - Target-related (days supply, investment, turns, customer service level, inventory accuracy level)
Inventory Planning	- Order-related (order quantity constraints and qualifiers) - Forecasting-related (alpha and beta factors) - Safety Stock-related (safety stock customer service %, alpha factor, number of standard deviations "=" 100% safety stock customer service %)
Inventory Control	- Cycle Counting-related (accuracy targets, acceptable deviations) - Container Standardization (size, weight, and capacity) - Equipment Standardization (type, operating characteristics) - Cycle Time Standards (receiving, issuing, handling, storage)

	CATEGORY	ELEMENT	POLICY	COMMENT(S)
08:00am 07/01/YY			POL— Surplus Inventory Management Policy	

	CATEGORY	ELEMENT	POLICY	COMMENT(S)
FROM:	Financial Inventory	Surplus	> 18 Month Supply	Inventory-planned parts only
TO:			> 12 Month Supply	
FROM:	STOCK $: $2,000,000	FINANCIAL $: $ 500,000	SURPLUS $: $ 23,000	
TO:	$2,000,000	$ 500,000	$ 100,000	
CHANGE:	$ 0	$ 0	$ 77,000	

	PART NUMBER	PART NAME	TOTAL BALANCE	SURPLUS BALANCE	PART COST	EXTENDED COST	% OF TOTAL
	63 parts					$100,000.00	100.00%
1	A123B456C	Volt Meter	34	20	$ 120.00000	$ 2,400.00	2.40%
2	B111C2234	Motor	6	2	$1125.00000	$ 2,250.00	2.25%
	V						
	V						
63	C555D4321	Resistor	450	425	0.01200	5.10	0.00%

PRINT	MODIFY	SUMMARY	$ SORT	PART SORT	WHAT-IF

Figure 5.13 Surplus Inventory Policies Details Screen

08:00am 07/01/YY   MGT—Customer Service Level (Based on Stock-outs)

Part Number:	XXXXXXXXXXX	Part Name: XXXXXXXXXX	Inv U/M: PCS
Safety Stock:	F—Fixed	Part Cost: $ 1.25	
Target Service:	95.0% (Minimum)	Date Set: 04/16/YYYY	

Formula: $\dfrac{\text{Total Planned or Unplanned Issues} <+ \text{Required Date}}{\text{Total Planned or Unplanned Issues}}$ ex. (22-2)/22=90.9% Jan.

MONTH	ISSUES <= REQD DT	ISSUES > REQD DT	UNPLANNED PORTION	SAFETY STOCK	SERVICE LEVEL	DEVIATION FROM TARGET	REQUIRED ADDED SAFETY STOCK
Jan.	20–1,000 PCS	2–30 PCS	1–10 PCS	40	90.9%	–4.1%	20–$25.00
Feb.	25–800 PCS	1–10 PCS	0–0 PCS	40	96.2%	+1.2%	0–$0.00
Mar.	40–1,200 PCS	0–0 PCS	0–0 PCS	40	100.0%	+5.0%	0–$0.00

PRODUCT	PART	GRAPH	MODIFY	WHAT IF	DETAILS

Figure 5.14 Customer Service Level Screen

portunities to provide service compared to the number of times service was not provided. One way to calculate this is to divide total issues which occurred on or before their required date by total issues for the part. If this meets or exceeds the target, then performance is acceptable. If not, additional safety stock investment may be required.

Two late issues occurred in January due to a stock-out sometime during the month. One was for 20 pieces of dependent demand and the other was for 10 pieces of independent demand (identified in the Unplanned Portion column).

This stockout occurred after the 40 pieces of safety stock had already been consumed. Therefore, an additional safety stock of 20 pieces would have satisfied the dependent demand, and 30 pieces would have satisfied both demands.

The minimum 95 percent Target Service at the top of the screen would have been achieved by covering either or both of the demands. In this case, it is less expensive to carry the extra 10 pieces needed to cover the independent demand. However, dependent demand should take priority over independent or unplanned demand. Therefore, the target service level would have been achieved with an additional 10, 20, or 30 pieces in safety stock. The company's customer service policy must establish which type of demand takes precedence when considering a change to safety stock level. *Note that safety stock is not normally used to cover dependent demand. However, in situations where companies promise product deliveries in less than the published lead times, safety stock will be dipped into.*

Part Master

Part numbers are typically added in one of two ways to the inventory system. Engineering creates a part master record when a new part is added to a bill of material. This record contains default data based on whether the part is initially identified as a purchased or self-manufactured part. Records for Maintenance, Repair, and Operating Supplies (MRO), R&D, and other parts not included on a bill of material are created on-line by the planner.

The part master screen (refer to Figure 5.15a) provides the capability to view information about any part. Dialogues enable the planner to display information, modify fields, add a part master record, and delete a part master record. "Selection" windows provide lists to ensure that only valid alternatives are selected. Units of measure, accounting classifications, planners, storerooms, part names, commodity codes, and so on, all lend themselves to lists. Edits are used for fields entered by the planner to ensure validity. This works for dates, unit of measure conversion factors, and so on. Part master data typically encompasses multiple screens.

Part master information is generally categorized as descriptive information, policy-related, planning-related, ordering-related, Safety Stock-related, Forecasting-related, and Control-related. Details for a field include such information as the last date the field was modified, reason the planner used for selecting one value over another, planner performing the modification, and date the part should be reviewed. Consider a case where engineering is in the process of modifying a part. The engineer can provide the inventory planner with a notification of the extent of change, target effectivity date, and effect on inventory for the part (see Details window in Figure 5.15b). Modifying the fields automatically sends an action message to the planner to review the changes.

The following part master fields are representative. Other fields used for ordering, safety stock, and forecasting are generally covered in later chapters.

Part Number—Unique alphanumeric designation for the part. Part numbers remain the same until form, fit, or function changes to the extent that a later re-

08:00am 07/01/YY		SKU—Part Master File			

Part Number:	xxxxxxxxxx	Part Name:		xxxxxxxxxxxx
Part Description:	xxxxxx xxxxx xxxxxxxx xxxxxxxxxx x xx xxxxxxx xxxxx xxxxx			
Commodity:	code–description	Normal Lead Time:		999 DAYS
Product:	code–description	Expedited Lead Time:		999 DAYS
Source:	code–description	Primary Supplier:		code–name
Inventory Planner:	code–description	Contract Type:		code–description
Inventory U/M:	code–description	Drawing Revision:	*	99
Purchasing U/M:	code–description	To Inventory Multiplier:		999.99999
Engineering U/M:	code–description	To Purchasing Multiplier:		999.99999
Supersede Part:	xxxxxxxxxx	Superseding Date:	*	mm/dd/yy
Phase Out:	code–description	Phase Out Date:	*	mm/dd/yy
Stock:	code–description	Inventory Class:		code–description
Pending:	code–description	Available Date:	*	mm/dd/yy
Consignment:	code–description	Inspection Code:		code–description
Alternate Part:	number–name–description			
Floor Stock:	code–description			
Planner Note:	xxxxxxxxxxxxxxxxxxxxxxxxxxxxxxxxxxxxxxxxxxxxxxxxxxxxxxxxxx			

PREV PART	NEXT PART	ADD	MODIFY	DELETE	DETAILS*

Note: The * indicates that there are additional details available (via the Details button) for the Drawing Revision.

Figure 5.15a Part Master Screen

Drawing Revision—04	
Engineer/Phone/Date:	D. Shore x5367 / 04/12/YY
Date of Current Revision:	02/23/YYYY Current Rev: 03
Effectivity Date of Next Revision:	07/21/YYYY Firm
Part on Hold:	NO
Reason for Change:	Additional details for Assembly
Effect on Current Inventory:	None; continue to use
Engineer's Comments:	Adjustment tolerances added
Planner's Comments:	

Figure 5.15b Part Master Details for Drawing Revision

vision cannot be used as a replacement for an earlier revision. Length may be 30 characters or more but is more commonly in the 10 to 20 range. Part numbers may incorporate a coding sequence which describes characteristics of the part. Other techniques include using the supplier's part number, the parent assembly and part item number on the bill of material, or a generic (sequential) number of some type.

Part Name—Common name of the part such as resistor, bolt, or motor. Following part name standards established by engineering enables report sorts to be made by part name. This minimizes the risk of adding duplicate parts under different part numbers. Part name is a shortened version of the part description (e.g., screw; for 10-16 × ½″ self-tapping Phillips head screw).

Part Description—Specific description of the part. Format should be consistent within part name to make reading lists easier. For example, listing name, volts, amps, phase, and shaft length for motors are easier to read if the sequence of descriptive information remains constant. Engineering should establish standards for the format.

Commodity—Castings, fabricated parts, motors, plastic injection molded parts, and so on, used by some companies to identify parts purchased by a particular buyer. Commodity can also be used to identify storage area (i.e., flammable, acid, base, refrigerated, security) or scrap percentages. Pricing multipliers may also be based on commodities such as metals where price changes follow market indicators.

Product—Identifier for a particular product family or line. Where the part is used for multiple products, the field indicates "multiple." The Details dialogue then provides a listing and related usage information such as quantity per product and percentage of total demand based on relative demand among products.

Source Code—Source indicates that the part or assembly is self-manufactured, purchased, or possibly obtained from a sister division. It determines the type of order processing for the part (i.e., production/work order, purchase order, or interdivisional order, respectively).

Normal Lead Time—Cumulative lead time for material, part, or assembly if obtained from the primary supplier. This is the time used in calculating replenishment lead time for order processing. The Details dialogue identifies the lead times for any additional suppliers on file. Lead time reflects the total duration from order release to Raw material receipt or Work in Process receipt if material is received directly to the point-of-use.

Expedited Lead Time—Normal supplier lead time includes backlog, cycle time, and normal shipment time. There are usually opportunities to expedite a part if necessary, constrained only by the actual manufacturing lead time and availability of components or materials. Expedited lead time provides an indication of how short a lead time may be achieved if the company is willing to pay a premium for overtime and air freight. This may also be the lead time if purchasing from a distributor in cases where the company normally purchases direct from the manufacturer.

Primary Supplier—The primary supplier identifies which supplier's lead times, order quantity constraints, and current costs will be used in the ordering logic.

Contract Type—Parts may be procured for specific customer contracts or procured based on specific contractual conditions negotiated with the supplier. The contract type may correspond to a specific storage area in cases where contract materials must be physically separated for accounting purposes. Engineer-to-order companies may have material purchased for one contract which cannot be considered as an available balance and used for another. Other types of supplier contracts (e.g., blanket contracts for inexpensive parts) may permit the receipt quantity to deviate from ordered quantity by some percentage or materials to be received early or late by some number of days.

Drawing Revision—Drawing revision identifies the current part engineering level in companies where product designs are subject to change. Before releasing orders to suppliers, the purchasing system should verify that lead times and pricing reflects the current engineering revision. If the purchasing supplier file indicates that the supplier has not received and confirmed the latest revision drawings and information for company-designed parts, the order cannot be released until the supplier receives updated information to prevent getting the old revision. There may also be a need to perform more stringent incoming inspection until the supplier is requalified for the part at the new revision.

Inventory Planner—The planner code acts as a sort field for messages and reports. Only the designated planner and inventory manager may be authorized to make changes to a part, depending on responsibility and authority levels established by the company.

Inventory Unit of Measure—Materials are stocked and issued per the inventory unit of measure. Standard cost and requirements are also based on the inventory U/M.

Purchasing Unit of Measure—Materials are purchased, received into the plant, and invoiced according to the purchasing unit of measure.

Purchasing to Inventory Multiplier[2]—The conversion multiplier is 1.00 where the purchasing U/M on a purchase order matches the inventory U/M. A conversion is required after receiving but before storage where there is a mismatch. This conversion is calculated as that multiplier which converts purchasing units to inventory units. For example, where wire is purchased 10 reels/carton and is issued by the reel, purchasing units of boxes × 10.00 = inventory units of reels.

Engineering Unit of Measure—Where the engineering U/M on a requirement matches the inventory U/M, no conversion is required. Where there is a mismatch, a conversion is required when MRP or the inventory subsystems convert requirements into orders. This conversion is calculated as that multiplier which converts engineering to inventory units. For example, where engineering specifies wire in inches, a requirement for 3,000 inches when inventory stocks in reels of 5,000 inches per reel is translated into a work order requirement of 0.6 reels in in-

---

2. There is typically no work order to inventory multiplier since inventory should be produced directly in inventory units.

ventory units. In this case, inventory will issue one reel, or perhaps the wire will be a floor stock item.

Supersede Part—The supersede part field identifies the new part number when a part has been replaced by another. Any service part orders or other requirements for the original part will automatically be assigned to the new number. The new number must meet form, fit, and function criteria. If statistical ordering techniques are used for the new part, it may be desirable to transfer historical usage patterns from the old to the new part to ensure that orders reflect anticipated usage. This is discussed in Chapter 8.

Supersede Date—When a part has been superseded, the supersede date field identifies the effective date. If this date is in the future, the original part may continue to be used. However, as of the supersede date, all usage of the original part ceases. Any residual stock must be applied to requirements for the new part number or disposed of, as applicable.

Supersede Reason—A short description of why the part is being superseded should be provided. A supersedure due to a safety reason is very important to broadcast to the organization and may involve changes to sold products. This and related information are available via the Details dialogue.

Phase Out Code—Parts are phased out once they are no longer needed for production or service requirements. The phase out code prevents the system from suggesting any replenishment orders. Once inventory reaches a zero balance through normal usage or disposition, the planner deletes the active inventory record.

Stock—Parts are procured or manufactured for stock (general inventory) or nonstock (specific customer orders). Nonstock parts are ordered on an order-for-order basis (lot-for-lot order quantity technique).

Pending—Adding new parts to engineering bills of material creates supporting part master records based on a minimal amount of default data. The new parts need to be identified as "pending" until the actual bill of material revision is approved for use. This ensures that no ordering action occurs until the required approvals are received.

Consignment—Consignment materials are stocked by the company but not paid for until the end of the time period (month) in which they are used. This is considered a "contract type" as discussed previously. With consignment materials, returns from production during the period offset issues up to the quantity which has been issued. Consignment quantity and inventory quantity (company-owned) stock balance fields must be maintained separately within the system since it is possible to have material in both classifications concurrently. Issue logic assumes that company-owned materials are issued prior to consigned material unless there are location, supplier, or other restrictions in effect. Consigned inventory is excluded from calculations of inventory value and inventory turns.

Alternate Part—When a given part is out of stock, there may be acceptable alternates. These tend to be higher-priced as compared to the standard part and so are used only as a replacement on an as-needed basis. Note that use of an alternate part constitutes an unplanned issue and so may cause safety stock of the unplanned item to increase, rather than that of the originally planned part.

Floor Stock—Parts which are classified as floor stock tend to have few, but large, issues. Floor stock materials may be stored in a single location in the production area, distributed throughout multiple production areas, or treated as a two-bin item with some material in production and some in the stock room. Such items are not issued individually on a pick list for a particular order. The inventory system will not treat a stock-out as an emergency replenishment since such issues are more similar to transfers to a point-of-use or point-of-fit location.

Inspection Code—The inspection code identifies the type of incoming inspection required for purchased parts. This may include 1—No Inspection, 2—Mechanical Inspection, 3—Electrical Inspection, 4—Mechanical and Electrical Inspection, 5—Test, and so on. Inspection generally refers to a visual inspection against specifications or drawings to verify dimensional or design characteristics. Test refers to some type of mechanical, electrical, metallurgical, or chemical test to verify material or operating characteristics. Where sample quantities are retained or destroyed by the testing method, sufficient extra materials must be ordered to compensate for inspection losses. From an inventory perspective, materials will be identified as in-plant but unavailable until after acceptance by inspection.

Characteristic 1-n—Parts may have a variety of specific characteristics which serve to further differentiate them from other parts. Characteristics include length/width/height/inside diameter/outside diameter, electrical properties such as volts, ohms, or amps, speed, materials, color, country of usage, and so on. A minimum of 4–5 special characteristic fields serve to complement the part name and description fields. Having individual fields also simplifies searches on special part characteristics (i.e., all 1-ohm resistors).

Characteristic Description 1-n—All parts cannot be described by the same standard characteristics. Rather than using generic "Characteristic 1" headings, the inventory system should provide the capability to customize the field headings per part. The planner should ensure that the same sequence of information is consistently used, such as always length/width/height, and so on. This is regulated by providing a selection list which identifies complete sets of headings for raw materials, mechanical parts, electrical parts, motors, and so on. These may also be selected automatically based on commodity code.

Standard Cost—In a standard cost environment, all inventory transactions are valued at the standard cost. This is typically several percentage points higher than expected actual cost. Formulas which use part cost use this cost. If a significant change occurs during the year, accounting may change the standard cost. Typically, however, standard cost is retained for a year and considered for change only at the end of the fiscal year.

Current Cost—In a standard cost environment, a cost must be developed for the next year's standard cost based on current costs and known or projected changes. The current cost will become the next year's standard cost at or around the end of the fiscal year.

Last Year's Standard Cost—In a standard cost environment, the previous year's standard cost may be retained for reference purposes. This enables significant changes in costs from year to year to be tracked.

Inventory Balances

The inventory system maintains stock balances by location for parts which are under inventory control. The system should additionally provide an indication of material which has been received but is not yet in inventory, in the case of purchased parts, or completed but not yet stored, in the case of manufactured parts. Refer to Figure 5.16.

The screen indicates that there is an available balance of 400 units out of a total stock balance of 1,000. There are 100 units in receiving which have not been moved to storage. Activating the Details dialogue with the cursor positioned on the receipt quantity of 100 identifies the purchase order number, date received, inspection requirements, if any, and so on. The system will not consider the 100 units as available until they have been stored (though MRP will recognize that

08:00am 06/28/YY		LOC—Part Location			
Part Number: XXXXXXXXXX		Part Name: XXXXXXXXXX Inv U/M: EACH			
Stock Balance: 1000		Avail. Bal.: 400* On Hold: 0			
Receiving Stock: 100*		Inspection Stock: 0 Disposition Stock: 0			
	AS/RS		SERVICE	ON HOLD	OVERFLOW
Bin Location:	LOC	C04231	PARTS	AREA	AREA
Stock Balance:	800	150	50	0	0
Cycle Count Discrepancy:	0	135	0	0	0
MTD Receipts:	300	0	0	0	0
MTD Returns for Credit:	0	0	0	0	0
MTD Planned Issues:	140	0	0	0	100
MTD Unplanned Issues:	10	0	0	0	0
MTD Transfer In:	0	[50]	0	0	0
MTD Transfer Out:	50	0	0	0	0
MTD Adj. Increase:	0	0	0	0	0
MTD Adj. Decrease:	0	0	0	0	0
MTD Scrap Issues:	0	0	0	0	0
MTD Service Issues:	0	200	0	0	0
MTD R&D Issues:	0	0	0	0	0
Begin Balance:	700	350	50	0	100
Date of Last Inventory:	06/05/YY	06/05/YY	06/05/YY		06/05/YY
Date of Last Issue:	06/30/YY	06/27/YY	05/03/YY		06/03/YY
Date of Last Receipt:	06/15/YY	06/15/YY	03/29/YY		05/18/YY
Date Stockout:				03/24/YY	06/03/YY
Bin Hold Date:				06/23/YY *	
PREV PART	RQMTS	HISTORY	DETAILS*	NEXT PART	

Figure 5.16   Part Location Screen

they are in-plant). Requirements for the 600 units are viewed via the RQMTS dialogue.

The columns indicate the quantity in each storage location. The AS/RS location may actually consist of multiple bin locations if the inventory system maintains only summary level data. Location C04231 indicates Conventional storage. Other columns may identify additional locations or areas such as service, on hold, and overflow.

Bin (Storage) Location—Unique identifier of each individual storage location. With an AS/RS which maintains the actual locations for storage and retrieval purposes, the bin location may be a general designation at the host level. General designations may also be used for inventory in laydown or floor stock areas where individual locations have not been specified. Bin location ID will typically identify warehouse or stockroom, area or aisle, bin and shelf, or location.

Stock Balance—Actual quantity in the location per the inventory unit of measure.

Cycle Count Discrepancy—Current cycle count discrepancy for the location, if any (the planner will have been notified of the discrepancy via an action message).

MTD Receipts—Month-to-date quantity received against purchase or work orders and stored in the location. Receipts do not include returns for credit.

MTD Returns for Credit—Month-to-date returns from production or customers for credit. Production credit is made against the original order number or department charge.

MTD Planned Issues—Month-to-date quantity issued to production/work orders based on previous allocations. Planned issues will not be considered in historical demand for calculating statistical safety stock. Planned issues are differentiated from unplanned issues since work or customer order fields are nonblank in the issue transaction. Note that companies may need to assign a time-fence to differentiate planned from unplanned issues. It is unreasonable to categorize an order added to the system the previous week as "planned" demand when the normal order lead time is greater than one week.

MTD Unplanned Issues—Month-to-date quantity issued to work or customer orders or departmental or other charges, where there was no prior allocation (or where the allocation was not made early enough). Unplanned issues must be forecasted in advance and are included in statistical safety stock calculations.

MTD Transfer IN—Month-to-date quantity transferred from one inventory-controlled bin location to another. Transfers are not normally considered accounting transactions since total inventory value remains the same. However, a transfer from regular to service parts storage may be an exception if accounting classification changes. Since there may be a time delay in getting material from one location to another, both the from and to locations should be maintained in the transaction. Bin location C04231 indicates that there are 50 units currently in the process of being transferred from another location (in this case, the AS/RS). The [brackets] will be removed when the transfer transaction is completed and the material has been stored.

MTD Transfer OUT—Month-to-date quantity transferred out of one inventory-controlled bin location to another. Transfers are used to move material from one storage area to another or to consolidate partial pallets. A transfer may also be used to maintain control of a retrieval from the AS/RS to a "logical" destination such as cycle counting or quality control where the material will be restored (though not necessarily in the original location).

MTD Adjustment Increase—Month-to-date quantity increase in a storage location. This occurs when one or more cycle counts result in a net increase.

MTD Adjustment Decrease—Month-to-date quantity decrease in a storage location. This occurs when one or more counts result in a net decrease. Note that adjustment transactions do not affect historical demand for forecasting or statistical safety stock purposes.

MTD Scrap Issues—Month-to-date quantity scrapped against an accounting scrap account. Scrap transactions do not affect historical demand for forecasting or statistical safety stock purposes.

MTD Service Issues—Month-to-date quantity issued to an accounting service account. Service part issues will be added to unplanned issues for purposes of calculating independent demand. Independent demand is used for forecasting and statistical safety stock purposes.

MTD R&D Issues—Month-to-date quantity issued to an accounting Research and Development (R&D) account. R&D issues will be added to unplanned issues for purposes of calculating independent demand used for forecasting and safety stock.

Beginning Month Balance—The beginning balance provides a reference point for calculating net changes over the course of the month.

Date of Last Inventory—Date on which the last cycle count transaction was processed for the bin location. The quantity may have remained unchanged.

Date of Last Issue—Date on which the last issue occurred. This includes planned, unplanned, scrap, service part, or R&D issues.

Date of Last Receipt—Date on which the last purchase or production/work order receipt was processed.

Date Stock-Out—Date on which the inventory balance was reduced to zero through an issue, adjustment, or transfer. Some systems will delete a nonprimary location automatically when there is a zero balance and no inventory is in the process of being transferred.

Bin Hold Date—Date on which a bin hold was set. In an automated system, this prevents automatic order processing from applying the materials in the bin to an order. However, there will be an override dialogue which enables a supervisor to retrieve materials on hold for inspection or scrapping.

Inventory Operating Transactions

Operating transactions increase, confirm, or reduce inventory balances. Transaction categories include issue, receipt, adjustment, and Transfer (refer to Figure 5.17). Paperwork transaction processing occurs after the physical activities so

08:00am 07/01/YY		TRN—Inventory Operating Transactions				
	PLANNED ISSUE	UNPLANNED ISSUE	RECEIPT	ADJUSTMENT	RETURN MATERIAL	SCRAP ISSUE	TRANSFER
Part Number:	required	required	required	required	required	required	required
Order Number:	required	----------	required	----------	required *	----------	----------
Order Suffix:	required	----------	required	----------	required	----------	----------
Order Item:	required	----------	required	----------	required	----------	----------
Quantity:	required	required	required	required	required	required	required
Inventory U/M:	required	required	required	required	required	required	required
Location From:	required	required	----------	required	----------	required	required
Location To:	----------	----------	required	----------	required	----------	required
Charge Number:	----------	required	----------	----------	required	required	----------
Return From:	----------	----------	----------	----------	required	----------	----------
PLAN ISSUE	UNPLAN ISSUE	RECEIPT	ADJUSTMENT	RETURN	SCRAP	TRANSFER

Note: Transaction headings are for the purpose of identifying required fields. Only required fields are displayed based on the button activated.

Figure 5.17   Inventory Operating Transactions Screen

there is always a risk of out-of-sequence errors. Companies have procedures to ensure that this risk is minimized. With bar code and RF systems, the paperwork is replaced with an electronic transaction. The electronic completion occurs at the same time as the physical completion.

Issue transactions indicate that inventory has been removed from the Raw material category to either:

- Production (as Work in Process charged to orders)

- Production (as Work in Process charged to floor stock, typically a department budget)

- Customers (as sales)

- Other departments (as a charge against a department account)

- Scrap (as a charge against a scrap account)

- Supplier (as a charge against a supplier account, where the supplier may be performing some type of process on the part prior to its return such as plating, painting, and so on)

Receipt transactions indicate that inventory has been added to the raw material or Finished Goods category, as applicable, from either:

- Suppliers (as a purchase order receipt)

- Production (as a production/work order receipt)

- Production (as a return for credit of excess or unnecessary inventory)

- Customers (as a return for credit of previously purchased inventory)

- Other departments (as a return for credit of previously issued inventory)

Adjustment transactions indicate that inventory has been counted in a particular location(s) and is either being:

- Increased (the actual count was greater than the computer balance)

- Decreased (the actual count was less than the computer balance)

- Accepted (the actual count matched the computer balance)

Transfer transactions track inventory being moved from one location to another. With conventional (noncomputerized) storage systems, a transfer usually indicates that material is being moved from one storeroom or warehouse to another or is being consolidated from one pallet onto another. Another possibility is that inventory is being transferred to repair. Inventory in repair will be excluded from the available balance but will be recognized by MRP. With automated systems, transfer transactions may additionally be used to indicate that materials are being removed from the AS/RS for cycle counting or inspection, with the intention of returning the materials to storage. This enables logical control to be maintained by the AS/RS control system even though the materials are not physically stored within the system. The operator is responsible for returning the material to storage. Quantity changes may occur to account for sample quantity removal or inventory adjustment.

Backflush transactions are a category of issue transactions. A bill of material explosion based on the number of products or assemblies produced is used to calculate the quantity of each part consumed in the process. This quantity and value are removed from Work in Process when the inventory is backflushed at the end of a shift, end of a day, or based on pay points within the process. Backflushing logic is incorporated into PAC/MES logic and eliminates having to process individual issue transactions.

Part Number—Unique identifier of the part. Edits verify that this is a valid number.

Order Number—For planned issues, order number is the production/work or customer order number. For supplier receipts, order number is the purchase order number. For manufactured receipts, order number is the production/work order number. For returned materials, order number is the order to be credited for the return of the material. If no order number is provided (refer to * in Return Material column), a charge number is required. Edits verify that the order number is valid for an open order or requirement.

Order Suffix—Some systems assign a sequential order suffix for each successive order. This allows the purchase or production/work order number to be the actual part number, while the suffix provides uniqueness. Using a generic sequential number as the order number requires additional information to identify the part number being ordered. Generic numbers are, therefore, less useful than numbers based on part number. Edits verify that the order suffix is valid for an open order or requirement.

Order Item—The item number identifies the specific bill of material line item for the part. This differentiates issues for orders where the same part number may be used multiple times in different assemblies or identifies the order number and item to be credited when material is returned. Edits verify that the order item is valid (part of a requirement).

Quantity—The actual quantity issued, received, or returned is identified. If the actual quantity does not match the supplier's packing slip, purchasing will account for the discrepancy. Adjustment transactions may vary, where the quantity is either the actual counted quantity (an absolute adjustment) or the difference (plus or minus) between the computer and actual balance (a net adjustment).

Inventory Unit of Measure—The inventory unit of measure is a verification that the operator has issued a quantity which matches the proper inventory unit of measure. The transaction will be rejected if the transaction and inventory unit of measures do not match.

Location From—Actual location the material was issued from, transferred from, or where the inventory balance was adjusted.

Location To—Actual location the material was received to or transferred to from some other location.

Charge Number—Accounting charge number material was issued to for an unplanned or scrap issue or credited for material being returned (if not being returned against a previous planned issue).

Return From—Department, customer, or individual returning the material, for reference and tracking purposes.

Inventory Activity

In an ongoing business, a record of past history provides an indication of future demand. A transaction history also provides a means of tracking changes against a part for cycle counting purposes. Note that the transaction file should identify the accounting month in the details in companies where monthly summaries are on an accounting month, rather than a calendar month basis. Knowing the month is important for statistical purposes since months vary in length. Translating demand into days is required for consistency purposes in order to smooth the effect of variable length months. Demand during an 18-workday month is only $18/22 = 82\%$ of a 22-workday month, for example. Refer to Figure 5.18, which shows past history leading up to the current month (July YYYY).

Month—Total issues, receipts, and adjustments for each month are summed. Display may be by calendar month or by most recent month first.

12-Months—Running total for the previous 12 months.

Straight Average/Month—Average per month of most recent *complete* 12 months.

08:00am 07/31/YY				ACT—Part Activity			
PART NUMBER: xxxxxxx PART NAME: xxxxxxxxxxxx INV U/M: xxxx							
CALENDAR MONTH	START MONTH QTY	RECEIPTS	PLANNED ISSUES	UNPLND ISSUES	NET ADJUST (+ / -)	SCRAP ISSUES	SERVICE PARTS ISSUES
January YYYY:	100	200	80	20	-10	5	15
February YYYY:	170	0	150	5	0	0	0
March YYYY:	15	200	125	15	0	0	10
April YYYY:	65	150	140	6	0	0	14
May YYYY:	55	200	100	25	0	0	25
June YYYY:	105	0	105	0	0	0	0
July YYYY:	0	0	0	0	0	0	0
August YYYY-1:	0	350	250	45	0	0	45
September YYYY-1:	10	200	100	15	0	0	10
October YYYY-1:	85	0	85	0	0	0	0
November YYYY-1:	0	150	130	20	0	0	0
December YYYY-1:	0	200	170	10	0	0	10
12 Months:	605	1,650	1,435	161	-10	5	129
Straight Avg/Mnth:	50	138	120	13		0	11

PREV PART	NEXT PART	GRAPHICS	HISTORY	DETAILS	MORE

Figure 5.18   Part Activity Screen

Inventory Storage and Handling

Material handling and storage requirements are a function of the type and quantity of containers received or used. This information is often *not* readily available or routinely maintained for parts in the inventory system. However, having such data makes it easier to perform storage and handling assessments as conditions change over time. Refer to Figure 5.19.

"Type" per the example screen indicates that materials are currently received in COP—Cartons on Pallets. The target container is a returnable tote (supplier catalog number 812) containing 100 pcs. Note (1) for the tote indicates that it has not been implemented due to financial considerations. When it is, the totes will be transported on plastic returnable pallets.

The Graphic dialogue provides a front, side, and top view of the load, as well as relevant specifications. The Storage dialogue provides the information required to size storage and staging areas or receiving and production markets (refer to Chapter 12). The Work Station dialogue provides the information required to size staging at the workstation(s) using the part.

Container Quantity—Standard quantity normally contained in each individual container for the part. Where a rounding quantity is used, the rounding quantity is either the standard container quantity or a calculation based on standard container quantity × containers per unit load.

08:00am 07/01/YY		CTN—Containerization and Storage Profile				
Part Number: XXXXXXXXXX		Part Name: XXXXXXXXXX		Date As Of: mm/dd/yy		
	CURRENT CONTAINER	TARGET CONTAINER	CURRENT UNIT LOAD	TARGET UNIT LOAD	UNITS	ON TARGET
Quantity:	115	100	5,520	2,000	pcs	HIGH
Containers/Layer:			12	10		HIGH
Quantity/Layer:	1,380	1,000			pcs	HIGH
Stack Height:	4	2	2	2		OK
Type:	COP	812-TOTE	GMA Pallet	Plastic Plt		(1)
Length (Into Rack):	12	12	48	48	inches	OK
Width (Down Aisle):	14	14	42	42	inches	OK
Height (Plus Pallet):	10	9	45	23	inches	OK
Tare Weight:	0	6	35	95	lbs	OK
Part Weight: 0.300	34.5	36	1,691	815	lbs	OK
Maximum Weight:	—	40	—	3,000	lbs	OK

Planner Notes: 2,000 Unit Load Quantity is 1-Week Supply
Part Orientation: Loose Fill   Packing Dunnage: NONE
Reason for Discrepancy: (1) NEW TOTE NOT ECONOMIC AT THIS POINT (04/17/YY)

Storage Indicator: AS/RS   Overhang: + 0.25" ALL DIMENSIONS
Bar Code ID: YES   Repack Reqd: Yes—From Carton to Tote
Owner: N/A   Company   N/A

	DAYS SUPPLY	FLOW RACK	PALLET RACK	AS/RS	FLOOR LAYDOWN	LAYDOWN SQ FT
Container Storage:	0	0	0	0	0	0
Unit Load Storage:	5	0	0	1	0	0
PREV PART	NEXT PART	GRAPHIC	STORAGE	WKSTN	DETAILS	

Note: Bottom details are actually portion of Storage and Workstation dialogue.

Figure 5.19   Containerization and Storage Information

Containers/Layer—Number of containers per layer on the unit load.

Quantity/Layer—Calculated as containers/layer × quantity/container.

Stack Height—Number of unit loads which can be stacked or containers on a unit load.

Container Type—Container type indicates the type of handling and storage which may be required. Type includes cartons (pieces), jugs (hopper-type parts), wire baskets (heavy metal or bulky parts), drums (liquids), kegs (hardware), bins-JIT containers (loosely packed parts in pallet quantities), and so on. The type should include unit load characteristics, where applicable.

Length—Container or unit load length (cross aisle; into the rack), in the designated unit of measure. Maximum pallet or carrier length, including allowable overhang, is critical in an automated storage system. Since loads are prevented from extending into the flue space at the back of the rack by stops, any overhang into the aisle beyond specified limits runs the risk of interfering with the normal travel of a loaded SRM. Load overhang is typically not allowed or limited to a very small amount in an automated system. In a conventional storage system, it is not a consideration.

Width—Container or unit load width (down aisle), in the designated unit of measure. Maximum pallet or carrier width (when facing the storage location) including allowable overhang is critical in an automated storage system. Any load overhang runs the risk of hitting a rack column if the load is stored off-center. With drive-through rack designs (load arms extend under the carrier but do not span the distance from upright column to upright), undersize carriers must be detected prior to storage as well. Undersize carriers may fall between the load arms if shifted too much to the right or left.

Height—Container or unit load total height, in the designated unit of measure. Unit load height is calculated as the standard pallet height (typically 5 inches plus slave pallet height, as applicable) plus container height × stack quantity. Automated systems may include sizing stations which detect loads which exceed various heights. In systems where there are multiple height bins, loads may be stored in any bin which meets *or exceeds* the load height. Overheight loads are rejected to an error correction station.

Tare Weight—Weight of the empty container, in the designated unit of measure.

Part Weight—Weight per part, in the designated unit of measure.

Weight—Calculated as the container quantity × part weight + container tare weight for an individual container. Ergonomic weights range from 35–45 lb. for general evaluation purposes. For unit loads, weight is calculated as the container weight (part weight × container quantity + container tare weight) × containers per unit load + unit load tare weight. With automated systems, any load which exceeds the design weight of the rack structure must be stored manually in a conventional storage area. Go/No Go checks on the inbound conveyor system will route any overweight loads to an error correction station.

Containers per Unit Load—Calculated as the containers/layer × stacking height.

Maximum Weight—Design or ergonomic maximums for containers and unit loads.

Planner Notes—Free-format notes provided by the planner.

Part Orientation—Specified if required. Orientation may be relevant for robotic or manual load or unload, for part identification if a bar code ID is in a specific location on the part, for ensuring a specific container quantity, and so on. Where important for the operation of the various production processes, part orientation is typically designed into the returnable dunnage used to transport the part.

Reason for Discrepancy—Where there is a discrepancy between target container quantity and current container quantity, a descriptive field identifies the reason. Common reasons include ergonomic weight limitations which prevent a certain "rounding" quantity from being achieved, robotic loading/unloading requirements which prevent a certain quantity pattern per layer from being achieved, and so on.

Packing Dunnage—Dunnage may be required to protect or separate parts or to ensure that parts are bagged in specified multiples. Dunnage is sometimes used to refer to the container itself.

Storage Indicator—Storage indicator identifies where the material is stored. Alternatives may include AS/RS, conventional storage (storeroom, flammable, and so on), or point-of-use storage. Storage indicator determines the routing when materials are received.

Bar Code Identification—In automated systems, the ability to receive materials which are already bar coded may offer a competitive advantage. Materials which are not bar coded upon receipt may involve "waste" to generate an in-plant bar code.

Repack Requirement—In operations where specific quantities must be presented to the line, "waste" in the form of repacking must be restricted to the receiving market. Identifying these parts enables the company to monitor repacking cost as a percentage of total parts received.

Owner—Returnable containers are owned by the company or the supplier. Ownership identifies responsibility with respect to maintenance, cleaning, repair, and replacement.

Data at the bottom of the screen refers to equipment and layout sizing. Relevant information may include totes per market flow lane and total totes on-hand at any time, which identifies the number of flow lanes required. In general, layout or storage space must be available for the full receipt quantity plus the level of stock in storage at the point of receipt. Quantity must be thought of in terms of increments of packaging, which will be either individual containers or full unit loads. Even a pallet with one container requires a full storage position until the final container is issued.

Inventory Reports

Inventory system reports fall into three basic categories. The first two will be included on the Reports Menu as shown in Figure 5.20. The system should additionally have a report generation program which a knowledgeable individual can use to obtain ad hoc reports using data from the inventory and other systems. Reports may be hard copy or on-line.

Operating Reports are generated automatically by the system to support daily operations. Special reports may also be printed on a weekly, monthly, quarterly, and annual basis. These reports are printed without changes in format, though the time frame covered by the report may be selectable.

Request Reports are used on a somewhat repetitive basis for assessing current operating conditions. Such reports may provide an opportunity to select one or more categories, sorts, or time frames, as well as overall summaries.

Ad Hoc Reports are used on a onetime or occasional basis to obtain information to support a specific decision. The system should provide the capability to select and sort and perform calculations and summaries.

Reports may be printed to the screen (client), to the report printer, or to a file.

08:00am 07/01/YY		RPT—Inventory Reports Menu
Daily	Automatic	Daily Transaction Listing
Daily	Automatic	Daily Reject Listing
Daily	Automatic	Part Master Advisory
Daily	Automatic	Order Advisory
Daily	Automatic	Messages from Other Systems
Daily	Automatic	Daily Cycle Counting Report
Daily	Request	Cycle Counting Control Group Report
Daily	Request	Part Number Listing
Periodic	Request	Month-to-Date Inventory Status Report
Periodic	Request	Inventory Investment Report
Periodic	Request	Inventory Accuracy Report
Periodic	Request	Inventory Turns Report
Periodic	Request	Service Level Report
Periodic	Request	ABCZ Classification Report
Periodic	Request	Stock Location Report by Part Number
Periodic	Request	Stock Location Report by Location
Periodic	Request	Requirements Report
Monthly	Request	Excess, Surplus, and Obsolete Inventory Report
TO SCREEN	TO PRINTER	TO FILE

Figure 5.20   Inventory Reports Menu

If the report can be customized, the planner will be prompted to identify, select, sort, and combine data before the request is accepted.

Daily Transaction Listing—Lists all transactions for the previous day, sorted by date and part number. These same transactions are available in the history file.

Daily Reject Listing—Lists all transactions which were rejected in the nightly run, with the nature of the reject. These must be corrected on-line by the planner or resubmitted the next night. The system integration screen also includes the same information.

Part Master Advisory—Lists all parts which require maintenance. For example, new parts added by engineering with default data will be included, as will any discrepancies identified by the system in normal processing. The system integration screen also includes the same information.

Order Advisory—Lists all inventory-planned parts which must be reviewed for ordering. The order advisory screen also includes the same information.

Messages from Other Systems—Lists all messages regarding inventory parts which were generated from other systems. This may include order quantity revisions made by purchasing, canceled orders, engineering changes, and so on.

Daily Cycle Counting Report—Daily listing of parts to count, based on the count frequency.

Cycle Counting Control Group Report—Compares test counts with computer balances to provide an overview of the previous day's counting, count accuracy, and causes of inaccuracy.

Part Number Listing—Current status and basic information for all part numbers.

Month-to-Date Stock Status Report—Summary by day of inventory transactions for each inventory-planned part. Beginning and ending balance is listed for each transaction.

Inventory Investment Report—Summary of investment by part and inventory category against target and magnitude of required improvement.

Inventory Accuracy Report—Summary of inventory accuracy against target and progress against causes of inaccuracy.

Inventory Turns Report—Summary of inventory turns by category against target.

Service Level Report—Summary of customer service level by part and category against target.

ABCZ Classification Report—Sorted listing by ABC category, including override parts.

Stock Location Report by Part Number—Lists all locations and stock balances (with categories such as consignment, as applicable) for all parts sorted by part number.

Stock Location Report by Location—Lists all locations and stock balances in location sequence to aid in verifying inventory by location.

Requirements Report—Lists all requirements for each inventory-planned part with an adjustment for independent demand, as applicable. This report may be available via the MRP system.

Excess, Surplus, Inactive, and Obsolete Inventory Report—Summary by category of *financial* inventory with date of last issue, forecasted demand, and so on.

System Integration

A paperless system is only paperless if there is an electronic means of transferring messages among individuals. An integral system automatically initiates screen changes and dialogues based on the type of message. New messages may be routed to another individual as an outcome of the process. This is accomplished via a subsystem specifically designed to transfer action messages among individuals, with the appropriate file modifications occurring based on the action taken.

Example: Consider a simple application where engineering adds a new purchased part number via the bill of material processing program. This automatically creates a part master record in inventory using default data. As a result of adding this new part, the inventory planner receives an action message to add the required data fields to the part master. The buyer receives a message to create the required supplier pricing record. Adding the actual records automatically deletes the system integration file action messages.

Example: A more complex example occurs when an operator tries to issue a particular purchased part for a production/work order and discovers a quantity shortage. A (cycle) count discrepancy message is added to the system integration file for the planner responsible for the part as shown in

Figure 5.21. Since the message relates to inventory adjustments, the planner will be immediately placed into the related cycle counting screens when the action button is selected.

The cycle counting screen identifies the current inventory status for the part, including all locations. When the planner is ready to either accept or change the count, the system integration subsystem provides a screen to complete the process. Assuming the count is accepted as is, the following process will be initiated:

- The inventory balance is updated.

- The initial adjustment transaction record is updated to show the date and time when the planner completed the adjustment. This adds the planner ID and cause of inaccuracy to the transaction.

- A message is added to the production planner's message queue who is responsible for the production/work order with the shortage. When activated, this message identifies when the shortage will be rectified, what the effect is on the order, and so on.

- A message is added to the buyer's message queue identifying the shortage, as required. When activated, this message identifies when the next purchase order is scheduled for receipt, who the supplier contact is, who the production planner is, and so on, so the order can be expedited.

- The inventory planner's message is deleted.

Date Added—Date the action message was added to the system integration subsystem. Sorting in date sequence identifies messages which have not been addressed from previous days.

Time Added—Time message was added.

Message Type—Abbreviated message type used for sorting purposes and general identification. Each subsystem (MS, MRP, inventory, purchasing, PAC, MES, and so on) will have a list of standard types.

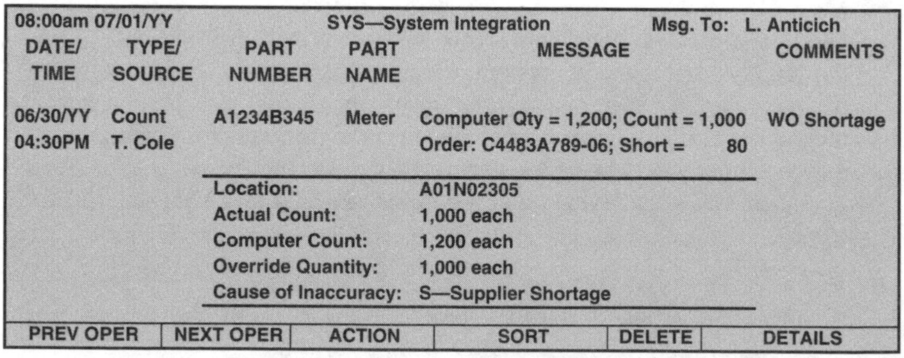

08:00am 07/01/YY			SYS—System Integration		Msg. To:	L. Anticich
DATE/ TIME	TYPE/ SOURCE	PART NUMBER	PART NAME	MESSAGE		COMMENTS
06/30/YY 04:30PM	Count T. Cole	A1234B345	Meter	Computer Qty = 1,200; Count = 1,000 Order: C4483A789-06; Short = 80		WO Shortage
		Location:		A01N02305		
		Actual Count:		1,000 each		
		Computer Count:		1,200 each		
		Override Quantity:		1,000 each		
		Cause of Inaccuracy:		S—Supplier Shortage		
PREV OPER	NEXT OPER	ACTION		SORT	DELETE	DETAILS

Figure 5.21 System Integration Screen

Source—Indicates actual source of the message. Names are included when an individual initiates the action message, such as with an adjustment or new part added to the part master. System-generated messages will identify the system, such as with a discrepancy discovered in normal processing within the order review program.

Message—Messages are customized based on the message type. The amount of data included is a function of the amount of data needed.

Comments—A comments field enables the initiator to include a short message or the planner to provide a short status if the message cannot be addressed immediately. This keeps others appraised of the current status.

SUMMARY

Traditional systems were designed to manage and display data. The basic design principle was to eliminate data redundancy. The basic operator interface displayed all of the data available so the user could make whatever decisions were required, whether the data was really needed for the decision or not. This type of system is the easiest to design because the system developers do not really need to understand much about the business or how decisions are made.

Companies probably have systems based on traditional design principles (1) if there is no paperless capability, (2) if there is no decision support capability in the form of graphs and "what if" analyses, (3) if there are no or few performance targets against which to automatically assess performance, and (4) if companies resort to category planning based on dollar value. The price companies pay for tools which do not adequately support the business is higher inventory investment levels. This ultimately translates into an even higher price—noncompetitiveness.

Systems based on traditional design principles are the least effective type for inventory management in an integral environment. This is because there are too many decisions to make without having some type of effective decision support capability. The focus of integral systems is on effective, timely decision-making based on an understanding of the products, processes, and parts. This requires a knowledge of cause and effect relationships incorporated into a Decision Support System.

Chapter 6

Zero-Tolerance Inventory Count Accuracy

No inventory strategy can be successful if inventory accuracy cannot be relied on for scheduling and promising decisions. Even knowing this, companies continue to use decades old inventory accuracy logic with accuracy targets below 100 percent. This has the effect of unintentionally setting inaccuracy targets greater than 0 percent. Management believes they are being flexible by allowing some parts to be inaccurate. The company can then use the time saved by not implementing corrective actions for more important things.

Setting an inaccuracy target is a choice to have scheduling and promising problems. The organization understands that an inaccuracy choice means that inventory accuracy is unimportant, regardless of any rhetoric to the contrary. In fact, the company intends to have inaccurate inventory since they are stopping short of the commitment required to ensure accurate inventory levels. Accurate inventory does not happen by mistake.

In an integral environment, every occurrence of inventory inaccuracy requires a corrective action. Having inaccurate inventory is not permitted. To address this message to the organization, management must understand how different departments view inventory accuracy. Everyone needs to hear the same message without interpreting it differently.

Accountants view inventory "accuracy" in terms of dollars. Inventory is by definition a company asset. Therefore, it is perfectly acceptable for overages (the financial value of actual counts in excess of computer count) to be netted against shortages. This has the added benefit of creating the appearance of very accurate financial inventory levels. The focus is on the dollar accuracy of high value items. B- and C-items get progressively less emphasis since they have less of an impact on financial accuracy.

Planners view inventory accuracy in terms of an acceptable percentage range. Accuracy tolerances are established by inventory category. Expensive parts require a higher level of accuracy than inexpensive parts. Planners use these ranges to relax certain count and dollar accuracy requirements in order to artificially improve the calculated inventory accuracy performance levels. This means that much more emphasis is placed on count accuracy of expensive parts and much less emphasis on inexpensive ones.

With either the accountant or planner approach, focusing on the high dollar items really only focuses on 5 percent or so of the parts. This does not really support production's need.

Production views inventory "accuracy" in terms of absolute count accuracy. More specifically, inventory must be 100 percent accurate when it is needed. Dollars of one part cannot be traded off against another in order to complete an order, so financial accuracy without count accuracy is immaterial.

This chapter covers the following aspects of inventory accuracy:

- Traditional views of inventory accuracy are in basic conflict with the requirements of an integral strategy. This basic conflict is grounded in the conflict between production's and accounting's view of inventory accuracy.

- There does not need to be any conflict if the company focuses on count accuracy. Count accuracy ensures dollar accuracy.

- The goal of an integral strategy is to eliminate the need to confirm count accuracy. However, the company must balance both proactive and reactive initiatives, projects, and programs to achieve this goal.

Inventory accuracy is a perfect example of a measure driving the results. If inventory is allowed to be inaccurate, it will be.

How *Accurate* Is Accurate?

Traditional inventory accuracy principles create a basic problem for the organization. Not knowing which parts are inaccurate while knowing that a certain number are permitted to be inaccurate makes *all* parts suspect. People on the shop floor do not know the difference between A, B, and C parts. Schedulers are not clairvoyant when it comes to guessing which of the parts the computer system says are available are really unavailable.

With inventory accuracy based on financial criteria, there is simply no way to tell which parts are accurate or inaccurate at any given time. This includes not knowing which parts will be inaccurate at the future point in time when they are needed. This promotes secret stockpiling by production supervisors of key parts which they had trouble getting in the past. This stockpiling then causes the very shortages they are protecting themselves against. Once it becomes enough of a problem, companies are forced to kit in advance in order to identify the shortages because they cannot believe the computer.

Until the organization can rely on the inventory system quantities, the gap shown in Figure 6.1 between 100 percent and any other percent will continue to cause problems throughout the company. The risk is that 80 to 95 percent of the

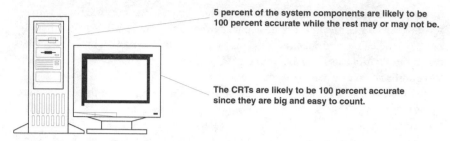

5 percent of the system components are likely to be
100 percent accurate while the rest may or may not be.

The CRTs are likely to be 100 percent accurate
since they are big and easy to count.

Figure 6.1   Comparison of Inventory Dollar vs. Count Inaccuracy

parts are as likely to be inaccurate as accurate simply because they are permitted to be inaccurate.

Companies are willing to settle for inaccuracy because of a perception that it is more expensive to ensure 100 percent count accuracy than to suffer the effects of inaccuracy. Cycle counting is usually considered an acceptable expense for correcting inaccuracies after they have occurred. Companies are often unwilling, however, to pursue and eliminate causes of inaccuracy because of the difficulty of backtracking history on the part and lack of time. Cycle count programs are often, therefore, simply cyclical counting programs. The real goal of such programs is actually to *not* detect any inaccurate parts. The fewer inaccurate parts identified, the higher the aggregate inventory accuracy measure/indicator.

What companies fail to realize is that every cycle count which identifies that a part is accurate is a total waste of time and effort. This effort could have been better spent locating and correcting inaccuracies and tracking down causes of inaccuracy. Every correct count is a missed opportunity to find and correct an inaccurate part (which the company knows exist since inaccuracy is permitted). The only effective cycle count is one which corrects a part count inaccuracy and identifies the cause of the inaccuracy. Any other count is a waste of the company's valuable resources.

Inventory accuracy levels are traditionally determined based on a month-end assessment, as shown in the following equation. The planner must ensure that a representative mix of counts is made among all of the cycle counting categories. This is determined by establishing a count cycle for each inventory category and ensuring that counts are made in that proportion. For example, an established mix may consist of 20 A-items, 45 B-items, and 150 C-items counted per week. As long as this proportion generally remains consistent over the course of the month, the accuracy of the counted materials is inferred to represent that of the total inventory.

$$\text{Inventory Accuracy Percentage} = (\text{A} + \text{B} + \text{C Accuracy}) \times 100\%$$

Where: A Accuracy = (A Counts − A Inaccuracies)/A Counts × 0.05
B Accuracy = (B Counts − B Inaccuracies)/B Counts × 0.15
C Accuracy = (C Counts − C Inaccuracies)/C Counts × 0.80

As previously discussed, every cycle count which identifies an inaccuracy reduces the overall calculated inventory accuracy level. The more diligent the inventory department is at finding inventory errors, the worse their measure of inventory accuracy performance. No credit is given for finding and correcting inaccuracies, since that only highlights failures within the organization's processes and procedures. Since people tend to do what they are measured on, the tendency is to ensure that many more parts are found to be accurate than are found to be inaccurate. The measure should really be based on the overall effectiveness of the process of locating and resolving causes of inaccuracy.

Manipulating inventory accuracy can be accomplished by counting more parts which are known to be accurate to offset the effect of any inaccuracies. When using financial measures, these are the A-items. Over the course of the month, the dollar value of accurate A-items can offset the effect of smaller dollar inaccuracies in B- and C-items.

Manipulating inventory accuracy performance can also be accomplished when the measure is based on the number of accurate vs. inaccurate parts. This involves counting parts which have a high probability of being accurate. Recounting previously counted parts is one technique. These are the A-item parts again. Processing zero counts when a part stocks-out is a second. If time permits, counting new receipt quantities and processing cycle counts along with the receipt transaction is a third. While these types of counts are included in the total counting profile for the month, they do not necessarily support the intent of the part's formal counting cycles established by the planner.

From a theoretical perspective, the need for accuracy increases the closer the actual available quantity matches the required quantity. If the stock balance is 100 units and today's demand is for 100 units, the inventory accuracy must be 100 percent. If the computer stock balance is 1,000 units of the same part, the actual stock balance can be as much as 900 units lower without affecting immediate production requirements. If short by 900 units, resolution of the shortage becomes an issue based on when the next requirement is due as a function of the replenishment lead time.

From a practical perspective, it is a waste of time to attempt to gauge the point where part accuracy is unimportant, somewhat important, and critically important. One of the directives in an integral environment is to reduce inventory of all parts to their target levels. Once this occurs, inventory accuracy becomes and remains critically important for all parts at all times.

Dollar Accuracy

Dollar accuracy is a function of how the company costs their inventory. With a standard cost system, dollar value is calculated as quantity × standard cost for each part. Since accuracy is reported in terms of dollars, a shortage of one part is allowed to offset an overage of another. In this way, individual parts can be inaccurate with respect to count, but inventory in total can still maintain a high dollar accuracy level. With a financial measure, companies can usually count on excellent A-item count accuracy and high B-item count accuracy. C-item count accuracy is always suspect.

Accounting views inventory from a four-wall perspective. This includes all Raw, WIP, and FG inventory in the facility. This may also include inventory in the logistics pipeline, depending on when ownership changes hands. Accounting is, therefore, concerned with the total dollar value of all inventory. The inventory department is only concerned with inventory over which it has either physical or logical control. Physical control begins once material is in the storeroom. Logical control begins when the incoming receipt transaction has been processed for a purchased part or production/work order completion transaction has been processed for a self-manufactured part.

Table 6.1 compares accounting vs. inventory areas of control and identifies typical causes of inaccuracy. As can be seen, there are many areas external to inventory's direct span of control which can adversely affect inventory accuracy. This is why inventory accuracy is a company, not an inventory department, problem and responsibility.

Companies traditionally set different dollar accuracy targets based on inventory category. Commonly used categories are based on ABC code. Table 6.2 identifies the acceptable inventory accuracy level using traditional parameters. Any total inventory dollar accuracy maintained at a level of 99.45 or above meets the traditional dollar target. Theoretically, 100 percent of the company's parts may be inaccurate on count, though in practice this situation should never occur. Nonetheless, this situation is permitted to occur, and that is the fallacy of inventory accuracy based on dollar measures.

Dollar and Count Accuracy, with Tolerances

According to a Pareto distribution, approximately 80 percent of a company's inventory in terms of number of parts consists of inexpensive items. In total, these parts may be only 5 percent of the company's total inventory value. Because of their low value, companies often consider a C-item part count as "accurate" if it is within some range of the computer balance. For A-items, the tolerance is zero. B-items might be +/–2 percent or $25.00, whichever is tightest. For C-items, the tolerance may be +/– 5 percent or $10.00, whichever is tightest.

Accuracy tolerances have two major advantages for the inventory department. The first is that receipts and issues need to be only generally accurate. This allows the use of scale and fill counts, which may be less precise than machine or hand counts. The second is that such inaccurate stock balances are considered accurate if they fall within the tolerance. Parts which are considered accurate do not penalize the inventory accuracy performance measure when an actual count disagrees with the computer count.

Example: A $2.50 B-item part can have an error of plus or minus ten pieces based on a $25.00 tolerance. The same part with a stock balance of 700 pieces can have an error of plus or minus 14 pieces based on a +/–2

Table 6.1   Accounting vs. Inventory Department Control

INVENTORY CATEGORY	ACCOUNTING CONTROL (TYPICALLY VIA "CHARGE" CATEGORIES)	INVENTORY CONTROL STATUS	CAUSES OF INVENTORY INACCURACY
Received Material	Upon "logical" receipt or Freight on Board (FOB) responsibility (Shipping Point or Destination)	Received but not "available"	Supplier-related errors: - Supplier overships - Supplier underships - Packing Slip quantity error - Material misidentified by packing slip - Supplier ships +/– packing slip quantity Shipping-related errors: - Loss during shipment - Damage during shipment Company-related errors: - PO Receipt data entry error - Inaccurate count upon receipt
Incoming Inspection	Raw material	In Inspection but not "available"	Quality Control (QC) error in specifying: - Loss due to destruct sampling - Loss due to sample quantity usage - Partial rejection quantity
Rejected Material	Raw material	In Disposition but not "available"	- QC error in specifying reject quantity
Disposed Material	Returned to Supplier or Scrapped	Unavailable	- QC error in specifying disposed quantity - QC error in specifying accepted quantity
Material in Transit to Stores	Raw material	Received but not "available"	- Material taken by Production without the proper paperwork update
Material in Stores	Raw material	Available	- Cycle count adjustment error(s) - Issue error(s) - Credit (returned materials) identification or quantity error(s) - Scale count error(s) - Receipt error(s) - Transfer error(s) - Damaged material - Lost/pilfered material - Misidentified material - Misplaced material - Misissued material - Incorrect unit of measure - Incorrect unit of measure conversion factor
Material Bin-Locked	Raw Material	In-stock but Not Available	

Table 6.1   *Continued*

INVENTORY CATEGORY	ACCOUNTING CONTROL (TYPICALLY VIA "CHARGE" CATEGORIES)	INVENTORY CONTROL STATUS	CAUSES OF INVENTORY INACCURACY
Kitted Materials	Work in Process	Issued	- Incorrect issue quantity - Incorrect part issued - Duplicate issue
Materials issued to Production (without Kitting)	Work in Process	Issued	- Incorrect issue quantity - Incorrect part issued - Duplicate issue
Production Loss	Scrapped	Issued	- Incorrect scrap quantity - Materials disposed of improperly - Lost or pilfered materials
Finished Goods in Warehouse	Finished Goods	Available	- Incorrect paperwork - Improper stacking pattern for quantity - Returned material without proper paperwork - See Material in Stores
Finished Goods in Shipping	Sales	Issued	- Incorrect issue quantity - Incorrect kitting - Incorrect paperwork

Table 6.2   Inventory Dollar Accuracy

INVENTORY CATEGORY	PERCENT OF INVENTORY $	MINIMUM ACCURACY PERCENT BASED ON $	MINIMUM $ PERCENT CONTRIBUTION
A	80%	100%	80% X 100% = 80.00%
B	15%	98%	15% X 98% = 14.70%
C	5%	95%	5% X 95% = 4.75%
TOTAL	100%		99.45%

percent tolerance by quantity. With both tolerances in effect, any actual count within +/−10 pieces when the inventory balance is ≥500 units is considered *accurate* (490 to 510). When the inventory balance is <500 units, the 2 percent tolerance by quantity constraint is used. Check the 500 line in the following table where both criteria are in sync.

ACTUAL COUNT	+2 PERCENT BASED ON QUANTITY	–2 PERCENT BASED ON QUANTITY	+$25 BASED ON VALUE (TEN PCS)	–$25 BASED ON VALUE (TEN PCS)
100	102	98	110	90
300	306	294	310	290
500	510	490	510	490
700	714	686	710	690

When an in-tolerance discrepancy is corrected by an adjustment transaction, the correction is made. The part is considered accurate both before and after the adjustment. If the company's inventory accuracy is inferred on the basis of 100 such parts, the company's inventory accuracy would be projected as 100 percent accurate. This is in spite of the fact that the inventory was 0 percent accurate in absolute terms by count.

One disadvantage of the use of tolerances from production's perspective is that the stock balance for 80 to 95 percent of the parts is not believable. This is aggravated by a tendency to sometimes overissue a part, rather than underissue. While this ensures that production has enough of a part to produce the order, it creates an inventory shortage. Once in production, the extra pieces must be disposed of, kept so they can be applied to a future shortage, or returned to the storeroom. In many environments, low cost parts are simply thrown away. Production personnel get paid to build products. They do not feel that it is their job to correct someone else's inventory mistakes. Keeping the parts in production creates a quality risk or a risk of using an old revision part on a new order.

From an inventory department perspective, a count or dollar tolerance enables a higher inventory accuracy to be claimed than can be demonstrated by actual part counts. If all 80 percent of a company's C-items are inaccurate but within tolerance, the inventory accuracy jumps from 20 percent (assuming that A- and B-items are accurate) to 100 percent. The greater the allowed tolerance, the higher the calculated inventory accuracy.

The cost shortage for a $10,000,000 10,000 part inventory, if every C-item is short by an average of $5, is an overall shortage of $40,000 (10,000 parts × 80% C-items × $5). Companies may risk this type of inventory valuation error if they believe that it costs more to cycle count, resolve problems leading to inaccuracy, delay orders due to C-item unplanned stock-outs, and promise customers delivery of parts and then shipping late due to unplanned stock-outs. If A- and B-items are also inaccurate to some degree, the $40,000 number becomes that much higher.

Check the cost accounting department and find out how much inventory gets written off each year because it has "disappeared." This means that it is on the accounting books as an asset but cannot in fact be located in inventory. Chances are, the inventory was issued to Work in Process without the proper transactions being processed. Another problem may be theft. This write-off number is usually a better justification for improving count accuracy than the argument in the previous paragraph.

INTEGRATION ISSUES ASSOCIATED WITH INVENTORY ACCURACY

100 percent inventory accuracy is more than a goal; it is production's right. It is inventory management's responsibility to ensure that target accuracy levels are achieved and maintained. The problem with making inventory management totally responsible is that many of the causes of inaccuracy are outside of their control as discussed previously. They can be held responsible for accuracy related to issuing, receiving, and adjustment processes. Other factors related to suppliers, receiving, incoming inspection, and handling are outside of their control. As a consequence, the company must come to terms with a number of issues related to how the company views inventory accuracy.

- Companies must clearly differentiate between traditional inventory accuracy levels and those required of an integral strategy. This means that the company must make a commitment to proactively pursue an accuracy improvement program. Relying on a reactive correction process of cyclical counting is only one element of the overall accuracy improvement process. Success is measured by the degree of trust the organization and customers have in inventory balances, as much or more so than by a mathematical projection of accuracy.

- Companies must trust their personnel to be contributors to the overall inventory accuracy improvement process. Many companies do not want their cycle counters to know how much inventory should be in a location prior to a cycle count. This is not a measure of trust. Operators who know how much of what type of inventory is supposed to be available are in a position to resolve a discrepancy if one occurs during the counting process. As likely as not, a counting mistake can be corrected immediately without causing any additional delay.

- The first logical place to check for an inaccuracy is upon receipt. Not catching a shortage at this point means that the company will pay once for inventory not received and again when the shortage quantity is reordered. Once non-receiving personnel have unrestricted access to an incoming shipment, it is very difficult to prove that there was a shortage upon receipt.

- Inventory inaccuracy can have subtle effects on forecast and safety stock calculations. If independent-demand material is physically issued but not properly accounted for via the issuing process, the usage rate is artificially lowered. This results in a lower forecast than is appropriate for the part. A lower forecast also lowers the statistically calculated safety stock. Both of these situations can reduce the customer service level. Any downward adjustment in inventory for an independent-demand part is likely to have an adverse impact on forecast accuracy if the material was actually required and issued since the effect is to show a lower consumption rate.

- Point-of-use or point-of-fit staging may have a different requirement for inventory accuracy than centralized storage. With supply measured in hours as opposed to days, weeks, or longer, finding errors on the line is too late. Centralized storage provides a time buffer if a problem is encountered. Therefore, when receipts bypass central storage, inventory accuracy must be guaranteed.

- Bar code and RF technologies are widely used to simplify and automate material identification, tracking, and counting. Such tools speed up counting processes and nearly eliminate data entry errors. Speeding up the process enables more time to be devoted to determining and correcting sources of error.

- Traditional inventory system designs are geared more to cyclical counting than to a comprehensive program of problem identification, resolution, and results tracking. If the existing system does not properly support the company's improvement initiatives, a PC-based tool can be developed and interfaced to the inventory database.

Inventory accuracy issues are usually related to the company permitting inaccuracy, people taking shortcuts, or people not having good tools or the time. All of these are management problems. Management is responsible for inventory accuracy.

PROACTIVE TECHNIQUES FOR IMPROVING INVENTORY ACCURACY

Inventory accuracy is a function of how well the causes of inaccuracy are eliminated or controlled. Some causes can be eliminated through process simplification or change. Other functions will always entail an inherent risk of inaccuracy. Therefore, from a proactive perspective, the company must eliminate those causes which can be eliminated, control those causes which cannot be eliminated, and minimize the impact of inventory inaccuracy on promising and scheduling.

Cyclically counting inventory to find and correct errors is a reactive element of the strategy. Proactive initiatives focus on preventing inaccuracy in the first place. These include minimizing quantities, making it easier to confirm the quantity, and simplifying processes and procedures.

Reduce Overall In-Plant Quantities

The lower the average inventory level, the easier it is to maintain inventory accuracy. This is part of the benefit of Just in Time and Short Cycle/Lean/Agile manufacturing. The risk of inaccuracy is greater, however, since the buffer is lower. The closer the inventory level is to zero, the easier it is to count.

However, more frequent receipts increase the opportunities for suppliers to make quantity and packing slip errors and for the company to make receipt processing errors. Using bar codes and electronic data interchange for information processing offset the likelihood of any errors. Dealing with certified suppliers minimizes procedural-related problems.

With certified suppliers, quality control can reduce the frequency of inspections. Fewer inspections reduce the risks of misstating sample, accept, and reject quantities. Less handling and open packages makes it easier to maintain incoming part quality levels during handling and storage.

Smaller quantities reduce the physical space needed to store materials prior to use. This makes it possible to stage the parts at the point-of-use (near the line) or point-of-fit (at the workstation). A single raw material bulk issue to Work in Process eliminates the potential for errors related to many individual issues. Since counting or transaction-related problems related to the issuing process are one of the primary causes of inventory inaccuracy, backflushing computerizes nearly the entire process. On the other hand, misstating the completed quantity in production results in an inventory error against every part used in the product. Therefore, correctly stating completed product quantities and mix and accurately accounting for scrap and rejected materials is crucial for maintaining Work in Process inventory accuracy.

Order in Round or Standard Supplier Packaging Quantities

Odd quantities which vary with every order make it difficult to establish an accuracy pattern. This is a common problem with economic and time-based order quantity techniques. Prepackaged standard quantities are easier to count and verify. This is part of the benefit of Kanban, fixed order quantity, two-bin, and simple numbering (refer to Chapter 12) techniques.

Placing orders for the same quantity all of the time allows opportunities to streamline the replenishment process. Orders which must account for variation in demand can still specify packaging in multiples of standard, easy to verify quantities. This can be accomplished by using a rounding quantity constraint with variable order quantity techniques.

Prepackaged standard quantities make it easier to count and issue materials. Six unopened packages of 100 each with one partial package means that less than 100 pieces must be counted to verify a 600+ total quantity.

Order in Ergonomic Quantities with Regard to Size and Weight

Ergonomic standards for lifting, carrying, pushing, or pulling are not established for purposes of ensuring inventory accuracy. The primary intent is to minimize the risk of injury to personnel, to lessen fatigue, and to establish design standards for workstation, material handling, and material storage equipment. However, containers which meet ergonomic standards for manual lifting or pushing contain less inventory than those which require mechanization such as forklifts for movement. Lower quantities are easier to count. This is part of the benefit of integrating organizational factors such as ergonomics with operational philosophies.

A container to be lifted on an occasional basis may be permitted to be greater than 35 to 45 lb., while one requiring more frequent lifting may be restricted to 40 lb. maximum. Small metal parts can easily weigh in excess of 40 lb. for a relatively small container. A unit load of such parts may weigh more than 2,000 lb. if the $4' \times 4' \times 4'$ cube is fully utilized. Setting ergonomic standards and then combining them with packaging multiples ensures that loads will meet ergonomic requirements and that prepackaged multiples can be distributed to workstations as required. One application, for example, is to receive the small metal parts packaged in units of a 4-hour supply. These packages can be buffered at the workstation in totes, with the number of totes indicating the number of half-shift supplies available.

Utilize Molded Returnable or Nonreturnable Dunnage

Dunnage refers to either the container itself or the protective packaging materials inside the container. Totes, plastic molded pallets or trays, inserts in tubs, wire baskets, and gaylords (4-sided cardboard containers with a top) are examples of dunnage. Disposable dunnage is disposed of prior to or after the parts are used in production. Cardboard, foam, and wooden pallets are common disposable dunnage materials. Materials may be either recycled or trashed. Returnable dunnage is reusable and must be returned to the supplier. The initial cost of returnable dunnage is higher than for disposable dunnage but pays for itself over its useful lifetime. Materials are usually plastic for molded dunnage or metal for unit load containers or racks carrying heavy cast metal or sheet metal parts.

Total cost must also consider the transportation costs required to return the dunnage. There is also a trend toward higher disposition costs for disposable dunnage, making returnable dunnage more attractive in some applications. With trucks making dedicated milk runs, the cost of returning dunnage is minimal since the truck is returning anyway.

Molded or compartmentalized dunnage is often specified by design engineering for part protection. Parts are physically separated to eliminate the risk of one part coming in contact with another. Precision machined gears can create a stress failure point if one part scratches another, for example. Other reasons may be to protect glass or paint from being scratched. With such dunnage, the only way to make a count mistake is to leave a compartment empty or to ship the wrong number of layers.

One of the benefits of molding compartments for protecting parts is that the molding pattern makes it easier to ensure that a specific quantity has been provided. This ensures that a specific quantity is provided per load which meets the ergonomic weight limits established for the part. For example, packaging 10 units per layer with 10 layers per pallet ensures a 100 unit quantity per pallet. At 100 Jobs Per Hour (JPH), eight pallets are required per shift, not accounting for the effect of complexity (different options).

With "generic" dunnage which can be used for a number of different parts (e.g., wire baskets or gaylords), dedication to a part and supplier may not be required. In this case, the correct number of containers based on the rate of usage must be returned to the supplier. Time at the supplier, in-transit, and at the company determines the pipeline quantity. The number of containers in the pipeline limits total inventory.

Logistics problems or build-ahead situations may require use of alternative containers and the related double-handling. Custom molded containers or specialty racks dedicated to a part and supplier must be staged and returned to the supplier on a regular basis. Since these containers can only be used for the part for which they are designed, any slowdown in the logistics pipeline may cause a problem with supply. This can be a special problem if the container is designed for robotic loading at the supplier, and the process cannot be run without the containers. Extra containers need to be available in the pipeline to account for transportation problems, cleaning, and repair.

Returnable dunnage is not restricted to a single part per container or load. Dunnage may be used for kits as well. Kit contents can be restricted to parts for a particular workstation. In this case, unit loads of kits are delivered to the workstation. The operator works from the unit load, or the individual kits are delivered via conveyor or some other means. Kits may also include parts for a number of workstations. These kits are delivered to the first workstation, travel with the product, and the empty is picked up at the last workstation.

Opportunity Count

Opportunity counts are not part of the formal cycle or cyclical counting program. They are simply opportunities to count the material while the operator is at a location doing an issue or receipt. This requires a little extra time for counting and transaction processing, while saving the longer time required to retrieve and store material.

Opportunity counts are not performed every time an issue or receipt occurs. Operators perform opportunity counts only when it involves little or no effort. This means that the inventory balance is low or zero or that the use of prepackaged quantities makes counting easy. Note that the operator must ensure that the cycle count transaction is processed directly after the issue transaction to maintain the proper sequence.

The inventory system design can facilitate opportunity counts when the operator uses an RF terminal to perform issues, receipts, and adjustments. In addition to identifying the issue, receipt, or adjustment quantity, the system also displays the new ending quantity. If the operator elects to confirm that quantity via an opportunity count, the system provides a screen or fields to do so. The operator can either confirm the quantity or enter the actual quantity as an override.

If the count matches the computer balance, the transaction is accepted. If there is a mismatch, the count discrepancy is displayed. The operator then recounts the material and either modifies or confirms the original count. An adjustment beyond the operator's authorization level sends an action message to the planner to identify the cause of the inaccuracy.

Opportunity counts result in relatively "free" cycle counts. They enable the operator to be more of a contributor in the overall inventory accuracy process.

REACTIVE METHODS FOR IMPROVING INVENTORY ACCURACY

Once an inventory inaccuracy has occurred, the company must use reactive methods to locate it and correct the count discrepancy. Reactive methods occur after the fact and are required because the root problem has not been eliminated. Reactive methods are a legitimate part of any improvement process, though they should not be the primary focus. Refer to Figure 6.2. Even with traditional cycle counting methods, the intent has always been to find the root causes of inaccuracy and eliminate them. Companies tend to shortcut the intent of the process by stopping after correcting the count discrepancy.

Count Material upon Receipt

There is no practical way to determine if an inaccuracy has been caused by the supplier or the company once material has been received and personnel have unrestricted access to it. Counting materials upon receipt may be the only way to de-

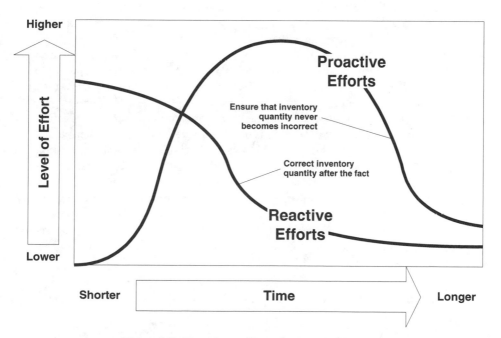

Figure 6.2   Reactive vs. Proactive Level of Effort

termine if the supplier is creating inventory inaccuracies that seem to defy identification once materials are stored.

The supplier can ship less material than the packing slip indicates. There may be an actual shortage in a single container or one or more containers may be missing. Once the shipping manifest is reviewed, the materials are unloaded, and the packing slip quantity is entered in the purchase order receipt transaction, the company is committed to paying for material it did not receive. This also closes the purchase order erroneously.

An overage quantity can be shipped. The packing slip quantity will either match the order quantity or reflect the overshipment. In this case, the purchase order receipt should reject the quantity if it is in excess of the tolerance allowed for the part. In this case, the material will be disposed of or returned. Disposition requires contact with the supplier. If the material is to be returned, the supplier will assign some type of return authorization number. If the part value does not warrant returning it, the supplier will inform the company to keep or scrap the materials.

If there is a future need for the material, the excess quantity can be accepted. The company may elect to wait until after any incoming inspection to determine the actual excess quantity. This permits rejected units to be replaced from the excess quantity.

The wrong part can be shipped. The packing slip part number may or may not match the actual part number shipped. The operator is more likely to miss the problem if the correct quantity of a similar part is shipped. To resolve the problem, the material must be checked against the purchase order, against identification markings on the material, or against drawings or specifications. Many parts, especially in the electronics industry, can only be differentiated by knowledgeable personnel. It may also be necessary to contact the supplier to determine which part was supposed to be shipped and if the incorrect parts are actually for a different purchase order number. If so, that receipt may contain the missing material (a double error).

With an RF system using bar code scanners, a flag can be set within the purchasing system to indicate when the operator should perform a part verification and count of an incoming receipt. This may only be required for suppliers which have a history of problems or for new suppliers. When the material identification bar code on the material is scanned or the packing slip quantity is entered via the keypad, a message on the RF terminal is displayed to count the material. After the operator enters the quantity, the computer matches the counted quantity against the supplier quantity. A match enables the receipt to be accepted, while a mismatch indicates to the operator to initiate corrective action. The flag may remain set until removed by the buyer or be automatically removed after a given number of accurate receipts.

Count Material Once It Is in Inventory

Counting to find and correct stock balances has the benefit of correcting erroneous quantities and improving the accuracy of scheduling and promising decisions. The real benefit, however, is to enable the planner to identify the cause(s) of inaccuracy if the discrepancy is detected before too much time has passed. This is the purpose of a control group which contains parts with a high risk of inaccuracy. Counting these parts frequently offers a higher probability of back-tracking to the source of any errors than for parts in the general inventory population.

Counting material has a geometrically increasing cost as higher accuracy targets are set and achieved as illustrated in Figure 6.3. This is the result when progressively higher accuracy levels are set without eliminating the root problems causing inaccuracies. For example, consider that it takes eight operators one hour each day to cyclically count inventory. This is equivalent to the cost of one operator per year doing nothing but counting material (many parts more than once). This may range as high as $50,000 to $65,000 per year in some companies when total costs are considered. This investment will achieve a certain level of inven-

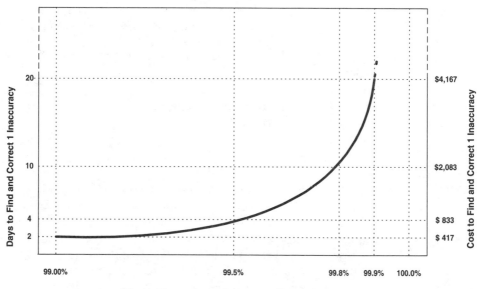

Target Inventory Accuracy Percentage

ACCURACY TARGET	COUNTS TO FIND 1 ERROR	DAYS TO REACH 1 ERROR at 50 COUNTS/DAY	COST TO FIND ERROR at $208.33/day
99.0%	1 in 100 counts (99/100)	2 days (100/50)	2 days = $417
99.5%	1 in 200 counts (199/200)	4 days (200/50)	4 days = $833
99.8%	1 in 500 counts (499/500)	10 days (500/50)	10 days = $2,083
99.9%	1 in 1000 counts (999/1000)	20 days (1000/50)	20 days = $4,167

Figure 6.3   Cycle Count Cost vs. Accuracy Level

tory accuracy. To increase accuracy levels from this point, progressively more counts must be performed. This requires more people and, therefore, higher costs.

The question a company must answer is whether the value associated with higher inventory accuracy is worth the expense of the increased cycle counting effort. If inventory accuracy by count is maintained at a 99 percent level and 50 counts per day are performed, counting finds and corrects one inaccuracy every two days on average. At an equivalent full-time operator cost of $50,000/year and 240 work days/year ($208.33/day), it costs $417 to find and correct each error (2 days/correction × $208.33/day). This does not include the planner's time to resolve the discrepancy or the buyer's time to expedite orders. To maintain a 99.9 percent accuracy level at steady state, the rate of correcting an inaccuracy is one every 20 days. This has a cost per inaccuracy of $4,167 (20 days/correction × $208.33/day). The effect of increasing accuracy targets on cost and days between "hits" (i.e., finding and correcting an inaccuracy) is shown by the graph in Figure 6.3.

Note that the $4,167 cost in the preceding example should not really occur. As inventory accuracy increases due to eliminating causes of inaccuracy, fewer counts per day are required to sustain accuracy levels. The cost per inaccuracy should actually fall below even the $417 level. However, if the company is performing cyclical counting without addressing the real causes of inaccuracy, the inventory accuracy level will plateau, as will the cost per finding and correcting each inaccuracy.

CYCLE COUNTING METHODOLOGY

Cyclical counting methods have developed along several different paths through the years. The two basic versions are cycle *Ac*counting (cyclical counting) and cycle counting. Cycle *Ac*counting involves counting inventory for the sole purpose of matching the computer count to actual count. In this respect, it is most similar to scheduling a physical inventory throughout the year through a process of cyclical counting. As a comparison, cycle counting additionally incorporates control group and related logic to enable causes of inaccuracy to be identified, tracked back to the source, and eliminated.

Cycle *Ac*counting (Cyclical Counting)

Counting inventory on a cyclical basis to ensure dollar accuracy primarily for cost accounting purposes can be referred to as cycle *Ac*counting. This methodology focuses on confirming the asset value of inventory. In this respect, there are many similarities to more traditional physical inventories. These similarities are compared in Table 6.3. What physical inventories accomplish in a week (and which the cost accounting department reconciles for months) is spread throughout the year with cyclical counting methods.

Maintaining an accurate asset value is accomplished by counting parts on a

Table 6.3 Comparison of Cycle *Ac*counting to Physical Inventory

INVENTORY CATEGORY	PERCENT OF TOTAL PARTS	JAN FEB	MAR APR	MAY JUN	JUL AUG	SEP OCT	NOV DEC	$ ACCURACY	PERCENT OF TOTAL VALUE
CYCLE *AC*COUNTING (spread throughout the year)									
A	5%	Count monthly to ensure that spot checks by Accounting will not detect "significant" $ inaccuracies						100%	80%
B	15%	Count quarterly to ensure that spot checks by Accounting will not detect "significant" $ inaccuracies						98%	15%
C	80%	Count annually to satisfy Accounting's need for an annual physical inventory count						95%	5%
		MON	TUE	WED	THURS	FRI			
(1 week) PHYSICAL INVENTORY									

```
08:00am 07/01/YY                                      ABC—Pareto Analysis

PART      ANNUAL    PART      ANNUAL        CUMULATIVE   CUMULATIVE   ABC    ABC
NUMBER    USAGE     COST      VALUE         VALUE        PARTS               OVERRIDE

A123456   10,000   $  5.00   $ 50,000.00   $50,000          1         A      A
B123456      400   $ 40.00   $ 16,000.00   $66,000          2         A      A
C123456    1,000   $ 15.00   $ 15,000.00   $81,000          3         A      A
  .
  .
D123456        1  $ 834.00   $    834.00   $ 100,834       80         A      A
AA12345      600   $  1.20   $    720.00   $ 101,554       81         B      A
 CALC. ABC  |   SUMMARY   |   ABC LIST   |   MODIFY   |   DETAILS   |
```

Figure 6.4 ABC Calculation Screen

frequency related to their individual and total inventory investment value. More expensive parts and parts having a significant investment due to their volume are counted more frequently than less expensive parts and parts with a lower volume. Inventory value is annualized to provide a consistent means of comparing parts where inventory balances vary over time. This is illustrated in Figure 6.4.

ABC categories are precise mathematical calculations which do not always reflect business conditions. This may be the case for a new part, one being superseded, or parts at the boundary between A- and B-items and B- and C-items. Planners override the system-generated ABC field by changing the ABC override field to a different value. Where the override field is nonblank, the inventory system uses the override field. Otherwise, the calculated value is used. In any event, both fields should have their own ABC date. The ABC override field should also allow a reason for the override to be entered.

The cyclical count frequency is typically determined based on three factors:

1. The inventory manager establishes a count frequency for each part based on inventory value (e.g., as associated with the ABC code). This frequency is typically weekly or monthly for A-items, monthly or quarterly for B-items, and semiannually or annually for C-items. This is illustrated in Figure 6.5.

2. The number of counts and the time per count determines the hours per day required for cycle counting. The count frequencies must be reduced if this is greater than the hours and personnel which can be committed. These reductions are more likely to be made for the B- and C-items, since a reduction in cycle frequency encompasses more parts. Another reason is that companies are reluctant to reduce cycles for A-items due to their value. Counting these items frequently plays a significant role in ensuring that a high inventory (dollar) accuracy performance level is maintained. The general method for determining the effect of count frequency vs. personnel is shown in Figure 6.6.

3. Any time an A-item error is identified, the part is typically counted more frequently for a period of time to ensure that the cause of the error does not recur. One technique is for the planner to manually request cycle counts on a daily or weekly basis. Another is to set a review cycle in the cycle counting selection logic based on the last cycle count date without an error. This permits the system to automatically schedule the counts and notify the planner via action messages of the result.

   For example, an A-item on a monthly count cycle may be counted weekly until four weeks have passed since the cycle count which required an adjustment. The part master would maintain two cycle count dates. The first is the date of last cycle count, and the second is the date of last cycle count with an error. This same logic might have a B-item counted monthly instead of quarterly and have no effect on a C-item.

Cycle *Ac*counting is easy to understand, easy to implement, forgiving on those days when it is just too inconvenient to perform counting, and easy to manipulate. Counting expensive items frequently will almost ensure at least an 80 percent inventory accuracy level by dollar. Offsetting dollar overages with shortages is

08:00am 07/01/YY			ACC—Inventory Accuracy Policies		
ABC CODE	INVENTORY $ PERCENT	WEEKS BETWEEN COUNTS	PERMITTED +/- $ DEVIATION	PERMITTED +/-COUNT DEVIATION	DATE ESTABLISHED
A	5%	4	$ 0	0%	MM/DD/YY
B	15%	12	$ 5	2%	MM/DD/YY
C	80%	50	$ 10	5%	MM/DD/YY
CALC. ABC	SUMMARY	POLICIES	MODIFY		

Figure 6.5   Cyclical Counting Policies Screen

| 08:00am 07/01/YY			CYC—Cyclical Counting Summary					
TOTAL INVENTORY $:	$10,000,000		TOTAL PARTS:		10,000		WEEKS/YR: 50	
TOTAL STOCK $:	$ 2,000,000		TOTAL STOCK PARTS:		8,000			
ABC CODE	INVENTORY $ PERCENT	DOLLAR BREAK POINT	NUMBER OF PARTS	TARGET DOLLAR VALUE	ACTUAL DOLLAR VALUE	COUNT FREQUENCY IN WEEKS	REQUIRED COUNTS PER YEAR	COUNTS PER WEEK
A	5%	$ 8,460	80	$ 100,000	$ 100,834	4	1,000	20
B	15%	$ 145	535	$ 300,000	$ 301,421	12	2,229	45
C	80%	$ 0	7,385	$ 1,600,000	$ 1,597,745	50	7,385	148
TOTAL	100%		8,000	$ 2,000,000	$ 2,000,000		10,614	213

Counts/Day:	43	Based on 213 Count/Week / 5 Days/Week
Average Minutes/Count:	5	Minutes/Count x 43 Counts/Day = 4.0 Hours/Day
Hours/Day for Counting:	1.00	7:30–8:30 am = 1-hour Counting Window
Required Personnel:	4	4 hours/day / 1-hour Counting Window

ABC LIST	SUMMARY	POLICIES	MODIFY		

Note: Nonstock parts are typically excluded from cycle counting, as they are purchased for a specific customer or master schedule-planned order.

Figure 6.6   Cyclical Counting Summary Screen

another way to achieve higher accuracy levels. Assigning accuracy tolerances further improves the company's ability to mask actual inaccuracies when calculating inventory accuracy performance. In fact, it is fairly easy to achieve dollar accuracy performance levels greater than 95 to 98 percent given all of the ways it can be manipulated.

In spite of all of the perceived benefits, there is a fallacy which eliminates this methodology from practical consideration in an integral environment. Dollar accuracy does not ensure the same level of count accuracy. Even a 100 percent dollar accuracy *does not* automatically mean a 100 percent count accuracy. As a consequence, production and customers do not have the same level of confidence regarding accurate promise and availability dates as accounting has regarding asset value.

Cycle Counting

Cycle counting is a methodology for identifying and eliminating causes of inventory inaccuracy. As such, it encompasses techniques for problem identification and corrective action and for accurately counting inventory. A successful cycle counting program will theoretically eliminate the need for itself over time. The reason it never seems to is that companies are constantly adding new product lines, parts and suppliers, and changing systems and personnel.

If problems are truly being eliminated over time, the company will be able to lengthen the counting cycle by reducing the counting frequency. Ideally, the cycle will lengthen until such time as no cycle count is required. Once all parts reach the point where no cycle counting is required, the company may find themselves back where they started in the 1970s–1980s. Accounting may still require a periodic sample count to verify accuracy levels for financial record-keeping purposes. The very success of a cycle counting program may reinstitute just the condition which the program was designed to eliminate—the annual physical inventory.

As shown in Figure 6.7, cycle counting is not a static process. There is little value in establishing generic cycles based on a projection of annual dollar usage unless dollar value is one of the key causes of inaccuracy. Rather, increased exposure to known causes of inaccuracy is the best way to catch and correct causes of inaccuracy. Logically this will vary by part and usage profile. Counting items more frequently which have a higher exposure to causes of inaccuracy then increases the chance of being able to track the causes of inaccuracy. Such causes get easier to track the shorter the time between cause and detection and the fewer other actions have occurred to cloud the occurrence.

With respect to a cycle counting program, a company must establish a three-pronged attack. The first addresses the need for an inaccuracy tracking system. This requires an understanding of how to identify causes of inaccuracy and track their effect through the use of control groups and transaction history files. The second addresses count frequency. Frequency is first established by part categories for simplicity purposes and is then progressively fine-tuned for individual parts. The third and most difficult area addresses the external (supplier) and internal (company) integration actions required to permanently resolve causes of inaccuracy. This can take far more time and personnel resources than the cycle counting process itself but has more far-reaching consequences than simply correcting count inaccuracies over and over again.

Cycle counting performance measures in an integral environment are a given.

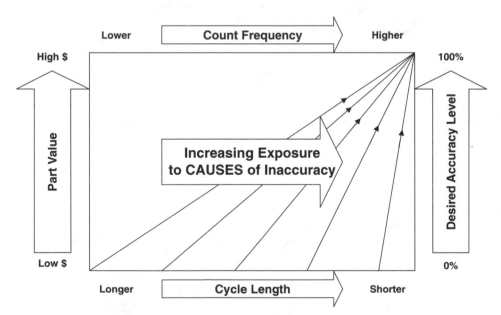

Figure 6.7 Cycle Count Frequency as a Function
of Exposure to Causes of Inaccuracy

The target is zero deviation from 100 percent count accuracy for all parts all of the time.

Inaccuracy Tracking System

An inaccuracy tracking system can become very complex if it is allowed to get out of hand. There are numerous causes of inaccuracy, oftentimes with a very random occurrence rate. A tracking system has three primary uses. The first is to provide a cross-reference among parts in order to identify similarities for purposes of establishing part categories. These categories can be used for establishing count frequency. The second is to provide a cross-reference among parts in order to see if a given cause of inaccuracy is also affecting other similar parts. The third is to provide a cross-reference among parts to see if a corrective action has been effective with other similar parts.

A representative screen for assessing and then tracking causes of inaccuracy is shown in Figure 6.8. The inventory system establishes the initial accuracy profile based on data normally generated for a part through receiving and issuing processes. The inaccuracy category is then assigned when the operator or planner enters the cycle count transaction into the inventory system, where one of the transaction fields is the category.

In the screen, the operator is provided with a trend column in English stating the current status. It is not left to the individual to have to figure out via numerical comparisons whether performance is improving or not. "On Target" indicates that for the Year-to-Date (YTD) there have been no assignable causes of inaccuracy for the particular category. For example, there have been no problems related to misidentifying the part on the packing slip. A positive trend indicates that there have been errors within the past year but that there are fewer errors this month than the average per month. A negative trend indicates that there have been more errors this month than the average month.

Note that a negative trend is an indication that performance may be getting worse. However, the trend may simply be the result of more opportunities for inaccuracy in a particular category this month than in an average month. The Accuracy Percent and YTD columns provide the totals. When dealing with company personnel, it is much more informative to deal with numbers than percentages. Knowing that the number of errors dropped from six (from history records) last month to two this month and that this is a continuing positive trend conveys more information than stating that causes of inventory accuracy have been reduced by some small percent.

Note also that the 94.7 percent figure is *not* the inventory accuracy percent for the part. This percentage applies strictly to all of the error categories selected for the part. Otherwise, the part could be set up as if a large number of error categories applied. When these categories did not have any errors assigned to them, their totals would sway the final results. Therefore, of all possible categories within which an error can occur for all parts, only those which actually apply to the particular part are selected for monitoring. This is done via a table in the data-

```
0:800am 07/01/YY              ITP--Inaccuracy Tracking Profile
Part Number: A123456789 Description: RD-12 Display Module Inv. U/M: Each
```

	OCCURRENCES			YTD OPPORTUNITIES	
	YTD	MTD	TREND	FOR ERROR	W/OUT ERROR
TOTAL FOR PART:	26	2	POSITIVE	492	466 = 94.7%
Supplier-related Errors:					
- Shipped Quantity Not = Packing Slip Quantity	1	0	POSITIVE	12	11 = 91.7%
- Shipped Parts Misidentified on Packing Slip	0	0	ON TARGET	12	12 = 100.0%
Receiving-related Errors:					
- PO Receipt Data-entry Error	0	0	ON TARGET	12	12 = 100.0%
Quality Control (QC) Errors:					
- Incorrect Sample Quantity Issue Error	0	0	ON TARGET	12	12 = 100.0%
- Sample Quantity Data-entry Error	1	0	ON TARGET	12	11 = 91.7%
- Incorrect Accept Quantity Error	1	1	NEGATIVE	12	11 = 91.7%
- Incorrect Reject Quantity Error	0	0	ON TARGET	12	12 = 100.0%
Inventory-related Errors:					
- Unknown	6	0	ON TARGET	6	0 = 0.0%
- Data-entry Error	3	0	ON TARGET	138	135 = 97.8%
- Issue Quantity Error	11	1	NEGATIVE	120	109 = 90.8%
- Receipt Quantity Error	2	0	ON TARGET	12	10 = 83.3%
- Credit (Returned Material) Quantity Error	0	0	ON TARGET	0	0 = 0.0%
- Transfer Quantity Error	0	0	ON TARGET	0	0 = 0.0%
- Lost/Pilfered Material	0	0	ON TARGET	0	0 = 0.0%
- Misidentified Material	1	0	ON TARGET	132	1 = 99.2%
- Misplaced Material	0	0	ON TARGET	0	0 = 0.0%
- Incorrect Unit of Measure	0	0	ON TARGET	0	0 = 0.0%

```
NEXT PAGE    |  GRAPH  HISTORY |  CATEGORY  |  TARGET  |  PREV PAGE
```

Note: Each supplier receipt transaction is subject to two supplier-related errors, one receiving-related error, four QC-related errors, and so on. No attempt was made to associate the mix of possible opportunities for error to the actual number of transactions processed for the part, though this information is available in the History File and could be displayed at the top of the screen for reference purposes.

Figure 6.8   Inaccuracy Tracking Profile

base by either selecting or deselecting a category. Over time, as few categories for a part should be selected as possible to enable the planner to focus on only those identified as a target for improvement.

As an alternative, the system could automatically display only those categories which have had errors assigned within the last year. This simplifies the category selection process for the planner, but tends to vary the categories on the screen from part to part. Another alternative is to provide a button so the planner can select to view *all* categories while another button enables display of only those categories which have had an error assigned.

Count Frequency

As a general statement, parts must be counted frequently enough that conditions which result in an inventory inaccuracy can be tracked and identified. The longer the count cycle and the greater the number of issue, receipt, transfer, and adjustment transactions (i.e., exposures to inaccuracy), the more difficult it becomes to assign a particular cause. This is illustrated in Figure 6.9. Even worse, there may be multiple causes of inaccuracy over time which further complicates the identification and resolution process.

Companies have thousands of parts requiring tens or hundreds of thousands of individual transactions. Each part has its own opportunities for inaccuracy. In such environments, it is unreasonable to believe that all parts can be counted as frequently as necessary to catch and track all individual causes of inaccuracy. Counting is a nonvalue-adding process and of low priority in a production environment. Therefore, what companies must do is rely on cyclically counting parts in the general inventory to correct inaccuracies after they have occurred (a reactive process), while counting parts in one or more focused control groups to identify general causes of inaccuracy (a proactive process). Control groups consist of parts which have a similar exposure to the types of errors the planner is attempting to isolate.

The cyclical counting methodologies previously discussed can be used to correct part inaccuracies. Inventory value is often inappropriate for determining count cycles, but this decision may not be totally under the inventory manager's

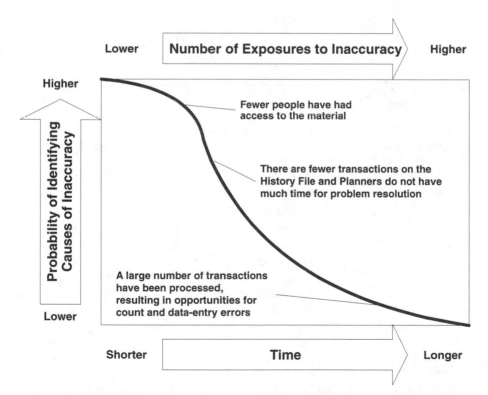

Figure 6.9   Probability of Identifying Causes of Inaccuracy Over Time

control. Accounting still needs some assurance that asset value is being correctly stated. A better cycle basis is to establish categories based on number of transactions (which entail both counting and data-entry risk) or risk of inaccuracy (i.e., inventory balances just sufficient to cover requirements). Establishing part categories is then based on similarity of reaction to inaccuracy drivers. This will vary by company and operating environment, including supplier relationships.

The first category always consists of those parts which do not need to be counted. The intent is for every part to end up in this category. This encompasses master schedule planned, final assembly planned, and other order-for-order (non-stock) parts which should theoretically never be inaccurate. These are the types of parts which are not considered stocked items. Therefore, they are not subject to many of the causes of inaccuracy or accounting requirements for cycle counting which apply to stock parts. Also included are parts which have demonstrated that they can be maintained at target accuracy levels and parts which do not need counting such as those in surplus, inactive, or obsolete categories where there are no transactions occurring.

Other categories are set up based on likely causes of inaccuracy. The planner will already know what some of the historical causes have been, including:

- Scale counting (resulting in scale tolerance errors)

- Many small issues (resulting in counting or data-entry errors)

- Many issues of inconsistent quantities (resulting in counting or data-entry errors)

- Incoming inspection (resulting in inaccurately accounting for sample quantity losses)

- Customer returns (resulting in quantity discrepancies or incorrect part identification)

- Supplier packing slip discrepancies (resulting in receipt quantity discrepancies)

In inventory systems which allow the ABC code to be set to a variety of values (greater than three), each category can be assigned a different value. This way, there may already be logic in the system for establishing counting cycles and for reporting results. Otherwise, some other field may need to be added or modified for use.

Once the parts are assigned to a category, a control group is selected for monitoring purposes. A control group is a subset of parts within the category, with no preference among parts. The group should be small enough that all of the parts can be counted on a frequent basis, no less than once per week and possibly daily. The inventory system should have a control group flag or allow an override ABC code of "Z" to differentiate control group parts from other parts. Problems found and fixed with these items should translate into improvements throughout the rest of the category. When the part is no longer part of the control group, the part returns to its default category.

Note that in companies where there are multiple storerooms having dedicated personnel, it makes sense to assign operators to count in other than their own storeroom. Individuals have difficulty at times in finding their own mistakes, especially mistakes bred from familiarity.

Corrective Actions

Once a problem has been identified, the proper resolution is usually fairly apparent. Resolution alternatives have been covered previously in the section on proactive actions for improving inventory accuracy. Of course, causes of inaccuracy can only be addressed when the real problem has been identified, and not one of its symptoms.

For example, receipts from a particular supplier may be consistently off by plus or minus 10 percent for the low value parts. This is determined by counting the received material and comparing to the packing slip. On the surface, the problem is that the supplier either cannot count material or cannot fill out a packing slip accurately. In fact, the supplier's contract with the company may permit the delivered quantity to vary by plus or minus some percent for these items. In such cases, the packing slip quantity will match the purchase order quantity in order to close out the order for each shipment. The company must either process a purchase order receipt for the packing slip quantity or have the capability to assign an invoice tolerance for invoice matching. Otherwise, orders will not close when the receipt quantity is less than the order quantity. This is a common situation for hardware or scale-counted parts and for parts or materials produced specifically to the company's specifications where some risk of over or underproduction exists.

As actions are identified, the company must establish relative priorities and plans. The priority should account for the level of improvement to be gained, as well as the ability of the company to effect the required changes. The plans should be realistic given the hours and personnel available to address the problems.

SUMMARY

With traditional financial inventory accuracy measures, companies make absolutely sure that the expensive items are accurate. This means frequent counting. This results in an approximate 80 percent dollar accuracy contribution. Getting the remaining 20 percent is then achieved by considering B- and C-items as accurate when they are only slightly inaccurate. If this is not quite enough, overages and shortages are netted to fine-tune the accuracy. Companies then give themselves credit for a high inventory accuracy level. The problem with financial inventory accuracy is that there is no assurance of count accuracy, which is what an integral strategy requires.

If inventory by count is not accurate, it is inaccurate. Cycle counting with control groups is a reactive method for correcting inaccuracies after the fact. Most companies stop short of actually using control groups and end up cyclically counting parts over and over again without ever resolving causes of inaccuracy. However, every count which simply confirms that the part is accurate is a wasted count knowing that there are still parts which are inaccurate.

Companies need to address higher inventory accuracy levels through infrastructural improvements. Standard containers enable materials to be packaged in standard, easy to count, and verifiable quantities. Bar coding reduces data-entry errors. RF terminals provide instant feedback to the counters regarding discrepancies. Processes must be streamlined and corrective actions taken on every occurrence of inaccuracy. The key is to prevent the very possibility of an error.

Chapter 7

Reorder Triggers

Planners have a choice of either time-based, quantity-based, or demand-based reorder triggers. Time-based reviews are typically planned to occur on a weekly or monthly cycle. All parts flagged for a time-based review are reviewed without regard to stock balance or demand profile. Quantity-based reviews are triggered by events which cause the projected net inventory balance to either dip into safety stock or reach zero before a new order can be received. Only parts which meet this condition are flagged for review in the next order review run. Parts may use both types of triggers. Between weekly and monthly reviews, for example, parts may be subject to quantity-based review logic. This identifies parts requiring immediate order action without waiting for the periodic review. Other parts using a lot-for-lot order quantity are never reviewed per se, only ordered as each individual demand is identified.

The review process itself is straightforward. Once a review is triggered, the system calculates whether an order needs to be released. The criteria is whether a stock-out will occur or safety stock will be dipped into if an order is not released during the current review period. If so, an order is suggested for planner action or released automatically. Other actions involve canceling orders, expediting or de-expediting orders, changing a requirement to specify an alternate part, and so on. Specifically how all of this is done or initiated depends on the methodologies or techniques chosen for the part, as well as the design of the MS, MRP, inventory, and related subsystems.

Note that automatic order release is the target in an integral environment. Automatic release without planner or buyer review occurs only when all order review edits are successfully passed. This means that those parts are operating within target control limits with respect to lead times and that all necessary information is available.

This chapter covers the following aspects of determining when to release a purchase or production/work order based on dependent- and independent-demand parts relationships:

- Order triggers vary based on part type (stock vs. nonstock vs. MRO). Time to receive material, once ordered, is a key criterion. This includes order review and release time, supplier lead and shipment time, and receiving and storage time. The reorder point technique encompasses the principles upon which the other techniques are based and is most applicable to independent-demand parts. This makes it less suitable in an integral environment than the time-phased reorder point which accommodates both dependent- and independent-demand.

- MRP is the primary planning tool used in an integral environment since it accommodates all order triggers and review techniques. Another advantage is that it is tightly integrated with the other order planning and scheduling subsystems and able to be responsive as a result.

- If production processes are streamlined sufficiently, order triggering and replenishment at the shop floor level can rely on visual techniques including two-bin and Kanban.

The ability of the planner to release orders on time for the right quantity requires a series of choices. Each choice either supports or hurts production's ability to meet the customer service targets. Any reordering strategy can be successful if the planner has the luxury of time and valid information for all parts all of the time. The reality is that this will not occur. The planner must be well-trained in evaluating and responding to the requirements of the business. The system must provide the necessary decision support information required to assess issues of order quantity, required dates, lead times, and demand variability.

REORDER METHODOLOGIES

The order review process is initiated automatically by the system. For those parts set up for automatic release and which meet established ordering criteria, actual ordering occurs automatically. Parts which are not on automatic release or which do not meet the ordering criteria require planner review and action. The entire review process is a methodology as opposed to a technique since action may vary based on knowledge the planner possesses with regard to the part, supplier, and business conditions. In general, however, the actual order review uses computerized techniques which provide a consistent starting point. Order action is usually consistent among planners if the replenishment lead time and available stock balance is sufficient to obtain materials without expediting. Order review methodologies are compared in Table 7.1.

Time-based reviews are controlled by logic within the system. One technique is to run a program which sets the review flag against every independent-demand (inventory-planned) part regardless of whether any action has occurred against it or not. Running Material Requirements Planning then causes every independent-demand part to be reviewed for order action.

Quantity-based reviews rely on reaching a specific stock balance in order to

Table 7.1 Representative Order Review Methodology Comparisons

METHODOLOGY AND PRIMARY TECHNIQUE	TIME-BASED TRIGGER (Planner Review)	QUANTITY-BASED TRIGGER (Issue)	DEMAND-BASED TRIGGER (Requirement)	KEY CHARACTERISTIC
Reorder Point—ROP	Weekly or Monthly	Stock Balance ≤ ROP Quantity	Not Applicable	Independent-Fixed Rate of Demand
Kanban	Not Applicable	Kanban Quantity Consumed	Not Applicable	Variation of ROP, Where ROP is equal to (Total Kanbans − 1)
Time-Phased Order Point—TPOP	Weekly or Monthly	Stock Balance ≤ TPOP Quantity	Not Applicable	Independent-Fixed and Dependent-Variable Rate of Demand
Two-Bin	Not Applicable	1st Bin Quantity Issued	Not Applicable	Manual "ROP" Method Independent of Type of Demand
Material Requirements Planning—MRP	Weekly (Regenerative)	Nightly (Net Change)	New Requirement	Independent-Fixed and Dependent-Variable Rate of Demand
Master Schedule Planned—MS	Weekly	Available/On Order Balance < Demand	New Requirement	All Products
Final Assembly Planned—FAS	Weekly	Available/On Order Balance < Demand	New Requirement	Individual Orders

trigger the review. The general theory is that this provides sufficient time to re-order before the available balance reaches the safety stock level or zero for parts with no safety stock. The review flag is set when an issue, addition of a new requirement, or other action results in the inventory balance reaching the point where an order must be considered for release within the current review period. The part is then reviewed on-line or in the nightly run via MRP, and one or more orders are suggested for planner review or released automatically.

Demand-based reviews are initiated by new requirements. The review flag is set whenever an order or bill of material explosion generates new requirements. The review flag is also set due to changes which affect the inventory plus on-order balance vs. demand rate ratio. Such changes include canceling an order, expediting or de-expediting an order, inventory adjustments, returned materials, and part supersedures.

Setting the review flag may be bypassed entirely if a lot-for-lot dependent-demand order is generated automatically as part of the MS, FAS, or MRP explosion process. This is a function of the system design. Generating the order directly is the more integrated approach, since there is no planning required. Note that an alternative to the review flag is simply to review every part every day, with dynamic plan update during the day.

REORDER TRIGGER ISSUES

Order review triggers are a function of the types of planning categories within the company. These categories are a function of the types of parts stocked for manufacturing, service, and operating support, the types of parts procured or manufactured on-demand, and the computer system logic used. Representative part categories identified by differences in the type of planner control applied include the following:

- *Inventory-planned* parts include independent-demand parts planned using inventory manager or planner specified logic. These consist of regular inventory parts, service parts, and MRO parts (Maintenance, Repair, and Operating supplies). The inventory system plans these parts in companies where the MRP subsystem does not have the imbedded logic to handle parts whose demand is not triggered by the MS. Such reviews are triggered by logic imbedded into the inventory transaction processing programs or via an order review program run periodically. The independent-demand is then fed to MRP in a similar manner as dependent-demand is fed by the MS/FAS.

- *MRP-planned* parts include dependent- and independent-demand parts planned within the MRP system. This is the preferred arrangement within an integral environment since all parts are reviewed and processed in a consistent manner as far as the planners and buyers are concerned.

- *Master schedule or final assembly planned* parts include lot-for-lot (non-stock) parts which do not require planning per se, since individual orders are created to match individual demands. Note, however, that even lot-for-lot parts should be checked to see if there is an available balance before an order is placed. There may be times when canceled orders, order quantity multiples, customer or production returns, or other actions result in having available stock which can be applied to the next order. This type of check is an MRP function.

Issues affecting order reviews are primarily time related. If the review occurs too early, average inventory levels may exceed the target. This is not a given though, since the actual date of projected stock-out or date when the safety stock will be dipped into can still be set as the required date. If the review occurs too late, a shortage may occur or additional costs may be incurred to expedite needed materials. Variability of demand in terms of both quantity and timing is the primary factor affecting the effectiveness of the trigger timing. This variability is what computer systems tend to ignore in their processing but which planners must consciously assess in their review. This is where a decision support capability which evaluates the effect of demand variability on the reorder decision is so valuable.

The order review triggers used by a company are dependent on the computer system and type of part. Most companies use either MRP triggers or some combination of MRP and inventory reorder triggers. In general, when a condition occurs which may indicate the need to place an order, the review flag is set for the part. Once set, the review flag is reset by performing the actual order review. With ordering performed via an inventory system, flagged parts are reviewed in the next ordering run. This is typically nightly but may be weekly with an older system. The sequence of review is not important with independent-demand parts, as compared with low level sequence for dependent-demand parts.

Note that MRP, MS, and FAS systems may not use flags per se. They review parts for ordering at each step in the explosion processes. Modern MRP systems may review every part for order action every day, with dynamic updates based on operational changes. This differs from MS and FAS systems which review only those parts within the bills of material being processed. Single-level MS systems have no need for flags, since every part which is MS-planned will be reviewed in each MS run. FAS-planned parts identified via an explosion for a particular customer order will typically consist of lot-for-lot parts at the higher levels and some combination of MRP and inventory-planned parts at lower levels as shown in Figure 7.1. Demand is time-phased via either MRP or Inventory logic. MS and FAS systems use primarily time-based reviews since the review occurs whenever the explosion program is scheduled to run.

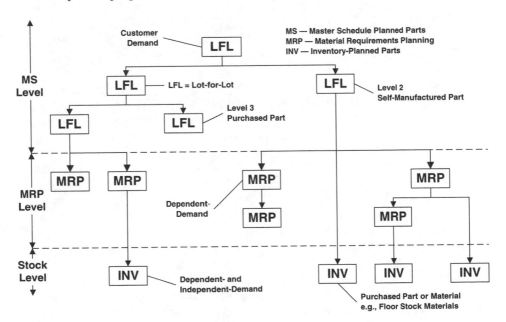

Figure 7.1   Master Production Schedule Explosion

Once a part is reviewed and one or more order actions are suggested, the issue is one of accepting or modifying the computer-generated recommendation. Accepting the recommended action is the simplest since it has the least effect on past or pending decisions. Computer recommendations are internally consistent, though they may not be practical. It may not be possible to expedite a particular order, for example. However, the computer will keep on recommending this action until the higher level demand is delayed or reduced in a case where the stock balance is insufficient to meet a particular demand.

Changing a recommended action and incorporating the effect with respect to other parts may not be handled on-line by some systems. In MRP, for example, a decision to decrease an assembly order quantity and change its due date may affect the quantity and timing of lower and upper level demands. Once the change is made, the planner should be able to see the effect of this change on the lower level parts immediately. This requires an on-line MRP recalculation capability.

Ideally, the planner should be able to analyze the effect before committing to the change. What commonly happens with older systems is that once the computer has performed the initial explosion in a nightly batch process, the effect of any changes must be assessed in the next nightly run. Therefore, changes at one level which affect another may not be incorporated into the overall plan for one or more days. This delay can result in actions taken on one day having to be modified on subsequent days if the planner's actions for parts at one level were not consistent with decisions for parts at others.

Example: Consider a product consisting of a printed circuit board at Low Level Code = 3 and components at Low Level Code = 4. The planner has an order action from the nightly batch review to order 25 printed circuit boards and 25 sets of components. The components are used on a variety of other printed circuit boards as well, so the suggested order quantities range from 25 to 500. The planner decides to increase the printed circuit board order quantity from 25 to 40 and does so. He and the other planners then order the other components in the quantities as originally suggested by the system (i.e., the quantities of the components were not adjusted to accommodate the increase in boards from 25 to 40). The next day, the system suggests some combination of ordering an additional 15 sets of components or rescheduling open orders. This could have been handled the previous day if the increase from 25 to 40 caused a dynamic recalculation of requirements. The effect is that the suppliers will receive two orders for the same parts due the same day, receive change orders to adjust quantities, or receive expedite requests to change order shipment dates.

The more a planner changes the computer-generated materials plan, the more work they create for themselves and others. The more they need to change the plan to reflect business conditions, *the more the system is not supporting the business.* The number and type of changes generated within the order review process is an indication of the level of control in the reordering process. The inventory manager should monitor these statistics to identify areas requiring improvement.

The forecast is typically calculated at the end of each week or month with independent-demand items. Any parts using the Reorder Point (ROP) technique are also automatically reviewed at the end of each week or month since updating the forecast causes the review flag to be set or independent-demand to be added to MRP, either of which creates a review condition. Modifying the forecast or adding a demand to represent a sales promotion or anomaly condition also sets the review condition. With the Time-Phased Order Point (TPOP) technique which includes dependent-demand, each new demand will also cause a review. Other activities which trigger reviews include:

Lead time changes trigger a review. Reducing a part's lead time delays the suggestion of new orders and may cause some orders to be de-expedited. Lengthening the lead time may initiate immediate order suggestions to cover the longer lead time horizon if there is an insufficient stock balance.

Changing safety stock level triggers a review. A increase in safety stock may initiate order expediting since the demand rate will cause safety stock to be dipped into sooner. A lower safety stock may cause orders to be de-expedited since the demand rate will dip into safety stock later than anticipated.

A stock balance change which causes a transition to occur from one side of the review point to the other triggers a review. Returning material to stores is an unplanned action which increases the available balance. This may initiate order de-expediting, depending on the quantity returned. Reducing the stock balance through a scrap issue or downward cycle count adjustment reduces the available balance. This can cause ordering or order expediting.

Note that order action for a phase-out part requires planner oversight. Order reviews which base demand on a forecast of continuing usage are inappropriate once the specific phase-out date is within the part's lead time. At the Reorder Point, the order review logic uses the phase-out date to initiate a special "manual review required" message to the planner. No order is suggested. It is up to the planner to determine whether an order is required or not, based on his or her knowledge of the part and reason for the phase-out. The computer's role becomes one of monitoring stock status. Messages are generated to the planner when action may be required.

REORDER POINT (ROP) TECHNIQUE

The Reorder Point technique is based on the principle that ordering must occur at the point where there is just time to receive material by the time the available stock balance reaches the safety stock level. Theoretically, safety stock will never be dipped into. On average, it can be expected to be dipped into half the time. However, these statements assume that forecasting and safety stocks are under statistical control and that the part conforms to a normal distribution. Planners must understand that using nonstatistical techniques clouds the issue of when safety stock will be dipped into when using ROP and TPOP techniques. The ROP technique is used for inexpensive independent-demand items where sufficient safety stock can be maintained to minimize the risk of a stock-out. Demand is typically based on either a statistical or fixed forecast. The Reorder Point equation is as follows:

$$\begin{array}{c} \text{Reorder} \\ \text{Point} \\ \text{(ROP)} \end{array} = \begin{array}{c} \text{Forecasted} \\ \text{Daily} \\ \text{Usage} \end{array} \times \begin{array}{c} \text{Lead} \\ \text{Time} \\ \text{Days} \end{array} + \begin{array}{c} \text{Safety} \\ \text{Stock} \end{array}$$

Demand over lead time may be calculated based on daily, weekly, monthly, or other demand profiles, depending on the computer system. The demand may also use a steady rate into the future or incorporate an increasing or decreasing trend.

In the preceding equation, the Forecasted Daily Usage is used to extend the forecast over the lead time. This is a better technique for a part required by manufacturing than using a forecasted monthly usage rate since the number of work days per month is not consistent. This is especially significant in months where there may be a planned one- or two-week shutdown as may be experienced for July and December in many companies. For service parts, however, the demand may not be a function of the number of company work days. The inventory system should provide a flag which indicates whether the demand over lead time is to be based on work or calendar days for purposes of calculating the Reorder Point. If the usage history consists of both service and manufacturing part demand for a part, a composite demand profile can be calculated if it is worth the effort.

When an inventory issue is processed which causes the sum of on-hand plus on-order balance minus safety stock to be less than or equal to the Reorder Point, the review flag is set against the part. If an order is required, the suggested order is added to the planner's order review screen or the order is placed automatically if all order review edits are passed. The three order review conditions (usage rate equal to, less than, or greater than the forecast) encountered by the planner are illustrated in Figure 7.2.

Demand may match the forecast. In this case, an order is suggested after the issue which causes the Reorder Point to be reached or passed. Theoretically, the degree to which the Reorder Point is passed is immaterial. Large issues are assumed to be offset by small ones, resulting in an average rate equal to the forecast. From a practical perspective, the timing of large vs. small issues may cause safety stock to be dipped into or consumed. However, a generally average usage rate equal to the forecast results in an inventory level generally equal to target.

Example: Consider a fuse with the following service part demand:

    3 Forecasted Daily Usage (FDU)
   40 Lead Time Days (LT Days)
   12 Safety Stock (SS)

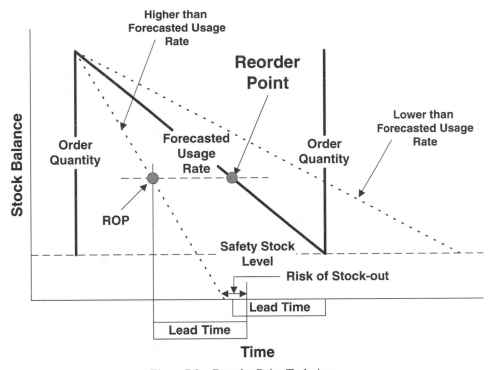

Figure 7.2 Reorder Point Technique

The ROP is calculated as the usage rate over the lead time plus safety stock. This provides sufficient time to reorder additional fuses once the Reorder Point is reached. The average usage rate over the lead time assumes that the inventory level will equal the safety stock quantity at the time when the next order is received. The 12-unit safety stock protects against an actual rate in excess of the average:

$$\text{ROP (132)} = [\text{FDU (3)} \times \text{LT Days (40)}] \times \text{SS (12)}$$

Demand may exceed the forecast. In this case, an order will be suggested after the issue which causes the Reorder Point to be passed. Safety stock will be dipped into before the next order is received if the higher usage rate continues since the Reorder Point was set based on a lower usage rate than is being experienced. If the rate is higher than can be protected by safety stock, the part will stock-out. This also results in an average inventory level less than the target. The planner needs to determine whether the actual usage rate will continue to be higher than forecast or whether it will average out to the forecast over time. This is a judgement call based on a knowledge of the part and its demand profile.

If the judgement is that the higher usage rate will continue or that the safety stock level is insufficient to protect the part from stock-out, the planner needs to expedite open orders and/or release the suggested order with a shorter than normal lead time required date. The need to expedite is determined by calculating whether the part will stock-out as indicated by the "risk of stock-out" time frame in Figure 7.2.

The inventory system can calculate a running average usage rate from the date of receipt of the last order. If this running average usage rate exceeds the forecasted rate upon which the Reorder Point is based, the part can be flagged for planner review. At this point, a new Reorder Point (ROP_1) can be calculated based on the higher rate. The system can monitor both reorder points and suggest an order review when the earlier point is reached. This provides the planner with forward visibility of a possible problem.

Example: Consider a fuse with the following service part demand:

    3   Forecasted Daily Usage (FDU)
    3.4   Current Daily Usage since receipt of last order (CDU)
    40   Lead Time Days (LT Days)
    12   Safety Stock (SS)

The revised reorder point is calculated as:

$$ROP_1 \ (148) = [CDU \ (3.4) \times LT \ Days \ (40)] \times SS \ (12)$$

Any rate in excess of that which can be covered by safety stock will cause a stock-out. This rate is calculated as:

$$Stock\text{-}Out \ Rate \ (3.3) = ROP \ (132)/LT \ Days \ (40)$$

The part can be expected to stock-out if the current usage rate of 3.4 fuses per day continues since safety stock will only protect against a 3.3 fuses per day rate.

Demand may be less than forecasted. An order will be suggested after the issue which causes the Reorder Point to be passed. Since the Reorder Point was set based on a higher usage rate than is being experienced, the next order will be received before the safety stock level is reached. This results in an inventory level in excess of the target. The planner should consider delaying the receipt in this case. The system should indicate that this is the current projection so the planner can consider a later required date for the order.

TIME-PHASED ORDER POINT (TPOP) TECHNIQUE

The Time-Phased Order Point technique is based on the principle that ordering will occur in time to receive material when the available stock balance reaches the safety stock level. It accounts for both dependent and forecasted (independent) demand over the lead time. The ability to handle dependent-demand differentiates it from the ROP technique. Including known demand enables the planner to account for sales promotions, seasonal conditions, or other customer orders in addition to the forecast.

TPOP logic is also useful when calculating distribution inventory requirements. Consider the case where a central Distribution Center (DC) receives orders from regional warehouses as well as directly from customers. Orders to manufacturing consist of dependent-demand in the form of regional warehouse orders and independent-demand in the form of customer orders. Material Requirements Planning and distribution requirements planning systems use this logic extensively, both with and without the addition of forecasted demand. The Time-Phased Order Point equation is as follows:

$$\begin{array}{c}\text{Time-} \\ \text{Phased} \\ \text{Order} \\ \text{Point}\end{array} = \begin{array}{c}\text{Independent-} + \\ \text{Dependent-Demand} \\ \text{During Lead time}\end{array} + \begin{array}{c}\text{Safety} \\ \text{Stock}\end{array}$$

Note that the same arguments for using a forecasted daily demand in combination with individual requirements as opposed to using a forecast monthly usage rate apply for TPOP as for ROP. The inventory system sets the review flag when an issue or other transaction (e.g., a downward adjustment caused by a cycle count) causes the total available quantity in stock and on order to be less than or equal to the Time-Phased Order Point quantity. The same conditions illustrated in Figure 7.2 for the Reorder Point technique also occur for TPOP.

Example: Consider a part which has both dependent- and independent-demand. The demand profile is shown following. A replenishment order is required to be released in the current period in order to prevent dipping into safety stock in Period 5.

LEAD TIME	AVAILABLE INVENTORY	SAFETY STOCK	OQ TECHNIQUE	UNIT OF MEASURE
5 Weeks	100	40	200 FIxed Quantity	PCS

		PERIOD (WEEK)					
		1	2	3	4	5	6
DEPENDENT-DEMAND		40	35	20	60	45	40
INDEPENDENT-DEMAND		20	20	20	20	20	20
GROSS REQUIREMENTS		60	55	40	80	65	60
SCHEDULED RECEIPTS		200					
PROJECTED AVAILABLE	60	200	145	105	25	160	100
NET REQUIREMENTS						40	
PLANNED ORDER RECEIPTS						200	
PLANNED ORDER RELEASES	200	----------	---------	----------	----------	--------^	

The top row of data regarding lead time, available inventory, safety stock, order quantity technique, and inventory unit of measure come from the inventory master data. The weekly demand and ordering time-phased profile comes from the requirements and open order files. The Dependent-Demand comes from requirements determined as a result of higher level bill of material explosions performed by MRP. The constant Independent-Demand forecast of 20 pcs comes from a forecast calculated from historical usage. The Scheduled Receipt row indicates that a released order is scheduled for receipt in Period 1.

The Projected Available inventory and the three following lines are calculated by the system based on the ordering technique selected by the planner. The same format is used for both purchased and self-manufactured parts and assemblies. Note that at some period in the future, the system may change the display from weekly to monthly buckets for screens and reports. The "period" should be a value which can be set by the planner for the display. An alternative is a "bucketless" display which shows individual requirements without grouping by period. An integral system should be capable of both types of display. Note also that the lines available in the display and the terminology will vary somewhat among systems. The preceding format was selected to reinforce the process of calculating a material plan from a combination of dependent- and independent-demand, available inventory, and open orders.

The logic followed by the system to review the part is as follows:

1. *Current Period:* There are 60 pcs available (100 Available − 40 Safety Stock). The system is suggesting that an order for 200 pcs be released for receipt in Period 5 based on the fixed order quantity. This matches the normal lead time of 5 weeks and will, therefore, require no expediting or special order action by the planner or buyer.

2. *Period 1:* The 40 pcs dependent-demand and 20 pcs independent-demand sums to 60 pcs of gross demand. "Gross demand" refers to the total demand for the period before accounting for any available or on-order inventory. There is an open purchase order for 200 pcs scheduled to be received in Period 1 (next week). This 200 pcs plus the 60 pcs of available inventory minus the 60 pcs of gross demand leaves 200 pcs available for Period 2.

3. *Period 2:* The 35 pcs dependent-demand and 20 pcs independent-demand sums to 55 pcs of gross demand. This can be satisfied from the 200 pcs of available inventory, leaving 145 pcs available for Period 3.

4. *Period 3:* The 20 pcs dependent-demand and 20 pcs independent-demand sums to 40 pcs of gross demand. This can be satisfied from the 145 pcs of available inventory, leaving 105 pcs available for Period 4.

5. *Period 4:* The 60 pcs dependent-demand and 20 pcs independent-demand sums to 80 pcs of gross demand. This can be satisfied from the 105 pcs of available inventory, leaving 25 pcs available for Period 5.

6. *Period 5:* The 45 pcs dependent-demand and 20 pcs independent-demand sums to 65 pcs of gross demand. This *cannot* be satisfied

from the 25 pcs of available inventory, leaving 40 pcs to be provided from a new order. Note that this net demand (i.e., remaining demand after accounting for all other sources of inventory, excluding safety stock) can be covered by the safety stock if the safety stock is still available by Period 5. This may not be a reasonable assumption. Therefore, an order is required to be received in Period 5. Since there are no open orders scheduled for receipt in Period 5 and none in later periods which can be expedited, a new order is required. The system backs off 5 weeks from Period 5 to determine the period (actually, a specific date) in which the order must be released. This is the current period. Assuming the order is received as scheduled, 160 pcs will be available for demand in Period 6.

7. *Period 6:* The 40 pcs dependent-demand and 20 pcs independent-demand sums to 60 pcs of gross demand. This can be satisfied from the 160 pcs of inventory *projected to be available,* leaving 100 pcs available for Period 7.

The system will continue to extend the demand and ordering profile to the end of the planning horizon. This should be longer than the longest cumulative product lead time. Actual demand will taper off over time and any forecast will continue to be projected at a constant, increasing or decreasing rate, as applicable.

TWO-BIN TECHNIQUE

Two-bin control is essentially a manual version of the Reorder Point technique. In application, the first bin represents the quantity which can be consumed without requiring any order action. The second bin represents the quantity which is sufficient to cover demand over the replenishment lead time plus safety stock. The point at which the second bin quantity must be used is the point at which a replenishment order is placed. In practice, the second bin quantity is usually generous enough to ensure a 100 percent customer service level. The concept is illustrated in Figure 7.3.

When the next order is received, the materials are separated into first and second bin quantities and kept segregated. This may be as simple as using separate bags or boxes in the same storage location. Some type of card or other indicator is typically used as a signal to the planner to reorder at the point where some or all of the second bin material is required to satisfy the next issue. This technique is used for stationary supplies, floor stock hardware, or other items purchased in bulk and issued or consumed on a random basis.

In theory, the inventory level prior to order receipt should be approximately equal to the safety stock level. In actual practice, this is the type of material which is often issued in bulk. Therefore, there may be no inventory in stock when the next order is received. There should, however, still be inventory in manufacturing if the demand rate and safety stock levels were correct. The intent when setting

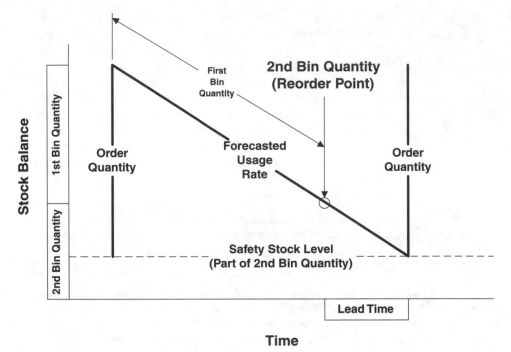

Figure 7.3   Two-Bin Reorder Point

the first and second bin quantities is not necessarily to prevent a stock-out as far as inventory management is concerned but to prevent a stock-out in manufacturing.

MATERIAL REQUIREMENTS PLANNING (MRP) TECHNIQUE

Material Requirements Planning is a computer subsystem for calculating a complete demand vs. ordering profile through the planning horizon. MRP can be used for every part within the company or at least for those designated as MRP-planned, depending on the capabilities of the software. The basic issue is whether the subsystem handles independent-demand parts (which is the assumption here). *Planner* in this usage refers to the MRP planner, not the inventory planner, though both positions may be integrated within the same individual(s).

MRP's primary advantage over a simple Reorder Point technique is its ability to customize ordering strategies for parts with variable demand profiles. This ability enables the planner to fine-tune the material plan based on differing product and part needs. The basic logic used is essentially the same as that used for the Time-Phased Order Point technique. The difference is that the software provides much more in the way of capabilities to review the source and magnitude of gross and net requirements and released, firm-planned and planned orders over time.

With ROP, each part is planned independently of the others. The effect of changing an order quantity or requested ship date on one part does not have to be evaluated with respect to any other part or parts. With MRP, changes to the material requirements plan for a part may affect the plans for parts at lower levels in the bill of material structure, as well as higher level work orders and customer promise dates. Therefore, part reviews must occur in a top-down fashion based on bill of material low level code and reconciled in a bottom-up fashion.

Low Level Code indicates the lowest level in the bill of material structure where the part appears for all products. For example, end-items are assigned a low level code of 0, items at the first bill of material level are assigned a 1, and so on. This is done automatically within the bill of material system. Because a part may appear at level 5 for one product and level 2 for another (refer to part 9 in Figure 7.4), Material Requirements Planning does not consider a part for further explosion until all possible higher level requirements are identified. In the case of the part which appears at both levels 2 and 5, the materials plan considers the part for ordering only after all level 0 through 4 parts have been reviewed. Otherwise, the plan for the part at level 2 (Product B in the figure) might have to be revised when the product with the part at level 5 is reviewed later in the same MRP run (Product A in the figure).

Note that MRP is an aggregation process. Requirements are normally combined in order to suggest fewer consolidated orders. If a particular part has an ordering technique of lot-for-lot, each individual demand will create an order regardless of the level. Possible exceptions to this include having to accommodate some type of order quantity constraint or the possibility of available inventory left over from some previous order.

If MRP has a weakness, it is in its aggregation of higher level requirements

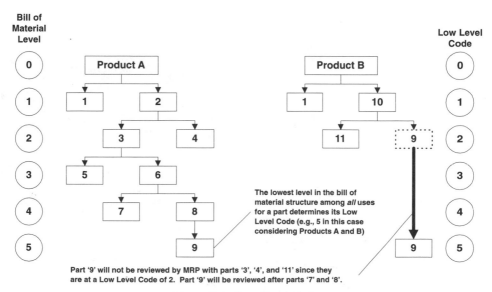

Part '9' will not be reviewed by MRP with parts '3', '4', and '11' since they are at a Low Level Code of 2. Part '9' will be reviewed after parts '7' and '8'.

Figure 7.4   Low Level Code

into lower level demand. While this is also its strength, the ability to aggregate higher level requirements tends to hide the actual source of the demand. This becomes a problem when there is a shortage of parts to satisfy demand. Where there is a shortage, the planner needs the ability to retrace demand back to the original requirements. This is referred to as having a "full pegging" capability. This enables safety stock and forecast demands at higher levels to be identified separately from actual customer requirements in order to revise the materials plan to something which can be supported by available inventory.

Example: Part XYZ has a total stock balance of 150 pcs. It is a child of part DEF which in turn is a child of part ABC. Assuming that parts ABC and DEF have no available inventory, the net demand for all three parts is shown in Figure 7.5. The 100 pc customer demand for ABC becomes the customer demand for DEF and XYZ (assuming that component quantities are one each). The forecast demand varies by part, possibly indicating service part demand. Safety stock is set individually by part. The net demand at each level is, therefore, a combination of types of demand from successively higher levels as well as unique to its own level.

Action messages from the MRP subsystem will indicate that open orders must be expedited for part XYZ and/or new orders placed to offset the shortage of 130 pcs (280 − 150). However, there will be times when existing open orders cannot be expedited. In these instances, the planner must have a knowledge of the higher level parts which created the demand in order to determine if certain demands can be delayed without affecting customer service.

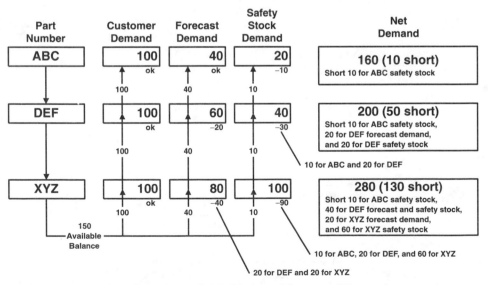

Figure 7.5   Example of a Variety of Sources of Demand

In this example, 150 units worth of higher level requirements can be satisfied. Therefore, the balance (200 – 150 = 50 of DEF and 160 – 150 = 10 of ABC) must be rescheduled at the ABC and DEF part levels to match the date when the next order of XYZ will be received. Otherwise, the MRP system will keep generating expedite action messages for part XYZ which the planner has already determined cannot be satisfied. The MRP subsystem should have a flag which the planner or buyer can set against a lower level order which cannot be expedited, in order to force the order action messages to reschedule (delay) the higher level order(s).

The result in this example is to satisfy 100 pcs of customer demand for parts DEF and ABC and 50 pcs of forecast demand for part DEF. This in turn satisfies an additional 40 pcs of forecast demand for part ABC and 10 pcs of safety stock demand for part ABC.

When considering parts for some type of order action, the planner has a series of decisions to make. These vary somewhat by the type of system used but generally relate to the review sequence, acceptance of the plan as-is, or revisions to the plan.

Review Sequence—MRP subsystems often list parts in numerical sequence for order review. This masks the low level code and also separates parts from their related products. This does not really matter if the planner makes no changes to the computer-generated plan. Sequence of review may be very important, however, when changes to the plan are required. This commonly occurs in situations when stock cannot be obtained per the schedule. A review by low level code may be more valuable to the planner in a shortage situation since changes at higher levels in the materials plan according to the bill of material structures can be more easily evaluated against parts at the lower levels. The higher the code (0 being the finished goods level), the greater the number of parts which are likely to be affected by deviations from the plan. If the planner considers making a change to a part, the system should identify which lower level parts will be affected through an on-line explosion. Reviewing by low level code ensures that the planner has not already taken action on parts which may be changed by later decisions.

Acceptance of Computer-Generated Plan—The system needs to provide some idea of the magnitude of change required to achieve the plan in order to enable the planner to assess its practicality. Some system designs make rescheduling someone else's problem. This means the buyer for purchased items or a production planner for manufactured items. There are many instances, however, when an order cannot be received on time, even with expediting. The dead giveaways are the parts which must be ordered and received on the same date. The problem becomes progressively more manageable as the provided lead time approaches the quoted lead time.

If the plan can be achieved, the planner will accept it as is. This requires some insight, however, based on experience. Plans based on lead times which are too short or on order expediting which cannot be achieved will simply result in getting the same action messages every time MRP is run (typically nightly). Other company personnel will continue to believe that the schedule is achievable until the planner reschedules the higher level production/work orders. The longer the planner waits when rescheduling is required, the greater the difficulty in resolving other problems. Waiting can sometimes reflect an organizational problem where the planner notifies the buyer that expediting is required and the buyer notifies the planner that the order cannot be expedited. Continuing to throw problems to someone else solves nothing. Sooner or later in the case where a particular lower level order cannot be expedited, the planner needs to reschedule orders at higher levels—preferably sooner.

The system can support the planner by providing the ability to review parts in multiple ways, as is indicated by the buttons on the bottom of the screen in Figure 7.6. If parts are independent of each other, the sequence is immaterial. However, the real function of planning should be to ensure that orders can be produced, not that parts can be individually planned. The system should, therefore, provide information which is consistent with the explosion path that the MRP, MS, FAS, or inventory subsystems used to generate the plan in the first place. In this way, the planner(s) and buyer(s) can coordinate their actions to ensure that production schedules and supplier commitments match the plan with no deviation from target.

The Order Action screen identifies the individual orders suggested by the system but not released automatically. Providing sort capabilities by low level code, buyer, required date, customer order number, manufacturing department, supplier, or priority based on some definition of criticality enables the planner to establish a course of action. Once the planner is ready to take action, the Details button provides access to additional information and the required ordering screens (refer to Chapter 9 for order quantity techniques).

Sorting by Order Number, with line skips, enables the scope of action by each customer or production/work order to be quickly viewed. Those orders having parts with a lead time problem will be readily apparent. The magnitude of the problem is indicated as shown for the second part in Figure 7.6. The plan is cur-

08:00am 07/01/YY			MSG—Order Action					Planner: J.B.
ORDER NUMBER	PART NUMBER	ORDER SUFFIX	PART NAME	ORDER ACTION	REQD QTY	REQD DATE	LD TIME PROBLEM	DEPT
Low Level Code 06--								
A284B114D03 16	1234567890	12	Bracket	New Order	150	08/21/YY	NO	Panel Assy
A284B114D03 16	23234A1329	02	Volt Meter	Expedite	200	08/21/YY	5 of 12 Wks	Panel Assy*
Low Level Code 07 ---								
B437D804D45 10	23234A1329	03	Resistor	De-expedite	200	08/12/YY	NO	PCB Assy
LOW LVL SORT	BUYER SORT	REQD DT SORT		ORDER SORT		DEPT SORT		DETAILS*

Figure 7.6 Message Action Screen—Order Action

rently based on receiving the second part in seven weeks, even though it has a 12-week lead time. This is a 5-week problem.

Before taking action on the first part knowing that there is a chance that the order may need to be rescheduled, the second part lead time problem must be resolved. Unless the system provides this insight via a decision support process, the planner may not realize the problem. The system needs to drive the review sequence in a case like this, not simply follow a part number sequence. This is especially important when some planners may be taking action on other parts without knowing that another planner has what may be an insurmountable problem on a part which affects their plan. The * at the end of the line indicates that there is additional information available. This information is accessed via the Details button, as shown in Figure 7.7.

The information contained in the order details and provided by the buyer indicates that 124 of the 200 units on the order can be obtained immediately. However, the remaining 76 for the order will not be available until 09/14/YY. The planner needs to review the MRP plan and determine if the order can be split. It may also be possible that by splitting the order, the remaining 76 units can be left at the normal lead time, depending on the demand profile. If the order is split, it may affect the timing of the first part as well in Figure 7.7 since it is for the same order number. There may also be other parts affected which are either under review or currently on order.

Plan revisions include revising due dates, increasing or reducing order quantities, canceling orders, deleting requirements, or substituting one part for another. If such changes are made without respect to their impact on other parts, the next MRP run may undo or change the affected parts. Processing parts in low level

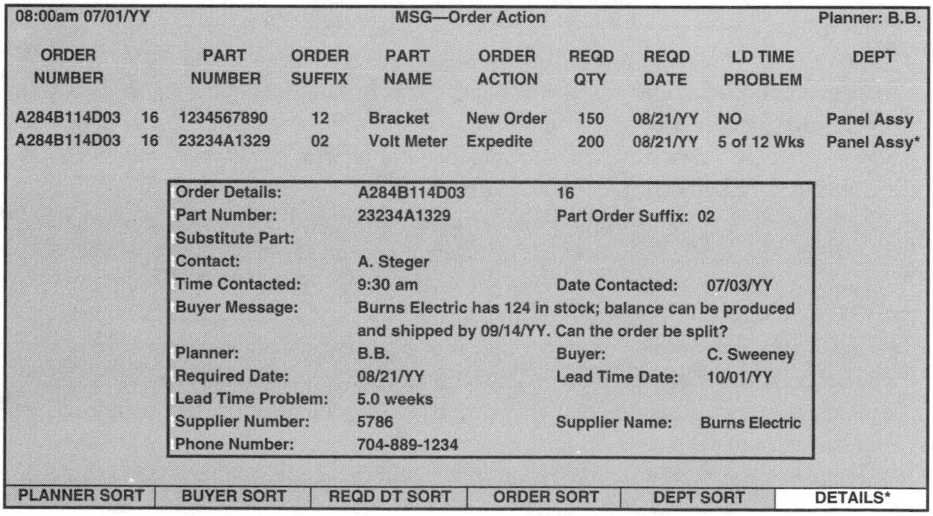

08:00am 07/01/YY			MSG—Order Action					Planner: B.B.
ORDER NUMBER	PART NUMBER	ORDER SUFFIX	PART NAME	ORDER ACTION	REQD QTY	REQD DATE	LD TIME PROBLEM	DEPT
A284B114D03 16	1234567890	12	Bracket	New Order	150	08/21/YY	NO	Panel Assy
A284B114D03 16	23234A1329	02	Volt Meter	Expedite	200	08/21/YY	5 of 12 Wks	Panel Assy*

Order Details:	A284B114D03	16
Part Number:	23234A1329	Part Order Suffix: 02
Substitute Part:		
Contact:	A. Steger	
Time Contacted:	9:30 am	Date Contacted: 07/03/YY
Buyer Message:	Burns Electric has 124 in stock; balance can be produced and shipped by 09/14/YY. Can the order be split?	
Planner:	B.B.	Buyer: C. Sweeney
Required Date:	08/21/YY	Lead Time Date: 10/01/YY
Lead Time Problem:	5.0 weeks	
Supplier Number:	5786	Supplier Name: Burns Electric
Phone Number:	704-889-1234	

PLANNER SORT	BUYER SORT	REQD DT SORT	ORDER SORT	DEPT SORT	DETAILS*

Figure 7.7   Message Action Screen—Order Action Details

code sequence and reexploding on-line changes keeps the lower levels in sync as the changes are made.

KANBAN TECHNIQUE

Kanban techniques provide a demand-pull level of control at the operator level in environments where the material flow is at least somewhat repetitive. A Kanban can be an electronic signal from a bar code or RF terminal or a physical signal such as a card, colored ball, empty container, or empty cart. It indicates that replenishment materials are required. The most common application is on the factory floor between producing and consuming stations. When the consuming station has taken the Kanban quantity, a signal to the producing station provides authorization to replenish the exact Kanban quantity.

In cases where there is complexity (multiple options), the consuming station may additionally have to identify the particular complexity required. The next Kanban quantity may not be a direct replenishment of the complexity consumed. This is typical of a production process where a changeover from one model to another occurs based on producing a batch quantity.

The Kanban quantity is essentially a fixed order quantity. The producing station is authorized to produce only in multiples of the Kanban quantity and only when replenishment signals have been received.

Some consuming stations will return a Kanban every time a Kanban quantity has been used. This return may be to an intermediate production market (Chapter 12) or directly to the producing station. Others will return Kanbans as a group. This is often a function of the type of Kanban. For example, with an electronic signal, an operator may use a RF (radio frequency) terminal or bar code to signal that a container has just been opened on the production line. This signal is routed via the computer to an operator in the receiving or production market to replenish the container during the next material delivery route. In this case, there are multiple reorder points equivalent to every container at the station. This same process is also used when one station directly feeds the next on an assembly line. In this case, however, visual signals replace computer signals since operators are within sight and direct communication with each other.

Other stations may not signal for a replenishment until two or more Kanban quantities have been consumed. This is more common for materials replenished via a route which is run less frequently than the rate at which the Kanban quantity is consumed. For example, running a route every two hours may involve replenishing four Kanbans at a time, where each Kanban is a one-half hour supply. The producing station may still replenish on an individual Kanban basis if there is an intervening production market. Otherwise, they will produce in multiples of four as well, since that is the transfer quantity.

With computerized dispatching, stations signal for a replenishment using some type of electronic means every time a container is opened at the line. The computer initiates an immediate replenishment or buffers the requests until a number equal to the transfer quantity is reached. For example, an AGV train may be capable of towing four dollies of racks, one rack per dolly, to the production line. In this case, the delivery route transfer quantity is always in a multiple of four racks. The computer buffers the individual requests for replenishment until four have been accumulated. At that time, a replenishment message is transmitted to the forklift operator in the receiving or production market via RF terminal. It authorizes the operator to load four racks of specific parts onto a train for delivery to the line. In this case, the quantity staged at the line is equal to the four racks plus an additional number based on the time it takes to load and move the next train.

Figure 7.8 illustrates a system where empty containers act as the replenishment signal. Routes are designed to pick up and deliver four containers at a time from a production market and deliver them to the consuming station. The producing station fills containers one at a time and moves them to the production market. With an emergency float of two containers (equivalent to the safety stock level in a traditional Reorder Point equation), the consuming station ROP =

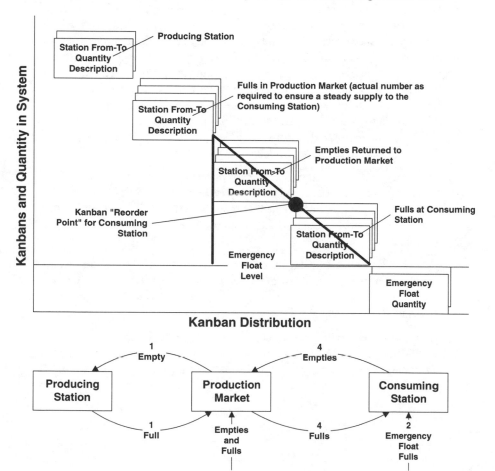

Figure 7.8   Kanban Reorder Point

4 + 2 = 6 containers. The next four containers will be received at or before the point of dipping into the emergency float. The actual number of containers/Kanbans in the system will then vary based on specific company factors related to hours supply and replenishment lead times.

SUMMARY

Regardless of the environment, determining when to place an order is a key planner activity. In many companies, this activity is largely computerized via straightforward methodologies and techniques. Much of the planner's actual time commitment is not spent in the review process itself, but in the need to address anomaly conditions when orders must be received in less than quoted lead time.

One of the problems companies face is that they overrely on the computer to solve problems which the planner should address. Simply implementing an integral strategy will not eliminate the lead time problems companies face. However, an integral strategy which focuses on supplier lead time reduction and delivery consistency, repetitive scheduling and demand-pull controls, manufacturing volume and mix flexibility, and integrated computer system decision support tools improves the chances for success. MRP is the planner's primary ordering tool. A computerized decision support capability which addresses order quantity and lead time issues is the planner's primary tool for dealing with anomaly conditions. Automatic order release is the target, since it is an indicator of the degree of control the company has over their ordering process.

The key issues related to ordering include the following:

- Determining when to review a part for ordering. This differs based on part cost, inventory category, and control methods. The lead time must be sufficient to perform the order review, release the order to the supplier, produce or procure the part, ship it to the company, and process the receipt and any incoming inspection.

- Determining how to deal with orders which are due in less than quoted lead time. Keep in mind that part of the lead time in the inventory system is internal to the company and can be ignored in situations where a part is being expedited.

Inventory systems will generally support all or some combination of Reorder Point (ROP), Time-Phased Order Point (TPOP), two-bin, and Material Requirements Planning (MRP). Kanban may or may not be supported but should be with any newer systems.

Chapter 8

Forecasting

Forecasting is a necessity for any parts, assemblies, or products where customers require delivery in less than the replenishment lead time. This is usually true of independent-demand parts and is often true of a company's finished goods (and related dependent-demand parts) and service parts. Once the forecast is established, it is used to establish order triggers, order quantities, and safety stock quantities. Other uses of the forecast are to determine excess, surplus, and inactive stock levels. If there is more inventory on-hand than is required over the "long-term," this balance becomes first excess, then surplus, and then inactive at the point when there is no more demand.

One of the biggest mistakes planners make with forecasting is in not reviewing the accuracy of the selected technique(s) over time. The tendency is often to continue using a particular method without questioning its continuing validity. This is a choice to delegate planning responsibilities to a computer which cannot respond very effectively to company-specific conditions over time. Safety stock is then relied on to cover deviations of actual usage in excess of forecast. The key is not so much to ensure that the forecast is accurate as to ensure that it is not too inaccurate. Planners cannot delegate their forecasting responsibilities to a computer. Computers perform forecasting calculations via techniques; planners perform forecasting via methodologies.

This chapter covers the following aspects of forecasting as it relates to improving customer service levels:

- Forecasting at part levels of detail is not required when customers are willing to wait for companies to procure and manufacture products. This case is more true of project and job shop manufacturers and less true of batch, line/repetitive, and continuous process manufacturers. The need for forecasting and the required accuracy level are, therefore, functions of the manufacturing environment.

- Forecasting accuracy improves for parts if the correct methodologies and techniques are used. It improves still further as the forecasting horizon shortens and as demand variability reduces. Techniques fall into statistical and nonstatistical categories.

- Safety stock and either excess inventory levels or stock-outs are the prices companies pay for the inability to accurately forecast demand. As the integral strategy enables the company to shorten dock-to-dock cycle times and achieve responsiveness targets in terms of product availability and delivery reliability, accurate forecasting becomes more critical to achieving target inventory levels.

Forecasting is not an easy or straightforward subject. Even though computers do all of the calculations, the inventory manager and planners need to understand the logic. All parts are not subject to the same demand profile, so changes must be made to accommodate unique requirements. Understanding the logic used by the calculations enables such changes to be made with an understanding of the effect on the actual forecast. What may be more complicated, however, is understanding the effect of the internal and external environment on product and part service levels. This is where the integral strategy needs to evaluate the interrelationships which affect forecast accuracy.

Equations and computers can do only so much. Companies which must forecast need to make a conscious effort to review their forecasts on a regular basis. Having a What-If capability simplifies this process tremendously. There is no possible way an individual can perform the variety and number of iterations related to forecast evaluation that a forecasting decision support system can do.

KEY FORECASTING PRINCIPLES PLANNERS MUST UNDERSTAND

Planners need to be well trained and educated in forecasting concepts, principles, methodologies, and techniques before attempting to fine-tune a company's forecasts. These are the same as used by the master planner for MS-level forecasting. While there are opportunities to apply nonstatistical forecasting methods for a particular sales promotion or other onetime activity, forecasts are primarily based on statistics. Planners need to understand at least the following forecasting principles as they relate to statistical techniques.

Statistical forecasts are an extension of the past into the future. If you visualize a forecast as being a "best-fit" line based on a scattering of actual demand points over time such as used for linear regression analysis in mathematics, that is *not* how a forecast is generated. The reason that historical usage points are not used directly is that forecasts are typically "smoothed" by weighting the effect of recent periods more heavily than earlier periods. This typically results in some type of curve over time rather than a straight line. Simple linear regression weights every period equally, no matter how old. However, the concept of fitting a forecast line to a scattering of actual usage points is a valid concept for understanding how a statistical forecast is determined as long as weighting is taken into consideration. Refer to Figure 8.1.

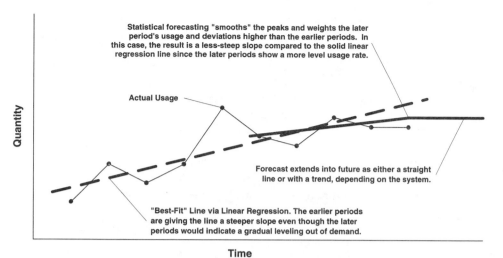

Statistical forecasting "smooths" the peaks and weights the later period's usage and deviations higher than the earlier periods. In this case, the result is a less-steep slope compared to the solid linear regression line since the later periods show a more level usage rate.

Actual Usage

Forecast extends into future as either a straight line or with a trend, depending on the system.

"Best-Fit" Line via Linear Regression. The earlier periods are giving the line a steeper slope even though the later periods would indicate a gradual leveling out of demand.

Quantity

Time

Figure 8.1   Weighted Forecast with Exponential Smoothing vs. Linear Regression Line

Weighting with exponential smoothing enables the deviation of actual usage from forecast in recent periods to determine more of the forecast than older periods. Exponential smoothing refers to successively greater weights being applied to recent periods, as opposed to weights evenly distributed to each period. The higher the Alpha (weighting) Factor, the fewer the number of historical periods required to determine the forecast.

Forecasts are based on a "period," commonly one month. Usage from previous months is weighted and summed to determine the new forecasted monthly usage. However, all monthly periods are not the same length. Consider the month of June as a full month compared to July which may include a one- or two-week shutdown. It is not reasonable to assume that June usage will apply to July without being factored. The historical and forecasted periods must be consistent in terms of production or service days, with days being the lowest common denominator.

Given the fact that forecasts will never be completely accurate, planners have a need to know when they become too inaccurate. A tracking signal can be used to monitor the deviation trend of actual usage from forecast. When the deviation exceeds a certain level, the system can flag the part for planner review. The problem with tracking signals is that the level where a forecast goes from accurate to inaccurate is totally subjective. Any part with a tracking signal above the cutoff is considered inaccurate while any value below the cutoff is considered accurate, or at least accurate enough. Planners need to understand how their system calculates the tracking signal.

When a tracking signal is used, systems should permit the planner to apply a dollar value to the deviation to differentiate expensive parts from inexpensive ones. It may be a better business decision to carry the required level of safety stock to accommodate a less-than-target level of forecast accuracy for those parts where the planner's time is better spent elsewhere. Also, some parts will never be able to be forecasted with any great degree of precision. Tracking signals should not be considered as the sole indicator that the forecast needs to be reviewed and changed. The customer service level provided by the part, including the safety stock, should also be considered. The tracking signal should also be capable of being calculated differently for different parts. The intent is not to force-fit all parts into the same mold but to be capable of responding to each part's uniqueness.

Depending on the system, forecasts may or may not incorporate a trending factor for future periods. Not incorporating a trend has the effect of extending the forecast into the future at a steady rate. This is essentially what the EOQ equation does when annual demand in the numerator is calculated as $12 \times$ forecast monthly usage. Where future periods are included in an order quantity calculation, the trend may be a significant factor.

FORECASTING TECHNIQUES

The inventory manager or planner selects which forecasting technique to use for individual parts, materials, assemblies, and products. This may be somewhat predetermined by part classification (MS, MRP, or inventory-planned; make-to-stock, assemble-to-order, or make-to-order) or other attribute such as part cost (expensive vs. inexpensive), usage type (steady or sporadic), physical size, or shelf life. Forecasting techniques covered in this chapter generally fall into either statistical or nonstatistical categories:

- Statistical Techniques using Exponential Smoothing
    - —Single-Smoothed Forecast
    - —Double-Smoothed Forecast
    - —Periodic (> 1 Month < 12 Months) Weighted Average Forecast

- Nonstatistical Methodologies
    - —Fixed Quantity Forecast
    - —MS and MRP (combination of actual and forecasted demand)

The planner indicates a part's or assembly's forecasting technique by setting the forecast code on the part master to one of the valid alternatives. Some techniques then require additional fields to be set, such as forecast quantity for the Fixed Quantity Forecast or time period for a Weighted Average Forecast.

Exponential smoothing is a statistical method of forecasting the future based on the past. It uses actual usage and deviations from forecast from previous time periods to establish a projection of demand into the future. The number of previous periods selected and weight applied to each period in terms of an exponential relationship is set by the planner through the selection of the Alpha Factor. The higher the Alpha Factor, the greater the weight given to more recent periods as compared to earlier ones. The process "smooths" the effect of increases and decreases from period to period when the new forecast is calculated.

Note that the smoothing process is based on the same principle as that used when companies use net overages to offset net shortages when calculating financial inventory accuracy levels. With forecasting, multiple periods of high usage are averaged with periods of low usage to create a forecast which falls somewhere in between.

Systems will do one of two things when a forecast is developed. Either each future time period (typically weekly or monthly) is assumed to have the same forecasted usage rate, or the system will incorporate a trend factor and increase or decrease each successive period accordingly. Some systems will additionally permit the planner to modify the forecast in a period to account for sales promotions or other exception conditions.

Nonstatistical methods base demand on a planner-specified quantity or on dependent-demands from higher level (MS and MRP) product explosions. None of these methods is based on historical usage rates necessarily, though the MS may incorporate statistical forecasting techniques for demand beyond the firm plan horizon. When future demand must be estimated, planners use heuristic methods based on some knowledge of the part, product, or product line.

The system should identify the individual who selected the particular forecasting technique and related field values. The Reason for Choice field provides a note area where the planner can record why the technique was selected. If the technique selection should be reviewed for change on a particular date, the Review Date is set. A common situation is for a new part being phased-in where a fixed quantity is selected during the ramp-up period. Once the product demand is more stable, a time period or statistical technique can be used. Refer to Figure 8.2.

```
09:00am 07/01/YY                    FOR—Part Forecast

Part Number:            A123456789      Part Name:        Fastener
Part Description:       Control cabinet A-120 wiring harness fastener
Date Set:               03/14/YYYY      Set By:           K. Wheeler
Forecast Code:          STA—Statistical Review Date:      --/--/----
Reason for Choice:      Independent-demand for Service parts plus dependent-demand.

-------------------------------------FIX—Fixed Forecast Fields-------------------------------------
Fixed Quantity:         0

-------------------------------------STA—Statistical Forecast Fields-------------------------------
Alpha Factor:           0.50            Weighted Periods:   6           with rounding
Single-Smoothed Forecast:  80           Usage Trend:        52.5
Double-Smoothed Forecast:  108          Forecast Trend:     +3.1        pieces/period

-------------------------------------TIM—Time Period Forecast Fields------------------------------
Time Period:            0 Months Issued Smoothed

  PREV PART  |  PART MSTR  |  ACTIVITY  |  MODIFY  |  DETAILS  |  NEXT PART
```

Figure 8.2 Inventory Part Forecast Screen

FORECASTING-RELATED ISSUES

Forecasting future part demand entails a risk of both over- and underforecasting. As risk managers, it is the inventory manager's and planner's responsibility to ensure that the forecast is within target accuracy limits. The greater the error in excess of actual demand, the greater the carrying cost for unsold parts. The greater the error under actual demand, the greater the lost opportunity for profits and the lower the customer service level unless safety stock can compensate. However, there is some tradeoff (but not typically one-for-one) between having excess parts and having unacceptable carrying costs. The less expensive the part and the higher the part's or product's contribution to profit, the greater the number of parts which can be economically held in inventory if the part is overforecasted. This is one of the reasons why companies carry sufficient safety stock of "C" parts to minimize the possibility of a stock-out.

Another element of risk entails whether the demand is a part, product, or service which can only be obtained from the company or whether alternatives in the marketplace exist. Internal "customers" (usually manufacturing but also including R&D and service) may not have an alternative; the inventory department may be the primary "supplier" for stocked parts. External customers may also have no choice for parts which are custom-designed for the project or product. Even so, a supplying company will often incur extra expenses for expediting and weekend handling in order to maintain satisfied customers. Future business and current customer satisfaction are definite forecasting considerations.

Replenishment vs. Marketing Lead Time Effect on Forecasting

A key forecasting issue affecting most parts and products is the difference between marketing lead time (quoted to customers) and cumulative lead time as shown in Figure 8.3. The greater this gap, the greater the risk and related investment in terms of excess inventory and safety stock. Expediting becomes a way of life. The reactive element of the integral strategy is to improve the ability of the company to accurately forecast over the duration of the cumulative lead time. The proactive element is to reduce the forecast duration through dock-to-dock initiatives and supplier lead time reductions and so reduce the need to forecast.

Companies measure forecast risk in terms of the dollar value of safety stock required to assure the desired level of customer service. This is a company-oriented measure in that the company determines the level of customer service they wish to provide in terms of a percentage. Customers, however, expect a 100 percent service level. Refer to Chapter 10 Safety Stock for a discussion of the difference between customer service level based on satisfied demands and safety stock service percent based on replenishment order exposures to stock-out. What safety stock does not account for very well is the opportunity for profit associated with lost sales if an unplanned stock-out can be prevented. The company should determine this value as part of any service level assessment.

Forecasting at the MS level has lower level inventory repercussions consistent with the part's bill of material level. Part of the Forecast Duration in Figure 8.3

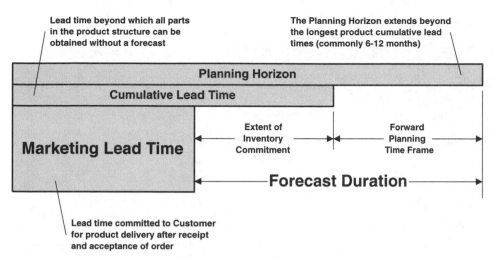

Figure 8.3   Product Forecast Lead Time

consists of the difference between cumulative lead time and marketing lead time. That is the extent of inventory commitment which the company must make in order to stock the parts which fall outside of the marketing lead time. Any parts in the product bill of material explosion which have an order release date in that portion of the forecast duration time frame must be purchased or manufactured based on the forecast. If the customer orders are not received as expected, the company will have excess inventory to carry into the next period. If more customer orders are accepted than forecasted, the company must have safety stock on-hand to cover the difference. Products with repetitive demand can absorb the risk of an overforecast easier than products with sporadic demand.

Lower vs. Higher Alpha Factor

The amount of weight applied to each historical period when calculating a statistical forecast is a variable. This variable is referred to as the Alpha Factor and is specified by the planner or inventory manager. The larger the Alpha Factor, the greater the weight given to the most recent periods and the fewer the number of historical periods essentially included in the forecast. Exponentially lesser weight is then given to each preceding period, until the weight becomes insignificant for the earliest periods. For example, a 0.20 Alpha Factor assigns a 20 percent weight to the most recent period, while a 0.50 Alpha Factor assigns a 50 percent weight. This does not mean that 20 percent and 50 percent of the forecast, respectively, comes from the previous period. Weighting with smoothing does not apply the Alpha Factor directly to the previous period usage, but to its difference compared to the forecast. This point is clearer when the equations are reviewed later in this chapter.

In actual practice, companies probably do not spend much time fine-tuning

Table 8.1   Number of Periods at 0.5 Alpha Factor
to Reach Various Percents of Forecast

PERIOD	WEIGHT/ 3 PERIODS	WEIGHT/ 4 PERIODS	WEIGHT/ 5 PERIODS	WEIGHT/ 6 PERIODS	WEIGHT/ 7 PERIODS	WEIGHT/ 8 PERIODS
0 (Current)	.5	.5	.5	.5	.5	.5
1	.25	.25	.25	.25	.25	.25
2	.125	.125	.125	.125	.125	.125
3	.0625	.0625	.0625	.0625	.0625	.0625
4		.03125	.03125	.03125	.03125	.03125
5			.015625	.015625	.015625	.015625
6				.0078125	.0078125	.0078125
7					.0039062	.0039062
8						.0019531
WEIGHT	.9375	.96875	.984375	.9921875	.9960937	.9980468
ROUND UP	.94	.97	.99	1.00	1.00	1.00

the Alpha Factor once it is set. In general, a part which is experiencing a small up-ward or downward trend may have a factor in the 0.10 to 0.20 range. A phase-in part which is experiencing growth or a phase-out part experiencing decline may use a factor in the 0.50 to 0.80 range. If usage is stable but subject to radical change based on random market conditions, the Alpha Factor should be set at 0.5 or higher. For parts with steady demand over a long time frame, Alpha Factor is essentially immaterial.

Table 8.1 illustrates the percentage of the forecast which is determined for a 0.5 Alpha Factor based on the number of periods of history available.[1] If actual usage was exactly 1,000 units per month over time, eight periods are sufficient to forecast a 998 part level without rounding. Note that Period 0 is the end of the current month.

This means that there is no restriction on the number of periods in the fore-cast, all things being equal. The more history there is up to a point (six periods for an Alpha Factor of 0.5 with rounding), the "better" the forecast. Beyond that, the weight applied to each additional older period is insignificant. For example, Periods 7 and 8 in Table 8.1 get closer to 100 percent than Period 6. However, with rounding up, all periods at six and above calculate the same forecast. From a purely mathematical perspective, therefore, the forecast never actually catches up to the actual usage. From a business perspective, computers round numbers up, and the forecast does actually reflect actual usage during our lifetime.

The lower the Alpha Factor, the less reactive the forecast is to deviation of ac-

---

1. The percentage of the forecast which is included by a given number of periods is cal-culated using the sum of the weights/period. As shown in Table 8.1 with an Alpha Factor of 0.5, six periods of history at a steady usage of 100 per month will calculate a forecast of 100 (99.2 rounded up, since any partial should be rounded up for forecasting purposes).

tual demand from forecast. As the Alpha Factor increases, the forecast tends to react to a greater extent to deviations, though after the fact. This can be a problem if the demand changes erratically each period, since extra materials are procured as demand is dropping and fewer materials when demand is increasing. In these types of situations where demand changes slope periodically, a lower Alpha Factor will tend to result in a smoothed forecasting rate as shown in Figure 8.4.

Moving Average

Consider a forecast based on a *moving average* where the oldest actual usage (i.e., Period 4 for an Alpha Factor of 0.5 as shown in Table 8.1) is replaced by the current period actual usage each period. In this case, three historical periods plus the current period are included and averaged for each new forecast. With a moving average based on the equation in Table 8.2, the forecast will never build up sufficient periods to rise above approximately 94 for a steady state usage of 100 units per period ($0.5 \times 100 + 0.25 \times 100 + 0.125 \times 100 + 0.0625 \times 100 = 94$). The periods required to achieve a 100 forecast (Periods 4–6) are always excluded. This is why moving averages based on a limited number of periods with Alpha Factor smoothing are inappropriate for statistical forecasting; they never catch up to actual demand.

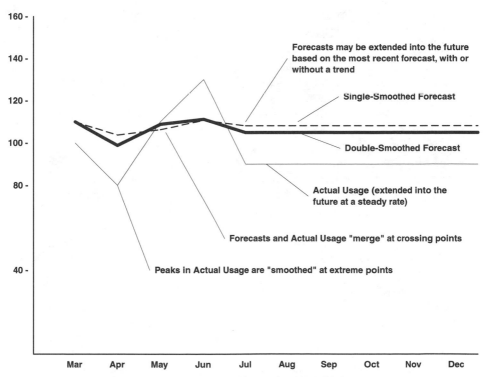

Figure 8.4   Effect of Smoothing Using a 0.2 Alpha Factor

Table 8.2 "Equivalent" Moving Averages for Varying Alpha Figures

$$\frac{\text{2-Alpha}}{\text{Alpha}} = \frac{\text{Number of Periods of Data in an}}{\text{"Equivalent" Moving Average}}$$

NUMBER OF (PREVIOUS) PERIODS IN "REPRESENTATIVE" EQUIVALENT MOVING AVERAGE	ALPHA FACTOR $\propto$	PERCENT OF WEIGHT WITHIN "EQUIVALENT" NUMBER OF PERIODS
3 (4 total including current)	0.500	93.8
4 (5 total including current)	0.400	92.2
5 (6 total including current)	0.333	91.2
6 (7 total including current)	0.286	90.5
7 (8 total including current)	0.250	90.0
8 (9 total including current)	0.222	89.7
9 (10 total including current)	0.200	89.3
12 (11 total including current)	0.154	88.6
19 (18 total including current)	0.100	87.7

Systems should use a weighted average using exponential smoothing to calculate forecasts. This enables the forecast to incorporate the effect of older periods but at a gradually decreasing contribution rate.

Table 8.2 identifies the Alpha Factor and number of periods required to achieve from approximately 88 to 94 percent of forecast for a new part which begins with a zero starting quantity. This is really only significant for parts which are being phased-in where no starting history is "created" for the part.[2] The planner should understand the risk that the forecast may continue for some time to be too low if there are insufficient historical periods to get close to a 100 percent level.

From a practical perspective for an inventory system using Single- or Double-Smoothing Forecasts, the number of periods associated with the forecast are essentially as many as the number of periods for which a statistical forecast has been calculated. However, the higher the Alpha Factor, the fewer the number of periods actually required to reach the "100 percent level." Forecasting is a nonissue if the actual usage rate is a constant. The more the actual usage rate varies,

---

2. A starting history is appropriate for parts with a step-function in demand. This may occur with a new product introduction or for a part superseding another.

the more important it is to build up a representative history for statistical forecasting and statistical safety stock calculations.

The previous discussions assumed a steady state actual usage rate simply as a reference. This makes it easier to verify the principles relating to the effect of weighting over time without complicating matters with variable demand.

Basis for the Calculation

With a 0.5 Alpha Factor, 94 percent of the forecast will be obtained from the most recent three historical periods plus the current period (four total). For a part with steady demand and an Alpha Factor of 0.5, six periods are required to achieve a 100 percent accurate forecast (with rounding up and steady state demand). The number of periods increases with lower Alpha Factors as illustrated in Figure 8.5.

Example: Consider a part where the planner wishes to compare the effect of rounding on the number of periods required to achieve 100 percent of the forecast. This provides a verification of the results included in Table 8.3:

0.5   Alpha (Smoothing) Factor
0 units   Old Single-Smoothed Forecast (SSF is a forecast of the previous period [month] based on a single-smoothing operation). A zero old forecast in this example indicates that the part has no history and is being phased-in.
10 units   Current Month Actual Usage and expected steady usage rate for the next year.

New SSF = Old SSF + ∝ (Current Period Actual Usage – Old SSF)

From the Figure 8.5 table, a new part's forecast will initially be five units after the first month's actual usage of 10. If usage remains steady at 10 units per month, the next month's forecast increases to 7.5. After four months, the forecast has increased to 94 percent (93.75 percent), but is still low by over 6 percent. This illustration is more for reference purposes regarding the SSF equation since forecasts and actual usage must be in integer quantities.

Example: Companies cannot receive or issue partial quantities based on the inventory unit of measure and so must round quantities up. Refer to the Figure 8.6 table which repeats the Figure 8.5 calculations *with* rounding. Note that the Single-Smoothed Forecast equation used here is covered in more detail later in the chapter. The Alpha Factor of 0.5 is not really basing 50 percent of the next month's forecast on 50 percent of the previous forecast. The Alpha Factor smooths the *deviation* from one month to the next and then adds it to the old single-smoothed value.

From the Figure 8.6 table, a new part's forecast will initially be five units after the first month's actual usage of 10. If usage remains steady at 10 units per month, the next month's forecast increases to eight (rounded up from 7.5). After three months (with the current month being the

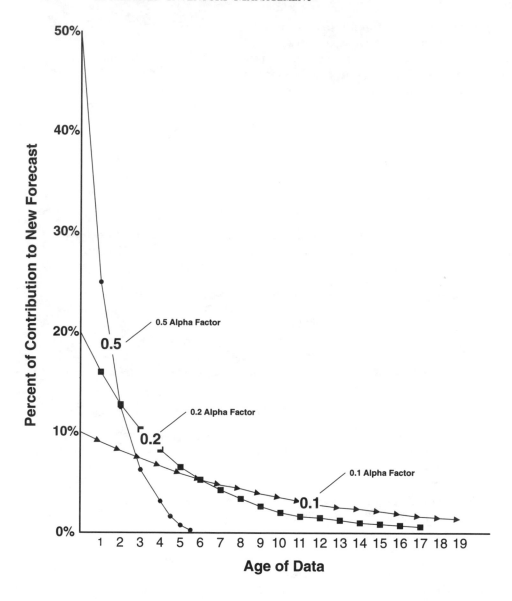

Single-Smoothed Forecast Without Rounding

PERIOD	NEW SSF	=	OLD SSF	+	(ALPHA FACTOR	X	[CURRENT PERIOD ACTUAL USAGE	OLD SSF])	WEIGHT CONTRIBUTION
0 (Current)	5.000 =		0.000 +		(0.5 x		[10.0 − 0.00])		50.00%
1	7.500 =		5.000 +		(0.5 x		[10.0 − 5.00])		25.00%
2	8.750 =		7.500 +		(0.5 x		[10.0 − 7.500])		12.50%
3	9.375 =		8.750 +		(0.5 x		[10.0 − 8.750])		6.25%

Figure 8.5 Weighting with Various Alpha Factors (values are from Table 8.3)

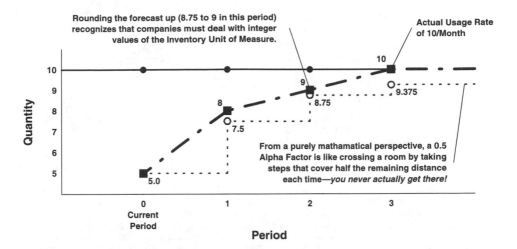

Rounding the forecast up (8.75 to 9 in this period) recognizes that companies must deal with integer values of the Inventory Unit of Measure.

Actual Usage Rate of 10/Month

From a purely mathamatical perspective, a 0.5 Alpha Factor is like crossing a room by taking steps that cover half the remaining distance each time—*you never actually get there!*

Single-Smoothed Forecast *With* Rounding

PERIOD	NEW SSF	OLD SSF +	(ALPHA FACTOR ×	[CURRENT PERIOD ACTUAL USAGE −	OLD SSF])	WEIGHT CONTRIBUTION
0 Current	5 =	0 +	(0.5 x	[10 − 0])		50%
1	8 =	5 +	(0.5 x	[10 − 5])		30%
2	9 =	8 +	(0.5 x	[10 − 8])		10%
3	10 =	9 +	(0.5 x	[10 − 9])		10%
4	10 =	10 +	(0.5 x	[10 − 10])		0%

Figure 8.6 Comparison of Forecasts With and Without Rounding

"fourth" month), the forecast has increased to 100 percent and remains there as long as demand remains steady at 10 units per month.

As long as the computer rounds values up to integer quantities, the forecast approaches actual usage rates with fewer periods of actual history. This addresses the confusion with tables such as Table 8.3 where it does not appear that forecasts reach 100 percent even after many periods of historical usage. Table 8.3 illustrates the basic mathematical relationships. Rounding represents the realities of a business situation where parts must be dealt with in integer quantities.

As the selected Alpha Factor for a part is decreased, the number of periods required to achieve a given forecast level of completeness (assuming a steady state usage rate) increases. Table 8.3 compares three different Alpha Factors. If the planner was to calculate the forecast manually using usage rates from previous periods, the table indicates the approximately weighting of each period. A better example of how an inventory system calculates the same forecast is illustrated later in the chapter.

Table 8.3   Weighting of Data with Various Alpha Factors

$$\text{Period Weighting} = \text{Previous Period Weighting} - \left(\text{Previous Period Weighting} \times \text{Alpha Factor } \alpha \right)$$

PERIOD	0.5 ALPHA FACTOR	0.5 WITH ROUNDING	0.2 ALPHA FACTOR	0.2 WITH ROUNDING	0.1 ALPHA FACTOR	0.1 WITH ROUNDING
Current	0.5000	0.50	0.2000	0.20	0.1000	0.10
1	0.2500	0.25	0.1600	0.16	0.0900	0.09
2	0.1250	0.13	0.1280	0.13	0.0810	0.08
3	0.0625	0.06	0.1024	0.10	0.0729	0.07
4	v	0.03	0.0819	0.08	0.0656	0.07
5		0.02	0.0655	0.07	0.0590	0.06
6		0.01	0.0524	0.05	0.0531	0.05
7			0.0419	0.04	0.0478	0.05
8			0.0336	0.03	0.0430	0.04
9			0.0268	0.03	0.0387	0.04
10			v	0.02	0.0349	0.03
11				0.02	0.0314	0.03
12				0.01	0.0282	0.03
13				0.01	0.0254	0.03
14				0.01	0.0229	0.02
15				0.01	0.0206	0.02
16				0.01	0.0185	0.02
17				0.00	0.0167	0.02
18				0.00	0.0150	0.02
19				0.00	0.0135	0.01
Weighting	94%	100%	89%	98%	88%	88%

Phase-In vs. Phase-Out Part Forecasting

The primary difference between phase-in and phase-out parts with respect to forecasting is that phase-in parts do not have any history and phase-out parts may have too much. Statistical-based forecasting techniques typically require some type of modification to account for history for both types of parts.

Consider a phase-in part which supersedes another (meaning it totally replaces it in terms of form, fit, and function). A system which supports statistical forecasting such as Double-Smoothing Forecast provides an opportunity to "transfer" the history from the old to the new part. By setting the Single-Smoothed Forecast, Double-Smoothed Forecast, and Usage Trend fields for the new part equal to those of the part being superseded, an instant "history" is created for the new part.[3] These fields are then recalculated each period as usage against the new part occurs. The effect is as if the new part were an old part. This is also an opportunity to reassess the particular values and parameters used. A reassessment may be especially important if the new part is replacing more than one old part, where a combined history may be required. Note that the Single-Smoothed Forecast related fields are discussed in more detail in the Single-Smoothed Forecast and Double-Smoothed Forecast subsections.

Example: Consider the data in Table 8.4 for a phase-in part. A *no history* approach is compared to one where a history is created by initializing the various forecast-related fields using the inventory system. The part has an initial 100 units per month demand, increasing at a rate of 10/month, and a 0.50 Alpha Factor. The purpose is to see if there is any value in creating a history for a phase-in part to improve its forecast.

The Single-Smoothed Forecast (SSF) lags both the Actual Usage and the Double-Smoothed Forecast (DSF) for both scenarios. Both of these are covered in more detail later in the chapter. What is of more interest, however, is that the No History part Double-Smoothed Forecast caught up to the Created History part DSF in Period 1 after two full periods of history. The No History part overshot the forecast while the Created History part remained within 0 to 2 units of Actual Usage over all periods. The most significant benefit of creating history for the part, therefore, is in getting the first period forecast closer to actual expected usage. Once this is

---

3. Computer systems do not need to actually maintain lengthy history files by part in order to calculate a forecast. The history is essentially rolled forward in terms of a few fields which simplify the computer calculation process. Once these fields are recalculated each month, the actual usage records can be moved to the History File. The fields include Single-Smoothed Forecast, Usage Trend, and Double-Smoothed Forecast. Note that the calculated fields are based on the particular Alpha Factor in use at the time. Changing from a 0.2 to a 0.5 Alpha Factor will not calculate a forecast as if a 0.5 Alpha Factor has been in use for the last six periods. The preceding named fields should *ideally* be recalculated from the History File if the Alpha Factor is changed.

Table 8.4   Phase-in Example With and Without History at a 0.5 Alpha Factor

PERIOD AND (ACTUAL USAGE)	NO HISTORY				CREATED HISTORY			
	SINGLE-SMOOTH FORECAST (SSF)	USAGE TREND	DOUBLE-SMOOTH FORECAST (DSF)	DSF MINUS ACTUAL USAGE	SINGLE-SMOOTH FORECAST (SSF)	USAGE TREND	DOUBLE-SMOOTH FORECAST (DSF)	DSF MINUS ACTUAL USAGE
Initialize	0	0.0	0	0	100	100.0	100	0
0 (100)	50	25.0	75	−25	100	100.0	100	0
1 (110)	80	52.5	108	−2	105	102.5	108	−2
2 (120)	100	76.3	124	+4	113	107.5	118	−2
3 (130)	115	95.7	134	+4	122	114.5	129	−1
4 (140)	128	111.6	144	+4	131	122.8	140	0
5 (150)	139	125.3	153	+3	141	131.7	150	0
Within %	93%		102%		94%		100%	

done, the following periods may remain a little more accurate as well, at least for parts with an increasing usage rate.

For a part being phased-out, the rate of phase-out will govern the changes to the statistical forecasting-related fields. An immediate phase-out requires the planner to set the fixed forecast equal to zero. A gradual phase-out forecast will tend to remain greater than actual usage if a low Alpha Factor is used. A higher Alpha Factor, an increase to the Usage Trend, or a decrease to the Single-Smoothed Forecast causes more recent periods to have a greater weighting. This calculates a greater rate of change.

Consider the comparison in Table 8.5 where one phase-out part has a 10-unit per period phase-out rate. The second part has an immediate reduction which reflects a discontinuance in manufacturing and then a gradual phase-out rate which reflects a reduction in service parts. The first part has a 0.2 Alpha Factor, and the second part has a 0.5 Alpha Factor.

The Single-Smoothed Forecast lags both the actual usage and the Double-Smoothed Forecast for both scenarios. The Double-Smoothed Forecast catches up to the actual usage faster with a higher Alpha Factor as shown for the second part. Phase-out parts should use a high Alpha Factor in conjunction with direct planner control for reordering based on a knowledge of business conditions.

Forecast Accuracy vs. Inaccuracy (What Level Is Enough?)

Forecasts are 100 percent accurate (i.e., zero deviation from target) when they accurately project 100 percent of the independent-demand for the period. For every 1,000 parts subject to independent-demand, there must be 12,000 100 percent accurate forecasts each year based on monthly forecast recalculations in order to achieve a zero deviation performance. For 10,000 parts, this is 120,000 accurate

Table 8.5   Phase-Out Example with Different Rates and Alpha Factors

PERIOD	Part 1 GRADUAL PHASE-OUT (0.2 ALPHA FACTOR)				Part 2 STEEP PHASE-OUT (0.5 ALPHA FACTOR)			
	SINGLE-SMOOTH FORECAST	USAGE TREND	DOUBLE-SMOOTH FORECAST	ACTUAL USAGE RATE	SINGLE-SMOOTH FORECAST	USAGE TREND	DOUBLE-SMOOTH FORECAST	ACTUAL USAGE RATE
Previous	110	110	110	110	110	110	110	110
Current	108	110	107	100	80	95	65	50
1	105	109	101	90	60	78	43	40
2	100	107	93	80	51	64	37	41
3	94	105	84	70	42	53	30	32
4	87	101	74	60	33	43	22	23
5	80	97	63	50	24	33	14	14
Within %	+38%		+21%		+42%		+0	

forecasts. Since demand is not under control of the company, zero deviation must really be considered from the company's customer service level perspective, not from the perspective of matching forecast to actual usage. Forecasting is, therefore, not considered as a stand-alone process within an integral strategy as is true with most other performance measures.

Where backorder situations exist, the company can track total customer demand and determine the level of customer service being provided. Customer service level can then be increased by carrying more safety stock in cases where underforecasts occurred.

However, the independent customer demand level is not always tracked or even possible to determine. One is a situation where orders are not accepted when a stock-out situation occurs. This may be the case with retailers or wholesalers who may not be able or willing to procure more of a particular product. Another case is when customers go elsewhere if the company cannot provide immediate or short-term service as occurs in retail or seasonal demand situations. In these cases, the company will issue (or sell) the available balance and then not accept any additional orders. For the seller, this has the effect of making demand appear to match the inventory balance, giving a false 100 percent accuracy reading to the forecast. For manufacturers providing products to these sellers, demand in excess of sales is invisible at their level in the logistics chain. All they can do is forecast the seller's demand (their buyer), not the market demand.

Companies must assess the effect of three scenarios when determining the level of acceptable forecast accuracy for a particular material, part, assembly, or product. The scenarios are (1) forecast is correct, (2) forecast is too high, and (3) forecast is too low. These are compared in Table 8.6 in inventory management terms.

The company's target is for the forecast to be 100 percent accurate. In cases

Table 8.6   Forecast Accuracy Considerations

FORECAST QUANTITY ACCURACY	CUSTOMER SERVICE LEVEL	DIP INTO OR CONSUME SAFETY STOCK	CARRYING COST LEVEL	EXPEDITNG LEVEL
Exact	100%	No	= Target	= $0
Too High	100%	No	> Target	= $0
Too Low But within SS	100%	Yes	< Target	= $0
Too Low and Consumes SS	< 100%	Yes	< Target	> $0

where the company has no control over demand, the probability of being 100 percent accurate for a part for all periods is essentially *zero*. This is where the value of having safety stock is imperative to the company's overall customer service level performance. The real issue is whether it is better to overforecast or underforecast and supplement the difference with safety stock and expediting.

An *overforecast* has the effect of maintaining a high customer service level. This comes with a higher inventory carrying cost due to having materials in excess of demand. This is less of an issue for inexpensive parts and many companies do not even consider carrying cost in such cases. Providing customer service is often an overwhelming factor compared to the cost or carrying, ordering, and expediting parts. Therefore, the cost of excess carrying cost due to some combination of overforecast and safety stock is worth the total inventory cost if it is less than or equal to the expediting costs and profit contribution of having the part in stock when required. From a practical perspective, the important financial consideration is the profit or customer service contribution of the part. Unfortunately, these are also among the most difficult part characteristics to quantify.

An *underforecast* becomes more of a problem as the quantity of the underforecast increases and the available safety stock is consumed. A small underforecast in one period may not be a problem until an underforecast in the next or some later period consumes the safety stock and results in a stock-out. Even this may not be an off-target problem if the stock-out falls within the acceptable safety stock service percent. This is calculated in terms of the number of "acceptable" stock-outs within a given number of exposures to stock-out. If statistical forecasting is being used in an upward-trending environment, underforecasting may occur on a continuing basis if the Alpha Factor is set too low.

The main problem with an underforecast is that companies typically cannot differentiate between a stock-out which falls within the parameters of an acceptable safety stock service percent and one which does not. When a needed part stocks-out, no one checks with the inventory department to find out if this is the time when it is allowed to stock-out. They expedite it immediately and blame the inventory system or department for the stock-out. Customers, whether internal or external, do not care about a company's acceptable stock-out levels because customers expect no stock-outs.

Therefore, company management must make a business decision with respect to forecast accuracy and actions which are to be taken in the event of a stock-out. Companies must either be willing to carry whatever level of inventory is required to provide 100 percent customer service levels as their customers define service, or they must be willing to expend whatever cost is required to expedite orders and absorb premium manufacturing and shipping costs to provide target service levels as the company defines service, or they must be willing to submit to the business repercussions of consciously providing a less than 100 percent customer service level. Note that any definition the company has of customer service which is not held by their customers is not likely to create an order winning/order qualifying environment over the long-term.

SINGLE-SMOOTHED FORECAST (SSF)

Single-smoothed Forecast is a weighted average forecasting technique. It is generally used for parts which cannot be relied on to continue any particular trend direction. Therefore, it may not be applicable for phase-in or phase-out parts which will trend up or down, respectively. The forecast period is typically monthly and is calculated as follows:

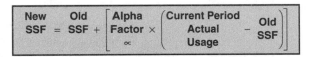

The Single-Smoothed Forecast is calculated via the following process (refer also to Figure 8.7). Note that the previous month refers to last month (i.e., May), and the current month (i.e., June) refers to the usage through the last work day of the month. The forecast is calculated via a monthly program run on the last work day after all of the inventory transactions have been processed.

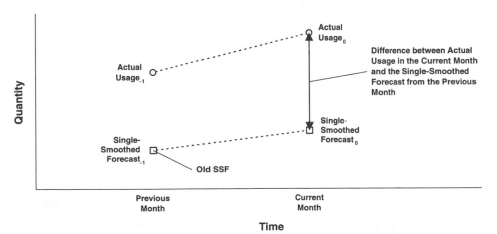

Figure 8.7   Single-Smoothed Forecast Calculation Process

1. The new "Current Month" SSF begins with the SSF from the previous month (month$_{-1}$). This was the quantity which was forecasted to be used in the current month.

2. The Current Period Actual Usage is calculated by summing all of the production issues for the month. This excludes scrap issues and issues for materials returned to suppliers due to quality reasons.

3. The forecast for the following month (and future time periods if a level forecast is assumed) is calculated by summing two factors. The first factor is the Single-Smoothed Forecast calculated the previous month. This factor incorporates the history developed for the part. The second is a factor calculated by weighting the difference between the Single-Smoothed Forecast from the previous month (Old SSF) and the Current Month Actual Usage. The closer the forecast is to actual usage, the smaller this second smoothed factor.

4. Though not specifically shown in the preceding equation, the system must finally adjust the New Single-Smoothed Forecast based on the number of days. Monthly periods are not equal in terms of workdays. Therefore, the SSF must be calculated in terms of a constant such as a 20-day work month. It can then be adjusted up or down when calculating the new SSF to account for the number of workdays in the current month.

Example: Consider the following (month$_{-1}$) information for an independent-demand part. The adjustment for workdays is not included, indicating that the Current Month workdays equals the Old SSF baseline workdays:

140 pcs   Old SSF (from Previous Period, month$_{-2}$)
0.20   Alpha Factor
120 pcs   Current Period (month$_{-1}$) Actual Usage (−14 percent deviation from Old SSF)

$$SSF = 140 + [0.20 \times (120 - 140)] = 140 - 4 = 136 \text{ pcs}$$
(−1 percent deviation from Old SSF)

For the Current Month (month$_0$):
136 pcs   Old SSF (from month$_{-1}$)
0.20   Alpha Factor
160 pcs   Current Period (month$_0$) Actual Usage (+33 percent deviation from Previous Month Actual Usage)

$$SSF = 136 + [0.20 \times (160 - 136)] = 136 + 5 = 141 \text{ pcs}$$
(+4 percent deviation from Old SSF)

This example illustrates that a relatively large change in Actual Usage from month to month (a 33 percent change) is smoothed to a much lesser change in forecast with a 0.20 Alpha Factor. As stated previously, the Alpha Factor smoothing occurs to the deviation, not to the Actual Usage itself. Therefore, forecasts are a based on a fine-tuning of the deviation between the forecast and actual usage.

The same example using an Alpha Factor of 0.50 yields a larger change:

Month 1   SSF = 140 + [0.50 × (120 − 140)] = 130 pcs
(−4 percent deviation from the Old SSF)

Month 2   SSF = 130 + [0.50 × (160 − 130)] = 145 pcs
(−9 percent deviation from Actual Usage)

Even when Single-Smoothed Forecasting is not used as the forecasting technique for a part, it may be advantageous to calculate and maintain it for comparison purposes using several values based on different Alpha Factors. More importantly, it is also one of the elements used in calculating the Double-Smoothed Forecast.

DOUBLE-SMOOTHED FORECAST (DSF)

Double-Smoothed Forecast provides a more accurate forecast than Single-Smoothed Forecasting for parts which are trending either upward or downward. The two techniques are compared in Table 8.5. While Single-Smoothed Forecasting will react to a trend, Double-Smoothed Forecasting reacts faster. It provides an equally accurate forecast for parts which have a steady demand rate. Because of this, companies are more likely to use a Double-Smoothed Forecast rather than a Single-Smoothed Forecast for independent-demand parts.

Double-Smoothed Forecasting uses the Single-Smoothed Forecast discussed previously and adds a second factor to account for the Usage Trend. The term *double-smoothing* (second order smoothing) comes from the fact that the forecast is a result of smoothing both the Single-Smoothed Forecast and the Usage Trend with the Alpha Factor. There are higher-order smoothing calculations available as well, which are not covered in this book. They are based on similar principles as discussed here.

$$\text{New SSF} = \text{Old SSF} + \left[\text{Alpha Factor} \propto \times \left(\text{Current Period Actual Usage} - \text{Old SSF} \right) \right]$$

$$\text{New Usage Trend} = \text{Old Usage Trend} + \left[\text{Alpha Factor} \propto \times \left(\text{New SSF} - \text{Old Usage Trend} \right) \right]$$

$$\text{New DSF} = (2 \times \text{New SSF}) - \text{New Usage Trend}$$

While the Single-Smoothed Forecast smooths the deviation of Actual Usage as compared to the Old SSF, the Double-Smoothed Forecast smooths the New SSF compared to the Old Usage Trend. In essence, the New SSF is used as the (new) Current Period Actual Usage. Refer to Figure 8.8. Smoothing it again has the effect of accentuating the trend. Therefore, if the New SSF has increased since the previous period, the New Usage Trend and the New DSF will increase as well and vice

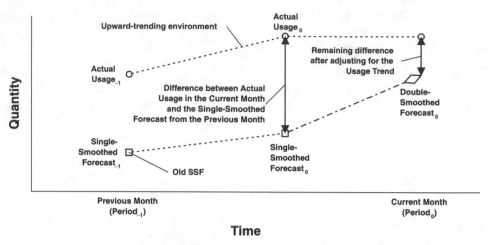

Figure 8.8   Double-Smoothed Forecast Calculation Process

versa. Since the New Usage Trend is less than the New SSF in an upward-trending environment, doubling the New SSF and subtracting the Usage Trend results in a forecast increase. The converse is true in a downward-trending environment.

The Double-Smoothed Forecast is calculated by first calculating the New Single-Smoothed Forecast, then calculating the Usage Trend, and then combining the two into the Double-Smoothed Forecast. This process is illustrated following. Note that the previous month refers to last month (i.e., May), and the current month (i.e., June) refers to the usage through the last workday of the month. The forecast is calculated via a monthly program run on the last workday after all of the inventory transactions have been processed.

1. The new Current Month SSF is calculated as discussed in the previous subsection.

2. The new Current Month Usage Trend is calculated by replacing the Actual Usage with the New SSF. The process is the same as that used to calculate the New SSF.

3. The new Current Month Double-Smoothed Forecast is then calculated by doubling the Single-Smoothed Forecast and subtracting the Usage Trend. In an upward-trending environment, the SSF is greater than the Usage Trend so a larger DSF is the result. The converse is true in a downward-trending environment.

4. As with Single-Smoothed Forecasting, the system must adjust the New Double-Smoothed Forecast based on the number of days. Monthly periods are not equal in terms of workdays. Therefore, the SSF, Usage Trend, and DSF must be calculated in terms of a constant such as a 20-day work month. The DSF can then be adjusted up or down to account for the number of workdays in the current and future months.

The inventory system should display both the Single- and Double-Smoothed Forecasts for reference purposes, regardless of the actual forecast technique used.

Tracking Signal

Like many other calculations within inventory management, statistical forecasts provide precise answers based on well-defined techniques. However, what the planner really needs in addition to such precision is an assessment of the accuracy of the forecasts.

In addition to the statistical forecast-related fields, an additional calculation referred to as the tracking signal should be provided. This signal provides an indication of the difference over time between the forecast and actual usage. A positive (+) value indicates that the forecast tends to exceed the actual demand. A negative (−) value indicates that the actual demand tends to exceed the forecast. Remaining either positive or negative over time is an indication that the forecasting technique is consistently high or low, respectively. This in itself may not be a problem as long as the magnitude of any deviations remain relatively small and manageable via safety stock.

The greater the magnitude of deviation (i.e., above 4 or 5), the greater the likelihood that planner review is required. The inventory system should provide a report which can be run based on the planner specifying a tracking signal limit. This enables the planner to sort parts in order of tracking signal. As discussed earlier, however, the tracking signal tends to be an arbitrary measure. Planners need to consider the accuracy of the forecast in conjunction with the safety stock and customer service level.

The general formula is as follows[4]:

$$\text{Tracking Signal} = \frac{\text{Running Sum of Forecast Errors}}{\text{Mean Absolute Deviation}}$$

The Running Sum of Forecast Errors is generated by subtracting Actual Usage from the forecast and summing over time. The ideal value of the RSFE is zero if periods of overforecasts offset periods of underforecasts. In actual practice, it tends to be positive in a downward-trending environment and negative in an upward-trending environment. The Mean Absolute Deviation is the absolute value of the sum of deviations between forecast and Actual Usage over time, divided by the number of forecast periods. The tracking signal, therefore, is really evaluating how closely the forecast is approximating actual usage over time.

Planners must be alert to three conditions with respect to tracking signals:

---

4. References differ somewhat regarding the tracking signal. Some use a normalized value ranging from 0 to 1 or −1 to +1. The purpose remains the same regardless of the actual calculation. Refer to your inventory system manual for details regarding the formula used by your company.

- The first is a condition where the signal remains positive or negative over time. This indicates that the forecast is consistently high or low, respectively. The inventory system should provide a set of fields which indicate the number of periods the tracking signal has been either positive, zero, or negative. The planner can then use some judgment regarding which parts to review if there is an unbalance.

- The second condition is one of magnitude. This is where the decision to review a part becomes rather arbitrary. The best thing to do is to set a limit and then assess the number of parts which need review. Those with the lowest tracking signals (in terms of negative value) should be reviewed first. These parts are the ones where the forecast is missing the actual usage the most and are potentially causing stock-outs. Those with the highest positive tracking signals are the ones potentially causing excess inventory levels.

- The third condition concerns the duration of history upon which the tracking signal is based. If the conditions affecting the tracking signal change over time, the inventory system should provide the ability to reinitialize the field to zero or some other value and start over again.

Example: Consider a part with a Fixed Forecast of 100 units per month (regardless of the number of workdays). The inventory system updates the MAD and RSFE each month when the new forecast is calculated as shown in the table. Note that as long as the forecast is adjusted for the number of workdays per month, the MAD and RSFE do not have to be adjusted.

PERIOD	FIXED FORECAST	ACTUAL USAGE (ADJUSTED FOR DAYS/ MONTH	DEVIATION (FORECAST— ACTUAL USAGE)	MEAN ABSOLUTE DEVIATION (MAD)	RUNNING SUM OF FORECAST ERRORS (RSFE)	TRACKING SIGNAL (RSFE/MAD)
1	100	100	0	0.0 (0/1)	0	0.00
2	100	90	10	5.0 (10/2)	10 (0 + 10)	2.00
3	100	80	20	10.0 (30/3)	30 (10 + 20)	3.00
4	100	120	−20	12.5 (50/4)	10 (30 − 20)	0.80
5	100	110	−10	12.0 (60/5)	0 (10 − 10)	0.00
6	100	100	0	10.0 (60/6)	0 (0 + 0)	0.00
7	100	80	20	11.4 (80/7)	20 (0 + 20)	1.75
8	100	140	−40	15.0 (120/8)	−20 (20 − 40)	−1.30
9	100	100	0	13.3 (120/9)	−20 (−20 + 0)	−1.50
10	100	130	−30	15.0 (150/10)	−50 (−20− 30)	−3.30
Check	1,000	1,050	150 absolute value	15.0 (150/10)	−50	−3.30 ok

Note: Mean Absolute Deviation is calculated as the absolute value of the sum of the deviations divided by the number of periods.

Whenever a tracking signal is provided as an output of the inventory system, make sure that other reference fields are provided as well. These include number of periods in the calculation, number of periods when the forecast was less than the actual usage, number of periods when the actual usage was less than the forecast, number of periods when the forecast equaled the actual usage, net deviation, Mean Absolute Deviation, and average deviation per period which would have resulted in a zero deviation over the number of periods in the calculation. Planners deal best with relationships based on a variety of perspectives and deal less well with numbers which do not indicate the values upon which they are based.

Things that make sense to a planner are that the forecast is consistently high or low, and by a given quantity. With the preceding table, the forecast was high three periods, low four periods, and correct three periods. Over that time frame, the shortage was a total of 50 units. What the planner needs to know is that the Fixed Forecast should have been 105 per period (on average) rather than 100. This is the type of information and insight which is provided by a Decision Support System.

Extending the Forecast

The Single-Smoothed and Double-Smoothed Forecast techniques previously discussed essentially calculate the forecast for the next period. In many systems, this value is extended indefinitely into the future to provide a demand profile to the end of the planning horizon. In periods where demand is trending up or down, simply extending the same forecast into the future is incorrect. Where a part is trending, the company needs to select from among several alternatives.

One alternative is to calculate a best-fit line based on the most recent periods. This should probably be in the 4–12 period range to ensure enough history to smooth anomaly conditions without getting too out-of-date. The slope quantity becomes an addition in an upward-trending environment or a subtraction in a downward-trending environment. Refer to the dashed line in Figure 8.1.

Another alternative is to use existing fields already being calculated for the Double-Smoothed Forecast. A factor can be calculated by subtracting the Usage Trend from the Single-Smoothed Forecast. This provides a subtraction in a downward-trending environment and an addition in an upward-trending environment. A variation is to calculate a weighted average in a similar manner as the Single-Smoothed Forecast is calculated. This has the effect of smoothing the rate of change over time.

There is nothing especially significant about any of these techniques. If the inventory system provides more than one alternative, all can be calculated and displayed on demand. The planner can then select the alternative which seems most reasonable for the part.

What the Planner Sees

With an inventory system, planners typically see the effects of the various forecasting calculations secondhand in the form of suggested orders. Fields maintained by the inventory system may or may not make a lot of sense when viewed individually or collectively. The integral system makes the forecasting relationships available to the planner in the form of graphs, tables, and figures in addition to providing the individual fields. Individual fields are used by the system; relationships are used by the planners.

Example: Consider the following June month end information (Figure 8.9) for an independent-demand part using Double-Smoothed Forecasting. Note that May and June are assumed to have the same number of workdays for this example. If there is a difference, an adjustment is required to reflect the effect of the difference in workdays from one period to the next.

103 pcs	Old DSF (from previous period [May], for reference)
106 pcs	Old SSF (from May)
108.1 pcs	Old Usage Trend (from May)
0.20	Alpha Factor
130 pcs	Current Period (June) Actual Usage (18 percent increase from 110 in May)

$$\text{New SSF} = 106 + [0.20 \times (130 - 106)] = 106 + 4.8 = 110.8 \ (111) \text{ pcs}$$
$$(5 \text{ percent increase})$$

$$\text{New Usage Trend} = 108.1 + 0.20 \times (110.8 + 108.1) = 108.6 \text{ pcs}$$
$$(0 \text{ percent change})$$

$$\text{New DSF} = (2 \times 111) - 109 = 113 \text{ pcs} \ (10 \text{ percent increase})$$

This example indicates that the part has an erratic demand since the SSF increased by 5 pcs while the New Usage Trend increased slightly. The Double-Smoothed Forecast increased by 10 pcs in response to a 20 unit increase in Actual Usage. Previous actual usage rates are tending to keep the Double-Smoothed Forecast Usage Rate increasing at the rate indicated by the most recent usage period. Another factor for change may also be the difference in the number of workdays per month. Total usage per month without factoring for the workdays does not provide a direct comparison from period to period. The Actual Average Daily Usage is also shown in Figure 8.9 for reference.

Figure 8.9 provides a screen format which enables the planner to evaluate a part's forecast history and projected future demand. The Details button provides transaction level detail and the Graph button (refer to Figure 8.6) enables a line or bar chart to be displayed. The screen indicates that after July, the forecast remains the same. This is a common technique for extending the forecast into the future. Activating the W/Trend button replaces the steady state forecast with one adjusted for trending, if the system provides one.

The lower the Alpha Factor, the less reactive the forecast is to deviation of actual demand from forecast. As the Alpha Factor increases, the forecast tends to

09:00am 07/01/YY						IDF—Independent-Demand Forecast						

Part Number:	123456789	Description:	Switch	BOM Revision:	2	Low Level Cd:	10
Forecast Qty:	CALC	FCST Technique:	DSF	Alpha Factor:	0.2	INV U/M	EA
Order Quantity:	CALC	OQ Technique:	Time Period	Time Period:	12 WKS	Stk Bal:	50
Safety Stock Qty:	10	SS Technique:	Fixed	Time Period:	N/A	Lead Time:	2 wk

Period: Month: Work Days/Month:	0 MAR (21)	1 APR (20)	2 MAY (22)	3 JUN (22)	4 JUL (18)	5 AUG (21)	6 SEP (20)	7 OCT (23)	8 NOV (18)
Actual Independent Usage	100	80	110	130	90	>>>	>>>	>>>	>>>
Actual Average Daily Usage	4.76	4.00	5.00	5.91	5.00				
Single-Smoothed Forecast	110	104	106	111	107	107	107	107	107
Usage Trend	110	108.8	108.1	108.6	108.0	108.0	108.0	108.0	108.0
Double-Smoothed Forecast	110	100	103	113	105	105	105	105	105
Double-Smoothed Forecast Accuracy Percent	+9%	+20%	−2%	−16%	+14%				
Ending Stock Balance									

MSG: Activate SCROLL < > buttons to extend demand horizon (12 history and 8 additional periods available)								
<SCROLL<	PART LIST	DETAILS	GRAPH	MODIFY	WHAT-IF	W/TREND	>SCROLL>

Figure 8.9   Double-Smoothed Forecast Screen

react to a greater extent to deviations, though after the fact. This can be a problem if the demand changes erratically each period, since extra materials are procured as demand is dropping and fewer materials are procured when demand is increasing. In these types of situations where demand changes slope periodically, a lower Alpha Factor will tend to result in a more level forecasting rate. There will be additional safety stock suggested, however, since the part will experience larger deviations between forecast and actual usage in an erratic environment.

GREATER THAN ONE MONTH WEIGHTED AVERAGE FORECAST

Parts which are subject to a periodic (greater than monthly) usage pattern may benefit from a weighted average technique which sums a given number of months' demand before the forecast is calculated. Otherwise, a monthly technique such as Single- or Double-Smoothed Forecasting tends to forecast low during periods of actual usage and high otherwise. The forecast will be representative only on average when considered over the part's usage cycle. Other products may have multiple peak demands based on seasonal buying patterns. A 12-month period is common for products which are specialty items related to holidays. Parts which are planned via two-bin logic and subject to a few large bulk issues spread over time are also candidates for a greater than one month usage pattern.

The inventory system should provide a forecast code and related logic for parts or products which are subject to a greater than one month profile. The

"Number of Month's Issues Smoothed" field default is 1 for other techniques. This field is changed to a number long enough that at least one period is included where activity occurs. To be most effective, the number should equal the period duration. If the length of the period is somewhat variable, additional months may need to be included in the weighted average.

Consider a part where the period repeats on a 3- to 4-month cycle. Selecting a 3-month cycle may miss any demand, while selecting a 4-month cycle may include two periods of demand. Either situation causes the forecast to be erroneous. In this case, selecting an 8-month cycle (Periods 0 through –7) includes two periods of demand as shown in Table 8.7 most of the time (but not if a 3-month cycle continues). Period 0 is the point at which the most recent demand has occurred, so the forecasting program will run at the end of the period. Forecasts in future periods must then accommodate the possibility of a 3- or 4-month usage profile. Planners need to pay special attention to parts with variable cycles or carry sufficient safety stock to make forecast deviations a nonissue.

Another usage pattern is illustrated in Figure 8.10. It is an almost every other month pattern except that no usage occurred in July. The average demand per month is 45. The Single-Smoothed Forecast tends to be higher than the Double-

Table 8.7 Weighted Average Forecast with Variable Time Frame Profile

	–8	–7	–6	–5	–4	–3	–2	–1	PERIOD 0
3-Month			■			■			■
4-Month				●				●	
3 and 4 Mix 4 and 3 Mix			■	●			● ■		

09:00am 10/31/YY				IDF—Independent-Demand Forecast Inquiry				

Part Number: 22222222   Description: Switch   Alpha Factor: 0.2   Low Level Cd: 10
Forecast Qty: CALC   FCST Technique: DSF   Time Period: N/A   INV U/M EA
Order Quantity: CALC   OQ Technique: Time Period   Time Period: 12 WKS   Stk Bal: 50
Safety Stock Qty: CALC   SS Technique: Fixed   Time Period: 4 WKS   Lead Time: 6 wk

Period: Month: Work Days/Month:	0 MAR (21)	1 APR (20)	2 MAY (22)	3 JUN (22)	4 JUL (18)	5 AUG (21)	6 SEP (20)	7 OCT (23)	AVG
Actual Independent Usage	120	0	150	0	0	0	90	0	45
Single-Smoothed Forecast	112	90	102	82	66	53	60	48	77
Usage Trend	110.4	106.2	105.3	100.5	93.4	85.2	80.1	73.6	
Double-Smoothed Forecast	114	73	99	63	37	19	40	22	59

MSG: Activate <SCROLL> buttons to extend demand horizon (12 history and 5 additional periods available)

<SCROLL<	PART LIST	DETAILS	GRAPH	MODIFY	WHAT-IF	W/TREND	>SCROLL>

Figure 8.10 Problems of Not Using a Greater than One Month Weighted Average

Smoothed Forecast in all periods. Total demand for the time frame shown is 360 units. Calculating the Double-Smoothed Forecast at the end of October (Period 7) is, therefore, based on having approximately one period of demand in every two. This has the effect of occasionally weighting a zero demand period as occurred in October with the Alpha Factor and calculating a lower forecast than is actually being experienced on average.

The equations for calculating the weighted average with exponential smoothing are shown following. The first step is to total and average the Total Productive Issues for the selected period duration. Productive issues exclude scrap, returns to the supplier due to a quality problem, and returns to the supplier for credit. Including nonproductive issues skews the usage rate and results in an over-forecast. The weighting period is the Number of Month's (or weeks or any other period) Issued Smoothed as selected by the planner. The equation reflects Single-Smoothed Forecasting. Double-Smoothed Forecasting can also be calculated if the part demand is trending, as explained earlier.

$$\frac{\text{New}}{\text{Average}} = \frac{\text{Total Productive Issues for Weighting Period}}{\text{Number of Periods Being Smoothed}}$$

$$\frac{\text{New}}{\text{[SSF]}}_{\text{Forecast}} = \frac{\text{Old}}{\text{[SSF]}}_{\text{Average}} + \frac{\text{Alpha}}{\text{Factor}} \times \left(\frac{\text{New}}{\text{Average}} - \frac{\text{Old}}{\text{[SSF]}}_{\text{Average}} \right)$$

The historical demand profile for the part is shown in Table 8.8 based on 2-month averaging of actual demand. The results can be compared to both the Single-Smoothed Forecast (average forecast of 77) and Double-Smoothed Forecast (average forecast of 59) in Figure 8.10 based on non time period averaging and weighting techniques. The straight average is 45.

In Figure 8.10, selecting a 2-month period for averaging incorporates several zero demand periods. Prior to running the order review program for parts with weighted average techniques, a computer program should be run to identify parts with zero demand time frames which exceed the Number of Months Issues Smoothed field selected for each part. The planner should review these parts and determine whether the Number of Month's Issues Smoothed field should be increased. Another consideration is whether to change the technique itself, though the timing may be too short to make a quick decision. As a minimum, the planner may need to manually override any computer-generated order quantities, forecasts, or safety stocks when the review occurs.

FIXED QUANTITY FORECAST

A typical candidate for a fixed forecast is a part being phased-out which has a history of usage. Setting the forecast quantity to zero overrides any calculation of gradually diminishing future usage based on historical data. This zero value is then also used by any order review, order quantity, and safety stock equations based on usage forecast.

Table 8.8   Weighted Average Profile for Demand in Figure 8.6

2-MONTH PERIOD	0	1	2	3	4	5	6	7	AVG
Actual Independent-Demand	120	0	150	0	0	0	90	0	45
2-Month SSF Calculated Monthly; 0.2 Alpha Factor	52	54	59	63	51	41	42	43	51

Period 0 Calculations:

```
    2      Month's Issues Smoothed
 50 pcs    Old Average (from previous period; given)
 0.20      Alpha Factor
120 pcs    Sum of actual issues (in Periods 0 and –1; given)
           New Average = Total Issues/2 = 120/2 = 60 units/period
```

New Forecast = Old Average + Alpha Factor (new Average – Old Average)
             50   +   0.20   (60   –   50   )
             = 52 (Period 0)

The planner selects the fixed forecast technique by setting the part master fore-

Calculations for the preceding table:

PERIOD	NEW FORECAST =	OLD AVERAGE +	ALPHA FACTOR ×	(NEW AVERAGE –	OLD AVERAGE)
0	52	50	0.20	(0 + 120)/2 = 60	50
1	54	52	0.20	(120 + 0)/2 = 60	52
2	59	54	0.20	(0 + 150)/2 = 75	54
3	63	59	0.20	(150 + 0)/2 = 75	59
4	51	63	0.20	(0 + 0)/2 = 0	63
5	41	51	0.20	(0 + 0)/2 = 0	51
6	42	41	0.20	(0 + 90)/2 = 45	41
7	43	42	0.20	(90 + 0)/2 = 45	42

Note: New Forecast values are rounded up.

cast code to the proper designation (i.e., FIX). The forecast quantity is then entered into the Fixed Forecast Quantity field. This technique forces a specific
forecast into the system.

A fixed forecast may also be used for a new part being phased-in where there
is no history. This prevents low usage during ramp-up from constraining the company's ability to forecast a steep enough usage rate.

Using the example from the previous section for weighted average, the planner can elect to use a fixed forecast of from 45 to 50 units per month based on the
45 "historical" average. A 50-unit fixed forecast is illustrated in Figure 8.11. Selection of the forecasting technique makes a difference because the order quantity based on forecast quantity per period will be calculated accordingly.

09:00am 10/31/YY					IDF—Independent-Demand Forecast Inquiry				

Part Number:	22222222	Description:	Switch	Alpha Factor:	0.2	Low Level Cd:	10
Forecast Qty:	50	FCST Technique:	FIX	Time Period:	N/A	INV U/M	EA
Order Quantity:	CALC	OQ Technique:	Time Period	Time Period:	12 Wks	Stk Bal:	50
Safety Stock Qty:	CALC	SS Technique:	Time Period	Time Period:	4 wks	Lead Time:	6 wk

Period: Month: Work Days/Month:	0 MAR (21)	1 APR (20)	2 MAY (22)	3 JUN (22)	4 JUL (18)	5 AUG (21)	6 SEP (20)	7 OCT (23)	WGT AVG
Actual Independent Usage	120	0	150	0	0	0	90	0	45
Fixed Forecast	50	50	50	50	50	50	50	50	50
Reference Fields									
Single-Smoothed Forecast	112	90	102	82	66	53	60	48	77
Usage Trend	110.4	106.2	105.3	100.5	93.4	85.2	80.1	73.6	
Double-Smoothed Forecast	114	73	99	63	37	19	40	22	59

MSG: Activate <<<<<or>>>>> buttons to extend demand horizon (12 history and 8 additional periods available)

<<<<<	PART LIST	DETAILS	GRAPH	MODIFY	WHAT-IF	W/TREND		>>>>>

Figure 8.11   Fixed Forecast Example

Table 8.9   Stock Balance Profile Based on Information in Figure 8.11

3-MONTH ORDER QUANTITY	0	1	2	3	4	5	6	7	AVG
Actual Independent-Demand	120	0	150	0	0	0	90	0	45
Single-Smoothed Stock Balance	0	274(1)	124	124	303	303	213	213	222
Double-Smoothed Stock Balance	0	235(2)	85	85	181	181	91	91	136
Fixed Forecast Stock Balance	0	150	0	0	150	150	60	60	82

(1) 90 + 102 + 82 April through June from Figure 8.11; (2) 73 + 99 + 63 April through June

Consider the three forecasting alternatives in Table 8.9. The order quantity technique in Figure 8.11 is time period, with a 12-week time period specified. An assumption of a stock-out and reorder is made at the end of Period 0 for this discussion. Since the system will ensure that there is sufficient quantity in stock to cover the forecasts in any period, the forecast quantity becomes an important consideration.

The 82-unit average inventory level for the 50-unit fixed forecast turns out to be better than Double-Smoothed. Part of what made it better was the fact that the inventory stocked-out in Period 2. Since the replenishment lead time is six weeks, no inventory was available to support demand in Period 3 (where demand was fortunately zero).

Another consideration regarding average inventory level is that the 60 units in Periods 6 and 7 are probably too low. A 60-unit inventory balance covers a one-month average demand. At the end of Period 6, however, the inventory system will recognize that the smallest demand for a period within the previous six periods has been 90 units. The average demand has been 120 units ([120 + 150 + 90]/3). Therefore, the inventory order review constraint logic should determine that 60 units is too small a quantity to prevent a stock-out the next time demand occurs. An order for 150 units will, therefore, be released in Period 6 for receipt in Period 8.

In systems where the forecast quantity can be individually set for each period, the planner accesses the current values via the Modify button (Figure 8.11). This causes a window (Figure 8.12) to be displayed with the current values and related information. Changing any of the values causes the updates to be implemented.

The display will contain as many future periods as are defined in the long-range planning horizon for the company. At any point where the planner leaves the forecast unchanged (i.e., 10 Oct in Figure 8.11), the system will begin calculating the forecast based on the current forecast technique selected. This type of manual override can be used with any type of forecast technique because it applies to future periods only. This concept is essentially the same as that used to create the master schedule, where each period quantity is set by the master scheduler.

DEPENDENT-DEMAND

Products and parts which undergo Master Schedule and then Material Requirements Planning explosions are referred to as being subject to dependent-demand. The end-items may be dependent- or independent-demand, but all of the lower level (children) quantities are calculated based on demand at the higher levels (parents). The sources of end-item demand may be some combination of customer orders, firm-planned orders, planned orders, forecast orders, and safety stock requirements.

In a make-to-stock environment, all MS-level demand may be forecasted. In

PERIOD	QTY	TECHNIQUE	SET BY	DATE	REASON
1 Jan	100,000	FIX	System	12/23/Y3	
2 Feb	50,000	FIX	JB	01/30/Y4	Draw down finished goods
3 Mar	30,000	FIX	JB	01/30/Y4	
4 Apr	30,000	FIX	JB	01/30/Y4	
5 May	70,000	FIX	JB	01/30/Y4	Summer ramp-up
6 Jun	100,000	FIX	KN	01/30/Y4	
7 Jul	140,000	FIX	KN	01/30/Y4	
8 Aug	120,000	FIX	JB	07/30/Y4	Fall ramp-down
9 Sep	80,000	FIX	NN	07/30/Y4	
10 Oct	50,000	WGHT'D AVG	MRB		
11 Nov	80,000	WGHT'D AVG			
12 Dec	120,000	WGHT'D AVG			

Figure 8.12   Modify Window to Set a Period-by-Period Fixed Forecast

a make-to-order or engineer-to-order environment, there may be little or no forecasted demand at the MS or Final Assembly Schedule (FAS) level. Assemble-to-order environments entail a combination of actual and forecasted demand at the MS level. The most complex environments for forecasting are those where a variety of demand types are scheduled and consolidated via Master Scheduling and Material Requirements Planning, where parts and materials are used across multiple products and bills of material levels and where some combination of dependent- and independent-demand exists.

Once a demand has been identified for a part or product via MS, FAS, or MRP processing, its source may not be easily identifiable from an inventory perspective. This is less of a consideration in an environment where inventory shortages rarely occur. It is more of a consideration when constrained resources must be allocated to demand which has the greatest value from the company's perspective. A typical priority is to apply available inventory to customer orders before applying it to orders which are based on forecasts. The problem with systems which aggregate demand is that it may not be easy to differentiate between customer orders, forecast orders, and safety stock replenishment at lower levels in the bill of material structure.

Differentiating between forecasted and actual demand is a moot point if the company always has enough inventory to meet demands at all levels of the bill of material explosion. It may also be immaterial if there is always sufficient materials and manufacturing capacity to produce what is planned. However, the source of demands is extremely important in environments where shortages result in the company's attention and resources being diverted to expediting, rescheduling, and even disassembly and reassembly in order to meet customer demands. In these environments, it may be very important to differentiate between customer and forecasted requirements in order to know which strategy to pursue. It may be acceptable to reschedule production of materials or products being produced to a forecast. Expediting or other tactics may be required if a customer order is involved.

Companies can differentiate between forecasted and actual demand at any level by exploding both types of demand and then summing only for evaluation purposes at each level. Before the next level of explosion occurs, the data is restructured into customer, forecast, and safety stock demand and the process continues. In this way, the portion of work and purchase orders due to customer demand vs. forecasts are clearly identified. This is referred to as "full-pegging." As shortages of certain parts occur, an assessment can be made of the effect on orders, expediting, and schedules by imploding from the part level up through the higher levels in the BOM. Shortages may affect all current orders (i.e., a shortage due to a stock-out), only forecast orders (i.e., a shortage less than or equal to the forecasted demand component), or both forecast and customer orders (i.e., a shortage greater than the forecasted demand). The company can then elect to prioritize actions based on those shortages affecting customer orders before focusing on shortages which affect forecasted demand. A priority report of this type should be available within the MS or MRP system.

Dependent-Demand Example—Child Part Has a Shortage

As the mix of demand changes over time, the ERP/MRPII system regularly compares available stock against demand. Until the point where stock is specifically allocated to a particular order, the highest priority orders (typically the earliest) will be serviced using available inventory.

When a shortage occurs, customer orders on a period-by-period basis should be serviced before any stock is allocated to forecast orders or safety stock replenishment. This becomes more of a consideration for parts and assemblies below level 0 (end-item level) which are children of multiple higher level assemblies or products.

Consider the simple parent-child relationship shown in Figure 8.13, where part Z is a child of parents X and Y. Either the order for part X (50 units total) or Y (15 units total) can be fully satisfied, but not both. The information for Z indicates that 50 units are available, but that customer demand (50 units) and forecast demand (15 units) sums to 65.

In shortage situations, a company must have a simple technique for differentiating among customer, forecast, and safety stock replenishment demand. Otherwise, it is difficult to select which order or orders to completely satisfy, partially satisfy, or delay. In this simple case, all customer demand can be satisfied *only* by splitting the Z part stock among products X and Y. Otherwise, if X is the older or higher priority order, no customer demand for product Y will be satisfied. If Y is the older or higher priority order, then order X will have a 5 unit customer demand shortage.

Systems should provide the capability to identify the effect of demand at higher levels on stock availability at lower levels. This is the function of MRP. What may not be a standard feature is including the capability to identify when the supplier has said that a particular part order cannot be expedited or increased. In this case, the system should provide an override function which enables the company to identify a shortage condition as an unchangeable factor. Otherwise, MRP keeps generating expedite messages for orders at lower levels which *cannot* be expedited. This wastes everyone's time and effort.

In the preceding case, once the planner identifies that 50 units of Z are all that are available, the system should generate action messages using implosion logic. An implosion is similar to finite scheduling logic which accounts for a capacity

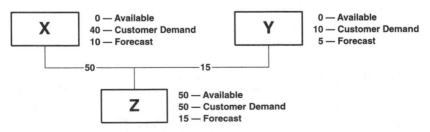

Figure 8.13   Demand for a Child with Multiple Parents

constraint. MRP treats the inability to expedite the lower level part as a constraint and instead recommends splitting the orders for X and Y to make use of the available stock.

An implosion is the reverse of an MRP explosion. The system begins with the available balance of the lower level part (Z) and determines how much higher level demand can be satisfied. With an implosion, customer orders are satisfied before forecast or safety stock orders.

Dependent-Demand Example—Parts Having a Multidemand Profile

In companies where one type of demand is "no different" than another, the traditional type of MS and MRP designs are applicable. These systems translate demand at one level into requirements and related orders at the next. For example, a 100-unit per week demand at one level may translate into an order for 200 units every two weeks at the next lower level.

Where lot-for-lot order quantity techniques are used, the source of the demand at lower levels is retained. This is commonly used in engineer-to-order environments where it is important to apply specific purchase or work orders to specific products due to revision, costing, lot traceability, serial number tracking, or other considerations. One of the most important considerations is simply the ability to prevent one master schedule, final assembly, or work order from "stealing" materials originally procured or manufactured for another order. One way this can occur, when not using a lot-for-lot order quantity technique, is when one order is received on a later date than the first but scheduled for shipment before the first one. Some systems will switch any materials soft-allocated to the first order to the second order based on the earlier shipment date. Poor planning and management level schedule changes are other ways material for one order can be redirected to another. Note that lot-for-lot order quantities cannot be "stolen," per se, only borrowed, since there is a specific need for the parts.

One technique for retaining order identity at lower levels is illustrated in Figure 8.14. The figure shows the product structure at the top, the bill of material in the middle, and the requirements records at the bottom. AAAAA is the end-item product, with parts at levels 1 and 2. One unique condition which some companies experience is having the same parts appearing at different levels and with different parents in the bill of material structure. This is illustrated with part EEEEE.

Material Requirements Planning records are created for the product and all of the parts when the bill of material explosion occurs. A pegging relationship is additionally created for each requirement with a full-pegging system as may be required in an engineer-to-order environment. This relationship enables the system and the inventory planner to associate any requirement with the end-item customer order and next higher level assembly work order. Having such a relationship enables an implosion process to occur in the event of a problem identified for a part at a low level in the bill of material structure.

Full-pegging is straightforward for lot-for-lot parts since requirements are not

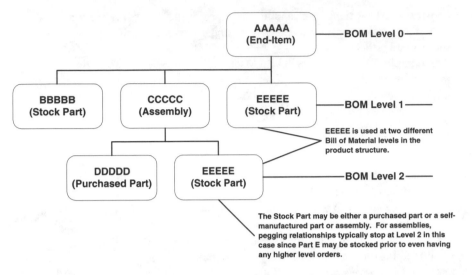

The Stock Part may be either a purchased part or a self-manufactured part or assembly. For assemblies, pegging relationships typically stop at Level 2 in this case since Part E may be stocked prior to even having any higher level orders.

BOM LEVEL	BOM ITEM NO.	PART NUMBER	PART DESCRIPTION	PART QUANTITY	BOM UNIT OF MEASURE	SERVICE PART INDICATOR
0		AAAAA	Printed Circuit Board Assembly			
1	001	BBBBB	Printed Circuit Board	1	EACH	
1	002	CCCCC	Buzzer Circuit	1	EACH	Y
2	001	DDDDD	Buzzer	1	EACH	
2	002	EEEEE	Resistor, 5 ohm, carbon	1	EACH	
1	003	EEEEE	Resistor, 5 ohm, carbon	1	EACH	

Bill of Material

Requirements Records

CUSTOMER ORDER NUMBER	CUSTOMER ORDER ITEM (FULL-PEGGING)	PART NUMBER	REQUIRED QUANTITY	REQUIRED DATE
C021345		AAAAA	1	10/15/YYYY
C021345	AAAAA–001	BBBBB	1	10/14/YYYY
C021345	AAAAA–002	CCCCC	1	10/13/YYYY
C021345	CCCCC–001	DDDDD	1	10/13/YYYY
C021345	CCCCC–002	EEEEE	1	10/14/YYYY
C021345	AAAAA–003	EEEEE	1	10/14/YYYY

The Customer Order Item identifies the Parent Part Number and the Bill of Material Item Number of the part on the parent BOM.

Figure 8.14   Pegging Relationships

combined across orders. Every bill of material assembly at one level generates individual requirements for all of its component parts or assemblies at the next lower level. The point at which inventoried or purchased parts are reached is where the explosion stops. These points were illustrated in Figure 7.1.

The point at which requirements at one level are combined in order to create an order at the next lower level is where full-pegging relationships are normally lost. For example, consider different products at the MS Level 0 which use the same Level 1 part. Generating a combined order for the Level 1 part loses the individual pegging relationships back to the end-item level at Levels 2 and below. Some system designs maintain these relationships where necessary to the operation of the business and maintenance of the materials plan. This is more common for engineer-to-order and project environments and less common for make-to-stock companies.

Traditional systems may contribute to two problem areas with respect to pegging. The first is that they may not easily enable a planner to differentiate among order priorities where certain customer orders should have a higher priority than others. This can happen when some customers have a "preferred" status of some type. The second problem is that the system may not stratify demand at lower levels to differentiate among customer, forecast, and safety stock requirements. The first problem area is related to using required date for priority as stated previously. Many orders can have the same required date, regardless of when they were actually added to the system. The second problem was illustrated in the Figure 7.5 example and is further detailed by the following discussion of Part ABC in Figure 8.15 which illustrates the basic methodology used to combine requirements in order to generate a planned order.

- The Fixed Order Quantity is 150 units. Each Planned Order Release is, therefore, for 150 units as shown in Periods 1, 3, and 6.

- The Safety Stock is 20 units. This quantity is not included in the "Available Inventory" row since it is not intended to be dipped into to cover "planned" demand. Any negative "Available Inventory" less than 20 can be covered by the Safety Stock if necessary. The negative values will be very visible to the planner.

- At the end of Period 0, the Available Inventory is 10. This indicates that Total Inventory is 30 (10 available plus 20 Safety Stock). Therefore, there is no need to replenish Safety Stock during this planning period.[5]

- The part Lead Time is two periods. Any Planned Order must be released two periods prior to the period in which it is required. The Planned Order required in Period 3 must, therefore, be released in Period 1. Note that Lead Time must allow for any internal order review and release and supplier shipping time, as applicable.

---

5. Check how your system handles safety stock in the matrix. It may or may not be treated as available inventory.

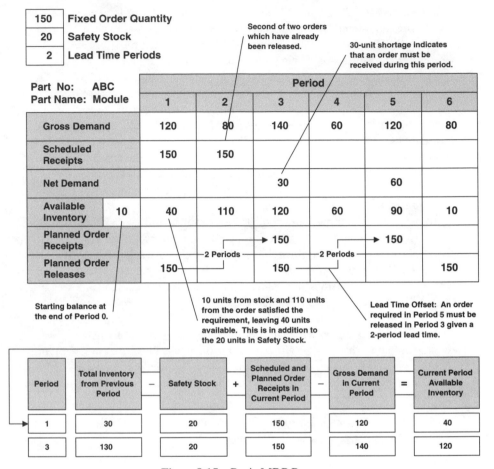

Figure 8.15   Basic MRP Process

- Gross Demand is the sum of any demand by customer, forecast, and safety stock replenishment orders at higher levels in the bill of material structure.

- Scheduled Receipts indicate that there are two orders which have already been released. The first is due for receipt in Period 1 and the second in Period 2.

- The Net Demand identifies the periods when the sum of available stock balance and Scheduled Receipts are insufficient to satisfy the Gross Demand. These are the periods when Planned Order Receipts are required.

- The Available Inventory row identifies the starting balance and the net Available Inventory which will remain in stock as of the end of the period.

This quantity does not include the Safety Stock. Therefore, any "Available Inventory" greater than or equal to −20 can be satisfied by the sum of Available Inventory plus Safety Stock.

- The Planned Order Receipts identify when receipts will occur if the orders are released when scheduled per the Planned Order Releases line.

- The Planned Order Releases line indicates when orders must be released in order to have materials available when indicated by the Net Demand line. Note that the system will assign actual required dates. Weekly increments are too general for actual material planning.

- The bottom rows in the figure provide the actual calculation routines for Periods 1 and 3. The difference between those calculations and the MRP process chart is that the rows begin with Total Inventory and subtract Safety Stock.

The screen in Figure 8.16 illustrates the type of information which is available for Product A within an MRP System which supports full-pegging. How the in-

09:00am 03/31/YY		DDI—Dependent-Demand Inquiry—Product: 448A330G01								
Part:	448A330G01	Description:	PCB Assy		Product Level:	0	Total Levels:	3		
Forecast Qty:	VARIABLE	FCST Technique:	MPS		INV U/M:	EACH	Level 1 Parts	15		
Order Quantity:	8-week	OQ Technique:	Time Period		Part:	FG	Parents:	0		
Safety Stock Qty:	10	SS Technique:	Fixed		Lead Time:	8 weeks	Stk Bal:	40		

Period: Month:	0 MAR	1 APR	2 MAY	3 JUN	4 JUL	5 AUG	6 SEP	7 OCT	8 NOV
Customer Demand/Rqmts	0	100	90	60	70	40	10	10	10
Forecast Demand/Rqmts	0	10	10	40	30	70	100	100	120
TOTAL DEMAND/RQMTS	0	110	100	100	100	110	110	110	130
Scheduled Receipts	0	210		200					
Available after SS	30	130	30	130	30				
NET DEMAND	0	0	0	0	0	80	110	110	130
Planned Order Receipts	0					190		240	
PLANNED ORDER RELEASE	0			190		240			
Due to Customer Demand	0			20	>>>>>	—[10] 20	—[10] >>>>>	—[10]	—[10]
Due to Forecast Demand	0			170	>>>>>	—[70] 220	—[100] >>>>>	—[100]	—[120]
Due to Replenishing SS	0								
Planned On-Hand (w/o SS)	30	130	30	130	30	110	0	130	0

MSG: Activate <Scroll> buttons to extend demand horizon (12 history and 5 additional periods available)								
DETAILS	BOM	DETAILS	GRAPH	MODIFY	WHAT-IF	W/TREND		

Figure 8.16   Dependent-Demand Screen for Product 448A330G01

formation is made available is subject to the particular system design. Customer demands decrease in the future as shown in Periods 6 through 8. Since the product is MS-planned (refer to the FCST Technique field), the master planner has added increasing forecast quantities in the later periods to compensate. There are currently two scheduled receipts for released orders of 210 and 200 units. The 210 order quantity comes from the time period technique for Periods 1 and 2, while the 200 order quantity comes from demand for Periods 3 and 4.

After accounting for a 10-unit safety stock, the starting available balance is 30 units as shown in the March Period 0 column. Adding 30 and 210 and subtracting requirements of 110 in April leaves an available balance of 130. The bill of material fields in the heading indicate that there are three levels (Levels 0, 1, and 2), that part 448A330G01 is at Level 0 (indicating that it is the end-item) and that there are 15 different assemblies, component parts, or materials at the next level (1).

There is no Net Demand which cannot be handled by existing or on-order stock until Period 5 (80 units). At that point, the system has indicated that orders must be planned for receipt in Period 5 (190) and Period 7 (240). These orders are suggested for release two periods earlier in Periods 3 and 5 respectively, based on their 8-week lead time as shown at the top of the screen. Note that the first Planned Order for 190 does not have to be sufficient to cover all 220 units of demand in Periods 5 and 6 since there is an available beginning balance of 30 units.

The "Due to" planning lines towards the bottom of the screen may not be available in a traditional inventory system. They are included here to show how the quantities for each type of demand are segregated by the system to support full-pegging. The quantities in brackets [ ] indicate how the quantity to their left is applied to the demand.

- There are two lines of information shown in the "Due to Customer Demand" line. The first line of data beginning in Period 3 indicates that 20 units of the 190 Planned Order is applied to Customer Demand. Of the 20 units, 10 are required in Period 5 and the other 10 in Period 6. The second line which begins in Period 5 indicates that 20 units of the Planned Order for 240 is being applied to Customer Demand. Of the 20 units, 10 are required in Period 7 and 10 in Period 8. This is based on applying the 30 units available in Period 4 to Period 5 Customer Demand and then 10 units per period in Periods 5 through 8.

- There are two lines of information shown in the "Due to Forecast Demand" line. The first line of data beginning in Period 3 indicates that 170 units of the 190 Planned Order is applied to Forecast Demand. Of the 170 units, 70 are required in Period 5 and the other 100 in Period 6. The second line which begins in Period 5 indicates that 220 units of the Planned Order for 240 is being applied to Forecast Demand. Of the 220 units, 100 are required in Period 7 and 120 in Period 8.

- There is no requirement to replenish safety stock as shown in the "Due to Replenishing SS" line.

- The bottom line identifies the Planned On-Hand inventory.

In all cases, customer order demand in a period is satisfied first, followed by replenishing safety stock and then forecast orders. Customer orders take priority over all other types of demand.

SUMMARY

Demand is either dependent or independent. Demand which comes from a forecast for end-items, service parts, raw materials, and inexpensive components is referred to as being independent. This really means that it is independent of any real control the company has. If demand is determined from a Master Production Schedule and Material Requirements Planning bill of material explosion, it is *dependent* (on the demand at the higher level). Most companies must perform some level of forecasting at product levels, so even seemingly dependent parts at lower levels may still be based on independent-demand.

Perhaps the most accurate statement to make about forecasting is that forecasts are rarely accurate. However, this does not provide an excuse for a company to fail to expend the necessary effort to develop as accurate a forecast as possible. The causes of inaccuracy need to be identified and either eliminated or their effect minimized in the same way the causes of inventory inaccuracy must be addressed.

Statistical forecasting is a calculation-intensive process. For parts and products where future demand can be predicted based on the past, statistical techniques remove this calculation burden from the planner. Otherwise, fixed or variable forecasts established by the planner can be used where there is no past history or where whatever history there is cannot be relied on to predict the future.

It is important to select appropriate forecasting techniques and variables. It is more important to provide the results and alternatives to the planner in the form of graphs, tables, figures, and specific recommendations. A simple display of fields without knowing the effect of conditions affecting past history is of little value in and of itself for decision purposes. The best forecasting tool is a decision support system designed to answer the planner's questions.

- Which technique is providing the best forecast?

- Which field values would have provided the best forecast in the past?

- Which parts are consistently being underforecasted or overforecasted?

- How is forecast inaccuracy contributing to excess inventory levels?

- How is forecast inaccuracy contributing to safety stock investment?

- At what point should the forecast for a part be reviewed for change?

- What will likely happen if a specific change is made (what-if)?

Forecasting is a complicated process. It can be significantly more complicated and difficult if the system does not provide the tools required to streamline the process. Forecasting is definitely a key knowledge and skill area where extra education and training is appropriate.

Chapter 9

Order Quantities

When a company orders too much material, inventory turns and order-related costs are reduced while carrying and storage-related costs are increased. Conversely, customer service level increases, while handling costs decrease. Determining how much inventory to order is a fairly straightforward decision. Any number of techniques can provide very precise order quantities. Knowing when and how to apply the trade-offs and when to use which technique is the key to ordering the correct quantity. "Correct" is defined as that quantity which satisfies all of the company's various targets.

It is up to the planner to determine which order quantity is most reasonable from business and operating perspectives given the specific objectives to be achieved. This assessment of reasonableness does not come from using techniques but from a knowledge and understanding of current business conditions and management inventory targets. As business conditions and inventory targets change, the planner may need to change the material, part, assembly, and finished goods order quantity techniques as well. The inventory system needs to support the planner's choices in this respect.

The application of order quantity techniques typically varies based on the planning category within which the particular part or part category falls. All planning categories do not make use of all techniques. Those shown in Table 9.1 are representative.

This chapter covers the following planning categories and their related order quantity techniques and issues:

- *Inventory-planned* parts include those parts not planned via the Material Requirements Planning subsystem. This could include all parts if the company does not have an ERP/MRPII system. Otherwise, this may include Maintenance, Repair, and Operating supplies (MRO parts), service parts stocked to support the existing customer base, and floor stock items. These are all independent-demand categories, and parts may be ordered via the MRP system if it handles all of the company's part ordering.

Table 9.1   Order Quantity Techniques vs. Planning Categories

PLANNING CATEGORY	ECONOMIC TECHNIQUE(S)	TIME FRAME TECHNIQUE(S)	QUANTITY TECHNIQUE(S)	DEMAND TECHNIQUE(S)
Inventory-planned	Economic Order Quantity	Period Order Quantity	Fixed	
MRP-planned	Economic Order Quantity Least Total Cost Part Period Balancing	Period Order Quantity	Fixed	Lot-for-Lot
MS-planned		Period Order Quantity	Fixed	Lot-for-Lot
FAS-planned			Fixed	Lot-for-Lot

- *Material Requirements Planning-planned* parts include those parts which are subject to higher level demand, typically from the Master Schedule. With an ERP/MRPII System, dependent-demand parts below the Master Schedule level will be MRP-planned, while independent-demand parts will be either MRP or inventory-planned. If there are no inventory-planned parts per se, the MRP subsystem must be capable of planning parts which have independent-demand or some combination of dependent- and independent-demand.

- *Master Schedule-planned* products include customer-demand products, options, and certain parts or assemblies which are planned by the master planner. Material Requirements Planning-planned parts are dependent on (subject to) this demand at the MS level.

- *Final Assembly Schedule-planned* parts are specifically associated with a particular order. Parts at higher levels in the bill of material structure typically use a lot-for-lot technique until the MRP or inventory-planned level is reached. Lot-for-lot enables requirements and their associated purchase or work orders to be pegged directly to the customer order and parent assemblies. Note that some companies use a FAS in conjunction with a MS, while others use a FAS in place of a MS.

Example: How effectively order quantities are used to control inventory levels may depend on who is doing the ordering. A new purchasing manager was complaining that even with a staff of six buyers, each having their own assistant, the company was up to 30 days late in placing orders. They needed temporary help to get the backlog of orders placed. This individual could not understand how they could be facing inventory shortages with all the excess inventory they had on hand.

The company had no dedicated inventory planners. Instead, each buyer performed the buyer/planner role. They would each get a weekly requirements printout, manually add up the requirements until they decided they had enough for an order, and then place the order. There were no suggested order quantities, no cutoff based on lead time, and no imbedded inventory order quantity policies. It should be no surprise that these buyers overordered on a regular basis in order to eliminate that part as a problem for awhile. The old purchasing manager had been the manufacturing manager previously. This individual had encouraged purchasing excess materials to prevent stock-outs. The company has just implemented a new MRPII system.

What this company was doing wrong is the subject of this chapter. The excess inventory could have been controlled by providing constraints to what the buyers were ordering. There was no way to set these constraints, however, since there was no inventory system interface to the Material Requirements Planning system. Order quantity policies could have been established for one or more order quantity techniques to enable the computer to calculate the order quantities. This would have saved the buyer/planners the time it took to manually add up requirement quantities and would have established some ordering consistency. The requirements should have been generated nightly, saving lost time. Finally, the company could have separated the buyer and inventory planner functions. There was enough of a reason given the excess inventory levels and the lateness of the orders. The buyer/planners were simply not properly trained in fundamental inventory management principles, methodologies, and techniques, and they did not have the time to be planners, given the purchasing environment.

ORDER QUANTITY TECHNIQUES

Order quantity techniques fall into four basic categories. Economic techniques have many variations, only a few of which are addressed in this chapter. The surface appeal of an economic technique is that ordering and carrying cost trade-offs are explicitly quantified via an equation. This can lead to erroneous stocking level decisions unless the cost fields accurately represent the cost elements associated with ordering and carrying inventory. The other three categories do not use cost fields in their determination of order quantity. This leads to the perception that no ordering and carrying cost trade-off is occurring. However, companies implicitly apply cost trade-offs via the selection of qualifiers such as rounding quantities and price breaks and constraints in terms of minimum and maximum days supply, quantities, and dollars.

The four basic ordering technique categories are identified in Table 9.2.

Table 9.2   Order Quantity Categories

TECHNIQUE	FIXED ELEMENTS	VARIABLE ELEMENTS
Economic	Costs	Time Frame and Order Quantity
Time Frame	Time Frame	Demand and Order Quantity
Quantity	Order Quantity	Demand and Time Frame
Demand	Time Frame and/or Demand	Order Quantity

Economic: The economic order quantity is at the point where ordering cost equals carrying cost. Both time frame and quantity vary. From a practical perspective, a quantity in the vicinity of the calculated quantity is acceptable, due to the normal variability of the various fields used to calculate the EOQ. Note that EOQ equations are generally not applicable with the use of MRP subsystems and Just in Time philosophies where demand is dependent on the Master Schedule. Even so, it is necessary to understand the economic principles behind carrying and ordering cost trade-offs since all of the ordering techniques use them either explicitly or implicitly.

Time Frame: Demand within the time frame is summed to determine the order quantity. Demand and order quantity are the variables. Time frame quantities are commonly used with systems which sum and review demand using buckets (daily or weekly) or with lower cost parts ordered on a monthly or less frequent basis.

Quantity: Each order is for the same quantity. Time frame covered by the order is the variable, based on variability in demand. Fixed quantities make sense when unit loads are sized specifically for a given quantity as with returnable dunnage or when purchasing all or a specific portion of a standard economical production run.

Demand: Each order covers a specific customer or forecast demand requirement. The time frame may also be fixed at one day to group individual demands into at least a one day order quantity. As many orders (or line items on multiple item orders) are placed as there are unique requirements. Quantity is the variable (equal to the demand). Lot-for-lot quantities enable specific purchase or work orders to be allocated to specific customer orders where it is necessary to ensure revision, contract, or other tracking.

Calculated order quantities may also be adjusted by conditions imposed by the supplier or management. These can be due to production line capacity or workstation design, packaging considerations and ergonomics, transportation distance and truck, rail, or air cargo quantity constraints, product life cycle, price, size, risk of obsolescence, and so on. The end result of using any technique, however, is a mathematically correct (though probably different) result using the same basic demand, safety stock, and costing data.

It is difficult to generalize regarding which techniques are used in which types of companies. Much of the choice depends on the type of Enterprise or Manufacturing Resource Planning (ERP/MRPII), Material Requirements Planning (MRP), or inventory systems used. However, many companies use more than one order quantity technique to accommodate different demand and ordering profiles.

Companies in an integral environment must focus on three aspects of order quantities. The first is on those conditions which require companies to modify a calculated quantity. This enables the inventory manager and planner to fine-tune aspects of the integral strategy which relate to order quantities. The second order quantity aspect concerns the value of having an automatic order release (no planner review) capability. Manual reviews of each suggested order are time-consuming and costly, especially when ordering is repetitive and consistent. The third order quantity aspect relates to the various types of order quantity techniques normally found in systems or the literature.[1] Selection of one technique over another relates to the types of orders normally used by the company and accommodated by the computer system.

ORDER QUANTITY-RELATED ISSUES

The inventory manager and planner must satisfy a variety of conditions when initially selecting an order quantity technique. These conditions may change over time and so must be reviewed on a regular basis. Two key areas relate to the company's business (i.e., low vs. high volume, make-to-stock vs. engineer-to-order, and so on) and their products. These areas are then modified as applicable based on the product life cycles, suppliers, and their geographic distance from the company and any inventory-related targets.

Phase-in parts have no history upon which to base a statistical order quantity. This makes the EOQ equation difficult to use, for example, since it uses Annual Forecasted Demand in the numerator. This is typically calculated based on historical demand. The planner must use nonstatistical techniques such as time period or fixed quantity to establish order quantities for parts being phased-in or must initialize the Monthly Forecast field at some value.

Phase-out parts which will continue to experience service part demand may require an order quantity technique more suitable to independent-demand. Statistical or time period techniques may be applicable.

High Volume parts lend themselves to a receipt frequency based on part cost. Low quantities and frequent deliveries can be cost justified for high value parts. Less frequent deliveries of higher order quantities may be appropriate for lower cost parts. Time period ordering may be most appropriate.

Low Volume part order quantities may cost less than the company's cost to place the order. In this case, a higher days supply can be justified using time period ordering or a minimum constraint. For more expensive parts, purchasing or

---

1. Note that this chapter places a fair amount of emphasis on economic ordering techniques. Relative to the other techniques, the economic ones are more complex from an equation and logic perspective. However, the detail is included not so much as a recommendation to use them, but as an aid in understanding them when they are an option in a company's inventory or MRP system. The use of all techniques incorporates economic aspects in either an explicit or implicit manner. If the ordering, setup, unit, and carrying costs are relatively accurate, economic order quantities can always be used as a comparison against quantities determined via other techniques. If large differences among calculated quantities exist, the planner may need to recheck the technique and variables being used.

manufacturing the parts only when there is an actual customer demand may be the appropriate lot-for-lot ordering strategy.

Price Breaks are sometimes available when the volume produced generates economies of scale for the supplier. If there is demand for the additional parts, it may be to the company's advantage to purchase the extra quantity. In this situation, it may not really be a matter of incurring additional carrying costs, since the additional parts are essentially procured at little or no cost to the company (i.e., at less than standard cost in a standard cost environment). For example, purchasing five individual parts for $1.00 per unit for a total of $5.00 or 6 for $5.00 may be an actual cost savings for the company. The planner must recognize, however, that a standard cost system will value the units in inventory as if they were purchased for $1.00, rather than for $0.83. The savings will not be recognized through any inventory system reporting but will receive a favorable variance in cost accounting.

Risk of Obsolescence is a consideration for low value forecasted parts where the part cost justifies a larger order quantity than can be used in the short-term or midterm. Companies which establish order quantity rules based on purchasing the number of parts which equal some "purchase order cost" risk exceeding a practical maximum days supply for the part. For example, consider a policy of purchasing 100 parts to offset a $25.00 "purchase order cost" based on a $0.25 part cost. Having a maximum days supply equivalent to 40 parts will immediately result in the remaining 60 pieces becoming excess and then surplus and inactive if they are not used.

Risk of Stock-out increases as the number of exposures to stock-out increases. The smaller the order quantity, the greater the risk of stock-out. With independent-demand parts, risk of stock-out is compensated for with safety stock based on the planner-defined safety stock customer service percent. With dependent-demand parts, risk of stock-out or process loss is either not compensated for (since other related parts will be equally affected), compensated for by overplanning at the MS level, or compensated for by a scrap or yield factor.

Alternate Parts can be used to satisfy demand if the primary part is stock-out. The detriment is that the alternate may be more expensive. Another drawback is that the primary part history will not show the proper demand profile, while the alternate part shows an excess demand. This may result in the primary part not carrying enough safety stock based on statistical techniques, while the alternate part may carry too much. This is probably not a serious consideration unless it occurs frequently.

Sales Promotions or *Strike Protection* require the planner to override normal order quantity calculations to accommodate exception conditions. With a sales promotion, the intent is to stock additional parts for a short duration, in which case no significant carrying cost penalty will occur. With strike protection (i.e., stocking extra parts in case the supplier goes on strike), the risk is that the supplier may *not* go on strike, in which case the material remains in the excess inventory category for some period of time. For the supplier, this means that orders will reduce until the company consumes the excess inventory. If the supplier does go on strike and there are no alternate suppliers, the risk for the company is that the duration will exceed that which can be accommodated by existing inventory.

Equation values such as carrying and ordering cost are always "givens" in textbooks. These must be calculated for each company and inventory category in order to ensure any degree of relevancy.

ORDER QUANTITY CONDITIONS (CONSTRAINTS AND QUALIFIERS)

Order quantity techniques always provide precise order quantities. This precision may not make sense at times when considered in light of related parts and business conditions. Establishing constraints and qualifiers provides the ability to impose a certain level of order quantity consistency and control over otherwise mathematically-correct values.

Constraint and qualifier policy variables may be left at default values or changed for each individual part category or even every part number. Default values either have no effect on the calculated quantity or apply equally to all parts. Setting a 9999999 Maximum Order Quantity has no effect on the calculated Order Quantity. Setting a 120-day Maximum Days Supply for the C-item parts provides approximately three turns per year for 80 percent of the company's inventory.

Order quantity constraints provide upper or lower macroadjustment limits to the calculated quantity (refer to Figure 9.1). These constraints ensure that quantities will be neither higher nor lower than specified values. Regardless of the calculated quantity, the final quantity is constrained between the upper and lower limits, inclusive. Upper limits prevent too many months' supply from being ordered. Lower limits prevent numerous orders for inexpensive parts from being placed. Constraints fall into the three general categories of quantity, cost, and days supply. The inventory manager establishes constraints by inventory category.

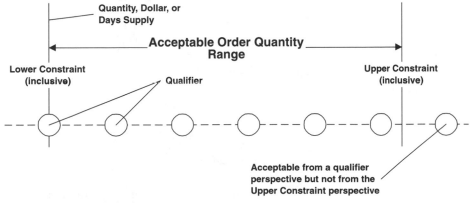

Figure 9.1 Order Quantity Conditions (Policy Decisions)

Order quantity qualifiers (if/then) provide a microadjustment mechanism to fine-tune calculated quantities. This enables the company to match order quantities with supplier or company-specified order multiples. Qualifiers also enable the planner to take advantage of price breaks. The inventory planners establish qualifiers by part.

Constraints take precedence over qualifiers. An 80-unit maximum order quantity (constraint) overrides a 100-unit rounding quantity (qualifier). However, if the 100-unit rounding quantity has been imposed by the supplier, an order for 80 units will result in a receipt and invoice for 100 units from the supplier regardless. The planner is responsible for ensuring that all order-related conditions are internally consistent with each other. As a minimum, the inventory system should provide a program which can be run on a periodic basis to check for discrepancies between constraints and qualifiers. A better alternative is to provide on-line edits to ensure consistency when the various field values are set.[2]

Table 9.3 identifies representative order quantity constraints and qualifiers. They are executed by the ordering program after the selected technique calculates the base quantity. The default values are set automatically for a new part in order to eliminate the constraint or qualifier from consideration.

Setting Constraints and Qualifiers by Category

Order quantity constraints and qualifiers are applied by inventory category or part. Any condition set at an inventory category level can usually be overridden at the part level. Systems do this by using the category value if the corresponding override field in the part master record is blank. Figure 9.2 illustrates constraint and qualifier conditions set by ABC category.

Setting both the minimum and maximum days supply to the same number has the same effect as setting a time period order quantity. Setting a Minimum $ Supply rounds the quantity up (if it is less than the minimum) until the order value matches the minimum. Setting a Maximum $ Supply either reduces the order quantity to the maximum (in which case multiple orders are suggested) or generates an action message to the inventory manager or other authorized individual with signature authority to approve and release the order.

Where different categories create conflicts with each other, the most rigid condition applies. However, the system design should prevent such conflicts by editing fields as they are entered or modified. Any conflicts are identified on-line as soon as the information is entered or forwarded to the planner or buyer via the message action system.

Setting Constraints and Qualifiers by Part

Once the category defaults are set by the inventory manager, the planner reviews them as they affect individual parts. The planner sets a different current value as

---

2. Note that order of precedence may vary among systems; the discussion here is representative.

Table 9.3 Order Quantity Constraints and Qualifiers

PART MASTER FIELD	TYPE	REPRESENTATIVE APPLICATIONS	DEFAULT
Minimum Quantity	Quantity Constraint	-Meet a supplier-specified minimum quantity -Meet a contractually agreed to minimum quantity -Set the minimum quantity to a specific price break quantity	1
Maximum Quantity	Quantity Constraint	-Meet physical storage restrictions -Meet physical shipping restrictions -Meet a supplier-specified maximum ordering quantity	9999999
Minimum Dollar	Cost Constraint	-Meet a part purchase order minimum charge -Meet a purchase order minimum charge -Establish an internal minimum purchase order value	$0.00
Maximum Dollar	Cost Constraint	-Establish inventory investment limits -Limit orders to defined signature authority levels -Establish cash flow limits	$999999
Minimum Days Supply	Time Constraint	-Prevent multiple orders in a time period -Reduce handling associated with frequent orders -Prevent many low value orders	1
Maximum Days Supply	Time Constraint	-Constrain the order quantity to meet inventory turns limits -Limit excessive purchases of low value parts -Limit parts with a shelf life to defined days supply	999
Price Break Quantity	Qualifier	-Take advantage of volume discounts if economical -Take advantage of shipping quantity economies -Order a minimum (price break) quantity	Y or N
Rounding Quantity	Qualifier	-Order in container multiples -Order in simple number multiples -Simplify cycle counting process	1
Minimum Demand Quantity	Qualifier	-Increase quantity to cover a complete requirement quantity -Increase quantity to cover a minimum or average "demand" -Increase quantity to cover a complete period quantity	1
Order Quantity Multiplier	Qualifier	-Adjust quantity to account for process scrap -Adjust quantity to account for destruct testing -Adjust quantity to account for inspection rejects	1

illustrated in Figure 9.3 if the category value does not strictly apply to the part. After that point, the planner should receive action messages to review any parts where there is a discrepancy between the category and part values whenever the category values change. A discrepancy may or may not interfere with the ordering process, depending on whether the particular constraint or qualifier applies or not. The Supplier column provides reference values related to the primary supplier, as applicable, or all suppliers, if selectable.

08:00am 07/01/YY	POL—Inventory Management Policies		
CATEGORY	ELEMENT	POLICY	COMMENT(S)
A - Daily	Minimum Days Supply	1	JIT parts from local suppliers
	Maximum Days Supply	1	
	Minimum $ Supply	$ 0	
	Maximum $ Supply	$50,000	
B - Alternate Days	Minimum Days Supply	2	JIT parts from milk runs
	Maximum Days Supply	2	
	Minimum $ Supply	$ 0	
	Maximum $ Supply	$20,000	
C - Weekly	Minimum Days Supply	5	Tote-size returnable dunnage parts
	Maximum Days Supply	5	
	Minimum $ Supply	$ 100	
	Maximum $ Supply	$ 500	
D - Biweekly	Minimum Days Supply	10	Overseas parts in container quantities
	Maximum Days Supply	10	
	Minimum $ Supply	$ 25	
	Maximum $ Supply	$ 250	
E - Monthly	Minimum Days Supply	20	Bulk unit load container parts
	Maximum Days Supply	40	
	Minimum $ Supply	$ 25	
	Maximum $ Supply	$ 100	
F - Quarterly	Minimum Days Supply	60	Hardware and inexpensive parts
	Maximum Days Supply	120	
	Minimum $ Supply	$ 25	
	Maximum $ Supply	$ 100	
CATEGORY	MODIFY		DETAILS	WHAT-IF

Figure 9.2   Inventory Category-Related Order Quantity Conditions

The following subsections provide an overview of the various order quantity qualifiers and constraints. Different systems handle them differently. Keep in mind that qualifiers are more likely to be set by the supplier or planner and constraints set by the inventory manager. Therefore, system edits treat qualifiers first. For example, if a quantity is rounded up and ends up exceeding a maximum order or dollar quantity constraint, the maximum constraint overrides the rounding.

Order Quantity Scrap or Yield Factors (Qualifier)

There are situations where losses result in less quantity output than raw material input. One way to account for this loss is to use a multiplier/divisor/adder with the original order quantity. The loss may be the result of the quality of material received from the supplier. Losses also occur within inspection, processing, or testing. Whatever the calculated quantity, it is factored before any other constraints or qualifiers are applied. The order quantity can then be increased but not reduced from this point.

08:00am 07/01/YY		Part-Related Order Quantity Conditions				
Part Number: 1234567890		Description: Switch			Inv U/M: EACH	
Raw Order Qty:	76	Adjusted OQ:	80		ORDER $: $52.00	
Supplier: Primary: 5607—ACME Electric						

Qualifiers:	Default	Current	Supplier	Last Update	Comments
Price Break Qtys:		Yes	Yes	03/24/YY	DO NOT increase OQ to take advantage
Rounding Qty:	1	10	10	08/14/YY	Parts come 10 per box
Order Qty Mult:	1.0000	1.0000		03/24/YY	

Constraints:					
Min Qty:	1	1	10	03/24/YY	Standard OQ > 10, so no problem
Max Qty:	9999999	99999999		03/24/YY	
Min $ Amt:	$ 0.00	$ 0.00		03/24/YY	
Max $ Amt:	$ 100.00	$ 100.00		03/24/YY	Orders >$100 req. mgmt. approval
Min Days Supply:	1	5		08/14/YY	1-week minimum
Max Days Supply:	240	90		08/14/YY	C-Item 3-month maximum

Supporting Information:

Supplier:	Primary—5687—Acme Electric, 880 Main Street, Grand Rapids, MI 49505-6098

Part Cost:	$ .65	PO $ Min:	$ 0.00
Lead Time:	5 Weeks	Part $ Min:	$ 0.00
Price Breaks:	Yes (10, 100, 500)		
Contract Minimum:	10 Units		

PREV. PART	PRICE BRKS	WHAT-IF	ALT. SUPLRS	DETAILS	NEXT PART

Figure 9.3 Inventory Part-Related Order Quantity Conditions

Process Yield—Processes which yield less than they start with must begin with a higher initial quantity. The starting quantity must allow for the full yield effect against both the starting quantity *and* the additional quantity added to offset the fallout. Yield uses a divisor.

Example: A process experiences a 3 percent process fallout (a 97 percent yield). To satisfy a 500-piece order quantity, begin with 516 units [500/(1 − 0.03)]. The product standard cost should include the yield factor since it is a cost of producing the product.

Destruct Inspection or *Testing*—Incoming, in-process, or finished goods may undergo destruct inspection or testing to confirm conformance to requirements or adequacy for usage. The specific quantity consumed by the testing process must be added to the initial quantity in order to ensure adequate required quantity levels. Destruct testing uses an adder or a table lookup value in the case of Acceptable Quality Level (AQL) testing.

Process Scrap—Scrap is an absolute, rather than a yield. It relates to the raw materials used for the part or product quantity produced. A common application of a scrap factor is for raw materials such as sheet steel or bar stock where the left-over materials cannot be used. The scrap factor is calculated knowing the original sheet or bar stock size and the usage quantity.

> *Example:* Experience has indicated that a certain printed circuit board is subject to a 5 percent scrap rate. Regardless of the order quantity, 5 percent (rounded up) is, therefore, added to the required quantity. For a 20-piece required quantity, the order quantity is 21 (20 + [20 × 0.05]).

Minimum Demand Quantity (Qualifier)

Some parts are almost solely subject to consistently large issues. These include two-bin parts where bulk materials are issued to floor stock, inexpensive parts where customers purchase in bulk quantities to obtain price breaks, and products subject to large production runs. With parts regularly subject to large issues, the system should ensure that at least as much inventory is ordered as may be required by a single large issue. This situation can be resolved by setting a high Fixed Order Quantity. An alternative is to let the system determine the Minimum Demand Quantity based on historical usage.

Largest (Average) Issue Quantity—The system can maintain fields which indicate the largest issue quantity of the part to date and the average issue quantity over the last n periods. If the planner elects to use them as a qualifier, a flag is set to include them in the order quantity constraint and qualifier logic.

Average Demand Per Period—For parts which are ordered infrequently, it may be advantageous to ensure that at least the average demand for a period (typically monthly) can be satisfied by an order. This average demand may be calculated via straight line or weighted techniques, based on productive issues.

Maximum Demand Per Period—For parts which are ordered infrequently, it may be advantageous to ensure that the maximum demand for a period (typically monthly) can be satisfied by an order. This demand is based on productive issues.

Rounding Quantity (Qualifier)

Regardless of the order quantity technique selected, there may be a need to round the calculated quantity. This may be imposed by the supplier (via the purchasing pricing file) or the planner (via the inventory part master). If the calculated quantity is not evenly divisible by the rounding quantity, the order is rounded up to the next rounding multiple.

Container Multiples—Many parts are purchased in standard container quantities but issued in individual units. This also applies to reels of wire issued in feet or inches, pounds of steel issued in sheets, 55-gallon drums issued in gallons, and to parts which may be repacked upon receipt or issue into standard containers. The rounding quantity is set to the purchase container size to ensure that even quantities are ordered.

Random Quantities—Order quantity techniques generate precise but random order quantities. Applying a rounding quantity in such cases simplifies the supplier's effort to fill the order and Receiving's effort to verify that the correct quantity was received.

Cycle Counting—It is much easier and faster to count standard versus random quantities. Cycle counting accuracy should increase if standard quantities are ordered and issued.

Price Break Quantity (Qualifier)

Suppliers may offer a price discount for large quantity purchases where economies of scale exist. These values should be considered by the order quantity logic for inventory-planned parts. If a price break is taken, the company obtains the benefit of lower unit costs. The risk is that a lower unit price may be obtained at a risk of surplus, excess, and inactive inventory costs. The decision to take advantage of a price break or not is based on total cost (quantity × price break price) for the order.

Maximum Days Supply (Constraint)

Maximum days supply is used to establish an upper order quantity limit. If the calculated quantity is greater than the maximum, the order quantity is replaced by the maximum. The standard cost should reflect this maximum in cases where the system would normally suggest a higher quantity, as may be the case for parts with low unit costs.

The 1-day demand is calculated by factoring forecasted monthly usage by days per month for independent-demand parts. The 1-day demand should ensure that a month with 18 workdays and a month with 22 workdays have the same "equivalent" monthly forecast.

Inventory Turns—A maximum days supply can be established for each inventory category in order to achieve a specific inventory turns target. This enables the planner to manage each part on an individual basis within the limits established for the various categories. For example, a particular product may have a 2-week average inventory target based on dollars. The planner is free to set maximum days supply in any manner for each part as long as the inventory turns target is achieved in total for the product.

Limit Order Quantity—Economic-based ordering techniques will typically result in large order quantities for inexpensive, high volume parts. This is unnecessary in many cases for parts which are obtainable in reasonably short lead times. The maximum days supply limits order quantities for these parts. For example, the EOQ for a part with a 100-unit demand per month, a unit cost of $0.10, an ordering cost of $25.00, and a 0.24 carrying cost factor is 1,582. A maximum days supply of 90 days limits the order to 300 units.

Shelf Life—Parts and materials which have a defined shelf life must be limited in quantity to something less. The maximum days supply must allow for the age of the parts or materials upon receipt since the aging process may have already started for parts shipped from supplier stock. A practical safety time based on normal demand variability should also be allowed to minimize the chance that the company will be left with material which has exceeded its shelf life. Pharmaceutical or food items commonly fall into this category. Machined parts may also have a one month or less shelf life dictated by the rust preventive coating applied during their final wash or packaging.

Minimum Order Quantity (Constraint)

The Minimum Order Quantity field establishes the lowest order quantity limit. If the calculated quantity is less than the minimum, the order quantity is replaced by the minimum.

Price Breaks—Where there are price breaks, the standard cost must at least reflect the cost at the minimum quantity in cases where the system will normally suggest a lower order quantity. For example, in cases where a supplier offers price breaks at 1, 10, 50, and ≥ 100 units, a minimum order quantity of 50 units should reflect at least a standard cost based on the 50-unit price break. However, the 100-unit price may be selected if orders will normally exceed 100-unit quantities.

Supplier Minimum—The supplier's minimum quantities should be entered into the Supplier's Minimum Order Quantity field in the purchasing pricing file. This ensures that the adjusted order quantity is greater than or equal to the supplier's minimum. Supplier minimums reflect normal production run quantities, container sizes, or simply economical transaction quantities. Supplier minimums typically apply to all customers. Figure 9.3 (in the Supplier column) displays a value for those suppliers with a stated minimum.

The purchase orders for a job shop using lot-for-lot may specifically state that the required quantity is to be supplied and not the minimum. These companies should be prepared to pay the full amount as if the minimum quantity is supplied unless another price is negotiated with the supplier. The cost per part is higher this way, but the company eliminates the generation of potentially excess or surplus stock. This can also occur when the maximum quantity, maximum days supply, or maximum order quantity is set at a lower level than the supplier minimum quantity.

Contractual Minimums—The company may have a contractual agreement with the supplier to purchase a minimum quantity on an order. This occurs with economies of scale, reserving capacity, agreeing to purchase a mill run quantity of a certain grade of steel, and so on. The purchase order will have a negotiated price and may entail some variability in actual delivered quantity based on process yields. These same minimums or prices may not apply to other customers who purchase in smaller quantities.

Minimum Dollar Amount (Constraint)

The Minimum Dollar Amount field establishes a lower order quantity limit. If the calculated order value is less than the minimum, the order quantity is increased. The intent is not to place a purchase or work order for less than a given dollar value.

Order Value Logic—Dollar minimums are typically established to get the most inventory for the money spent. The theory says that any order placed for less than the "cost" to place an order is not worth the time and effort. Therefore, at least as much inventory should be ordered as can be purchased for the minimum order cost. For example, consider a $25.00 minimum order cost imposed by a supplier for a part with a $5.00 setup per order. Ordering one unit results in an actual part "cost" of $20.00, two units cost $10.00, four units cost $5.00, five units cost $4.00, and 20 units cost $1.00 each for any parts costing $1.00 or less if purchased in higher quantities.

Part Purchase Order Minimum—There are cases where a supplier establishes a minimum purchase order charge for one or more parts or commodities but not as a general rule for all orders. In these instances, a minimum dollar amount can be established for the affected parts. Whenever the part is ordered from the supplier, the order quantity logic will ensure that at least as many parts are ordered as the minimum cost justifies.

Purchase Order Minimum—The planner or buyer can elect to order multiple line items on the order to satisfy the purchase order minimum where the minimum does not apply to a particular part. If the total is still less than the minimum, individual part order quantities can then be increased on a selective basis by the planner to get full value. If there are a limited number of high demand parts procured from the supplier, the planner may simply assign the purchase order minimum to each part.

Note that any minimum quantity or dollar constraint may result in being charged a higher actual part cost than is reflected in the standard cost. This has the appearance of a lower inventory investment based on standard cost while actually paying more for the material.

Maximum Order Quantity (Constraint)

The Maximum Order Quantity field establishes an upper order quantity limit. If the calculated quantity exceeds the maximum, the order quantity is replaced by the maximum. The standard cost should reflect this maximum quantity in cases where a higher quantity and more favorable price break would normally be used. For example, in cases where a supplier offers price breaks at 1, 10, 50, and ≥ 100 units, a maximum order quantity of 50 units should reflect at most a standard cost based on the 50-unit price break, rather than the more favorable cost based on a ≥ 100-unit price.

Supplier Maximum—Suppliers do not typically establish a maximum order quantity. However, there may be instances where raw materials are in short demand. This can be a situation where a new production process is just coming online, where an existing line is at maximum capacity, where production output is limited due to poor yields, where a new product is being protected from buyout by a small number of customers during a shortage situation, where promotional quantities are being limited to ensure broader availability, and so on. Companies try to get around these limitations by placing multiple orders. The supplier can then prioritize and sequence deliveries based on their marketing and sales strategy.

Storage Restrictions—Traditional carrying costs based on an average of all materials does not adequately account for the part's size in economic trade-off equations. The Maximum Quantity field can be used to ensure that each order fits allocated storage capacity in terms of unit load or individual container storage space. Economic criteria does not account for physical size, but unit loads of inexpensive parts take up as much space as expensive parts.

Figure 9.4 illustrates the total cubic feet required by standard $4' \times 4' \times 4'$ unit loads when rack spacing and access is included. Given a 48″ deep load and a rack system with a 6-inch flue space (pallet back-to-back dimensions), the following storage profile refers to the maximum size load. Storage density becomes progressively underutilized as the load gets smaller without a corresponding reduction in storage location height and as the storage aisle gets wider.

The aisle cubic footage is the amount of space required to obtain access to the pallet. It includes the full pallet and rack face dimension but is split 50/50 with the pallet across the aisle. With a 9.0-feet wide aisle, each pallet is allocated approximately 104 cubic feet (56″ width × 59.5″ height × 54″ aisle).

The unit load square feet does not include the pallet. For a maximum 48″ × 48″ × 48″ load minus a 5-inch height pallet, the material consumes 57.3 cubic feet per pallet.

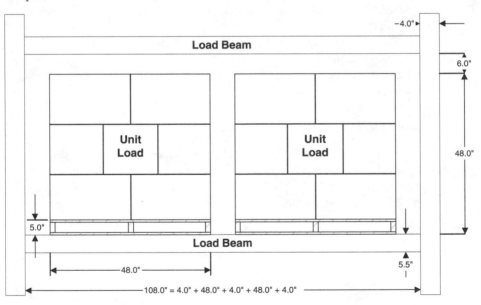

Rack Storage Utilization for a 9′ Storage Aisle

AISLE CUBIC FT	UNIT LOAD CUBIC FT	PALLET CUBIC FT	AIRSPACE CUBIC FT	RACK STRUCTURE CUBIC FT	UTILIZATION CUBIC FEET
104.0	57.3	6.7	24.1	11.6	58/204.4 = 28%

Figure 9.4   Representative Storage Space Requirements

The pallet cubic feet for a maximum size load are approximately 48 inches wide (down aisle) by 48 inches deep (cross-aisle or into the rack) by 5 inches high. Pallets, therefore, consume 6.7 cubic feet.

Airspace around the pallet requires approximately 4 inches on either side (the middle 4 inches is split between the two pallets), approximately 6 inches between the top of the pallet and the load beam, and 3 inches of flue space at the rear of the pallet. Note that flue space is subject to fire code requirements as dictated by insurance criteria and may also be affected by column dimensions. Airspace, therefore, consumes a minimum of 24 cubic feet per pallet.

The rack structure itself consists of uprights and load beams. Dimensions are subject to the load weight and height of the system. Given 4-inch wide uprights and 5.5-inch high load beams (including the dead space under the pallets and between the uprights), racking consumes approximately 12 cubic feet per pallet.

This scenario results in an overall utilization of approximately 28 percent before accounting for all other considerations. These considerations include crossing aisles, office space, and dead space lost to columns or other facility-related conditions. Therefore, even a well-utilized conventional storage system is likely to use only about 20 percent of the total cube for actual material. This is why it may be very economical for companies with a large unit load or miniload storage requirement to invest in Automated Storage and Retrieval Systems which make much better use of available height than conventional systems. Aisle widths alone will be half or less than that of a conventional pallet storage system.

Maximum Dollar Amount (Constraint)

The Maximum Dollar Amount field establishes an upper order quantity limit. If the calculated order value is greater than the maximum, the order quantity is constrained to the maximum dollar amount. The standard cost should reflect this maximum in cases where the system would normally suggest a higher quantity at a lower standard cost.

Cash Flow—For companies implementing a strict cash flow management strategy, reducing order quantities is an effective technique for reducing cash tied up in inventory. This can be accomplished by setting a maximum dollar limit on all or selected parts and forcing manual review of all orders. This will not eliminate demand or the need for the inventory but will spread the purchase dollar commitment over time in a manner which more closely matches cash inflow from sales. This policy generates more replenishment orders than normal and increases ordering and handling-related costs.

Exception Management—Setting a maximum dollar limit can be used to control the level of financial commitment being made with a new supplier, an alternate supplier, or a supplier under some type of quality sanction. Since the issue is financial in nature, using a maximum order quantity is inappropriate since quantity is not the real limiter.

Minimum Days Supply (Constraint)

The Minimum Days Supply field establishes a lower order quantity limit. If the calculated quantity is less than the minimum, the order quantity is replaced by the minimum. The standard cost should reflect this minimum in cases where the System would normally suggest a lower quantity, resulting in a higher standard cost where price breaks are available.

Single Orders Per Time Period—It is possible to suggest multiple orders due within the same period (which could be the same day) with ordering techniques which do not explicitly account for time period duration. Lot-for-lot parts can easily experience this problem. This is also a problem in systems where orders are reviewed on a weekly or monthly basis. For example, any fixed order quantity which is less than the time period demand will create a minimum of at least two suggested orders. Setting a minimum days supply ensures that unreasonable numbers of orders are not suggested, based on the part, demand profile, and supplier relationship.

Handling (and Freight) Reduction—Frequent receipts may result in higher freight costs and greater receipt processing, invoicing, handling, and storage or staging activities than the company considers reasonable for a particular part. This effort has a real cost which may not be adequately accounted for in economic-based ordering techniques based on average ordering and carrying costs. Companies address these types of costs through point-of-use staging, standard containers, returnable dunnage, supplier unloading, automated storage and handling, facility relayout to reduce handling distances, and so on. Setting a specific minimum days supply ensures that orders and receipts will be spread over time.

TYPES OF ORDERS

One of the issues companies face is whether to allow automatic release of purchase orders without planner or buyer review. Doing so is a management choice, though every system may not support the capability. Companies which use automatic release significantly reduce planner and buyer review times and minimize order release cycle times for repetitive purchases.

> *Example:* Consider a company with a volume of 20,000 purchase orders per year. Releasing 80 percent of the orders automatically means 16,000 purchase orders being released with no buyer review and little or no planner review. At 15 minutes per order, this adds up to 4,000 hours saved per year, which is two full-time people.

The disadvantages of automatic release are mostly a perception that control of the ordering process will be lessened or lost if an actual individual does not perform the review. This is a misconception, since a series of edits must be passed before a suggested order can be automatically released. These include the type of edits which the planner, inventory manager, buyer, and purchasing manager have already established and approved. If there is a need for the planner to manually review suggested order quantities, then perhaps inappropriate order quantity techniques are being used. In any case, a manual review can be forced by not setting the automatic release flags in the inventory and purchasing subsystems.

Companies exercise control over order quantities via a time-phased planning process. Once the order quantity technique and constraints are established, Material Requirements Planning systems migrate orders through a variety of phases. Each phase provides an opportunity to revise order quantities and dates. The phases are illustrated in Figure 9.5.

Planned Orders are created by the Material Requirements Planning subsystem in order to extend orders from the firm-planned horizon to the end of the planning horizon. The system may change order quantity and required date in each planning run. Planned orders may be added or deleted automatically. New orders may be created as new requirements are generated, as existing requirements change required dates, or as orders are released or replanned. Planned orders provide forward-planning visibility to both the company and the suppliers.

A *Firm-Planned Order* is a planned order which has entered the firm-plan horizon. This means that the required date is within a time frame where management has determined that the system can no longer change quantities and dates automatically. The closer to actual production that the system is allowed to change quantities and dates, the greater the system "nervousness" since orders may already be released for the lowest items in the bill of material structure. For example, an assembly with a 2-week manufacturing lead time may include a part with a 12-week lead time. Without a firm-planned horizon, the system may continue to modify the assembly order quantity and required date for 10 weeks after the purchase order for the long lead time part order has been released. Each change, no matter how minor to the assembly order, causes expedite, de-expedite, and order quantity modification action messages to be generated for the part.

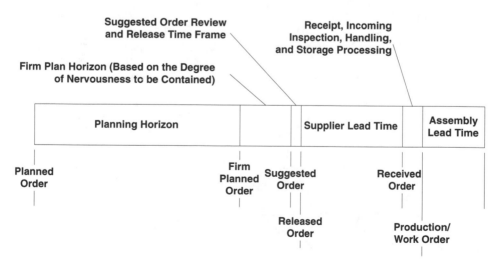

Figure 9.5   Order Phases Related to Timing

Nervousness is defined as numerous small changes to required dates and quantities of released orders. Nervousness increases in direct proportion to the cumulative lead time and the number of bill of material levels.

A *Suggested Order* is typically a firm-planned order which has become due for release. However, suggested orders may have been system-generated as a reaction to an anomaly condition such as a stock-out or excessive rate of usage. The mere fact that a suggested order exists on the planner's order action queue is proof that either the part is not set up for automatic release within the inventory system or that one or more automatic release edits failed. Suggested orders are reviewed and released via an ordering screen such as that shown in Figure 9.6.

If the planner makes no change to quantity or required date of a suggested order, no action is required regarding other orders. However, if any order quantity or date change is made by the planner, the system should immediately replan any affected firm-planned or planned orders to compensate. Note that a delay may also require replanning of higher level orders.

A *Released Order* is one which has been approved for purchase or manufacture by the MRP or inventory planner. If the suggested order cannot be converted directly into a purchase order via automatic release processing, the requisition is added to the buyer's queue and an intermediate classification of "pending release" may exist. This is updated to "released" once the requisition is converted into an order.

When reviewing a suggested order for release, the planner must verify that the lead time does not present a problem. The system should perform this check automatically. Figure 9.6 indicates that there is no lead time problem since the Required Date is later than the 4-week lead time. If there was a lead time problem, the magnitude of the problem would be displayed, along with the appropriate date. In such a case, the buyer should contact the supplier and verify that the shorter date can be achieved.

In an integrated system, automatic purchase order release is either enabled or disabled on a individual part basis. Failing any release edit adds the suggested order to the planner's order queue or to the buyer's queue, depending on whether the failed edit related to inventory or purchasing fields. Once all edits are passed, the order may be printed immediately or sent via electronic means (i.e., Electronic

```
08:00am 03/18/YY                    MSG—Suggested Order

Part Number:    1234567890  Description:   Switch            Inv U/M:   EA
Auto Rel Cd:    NO          Lead Time:     4 WKS
OQ Code:        Period OQ   Set Date:      01/12/YY  Reason: xxxxx xxx xxxxxxx x
Period:         Week        Receive Day:   Thursday
Forecast Usage: 20/day

ORDER SUFFIX    QUANTITY    REQD DATE          LD TIME PROBLEM
   120            100        04/24/YY               NO
  PREV. PART  |  RELEASE  |  OPEN ORDERS | REQUIREMENTS | HISTORY | NEXT PART
```

Figure 9.6   Suggested Order Release Screen

Data Interchange—EDI) to the supplier. A message is then added to the daily order log to confirm completion of the ordering process.

The following edits and action messages are representative of the automatic purchase order release process (refer to Table 9.4):

- The *Inventory Automatic Release Code* on the Inventory Master File must be set to "YES." If not, the suggested order is added to the Planner's Suggested Order Queue.

- The *Purchasing Automatic Release Code* in the Purchased Part File (part-specific) or Vendor Master File (vendor-specific) enables or disables automatic purchase order release processing. If not set, the buyer must manually review the requisition in order to release the order.

- A *Preferred Supplier* must be identified in the (Purchasing) Purchased Part File. Otherwise, there is no source for the order or supplier-specific data such as part cost, lead time, rounding quantity, and so on. An action message is added to the buyer's queue to specify a preferred supplier and the requisition is added to the Buyer's Order Queue.

- A *Unit Price* must be on the Purchasing Price File or standard cost in the Inventory Part Master File. If there are price breaks identified, the order quantity must fall within one of the defined price breaks. Otherwise, an order quantity which is less than the lowest price break quantity will fail the edit. For example, a supplier with a minimum order quantity of 10 will quote at least a 10-unit price. Any attempt to order a quantity less than 10 will result in a failed edit since there is no corresponding price for quantities from 1

Table 9.4   Effect of Failing Automatic Purchase Order Release Edits

Automatic Release Edits	Add Message to Planner's Message Action File	Add Suggested Order to Planner's Order Queue	Add Message to Buyer's Message Action File	Add Requisition to Buyer's Order Queue
Inventory Automatic Release Code = NO		X		
Purchasing Automatic Release Code = NO				X
Preferred Supplier Not Identified			X	X
Unit Price Mismatch with Quantity			X	X
Required Date Invalid	X	X		
Dollar Limit Mismatch	X	X		
Bill of Material Revision Mismatch			X	X
Unit of Measure Conversion Factor Mismatch	X	X		
Date of Last Order > 1 Year				X
Price Review and Verification > 1 Year			X	X

through 9, even though there is a "price" on file for quantities above 10. Not having a price on file which corresponds to the quantity creates an action message to the buyer to add one and adds the requisition to the Buyer's Order Queue.

- The *Required Date* must fall within some defined tolerance of the lead time (i.e., minus no more than one week). This tolerance should be specified on the Purchasing Price File for the part or as a general override on the Supplier Master File for all parts from that supplier. It indicates the minimum lead time the supplier will accommodate without specific prior agreement with the buyer. Forcing the buyer and planner to address the problem immediately prevents problems from escalating when the material becomes overdue.

- Any suggested order which exceeds the *maximum order quantity* or *dollar limit* will be added to the Planner's Order Queue for manual review and release. This may entail a second level of manual review and release by the buyer. Since it is possible to release multiple orders for small quantities to bypass the dollar limit edits, management may need some type of oversight report to track dollars by part or supplier.

- The Purchasing Price File should contain a reference field identifying the latest *bill of material revision* submitted to the supplier for pricing. If there is a discrepancy between this revision and the latest engineering revision, an action message is added to the Buyer's Order Queue to furnish the current drawings and information to the supplier. The requisition is added to the Buyer's Order Queue pending either new or confirmed pricing. Since all parts are not subject to revision control, there should be an additional field which indicates whether this edit is enabled or disabled.

- The Inventory Unit of Measure on the Inventory Master File must match or convert to the Purchasing Unit of Measure. If the two units of measure are not equal and there is no *Conversion Factor* on the Inventory Master File, an action message will be added to the Planner's Order Queue. For example, the Inventory Unit of Measure may be *feet* while the Purchasing Unit of Measure is *reels*. The Unit of Measure (U/M) Conversion Factor must convert the inventory units to purchasing units, such as Inventory U/M (Feet) $\times$ 500 Ft/Reel = Purchasing U/M (Reels).

- If the *Date of Last Order* is greater than some specified time duration (i.e., 1 year), the original conditions under which the Automatic Release code was set may no longer apply. In this case, a planner and buyer review can be forced just to make sure that conditions have not changed significantly.

- If the *Supplier Quotation* is no longer valid, the system can force a pricing verification. If the price has not changed, the order will continue to reflect the old price. If the price has changed, the order will reflect the new price. In either case, the *Price Valid Until Date* on the Purchasing Pricing File is updated to the current date to restart the Automatic Release Duration.

LOT-FOR-LOT (LFL OR L4L) ORDER QUANTITY

Companies needing to exactly match order quantity to individual customer requirements use the lot-for-lot technique. The order quantity exactly equals the requirement quantity. The order required date equals the requirement date as offset by receiving, incoming inspection, handling, storage and kitting, or issuing time, as applicable.

Depending on the system, all order quantity constraints and qualifiers are either bypassed or applied. Since lot-for-lot is essentially a direct match of order quantity to the requirement, any other conditions should normally be bypassed. A note may also appear on the purchase order specifically stating that the exact quantity must be supplied. This indicates to the supplier that the part is for a customer order and not for general stocking purposes. An overshipment may be returned to the supplier at their cost. An undershipment is not generally acceptable, though acceptance of a partial shipment may be authorized so production can begin while awaiting the balance.

The conditions under which the LFL technique may be considered include the following:

- Materials are purchased for a specific customer order or government or other type of contract. These materials cannot be applied to another order without a formal accounting transfer to track costs and ensure proper replacement.

- Parts may regularly undergo engineering revision changes over time in an engineer-to-order environment. Using the LFL technique ensures that only sufficient quantities of each revision are procured as are needed at that time.

- A company may generate orders directly from the Master Schedule for MS-planned parts or assemblies or from the Final Assembly Schedule subsystem. Such orders do not go through the MRP netting process and, therefore, directly match the individual requirements.

- Requirements may be filled on a one-for-one basis when a part is being phased-out. This limits any risk of generating excess, surplus, inactive, and obsolete inventory. This is more cost effective for expensive parts than inexpensive parts from an economic ordering perspective. However, phase-out parts do not conform to economic order quantity logic since demand is not continuing into the foreseeable future.

Perhaps the biggest advantage of lot-for-lot over other techniques is the ability to bypass MRP and generate orders directly from the bill of material explosion process. A company producing a control unit for a military application had a product with 600 purchased parts. Before the MRPII system was installed, each purchase order had to be manually typed, reviewed, and released. With the requirement for unique notes and government-related processing, the process required 6–8 weeks before the last order was placed.

After the MRPII system was implemented, special part notes and negotiated pricing was added to the purchasing system. The nightly Final Assembly Schedule system order explosion process generated all 600 purchase orders automatically in a mailer format. This consisted of a multipart 8½" × 11" form with a pre-stamped envelope on the outside and the purchase order, acknowledgment, and terms and conditions copies on the inside. The purchasing clerk's only task was to remove and file the top copy, leaving the preaddressed and postage-paid purchase orders to be mailed. This provided as much as a 6-week lead time reduction on many of the parts and significantly improved the company's ability to meet schedule commitments.

FIXED ORDER QUANTITY (FOQ)

The Fixed Order Quantity technique is the only one which places order quantity determination under full control of the planner. There is no logic other than that which the planner elects to use. The technique can be used with any safety stock and forecasting technique and can be varied at any time. The greater the demand, the more frequently the part is ordered. To use the technique, the planner sets the Order Type Code on the Part Master File to "FOQ" and enters the fixed quantity and related reference note, as applicable. Note that full control does not imply that the system order quantity constraints and qualifiers are bypassed.

Order, setup, unit, and carrying costs are not explicitly considered when setting the Fixed Order Quantity. However, the planner incorporates these costs implicitly in the determination by setting the fixed quantity lower for expensive parts and higher for inexpensive ones. The EOQ may be used as a comparison for a reasonableness check.

The conditions under which the FOQ technique may be considered include the following:

- Quantity may be fixed at a standard container (carton or tote), unit load (pallet, basket, or shipping rack), or shipping load (truck or shipping container) capacity.

- A Fixed Order Quantity may correspond to a specific financial target for purposes of managing cash flow or limiting financial risk. This provides a simple override to a calculated quantity. The alternative is to artificially change carrying cost, order cost, and other equation fields in order to force a particular order quantity result.

- There may be a requirement to purchase a supplier's standard production lot size. A fixed quantity prevents variation in demand from changing this standard quantity.

- The company may elect to take advantage of a particular supplier price break. The fixed quantity can be set at the associated price break quantity to prevent variation in demand from changing the order quantity.

- A new part having independent-demand may not have any past history upon which to base a forecast. Using a fixed quantity provides some stability for the supplier and manufacturing until such a history is established.

- A *Kanban* is essentially a fixed quantity. Each card or empty container is authorization to produce a specific quantity.

- Each part is ordered as a fixed quantity or multiple of the fixed quantity with a simple number scheme. Simple numbers are discussed in detail in Chapter 12. They are essentially numbers which divide evenly into the production schedule quantity.

One drawback of fixed order quantities is that they do not get reviewed and updated when conditions change. The additional Fixed Order Quantity related fields which address this problem include the following:

- *FOQ Date* is the date the fixed quantity was set.

- *Reason* is a note field used to identify why the planner elected to use the particular fixed quantity.

- *Reassess Date* is the date when the Fixed Order Quantity or technique selection decision should be reviewed. A report can be run periodically to identify those parts up for review. If the fixed quantity is left as is, the planner can set a new Reassess Date (a blank indicates that no planned reassessment is required).

The two-bin technique is a common usage of a Fixed Order Quantity technique. With a two-bin scheme, a reserve quantity is kept separated (but possibly in the same stocking location) from the regular inventory. When the last of the regular ("first bin") stock is issued, the reserve bin quantity ("second bin") is used. The reserve quantity is essentially the reorder point for the part and usually includes a generous safety stock. A card or some type of computer transaction is used to initiate the reorder process. Any order quantity technique may be used to establish the order quantity, but a fixed quantity is often the easiest. In this way, order quantity remains fixed. This makes it easier to separate the reserve from the regular stock when the new material is received. The time frame varies based on the demand rate.

PERIOD ORDER QUANTITY (POQ)

A Period Order Quantity covers the total demand for a specified number of periods. The time period remains constant while the order quantity varies since demand may vary from period to period. POQ is the opposite of the Fixed Order Quantity technique. Any safety stock or forecasting techniques may be used.

To use this method, the planner sets the Order Quantity Code to "POQ" and enters the selected time period in the Period field on the Part Master File. Periods may be selected as shifts, days, weeks, months, quarters, and so on. All requirements during a period are summed and ordered together. If there are no requirements, there is no order.

Period starting and ending points are normally associated with workdays or shifts. Weeks begin on Monday and end on Friday (or Sunday). Months begin on the first and end on the last day, and so on. However, for companies where it is necessary to schedule shipments to be received on specific days, periods may have some other type of cycle specified. For example, a part may have a 1-week period but be scheduled for receipt every Thursday. Demand in this case encompasses a Friday through Thursday time frame (assuming no emergency float beyond what is available by receiving one day ahead of time). For each day of additional float required, back off the receipt date by one day.

Period ordering is used in situations such as the following:

- *Regular Deliveries* or milk runs require a time period equal to the delivery or pickup cycle.

- *Part Sets* are established by ordering all demand for a period. Economic-type equations do not create part sets since part interdependencies are not considered. Setting the same Period Order Quantity for all parts for a product resolves this. This is one of the primary benefits from using a Material Requirements Planning system.

- *Inventory Investment* may be managed by setting order quantities equal to one or more periods (typically days, weeks, or months). A relevant safety stock can be established to ensure that the part will be reordered before it runs a risk of stocking-out.

Selecting time-dependent periods is essentially saying that time, rather than ordering cost vs. carrying cost economics, is the primary order quantity driver. The logic is intuitive and easy to understand. Order reviews occur on a regular basis. Demand for a period is considered when the lead time for each part falls into the order review window. If there is no demand, no order is suggested. Otherwise, the planner simply places an order to cover the demand in that period. In practice, however, planners tend to select shorter periods for expensive parts and longer periods for inexpensive parts. This implicitly applies economic conditions to the order quantity.

Time period logic lends itself to cases where the company and supplier have an agreement that the supplier will ship on a specific schedule. The supplier has visibility of future requirements, and the company can schedule receiving processes and related transportation. This is very consistent with Continuous Flow Manufacturing and Just in Time operating philosophies. Techniques which vary the order quantity and timing make this type of relationship more difficult to manage.

Note that orders are for the time period and are, therefore, scheduled to be received prior to the beginning of the time period. This may involve additional carrying costs if the demand is actually near the end of the time period. Keeping the time period short minimizes the carrying cost impact in this type of situation.

ECONOMIC ORDER QUANTITY (EOQ)

The logic used by the EOQ equation has good surface validity. Minimum total costs are achieved at the point where the cost to order material matches the cost to carry it. That is, carrying cost for material may be incurred up to the point where it becomes more economical to place another order.

The EOQ equation is used primarily for independent-demand parts where part dependencies do not exist. These parts are procured based on a forecast and there is no guarantee that materials will be used in the near term. Carrying cost, therefore, becomes an issue.

Dependent-demand environments which synchronize the flow of inventory with the rate of production are less concerned with balancing carrying and ordering costs. These parts have some assurance of being used in the near term. This does not invalidate the concept of trading-off ordering with carrying costs. However, these costs are not always the only or most relevant considerations.

EOQ or one of its derivatives can be used where other techniques are felt to be less appropriate. This is the inventory manager's or planner's decision. Perhaps the most appropriate use is as a comparison to order quantities calculated by other techniques. If there is a large difference between the EOQ and order quantities determined via other techniques, the planner can check to see if the other technique is using the most appropriate parameters. One of the reasons why economic equations are currently out of favor is that companies often do not know their own ordering and carrying costs with much accuracy. This reduces the credibility of any economic order quantity decisions.

The intent of this and the following subsections is to provide some understanding of several economic ordering techniques. Specifically, the subsections focus on the differentiators identified in Table 9.5:

The conditions under which the EOQ equation or one of its derivatives may be used are as follows:

1. The part demand can be extended (fairly) accurately over the part's planning horizon and potentially through the next 12 months. Demand is an approximation and may be steady, increasing, or decreasing.

2. Order and setup costs can be accurately determined for the part. In practice, one standard value tends to be applied for all parts. However, the requirement of accuracy per part or category implies an activity-based costing type of analysis. This enables realistic values to be assessed for each

Table 9.5 Economic Ordering Techniques

TECHNIQUE	TRADE-OFF	DIFFERENTIATOR FROM OTHER TECHNIQUES
EOQ—Economic Order Quantity	Ordering vs. Carrying Cost	Assumption of Steady Demand Usage Per Period
LTC—Least Total Cost	Ordering vs. Carrying Cost	Assumption of Variable Demand Usage Per Period
PPB—Part Period Balancing	Ordering vs. Carrying Cost	Fine-tuning of Variable Demand with Look-Forward/Look-Back Feature

part based on the actual variable ordering and carrying costs incurred. Order and setup costs are approximations.

3. Unit cost can be accurately determined for the part. Typically, standard cost is used if accounting uses a standard cost system. This places the accuracy within several percentage points of the actual purchase cost. The extra percentage accounts for related processing costs allocated to each part by cost accounting. Otherwise, actual cost from the Purchasing Pricing File for the price break quantity range is used. In either case, cost is usually accurately known.

4. Carrying cost can be accurately determined for the part. In practice, one standard value tends to be applied for all parts. Again, the requirement of accuracy per part implies an activity-based costing type of analysis and must satisfy the same arguments as order and setup costs as previously mentioned. Carrying cost is an approximation.

Note that information provided later in this section illustrates a technique for actually calculating ordering and carrying costs. These costs are always "givens" in classes on inventory management.

If the preceding conditions are met, an economic order quantity may still not be an obvious choice. Other factors which should be considered include the following:

- A random order quantity must be acceptable to both the company and the supplier. While order quantity qualifiers and constraints may be used to modify the EOQ, the implication is that the economic order quantity can be efficiently received, containerized, handled, stored, controlled, cycle counted, and issued.

- The carrying and ordering costs must accurately reflect all of the relevant order quantity costs. If the part deviates from the average used for the carrying and ordering costs, the EOQ will be inaccurate. Freight cost is always an area to check, especially if air freight or returnable dunnage is involved. Parts on automatic release cost significantly less to order than parts which require planner and/or buyer review and approval.

EOQ is easy to use. Trading-off carrying with ordering cost makes sense. Since companies often do not know what their real carrying and ordering costs are, it becomes easy to make an assumption that mistakes on the high side on some parts will be offset by mistakes on the low side on others. If this sounds like cycle counting logic, it is. Both have the primary purpose of balancing costs, not ensuring absolutely correct quantities.

Therefore, EOQ tends to be used for parts and operating environments where it is not the most appropriate. With the advent of MRP, JIT, Short Cycle/Agile/Lean Manufacturing, and so on, there are better techniques for synchronizing order quantity with demand. However, independent-demand parts will always require forecasting and some degree of economic decision-making regarding ordering and carrying cost trade-offs.

The most common version of the EOQ equation is shown following:

$$EOQ = \sqrt{\frac{2 \times \text{Annual Usage} \times (\text{Ordering Cost} + \text{Setup Cost})}{\text{Unit Cost} \times \text{Decimal Carrying Cost / Year}}}$$

Annual Usage is the projected usage over the next 12 months. Theoretically, the EOQ may be calculated once per year. However, companies often recalculate the annual usage on a monthly basis as (12 × Forecasted Monthly Usage). The more stable the forecast monthly usage, the more stable the EOQ.

Order Cost is the calculated cost of placing a purchase or production/work order. Separate costs by inventory category may be provided by cost accounting as described in later subsections.

Setup Cost is the supplier or manufacturing-provided cost to process each order or setup for each production run for the part. If applicable, this cost is quoted separately by the supplier and is incurred regardless of order quantity.

Unit Cost may be the part's standard cost or actual cost quoted by the supplier. If actual cost is being used and there are price breaks available, the price associated with the calculated quantity is used.

Carrying Cost is the annual decimal multiplier of the cost to carry one unit of inventory for one year. Companies commonly use values which are evenly divisible into months (e.g., 0.24) or values which are easy to multiply (e.g., 0.20 or 0.25). However, this negates the value of the field if the resultant carrying cost is not representative of the company's actual carrying cost. A carrying cost does not imply that a part has increased in value if held in inventory for one year (i.e., its value is now 1.24 × Unit Cost). Carrying cost indicates the level of expenses the company incurs to keep the part in inventory for one year. Note that if some value other than an annual value is used, the Annual Usage field must be changed accordingly. For example, if a 6-month usage is used in the numerator, a 6-month carrying cost rate is used in the denominator (e.g., 0.12 for a 0.24 annual rate).

A clear indication that the EOQ equation is invalid for a part is where the ordering and carrying costs are selected arbitrarily by the inventory manager. A second indication is when the equation values are manipulated by the planner in order to force a particular order quantity to be calculated.

Figure 9.7 indicates that the cost curve is fairly flat to either side of the mathematically calculated EOQ. This is a characteristic of the EOQ equation. It essentially means that any quantity near the calculated economic order quantity is still a relatively economic trade-off between the ordering and carrying cost. The flatness of the curve indicates that minor changes caused by rounding or other conditions may not have a significant effect on basic cost trade-offs.

Early in the JIT era, a high carrying cost in the EOQ equation was used as an argument to justify smaller order quantities and more frequent deliveries. This was used since existing computer systems could not accommodate JIT ordering

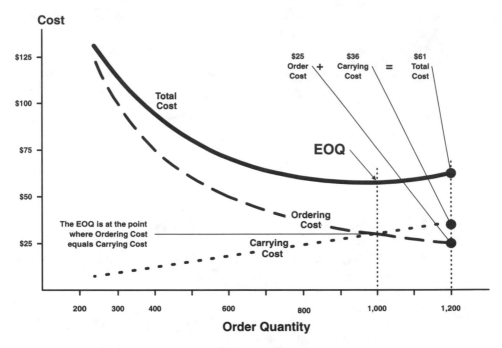

EOQ = ((2 X 1200 X [$20.00 + $5.00])/($0.25 X .24))$^{0.5}$ = 1,000 Units

ORDERS/YR	ORDER QUANTITY	ORDER COST	AVERAGE INVENTORY	CARRYING COST	TOTAL COST
1	1,200	$25	600 x $0.25 = $150.00	$36	$61.00
1.2	1,000	$29	500 x $0.25 = $125.00	$30	$59.00
2	600	$50	300 x $0.25 = $75.00	$18	$68.00
3	400	$75	200 x $0.25 = $50.00	$12	$87.00
4	300	$100	150 x $0.25 = $37.50	$9	$109.00
5	240	$125	120 x $0.25 = $30.00	$7	$132.00

Figure 9.7   Economic Order Quantity

logic. However, arbitrarily varying equation parameters cannot be considered as an engineered or economic justification of lower order quantities.

Example: Consider the effect on order quantity of substantially increasing the stated carrying cost for a part. Table 9.6a indicates that the carrying cost must be very high in order to justify weekly or daily receipts for an inexpensive part. It is less for a more expensive part as shown in Table 9.6b. In either case, manipulating the order quantity by changing the carrying cost is not a valid technique for supporting lower order quantities as was done for JIT. The benefits came in areas related to higher quality levels and shorter cycle times.

Table 9.6a   Effect of Carrying Cost on Order Quantity for an Inexpensive Part

0.24 CC	0.90 CC	1 Week OQ	1 Day OQ
548 units (5.5 months)	283 units (2.8 months)	Carrying Cost = 125	Carrying Cost = 3,125

Table 9.6b   Effect of Carrying Cost on Order Quantity for an Expensive Part

0.24 CC	0.90 CC	1 Week OQ	1 Day OQ
87 units (0.9 months)	45 units (0.5 months)	Carrying Cost = 3.125	Carrying Cost = 78.125

Annual Demand: 1,200 (100/month, 24/week at 50 weeks/yr, 4.8/day at 5 days/week)
Ordering Cost: $10.00
Setup Cost: $5.00
Unit Cost: $0.50 (inexpensive part) and $20.00 (expensive part)
Carrying Cost: 0.24 compared to 0.90 for the left-hand side in Tables 9.6a and 9.6b and calculated for the right-hand side as required to achieve stated time period order quantities.

Using the preceding example fields for an inexpensive part, increasing the carrying cost from 0.24 to 0.90 has the effect of nearly halving the order quantity. Establishing a period order quantity of one week or one day can be duplicated only by setting the carrying cost to 125 and 3,125 respectively. Clearly, short time frame coverage for an inexpensive part cannot be justified in terms of high carrying cost via the EOQ equation. It is probably not reasonable for the carrying cost to exceed 30 percent (0.30), much less the values shown in the right-hand side of the table.

Using the preceding example fields for an expensive part, increasing the carrying cost from 0.24 to 0.90 has the effect of roughly halving the order quantity. This is independent of part cost, since the same effect was determined in Table 9.6a. Establishing a period order quantity of one week or one day can be duplicated only by setting the carrying cost to 3.125 and 78.125 respectively. Again, the short time frame coverage for an expensive part cannot be justified in terms of carrying cost savings via the EOQ equation.

Carrying and Ordering Costs

The concepts of carrying and ordering costs at least used to be among the foundation principles of inventory management. Carrying cost is time and quantity dependent. The longer inventory is carried in inventory and the higher the part costs, the greater the carrying cost and the lower the ordering cost. The more frequently material is ordered, the more receiving-related costs are incurred and the lower the carrying cost. At some point, the cumulative cost to carry one more unit of inventory exceeds the cost to place another order. This point is the Economic Order Quantity (EOQ).

The EOQ equation has outlived its usefulness in companies with primarily dependent-demand. This raises a basic question. Are companies abandoning the principle of carrying and ordering cost trade-offs?

The easy answer is that materials should be received frequently and in small quantities. Carrying cost savings will then offset extra ordering costs. In short, companies should receive all materials Just in Time. The example in the previous subsection demonstrated the fallacy in this with respect to carrying and ordering costs.

> *Example*: One division of an automotive company began with a target of receiving all components daily. The analysis considered this delivery frequency in conjunction with a returnable dunnage program. The analysis results determined that a 100 percent Just in Time program would increase freight costs 250 percent over existing levels. The carrying cost savings were no where near this multimillion dollar freight cost increase. This did not even include the increased handling due to receiving partial pallets of material, rather than full unit loads.
>
> This was an unacceptable increase in freight costs. Therefore, the shipment frequency target was revised to receive materials in a profile covering daily, every other day, weekly, monthly, and quarterly shipments. The target was revised such that projected freight cost approximated existing levels. This allowed savings obtained via the returnable dunnage program to offset more frequent receipts of certain parts. The result was acceptance of JIT in principle, while recognizing the economic trade-offs of carrying and ordering costs.

Companies tend to forget that carrying and ordering costs are accounting constructs and not actual costs. They are an attempt to allocate period costs to parts and orders which are difficult to determine on an individual basis. As a consequence, they do not apply equally well to all parts at all times.

Carrying cost is an attempt to identify the company-related costs of having material in stock. The cost of money is the most significant portion of this cost. Perhaps the most important element which carrying cost does not consider is the value of having a part in stock to support the company's production requirements and customer service target. This factor must be considered separately. It is difficult to argue that stocking a year's supply of a part which has a 60-day lead time is providing any significant value to the company.

Note that ordering cost is not the average calculated by taking total purchasing, receiving, and storeroom departmental costs and allocating them across the orders for individual parts. For example, a $10 ordering cost calculated as the result of taking total annual departmental costs of $250,000 per year and dividing by the 25,000 orders placed per year is not a valid order cost for the EOQ equation.

Both carrying and ordering costs are based on variable elements. The test for variability is based on the costs which would be incurred if business levels increased by a given percentage. Fixed costs are not considered since they will exist regardless of any decision to place more or fewer orders.

Theory Behind Calculating Carrying and Ordering Costs

Carrying and ordering costs are company-specific. They consist of actual costs incurred to implement the inventory strategy. The general theory upon which carrying and ordering costs are based for purposes of calculating an Economic Order Quantity is described following:[3]

1. The most economic size for a replenishment order is developed by minimizing the total of carrying costs and ordering costs. The optimum order size is the EOQ.

2. Only variable elements of ordering and carrying cost are incorporated into the cost factors used in the EOQ formula. For purposes of defining included costs, a sustained increase in inventory level or ordering activity must be considered. An increase of 25 percent is used in this book, though an increase requiring an addition of one more person is as valid. Costs which fluctuate within this range are considered variable and are included when calculating ordering and carrying costs. If, for example, heat, lighting, and equipment-related costs do not vary, they would not be included. If existing personnel cannot handle a 25 percent increase in workload with casual overtime, additional labor cost would be included.

3. Semivariable ordering and carrying cost factors are excluded from the EOQ formula since they may or may not apply to a particular ordering decision. These factors include supplier quantity or dollar minimums, order quantity rounding amounts, price breaks at various order quantities, setup reductions if certain parts are ordered together, and order quantity limiters due to truckload, railcar, or other in-plant physical space limitations. The effect of these types of conditions is evaluated as order quantity adjustments after the EOQ is calculated. Relatively small changes do not cause a significant cost penalty since the EOQ curve is fairly flat around the actual EOQ point.

4. Consideration must be given to the fact that action based on these carrying and ordering costs will take place in the future. Therefore, the costs used should be based on expected future costs and not solely on historical data. This is especially significant in companies where new product lines will be added or existing lines expanded during the coming year. Carrying and or-

---

3. The basis of this information for calculating carrying and ordering costs came from work with Westinghouse Electric in the 1970s prior to the use of MRP. In those days, the controller's manual contained the equations or tables for calculating costs needed for the EOQ equation. The tables on the following pages are representative; each company would either have their own or would use values based on some other means of calculation.

dering costs must represent the time period during which the ordering decisions will be made. With the EOQ equation, this typically encompasses a 1-year time frame.

5. Costs may vary among Raw, WIP, and FG inventory categories. As long as the costs for each individual category are within approximately 10 percent of the value calculated for total inventory, the total inventory average may be used. A 10 percent variability is reasonable given the normal variability of the cost elements used to develop the ordering and carrying costs. Separate category rates should be used beyond the 10 percent range. The inventory system should accommodate unique ordering and carrying costs by inventory category.

6. Carrying and ordering costs may vary significantly from one part, product, product family, or product line within an inventory category. For example, the risk of obsolescence is much greater for products and parts being phased-out than for those being phased-in. With this as a carrying cost element, parts being phased-out have a higher carrying cost than similar parts being phased-in. It may also be necessary to exclude such parts or products from the category calculation so as not to skew the results. A common sense rule should also be applied for parts or products which are not truly represented by the category averages. Very high dollar items fall into this category. These types of items tend not to be purchased based on a trade-off between carrying and ordering costs. The planner must be aware that averages across a large mix of parts may not be truly representative of the outlying points.

7. Setup costs must be considered separately for purchased parts if the supplier states them separately. This cost should be in the Purchasing Pricing File in the purchasing subsystem. Note that one supplier for a part may include the setup cost in the unit cost while another may specify it as a separate setup cost. This may indicate the difference between a distributor who stocks the part and the actual manufacturer who produces it to order. The setup cost may even be unknown to the planner if it is identified in the purchasing system and appears on the supplier invoice as a separate line item. The planner should make a buy decision knowing the total cost, not just the unit cost.

8. Costs should be used based on those for the preferred supplier. This may not always be apparent at an inventory level if the company does not automatically pass purchasing costs to the inventory system. For example, in a standard cost environment, all suppliers appear to have the same unit cost since ordering decisions are based on the standard cost. The assumption is that the standard cost represents the preferred supplier's price and that the part will be purchased from the preferred supplier. Any difference is accounted for as a cost variation by accounting. If pricing from a particular supplier differs significantly from the standard cost, there must be a way to account for it. Otherwise, as much as a year's worth of ordering decisions (in companies where standard cost is revised once per year) will be made based on erroneous cost data.

Important Note

The balance between carrying and ordering cost becomes less applicable to ordering decisions as companies rely more on lot-for-lot, time period, and fixed order quantity techniques. Costs become less variable and more fixed as the level of automation and computerization increases in an integral environment. As carrying and ordering cost trade-offs become less relevant because of volume flexibility provided through the integral infrastructure, so does the validity of the EOQ equation. This is the reason why some companies can use other techniques without incurring the substantial ordering or carrying cost penalties suggested by the EOQ equation. Keep in mind, however, that frequent ordering may still incur a very real freight cost penalty. Therefore, companies are not incurring ordering versus carrying cost penalties if their infrastructure provides the flexibility required to accommodate volume changes. However, they may still be incurring inefficiency-related cost penalties due to not using automatic order release and double-handling materials.

Periodic Update of Carrying and Ordering Costs

Carrying and ordering costs must be reviewed and updated on a periodic basis. This should incorporate any business or strategic changes being considered for the coming period, as well as reflect demonstrated historical costs.

1. Companies typically revise carrying and ordering costs on an annual basis. The timing coincides with update of the standard cost in standard cost environments. A cost change may also occur due to adding a new product line or making a facility expansion.

2. A rate of return for investing capital in inventory must be established for the coming year. This borrowing rate varies among companies based on their financial situation. It is inappropriate to increase the straight borrowing rate used in the carrying cost calculation to reflect an internal rate of return consistent with capital budgeting and justification guidelines. Inventory and capital investments are not equivalent.

Note that if insurance is a fixed cost negotiated with the insurance carrier on an annual basis, it is excluded from the carrying cost. As a fixed rate, insurance is not affected by inventory level. Only variable costs are included.

Carrying Cost Worksheets

The easiest way to calculate carrying and ordering costs is to create a spreadsheet or database application. Downloaded values from the inventory database provide the required monthly averages by inventory category. Other management parameters or operating values are then applied as applicable. Once the results are calculated, they are uploaded to the Part Master File via a conversion program.

Table 9.7   Carrying Cost (Dollars in Thousands) per Inventory Category

CATEGORY	NOTE	MATL (000's)	PURCH. PARTS (000's)	MANUF. PARTS (000's)	FG IN PLANT (000's)	MRO SUPPLIES (000's)	TOTAL (000's)
I. INVENTORY INVESTMENT							
A. Average Inventory	(1)	100	1,900	300	1,000	100	3,400
II. CARRYING COST							
A. Storage Costs							
1. Rent	(2)	0	0	0	0	0	0
2. Maintenance	(2)	0	0	0	0	0	0
3. Utilities	(2)	1.00	5.00	0.50	3.00	0.50	10.00
4. Operators (issuing-related)	(3)	1.25	125.00	25.00	25.00	2.500	178.75
B. Inventory Dollars							
1. Rate of Return	(4)	15.00	285.00	45.00	150.00	15.00	510.00
2. Taxes	(5)	5.05	95.95	15.15	50.50	5.05	171.70
3. Obsolescence	(6)	0.25	15.00	0.25	00	0	15.50
C. Part Master Maintenance							
1. Cycle Counting	(7)	0	11.78	0.62	0	0	12.40
D. Total Annual Carrying Cost (A + B + C)		22.55	537.73	86.52	228.50	23.05	898.35
III. CARRYING COST RATE (IID/IA)(10)		0.23	0.28	0.29	0.23	0.23	0.26

Note: Values are for example purposes only.

Representative worksheets are provided in the following pages for reference purposes.[4] Table 9.7 provides the summary level worksheet. The inventory accounting categories vary by company but may include:

- Material (sheet steel, bar stock, liquids, and so on, used to manufacture parts)
- Purchased Parts (purchased parts and assemblies)
- Manufactured Parts (manufactured parts and assemblies)
- Finished Goods in Plant (finished goods stored within the plant; an alternative might be finished goods stored in a remote warehouse)
- Supplies (maintenance, repair, and operating supplies)

The test for variability in the following worksheets is whether an increase of 25 percent causes the company to incur additional variable costs. All costs are annual costs and exclude those of an abnormal or nonrecurring nature such as may be a result of temporary warehousing during a construction phase or inventory buildup to cover an anticipated strike or material shortage.

Values may be factored up or down based on any specific knowledge of the upcoming year if historical trends are not expected to hold. All ordering is assumed

---

4. Note that the work sheets apply to calculation of ordering and carrying costs for the EOQ equation. The same principles can be applied to support an Activity Based Costing analysis. The key is to assign realistic costs to the proper categories as required to support the decision processes of the company.

to be via the EOQ equation. To do this, if applicable, the inventory system should maintain the following set of fields for both carrying and ordering cost:

- Carrying and Ordering Cost by Category
- Override Carrying and Ordering Cost (Category Cost × Multiplier)
- Multiplier (default = 1.00) if the Category Cost should be modified
- Reason for selecting a multiplier other than 1.00
- Name of individual who changed the Multiplier
- Reassess Date upon which the Multiplier should be reviewed for change

The summary sheet indicates that carrying cost ranges from 23 to 29 percent for the categories indicated. The overall average is 26 percent. As 26 percent is approximately +/–10 percent of the upper and lower values, the company can elect to use either the individual carrying costs by category or the 26 percent average for everything.

(Check company controller's manual for specifics if company uses EOQ.)

1. *Average Inventory*—The easiest method of calculating average inventory is to take the average of month-end inventory for the preceding 12 months. Since carrying cost is applied to future orders, a more appropriate value may be the target month-end inventory for the coming 12 months. Either the historical average may be factored as shown at the bottom of the worksheet, or the actual monthly targets may be used as is. Month-end values are typically used as opposed to higher midmonth values since financial record-keeping is based on financial month-end closings. Month-end values which approximate calendar months are likely to be more readily available than averages based on other criteria. Refer to Table 9.7.1.

2. *Rent, Maintenance, and Utilities*—The variable portion of rent, maintenance, and utilities is included. This may be significant if rented warehouse space is required or zero if existing facilities can accommodate the "25 percent" increase. Any requirement to operate additional hours or extra shifts is considered a variable expense only if maintenance and utilities relate to actual hours of operation. Companies which do not know the specific amount related to carrying and ordering cost functions may allocate total company costs to purchasing, receiving, inspection, stores, and so on, based on floor space. Refer to Table 9.7.2.

3. *Operators*—The variable portion of operator costs associated with processing issues is included. Other operator duties are encompassed by ordering cost or other aspects of carrying cost (see notes 8 and 9). Refer to Table 9.7.3.

4. *Rate of Return*—Management specifies the rate of return as a percentage. This percentage is then multiplied by the average inventory by category to develop a projection of the cost to borrow money and invest it in inventory. Refer to Table 9.7.4.

Table 9.7.1   Average Inventory Worksheet

MONTH (Either Calendar or Fiscal Year)	MATL (000's)	PURCH. PARTS (000's)	MANUF. PARTS (000's)	FG IN PLANT (000's)	MRO SUPPLIES (000's)	TOTAL (000's)
January	$100	$1,900	$300	$1,000	$100	$3,400
February	100	1,900	300	1,000	100	3,400
March	100	1,800	300	1,000	100	3,300
April	100	1,800	400	1,100	100	3,500
May	110	1,900	400	1,100	100	3,610
June	110	1,900	300	1,000	100	3,410
July	100	2,000	300	1,000	100	3,500
August	100	2,000	200	900	100	3,300
September	90	1,900	200	900	100	3,190
October	90	1,900	300	1,000	100	3,390
November	100	1,900	300	1,000	100	3,400
December	100	1,900	300	1,000	100	3,400
Total / 12	100	1,900	300	1,000	100	3,400
Multiplier	1.00	1.00	1.00	1.00	1.00	1.00
AVG. INV.	$100	$1,900	$300	$1,000	$100	$3,400

Table 9.7.2   Rent, Maintenance, and Utilities Worksheet

	%	RENT	%	MAINT.	%	UTILITIES
Company Total	100%	0	100%	0	100%	$100,000
Variable Portion	0%	0	0%	0	10%	$10,000

ALLOCATION:
  Raw Material
  Finished Purchased Parts
  Finished Manufactured Parts
  FG in Plant
  MRO Supplies
	
	60%
	10%
	3%
	20%
	7%
		
		0
		0
		0
		0
		0
			
			60%
			10%
			3%
			20%
			7%
				
				0
				0
				0
				0
				0
					
					60%
					10%
					3%
					20%
					7%
						
						1,000
						5,000
						500
						3,000
						500

Note: For this example, rent and maintenance costs will not increase with a 25 percent inventory increase; utilities will increase 10 percent to accommodate overtime.

Table 9.7.3   Operator Worksheet

ISSUE PROCESSING	MATL	PURCH. PARTS	MANUF. PARTS	FG IN PLANT	MRO SUPPLIES	TOTAL
Issues/Year	$1,000	$100,000	$20,000	$20,000	$2,000	$143,000
Hours/Issue	0.05	0.05	0.05	0.05	0.05	
$/Hour	25	25	25	25	25	
$/Year	1,250	125,000	25,000	25,000	2,500	178,750
Multiplier	1.00	1.00	1.00	1.00	1.00	1.00
OPER. $/YR	$1,250	$125,000	$25,000	$25,000	$2,500	$178,750

Note: A full 25 percent increase is included as a variable cost.

Table 9.7.4   Rate of Return Worksheet

	MATL (000's)	PURCH. PARTS (000's)	MANUF. PARTS (000's)	FG IN PLANT (000's)	MRO SUPPLIES (000's)	TOTAL (000's)
Average Inventory	$100	$1,900	$300	$1,000	$100	$3,400
@15%	$15	$285	$45	$150	$15	$510

Note: A full 25 percent increase is included as a variable cost.

5. *Taxes*—Consider state and local taxes if either or both are based on an average inventory value such as average monthly balance or average yearly balance. Refer to Table 9.7.5.

6. *Obsolescence*—The risk that inventory will become excess and then surplus, inactive, and/or obsolete[5] is greater the larger the order quantity and the lower the demand. It is also greater for nonstandard parts where there is less opportunity to reapply overages from one product to another. One way of estimating the upcoming year's obsolescence is to use a multiyear average. This is calculated by taking the current inactive balance less the previous year's inactive, plus the previous year's scrap charges and developing an average. Note that delaying the inevitable (i.e. not scrapping materials which are obsolete) causes the carrying cost to increase over time. This can penalize future order decisions based on decisions which occurred years ago. Refer to Table 9.7.6.

7. *Cycle Counting Inventory*—Include the cost of operator, planner, manager, and cost accounting personnel time to take and reconcile inventory bal-

---

5. Excess, surplus, inactive, and obsolete are accounting categories which change over time as a part progresses through the phase-out process. These categories vary by company. Refer to the controller's manual.

Table 9.7.5 Taxes Worksheet

TAXES		MATL (000's)	PURCH. PARTS (000's)	MANUF. PARTS (000's)	FG IN PLANT (000's)	SUPPLIES (000's)	TOTAL (000's)
Avg. Inv. $	A	$100	$1,900	$300	$1,000	$100	$3,400
State Tax %	B	5%	5%	5%	5%	5%	
State Tax	D = A x B	$5	95	15	50	5	170
Local Tax %	C	1%	1%	1%	1%	1%	
Local Tax	E = A x C	$0.05	0.95	0.15	0.50	0.05	1.70
Total Tax	D + E	$5	$96	$15	$51	$5	$172

Table 9.7.6 Obsolescence Worksheet

INACTIVE	MATL (000's)	PURCH. PARTS (000's)	MANUF. PARTS (000's)	FG IN PLANT (000's)	MRO SUPPLIES (000's)	TOTAL (000's)
YEAR 1 (Past Year) Year 1 Inactive $ − Year 2 Inactive $ + Year 2 Scrap $						
YEAR 2 Year 1 Inactive $ −Year 2 Inactive $ + Year 2 Scrap $						
YEAR 3 Year 1 Inactive $ − Year 2 Inactive $ + Year 2 Scrap $						
3-Year Average	1	60	1	0	0	62
@25%	0	15	0	0	0	16

Note: Just the 3-year average is shown. Not scrapping inactive and obsolete inventory increases the "financial" inventory level and reduces inventory turns (refer to Chapter 2).

ances. These costs are spread throughout the year. Refer to Tables 9.7.7a and 9.7.7b.

One of the historical problems with the application of carrying costs is that the allocation process is based on part cost. With the EOQ, carrying cost is in the denominator of the equation and is calculated as Part Cost × Carrying Cost Decimal. This has the effect of assuming the following:

- Expensive parts incur proportionately more storage-related costs than less expensive parts. This means that expensive parts require more storage space

Table 9.7.7a Cycle Counting Worksheet

CATEGORY	NO. OF PERSONNEL	% OF TIME	$/YEAR	TOTAL ANNUAL COST
Operator	10	12.5%	$30,000	$37,500
Planner	2	10.0%	$40,000	$8,000
Inventory Manager	1	2.0%	$80,000	$1,600
Cost Accounting	1	5.0%	$50,000	$2,500
TOTAL × 25%				$12,400

Note: Full 25 percent increase included as variable.

Table 9.7.7b Cycle Counting Costs by Inventory Category

	MATL (000's)	PURCH. PARTS (000's)	MANUF. PARTS (000's)	FG IN PLANT (000's)	MRO SUPPLIES (000's)	TOTAL (000's)
Average Inventory	$100	$1,900	$300	$1,000	$100	$3,400
% by Category	0%	95%	5%	0%	0%	100%
@ 12,400	$0	$11,780	$620	$0	$0	$12,400

Note: A full 25 percent increase is included as a variable cost.

(i.e., incur a larger portion of the rent, maintenance, and utilities expenses) and incur more issuing-related costs than less expensive parts. This is a very questionable assumption.

- Expensive parts incur proportionately more financial-related costs than less expensive parts. This is certainly true with respect to rate of return and taxes but may not be true for obsolescence.

If the preceding assumptions are not reasonable for certain parts, then the carrying cost established via the allocation process is invalid. Justifying manufacturing investments on the basis of reducing such costs will also be invalid. If it is extremely important to have a correct carrying cost for a part, a weighting scheme based on storage costs and inventory dollars should be developed. In this way, a bulky but inexpensive part is assigned a greater proportion of storage costs but a lesser proportion of rate of return dollars, for example. A small but expensive part is assigned a lesser proportion of storage costs and a greater proportion of rate of return dollars.

As a justification for carrying cost, consider the following. One of the basic premises of carrying cost is that costs are or will be incurred for the inventory if a significant increase in inventory level were to occur. One of the major cost elements is rate of return. If a company delays payments to suppliers long enough that customer payments partially or largely offset the supplier payments, should

Table 9.8   Purchased Part Order Cost

CATEGORY	MATL	PURCH. PARTS	FG IN PLANT	TOTAL
I. ORDER PLACEMENT COST A. Inventory Control (Planner)	5% $384	93% $7,142	2% $154	100% $7,680

B. Purchasing
  1. Placing Order
  2. Writing Order
  3. Filing Orders
  4. Materials
  5. Total
	5,000	93,000	2,000	100,000

C. Total Annual Variable Placement Costs (A + B5)	5,384	100,142	2,154	107,680

II. ORDER RECEIPT COST
A. Purchasing
  1. Expediting
  2. Expedite Reports and Related Processing
  3. Invoice Approval
  4. Communications
  5. Total
	1,250	23,250	500	25,000

B. Receiving and Incoming Inspection
  1. Receive Materials and Remove Paperwork
  2. Incoming Inspection/Disposition Processing
  3. Purchase Order Receipt Processing
  4. Material Handling from Receiving to Storage
  5. Total
	8,700	161,820	3,480	174,000

C. Storeroom
  1. Store Materials
  2. Process Inventory Receipt
  3. Total
	4,950	92,070	1,980	99,000

D. Inventory Control (Planner) Daily Maintenance	704	11,904	192	12,800

E. Accounting
  1. Match Receipts to Invoices
  2. Documentation and Invoice Payments
  3. Materials (paperwork, reports, checks, and so on)
  4. Total
	2,136	40,920	944	44,000

F. Total Annual Variable Receipt Cost (A5 + B5 + C3 + D + E4)	17,740	329,964	7,096	354,800
III. NUMBER OF PURCHASED PART (STOCK) ORDERS (CURRENT VOLUME × 25%)	250	5,000	125	5,375
IV. ORDERING COST A. Total Annual Variable Cost (IC + IIF) B. Variable Cost per Order (IVA / III)	$23,124 $92	$430,106 $86	$9,250 $74	$462,480 $86

rate of return be excluded from carrying cost since it is no longer a factor? The effect would be to reduce carrying cost and increase economic order quantities. This in turn would then cause inventory levels to increase above the rate which could be sold before payment was due. This higher inventory level would then incur the rate of return portion of carrying cost. Therefore, carrying cost is a real consideration when considering how much to order.

Ordering Cost Worksheets

As with carrying costs, the criteria used to determine ordering cost variability is whether a 25 percent volume increase causes the company to incur additional costs. Refer to the summary sheet in Table 9.8.

Table 9.8.1 Inventory Order Placement and Receipt Costs Worksheet

ORDER PLACEMENT AND RECEIPT COSTS	NO. OF PERSONNEL	% OF TIME	AVERAGE ANNUAL SALARY	TOTAL ANNUAL COST
ORDER PLACEMENT $:				
Inventory Control (Planner)	4	60%	$32,000	$7,680
Purchasing	8	25%	$50,000	$100,000
ORDER RECEIPT $:				
Purchasing	10	5%	$50,000	$25,000
Receiving and Inspection	6	130%	$29,000	$174,000
Storeroom	8	44%	$28,000	$99,000
Inventory Control	4	10%	$32,000	$12,800
Accounting	2	50%	$44,000	$44,000
TOTAL				$354,800

Note: An assumption is made that a 25 percent increase will be a direct variable cost.

Note that the more integrated the system, the more automated the ordering process will be. The more automated the ordering process, the less likely a 25 percent increase in ordering volume will affect operating costs.

1–2. *Stock (Inventory) Order Placement* and *Receipt Costs*—Order-related costs are those incurred from the point of determining that an order is required through storage of the material and completion of receipt processing. Note that ordering costs are *not* the average total cost per order calculated as total purchasing department costs divided by total orders per year. The ordering cost factor is the variable cost related to placing orders, receiving materials, and data processing. This excludes fixed expenses such as supervisory, secretarial, floor space, equipment, maintenance, and so on, which are not dependent on the number of orders placed. Salaries are for the coming year. Refer to Table 9.8.1.

3. The *Number of Purchased Part Stock Orders* (orders for inventory-planned parts) is calculated by multiplying the annual number of inventory orders processed by 25 percent (or whichever volume increase was used to determine the test for variability). The number of orders must match the number used to calculate the effect of a change in volume. Refer to Table 9.8.2.

4. *Ordering Cost*—Once the total annual stock order variable costs are calculated, dividing by the total annual number of stock orders provides the order cost.

Note that the preceding process used to calculate purchase order cost can be followed for self-manufactured parts.

Table 9.8.2   Inventory Orders Worksheet

ORDER PROCESSING	RAW MATL	PURCH. PARTS	MANUF. PARTS	FG IN PLANT	SUPPLIES	TOTAL
Annual Orders	1,000	20,000	4,000	500	500	26,000
Order Volume × 25%	250	5,000	1,000	125	125	6,500

"ACCEPTABLE" ORDER QUANTITY

The Economic Order Quantity is still reasonably "economical" where the curve flattens out. Therefore, it is advantageous to consider an ordering range when using the EOQ, rather than a single value. Any value within this range is considered an acceptable order quantity[6] for discussion purposes. Planners can set such a range within an integral system as a means of evaluating the economic validity of various order quantity techniques compared to the EOQ.

Note that any deviation from the EOQ theoretically carries a cost penalty in terms of excess ordering cost (left of the EOQ point) or carrying cost (right of the EOQ point). However, in actual practice, the likelihood that any actual out of pocket costs will be incurred is not worth considering for minor deviations. This is due to the fact that most fields used in the EOQ calculation are themselves approximations or averages. To illustrate this point, consider Table 9.9 and the following discussion.

The first line calculates the EOQ as the system will. The second line assumes that all fields except unit cost are increased by +10 percent in the numerator and –10 percent in the denominator (a maximum increase in EOQ). Unit cost is left as is since it is the only field used within the EOQ equation which is typically accurately known. The third line assumes that all fields are decreased by 10 percent except unit cost in the numerator and increased by 10 percent in the denominator (a maximum decrease in EOQ). A +/–10 percent error in the fields comprising the EOQ is equivalent to a +16 percent ([626 – 540]/540) and –14 percent ([464 – 540]/540) order quantity range. For system purposes, a +/–10 to 15 percent range could be established as the acceptable order quantity range.

When the planner accesses the ordering screen, a request to compare order quantity techniques displays the type of information in Figure 9.8. The assumption is that reference fields must be on file for all of the order quantity techniques even though they may not be used at the time by the "active" technique.

A graph makes it easy to compare the various order quantities by technique, as well as the effect of any constraints. The period order quantity established by the planner and currently active for the part (refer to the top portion of the screen) is 250 pcs. A POQ of 250 pcs is less than the EOQ of 540 pcs and also less

---

6. Note that this is not intended as a recommendation for a new order quantity technique. It is included as a decision support example to illustrate how the planner can compare order quantities determined using various order quantity techniques.

Table 9.9   "Acceptable" Order Quantity

SCENARIO	ANNUAL USAGE	ORDER COST	SETUP COST	CARRYING COST	UNIT COST	EOQ
Standard EOQ	1,000	$25.00	$10.00	0.240	$1.00	540
+ 10% error	1,100	$27.50	$11.00	0.216	$1.00	626
− 10% error	900	$22.50	$9.00	0.264	$1.00	464

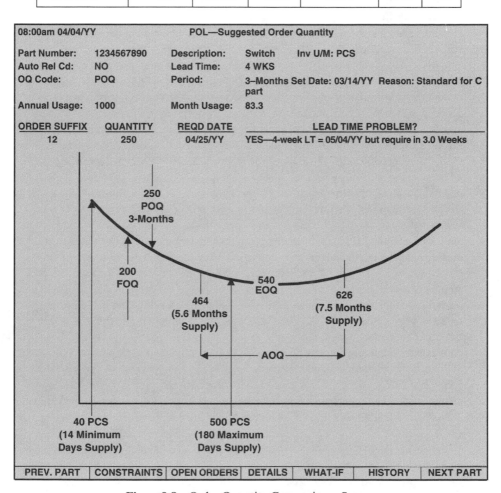

Figure 9.8   Order Quantity Comparisons Screen

than –10 percent of the EOQ. Therefore, the POQ is outside the lower Acceptable Order Quantity (AOQ) range limit. If the ordering and carrying costs are correct for the part, higher ordering costs will be incurred than are "economic."

The POQ quantity does, however, fall between the minimum and maximum days supply set by the inventory manager, while the EOQ does not. If the EOQ were being used, the quantity would be adjusted down to the maximum days supply of 500 pcs.

Least Total Cost (LTC) Quantity

Part period-based order quantity techniques are a special case of the Economic Order Quantity calculation. They are used when there is either a record of known future demands or when there is variability in forecasted demand per period. The annual usage field in the EOQ equation is replaced by a profile consisting of some combination of known and forecasted demand. The Least Total Cost technique considers the cost of carrying each additional demand quantity in inventory and suggests a new order when the cost will be less to place a new order than to carry the material.

If this technique is used, it makes sense to consider summing individual requirements within a period (daily, weekly, or monthly) to produce a period "demand." This eliminates the possibility of splitting demand within a period among multiple orders.

A "part period" is the basic unit in this technique. It is equivalent to the cost to carry one part for one period. A period is typically one day. Therefore, ordering 10 additional parts on an order and carrying them for two additional days until they are required is equivalent to 20 (10×2) part periods. This is done if it is less expensive to carry the 10 parts for two periods than to place an additional order to receive the 10 parts on their required date and incurring the extra setup and/or ordering costs. This same logic is used on each successive requirement until cumulative carrying cost exceeds ordering cost, at which time a new order is suggested.

Note that the first requirement must be assessed a carrying cost if the order is received prior to the actual requirement date. This often occurs with parts where the purchase order receipt date is scheduled earlier than the required date to accommodate receiving, incoming inspection, handling, and storage processing.

The same discussion regarding costs used in the EOQ equation apply to the LTC as well. The planner must be confident that ordering and carrying cost are known with enough precision that both can be reduced to a specific dollar figure. Table 9.10 indicated that a +/–15 percent change in order quantity resulted from +/–10 percent cost accuracy variation. This same logic has the effect of reducing or increasing the K-Factor (discussed later in this section), which determines how many parts can be carried for how many days. This in turn reduces or increases the LTC order quantity respectively.

The LTC technique may be used with any of the ordering methodologies and safety stock and forecasting techniques discussed in this book. It can be used as a direct replacement for the EOQ equation as well. Both techniques calculate the same order quantity when using an annual demand or unchanging forecasted monthly usage rate.

The conditions under which the LTC technique may be considered include the following:

- Demand may be dependent or independent. Either type may vary in quantity each period. Demand may be stated in daily or other quantities or may be based on individual order requirements. To prevent two requirements within the same day from being split into two orders, a minimum days supply constraint can be used to summarize requirements into daily (or longer) increments.

- A firm-plan time fence may need to be used to prevent new requirements from causing order quantities to be recalculated. This reduces "nervousness" and generation of expedite and deexpedite action messages. Forecasted demand can be used to extend the horizon into the future beyond the known demand.

- Order quantity will vary from order to order.

The LTC technique is dynamic in nature since new requirements and changes in forecasted demand will cause the order quantity to change over time.

The six-step process for calculating the LTC order quantity is as follows:

1. *Calculate the "K-Factor":* This is an upper limit to be used in deciding whether to include an additional future demand in the order quantity. The K-Factor is the total number of part periods which one or more parts can be carried in stock before the carrying cost exceeds the cost to place a new order.

$$\text{K-Factor} = \frac{\text{Order Cost} + \text{Setup Cost}}{\text{Unit Cost} \times (\text{Decimal Annual Carrying Cost} / 365 \text{ days} / \text{yr})}$$

For example, consider a part with a unit cost of \$152.08. If the cost to carry the part is \$0.10 per day (\$152.08 × .24/365) and the order cost is \$6.50, carrying one unit for 65 days is equivalent to carrying 65 units for one day or 65 part periods. The K-Factor is 65. After the first requirement is issued upon receipt (with or without incurring any part period cost, as applicable[7]), the next requirement is considered and compared to the full remaining 65 part periods. If the Required Quantity × Days Carried in inventory is less than 65, it is included in the existing order. If Required Quantity × Days Carried in inventory is greater than 65 days, it is more economical to place a new order.

2. *Calculate the Base-Day:* The Base-Day is the date on which the selected order review methodology calculates that the sum of available and on-order

---

7. From a practical perspective, material may be received prior to the actual required date in order to allow for receiving, incoming inspection, handling, storage, and kitting processing. If so, the entire order quantity must be assessed a carrying cost. To simplify the example, the balance of the discussion assumes that the first demand quantity is issued upon receipt and so does not incur a carrying cost.

balance minus safety stock is projected to be negative. This indicates that the demand at that point cannot be satisfied by on-hand plus on-order inventory. The order due date is then typically set at some number of days earlier to accommodate receiving, incoming inspection, handling, and storage processing.

3. *Calculate the Initial Order Quantity:* The initial order quantity (not necessarily the final one which will be suggested for ordering) is the quantity required to establish a zero or positive net inventory balance. If the net inventory is (-8) for example and another demand exists within the same period for 10, 18 becomes the initial order quantity. This quantity is not assessed a carrying cost penalty since it will be issued upon receipt.

4. *Determine whether the next demand should be included:* First, determine the number of days separating the demand Required Date and the Base-Day. This is the number of total elapsed days for which carrying cost will be incurred, including weekends and holidays, and is referred to as Delta. Second, multiply Delta by the demand quantity to determine the number of part periods involved. For example, carrying 12 pieces (the demand) for two days (Delta) is 24 part periods; carrying 40 pieces for one week (7 days) is 280 part periods.

   Multiple demands for the same period should be summed for this step. This prevents carrying inventory for a particular day while receiving an order covering additional demand for the same day.

5. *Compare the result in Step 4 to the K-Factor:* If the (sum of the) part periods calculated in Step 4 is less than the K-Factor, it will cost less to carry the parts than to place a new order. Add this demand's part periods to the previous and repeat Step 4 for the next demand. Repeat this process until the sum of the part periods exceeds the K-Factor. This demand is the final one to be included in the order quantity.

   Note that it would have been as valid to say that this demand should be included in the next order. From a practical perspective, it is probably better to err on the side of having inventory in-house rather than on-order. This trades-off carrying costs with having the additional flexibility to accommodate date and quantity changes rather than having to expedite existing orders or place new orders.

6. *Repeat until all demand within the planning horizon is covered:* If there is additional demand which is not covered by an order, repeat Steps 2 to 5. Demand within lead time will cause one or more suggested orders to be generated. Demand beyond lead time for which an order does not have to be placed in the current ordering period will generate planned or firm-planned orders to the end of the demand horizon. These orders will be used for reference purposes until the next ordering period, at which time they may be recalculated if demand has changed.

The following example illustrates the points discussed previously. Specifically, it covers basic Least Total Cost logic in an environment where both dependent- and independent-demand exists. Independent-demand is forecasted at two units per day in addition to any customer demand.

Example: On July 1, the MRP subsystem has determined that part 1234567890 has demand within the order horizon which is not covered by any released or firm-planned orders. The part is not on automatic release so the planner has the option of reviewing and adjusting the order quantity before the order is released. The system has generated a suggested order and notified the planner via the message action subsystem that the order has been added to the planner's Order Review Queue.

The planner observes from the Message Action Screen that part 1234567890 has demand which falls within the lead time. Such parts need to be reviewed immediately.

The Message Action Order Review Queue screen provides a listing of all suggested orders which require planner review. This includes orders which are either not set up for automatic release or orders which failed one or more automatic release edits. Refer to Figure 9.9. The Magnitude of the Lead Time Problem column indicates the extent of the problem (4 weeks in the case of the second order). "No Price" indicates that the purchasing system has no price related to the 200 piece quantities for part 23234A1329, even though there may be a standard cost on file. For this example, the planner positions the cursor on the top item (1234567890–12) and activates the Detail button. The Inventory Order Screen is displayed as shown in Figure 9.10.

The demand from July 1–July 27 was summed for example purposes. The Base-Day is determined by the system to be July 31. This is the date on which the net inventory goes negative. With a K-Factor of 44, the orders suggested by the system are calculated as follows:

1. Order 1 (Suffix 12) begins at 30 to cover the demand on July 31. These 30 pieces are assigned a zero carrying cost as the order is assumed to be received on July 31.

08:00am 07/01/YY			MSG—Order Review Queue				Planner: P. Mittner		
PART NUMBER	ORDER SUFFIX	REQUIRED QUANTITY	REQUIRED DATE	LD TIME PROBLEM	MAGNITUDE OF LT PROB	DATE ADDED	PLNR ID	AUTOMATIC RELEASE	
1234567890	12	95	07/31/YY	YES	1 DAY	06/30/YY	JJ	MANUAL	
23234A1329	02	200	08/12/YY	YES	4 WEEKS	06/28/YY	JJ	NO PRICE	
23234A1329	03	200	09/12/YY	NO		06/28/YY	JJ	NO PRICE	
PRIORITY SORT	PLNR SORT		RQD DT SORT		DETAIL		DELETE		

Figure 9.9   Message Action Screen—Order Queue

08:00am 07/01/YY				ORD—Order Details					K. Nimmo
Part Number	1234567890	Description:		Switch	Inv U/M:		PCS		
Auto Rel Cd:	NO	Lead Time:		4 WKS	Ld Time Date:		Aug. 01, YYYY		
OQ Code:	LTC	K-Factor:		44 Part Periods ($6.50/($194 × 0.28/365)					
Set Date:	03/14/YY	Reason:		B part with variable demand					
Unit Cost:	$ 194.00	Available Balance:		236					
Order Cost:	$ 6.50	Days Supply:		30	Independent Demand: 2.00 PCS/DAY				
Setup Cost:	$ 0.00	Safety Stock:		00					
Carrying Cost:	0.28	Dep. Demand w/in LT:		160					

PART NUMBER	ORDER SUFFIX	REQUIRED QUANTITY	REQUIRED DATE	LD TIME PROBLEM	MAGNITUDE OF LT PROB	DATE ADDED	PLNR ID	AUTOMATIC RELEASE
1234567890	12	95	07/31/YY	YES	1 DAY	06/30/YY	JJ	MANUAL

DATE	DEPENDENT DEMAND	INDEPENDENT DEMAND	TOTAL DEMAND	NET AVAIL.	PART PERIODS	REMAINING K-FACTOR	ORDER SUFFIX -QTY
07/01–07/25	150	34	184	52	0		
07/28	18	2	20	32	0		
07/29	18	2	20	12	0		
07/30	10	2	12	0	0		
07/31–BASE	28	2	30	–30	0 3 30 = 0	44	12 - 95
08/01	28	2	30	–60	1 3 30 = 30	14	
08/04	33	2	35	–105	4 3 35 = 140	–126	
08/05	0	2	2	–107	0 3 2 = 0	44	13 - 61
08/06	0	2	2	–109	1 3 2 = 2	42	
08/07	0	2	2	–111	2 3 2 = 4	38	
08/08	53	2	55	–166	3 3 55 = 165	–127	
08/11	33 + 28	2	63	–229	0 3 63 = 0	44	14 - 143
08/12	0	2	2	–231	1 3 2 = 2	42	
08/13	0	2	2	–233	2 3 2 = 4	38	
08/14	0	2	2	–235	3 3 2 = 6	32	
08/15	0	2	2	–237	4 3 2 = 8	24	
08/18	40 + 30	2	72	–309	7 3 72 = 504	–480	

GRAPH	TIME-PHASE				

Note: Headings will remain displayed while details can be viewed by scrolling up or down

Figure 9.10 Order Details Screen for Least Total Cost

2. The forecast of Independent-Demand is two pieces per day. On August 1, Independent-Demand accounts for two and Dependent-Demand accounts for 28 pieces. One day of carrying cost is equal to 30 of the available 44 part periods. This leaves 14 part periods, so the next requirement is added to the order.

3. The next requirement of 35 is carried for four days. This causes the Remaining K-Factor to drop below zero, resulting in an order of 95. The new Base-Day for the next order is August 5. The initial order quantity is two pieces.

4. Demand on August 6 and August 7 is for two pieces per day. This calculates to two and four part periods, respectively. This results in a Remaining K-Factor of 38.

5. A 2-piece Independent-Demand and 53-piece Dependent-Demand quantity is required on August 8. Fifty-five pieces for three days is 165 part periods which, with the six part periods from Step 4 is greater than the K-Factor. A planned Order (suffix 13) is suggested for 61 pieces.

6. The next Base-Day is August 11. The initial quantity is 63 pieces to cover the two Dependent- and one Independent-Demands.

7. The demand from August 12 through 15 is for two pieces per day. This is 20 part periods. Since this is less than the K-Factor of 44, the August 18 demand for 72 pieces carried for seven days is added to planned Order suffix 14. This results in an order for 143 pieces.

Note that on August 18, the first demand of 40 is sufficient to cause the part periods to go below zero. Without combining demand within the daily periods prior to performing the K-Factor check, the second demand of 30 would have caused an order to be due the same day.

Least Total Cost has some problems. In some cases, it is better to include additional (small) requirements to an order to reduce carrying costs incurred by the next order. This is addressed by Part Period Balancing.

PART PERIOD BALANCING (PPB) QUANTITY

Part Period Balancing is a fine-tuning technique using Least Total Cost (LTC) as the basis. What it essentially does is consider whether certain later demands should be included with or excluded from the existing order. The general effect is to include small demands which might normally be included in the next order. This positions large demands encompassed by the next order closer to the order receipt date. The key is to minimize the effect of carrying costs among the various requirements.

The basic PPB starting criteria is the same as for LTC. The PPB-specific question is whether to include or exclude additional smaller demands in order to achieve a better balance among orders. Therefore, PPB considers the effect of one order on another while LTC considers orders individually. Refer to Figure 9.11 for the basic concept.

Example: Consider the requirements data from Figure 9.10. Part Period Balancing generates a different set of orders than Least Total Cost as shown in Figure 9.12 because the requirements are combined differently. For example, the order due on July 31 for 101 pieces includes the August 5 through August 7 demand which LTC excluded. It is less expensive to carry these six parts as part of Order suffix-12 than to carry the 55 parts on August 8 as part of Order suffix-13. Using this same logic, Part Period Balancing logic suggests an order due on August 8 for 126 pieces and on August 18 for 72+ pieces.

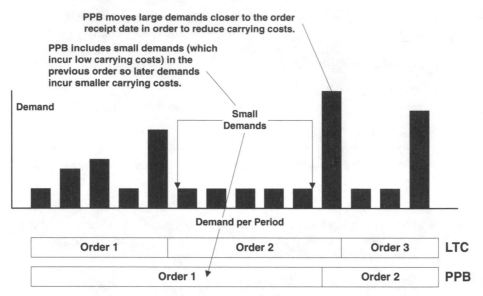

Figure 9.11   Least Total Cost vs. Part Period Balancing Comparison

Table 9.10 compares the Least Total Cost and Part Period Balancing techniques for this example. With a system which supports what-if capability, the planner should be able to manually combine demand among periods and have the system compare the cost among alternative scenarios. Once the planner is satisfied with the order coverage, the suggested order can be released and any orders which were manually adjusted can be firm-planned.

The table indicates that a technique where the effect of one order on the others is considered has the potential of substantially reducing total costs. In this example, the savings is $63.90. This example also points out the fallacy of relying on a single technique for all situations. Least Total Cost does not perform as well as Part Period Balancing where a few large demands are intermixed with small steady demands. Both perform equally well if demand is steady.

SUMMARY

Inventory part planning categories fall into inventory-planned, MRP-planned, MS-planned, and FAS-planned. To support these part categories, the planner can use economic, time frame, quantity, and demand order quantity techniques.

All techniques encompass economic aspects. Economic techniques explicitly account for ordering and carrying cost trade-offs via equations. The other techniques implicitly account for such trade-offs via the qualifiers and constraints established by the planner.

08:00am 07/01/YY				ORD—Order Details					E. Mittner

Part Number	1234567890	Description:	Switch	Inv U/M:		PCS			
Auto Rel Cd:	NO	Lead Time:	4 WKS	Ld Time Date:		Aug. 01, YYYY			
OQ Code:	PPB	K-Factor:		44 Part Periods ($6.50/($195 × 0.28/365)					
Set Date:	03/14/YY	Reason:		B part with variable demand					

Unit Cost:	$ 194.00	Available Balance:		236					
	$ 6.50	Days Supply:		30	Independent Demand: 2.00 PCS/DAY				
Setup Cost:	$ 0.00	Safety Stock:		0					
Carrying Cost:	0.28	Dep. Demand w/in LT:		160					

PART NUMBER	ORDER SUFFIX	REQUIRED QUANTITY	REQUIRED DATE	LD TIME PROBLEM	MAGNITUDE OF LT PROB	DATE ADDED	PLNR ID	AUTOMATIC RELEASE
1234567890	12	95	07/31/YY	YES	1 DAY	06/30/YY	JJ	MANUAL

DATE	DEPENDENT DEMAND	INDEPENDENT DEMAND	TOTAL DEMAND	NET AVAIL.	PART PERIODS	REMAINING K-FACTOR	ORDER SUFFIX -QTY
07/01–07/25	150	34	184	52	0		
07/28	18	2	20	32	0		
07/29	18	2	20	12	0		
07/30	10	2	12	0	0		
07/31–BASE	28	2	30	−30	0 × 30 = 0	44	12 - 101
08/01	28	2	30	−60	1 × 30 = 30	14	
08/04	33	2	35	−105	4 × 35 = 140	-126	
08/05	0	2	2	−107	5 × 2 = 10	-136	
08/06	0	2	2	−109	6 × 2 = 12	-148	
08/07	0	2	2	−111	7 × 2 = 14	-162	
08/08	53	2	55	−166	0 × 55 = 0	44	13 - 126
08/11	33 + 28	2	63	−229	3 × 63 = 189	-145	
08/12	0	2	2	−231	4 × 2 = 8	-153	
08/13	0	2	2	−233	5 × 2 = 10	-163	
08/14	0	2	2	−235	6 × 2 = 12	-175	
08/15	0	2	2	−237	7 × 2 = 14	-189	
08/18	40 + 30	2	72	−309	0 × 72 = 0	44	14 - 72+

GRAPH	TIME-PHASE			

Note: Headings will remain displayed while details can be viewed by scrolling up or down.

Figure 9.12 Order Details Screen for Part Period Balancing

Table 9.10 Comparison of LTC and PPB Examples

	COST ELEMENT	LEAST TOTAL COST LTC	PART PERIOD BALANCING PPB
Order Cost	$6.50	3 Orders × $6.50 = $19.50	3 Orders × $6.50 = $19.50
Carrying Cost	$0.15 per Part Period	865 Part Periods× $0.15 + $129.75	439 Part Periods × $0.15 = $65.85
Total Cost		$149.25	$85.35

There is a very real point at which the frequency of ordering, receiving, processing, handling, and storing material exceeds the cost to carry the same material for longer periods of time. The integral strategy determines this point and then develops an infrastructure in terms of facilities, equipment, systems, and technologies to ensure that the cost is minimized. The inventory manager and planners ensure adherence to the strategy.

Chapter 10

Safety Stock

In spite of all of the company's attempts to quantify and time-phase customer demand, there are a number of forces at work which result in random demand both above and below this number. This applies to both dependent- and independent-demand parts. Safety stock is intended to protect the company's plans and schedules from the nervousness associated with a given level of actual demand in excess of the forecast.

Customers are not the only source which can create a condition where demand exceeds the forecast. Suppliers may not ship the quantity ordered, thus creating an unplanned shortage. Incoming inspection may reject some or all of a receipt. Destruct testing methods may render sample quantities unusable. For materials which have a shelf life, samples may be retained for periodic testing. Loss may occur while in storage due to damage or pilferage. Damage may occur within the production, storage, or handling processes. Infant mortality or design problems may cause failures in testing. R&D usage may consume materials for new product development. Service part requirements siphon off parts for the installed customer base. Random unplanned usage may occur if a given part is a designated alternate for another part which stocks-out.

Stock-outs are not to be mistaken for "out-of-stock" conditions. An out-of-stock condition is planned. A zero inventory during times when there is no demand is desirable. Stock-outs are unplanned and any zero inventory condition may be undesirable. Stock-out conditions are somewhat more complicated than simply determining whether there is no inventory. Many companies have a part safety stock strategy which results in specifying a zero or low safety stock quantity. In this case, a certain number of stock-out occurrences per year may be acceptable to the company. This occurs when the safety stock service percent is set low enough that one or more stock-out situations are statistically likely to occur.

The critical choices of a safety stock strategy relate to safety stock level, safety stock investment, customer service level, and risk of stock-out vs. value to the company of not stocking-out. The inventory policy-setting area is involved with establishing the investment and service level policies. Inventory planning then selects the techniques and variables used to determine safety stock quantities and provides the decision support data used over time to assess the ability of the selected technique to meet the policy targets. Inventory control actions address the problems caused by stock-out conditions as they occur.

This chapter addresses the following elements of safety stock and related issues:

- "Customer Service" is a term used to refer to two different types of service. This can be confusing at times. Customer service level from an inventory target perspective refers to the percentage of demands completely filled based on required date and quantity as compared to total demands. The safety stock customer service percent refers to the number of orders received without a stock-out compared to the total exposures to stock-out. Setting a lower safety stock customer service percent may still result in a fairly high customer service level, but the two terms are definitely not the same.

- There are three primary techniques used to calculate or set a safety stock. Statistical, fixed, and time period techniques are reviewed with respect to their different areas of application.

- Traditional inventory systems support the preceding alternative safety stock techniques. Integral systems additionally calculate reference fields based on what the various equation fields would have to be in order to achieve given levels of service. This provides the planner with a common sense insight into the effectiveness of the various techniques given actual vs. forecast usage profiles. Mathematical equations and smoothing parameters tend to mask what is really occurring from a planner perspective unless some type of decision support is provided.

If operational inventory needed to conduct business is considered "waste" from a traditional perspective, then safety stock which is only needed in peak demand situations must be considered "toxic waste" by comparison. This is not such an uncommon view of safety stock. It is easier to realize the value of safety stock as one element of an integral strategy if the principles behind the calculations are understood and if the conditions leading to safety stock within the company are recognized. That is the focus of this chapter.

COMMON MISUNDERSTANDINGS
RELATED TO SAFETY STOCK

Of the various methodologies and techniques used within inventory management, safety stock is perhaps the most difficult to understand. The following are probably the most misunderstood aspects of statistical safety stock as they relate to the mathematics and application in various environments.

1. Students are taught that a 100 percent safety stock customer service percent can *never* be provided. This can be proven mathematically based on the standard

deviation relationships covered later in this chapter. However, in actual practice this translates into a perception that even an infinite safety stock quantity cannot protect a part from stocking-out. There are many companies (perhaps even an infinite number) that would like to have this problem. Consider having so much demand that even an infinite safety stock is too little.

While companies have many problems, having an infinite amount of business is not one of them. "Business math" is based on finite considerations. There are levels of safety stock which can provide a 100 percent safety stock service level for every part. This means that companies can by definition establish the number of standard deviations which will provide a 100 percent service level for every part. This number is based on deviations actually experienced in the past and on a projection of future demand. The fact is, companies must establish the level associated with a 100 percent service level. Computer systems require a relationship between 100 percent and some number of standard deviations for those times when the planner sets a 100 percent safety stock customer service percent. The answer cannot be "infinite."

Consider a part with an average usage of 10 per month and a standard deviation of two. History has shown a maximum deviation to date of eight. A reasonable definition of a 100 percent safety stock customer service level is, therefore, four to five standard deviations. This provides a safety stock of 8 to 10 units. This is a far cry from an infinite safety stock level. Business math takes a much more practical view of the needs of the company than theoretical math.

Planners question the validity of a statistical technique which is incompatible with their actual experience. In such cases, it is not the technique which is the problem but rather the incorrect application of a particular mathematical relationship to a particular business environment. *Do* establish a 100 percent safety stock service percent target relationship for each and every part subject to a statistical safety stock calculation. *Do not* confuse this with an infinite safety stock quantity. Set the target to 100 percent when it makes business sense.

2. The second area of confusion is whether safety stock is even needed. Usage is as likely to be greater than forecast as less, assuming a normal distribution. One might think that inventory not issued in the periods when demand is less than forecast can be used to offset demand during the periods when demand is greater than forecast. This results in a complete offsetting of demands so safety stock is not really needed at all on average. With a forecast of 50 units per month, using 40 last month and 60 this month nets to 50 per month. Since average usage equals 50 and the forecast is 50, there seems to be no need to carry 10 units in safety stock.

The fallacy with this is that high and low demand periods net to the forecast only when considered over a long period of time and only when the forecast tracks actual usage accurately. In the short-term, every period with low usage does not fortuitously precede a period with high usage. In an upward-trending environment, periods of high usage follow each other. Therefore, while there may be periods where safety stock is not required, there will be others when having it is the only way to provide the target customer service level.

3. Statistical safety stock is commonly based on parts having an actual demand profile which corresponds to a normal distribution (covered later in the chapter). Assuming a normal distribution for every part permits a statistical forecast to be generated and standard deviations to be calculated. In reality, this simplification does not hold true for all parts. Companies, however, often assume that all parts adhere to a normal distribution for simplicity. Therefore, planners can end up spending an inordinate amount of time "fine-tuning" the statistical variables for a part which does not seem to be tracking to forecast very well. The problem may be that the base assumption of a normal distribution is incorrect from the beginning.

4. Standard and mean absolute deviations are based on deviation of actual usage vs. forecast for a period. If the company does not adjust their monthly forecast for the difference in days per period as was discussed in Chapter 8, Forecasting, deviations will be incorrectly calculated as well. "Equivalent" periods based on a 20-day month should be used for forecasting, if weekly or other "standard" periods are not used. Deviation calculations related to safety stock then require no additional adjustment.

COMPARISON OF SAFETY STOCK TECHNIQUES

Safety stock level is a management policy (business level) decision. There are three techniques which companies commonly use at a part level:

- *Statistical*—Safety stock is calculated via statistical methods based on the historical deviation of actual from planned usage.

- *Fixed*—Safety stock is set at a fixed quantity, regardless of the usage rate.

- *Time Period*—Safety stock is set based on covering 100 percent of some number or portion of future periods' demand.

The selection of a part level technique is based primarily on the type of part (demand- vs. independent-demand), type of demand to which the part is subject (consistent or sporadic), and degree of variability to which the part is subject (low vs. high). Other factors such as replenishment lead time, target customer service level, availability of history, part cost, number of time periods to protect from stock-out, impact on production or service of a stock-out, and MRP or inventory subsystem designs affect the choice. In addition, companies also overplan at the Master Schedule level in order to create sets of parts for products in case product level demand is greater than forecasted or to provide option mix flexibility.

The problem companies face with regard to safety stock, however, is *not* which technique to use. The problem is determining how much to carry of which parts at any given time, based on the product life cycle, competitive environment, and customer commitments. The selected technique then becomes an element within the company's integral strategy. Table 10.1 provides a comparison of safety stock techniques based on various company conditions.

Table 10.1   Comparison of Safety Stock Techniques

CONSIDERATION	STATISTICAL	FIXED	TIME PERIOD
Phase-In Part	Ineffective for a new part unless new part picks up history from superseded part	Set high enough to prevent stock-out	Set demand (Forecasted Usage) high enough to prevent stock-out
Phase-Out Part	Set Customer Service Percent to 0	Set Fixed Safety Stock to 0	Set Time Period demand to 0 or a low quantity
Demand Profile (dependent, independent, or some combination)	Any demand profile, though erratic demand profiles will be smoothed	Steady or decreasing demand profile, since technique does not adjust to changing conditions	Any demand profile, since technique is based on demand in future periods
Variability Profile (demand, lead time, yield, and so on)	Any variability profile, though peaks will be smoothed	Any variability profile, with the Fixed Quantity set high enough to cover one or more peak conditions	Any variability profile, with the Time Period demand set high enough to cover one or more peak conditions
Typical Usage	Independent-demand parts where coverage is based primarily on part Safety Stock Customer Service Percent	Dependent-demand parts where safety stock coverage is set to zero or inexpensive independent-demand parts where excess coverage to provide a 100 percent Customer Service Level is desired	Dependent-demand parts where coverage is based primarily on days or weeks supply for a product

SAFETY STOCK TECHNIQUE-RELATED ISSUES

Prior to selecting a particular safety stock technique, the inventory manager and planners must resolve a number of issues. This process is facilitated by having a defined integral strategy which provides the focus and boundaries.

- What is the benefit to the company and customer of having safety stock? Parts required by production or service are two of the highest priorities. Other types of internal usage may be a lower priority. An assessment should be made over time of the accuracy of the forecast vs. actual unplanned usage rates and frequency of stock-outs. The safety stock should be set at a quantity which reduces the number of occurrences of stock-outs to an acceptable target level. Once the frequency and magnitude of stock-outs are determined, the safety stock quantity can be set appropriately. The problem, of course, is determining the "acceptable" stock-out level.

- Once the safety stock level is determined in terms of service level, the parameters required to calculate the quantity must be identified for each part. These will vary by safety stock technique, part cost, dependent- or independent-demand, and so on. Establishing a statistical safety stock requires initializing and maintaining more fields than do either the fixed or time period safety stock techniques.

- Once the acceptable frequency of stock-outs is determined, a reassessment must be made based on the likely effect of stock-outs at the given frequency. If the company's reaction will be to allow the replenishment order to be received late, then the safety stock level may be okay. If the company's reaction will be to expedite the order and incur the related costs associated with a higher priority stock-out, perhaps a higher safety stock investment should be considered.

- Other considerations include the following:

   —Is there safety stock of the finished good for which the part is used? This reduces the necessity to carry additional safety stock of each part.

   —Can another part be substituted, thus allowing lower or no safety stock on the first part? Substitute parts may be more expensive on a one-for-one basis but may be very economical when compared to consolidating safety stock levels across parts.

   —What level of investment in safety stock is justified based on the profitability of the product or support of strategic customer service objectives? Conversely, what higher level of profitability can be achieved if safety stock is readily available to take advantage of increases in actual usage over forecast?

- Once an individual part's safety stock is set, a consistency check should be made regarding other similar parts or parts used for the same products or product lines. Not protecting all related parts to a similar level negates the higher protection provided by some parts. Where parts cannot be easily associated with products, other relationships may include parts for key customers, parts which are difficult to obtain, or parts from a particular supplier.

Note that stock-outs can become an emotional issue within a company. No one responsible for an order wants to deliver late when expediting can be used to deliver the product on-time. No one in inventory wants to have a stock-out condition prevent an on-time production order or customer shipment. However, reality may mean living with stock-outs every day. Given an inventory of 10,000 parts, a stock-out once every two years for each C-item still adds up to 4,000 stock-outs per year (10,000 × 80%[C-items] × 1 stock-out/2 years). This is approximately 15 new stock-outs per day. If the stock-out duration lasts an average of two weeks, this is 150 stock-outs at any given time. The other problem is that no one knows whether a particular stock-out is one of the "acceptable" ones or not. Therefore, all stock-outs with one or more requirements pending tend to receive the same consideration with respect to expediting and special processing. This example illustrates why companies attempt to maintain sufficient inventory of C-items; it may be less expensive in terms of money and disruption to spend the money for additional safety stock.

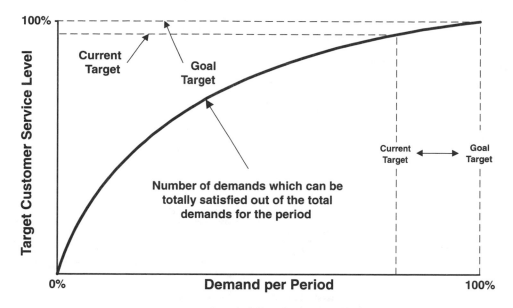

**Forecast for the Period Plus Safety Stock Quantity
and Related Investment**

Figure 10.1   Customer Service as a Function of Safety Stock

Customer Service Level

The reason for maintaining safety stock is to enable the company to achieve and sustain a target level of customer service. "Customer Service" in this case is defined as the number of inventory demands which can be fully satisfied out of the total demands during a period as shown in Figure 10.1. This definition is, however, *not* the definition of the field used in statistical safety stock equations. Do not confuse the two.

Instead statistical safety stock equations incorporate a safety stock service percent factor based on the number of permitted stock-outs during a given number of order replenishment cycles. The customer service level percent is, therefore, based on satisfying individual demands while the safety stock customer service percent is based on not stocking-out more than "x" times out of 100.

These two views of safety stock have similarities. A high customer service level based on demand probably also indicates that a high safety stock service percent is being achieved. A high safety stock service percent may also indicate that a high customer service level is being achieved as long as stock-outs are infrequent and of short duration. These two measures are not the same, however. A part can stock-out, giving a less than 100 percent safety stock service percent. If no demands occurred within the time it takes to replenish the stock, customer service level remains at 100 percent (refer to Figure 10.2).

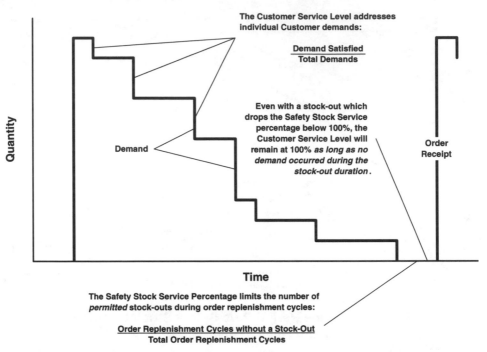

Figure 10.2   Customer Service Level Relationship to Safety Stock Service Percent

The first problem a company has with safety stock determination, therefore, is in understanding that customer service level based on demand cannot simply be set as a parameter used by statistical safety stock equations. Customer service level is a performance-related "result" while safety stock service percent is a "field" used in calculating a statistical safety stock.

A related problem is in really understanding the relationship between safety stock service percent and safety stock quantity relative to the value to the company of ensuring a given number of reorder periods without a stock-out. Does a 98 percent safety stock service percent mean the same thing for an item received twice per year as compared to one received weekly? What if the percent is 97.9 percent or 98.1 percent? How sensitive is the safety stock quantity to safety stock service percent? Can customers (both external and internal) wait until the next shipment is received (i.e., how absolute are required dates)? What amount of part level and total safety stock investment is really appropriate for the business? What level of investment is required to support the integral strategy?

While the mathematical relationship of safety stock service percent may not be completely understood by those who use it, company management understands very well how to calculate the dollar value of safety stock. They also understand that on average, safety stock is not intended to be used. It is an insurance policy against stocking-out. For every part which dips into safety stock due to an underforecast or anomaly condition, there is a part which does not use the forecasted quantity. Management needs to be confident that the $200,000 investment in safety stock, for example, is the best application of that money, considering the alternatives. Once set, how it is invested among parts is the responsibility of the inventory manager and planners. Whether an investment in better forecasting and safety stock decision support software will provide a justifiable return on investment in terms of reducing the investment in safety stock is an infrastructural decision.

Product Life Cycle

The basic problem with unplanned usage is that no one can accurately predict which specific parts will have unplanned usage in any given time period. Therefore, all parts subject to unplanned usage must be considered for protection by safety stock in order to protect the significant few from an unacceptable stock-out condition. What is "unacceptable?" Which parts of all of those subject to unplanned usage require safety stock?

The question of "what is unacceptable" differs by product line and perhaps even product. For new products in the introduction and growth stages, there is little risk in stocking sufficient materials to provide a very high customer service level since the parts will be used in the near term (refer to Figure 10.3). The primary risk is for parts which may be superseded via engineering changes if the product is still undergoing modifications. This changes for products being phased-out. Any stock which cannot be sold or applied to another product or service part demand becomes first excess, then surplus, then inactive, and ultimately obsolete/scrap.

Introduction, growth, and decline stages are, therefore, special cases with respect to safety stock. The primary risk associated with a safety stock dollar investment is during the maturity phase when the largest investment in safety stock must be made and then sustained to support the volume of business. This is the point where companies experience the most conflict between safety stock investment and customer service level. The tendency is to want to reduce safety stock and free up investment while relying on production volume and mix flexibility to accommodate unplanned demand.

Safety Stock Service Percent

The inventory manager and planners establish the number of acceptable stock-outs relative to the number of exposures to stock-out for each part, based on the product level strategy. The inventory system then maintains the fields necessary to monitor performance over time as shown in Figure 10.4 for the safety stock service percent.

Service level based on stock-outs really covers two types of situations as shown in Figure 10.4. The first is number of stock-outs per number of exposures to stock-out. This is the more traditional way of looking at safety stock service percent. The second situation is days stocked-out as compared to target. This may be more critical to customer service.

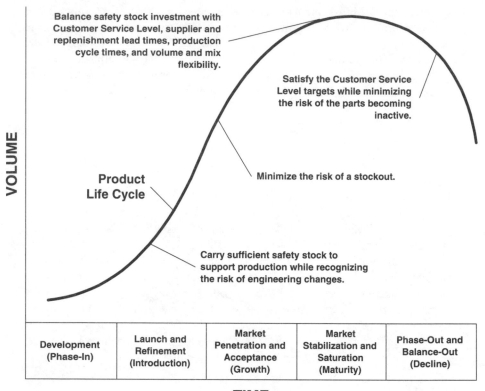

Figure 10.3   Safety Stock as a Function of the Product Life Cycle

08:00am 07/01/Y2		Safety Stock Service Percent		Planner: R. Delmerico
Part Number:	1234567890	Part Description:	Meter	
Receipt Frequency:	Weekly	Performance to Target:	98.2%	(96.2/98.0)
		Deviation from Target:	−1.8%	([96.2 − 98.0]/98.0)
	Deviation from Target based on Days Stock-Out:		−1.9%	([254 − 259]/259)

SAFETY STOCK SERVICE % BASED ON EXPOSURES TO STOCK-OUT----------------------------

Target Service Level:	98.0%	Actual Service Level:	96.2%	
Target Exposure to Stock-Out:	51/52	Actual Exposures to Stock-Out:	52	Since 07/01/Y1
		Actual Stock-Outs:	2	Since 07/01/Y1
Target Stock-Outs:	≤1/52	Actual Acceptable Stock-Outs:	1	Since 07/01/Y1
		Actual Unacceptable Stock-Outs:	1	Since 07/01/Y1
Target Periods without a S/O:	51/52	Actual Periods without a S/O:	4	Since 06/01/Y2

SERVICE LEVEL INDICATOR BASED ON DAYS STOCK-OUT----------------------------

Target Stock-Out Days	≤1/260	Actual Days Stock-Out:	6/260 Since 07/01/Y1	
		Days Stock-Out > Target:	5 (6 − 1)	
		Avg Days Stock-Out/Occurrence:	2.5 (5/2)	
Target Stock-Out Days %:	≤0.38%	Actual Stock-Out Days %:	1.54%	

PART LIST	PRODUCT LIST	GRAPH	HISTORY	WHAT-IF	DETAILS

Figure 10.4   Safety Stock (SS) Service Percent

In the screen, a 98 percent target safety stock service percent has been set for a part which has a weekly receipt frequency. This translates into a minimum of 51 out of 52 weeks per year without a stock-out. With this as the target, the actual number of stock-outs (2) exceeded the target (1) by 1 (2 − 1). In the screen, the first stock-out is acceptable, but the second is unacceptable. Therefore, the actual service level is less than the target by 1.8 percent.

With a parameter of days stocked-out as compared to target, the system must track the number of days stocked-out per stock-out. This may not be a typical condition monitored by a traditional inventory system. With respect to customer service level, however, the number of days stocked-out may be as or more important than the number of stock-outs. If a company can absorb a 1-day stock-out per year but experiences six, the impact on production may be considerable in terms of lost production or rescheduling, overtime, or lost sales. One or two stock-outs per year may not seem like much when considered without accounting for duration. A 6- or 7-day stock-out may mean a week of lost production if it affects a constrained operation. This is approximately $1,000,000 for a $50 million per year operation.

Safety Stock (SS) Service Percent (used in calculating a statistical safety stock) is based on allowing an acceptable number of stock-outs within a given number of *exposures* to stock-out. An exposure to stock-out occurs at the point where stock is the lowest just prior to receiving the next order quantity. For a part with 10 orders per year and a 90 percent safety stock service percent, the part can be expected to stock-out one of every 10 order cycles if demand variability and usage rate remains consistent with historical experience.

Customer service level is based on the number of demands which cannot be satisfied on or before their required date as compared to total demands. Therefore, customer service level remains at 100 percent until the point at which safety stock is unable to cover a requirement. At this point, customer service level becomes 0 percent until the next receipt. The aggregate then becomes the number of satisfied demands divided by the total number of demands, as shown in Figure 10.5. When the next order is received, both safety stock service percent and customer service level are back to 100 percent until the next stock-out.

Note that statistical service level logic is based on having no outside factors affecting results. However, companies monitor usage rate on a regular basis. If the actual usage rate is trending such that the forecasted rate will be insufficient to cover demand, orders may be increased or expedited. This has the effect of improving safety stock service level and customer service level above that which would have occurred without any intervention. This is one of the key advantages of including independent-demand parts in the dynamic MRP review process and not waiting for weekly or monthly reviews. Companies that react based on trends which differ from their original projections and do not wait for an actual stock-out will achieve higher than expected customer service levels.

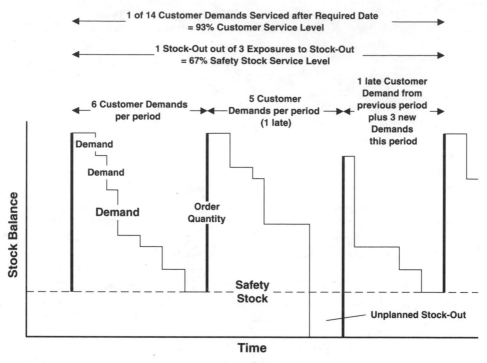

Figure 10.5   Customer Service Level vs. Safety
Stock Service Level Percent Example

Stock-Out Duration

The number of exposures to stock-out to which a part is subject does not consider duration of stock-out. Safety stock service percent does not consider duration. Customer service level based on the number of demands during a period which are fully satisfied on either the original or current required date does. The longer the stock-out duration, the greater the number of demands which cannot be satisfied and the lower the customer service level.

> *Example:* A part has a fairly constant usage rate and a risk of 10 exposures to stock-out per year (i.e., 10 orders per year). No more than one stock-out per year is desired (i.e., a 90 percent safety stock service percent). If the duration of the stock-out lasts for the durations listed in Table 10.2, a variety of customer service levels will be achieved. Assume 50 production weeks per year at one customer order per week equals 50 *demands* per year. Safety stock service percent remains the same regardless of the duration since only one stock-out has occurred in each scenario. The single stock-out condition may last for as long as five weeks before the customer service level drops to the safety stock service percent. The key point to note here is that customer service level can be expected to be significantly

Table 10.2   Customer Service Levels with Steady Demand/Week

STOCK-OUT DURATION	% OF PART USAGE (CONSTANT RATE)	SAFETY STOCK SERVICE %	CUSTOMER SERVICE LEVEL
1 week	1/50 = 2%	90%	1 - 1/50 = 98%
2 weeks	2/50 = 4%	90%	1 - 2/50 = 96%
5 weeks	5/50 = 10%	90%	1 - 5/50 = 90%

Table 10.3   Customer Service Levels with a Peak Seasonal Usage Rate

STOCK-OUT DURATION	% OF PART USAGE (SEASONAL RATE)	SAFETY STOCK SERVICE %	CUSTOMER SERVICE LEVEL
1 week	1/15 × 80% = 5.3%	90%	1 - 0.053 = 95%
2 weeks	2/15 × 80% = 10.7%	90%	1 - 0.107 = 89%
5 weeks	5/15 × 80% = 33.3%	90%	1 - 0.333 = 67%

Table 10.4   Customer Service Levels with a Nonpeak Seasonal Usage Rate

STOCK-OUT DURATION	% OF PART USAGE (SEASONAL RATE)	SAFETY STOCK SERVICE %	CUSTOMER SERVICE LEVEL
1 week	1/35 × 20% = 0.6%	90%	1 - 0.006 = 99.4%
5 weeks	5/35 × 20% = 2.9%	90%	1 - 0.029 = 97.1%
16 weeks	16/35 × 20% = 9.1%	90%	1 - 0.091 = 90.9%

higher than the safety stock service percent for a part with a steady usage and small number of demands, if the stock-out durations are kept short.

Example: Consider a second part which has a seasonal distribution where the stock-out occurs at a time when demand is peaking. The customer service level is impacted to a greater degree in a much shorter duration stock-out condition than in the previous example. Assume a seasonal rate of 80 percent of annual demand occurring over a 15-week time frame during the peak usage period as shown in Table 10.3. It does not take long for the customer service level to drop below that of the safety stock service percent if a stock-out occurs during the peak demand period. A company's stock-out window may be only 40 percent of that for a steady demand case (two vs. five weeks in these two examples). Stock-out duration is a definite factor when determining customer service level, while being immaterial with respect to the safety stock service percent.

A stock-out condition which occurs during a nonpeak period can absorb a much longer duration before the customer service level drops below the safety stock service percent. This is illustrated in Table 10.4. Customers may not agree with this type of math, however. To customers, stock-out duration is *very* important and transcends any math a company may use to justify service levels. For some parts, stock-out duration in terms of maximum lateness of shipments may need to be part of overall customer service performance in order to provide a realistic measure from the customer's perspective.

Note that stock-outs are not always clear indicators of lower performance. The planner must recognize differences among parts. For example, a part issued in bulk to the floor is actually only an intermediate issue. Being *stock-out* in inventory but *in-stock* on the floor is not a cause for alarm when the calculated safety stock service percent drops below the target. It may be necessary to consider floor stock parts differently from other parts with regard to customer service level. There should be a Floor Stock Indicator Flag in the Inventory Master File for such parts.

Overplanning at the Master Schedule Level

Overplanning at the Master Schedule level provides safety stock at part or subassembly levels in terms of sets. The company will only produce these extra products if there is demand. Otherwise, the parts become safety stock. Overplanning individual options creates excess demand for selected elements of the bill of material. For example, a quantity of a particular subassembly which has a complexity of two (i.e., two options or variations) may be planned as 60 percent of the first variation and 55 percent of the second. If the actual usage turns out to be a 50-50 split, the overplanning effectively provides a safety stock of 10 units and 5 units, respectively. The effect is to leave a given number of part sets in inventory which can be converted to finished goods as required.

With overplanning, any parts or subassemblies left in stock become "available" during the next MS run. From the inventory manager's perspective, these parts may be considered excess inventory or safety stock, depending on the business category established (see Chapter 2). This inventory is the responsibility of the master planner, since it was generated via a dependent-demand relationship.

Safety Stock vs. Safety Lead Time

One alternative to carrying safety stock is to use a technique where materials are received earlier than actually required. Since the highest risk of a stock-out is just prior to the next order being received, ordering and receiving earlier than required provides extra material at the high risk times. This is referred to as a Safety Lead Time and is illustrated in Figure 10.6.

All things being equal, safety lead time does not differ from having a safety stock. The amount of material on-hand when the new materials are received is in essence the safety stock level. Since the new order is received with material on-hand, this on-hand quantity becomes the "pseudo" safety stock level. Using this technique eliminates having to calculate a statistical or fixed safety stock. However, since the amount of time the material is received early is not likely to change once it is set, the risk is that the actual deviation for some number of parts will

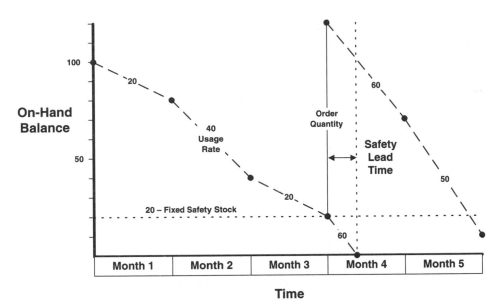

Figure 10.6 Safety Lead Time

not be adequately covered by the average safety lead time. A safety lead time is equivalent to a time period safety stock.

Safety lead time is also used for parts which do not carry any safety stock (i.e., have a fixed safety stock of 0). Receiving material earlier than required provides some schedule flexibility or a small protection against late shipments. Systems provide the planner with the capability to receive parts early by establishing a receipt processing duration as part of the cumulative part lead time. The longer the duration, ostensibly for receiving, incoming inspection, handling, and storage, the longer the safety lead time.

BASICS OF STATISTICAL DEVIATION CALCULATIONS

The basic premise behind a statistical safety stock is that the level of safety stock required to prevent a given number of stock-outs based on exposures to stock-out can be mathematically determined. Deviation can be defined in terms of standard deviation or mean absolute deviation, both of which can be related to a safety stock quantity. The typical distribution model used to determine deviation is the Normal Distribution, illustrated in Figure 10.7. With the normal distribution, the forecast is assumed to be representative of the actual usage rate on average. Deviations above and below the forecast are assumed to be relatively proportional on average. Conditions affecting success (defined as not stocking-out) are assumed to be constant as well. Therefore, when a standard deviation is calculated, it is assumed to be representative of the deviation to be encountered in the future on average. The greater the deviation, the greater the number of standard deviations which must be covered.

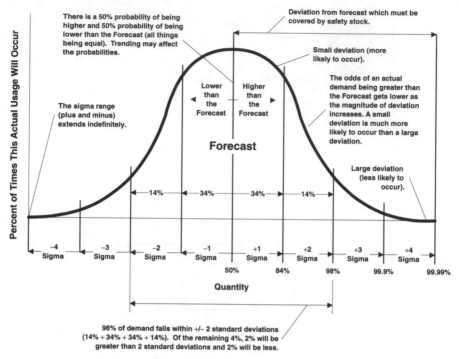

Figure 10.7   Normal Distribution

With a normal distribution, the midpoint is the forecast, also referred to as the *mean* or average value. The downward sloping curve on either side of the average value indicates that the probability of having a specific actual usage which deviates from the forecast gets less and less as the deviation from the forecast gets larger and larger. For example, while there is a 16 percent (100% - 84%) probability that actual usage will deviate beyond +1 sigma, there is only a 0.1 percent probability that actual usage will deviate above the forecast beyond +3 sigma. The right-hand side of the curve is where usage exceeds the forecast. This is the usage which must be covered by on-hand, on-order, and safety stock inventory.

In practice, most companies calculating a statistical safety stock apply the normal distribution[1] logic to all independent-demand parts. Variables within the

---

1. The Poisson Distribution is an alternative to the Normal Distribution where deviation is skewed to one side or the other. For example, a part with a forecast demand of two cannot fall below a zero demand (deviation = −2) but may have demand of 10 (deviation = 8). The integral system can monitor parts where the calculated deviation tends to be significantly less than the experienced overdeviation and flag the planner to review the logic. Note also that the Normal Distribution may be positively or negatively skewed as well and is not always in the bell shape.

equations are then used to fine-tune the results for specific parts. The width of the bell-shaped curve in Figure 10.5 varies from part to part based on the deviation each experiences. A part with small deviations will have a small sigma (σ) and, therefore, a skinny distribution curve. A part with large deviations will have a large sigma (σ) and, therefore, a fatter curve. The width of the curve is a direct indication of the quantity of safety stock which must be held to compensate for the deviations.

Sigma corresponds to a particular quantity based on an average of the deviation. If there is a forecast of 50 and there are 50 units in stock, there is a 50 percent chance of satisfying demand for the period without any safety stock. If safety stock includes a quantity equal to one standard deviation (as factored for order quantity, alpha factor, and lead time which is covered later in this chapter), there is an 84 percent chance of satisfying demand for the period. This percentage (which is the safety stock service percent) increases as shown in Figure 10.5 as safety stock is provided for each additional increment of the standard deviation or any portion thereof.

Another way of looking at standard deviation is to consider ranges. There is a 68 percent ($2 \times 34\%$) chance that actual usage will equal the forecast plus or minus one standard deviation quantity. Therefore, if the forecast is 50 and the standard deviation is five units, there is a 68 percent chance that actual usage will range from 45 to 55 units.

Regardless of the magnitude of the deviations, the relationship of sigma to the percentages at the bottom of the figure remains the same. For practical purposes, covering four standard deviations (99.99685%, also equivalent to 5 mean absolute deviations (MADs)) is essentially equivalent to a 100 percent safety stock service percent once calculated quantities are rounded up. Mathematicians, however, will point out that 100 percent can never be reached from a safety factor perspective (check out 5 and 6 sigma deviation factors in Table 10.7). At some point, though, the company needs to equate 99.99xxx with 100 percent for practical business math purposes. Even so, additional coverage even beyond this level may still be appropriate if there is a chance that future deviations will be greater than those experienced to date, as may occur with a part being phased-in. Statistical relationships are a projection of the past into the future; such projections are not a business certainty!

Note also that smoothing the deviation over time using the alpha factor tends to reduce the maximum coverage to something less than the potential maximum peak deviations. This means that it is possible that the safety stock may not cover an actual historical deviation level. Smoothing has an advantage when usage less than forecast tends to be greater than usage higher than the forecast. The integral system should maintain the magnitudes of the maximum deviations and their related dates over some number of previous periods as a direct check for the planner against the calculated quantities. Safety stock should not be relegated to the computer, just calculated by it. The planner needs the ability to check on the validity of safety stock calculations on a part by part basis.

Calculating the Standard Deviation (σ)

Standard Deviation (σ) is a measure of the spread of a probability distribution. Consider two parts which have the same forecast usage rate. The one which experiences the greater deviation of actual usage from the forecast rate has a greater spread. The smaller the standard deviation, the higher the probability of the actual usage rate approximating the forecast usage rate.

Within statistics, both simple and integral mathematics are required to fully understand probability distributions. For inventory planning purposes, the mathematics are simplified by accepting the concept that all parts conform to a normal distribution. This allows a table (refer to Table 10.7) to be used to represent the probability that a part will be in-stock (a success) out of a given number of replenishment cycles (number of trials).

Having the table eliminates the necessity to calculate the actual normal distribution function, which is an integral equation. A value of 84.13, which applies to a standard deviation equal to 1.0, indicates that there is an 84.13 percent probability that the actual usage for a period will not exceed the forecast usage plus one standard deviation quantity of safety stock. This is also equivalent to saying that the probability of exceeding one standard deviation on the high side of the forecast is less than 16 percent. This corresponds to the area under the bell-shaped curve shown to the right of 1 sigma in Figure 10.5.

> *Example:* Consider a part with a forecast of 25 units per month, a time period order quantity equal to one month's supply and a standard deviation of three units. There is a 50 percent probability that usage will be 25 or less units per month as well as a 50 percent probability that usage will be 25 or more units per month. There is a 15.87 percent (100.00 − 84.13) probability that usage will be greater than 28 units (25 + [1 standard deviation × 3]). Due to the slope of the curve, there is only a 2.28 percent (100.00 − 97.72) probability that usage will be greater than 31 (25 + [2 standard deviations × 3 units]).

When forecasting by period, it is necessary to ensure that one period is equivalent to any other period. Using a weekly period where the week is always a "work week" consisting of five workdays is a common period used in MRP. With independent-demand parts, a monthly forecast is more common. Since each calendar month varies in terms of number of workdays, it is not mathematically correct to simply treat each as a "period" with respect to the others. A month with 15 workdays would be expected to have less demand than one with 22, all things being equal. Therefore, applying an equivalent workdays factor based on 20^2 as the norm enables the forecast to more closely reflect workday differences within the month. Note that this means that a forecast in the current month cannot be

---

2. Twenty is a reasonable norm based on there being approximately 240 workdays in a year (240 workdays/12 months = 20 days per average month).

simply extended into some number of months into the future. Each future month must be factored as well. Refer to Figure 10.8.

For the workday profile illustrated in Table 10.5, therefore, an equivalent number of workdays has been established by calendar month. The forecast of 100 per normal 20-day period has been adjusted accordingly in Column 3. The deviation is then determined by subtracting actual usage from "factored" forecast usage.

The standard deviation (σ) is calculated as the square root of the sum of the deviations squared divided by the number of periods minus one:

$$\sigma = (1450/(12-1))^{0.5} = 11.48$$

Based on the variability within this sample, only one period (June) actually exceeded one standard deviation (11.48) when considering only those periods where actual usage exceeded forecast. Three of the 12 periods (January, May, and June) exceeded one standard deviation when considering all deviation from the forecast.

It may not appear to make much sense to include deviations which are less than the forecast since no safety stock is required in those periods. However, both standard and mean absolute deviation consider underdeviations and overdeviations. This is based on the normal distribution assumption that actual usage is equally likely to be higher than forecast as lower. Therefore, any and all deviations must be summed and then averaged in order to develop a representative deviation profile. Table 10.5 contains the data needed to calculate three different types of deviations. The "Deviation" column is used to calculate the mean absolute deviation. The "Deviation^2" column is used to calculate standard deviation. The

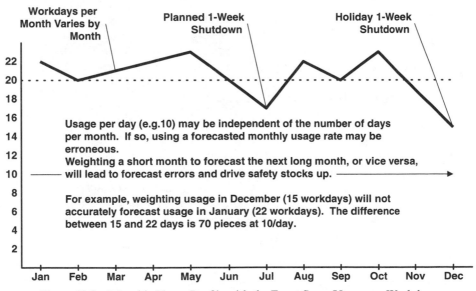

Figure 10.8 Monthly Usage Profile with the Exact Same Usage per Workday

Table 10.5   Calculating Standard and Mean Absolute Deviation

PERIOD	EQUIVALENT WORK DAYS (20 = AVG)	FORECAST USAGE (FACTORED)	ACTUAL USAGE	DEVIATION (FORECAST— ACTUAL)	DEVIATION²	OVERDEVIATIONS ONLY
Jan	21/20 = 1.05	105	85	20	400	
Feb	20/20 = 1.00	100	105	−5	25	−5
Mar	21/20 = 1.05	105	105	0	0	
Apr	22/20 = 1.10	110	100	10	100	
May	22/20 = 1.10	110	90	20	400	
Jun	21/20 = 1.05	105	120	−15	225	−15
Jul	15/20 = 0.75	75	70	5	25	
Aug	21/20 = 1.05	105	100	5	25	
Sep	20/20 = 1.00	100	110	−10	100	−10
Oct	23/20 = 1.15	115	110	5	25	
Nov	18/10 = 0.90	90	100	−10	100	−10
Dec	15/20 = 0.75	75	80	−5	25	−5
				Abs 110	1,450	Abs 45
Abs Avg				9.17		9.00

Note: Abs refers to the absolute value. When calculating deviations, positives do not net against negatives.

"Overdeviations" column is used to calculate an alternate to the standard or mean absolute deviation where only overdeviations are considered.

For the data in Table 10.5, calculating MAD based on all overdeviations and underdeviations and just overdeviations, equals nine. This indicates that the forecast is tracking actual usage fairly accurately on average.

Calculating the Mean Absolute Deviation (MAD)

Mean absolute deviation is an approximation of the standard deviation. It is the sum of the absolute deviations between the forecast and actual usage divided by the number of periods. The number of periods included in the average is important to the result. If the planner recently made a correction to synchronize the forecast with the actual usage rate, the system will continue to calculate a higher deviation until the smoothing process has compensated. From Table 10.5, mean absolute deviation is calculated as:

$$MAD = 110/12 = 9.17$$

In order to use statistical tables derived from the standard deviation, standard deviation can be approximated as shown following. Multiplying MAD (9.17) by 1.25 to obtain the standard deviation equals 11.46. This is within 0.17 percent of the calculated standard deviation ([11.48 – 11.46]/11.48). Anything this close will not significantly affect the safety stock quantity regardless of which of the two techniques is used.

$$\sigma = \text{MAD} \times 1.25 = 11.46$$

Example: The information in Table 10.5 can be used to verify the 1.25 factor which relates standard to mean absolute deviation:

$$\text{MAD} = 110/12 = 9.17 \quad \sigma = (1450/[12 - 1])^{0.5} = 11.48$$

$$11.48/9.17 = 1.252$$

If only the periods where actual usage exceeded forecast are included as shown in the last column of Table 10.6, MAD = 45/5 = 9.0 and σ = 11.25. This is a valid technique to use for parts where actual usage can exceed forecast to a greater extent than forecast can exceed actual usage. A part with average usage equal to two per period cannot have less than a zero demand, for example. This is a –2 deviation at most. However, a demand greater than +2 may be very likely and is really the condition which must be covered by safety stock. Using this technique reduces the impact on averaging of including those periods where demand is zero or one. Periods of small deviations will tend to reduce the standard or mean absolute deviation. The integral system can monitor deviation history against such parts and identify those where the planner may need to perform a manual review or change to some distribution other than normal. This is a common occurrence with phase-out parts.

A check on this technique is to compare the resultant MAD with that calculated by including both underdeviations and overdeviations. The planner can review any parts where the discrepancy between the two calculations differs by a given percentage. Another check is to review any parts where the forecasted usage is five (pick a number) or less per month.

STATISTICAL SAFETY STOCK VIA MEAN ABSOLUTE DEVIATION

Statistical safety stock provides the highest degree of management control in terms of being able to fine-tune variables in order to affect the calculated safety stock quantity. This is not to be mistaken for an increase in precision necessarily, though this is the intent as compared to the other techniques.

Mean absolute deviation is traditionally used in inventory systems as compared to standard deviation. From a practical perspective, the integral system can use either technique for determining deviation. This section uses MAD to illustrate the technique since it involves the extra steps required to first approximate standard deviation. The equations used for illustration lend themselves to update once per period, which is assumed to be monthly.

When to Select the Statistical Safety Stock Technique

A company selects the statistical safety stock technique over fixed or time period in the following representative situations:

- The part has some unplanned demand but is primarily a dependent-demand part. Only the unplanned portion of demand is considered for safety stock purposes.

- The part has a large volume and stable demand from period to period. In this situation, statistical safety stock provides for a very minimal or possibly even zero safety stock based on the safety stock service percent selected. Fixed and time period safety stock techniques may provide too large a safety stock for such parts.

- For parts having deviations within a predictable range, statistical safety stock can be structured to provide a given level of safety stock service percent. Extending the current usage rate into the future via the time period method tends to shortchange these items in periods where increases follow decreases.

- Parts are not used as sets, and stock balances do not need to be maintained in sync with those of other parts.

- The part being phased-in is superseding another part which has a usage history. Initializing the mean absolute deviation related statistical fields to reflect history of the part being superseded automatically transfers the history of the old part as required to calculate a statistical safety stock for the new part.

Pros and Cons of a Statistical Safety Stock

Statistical safety stock equations calculate a precise answer for situations which may not be all that precise. However, the basis for the calculations is well-grounded in mathematics and statistics. Some attributes or problems of statistical safety stock which the planner must account for include the following:

- Certain parts may have a zero calculated safety stock even when a safety stock service percent is set. The combination of a part's deviations and low enough safety stock service percent may be such that no actual safety stock is required. Therefore, merely specifying a safety stock service percent is no guarantee that there will be some quantity of safety stock.

- The equations and logic used to calculate a statistical safety stock are complicated for those who are not mathematically inclined. While being fairly straightforward once an individual knows how they are used, they do require a basic knowledge and understanding of mathematics and statistics to know when to bend or break the "rules" regarding their application. Many individuals distrust calculated values where the basis is not understood.

With an integral system, the calculated values can be compared to the actual values over time to determine how close they are. Systems should not be designed in a manner where the users must take a calculated value on faith. Also, there are fields in the statistical safety stock equations which can be modified to fine-tune the results. These fields should be calculated as a reference when a change can improve accuracy levels so the planner does not have to perform the mathematics manually.

- Safety stock is dependent on the number of orders (i.e., exposures to stock-out) being protected against a stock-out. Placing more orders to reduce average inventory may require an increase in safety stock in order to protect a part from stock-out for a given time frame. Alternatively, safety stock decreases as lead times are reduced because the deviation over lead time is smaller. Therefore, Just in Time initiatives which couple frequent receipts with short replenishment lead times somewhat offset two competing safety stock conditions. The number of exposures to stock-out is encompassed by the Safety Factor (Table 10.7).

- Keeping the safety stock service percent low in order to reduce safety stock implies that a certain number of stock-outs are acceptable out of a given number of replenishment cycles. This can become more of a problem in assemblies that use many parts which are independently planned. In such a case, the probability of having all of the components at any given time is directly related to the safety stock service percent. For example, consider a printed circuit board consisting of a board and 10 components where all have a 90 percent safety stock service percent and all eleven items are independently planned. The probability of having all parts in stock at the same time is $90\%^{11} = 31\%$ (0.9 multiplied by itself 11 times, one each for the board and components). In actual practice, companies seem to be able to produce such products in spite of the low odds. They expedite stock-outs, reschedule open orders, and carry safety stock. Pure statistical averages are not necessarily applicable in cases where the company takes proactive actions to address problems.

Calculating Safety Stock Via Mean Absolute Deviation (MAD)

The previous examples used a 12-month table to illustrate how to calculate the standard and mean absolute deviations. It is not necessary to maintain this level of history with an inventory system which calculates Mean Absolute Deviation (MAD) at the end of each (monthly) period. The period activity (total quantity of actual unplanned productive issues) is compared to forecasted activity to determine the absolute deviation. This value is then smoothed with that of historical activity via a weighting factor to determine the statistical safety stock. Therefore, the maximum peaks will be smoothed to a lesser value.

Smoothing prevents a large one-time deviation (whether underforecast or overforecast) from causing a significant change in the safety stock quantity. For example, an alpha factor of 0.20 bases the calculated new mean absolute deviation on 20 percent of the current period's deviation and 80 percent of historical usage and deviation. This "smooths" the effect of deviation of actual from forecasted usage in the current month, which may be higher or lower than average. With an average deviation of 40 and a current month deviation of 60, a 0.20 alpha factor uses only 12 (0.20×60) as the current month contribution and 32 [$(1 - 0.20) \times 40$] as the historical contribution for a new MAD of 44. The "60" deviation was smoothed into the historical deviation history. Even if this deviation was due to actual usage being less than forecast, the MAD will still increase. However, the reduction in usage will be accounted for by a reduction in the new forecast, which will be used in next month's safety stock calculations.

Once the calculation process is completed, the previous set of MAD-related fields is replaced by the current values. The unplanned issue transactions from the current month can then be moved from the active database to the history file. In this way, a small number of fields are maintained in the inventory part master file as opposed to what may be a lengthy number of transactions in the part activity file. The Part Activity Screen can then display the monthly statistics related to forecast (factored for the 20-day month), actual unplanned usage, maximum deviation, smoothed deviation, and so on.

Example: Consider the following data for an independent demand part:

60 Days   Lead Time, at 20 workdays per standard month
90%   Safety Stock Service Percent ($\geq$ 9 of 10 replenishments protected from stock-out)
0.20   Alpha Factor (for trending purposes; see Chapter 8 Forecasting)
40 pcs   Order Quantity (indicating multiple orders per month)
125 pcs   Past Month's Actual (Unplanned) Usage Rate
100 pcs   Past Month's Forecast (Unplanned) Usage Rate
1.00   Mean Absolute Deviation[3]

In the monthly inventory run, the following sequence of calculations is performed to determine the statistical safety stock. Date is as of the end of business the last workday of the calendar month.

1. Absolute Deviation (absolute value) equals 25 pcs. This is the actual usage difference (either plus or minus) from forecast.

$$\text{Absolute Deviation (25)} = \text{ABS} \left[\text{Past Month's Forecast Usage (100)} - \text{Past Month's Actual (125)} \right]$$

2. New Mean Absolute Deviation equals 5.8 pcs (this becomes next month's Old MAD). The Alpha Factor is a weighting factor. The higher

---

3. The Mean Absolute Deviation is rounded up to 1.00 if less than 1.00. This prevents MAD from being set to zero.

the Alpha Factor, the more weight is given to the most recent period. Refer to Chapter 8, Forecasting, for more detail. The MAD is an average of deviation over some number of periods into the past.

$$
\underset{(5.8)}{\text{New MAD}} = \left(\underset{(.20)}{\text{Alpha Factor}} \times \underset{(25)}{\text{Absolute Deviation}} \right) + \left(\left[1 - \underset{(.20)}{\text{Alpha Factor}} \right] \times \underset{(1)}{\text{Old MAD}} \right)
$$

Note that an equation such as this is an alternative to maintaining an on-line period-by-period history of forecast vs. actual usage in order to calculate the Mean Absolute Deviation as described in a previous section. The smoothing factor (Alpha Factor) has the same effect as adding up various deviations from a table and dividing by the number of periods to obtain an average. The advantage is that deviations in older periods are assigned a lower weight than more recent deviations. *Note that the company may want to use a separate weighting factor than is used for forecasting.*

3. Standard Deviation calculated from MAD equals 7.25 pcs. Standard Deviation is used as a reference for statistical tables which are based on standard deviation.[4]

$$
\underset{(7.25)}{\text{Standard Deviation}} = 1.25 \times \underset{(5.8)}{\text{New MAD}}
$$

4. Lead Time Deviation equals 12.6 pcs.

$$
\underset{(12.6)}{\text{Lead Time Deviation}} = \underset{(7.25)}{\text{Standard Deviation}} \times \left(\underset{(3.0)}{\text{Lead Time Months}} \right)^{.5}
$$

The preceding formula extends the standard deviation over some portion of the lead time for parts with a forecast review period which does not match the part's lead time. In this example, the calculated standard deviation is based on a 1-month forecast period, though the part has a 3-month lead time. Theoretically, an order for the part can be released and then the part can experience three months in a row of higher than forecasted demand. Safety stock based on this worst-case scenario would assume that the average deviation would occur for three months in a row. This part would then have to be protected at three times the

---

4. Note that standard deviation may be calculated directly by some systems, in which case Mean Absolute Deviation is not required.

level of a similar part with a 1-month lead time. In practice, this is probably not a reasonable assumption. Therefore, the Lead Time Deviation applies a factor to account for some portion of deviation over the lead time but not worst case. The full equation is as follows:

$$\underset{\text{Deviation}}{\underset{\text{Time}}{\text{Lead}}} = \underset{\sigma}{\text{Standard}}_{\text{Deviation}} \times (LT/F)^{\beta}$$

LT   Lead Time in months (3 months in this example)

F   Forecast interval (1 month in this example)

β   Beta factor—the increase in safety stock is not directly proportional to the increase in lead time. Beta is typically set in the 0.5 to 0.7 range (0.5 is commonly used as it is the square root formula). Setting Beta to 1 is equivalent to the worst case scenario.

Table 10.6 identifies the multipliers used based on lead time vs. Beta for various combinations. The decision support element of the integral system should calculate the deviations which have actually been experienced in the past based on the lead time. These deviations can then be used to support the planner's selection of an appropriate value for Beta.

4. Safety Factor equals 1.28 based on σ (or 1.60 based on MAD). The Safety Factor is the number of Standard Deviations (or Mean Absolute Deviations) associated with the Safety Stock Service Percent. The system uses a lookup table such as that shown in Table 10.7 to assign the Safety Factor.

5. Safety Stock equals 17 pcs (rounded up from 16.1) based on standard deviation.

Table 10.6 Lead Time/Beta Multipliers for Forecast Period Equal to 1 Month

β	ACTUAL LEAD TIME					
	0.25 MONTHS	0.5 MONTHS	1 MONTH	2 MONTHS	3 MONTHS	4 MONTHS
0.5	0.50	0.71	1.00	1.41	1.73	2.00
0.6	0.44	0.66	1.00	1.52	1.93	2.30
0.7	0.38	0.62	1.00	1.62	2.16	2.64
0.8	0.33	0.57	1.00	1.74	2.41	3.03
0.9	0.29	0.54	1.00	1.87	2.69	3.48
1.0	0.25	0.50	1.00	2.00	3.00	4.00

Table 10.7   Safety Factors Based on a Normal Distribution

SAFETY STOCK SERVICE PERCENT FOR INVENTORY PURPOSES	ADDITIONAL SAFETY STOCK SERVICE PERCENTS FROM STATISTICS TABLE	SAFETY FACTOR FOR STANDARD DEVIATION (σ)	SAFETY FACTOR FOR MEAN ABSOLUTE DEVIATION (MAD) ($\sigma \times 1.25$)
50%	50.00%	0.00	0.00
80%	79.95%	0.84	1.05
85%	84.13%	1.00 σ	1.25
90%	89.97%	1.28	1.60
	94.52%	1.6	2.00
95%	95.05%	1.65	2.06
	97.72%	2.00 σ	2.50
98%	97.98%	2.05	2.56
99%	99.01%	2.33	2.91
	99.18%	2.40	3.00
	99.87%	3.00 σ	3.75
	99.93%	3.20	4.00
"100%"[1]	99.99685%	4.00 σ	5.00
	99.999971%	5.00 σ	6.25
	99.999999%	6.00 σ	7.50

Source: Normal Distribution Function Table and "The Nature of Six Sigma Quality"
[1]The planner needs to specify the number of sigma "equivalent" to 100 percent service by part. The system default may be 4 sigma. The actual may be set from 3 to 6 based on actual deviations experienced in the past.

```
Safety         Safety      Lead Time
Stock    =    Factor  ×   Deviation
 (17)         (1.28)       (12.6)
```

The same calculation using MAD provides a safety stock of 1.6×10.05 = 17 (rounded up from 16.1). Table 10.8 identifies the quantity of safety stock which is required at various Safety Stock Service Percents for this example. Figure 10.9 then graphs these values to illustrate the geometric relationship of safety stock quantity to Safety Stock Service Percents.

Note that the Safety Factor is related to replenishment frequency. A

Table 10.8 Example Safety Stock at Various Safety Stock Service Percents

FACTOR	SAFETY STOCK SERVICE PERCENTS					
	80%	90%	95%	97%	99%	100%
New MAD	5.80	5.80	5.80	5.80	5.80	5.80
Standard Deviation	7.25	7.25	7.25	7.25	7.25	7.25
Lead Time Deviation ($\beta = 0.5$)	12.60	12.60	12.60	12.60	12.60	12.60
Safety Factor Based on σ	0.84	1.28	1.65	1.88	2.33	4.00
Safety Stock	11	17	21	24	30	51

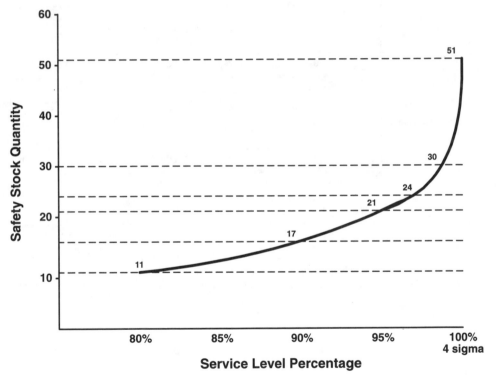

Figure 10.9 Example Safety Stock at Various Safety Stock Service Percents

Safety Stock Service Percent of 90 percent relates to nine orders out of 10 without a stock-out. If there are 10 orders per year, this relates to at most one permitted stock-out per year. At one order per week, this is at most one permitted stock-out every 10 weeks. At a 99 percent level and weekly replenishments, this is at most one permitted stock-out approximately every two years.

Example: To calculate the Safety Stock Service Percent required for a given protection level in terms of at most "x" stock-outs per time, use the following example for a part received daily:

Periods without a Stock-Out/Replenishment Periods

239 Days without a Stock-Out/240 Days per Year = 0.9958

This is very close to four standard deviations in Table 10.7. Therefore, set the Safety Factor to 100 percent. Since the planner must define what level of protection is related to 100 percent, set the "Standard Deviation related to 100 percent for the Part" equal to 4.00 Standard Deviations in the Part Master.

Table vs. Smoothed MAD Calculation

As a check between using a smoothing equation for the MAD as discussed previously or a table calculation as was illustrated in Table 10.5, consider the following comparison. Table 10.9 contains the Table 10.5 source information, along with two different calculations for MAD. One uses a 0.2 Alpha Factor and one uses a 0.5 Alpha Factor. Since the smoothed MAD equation requires one period of initial data for the old MAD, the Table 10.5 value of 9.17 was used.

The 0.2 "smoothed" MAD was lower than the Table 10.5 (averaged) MAD in

Table 10.9   Calculating Mean Absolute Deviation via Smoothing Technique

PERIOD (TABLE 10.5)	EQUIVALENT WORK DAYS (20 = AVG) (TABLE 10.5)	FORECAST USAGE (FACTORED) (TABLE 10.5)	ACTUAL USAGE (TABLE 10.5)	DEVIATION (FORECAST— ACTUAL) (TABLE 10.5)	MAD CALCULATED USING 0.2 ALPHA FACTOR	MAD CALCULATED USING 0.5 ALPHA FACTOR
Initial					9.17	9.17
Jan	21/20 = 1.05	105	85	20	11.34	14.59
Feb	20/20 = 1.00	100	105	−5	10.07	9.80
Mar	21/20 = 1.05	105	105	0	8.06	4.90
Apr	22/20 = 1.10	110	100	10	8.45	7.45
May	22/20 = 1.10	110	90	20	10.76	13.73
Jun	21/20 = 1.05	105	120	−15	11.61	14.37
Jul	15/20 = 0.75	75	70	5	10.29	9.69
Aug	21/20 = 1.05	105	100	5	9.23	7.35
Sep	20/20 = 1.00	100	110	−10	9.38	8.68
Oct	23/20 = 1.15	115	110	5	8.50	6.84
Nov	18/10 = 0.90	90	100	−10	8.80	8.42
Dec	15/20 = 0.75	75	80	−5	8.04	6.71
				Abs 110		
Abs Avg				9.17		

Note: Abs refers to the absolute value. When calculating deviations, positives do not net against negatives.

December by about 12 percent (8.04 vs. 9.17). The 0.5 smoothed MAD was 27 percent lower (6.71 vs. 9.17). Both of the "smoothing" equations using the Alpha Factor recognized that the 15 to 20 magnitude deviations experienced by the part occurred further in the past and that the more recent deviations were all in the 5 to 10 range. As is shown in Table 10.9, both the 0.2 and 0.5 Alpha Factors reacted at the time of the larger deviations. Over time, however, the smaller 5 to 10 magnitude deviations caused the smoothed MADs to be reduced. The difference, therefore, between the Table 10.5 (average) calculation and the smoothed calculations is that the table calculation weighted all period deviations equally, without accounting for the age of the data. Smoothing reacted more heavily to the most recent trend toward lower deviations.

Table 10.10 compares the three MADs with respect to the safety stock required at a 100 percent Safety Factor level (4σ). A 3-month replenishment was assumed. A 0.2 Alpha Factor results in approximately 12 percent less safety stock than the table calculation ([80 − 70]/80). The 0.5 Alpha Factor results in approximately 26 percent less ([80 − 59]/80). Selecting either of the smoothed values results in a reduction in safety stock investment in this case.

FIXED SAFETY STOCK

A fixed safety stock provides a means for the planner to specify a part's safety stock quantity separately from any system calculations. This technique is used for parts which require some type of special oversight or for parts where a zero safety stock is desired. For example, phase-in and phase-out conditions may require a manual override to keep pace with changing demand patterns. Consider dependent-demand parts where safety stock is not required or is set at the Master Schedule level in the form of overplanning. It may be desirable to force any additional calculation of safety stock to zero. The fixed quantity remains in effect until changed by the planner.

Figure 10.10 illustrates a part with variable demand which has a fixed safety stock quantity of 20. When considering the on-hand balance for ordering pur-

Table 10.10   Comparison of Safety Stock at Various MAD Calculations

FACTOR	100% SAFETY STOCK SERVICE PERCENTS (DECEMBER)		
	TABLE CALC.	0.2 ALPHA FACTOR	0.5 ALPHA FACTOR
Old MAD	N/A	8.80	8.42
New MAD	9.17	8.04	6.71
Standard Deviation ($\times$ 1.25)	11.46	10.05	8.39
Lead Time Deviation ($\beta = 0.5$)	19.85	17.41	14.53
Safety Factor Based on σ	4.00 (100%)	4.00 (100%)	4.00 (100%)
Safety Stock	80 (79.4)	70 (69.6)	59 (58.12)

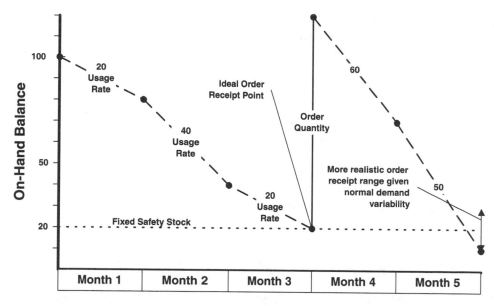

Figure 10.10   Fixed Safety Stock

MONTH	USAGE	FIXED SS	BEGIN MONTH	END MONTH	RECEIPT
1	20	20	100	80	
2	40	20	80	40	
3	20	20	40	20	100
4	60	20	120	60	
5	50	20	60	(10)	100

poses, the reorder point considers the 20 as unavailable. Any usage which dips into safety stock must be replenished by the next order, as happened in Month 5. The planner bases the fixed quantity on some knowledge of past usage and expected future usage.

A fixed safety stock may be used in the following representative situations:

• A new part being phased-in has no history (as opposed to one which is superseding another). Therefore, a calculated statistical safety stock may be too low for the amount of stock the planner feels is required until sufficient history is available. Establishing a fixed safety stock enables the planner to protect the part from stock-out during the introduction phase.

• There may be a long history of usage for a part being phased-out. Both the statistical safety stock and time period safety stock techniques will continue to calculate a gradually-reducing safety stock over time. This will occur at the same time the company is consciously trying to deplete the on-hand balance to zero. To counter this, the planner sets the fixed safety stock to zero and manually monitors usage against stock balances.

• Dependent-demand parts which do not have any unplanned usage are fully planned via the MS and MRP systems. The planner eliminates any possibility of the system generating a safety stock by setting the safety stock technique to fixed and the safety stock quantity to zero.

To use this technique, the Safety Stock Code is set to F—Fixed, and the safety stock quantity is set to the fixed quantity in the Part Master File. The date should also be set and a comment added as to why the particular technique or quantity was selected. If the selection should be flagged for reevaluation on a particular date, that date should also be specified.

TIME PERIOD SAFETY STOCK

A time period safety stock provides a level of safety stock equal to the usage over the specified (future) time frame. The period may be a decimal (i.e., 0.5 equals 2 weeks, where periods are months). As dependent- or independent-demand increases, safety stock increases in direct proportion, and vice versa.

At 1,000 finished goods products per day and a 2-day time period safety stock, the safety stock quantity for any component is equivalent to 2,000 units (or some multiplier, based on the bill of material quantity for the product). Where demand varies over time, the safety stock time period applies to the period following the review period.

Time period safety stock is calculated based on forecasted demand, actual demand, or a combination. Inventory systems which base demand on a monthly forecast extend the forecasted monthly usage by the number of time periods as shown following. This is based on an assumption of steady usage in future time periods, as occurs with a forecast of independent-demand parts where forecasting is based on statistical or fixed quantity techniques. A variation is to account for trending in future periods by adjusting the forecasted monthly usage accordingly. In any case, the forecast should be adjusted for the number of days per period such as when months vary in terms of workdays.

$$\begin{array}{c} \text{Time} \\ \text{Period} \\ \text{Safety} \\ \text{Stock} \end{array} = \begin{array}{c} \text{Forecast} \\ \text{Monthly} \\ \text{Usage} \end{array} \times \begin{array}{c} \text{Safety Stock} \\ \text{Time} \\ \text{Period} \end{array}$$

Example: Consider the following data for an independent-demand part where a statistical forecast is calculated each month. Note that the forecast monthly usage in future periods must also account for the variation in the number of days in the month.

2 weeks   Safety Stock Time Period
40 pcs   Forecast Monthly Usage
1 month   Review Period, with 20 days being the average period length

$$\frac{\text{Time Period}}{\text{Safety Stock}} = \frac{2 \text{ weeks}}{4 \text{ weeks/month}} \times \frac{40 \text{ pcs}}{\text{month}} = 20 \text{ pcs safety stock}$$

Future demand must be calculated and summed when demand in future periods varies. This is common for parts subject to both dependent- and independent-demand. Variable demand also occurs for parts or products with cyclical demand patterns as occurs with seasonal products. In this case, the time period safety stock sums the actual dependent- and independent-demand over the safety stock time period to determine the safety stock.

Example: Consider a part with a usage of 100 units in Period 1 and 140 units in Period 2. A 2-period time period safety stock results in a 240-unit safety stock. Each period, the safety stock is subject to change to reflect the changing demand patterns in the future.

Note that a time period safety stock includes both dependent- and independent-demand unless specifically restricted to independent-demand. If the intent is to cover only the independent-demand portion of demand, the inventory system must provide a way to differentiate between the two types.

Figure 10.11 illustrates a part with variable demand which has a 2-week time period safety stock quantity. In this case, a monthly run calculates the safety stock quantity as one-half (2/4 weeks) of the next month's forecasted usage. The quantity varies directly as the sum of the planned and forecasted usage varies. When considering the on-hand balance for ordering purposes, the reorder point considers the safety stock quantity as unavailable. Any usage which dips into safety stock must be replenished by the next order, as happened in Month 5.

The time period safety stock technique is typically used for two different types of situations. The first is for inexpensive independent-demand parts where the cost of a stock-out more than offsets the expense of carrying excess safety stock. The level can be set at a quantity which should ensure that the part rarely or never stocks-out. The second is to cover a given number of hours or days supply of production. In this case, both dependent- and independent-demand parts are covered equally. In the second case, there may not be many independent-demand parts except as required to support customer service.

- A time period safety stock enables the planner to synchronize safety stock levels with the usage rate when demand is either increasing or decreasing. In this respect, it is similar to a leading capacity strategy which attempts to synchronize capacity with expected, rather than current, requirements. A fixed safety stock quantity during periods of increasing demand is likely to provide insufficient stock as demand increases, while providing excess stock as demand decreases. From a practical perspective, however, any part where a

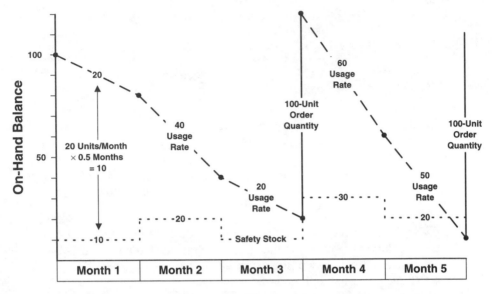

MONTH	MONTHLY FORECASTED USAGE	2-WEEK SAFETY STOCK	BEGIN MONTH	END MONTH	RECEIPT
1	20	10	100	80	
2	40	20	80	40	
3	20	10	40	20	100
4	60	30	120	60	
5	50	20	60	(10)*	100

Note: The negative balance in Month 5 of 10 units is covered by the 20-unit safety stock.

Figure 10.11   2-Week Time Period Safety Stock

fixed safety stock applies probably does not require a very dynamic review process as related to safety stock.

- When the time period order quantity technique is used to order materials, time period is also the logical choice for the safety stock technique. Where reordering occurs monthly, the safety stock is typically set for one or more days, weeks, or months. For inexpensive parts, for example, the safety stock quantity may be set as the sum of the demand during the review period (i.e., time between review periods) plus demand during the replenishment lead time. This accounts for the worst case situation where a stock-out condition occurs immediately following a monthly order review when no replenishment order was placed (i.e., the stock balance was greater than the reorder point). Safety stock must cover that entire month plus the time to receive parts when ordered in the end-of-month order review.

$$\begin{array}{c}\text{Safety Stock}\\\text{Time}\\\text{Period}\end{array} = \begin{array}{c}\text{Periodic}\\\text{Review}\\\text{Cycle}\end{array} + \begin{array}{c}\text{Replenishment}\\\text{Lead}\\\text{Time}\end{array}$$

Note that this is somewhat of an extreme case. If a stock-out occurs at any time between order review cycles, the planner should reorder immediately.

Example: Consider the following "worst case" data for the part in Figure 10.12 where ordering is considered only at the end of the month:

100 units   Demand per month (25 per week)
6 weeks   Lead Time
Monthly   Order Review Cycle
150 units   Demand during the replenishment lead time is 150 ($100 \times 6/4$)

The Time Period Safety Stock = 250 units (100 + 150)

During a particular monthly order review, there was sufficient stock that no reorder was suggested (i.e., the stock balance was greater than the Reorder Point). The Reorder Point of 400 is calculated as Demand During Lead Time (150) plus Safety Stock (250). However, the day following the review, an issue dropped the available inventory level just below the Reorder Point. As long as the available stock balance is between the ROP of 400 and the Safety Stock of 250 and demand remains within forecast parameters, the part does not need to be reordered until the next monthly review cycle. At that time, 100 additional units will have been issued, leaving 150 to cover the lead time duration until the next order is received.

```
08:00am 07/01/Y1                    Safety Stock Technique Details

Part Number:              4482A19AAA   Part Name:              Bracket    Inv U/M:              PCS
Replenishment Lead Time:  6 Weeks      Forecast Monthly Usage: 100/Month  Review Period: Month

Safety        Demand        Replenishment    Planner          Safety       Standard
Stock    =    During    +   During       x   Adjustment       Stock    @   Cost
Quantity      Review Period  Lead Time        Multiplier       Investment

  250    =     100      +   150(100 x 6/4) x    1.00           $ 125.00     $ 0.50

Safety Stock Code:        T—Time Period  Reason for Selection:   Consistent with Time Period OQ
Safety Stock Date:        08–Aug–YYYY    Reevaluate Date:        12/01/Y1             By: T. Allen

Statistical Safety Stock Reference Information-----------------------------------------------------
Service Level:            100%    99%    97%    95%    90%    80%
Ref. Statistical Qty:     300     170    143    105    87     54

   PART LIST    PRODUCT LIST      GRAPH         HISTORY        WHAT-IF        RETURN
```

Figure 10.12 Time Period Safety Stock

The company can eliminate the extra 100 units in stock which covers the duration from a stock-out during the month until the end of the month if the planner reorders immediately upon a stock-out. This reduces the Time Period Safety Stock to 150 units.

With an inexpensive part in regular usage, the safety stock should be set to a high enough quantity that the risk of stock-out is negligible. As shown in the reference information at the bottom of the screen, demand variability is such that a "100 percent" statistical safety stock quantity has been calculated at 300 pcs. The planner has decided not to set the Planner Adjustment Multiplier to 1.2 (300/250) as required to calculate a Time Period Safety Stock equal to the 100% Statistical Safety Stock quantity. The planner will be prompted to review the safety stock-related logic for this part on 12/01/Y1.

COMPUTER-BASED DECISION SUPPORT FOR SAFETY STOCK EVALUATION

It is often difficult to select the most appropriate safety stock technique for a given part and competitive environment. The difficulty is not so much in selecting the technique. There are not that many. The problem is in selecting a technique which provides the level of service required and informative feedback with respect to service level performance over time. Selecting a technique is more critical for an expensive part than for an inexpensive one from the perspective of inventory investment. However, cost may not be the relevant factor when considering the criticality of the part itself and risk of halting production. Once the technique is selected, specifying the relevant variables such as time period, Alpha Factor, and safety stock service percent become the planner's task.

There is often a natural resistance against changing a technique once it becomes ineffective. The first problem is in being able to determine when this occurs. Normal forecast variability and permitted stock-outs tend to obscure this point. The second is to change to what. The inventory system should provide a comparison among techniques to enable the planner to assess the relevance of each technique over time with respect to the company's customer service target. This includes variables within a technique, as well. In order to do this, the system must maintain a history by part of demand, safety stock level, and service level. What is more, the system should maintain reference data such as Alpha Factors used over time, overdeviations and underdeviations, Alpha Factor which would have provided a range of service levels, and established targets.

With targets set by the planner, the inventory decision support system can monitor performance over time and identify those parts which need to be reevaluated, what the problem areas seem to be, and what the alternatives are. The system should additionally calculate what the variables would have been in order to achieve the service targets in periods where they are missed. This eliminates the planner having to do it manually.

Figure 10.13 identifies several of the screens most applicable to the safety

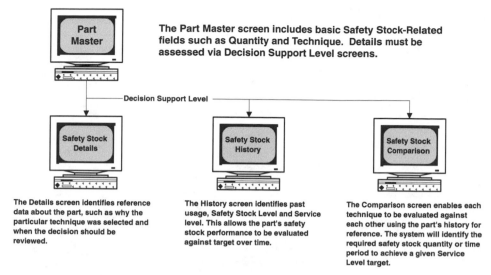

The Part Master screen includes basic Safety Stock-Related fields such as Quantity and Technique. Details must be assessed via Decision Support Level screens.

The Details screen identifies reference data about the part, such as why the particular technique was selected and when the decision should be reviewed.

The History screen identifies past usage, Safety Stock Level and Service level. This allows the part's safety stock performance to be evaluated against target over time.

The Comparison screen enables each technique to be evaluated against each other using the part's history for reference. The system will identify the required safety stock quantity or time period to achieve a given Service Level target.

Figure 10.13   Inventory System Safety Stock-Related Screens

stock area within an inventory decision support system. A representative Details screen was used in the example in the Time Period subsection (Figure 10.12). Other screens support the type of decisions the planner must make with regard to selecting a particular safety stock technique or changing from one technique to another.

In the Figure 10.14 screen, the company made a change from 98 percent target customer service level to 100 percent in February. Even with 295 units in safety stock, a stock-out occurred, resulting in providing only a 99.8 percent customer service level. This stock-out may have been within the parameters established for the safety stock service percent in terms of allowable number of stock-outs compared to exposures to stock-out. However, once a 100 percent customer service level is established, the safety stock service percent must be "100 percent" as well (with 100 percent based on a specified number of standard deviations for the part).

Other information on this screen indicates the number of periods when safety stock was actually used. Ideally, this should be approximately 50 percent of the total replenishment periods being reported. If it is much higher (this is a judgment factor), the forecast may be too low. If it is much lower, the forecast may be too high. In this case, safety stock has been used in 71 percent of the periods displayed, which indicates that the forecast may be too low.

Requirements fall into categories of dependent- (Planned Usage column) and independent-demand (Forecast Unplanned Usage column). Theoretically, dependent-demand parts do not require inventory-planned safety stock since demand is a function of higher level bill of material explosions. Any required safety stock (in the form of business inventory) is specified at the MS-level by over-

08:00am 07/30/YY	Safety Stock History

Part Number: 4482A19AAA Part Name: Bracket Inv U/M: PCS
Replenishment Lead Time: 6 Weeks Forecast Monthly Usage: 100/Month Review Period: Month

Safety Stock Quantity	=	Demand During Review Period	+	Replenishment During Lead Time	x	Planner Adjustment Multiplier	Safety Stock Investment	@	Standard Cost
325	=	100	+	150(100 x 6/4)	x	1.50	$ 162.50		

PERIOD	PLANNED USAGE	FCST UNPLANNED USAGE	SAFETY STOCK	SS TECHNIQUE	TARGET SERVICE	ACTUAL CUST. SERVICE	STOCK-OUTS	SS STK USED	MEET TARGET
Jan	100	99	287	Statistical	98%	100.0%	0	150	Yes
Feb	120	98	295	Statistical	100%	99.8%	1	295	No
Mar	90	100	300	Fixed	100%	100.0%	0	240	Yes
Apr	110	100	300	Fixed	100%	100.0%	0	40	Yes
May	100	80	300	Time Period	100%	100.0%	0	0	Yes
Jun	105	90	338	Time Period	100%	100.0%	0	0	Yes
Jul	125	110	325	Time Period	100%	100.0%	0	275	Yes
Aug	80	100	325	Time Period	100%				
Sep	60	100	325	Time Period	100%				
Oct	50	100	325	Time Perod	100%				
Nov	20	100	325	Time Period	100%				
Dec	0	100	325	Time Period	100%				
HIST AVG	107	97	264		100%	99.97%	1	71%	

PART LIST	PRODUCT LIST	SS TECHNIQUE	WHAT-IF	DETAILS	HISTORY

Figure 10.14   Safety Stock History

planning particular products or options. However, even dependent-demand parts may still be subject to damage, loss, shortages, and service part issues.

Assessing past customer service level is a little more complicated. It requires a knowledge of whether inventory was available to satisfy a requirement at the time the demand was due. The simplest solution may be to flag any demand required during a period when the part was stocked-out. This flag is set within a transaction field by a system program which runs automatically once per day. When the transaction is finally moved to the history file, any transaction which had a required date during a day when the part was stocked-out can be determined.

Note that this type of logic should not be accepted blindly. Take, for example, a dependent-demand part where the material was received four days after the required date. This logic indicates that safety stock is required for the part. While having safety stock would have enabled the part to be issued on schedule, the company may be able to accept a timing availability tolerance in certain situations for certain types of parts. The real focus should be on receiving the material on schedule, on establishing a reasonable required date, or some combination. However, if late issues are an on-going problem, some type of safety stock may be appropriate. This type of analysis identifies those parts and products which should at least be evaluated.

Once the requirements are established for a period and the Stock-Out Flag is either set or not set on each transaction, the customer service level percent can be calculated. For example, consider a part with 100 requirements in a time period, where two could not be satisfied due to a stock-out condition. The customer service level for that period is 98 percent ([100 – 2]/100).

The same type of equation as is used to determine the new mean absolute deviation over time (refer to the statistical safety stock subsection) can be used to establish a customer service percent over time. It is based on weighting the current period using an Alpha Factor and then smoothing previous periods into an overall weighted customer service level. The weighting may be heavier than used for statistical safety stock (i.e., an Alpha Factor of 0.5 vs. 0.2). This weighted percent can be compared against the current level to ensure that trends are improving or at least remaining constant.

$$\begin{matrix} \text{New} \\ \text{Service} \\ \text{Level} \end{matrix} = \left(\begin{matrix} \text{Alpha} \\ \text{Factor} \\ (.50) \end{matrix} \times \begin{matrix} \text{Current} \\ \text{Service} \\ \text{Level} \end{matrix} \right) + \left(\left[1 - \begin{matrix} \text{Alpha} \\ \text{Factor} \\ (.50) \end{matrix} \right] \times \begin{matrix} \text{Old} \\ \text{Service} \\ \text{Level} \end{matrix} \right)$$

Figure 10.15 illustrates a comparison between the Service Level Percent at various levels and the equivalent Statistical Safety Stock. This is contrasted to the Time Period Safety Stock Period required to provide the same quantity. For example, a 98 percent Statistical Safety Stock is equivalent to a 0.09 Time Period Safety Stock. The quantity listed under each Safety Stock Service Percent is also the required Fixed Safety Stock Quantity to provide that level of service. For example, for a Safety Stock Service Percent of 95 percent, the safety stock quantity is three units. To obtain the same safety stock quantity via the time period technique, the period must be set to 0.03 (3/100 units/month) and the Fixed Safety Stock Quantity must be set to 3 pcs.

When a stock-out occurs, the planner can quickly assess historical service level trends. If the current safety stock technique is not providing at least the Target Service Level Percent (98 percent in this case), a change of some type is required. This may involve changing the technique, changing variables, or changing the safety stock quantity. The converse is also true. If service levels are consistently higher than target, it may be advisable from a financial perspective to reduce safety stock levels to some lesser quantity (though providing higher than target service is not considered a negative by customers). A graphical display as shown in Figure 10.15 provides an easy way to compare safety stock levels at various service level percentages.

SUMMARY

From one perspective, safety stock is simply a reaction to a company's inability to accurately forecast independent-demand. As a reactive component of the integral strategy, the emphasis is to increase the accuracy of the forecast and so reduce the investment in safety stock. To a certain extent, perhaps this can be done

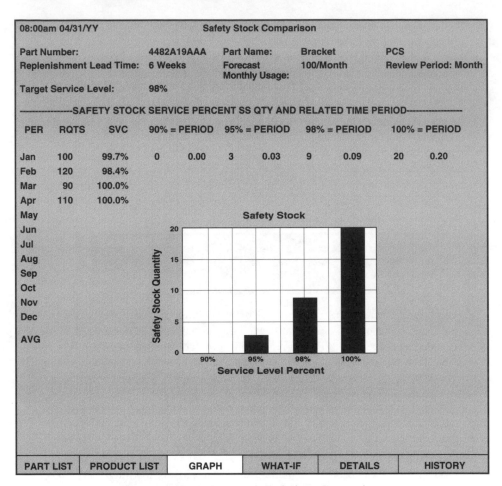

Figure 10.15   Safety Stock Technique Comparison

by improving the methodologies and techniques used. However, safety stock cannot be considered as the penalty companies must pay for poor forecasts. Forecasts will always be approximations of actual demand and will always have deviations.

From another perspective, safety stock may be considered a proactive element of the integral strategy aimed at improving the company's ability to provide the level of service its customers demand and deserve. This does not negate the need in any way to improve the accuracy of the forecast, but companies have more control over their inventory than over the accuracy of the forecast.

Therefore, whatever the perspective, an element of any integral inventory strategy is to improve the company's ability to forecast accurately and determine target safety stock levels. The inventory system must provide the ability to extend historical demand into the future, extend trends into the future, accommodate known product and part changes in future periods, accommodate sales promotions or other anomaly conditions in future periods, and in general assess the effect of deviations in this future demand on safety stock and customer service level. When this ability exists on a part-by-part basis such that risk of stock-out can be compared to the value of investing in additional levels of safety stock via the design of the system itself, then the company has a tool which can be used to target and track improvements in service.

Without effective decision support tools, safety stock has a risk of becoming a mathematical exercise which few understand in many companies. Customer service level then becomes a by-product of the company's actions or, perhaps worse yet, inactions. Safety stock needs to be the result of a proactive series of strategic and tactical initiatives, projects, and programs. Companies with parts subject to independent-demand and deviation from forecast need to carry safety stock in order to ensure high levels of customer service.

- Safety stock can be specified via statistical, fixed, or time period techniques.

- Customer service level is either measured as the number of demands satisfied divided by the total number of demands or the total quantity of a part issued divided by the total quantity ordered. These are not equivalent measures and must be selected by a company based on how their internal or external customers measure performance. Note that neither of these measures is the safety stock customer service percent used in the statistical safety stock calculations, which is yet a third measure of service.

- A company's investment in safety stock is an investment in customer satisfaction. It is too important a process to leave to chance. Computers do the mathematics. However, it takes a planner to know the company's customers, internal production processes, and market conditions. Simply knowing is not enough, though. Planners need a decision support capability which translates data into information and information into choices.

Too many companies place safety stock calculations in the same category as order quantity and forecast calculations. The computer calculates the values and becomes the defacto determiner of company policy. If the company is consistently sustaining target inventory turns and customer service levels, it is probably because highly skilled inventory professionals are managing the safety stock levels.

Chapter 11
AS/RS Project

All projects have similarities in the form of beginning and ending points. It is what is in between that makes them interesting and unique. They require a formal process of requirements definition, development, implementation, acceptance testing, and training. How they are managed differs based on their scope and whether the majority of effort is internal to the company or performed by suppliers. A favorite ISO 9000 saying is that "a process is a process, except for uniqueness." Projects all have a similar process as covered earlier in this book. It is the type of project that makes them unique.

Companies often choose to delegate the design of systems to engineering firms, consultants, or material handling companies, while not making them privy to the company's long-term goals and objectives. With a vision which extends no further than the end of the project, there is little reason to focus on any strategic aspects of the system. Low purchase price becomes the (or a primary) order winner. Competitiveness objectives in terms of flexibility, responsiveness, and reliability are relegated to some average throughput rate.

Companies have a much better chance of making a major project an integral element of the manufacturing or distribution strategy if they follow a design/ build approach and partner with their major suppliers. The design/build approach directly involves the company in the overall design of the system. The company provides the product, process, and business knowledge and expertise. The supplier partners provide the construction, engineering, system, and project management knowledge and expertise. Suppliers develop costs and schedule while being a contributing party to the design and evaluation process. This is a much better risk management technique than having to develop firm fixed prices to support a too short implementation schedule in a 3 to 4 week proposal period after having little interaction with the company and no involvement with the design.

There are three key elements of a successful integral system project:

1. *Use a Design/Build as opposed to a Bid Spec approach.* Design/build is a concurrent engineering approach specifically designed for situations where a variety of trade-off decisions and choices must be evaluated.

2. *Develop an Integral Specification* describing *how* the system will operate, in addition to *what* functions are supported. Integral systems are too complex and involve too many changes within the company to leave the *how* as an afterthought to supplier personnel who will not be intimately involved in the day-to-day operation of the system.

3. *Be realistic about the budget and schedule.* Manage the project in a professional manner. If there is such a thing as the "one" mistake companies make after a project starts, it is allowing the schedule to slip. Projects which remain on schedule have a better chance of remaining within budget than projects which experience delays. There are times, however, when delays are inevitable. Accept the consequences in a realistic, businesslike manner regarding budget and end-date and get on with the project.

This chapter uses an Automated Storage and Retrieval System (AS/RS) project to represent any project in an integral strategy.

- *Getting Started* compares the traditional and design/build approach. Stand-alone systems may be implemented using a traditional approach, but integral systems require a design/build approach. Systems do not somehow "become integral" after the fact.

- *Issues* fall into project, functional, physical, and logical categories. The most significant issues relate to capacity, load configuration, host computer interface, and equipment interfaces and integration.

- *Project Phases* are generally sequential but may overlap to accelerate the schedule. They begin with scope definition and end with integration and final acceptance.

- An *AS/RS* has a number of standard equipment elements. An understanding of the major elements and related terminology helps to understand what a material handling company considers when system designs are developed.

- The *AS/RS Computer System* maintains inventory control of Stock Keeping Units (SKUs), carriers (pallets, totes, and so on), and locations. It differs from a host inventory control system in the real-time interface required to integrate the various equipment and subsystem elements. Host systems "move" data; AS/RS computer systems move machines and loads.

An AS/RS project embodies many of the elements inherent in an integral inventory strategy, whether the need is to store or simply buffer materials. Such a project often begins with a generally defined need and a relatively undefined solution. Timing and costs are issues. Space is at a premium. Technologies which might be unfamiliar to the company are involved. There are multiple apparently valid alternatives. Incremental changes have taken the company as far as they can go. Success is measured in terms of improved operational responsiveness and flexibility, in addition to financial justification elements. Organizational changes are required. These are the situations where design/build is not just the right business approach; it may be mandatory.

GETTING STARTED WITH AN AS/RS PROJECT

Companies have two basic alternatives when it comes to AS/RS project approaches. With a traditional approach, the company defines the type of system they want in the form of a bid spec which they or a third-party develop. As an alternative, a design/build approach requires selecting the suppliers first and then jointly developing the system specification. Table 11.1 provides a comparison among the eight areas of integration.

Traditional Bid Spec Approach (Not Recommended for an Integral System)

Bid specs are developed for projects where the company or their consultant is able to explain exactly what they want. In many cases, these specifications go well beyond specifying functionality, interfaces, and performance. In fact, many bid specs get so detailed as to tell the suppliers mechanical, electrical and controls components, paint thickness, design practices, labeling practices, component dimensions, and so on. They often contain so much detail that they cannot possibly apply to any one supplier's equipment or systems. This increases costs unnecessarily to the company without any increase in functionality or performance.

The traditional bid spec approach for an AS/RS project is not conducive to an integral strategy. With a bid spec, system sizing requirements are often based on a static calculation of average or peak loads per time. An integral strategy bases sizing requirements on the amount of inventory required to meet the company's inventory turns objective at a given manufacturing cycle time and customer service level. With a bid spec, manual interfaces may be specified as opposed to automated delivery to the point-of-use or fit to constrain the scope to as small an area of the company as possible. This stand-alone mentality results in the system being located at an outside corner of the facility, for example. An integral strategy distributes materials among buffers (markets) and centralized storage in order to optimally locate materials to the receiving, shipping, and production operations. Refer to Figure 11.1.

The traditional approach has grown out of a historical reliance on bid specs and proposals to arrive at a system design and price. This works well for standard products and focused systems which lend themselves to such definition before the general and detail design processes have been undertaken. However, even with systems entailing little performance, budget, and schedule risk, a bid spec devel-

Table 11.1 Integration vs. Traditional Approach for AS/RS Project

INVENTORY MANAGEMENT AREAS OF INTEGRATION	INTEGRATION DESIGN/BUILD APPROACH	MORE TRADITIONAL BID SPEC APPROACH	MORE TRADITIONAL BID SPEC RESULT
Materials Management	Inventory turns are translated into the number and size of locations per part. This allows an accurate storage profile to be developed (number of storage locations per carrier height).	Number of (minimum) locations per height are specified in Bid Spec, as is maximum weight of pallet. A generous safety factor is included to account for lack of a structured analysis.	Rack is designed for the maximum pallet weight and one or more carrier heights. System is designed for future expansion in case sufficient number of storage locations has not been specified (or in expectation of increased business).
Information Management	Real-time Host interface is specified in terms of specific fields, lengths, edits, and so on, prior to the System development process.	Host system may not be well defined; actual interface is described in general functional terms, with little or no structure.	Host interface is driven by AS/RS design, reducing time company has to incorporate modifications to Host to meet schedule.
Product Management	Storage and handling profiles are defined in a fashion which ensures that the system is *integral* to the company's receiving, production, and shipping processes.	Storage and handling profiles are defined in a fashion which ensures that the system is (fairly) independent of the company's receiving, production, and shipping processes.	Storage and handling system is designed in a stand-alone fashion, with primary reliance on operator vs. automated interfaces.
Process Management	System Integral Specification specifies material and information flows, rates, volumes, peak conditions, tolerances, timing, handling and storage requirements, and exception conditions.	Brief description of material flow is based on average conditions for a shift or day. A system concept must be developed and firm-fixed priced in a short period of time by the supplier and accepted by the company (with little time for review), as part of the Proposal process.	Software Functional Specification briefly describes functions and screen formats; no integrated system description of operation is developed covering modes of operation and standard and exception conditions.
Quality Management	High-quality pallets, equipment, controls, and software are specified to maximize safety, ergonomics, reliability, maintainability, and system performance.	Same as integration approach.	Low(est) cost system is purchased, with initial perceived savings consumed by additional spare parts, maintenance, and operating costs which were never considered when selecting the supplier.

(continued)

opment and proposal evaluation process can easily add months to the lead time. This increases costs and delays system benefits.

The issue with bid specs for an integral system AS/RS project is one of trust. The company believes that a very detailed bid spec developed by a nonmaterial handling supplier will nonetheless provide all of the specifics needed by the sup-

Table 11.1 *(Continued)*

INVENTORY MANAGEMENT AREAS OF INTEGRATION	INTEGRATION DESIGN/BUILD APPROACH	MORE TRADITIONAL BID SPEC APPROACH	MORE TRADITIONAL BID SPEC RESULT
Organization	Company integrates AS/RS training with ongoing in-house or company-sponsored training program encompassing mechanical, electrical, controls, computer, pneumatic, and hydraulics to ensure that personnel are fully qualified to operate and maintain the system.	System operator, maintenance and system administrator training is left up to the material handling company to specify and conduct.	Company personnel are trained in the basic operation and maintenance of the system. They are assumed to be experienced in the PLCs, controls devices, motors, and so on, incorporated in the system.
Facilities and Equipment	Standard equipment is specified. Nonstandard or company-specific specifications may be incorporated as a cost adder if the extra cost is justified.	Companies overspecify systems in an effort to standardize on characteristics of systems purchased in the past or to save time by consolidating specifications accumulated over time on a variety of projects.	Overspecified equipment performs the same functions as standard equipment but costs more.
Systems and Technologies	Bar code carrier ID and material ID labels and format (or specific RF requirements) are prespecified, including size and location tolerances which meet or exceed normal material handling and identification requirements.	Company requires use of bar code labels but has no clear format or specification.	Bar code specification is developed as part of the control system design with the focus on minimizing scanner costs, not necessarily on meeting the company's needs (since they are not well-defined).

pliers. They further believe that such a specification will be equally applicable to all suppliers. The theory is that some third-party who they are paying thousands of dollars to for a bid spec will protect their interests better than the supplier with whom they will be spending millions of dollars. In such instances, company or third-party specifications should be kept at a performance level and stay away from a level which designs the supplier's equipment for them.

There are nearly always omissions and scope changes in a project. No bid spec developed before a supplier is even selected can possibly anticipate all of the design, operational, organizational, and project issues which will be encountered. With a bid spec, companies and suppliers deal with unresolved issues via the use of a project contingency account. Note that an aberration of project work is that without a contingency account, project managers are given responsibility to manage multimillion dollar projects but are often not given authority to quickly

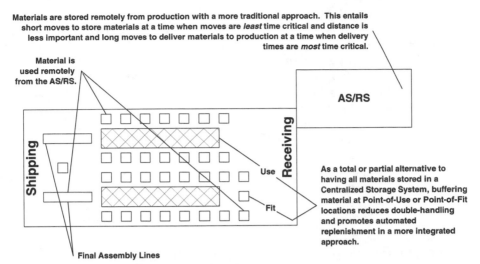

Materials are stored remotely from production with a more traditional approach. This entails short moves to store materials at a time when moves are *least* time critical and distance is less important and long moves to deliver materials to production at a time when delivery times are *most* time critical.

Material is used remotely from the AS/RS.

AS/RS

Shipping

Receiving

Use

Fit

As a total or partial alternative to having all materials stored in a Centralized Storage System, buffering material at Point-of-Use or Point-of-Fit locations reduces double-handling and promotes automated replenishment in a more integrated approach.

Final Assembly Lines

Figure 11.1   Problems with a Traditional Approach to AS/RS Applications

evaluate and make decisions involving only hundreds or thousands of dollars. Authority should match responsibility.

What companies need to be aware of is suppliers who lowball a proposal cost in order to get the contract, with the intention of "getting healthy" through change orders. Companies can end up paying 10 to 25 percent for such learning experiences. An interesting evaluation criteria is the price at which the supplier won several similar projects, the final total cost, and the conditions which caused the increases. Use percentages if dollars are confidential. One supplier won a contract with a 10 percent lower cost than another. After award of the contract, a general design effort was initiated to finalize the overall system design. In less than two months, the change orders wiped out and then exceeded this 10 percent savings based on the second company's more realistic bid. Low purchase cost is not necessarily low final price when dealing with bid specs. A company's best protection is to deal with other professional companies. This is the focus of the design/build approach; select the supplier and then develop the system.

Design/Build Approach (Recommended for Any Type of System)

Companies with a solid justification for the system view *any* time wasted as a lost opportunity to gain the financial, operational, and competitive benefits of the system. Such companies approach major integration projects from a design/build perspective. Automotive companies could not bring car designs to market as fast as they do without design/build, for example. With a design/build approach, the company evaluates the material handling suppliers in terms of their products and services, cost competitiveness, project management capabilities, design standards, personnel, financial stability, ISO 9000 certification, and professionalism prior to initiating the project. The one best suited to the project and company is selected as the partner. Material handling, facility, engineering, computer system, and other business partners are teamed in this manner to focus engineering, project management, simulation, manufacturing, installation, and operational support resources on the material storage, buffering, and handling system need.

With a design/build approach, activities occur in parallel to the greatest extent possible. Multiple designs may be evaluated to assess alternatives. Use of analyses, models, simulation, and prototypes are used to evaluate key design and operational issues. Contractual terms are negotiated with regard to changes in scope, dollars per hour by labor category, and so on. The company makes a commitment to pay the legitimate costs of the project, and the suppliers make a commitment to meet project targets and protect the business interests of the customer in terms of budget and schedule. Regularly scheduled meetings of all partners ensure that communication occurs in a face-to-face manner and that the full resources of the team are focused on identifying and resolving open issues and problems.

The primary emphasis of a design/build approach is to look past the simple concept of order winning and qualifying criteria. The company's intent is to determine how to partner with leaders in the industry to support the achievement of a competitive advantage. This permits the company to establish a design to cost target which maximizes the functionality which can be provided at the target cost. For an AS/RS, this encompasses the elements in Figure 11.2.

Open communication is a key benefit for all parties of the design/build ap-

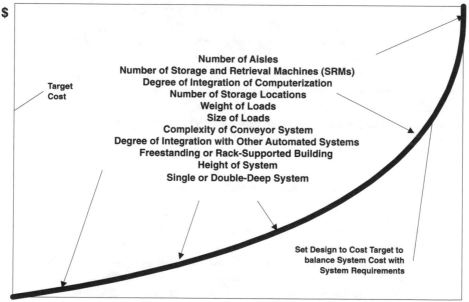

Figure 11.2   AS/RS Design to Cost Target

proach as compared to the traditional approach. This cannot be emphasized enough! Talking saves money when it brings issues to the team for resolution in a timely manner. One company was going to use scissor lifts and special lift/lower deck Automated Guided Vehicles (AGVs) to compensate for a height differential from the AS/RS to the many delivery points in the facility (an expensive solution). The material handling supplier suggested placing the AS/RS floor level at a lower level than the rest of the floor (which also took advantage of a slope on that side of the facility). As a consequence, all material handling transfers were at the same height, eliminating the need for any special equipment.

System capacity and throughput are two of the key considerations for an AS/RS. The bid spec approach as discussed in the last section by definition informs the suppliers that the company has already performed a complete assessment of their material handling and storage needs. Capacity has every appearance of being an absolute requirement, like all other requirements in a bid spec. Experience indicates that capacity tends to become a variable when the company learns the total system price and must search for ways to cut costs. With an integral strategy, capacity and other system requirements are set in relationship to the operation itself (refer to Figure 11.2).

AS/RS PROJECT-RELATED ISSUES

AS/RS project issues are generally categorized as either project-related, operating-related, facility and equipment interface-related, or computer control-related. Project issues primarily deal with scope, budget, and schedule. Operating issues deal with system operation and performance. Facility and equipment issues deal with physical interfaces. Computer and control system issues deal with system communications and control. Issues should be identified and resolved during the design/build process.

Project-Related Issues

Maintaining budget, schedule, and effective communications are the three primary project-related issues areas. Budget and schedule are defined at the beginning of the project. These are updated over time if scope changes or delays or accelerations occur. If scope or other changes occur, a formal change process requiring review and approval prior to beginning any work is followed.

The most common types of issues which occur on any major project involving construction, equipment, and computerization relate to scope changes. These fall into two basic categories. The first includes reassignment of known scope from one company to another. Companies often find that they cannot perform some of the scope they originally assumed due to timing or manpower problems. The second type of scope change relates to layout changes, addition or deletion of equipment, and so on. These are all typical for any major project where there is no possible way to have perfect foresight. Because of this, companies should allocate a contingency budget to be administered by their project manager.

Five to ten percent is a reasonable rule-of-thumb for a contingency budget. This covers oversights as well as items which are difficult to quantify until the engineering is completed. Note that software is a common area for changes since code can often be placed at the host (customer) or AS/RS (supplier) level to perform the same function. Another common area relates to facility-related (physical) interfaces, especially when a new facility is being designed concurrently with the AS/RS and other equipment.

Communication of status occurs on a monthly basis in the form of a written report. At specified milestones, plans, specifications, and drawings communicate design requirements. Manuals communicate operating and maintenance requirements for the installed system. The project manager maintains the Master Project File.

Note that one of the most common mistakes companies make is in not reviewing and approving specifications and plans within the required time frame. This can result in delay charges due to extended schedules. Adhere to the contractual relationship, within the confines of a fair and equitable business relationship.

Operating-Related Issues

A unit load AS/RS is typically purchased primarily for storage density and computerized control of inventory. The overriding functional issue typically deals with system throughput. This refers to the number of loads which may be stored and retrieved in an hour. A dual cycle consists of picking a load from the inbound pick position, storing it in a storage location, moving to another storage location and retrieving a load, and depositing it on the outbound drop position. A single cycle is a complete store or retrieve. A large unit load (pallet) system may perform 25 dual cycles per hour per aisle, while a small miniload (tote or carton) system may perform 100 single cycles or more per hour. These smaller systems are primarily buffer systems to support receiving, incoming inspection, sequencing, and Work in Process activities.

Operating Profile

Operating profile refers to the number, type, and timing of stores and retrieves during the shift or day. The daily profile may be one, two, or three shifts per day, with breaks, startup and shutdown periods. The premise behind dual cycles (refer to Figure 11.3) is that a store will always be available to match with a retrieve and that retrieves have a higher priority than a store. This premise may not be valid at times during the day if there is a rate differential among storage, retrieval, cycle counting, quality control, and quality assurance functions. Load location (zoning) is also a factor. Shorter cycles are involved with loads which are closer to the pick and drop stations and for those which require less vertical movement.

Some type of level loading over time is required if there is a significant mismatch between average throughput and the operating profile. A system which can support operations "on average" may not be able to handle peak demands. Truck schedules are a common area where bid specs fail to account for system per-

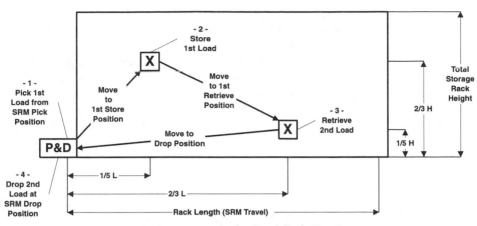

Figure 11.3   Representative Dual Cycle Test Pattern

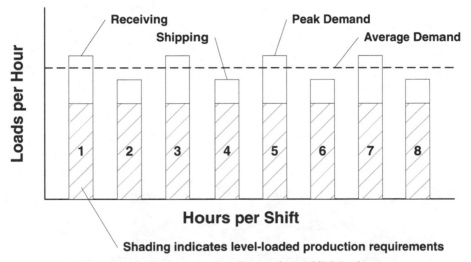

Figure 11.4   Peak vs. Average Demand on AS/RS Performance

formance requirements. Loading or unloading 20 to 40 pallets in a short period of time while also supporting production-related stores and retrievals is a significant peak demand over a 30 to 60 minute time frame. Refer to Figure 11.4. Make sure that the system is not designed on the basis of average rates when peak rates cannot be leveled to the average. Identify both scenarios to the supplier.

System Capacity

From a physical perspective, system capacity is a function of the number of aisles, total storage locations per aisle, and lost locations due to personnel egress aisles, environmental control ductwork, and pick and drop stations. A rule of thumb is to reserve 5 to 15 percent of the available storage locations for normal overflow and peak conditions. This should be evaluated against the operating and growth needs of the business.

Some assessment of the number of parts, number of zones, mixed loads, number of loads, and partial loads is required to size the system. Determining this number with a high level of confidence is frequently a problem during the design process. Companies need to determine the required storage volume for each product, the number of days supply required to support supplier shipment quantities and manufacturing or distribution mix and rate profiles, and the effect of mixed loads and picking operations. This is an analysis and modeling process.

Zoning

Zoning permits materials with similar characteristics to be grouped and separated from those with dissimilar characteristics. Some materials may need to be physically separated due to contamination precautions. Liquids may need to be stored in lower storage locations to prevent leaks from affecting other materials. Splitting lots among aisles provides a backup capability if one aisle is out of service for any reason. Only as much material of a certain type can be stored as the number of storage locations in the zone permits, unless the storage logic permits loads to be stored in another zone once the primary zone is full. Zoning is a logical constraint, however, and may be modified via a computer terminal at any time.

Figure 11.5 illustrates a representative zoning profile. The AS/RS computer system enables the system administrator to assign any storage location to any

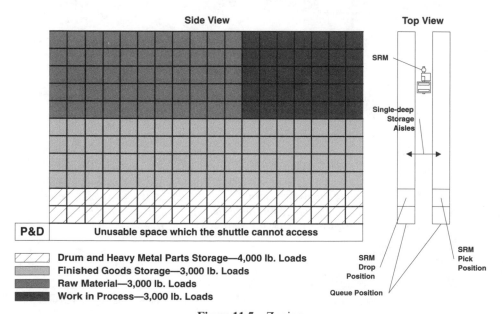

Figure 11.5   Zoning

zone. Note that locations do not need to be adjacent to each other since they are a "logical" assignment. With velocity zones, horizontal speeds are faster than vertical speeds. Therefore, the SRM may be able to get to a further storage location in terms of horizontal distance in less time than to a closer one in terms of vertical distance. Note also that velocity zones are of less consideration for an AS/RS than for conventional storage because the SRMs are much faster than other man-ride forklifts or turret trucks.

Mixed Loads

Mixed loads containing multiple Stock Keeping Units (SKUs) or SKUs/Lots is a computer system issue. The system keeps track of the individual parts and quantities no matter where the load is moved. This is done by associating the parts and quantities to a carrier (pallet or tote) ID and then tracking the location of the carrier. Whereas a carrier is often issued in full when it is retrieved to an outbound station in operations where the entire unit load is shipped or issued to production, carriers with mixed loads require an operator to perform a picking function. This logic may also involve customer-specific host transactions related to Raw, WIP, FG, scrap, transfer, or other transactions. Note that material handling companies may not recognize the need to differentiate among types of issue transactions for accounting purposes; to them, an issue simply means the material is no longer in the AS/RS. If the AS/RS contains different accounting classifications of material, identify this during the design stage.

Mixed loads also relate to the zoning issue. For those parts which may be stored as mixed loads, the limiting factor is that each part on a carrier must have the same zoning requirement as the first (initial) item. The system will reject any attempt to add a part to the carrier which cannot be stored in the same zone.

Future System Expansion

The most common method of expanding an existing AS/RS is to add additional aisles. Companies should not locate site underground or overhead utilities in areas which may be used for future expansion. The computer system should be configured to allow future aisles and stations to be added.

Random Storage

Random storage is the normal method used within a unit load AS/RS. With a maximum-size system where all locations are the same size, any load can be stored in any location. With random storage, the storage algorithm uses the "closest" available storage location unless modified by aisle selection, zoning, or other criteria.

Facility and Equipment Interface-Related Issues

An AS/RS generally consists of the rack structure, in-rack fire protection system, Storage and Retrieval Machine(s), and conveyor system or some type of pick and drop (P/D) station arrangement at the end of aisle. Figure 11.6 provides a typical layout for a two-aisle system. Note that the forklift interface may be replaced with an Automated Guided Vehicle (AGV), Automated Electrified Monorail (AEM), or conveyor system interface as well. Note that even with automation, a manual backup capability which enables a forklift to access the Pick and Drop conveyors is desirable. Physical issues deal with overall length, width, height, and related tolerances, as well as the carrier, vehicles, equipment, controls, and operator interfaces from one system element to the next.

Carriers

A "carrier" is a general term for slave pallets, wooden pallets, captive metal pans with compartments for different part numbers, totes, or product-specific pallets of some type. The carrier dimensions, conveyability characteristics, and fully-loaded weight and deflection while in storage are the primary physical characteristics which drive the balance of the system design.

Slave pallets may be 3/4″ or thicker plywood sheets with or without metal cladding. Washable aluminum pallets may be used in pharmaceutical environments. The advantages of slave pallets are the ability to provide a uniform load footprint regardless of the size or quality of the pallet and to ensure conveyability. Individual bar code or RF tags can also be applied in consistent locations for permanent identification. Slaves are larger than the load placed on them and so accommodate a certain amount of carton overhang on the pallet. Carton overhang may be due to how the cartons were placed on the pallet or due to load shifting (especially at the top of the load) at normal conveyor and SRM operating

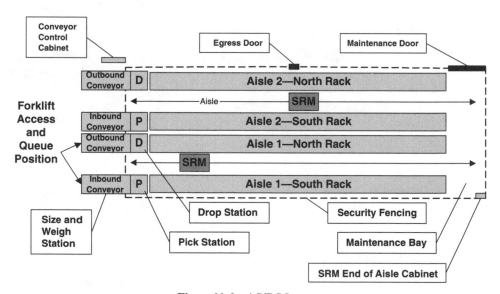

Figure 11.6   AS/RS Layout

speeds and when stopping. Slave pallets also accommodate a variety of pallet sizes and types in environments where pallets are not standardized.

Companies are often reluctant to use slave pallets due to the initial purchase cost and cost of slave pallet accumulators and dispensers. Accumulators automatically stack slaves after retrieval, and dispensers automatically position slaves on the inbound conveyor for pallet loading. Such equipment is typically integrated with the conveyor system to eliminate manual handling of slave pallets. The decision is usually based on whether the supplier pallets are of a uniform size, whether they are designed for an automated system, and the cost to re-palletize. The alternative is to impose pallet standards on suppliers who may pass their cost back to the company. This may be acceptable in order to eliminate the costs associated with repalletizing.

Freestanding System or Rack-Supported Building

The primary facility-related issue with a unit load AS/RS is the subject of a freestanding rack versus a rack-supported building in cases where a significant volume of storage is required. While automated storage systems may be freestanding as is typical with conventional storage racks, systems over a certain height commonly use the racks to provide support for the roof and siding. With rack-supported buildings, rack and floor-loading calculations must consider the weight of the roof and siding, as well as snow and wind loads. Both types must consider seismic conditions.

Location of the AS/RS is also a factor since low adjacent or nearby structures may need to have their roofs reinforced. The effect of snow accumulating against the side of the rack building on an existing roof may well exceed design guidelines for the existing roof structure. In this case, a physical separation is an alternative to reinforcing an existing structure.

A freestanding rack structure is less expensive if the building is not a consideration. While there is no specific height at which one system is used over another, typical high bay manufacturing facilities of 40 feet can support a freestanding rack structure. Rack-supported buildings of 80 to 100 feet and higher are common.

Floor Levelness

Floor levelness must be fairly precise for an AS/RS, since locations (ideally) need to be consistent in the horizontal and vertical direction. If they are not, extra commissioning and programming effort is required to individually identify the X-Y coordinates of out-of-tolerance bin/storage locations. Shimming is used under the rack support base plates to compensate for floor slope. Shimming must be held to a certain maximum height in order to ensure structural integrity and is typically specified as 1 inch maximum. A greater shimming tolerance may be permissible for lower height than for higher systems, all things being equal.

Anchor bolts are used to lag the support base plates to the floor. The reinforcing rod in the floor must be located at a depth where the drilling will not cut the rods. This issue must be coordinated between the material handling and rack suppliers and the construction manager. Drilling through the rebar under certain conditions may be permitted but at a risk of weakening the slab. If the rebar is deep enough in the slab, this is not a problem. Due to the special drills and time required, there is a cost increase to drill through rebar above a certain percentage of total holes.

Fire Protection

The company's insurance carrier will define the fire protection class based on the type of materials to be stored. This is used by the fire protection supplier to define the number and pattern of in-rack sprinklers required. Sprinkler heads may be located in the flue (between back-to-back racks), along the aisles at the face of the racks, and in the ceiling. The fire sprinkler design affects the rack tier (vertical) spacing since spacing must accommodate piping runs and sprinkler head placement. This means that there will be extra height between some tiers. The sprinklers may also be fed by different lines in an interleaved fashion to allow part of the system to be shut down for repairs without sacrificing fire protection. Note that failure to account for the effect of in-rack fire protection and down-aisle rack ties is a common mistake companies make when calculating the number of storage locations within a given height system as part of a bid spec.

Lighting and Roof Hatches

Lighting serves two purposes in an AS/RS. The first is to enable an operator to troubleshoot problems within the system or to enable a video camera to monitor aisles and key interface points. The second is to provide increased levels of lighting in the maintenance bay end of the system for maintenance, repair, replacement, and overhaul work. One lighting consideration is access to the lights if they are hung from the ceiling. Access may be via catwalks or some combination of the SRM and racks. Light access for replacement purposes should be considered during the concept and design process due to the height of the ceiling and limited access. Otherwise, lighting is not required in normal operation with an automated system.

Access to roof hatches is a similar problem as the lighting. The SRM should not be used as a means of access since a person can be trapped on the roof if the machine is moved. A safety ladder mounted to the wall in the maintenance bay, possibly with one or more platforms at various heights, may be required.

Doors

Since the system operates under automatic control, the AS/RS aisles must be fenced or walled. The maintenance door is the primary access point. There may be additional egress doors which open only from inside the high bay area for use in the event of an emergency. These will be spaced along an outside wall with access through the rack. Doors should have *Exit* lighting, and egress aisles should be lighted.

All doors providing access to the SRM aisles must be interlocked with the End-of-Aisle control cabinet to initiate an E-Stop (emergency stop) if the doors are opened without first setting the system into Man-in-Aisle mode. Man-in-Aisle mode prevents the computer system from automatically moving the SRM when someone is in an area where moving equipment creates a risk of injury. Man-in-Aisle mode is controlled by a key which must be removed from an outside control panel and taken into the AS/RS area whenever anyone enters the aisle. This key permits the individual to operate the equipment in manual mode while in the aisle. When the individual leaves, the equipment is reset to automatic mode and the key is returned to its normal (outside) location. Pressing a Reset button then reinitiates computer control.

Fire doors may be located at conveyor inbound and outbound points if the AS/RS is in a totally enclosed area. These doors normally remain open and close automatically if the fire alarm is triggered for any reason. A short delay of approximately one minute will enable a load to be indexed past the fire door to ensure that the door will close properly. Note that fire doors activated by a fusible link may actually close on a load, rendering them ineffective as a fire door. If this situation occurs, a separate controls interlock should set off an alarm if the door fails to close completely.

With environmentally-controlled warehouses, rapid-roll doors may be installed at conveyor inbound and outbound points to maintain temperature and humidity levels.

Pick and Drop Stations

The inbound and outbound conveyors move loads to and from the SRMs. The transport conveyor (if used) connecting all of the aisles moves loads to and from the aisles, while one or more loads queue at each End-of-Aisle pick (inbound) and drop (outbound) station. Conveyor subsystems may be located at one or both ends of the system, as required to support operations. Double-ended systems have a reduced overall throughput since there are deadhead moves to get from one end of the aisle to the other. To conserve floor space and make more productive use of the cube, the inbound conveyor may be located on a mezzanine over the outbound floor level conveyor, or vice versa. Side port delivery at floor level or at multifloor levels is also possible for picking or delivery operations. The floor level interface may also be via Automated Guided Vehicles (AGVs) or forklifts, with an Automated Electrified Monorail (AEM) interface at the mezzanine.

Computer Controls-Related Issues

The more a company's requirements causes a supplier to change their baseline software or the later in the process the change request occurs, the higher the cost. A key element of an integral specification (as opposed to a traditional functional specification) is to incorporate screens where they belong in the process so company personnel clearly understand the primary operator interfaces. The key computer and controls-related areas to consider encompass identification (carrier and material IDs), timing (of status uploads to the host computer and order downloads), backup operation (semiautomatic and manual modes), and primary inventory data location (AS/RS computer system or host).

Identification

Carrier identification is typically in the form of bar code labels on one, two, or four sides of the carrier. Placing permanent or temporary bar code labels on opposite sides of the pallet (centered or on opposite corners) allows the carrier to be placed into storage in different orientations and still have a label aligned with the scanner. This is especially important with a double-ended system where a carrier may be inducted at one end and retrieved at the other. The edge of the pallet must be positioned fairly precisely (e.g., 4 to 6 inches) at the points where scanning occurs to minimize scanner costs. Scanning points include inbound, divert, and outbound locations where routing decisions are made or where database updates occur. Less precision on location of the bar code labels, smaller labels, or a longer scanning distance requires more expensive scanners to compensate.

Generating separate material identification labels as part of the receiving process in addition to the carrier labels may not be required for actual operation of the AS/RS. However, they may facilitate the creation of expected receipts (records indicating which materials are to be stored on which carriers), issues, receipts, and transfers. Scanning the material ID label and then the carrier ID label "marries" the load information to the carrier for inventory control and tracking purposes. Material information becomes cross-referenced in the computer system by either SKU or carrier ID.

Computer System

Since an AS/RS is controlled in "real-time," a real-time transaction or file interface to the host is preferred. This provides the most flexibility and responsiveness with regard to adding orders, modifying orders, deleting orders, changing priorities, and updating status.

The location of the company's "official" inventory records is either at the host, Warehouse Management (WMS), or AS/RS (Warehouse Control System) level. When records are maintained in two or three systems, the highest level records are the official inventory. Successively more detailed records are then maintained at the lower levels as required for execution and control purposes. For example, the host may maintain inventory in total (e.g., 1,000 units), the WMS may maintain inventory by storage system (conventional [300 units] and automated [700 units]), and the AS/RS may maintain inventory by carrier and location (500 units on Carrier 001876 and 200 units on Carrier 001595). With today's system configurations, it is possible to have inventory records in three or four places (including hard copy), each maintaining a different level of detail.

The value of having a certain amount of SKU and order redundancy between the systems is that storage, retrieval, QC, QA, and cycle counting functions can continue to operate if the host is not communicating. Some companies will leave equipment-level control at the AS/RS computer system level and have all decision-related and inventory balances at the host level. Others will incorporate required warehouse management functions, inventory details, and equipment control in the AS/RS computer system, while leaving inventory summary balances and planning at the host level.[1]

The decision of where to locate the data and related system logic must be based on a realistic business assessment of costs, capabilities, and risk. AS/RS computer systems can be an expensive element of the overall cost (10 to 20 percent). On the surface, it often seems like it should be easier to enhance an existing Level 5 host system than to add a completely new Levels 3 and 4 AS/RS. In fact, there are many internal MIS departments which aggressively promote this approach. The thinking is that the AS/RS computer system only has to initiate the actual storage and retrieval processes and the host will do the rest. The money saved can be reallocated to the MIS department for the host upgrade.

More than one company has failed with this approach. The internal staff must have the experience and time to devote to a host upgrade communicating to a real-time AS/RS. The staff must have demonstrated that they can develop, test, install, and commission such a system within the required budget and schedule. The risk is that a failure of the internal staff to meet schedule will result in a project overrun and schedule delay which may be totally unacceptable.

Another problem with moving certain functions and controls to Level-5 (host) is that major cost reductions may not be realized. Material handling companies use baseline software to develop systems which they customize somewhat for each customer. Merely moving the responsibility for stores and retrievals to the host does not mean that major cost reductions in the Level 3 (System) and Level 4 (Facility) AS/RS computer system will be achieved. Much of the database structure and functionality needed to operate the system in semiautomatic mode (operator control) cannot be eliminated from the baseline software, especially with relational databases. There is often no large pool of savings which can be created by having the host perform functions normally performed at Levels 3 and 4.

PROJECT PHASES

All projects involve a phased approach. The value of a design/build process is that all of the company's time and effort is targeted specifically at the requirements definition, analysis, design, and implementation efforts. This makes most efficient use of the available schedule by eliminating multiple iterations of bid specs which can consume months of valuable time and effort.

Integrated system projects entail eight unique phases. The phases and areas of focus shown in Table 11.2 and Figure 11.7 are representative of those required for

---

1. System levels are discussed in Chapter 5.

Table 11.2   Project Phases and Representative Areas of Focus

PHASE	COMPANY FOCUS	MATERIAL HANDLING COMPANY FOCUS
1 Scope Definition	Define system requirements Establish system scope and boundaries Select material handling company	Specify deliverables Establish schedule and price Select subcontractors or partners

2
Preliminary Design
	Integrate AS/RS with facility and
	  site
	Resolve operational issues
	Define in-house scope of work
		Develop project plan
		Develop general arrangement
		  layout
		Develop integral specification

3
General Design
	Layout site utilities
	Develop floor slab specification
	Develop facility-related
	  specifications
	Develop bar code specification
		Develop equipment specifications
		Develop controls specifications
		Develop software design notes
		Develop host protocol
		  specification

4
Detail Design/
Procurement
	Design mechanical systems
	Design electrical systems
	Design HVAC and fire protection
	  systems
	Design pneumatic and hydraulic
	  systems
	Define host software changes
		Configure SRM
		Design rack and building
		  interfaces
		Design fire protection
		Design transportation subsystem
		Develop computer/controls
		  architecture

5 Manufacturing/Software Development	Complete site work Install floor slab and utilities Code host software changes	Manufacture equipment Manufacture control cabinets Write software

6
Installation/
Implementation
	Provide lay down area and secure
	  storage
	Provide unrestricted facility access
	Ensure that required support is
	  available
	Purchase spare parts
		Install racks and fire protection
		Install SRM and equipment
		Field wire controls
		Install computer system

7 Commissioning/ Acceptance	Provide test materials Provide support personnel	Verify equipment operation Verify subsystem operation Verify integrated system operation

8
System Startup/
Operational Support
	Operator training
	Maintenance training
	Supervisory training
	System administrator training
		Conduct classroom and hands-on
		  training
		Provide operation/maintenance
		  manuals
		Provide warranty support
		Monitor system performance

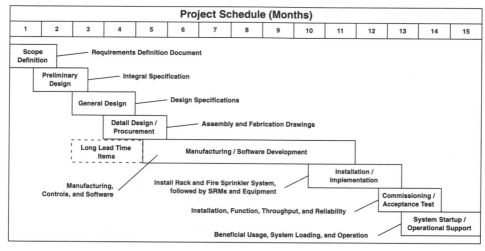

Figure 11.7   Representative Project Phase Durations

a rack-supported building where the company is (or hires) the general contractor. These phases usually overlap to some extent. In particular, the design phases will not coincide between the company and material handling supplier because site and facility work must be completed prior to system installation. Note that without general construction, time frames for a freestanding unit load storage system are most commonly in the 10 to 12 month range.

Phase 1—Scope Definition (2 to 12 months, commonly 3 to 6 months)

Phase 1 focuses on the establishment of business and working relationships between the company and the material handling supplier. Companies following a traditional approach develop a bid spec detailing the requirements of the system. This is then distributed to those material handling companies on the bidders list. A process of submitting questions for clarification continues for some number of weeks. Periodically, the company develops written responses to all questions and distributes them in the form of addendums to all suppliers who have indicated an interest in bidding.

The proposal development and review process can easily take 2 to 3 months after the original bid spec is developed. The process can be delayed even further if the company underestimated the cost of the system and must obtain additional funding authorization or reduce the system scope and rebid again. A design/build approach combines the Scope Definition, Preliminary Design, and part of the General Design phases and eliminates the bid spec and proposal development and review processes.

Phase 2—Preliminary Design (1 to 3 months, commonly 1 to 2 months)

Once selected, the material handling suppliers' project manager develops a project plan. The systems engineer translates the project requirements into an integral or system functional specification. During the same time, the system integrator ensures that the AS/RS layout is integrated with the facility and site layouts. Any discrepancies on the master general arrangement layouts are then resolved among the various companies. Issue resolution must occur on a timely basis in order to maintain the schedule, so more frequent meetings are required during this phase than during the later phases.

Phase 3—General Design (2 to 4 months, commonly 2 to 3 months)

Once the integral or system functional specification is completed, reviewed, and approved, it becomes the basis for the various design specifications needed for the system detail design. Time and effort to develop these specifications is a function of the degree of standardization of the systems and equipment. The more complex the system and interfaces or the greater the deviation from supplier standards to accommodate unique company requirements, the greater the level of effort and time required.

Phase 4—Detail Design/Procurement (2 to 4 months, commonly 2 to 3 months)

Detail Design begins with the development of assembly-level drawings for the project. Other drawings, schematics, and so on, are then developed down to the level where standard assembly and manufacturing drawings can be incorporated. Purchase orders for long lead time items are released as such items are identified. Major AS/RS subcontracts typically include rack, fire protection, construction and installation and specialty equipment.

Phase 5—Manufacturing Software Development (6 to 12 months, commonly 7 to 8 months)

Software development begins once the software design notes/specification is approved. In addition to customization and reconfiguration of the baseline software, activity also encompasses elements related to hardware configuration and the database, operating system, and network.

Equipment manufacturing is typically backscheduled from the shipment date. This minimizes the length of time equipment must be stored prior to shipment since its size takes up a large amount of production or storage space. The SRM shuttle mechanism and drives and any other long lead time elements are advance ordered to begin procurement of long lead time parts and reserve manufacturing capacity.

Phase 6—Installation and Commissioning (2 to 3 months, subject to scope and weather)

Rack installation begins after the floor slab cures. Suppliers use various installation techniques based on the rack type and height. One technique is to bolt the uprights together in blocks of perhaps six each and then erect them as an integral unit. This differs from post-and-beam systems normally used for conventional storage where the uprights are installed and then the beams are attached in a progressive sequence. Plumbness (vertical) and alignment (horizontal) are verified as part of the erection process. The roof deck, roof, and siding are then installed for a rack-supported building. The SRM top guide is attached to supports which span the aisles at the top of the rack, and the floor rail is shimmed, lagged, and grouted. The fire protection system is installed and tested once the rack is completed, though it may not be charged until system acceptance. In any event, a wet system cannot be pressurized until the facility is fully enclosed and there is no possibility of freezing.

The SRM should be erected before the final building roof deck and/or siding is installed. Otherwise, an area of roof deck or siding may have to be removed and reinstalled. This is a critical scheduling milestone, since the SRM may easily be 80 feet or more.

With the rack in place, Pick and Drop (P&D) stands and other conveyors or equipment are mechanically installed. The control cabinets are moved into position once they will not interfere with the other mechanical installation activities. The cabinets may be placed on concrete "housekeeping" pads to get them up off the floor. Wiring and certain control devices such as photoeyes and limit switches are installed on-site.

Near the end of this process, the computer system is installed, and the controls and host interfaces are verified. Commissioning is the process of ensuring that all equipment, vehicle, and subsystem elements are operational in stand-alone mode and that all communication interfaces between equipment, controls, the AS/RS computer system, and the host computer system are fully operational.

Phase 7—Integration and Acceptance (1 to 4 weeks, subject to scope and requirements)

Integration consists of three levels of system checkout. The first involves final inspection of the installation and verification that the safety devices operate properly. The area must be cleaned up and the installation verified against project requirements. The second level involves full subsystem operation on a nonintegrated basis. This verifies semiautomatic and manual modes of operation, sizing and weight checks, E-Stops, and startup and shutdown. At this point, basic storage, handling, and other functions are verified. The third level verifies full system operation in automatic mode.

A three-stage acceptance test verifies to the customer that the system operates per the integral specification. The system function test verifies that storage, retrieval, and other basic functions of the equipment, control system, and computer system operate properly. Throughput testing verifies that the hourly dual-cycle rate can be achieved. The reliability test verifies that the average dual-cycle rate can be achieved over a 1-shift or longer time frame.

MATERIAL HANDLING SUPPLIER DOCUMENTATION

While effective communication is no guarantee of project success, ineffective communication will certainly result in schedule delays, overruns, inefficiency, disagreements, and disputes. Face-to-face discussions are the best way to reach mutual understanding and resolve issues related to the project. Documentation is the best way to formally communicate requirements and agreements among the various companies and personnel involved with the project. Unfortunately, such documentation is often produced by personnel who view it as a chore, rather than a tool. Refer to Figure 11.8 for some of the more typical project documentation.

To be of practical use, documentation must be consistent, accurate, and complete. Consistency refers to both internal consistency within the document itself and external consistency with other system documentation. Accuracy refers to being factual, clear, and understandable by the audience for which the documentation is intended. Completeness refers to possessing a level of detail which eliminates misunderstandings due to having to interpret documentation or make assumptions about its meaning. When documentation fails to meet these requirements, it is often due to the author failing to completely understand certain areas or failing to recognize the reader's need to understand areas which the author already understands.

System documentation falls into four basic categories as shown in Table 11.3. Plans (1) cover the management, scheduling, and control aspects of the project and communicate work standards, requirements, and scope to core team, support, management, and company personnel. Specifications (2) indicate how quantitative and qualitative project requirements and functional, physical, and logical issues have been resolved and translated into operational and design standards and guidelines. These are then used to produce drawings (3) and related engineering documentation as required to either manufacture, procure, develop, or install equipment, controls, and software. The final set of documentation consists of manuals (4) and operator instructions used to operate, maintain, and service the system.

The key difference between a bid spec and an integration approach is with the specifications. A bid spec approach relies on functional specifications to define the project requirements to the various team members. These describe what is to be performed in terms of functions, without specifically describing how. The how is left to the detail design specifications. An integration approach consolidates the what and how details into a single integrated document written from the operator's perspective.

With separate specifications, team members must refer to a number of different specifications to obtain a complete understanding of how the system operates. For example, the system functional specification will describe the basic storage, retrieval, and other functions in function sequence. To determine how a pallet is actually conveyed to the SRM, the reader refers to the conveyor specification. To determine how the actual transaction is recorded, the reader refers to

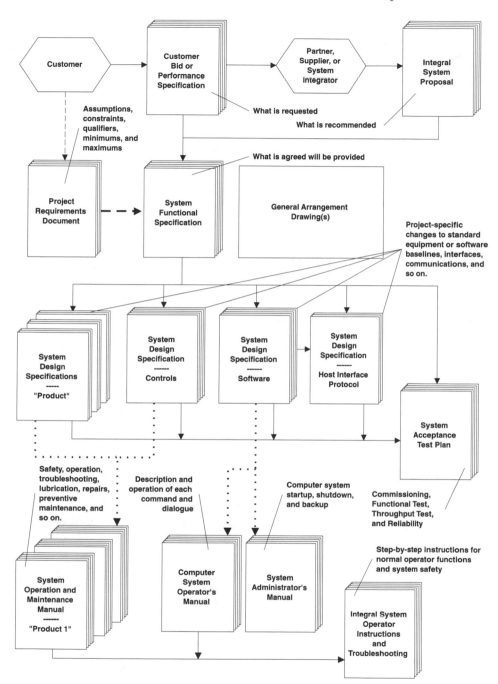

Figure 11.8   Typical Project Documentation

Table 11.3   Representative System Documentation

PROJECT FOCUS	PLANS	SPECS	DRAWINGS	MANUALS
System Design	- Project	Integral (Functional) Specification Design Specifications: - System - Software - Equipment - Host Protocol	- General Arrangement - Elevation - Interfaces	
Subsystem Design	- Quality Assurance	- Bar Code - Carrier/Pallet - Lighting - Racks - Fire Protection	- Rack - Fire Protection - Equipment - System Architecture - Controls	
Manufacturing	- Quality Control	- Finish - Tolerances	- As-Built	
Installation	- Installation - Safety	- Installation	- Installation - As-Installed	
Commissioning	- Commissioning			
Acceptance	- Acceptance Test		- Test Storage Locations	
System Operation	- Operational Support - Training - Warranty		- Layout - Adjustment - Lubrication - Repair	- Operator Instructions - Computer - Maintenance - System Administrator

the conveyor, SRM, host, and software specifications. This can get pretty unwieldy for a complex system supporting many functions and modes of operation.

The problem with this approach is not so much that information appears in so many documents. This is the traditional approach and companies are used to it. The problem is that the design specifications are developed after the functional specification has been approved by the customer. The customer does not even have the details necessary to understand specifically how the system will operate at the time of sign off of the system functional specification. The supplying company knows to a greater or lesser extent what they are providing, based on the degree of custom design involved. When companies finally reach the point in the project where they understand what they are getting and how the system operates, disagreements in perception are finally identified. This is a communication problem which can be solved by use of an integral specification.

Integral Specification

Integral systems commonly consist of standard and custom equipment, vehicles, controls, screens, and technologies. They involve layout, operational, and organizational changes. Justification is based on flexibility, reliability, and other capability improvements in addition to return on investment. In such systems where there may well be no other system in the world just like it, what is being performed is much less of an issue than how. What is a one-time design issue. How is an everyday operating issue.

Really understanding an integral system requires an integral specification (refer to Figure 11.9). This is a document which integrates the how from all of the project specifications into a single document. The functional descriptions include all of the screens, figures, tables, control cabinet layouts, and equipment drawings as required to understand the operation from the operator's perspective. Therefore, effort normally delayed to the Detail Design phase such as screen formats and control cabinet layouts must be pulled forward in time.

The integral specification is the mechanism by which the project scope and requirements are translated into a system definition. It is intended for all management and engineering team members, whether they work for the customer, company, or key suppliers. Detailed subsystem design specifications, as a comparison, are primarily for engineering personnel involved in actual development and design processes. A representative integral specification includes the following:

- The *Executive Overview* section identifies the scope of the system and key business benefits to be achieved. These system benefits establish the overall system design and operating targets.

- The *System Overview* section identifies the various elements of the system and their location within the facility or on the site. The key interface points or relationships are identified using drawings, diagrams, figures, tables, or charts. The intent is to orient the reader to the complete scope of the system.

- The *Design Considerations* section identifies the shift hours of operation, rates (average/peak), volumes, load configurations, types of loads and related characteristics, storage and handling requirements, facility and layout considerations such as clear height and available space, constraints and assumptions, and modes of operation. This is the type of information required to understand the difference between design and operating requirements in absolute and relative terms.

- The *System Performance* section identifies the performance requirements. This is defined by the contract or design/build criteria in system terms. Simulation, modeling, and analysis are then used to quantify specifics related to individual equipment or vehicle performance. This information is an input to the Acceptance Test plan. For example, Figure 11.3 identified a representative dual-cycle pattern commonly used in throughput testing. A mathematical-based analysis which incorporates distance, height, speed, acceleration/deceleration, and fork cycle times is used to calculate the number of dual-cycles (stores and retrieves) which can be performed in an hour at a given utilization factor (commonly 85 percent for a storage system).

- The *System Configuration* section identifies how the software will be configured in terms of operator profiles, equipment, aisles, stations, and storage

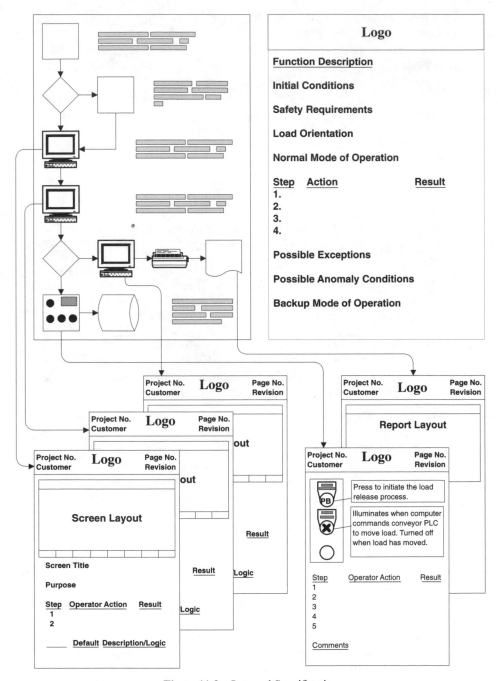

Figure 11.9   Integral Specification

location mapping (zoning). This provides a common set of terminology and descriptions for the system.

- The *Function* sections identify the step-by-step processes for receiving, incoming inspection, quarantine and disposition, storage, retrieval, cycle counting, shipping, wave planning, error correction, and so on, as applicable. Each section describes each mode of operation in terms of normal (ongoing), exception (infrequent), and anomaly (fault or error) conditions. Operator, equipment, and system actions are defined in terms of functional flows, screen layouts, control cabinet layouts, material flows, pallet flows, vehicle flows, information flows, logic, edits, or other relationships. The level of detail is representative for those portions of the system which are not yet designed. Otherwise, actual screen layouts, facility layouts, or equipment characteristics are used. Additional sections as required for the project may also be included for the various equipment and controls subsystems, rack, SRM, bar code labels, RF system, conventional storage systems, and so on. The intent is to have as comprehensive an understanding of the process as possible, from the operator's perspective. This same documentation can then be used for training in a "slimmed-down" version.

A representative table of contents for the storage function is shown following (with some of the detail missing). Note in the example that in normal operation, the operator simply places the pallet onto the inbound conveyor and presses the Start push button. This initiates the storage process. A variety of sizing and weight checks are then made automatically prior to storing the load. The integral specification describes this process in its entirety for all modes of operation and for normal, exception, and anomaly conditions. The description is in terms of the normal mode, with the others described in terms of their differences from normal mode. The intent is to communicate an understanding of the operation is sufficient detail that the design specifications are simply a reflection of everyone's understanding.

Storage Function
(Store a Pallet/Carrier in the AS/RS after an Expected Receipt is on File)

1.0 Storage (carriers may be pallets, pans, bins, baskets, racks, and so on)
    1.1 Comparison of Modes of Operation (how do the various modes differ)
        1.1.1 Automatic Storage Process (host computer provides receipt data)
        1.1.2 Semiautomatic Storage Process (operator enters receipt data)
        1.1.3 Manual Storage Process (operator actually operates equipment manually)
    1.2 Create Expected Receipt (so the operator does not have to enter any information)
        1.2.1 Valid Bar Code Carrier ID
        1.2.2 Invalid Bar Code Carrier ID
        1.2.3 Expected Receipt Already on File
        1.2.4 Adding a Part to the Carrier which Meets the System Edits for Combining Parts

RACK AND RELATED EQUIPMENT

Storage capacity is a function of the number of *net* storage locations. The number of tiers represents the number of vertical levels. This is (typically) consistent from one end of the system to the other, unlike that in conventional storage systems where tiers may vary on an individual bay basis. Each set of uprights is one bay. Refer to Figure 11.10 for a comparison. Each AS/RS aisle consists of two rows, one on each side. Rows vary in depth. For example, single-deep storage systems allow one carrier to be stored in a location, while double-deep systems allow two, one behind the other. There are numerous variations based on the application, including deep-lane storage.

Storage capacity is calculated as shown in Figure 11.11. The number of net locations may be reduced from the gross by losses due to unusable locations. Locations become unusable due to air-conditioning ductwork, insufficient overhang at the back of the storage locations due to a building column, need for space to mount bar code scanners inside the rack structure at P&D (Pick and Drop) positions, built-in access platforms for lighting or roof hatches, and so on. These locations are deleted from the SRM PC/PLC and are logically removed from the computer system storage location files. Personnel egress aisles through the rack structure included for fire safety purposes use one or two locations high. Storage locations may also be missing where the P&Ds are located in systems where storage space is being maximized by cantilevering the rack over the Pick and Drop positions.

Automated unit load (pallet) systems typically use a drive-through type of rack design. In a conventional storage system, drive-through racks allow a forklift to be driven into the storage opening for deep-lane storage. Except for the down-aisle ties at various heights for structural support, there are no cross beams.

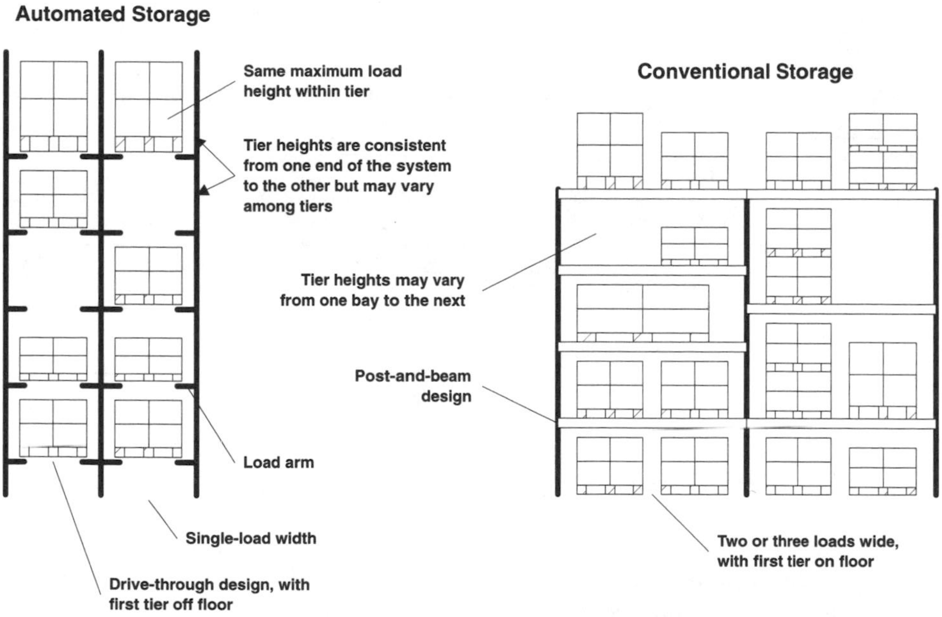

Figure 11.10   Comparison of Automated vs. Conventional Storage

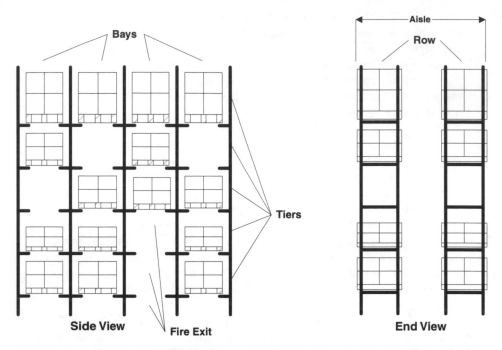

CONFIGURATION	DESCRIPTION	EXAMPLE
Tiers	Vertical levels	15
Bays	Horizontal positions (figured based on the top tier)	30
Locations/Row	Tiers (15) x Bays (30)	450
Aisles	Aisles (each aisle has 2 rows: left and right, east and west, or north and south)	10
Gross Locations	Aisles (10) x Rows/Aisle (2) x Locations/Row (450)	9,000
Loss Due to Fire Exits	Storage locations lost due to 2 egress aisles (2-high) through 19 rows	(152)
Net Locations	Available storage locations (with 15 percent safety factor for variability and growth)	8,848
Average Utilization	Net Locations x 85 percent (design for normal operations; 15 percent for peaks)	7,521

Figure 11.11   Calculating System Capacity

Carriers are supported in the storage location by load arms which extend from each upright but do not span the distance between uprights. This empty space provides room for the fork shuttle mechanism. Alternatives include horizontal load beams with standoffs to provide room between the load beam and load for the shuttle fork, cantilever racks for roll storage, and so on.

Customers have three primary areas of responsibility with respect to system tolerances. The first responsibility is to provide carriers (wooden pallets, slave pallets, pans, totes, and so on) which meet minimum and maximum size specifications and are in good physical condition. Minimum width ensures that a carrier cannot slip between the load arms if the load is not centered in the storage location. Maximum width ensures that a load can be stored in the storage location and transported on the SRM and conveyor system without jamming. Maximum depth ensures that loads will not project too far into the aisle or flue, while maximum height ensures that the fork shuttle mechanism will not hit the top of a load when accessing the storage location above. Overhang tolerances are intended to ensure that loads do not overhang the pallet and trip the sizing photoeyes on the inbound conveyor or on the SRM itself.

The second responsibility is to ensure proper placement of the bar code or other means of automatic identification. Variability in placement beyond tolerances which can be accommodated by the scanners will cause a load to be rejected. Use of slave or captive wooden pallets allows consistent bar code placement as opposed to labels which are generated for each receipt.

Table 11.4 provides a listing of common rack-supported building terminology, while Figure 11.12 provides a graphical illustration of some of the elements.

The third responsibility is to ensure that weights do not exceed the design maximum. While the SRM and rack design allow for a safety factor, the factor is not intended to allow excess weight loads to be stored. Another consideration is "wet" vs. "dry" load weight. If the fire sprinkler system is activated, load weights will increase based on the amount of water absorbed or weight of water which is retained in the containers. Systems may need to use a 30 to 100 percent safety factor for wet loads for planning purposes. The actual factor may need to be determined by experimentation. In any event, it may increase the rack cost. Pans and totes should be designed with holes or slots for water drainage.

The preceding size and weight conditions can be checked by size (dimensions)/scan (bar code)/weigh stations prior to storage. Any problem causes the load to be rejected. With Pick and Drop stands or conveyor spurs, the SRM may simply transfer the load from the pick to the drop station so the operator can remove the load and resolve the problem. Note also that the top of the load may shift or skew due to transport on any of the system conveyors or vehicles after passing the sizing checks. This varies based on load materials and stacking profile. If no (or minimal) overhang of the load over the edge of the pallet is allowed, the customer must ensure that all loads subject to skewing allow 1 to 2 inches clearance from the edge of the pallet, based on the type of load. Experience will ultimately dictate what the allowance needs to be. The SRM should have overheight and overhang photoeyes to verify that load integrity has been maintained prior to storage.

Rack design cannot use the floor for storage as in a conventional storage system. The low shelf height is dependent on the type of SRM selected. Thirty inches or so is a reasonable allowance for initial planning purposes. In general, the greater the load weight and larger the machine, the higher the low shelf height. As a general design consideration, throughput is improved by locating the

Table 11.4   Rack-Supported Building Terminology

ITEM	ELEMENT	DESCRIPTION
1	Frame Uprights	Uprights transmit the weight of the roof and loads to the base plates. Uprights are generally tubular steel, fixture-welded, or bolted to ensure consistency and accuracy.
2	Diagonal Bracing	Bracing between legs of the uprights to provide structural rigidity.
3	Load Supports or Arms	Load arms are welded to the uprights and support the carriers. With drive-through racks, load arms do not span the uprights. With post-and-beam construction, beams attach to the uprights.
4	Load Support End Stops	End stops welded to the load support prevent the carrier from being pushed into the flue space.
5	Flue	The flue is the space separating the back of one rack/carrier from the next. Some of the in-rack sprinkler heads may be located in the flue.
6	Down-Aisle Ties	Down-aisle ties are spaced at various vertical levels in the rack to tie frame uprights together. This provides lateral support from one upright to the next. Since extra vertical space is required at each tie, sprinkler heads may also be located at these levels to take advantage of the lost height. Aisle electrification for the SRM is either located below the lowest storage location or at a down-aisle tie positioned high enough to provide personnel aisles through the rack structure.
7	Cross-Aisle Ties	Cross-aisle ties connect the uprights at the top of the rack structure to provide structural rigidity. These ties also provide a mounting for the SRM Top Guide (an I-beam or other structural member which guides the top of the SRM).
8	Girts	Siding is attached to either horizontal (shown in Figure 11.12) or vertical girts cantilevered off the outside rack uprights.
9	Purlins	The roof decking is supported by purlins, which are the upper structural elements of the roof trusses.
10	SRM Top Guide	The SRM top guide consists of a structural I-beam or tube steel mounted beneath the cross aisle ties. The SRM upper truck guide roller assembly engages the guide. With a transfer car system, the SRM disengages from the top guide as it travels fully onto the transfer car. It reengages the top guide in the new aisle when it moves into position.
11	Base Plates	Base plates welded to the bottoms of rack columns distribute the load to the floor. Rebar in the floor must be at a level or position where the anchor bolts will miss them.
12	Runout Support Steel Framing	Runout support steel framing supports the SRM top guide beyond both ends of the rack where the mast can no longer be supported by the cross-aisle ties.

Table 11.4   *Continued*

ITEM	ELEMENT	DESCRIPTION
13	Power Buss Duct and Supports	The power buss duct, which provides electrical power to the SRM, is supported at one of the down-aisle tie levels or below the bottom tier.
14	Roof Decking	Roof decking is attached to the purlins. Roofing materials are then attached to the decking.
15	In-Rack Sprinkler	An in-rack sprinkler system provides fire protection as required by the company's insurance carrier via sprinkler heads spaced throughout the flue and/or along the aisle.

lowest height loads at the lower tiers and highest height loads at the upper tiers in systems where tier height varies. The logical tier to allow for a few tall loads is the one at the top of the system since extra height is required for the upper guide rail and related SRM assemblies.

COMPUTER SYSTEM

The AS/RS computer system typically encompasses Level 4 (facility) and Level 3 (equipment subsystem) software, with Level 2 being PC/PLC control of the conveyor system and SRM. There are two basic approaches to data management. The first is to stratify the Part/SKU data between the host and AS/RS. This enables independent operation of the AS/RS under operator control (referred to as semiautomatic mode) in the event the host computer (ERP, MRPII, or WMS) is not communicating for any reason. Since there is some degree of data duplication among systems with this approach, the host maintains the "official" inventory balances, which may or may not include the actual storage/bin locations.

The second approach is to maintain all database functions and control at the host level. Only the equipment-level operations (Level 3) are directed via the AS/RS computer system. The host in this case may be a Warehouse Management System (WMS) which in turn feeds summary totals to the company's ERP/MRPII system. In this case, the equipment performs a function and then must wait for the host to send the next mission.

Note that companies may do themselves a disservice by creating a specification where all communications among subsystems are forced to go to the host first. Find out what options are available from the suppliers before setting a direction in concrete. Real-time processing is not the same as normal host-level transaction processing. Throughput may be reduced if all communications must go through a host.

With the host performing the role of traffic cop, for example, the SRM may retrieve a pallet and place it on a P&D (pick and/or drop stand). A confirmation to the host enables the host to update the inventory record and request an AGV to pick up the pallet. When an AGV becomes available and is in the vicinity, it is di-

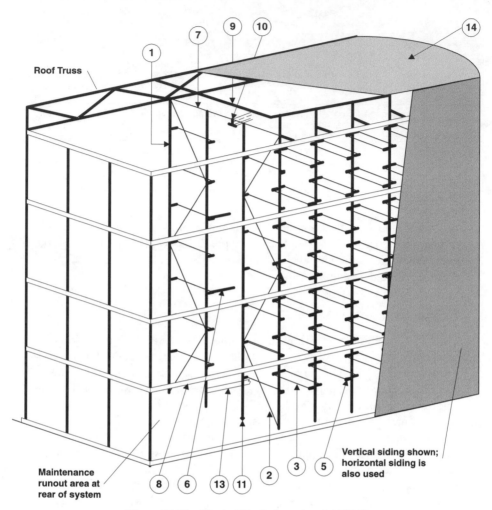

Figure 11.12   Typical Rack-Supported AS/RS[2]

rected to pick up the pallet and move it to a production line P&D. A confirmation to the host updates the location. The host requests the shuttle car to pick up the pallet and move it to the proper workstation. When the shuttle car completes its current move, it picks up the pallet and moves it to the workstation. A confirmation to the host updates the location and a signal is sent to the workstation controller to perform the next operation.

The greater the level of automation and need for integration, the more such a process as just described becomes a "manually automated" system. The control system is treating the automation like operators on forklifts who have to be told every single move. When they get done with one task, then and only then are they

2. Acknowledgement: Figure is a composite from Rapistan Systems documentation.

given the next. Imagine trying to optimize the operation of millions or tens of millions of dollars worth of automation this way. This is the type of architecture which is used when automation is purchased from a number of companies where there is no peer-to-peer communication among the subsystems. This is not a definition of an integral system but rather a loosely *integrated/interfaced* system.

In order for such a system to work, the number of missions (from/to moves) in process at any time must be kept to an absolute minimum. This makes the recovery logic easier in the event of an anomaly condition (e.g., an equipment breakdown). There is little or no forward visibility at the equipment level. What is lost is the ability to optimize operations and improve throughput which a peer-to-peer communications capability permits. It is rather like having two people who are standing next to each other refusing to talk directly and only communicating through a third person. The first person tells the intermediary something, who tells the second. The second person then does something and tells the intermediary, who in turn tells the first. The real-time system slows down to the rate of the host processing. Note that the host is also printing reports and packing slips, exploding bills of material, generating purchase orders, paying invoices, and so on.

As an alternative, the host in a tightly integrated system generates all of the transactions required for a wave (e.g., in a distribution center) or a build schedule or work order in manufacturing. The Level 4 integral system software then optimizes the operation of all of the subsystems based on the forward visibility provided by the host. The SRM determines the storage locations based on FIFO logic. AGVs are automatically routed based on priority schemes and the level of work throughout the facility. Load movement is monitored and verified at each subsystem interface. The host is updated only when loads reach their final destination, when inventory accounting classifications changes (e.g., from Raw to WIP), and when order statuses change.

With an integral system and a distributed architecture, the host focuses on business and operational planning functions while the integral system focuses on control and execution functions. The host deals with on-line transaction rates (seconds per operator transaction) while the integral system deals in real-time. The ability to optimize based on forward planning and real-time response rates are the primary advantages of systems using peer-to-peer communications.

The architecture shown in Figure 11.13 is representative of a system encompassing inbound and outbound conveyors, shuttle cars, and multiple SRMs. The workstation includes a terminal and bar code printer. The computer room includes the primary and backup computers, console terminal, log printer, and report printer. With an integral system, each subsystem has Level 3 software resident in the primary computer for direct peer-to-peer communications. With a loosely integrated system, each subsystem probably has a separate computer networked to the host.

With redundancy between or among the databases, the host interface supports upload of inventory balance and status information and download of orders, expected inventory receipts, and file adds and modifications. Material handling companies have a standard interface protocol specification. This may

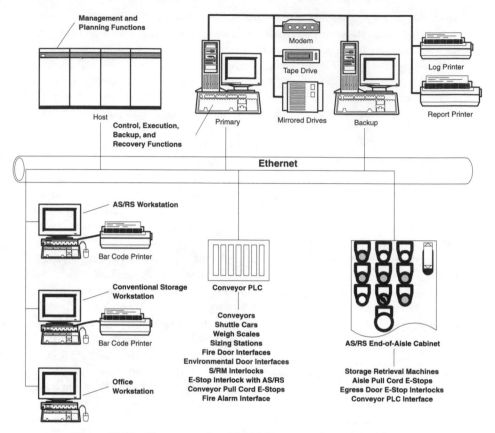

Figure 11.13   Representative AS/RS Computer System Architecture

need to be customized for the specific application based on the customer's host computer hardware, software, and unique needs.

Host Interface

Host transactions fall into 10 basic categories. These transactions are the types which may be performed via the host computer in automatic mode of operation or performed at the AS/RS computer level by operator entry in semiautomatic mode, for upload to the host.

1. *Retrieval*—Materials may be retrieved via one of three basic dialogues. The first and most common is by SKU or by SKU/lot number. Orders typically specify some quantity, and the AS/RS logic retrieves as many carriers in (generally) FIFO sequence as are required to fill the order demand. Alternative retrieval methods include retrieve by carrier, when the carrier ID is known, or retrieve by location. Either method is typically used to accommodate anomaly conditions. In unit load systems where the host

maintains the inventory by location, retrieve by carrier or location is equally valid since there is only one carrier per location. Note that "generally FIFO" sequence refers to double-deep or deeper locations, where the front load is issued before the back load, even though it may not be quite as old.

2. *Storage*—Expected receipts identify materials to be stored, as identified by purchase order receipts, QC or QA releases, or work order completions. Materials may be stored one SKU per carrier or mixed with other materials which share the same zone. The expected receipt contains all of the data which the AS/RS computer system is required to maintain, beyond carrier ID and date/time. This might include lot number, quantity, SKU, and QC status, for example.

3. *Recovery*—With automated systems, there is a need for transactions which recover from ones which are initiated but not completed for some reason. This may include aborts of current missions, recovery from full bin errors (onboard sensors identified that the SRM attempted to store a carrier in a full storage location), identification of overweight or oversize conditions, and conditions where loads jammed or power was lost.

4. *Order*—Production, shipping, quality control, scrap, and cycle counting orders are the mechanisms used to retrieve materials from the AS/RS. Orders may be single or multi-item. Placing an order on hold prevents any additional automatic retrieval processing but allows active missions for already-released line items to complete. If the active missions complete the order, the hold is ignored and the order status is updated to "complete." Missions only become active just prior to the SRM retrieving a load from storage or once a carrier is released on the inbound station.

5. *Carrier*—Materials are stored on carriers (slave pallets, pallets, or pans). Carrier records may be deleted, the location updated to reflect moving or storing a carrier in manual mode, or quarantine status modified (hold or release from quarantine hold).

6. *Storage/Bin Location*—One carrier is stored per storage location. Carriers may be retrieved by knowing the storage location in order to resolve a full bin error (i.e., the location is known but not the carrier ID), to retrieve carriers which may have been contaminated by leakage, or to free up locations for maintenance or other purposes. Storage locations are also associated with zones. Zoning profiles may be modified as required to accommodate storage requirements such as fast or slow movers, separation of acids from bases in pharmaceutical companies, heavier loads in the bottom tiers, tall loads in the top tier, and so on.

7. *Cycle Count*—Cycle counts are performed on a SKU or SKU/lot basis. All materials on a mixed load carrier may also be counted as an "opportunity" cycle count once the carrier has been delivered to the cycle count

area. When there is a quantity discrepancy, the key to maintaining count accuracy is to prevent issues of materials until the discrepancy is resolved. Otherwise, carrier quantities may be erroneously zeroed out, which may cause the carrier record to be deleted from the AS/RS database. The AS/RS should not maintain or permit negative inventory balances.

8. *Quality Control*—Incoming purchased or manufactured materials may require some type of inspection or testing prior to release for production or shipping. An Acceptable Quality Level (AQL) type of statistical test bases sample quantity on the total quantity received. Within the sample, if a certain number of parts fail out of the total inspected, the lot fails. If the sample is destruct-tested or retained for other purposes or if only the accepted items are returned to the carrier, the unreturned quantity must be issued to a QC charge number. If inspection or test fails, the carrier (plus all others for the lot) must be placed on QC hold until disposition is determined. In any event, the carrier quantity must reflect the removal of any sample quantities not returned or returned to a different carrier.

9. *Quality Assurance*—If materials are rejected by QC, QA may need to specify the proper disposition. Rejected materials are placed on hold pending rework or a decision to scrap or return the material. If a certain quantity is required for short-term production needs, a decision may be made to perform 100 percent inspection or test to obtain at least the quantity of materials needed for immediate requirements. Accepted material is then released for general usage or categorized for areas of use such as for certain products or geographic markets.

10. *Database*—The SKU table can be considered a subset of the inventory part master file. Additional fields specific to AS/RS operation such as zone, carrier height (in systems with carriers of varying heights), and storage indicator (single item or mixed carrier constraint) are included.

Table 11.5 identifies some of the transactions between Level 4 (Facility) and Level 5 (Host) used to synchronize inventory records.

AS/RS Computer System Functional Areas

An AS/RS computer system can be segregated into six basic areas from an operational perspective. The first relates to configuration, initialization, and startup activities, and the second relates to general operation, recovery, and system service states. These areas then provide support for the storage, retrieval, QA/QC, and cycle counting functional areas.

Configuration, Initialization, and Startup Activities

System configuration is the responsibility of the material handling supplier. The configuration scope encompasses all of the site-specific elements required to logically represent and control the physical system. System entities which must be

Table 11.5   Representative AS/RS—Host Transactions

TRANSACTION	DESCRIPTION	DIRECTION
Retrieve by Carrier	Issue all material on carrier	Host to AS/RS
Retrieve by Location	Issue all material on carrier in designated location	Host to AS/RS
Retrieve by SKU	Issue designated SKU quantity (FIFO sequence)	Host to AS/RS
Retrieve by SKU/Lot	Issue designated SKU and Lot quantity (any location)	Host to AS/RS
Create Expected Receipt	Confirm purchase order receipt/work order completion	Host to AS/RS
Store Complete	Confirm storage location in which carrier is stored	AS/RS to Host
Abort Mission	Stop current store or retrieval	AS/RS to Host
Add Order	Add order and line item(s) to retrieval queue	Host to AS/RS
Update Order Quantity	Update order line item quantity	Host to AS/RS
Delete Order	Delete order and all open line items	Host to AS/RS
Hold Order	Stop all retrievals which have not been initiated	Host to AS/RS
Hold Carrier	Prevent automatic order processing of carrier materials	Host to AS/RS
Storage Location (Bin) Lock	Prevent automatic processing of materials in storage location	Host to AS/RS
Storage Location (Bin) Unlock	Allow automatic processing of materials in storage location	Host to AS/RS
Cycle Count Match	Confirm that actual matches computer count	AS/RS to Host
Cycle Count Mismatch	Confirm that actual count does not match computer count	AS/RS to Host
QA Lot Hold	Prevent automatic processing of all SKU/Lot materials	Host to AS/RS
QA Lot Release from Hold	Allow automatic processing of all SKU/Lot materials	Host to AS/RS
QC Inspect Pass	Release SKU/Lot from inspection hold	AS/RS to Host
QC Inspect Fail	Prevent automatic order processing of SKU/Lot pending disposition	AS/RS to Host
QC Sample Quantity Issue	Issue QC sample quantity to QC charge number	AS/RS to Host
SKU Scrap	Issue SKU quantity to scrap charge number	AS/RS to Host

(*continued*)

Table 11.5 *Continued*

TRANSACTION	DESCRIPTION	DIRECTION
SKU Transfer	Transfer SKU quantity from one carrier to another	AS/RS to Host
Carrier Transfer	Transfer carrier from one storage location to another	AS/RS to Host
Add SKU	Add a new SKU master file record	Host to AS/RS
Update SKU	Update an existing SKU master file record	Host to AS/RS
Delete SKU	Delete a SKU record from the AS/RS database	Host to AS/RS

Table 11.6   Storage Location Naming Conventions

AXXSHHHVV	DEFINITION	DESCRIPTION	
A	Storage Area	A—AS/RS C—Conventional Storage F—Flammable Storage M—MRO Storage S—Steel Storage	B—Bulk Storage E—Empty Rack Storage L—Liquid Storage R—Returnable Dunnage Storage
XX	Aisle Number	01–99	
S	Side/Row	N—North S—South E—East W—West	
HHH	Horizontal Bay	001–999	
VV	Vertical Level/Tier	01 (lowest)–99 (highest)	

named for control purposes include storage locations (refer to Table 11.6), carrier IDs (alphanumeric), warehouse areas (logical destinations such as assembly, shipping, and so on), stations and queue positions (as related to physical conveyor, Pick and Drop positions), and vehicles (SRMs, shuttle cars, and AGVs, as applicable). Representation of the physical system is accomplished by configuring software baselines for the actual project. This may also involve adding fields and/or logic specific to the customer's environment.

System operating rules are also defined during the system configuration process. Order priorities define the relative importance of one type of order over another. An internal retrieve which is performed automatically by the system to resolve an anomaly condition such as full bin error is the highest priority. QC orders to support inspectors who are waiting for materials are the next likely priority. Production or shipping orders are considered next if the AS/RS is not directly feeding a production line or distribution system, and cycle count orders are lowest in priority. However, since each type of order is associated with a logical destination (e.g., production, shipping, cycle counting, or inspection), priorities can be overridden by setting certain logical destinations Out of Service.

Other factors will also affect priorities. Normal order priority for any type of order may be overridden to reflect emergency retrievals. These typically operator-generated orders are sequenced after the few missions already in progress are completed.

System action in the event of a fire alarm is typically dependent on the physical layout. One alternative is to complete the current missions (stores and retrieves) and stop. If this results in the SRM blocking a fire exit or system access point, additional computer logic may be required which returns the SRM to some designated "home" position.

System initialization is the responsibility of the customer. This includes entering part-related fields and synchronizing the AS/RS and host system databases. The operator profile establishes operator IDs and passwords, as well as authorization levels on a dialogue basis. Table 11.7 identifies typical functional areas and related dialogues. Authorization levels are established in terms of system administrator (all dialogues), supervisor (all nonadministrator dialogues), operator (all nonadministrator and nondelete or abort dialogues), maintenance (aisle, station, and equipment In and Out of Service dialogues), and casual users (all display dialogues) categories, for example. Note that, except for operator profiles and SKU master records, the majority of system initialization occurs as a natural function of storing materials in the system.

An individual obtains access to dialogues by logging on to one of the workstation terminals or to the console (computer room) terminal. All dialogues for which the individual is authorized are accessible via the menu structure. All those which are not authorized are either not displayed, displayed in some visual manner which differentiates authorized from unauthorized dialogues, or the system will display an error message indicating that access is not authorized if the operator attempts to activate one.

Note that having a multi-logon capability is advantageous where system terminals are physically separated. This allows the system administrator to remain logged on in the computer room and also troubleshoot a problem on the terminal located at the AS/RS. This capability is a necessity in a system with RF terminals on forklifts where an individual logged on to a terminal in their office also needs to log on to a forklift terminal occasionally.

General Operation, Recovery, and System Service States

The second basic functional area of an AS/RS computer system encompasses general operating characteristics. This includes display and reporting functions, log messages, system-related maintenance and recovery from anomaly conditions, setting service state of system elements, and system administration.

Perhaps the largest single difference between Level 5 host processing and Levels 3 and 4 is the importance of timing. Automatic material handling and storage missions must be physically completed before certain updates can be performed

Table 11.7   Representative AS/RS Functions and Dialogues

FUNCTION	DIALOGUE	DESCRIPTION
Operator	Add Operator Modify Access Delete Operator Copy Operator Change Password	Add new operator profile to system Modify dialogues to which operator has access Delete operator profile from system Copy an existing operator profile to a new operator Allow operator to change their password
Logging	Display Log File Print Log File Enable/Disable Messages	Display selected log file records Print selected log file records Select log categories and/or messages to file
Equipment	Display Equipment Status Change Service State (In or Out)	Display service state and carrier ID Toggle service state (In to Out or Out to In)
Aisle	Display Aisle Status Change Service State (In or Out)	Display service state and number of pending retrieves Toggle service state (In to Out or Out to In)
Destination	Display Destination Status Change Service State (In or Out)	Display service state in-transit counts Toggle service state (In to Out or Out to In)
Station	Display Station Status Change Service State (In or Out)	Display service state and error condition Toggle service state (In to Out or Out to In)
SKU/Part	Display SKU Master Data Display Inventory by SKU/Lot Retrieve Inventory by SKU/Lot Place SKU/Lot on Hold Release SKU/Lot from Hold Print SKU/Lot Bar Code Label Print SKU/Lot Report Print Aged Analysis Report Print Days Supply Report	Display SKU fields and control codes Display quantity by status (available, hold, allocated, and so on) Create order for SKU/Lot for specific quantity Place all inventory for SKU or SKU/Lot on hold Release all inventory for SKU or SKU/Lot from hold Print replacement SKU/Lot bar code label Print report of all information by SKU/Lot Print inventory by receipt date Print days supply by SKU
Carrier	Display Carrier Status Update Carrier Location Transfer Inventory to 2nd Carrier Delete Carrier Retrieve Carrier Place Carrier on Hold Release Carrier from Hold Print Carrier Bar Code Label Print Carrier Report	Display carrier ID, height, location, receipt date/time, and status Change carrier location to reflect a manual move Transfer inventory quantity from one carrier to another Delete a carrier from storage (and issue its inventory) Retrieve a carrier by specifying its ID Place a carrier and all of its inventory on Hold Release a carrier and all of its inventory from Hold (Re)Print a carrier bar code identification label Print a report of all carriers, locations, and inventory
Location	Display Location Status Retrieve Carrier by Location Change Service State (In or Out) Print Location Report Print Empty Location Report Print Space Management Report	Display location size, carrier ID, time/date, and error reason Retrieve whatever carrier is in the location Set a location In or Out of service Print report in location sequence of carriers Print report in location or zone sequence of empty locations Print report of full vs. empty locations by zone
Expected Receipts	Display Expected Receipts Status Add Expected Receipt Delete Expected Receipt	Display pending supplier and production receipts Add an expected receipt record Delete an expected receipt record
Order	Display Order Status Display Line Item Details Modify Line Item Delete Line Item Place Order on Hold Release Order from Hold Delete Order Print Order Report	Display order type, priority, destination, date/time, and status Display line item requested, in-transit, and completed quantity Change line item requested, in-transit, and completed quantity Delete a line item (and the order if only 1 line item) Place order on hold (current missions will complete) Release order from hold (and all line items) Delete order and all line items Print report of orders and line items
Mission	Display Mission Status Pick SKU/Lot Order Line Item Abort Mission	Display mission ID, status, source, destination, and order Pick required quantity from carrier Abort mission

(continued)

Table 11.7   (*Continued*)

FUNCTION	DIALOGUE	DESCRIPTION
QC/QA	Display QC/QA Status Issue Sample Quantity Modify QC/QA Status Issue Rejected Material to Scrap Return Rejected Material to Vendor Print QC/QA Report	Display hold/release/inspect/accept status by SKU/Lot Issue quantity used for inspection/test to QC charge number Change QC/QA status from one designation to another Issue rejected material to a scrap charge number Issue rejected material to a returned material charge number Print report of SKU/Lot by QC/QA status code
Cycle Count	Display Cycle Count Status Update Cycle Count Quantity Adjust Carrier SKU/Lot Quantity Print Cycle Count Report Print Cycle Count Disprepancies	Display inventory by cycle count status (due, hold, and so on) Record actual cycle count quantity (vs. computer count) Override computer count with actual count and release hold Print cycle count report by SKU/Lot, carrier, location, and so on Print records on hold due to a cycle count discrepancy

at Levels 3 and 4. This equipment-related synchronization element of computerized processing is not a factor when performing data transactions at Level 5. This timing factor also introduces the need for recovery logic when the physical action is not completed, which is not required at Level 5. This is one of the primary reasons why host systems which are not specifically sized and designed for real-time processing must be front-ended with a Warehouse Management System or by a Level 3 and 4 Warehouse Control System (WCS) provided by the material handling supplier.

Displays and Reporting

Displays provide current information regarding carriers, storage locations, orders, missions, and expected receipts. Information may be displayed via terminal or printed via report. Note that there may at times be discrepancies between AS/RS and host system records due to either timing of updates or discrepancies between edit checks. Note, though, that with a real-time interface, timing discrepancies are rarely an issue. If updates are via batch processing, the interval between updates determines the magnitude of risk of having discrepancies. Edit checks may be handled differently between the AS/RS and host system because the AS/RS is carrier-focused while the host is SKU-focused. If a discrepancy develops, a transaction may be accepted by the AS/RS but not by the host. For example, the AS/RS will accept an issue of 100 pcs from a carrier containing 100 pcs. If the host inventory is 90 pcs, the host issue will be rejected if negative inventory balances are not allowed. A discrepancy will exist for the amount of time it takes to resolve the discrepancy and synchronize inventory balances.

Log Messages

Log messages provide a tracking mechanism of system actions in response to system commands. To be most useful, these messages should be added to a database and configured such that they may be sorted by carrier, date, time, SKU/Lot, storage location, order number, error type, and so on. Categories (refer to Table 11.8) may include host (SKU balances and host communications), programmer

Table 11.8   Printer Log Messages

CATEGORY	USE	NORMAL	EXAMPLE
Host	Upload and download transactions	Off	Order Add or Delete Order Complete Cycle Count Adjustment
Programmer	Transaction intensive to assist in Commissioning and Problem Resolution	Off	Fork Shuttle Cycle Complete Move to Drop Position Complete Drop on Outbound Stand Complete
Operator	Specific error condition requiring operator intervention	On	Oversize Overweight Carrier Missing or Unreadable Bar Code
Information	Normal system changes	On	Physical Equipment In or Out of Service Logical Destination In or Out of Service Operator Log on or Log off
System Administrator	Inventory-related errors or inconsistencies which system logic resolved automatically	On	Full Bin Error (unknown carrier retrieved) Zone Full (carrier not stored) Empty Bin Error (carrier not retrieved)
Maintenance Operator	Anomaly conditions requiring maintenance operator action	On	Shuttle Time-out Fault P&D Full Error

Note: All log messages print to the daily file. Only those requiring some type of action should be printed on the log printer to separate the significant few from the trivial many.

(commissioning and problem resolution related to software), operator (condition requires operator intervention such as a missing bar code), information (system-related changes during normal operation such as service state changes which indicate whether a particular SRM or aisle is In or Out of Service), system administrator (errors or inconsistencies which system logic resolved automatically such as recovery from a full bin error), and maintenance (occurrences requiring Out of Service actions such as may be required to fix a jammed or oversize load).

Messages may be enabled or disabled for the entire category or by individual message. Enabling the message causes it to print to the log printer while disabling it prints to the log file but not the printer. Once the system is in operation, programmer-related messages are disabled, for example, since they are primarily for commissioning and debug purposes and not for normal operation. The only messages which should print are messages requiring some type of action or messages which convey important system information such as action taken automatically as a result of a full bin error.

Database Maintenance encompasses those database-related functions used to routinely maintain existing information. The host maintains certain fields on an ongoing basis via downloaded transactions. The AS/RS computer system maintains the rest, as well as provides a backup capability in case the host is not communicating. Recovery functions encompass nonroutine maintenance of items normally performed automatically by the AS/RS computer system. These types of actions may be due to anomaly conditions or to having performed handling in manual mode which requires the operator to record the new carrier location. Maintenance and recovery areas include carrier, mission, orders, and expected receipts.

Carriers are normally tracked automatically from inbound station to storage location or storage location to outbound station. If a carrier does not complete automatic handling, the operator updates the location in the computer system via a manually-entered transaction. Once the carrier is physically removed from the system, the carrier record is deleted. This is accomplished by either issuing the related inventory to a specified charge number and deleting the carrier record or by performing a zero cycle count transaction which deletes the carrier record if there is no more inventory on the carrier. Another alternative is to delete the carrier ID, but this should be done only if it does not impact inventory control record-keeping processes.

Missions apply to automated systems but not to conventional storage. A "mission" is a logical tracking record created by the system to control and monitor carrier movement. Each carrier is assigned a mission number (which may be the same as the carrier ID/bar code identifier) prior to any type of movement. Missions remain in existence until confirmation that the load has been stored (via the SRM interface) or until the carrier has reached the outbound destination in the case of a retrieval. Where carriers transfer from control of one subsystem to another as may occur when transfer progresses from the SRM to a conveyor and then to an AGV, each subsystem has its own mission record. The facility manager maintains a single overall mission.

Missions may be aborted if some anomaly condition occurs which prevents the carrier from actually reaching its destination under automatic control. An example may be a jammed load which had to be moved and stored in manual mode. The system provides a dialogue so the operator can add a carrier to a storage location if the load was actually stored. Edits will ensure that the location is empty and that the carrier ID does not exist elsewhere in storage or in an expected receipt. Failure to update the location prior to restarting automatic operation may result in a full bin error at some later time.

The carrier ID may also be quarantined irrespective of the inventory it contains or the location in which it is stored. This provides warehouse personnel with a quarantine capability which is independent of QC/QA. Situations where this may be needed include when a load is contaminated by leakage from loads above or when materials have been damaged by handling. Note that quarantining a carrier may not be permitted if an active mission is in process to retrieve it. Doing so without any active missions restricts any inventory on the carrier from consideration for automatic order processing. Removing the quarantine returns the inventory to automatic usage consideration. Note that a quarantine does not prevent an authorized operator or supervisor from retrieving the carrier using a workstation terminal in semiautomatic mode. The intent of a quarantine is to prevent the host from automatically applying quarantined material to an open order.

Order Maintenance encompasses adding line items, modifying line item quantities, placing orders on hold, releasing orders from hold, deleting line items, and deleting orders. There are restrictions regarding when certain actions can be taken. For example, an order cannot be deleted while an active mission is in process. The retrieval or pick mission must be allowed to complete in order to properly close out the database records. There is also the possibility that an action will be accepted but then later modified by the system automatically. For example, an order may be placed on hold when an active mission is in process. A hold status prevents further (new) automatic processing of other line items. However, if actual completion of an existing mission results in the order being completed (i.e., a mission to pick/complete the final line is in process), the hold is overridden by the completion status. The operator should be notified via a log message when this situation occurs.

Expected Receipts are records generated via purchase order receipt or production/work order completion processing. They relate quantity and data fields such as lot number, supplier, and date to the carrier ID. This simplifies the actual storage process since the operator does not have to enter the data manually when the carrier is actually stored in the AS/RS. In fact, if the carrier ID can be scanned automatically via bar code prior to storage, the entire storage process can be automated. Maintenance involves adding or deleting expected receipt records manually as a backup to automatic processing. When expected receipts are incorporated into an AS/RS, they are used to differentiate between "authorized" and "unauthorized" stores. Unauthorized stores (those entered manually by an operator) may require some type of QC inspection before the material can be used. Having the expected receipt records already on file as a function of purchase or production/work order processing simplifies the process of entering storage receipt data and also identifies materials which have been received or completed but not yet stored.

Service State defines whether each vehicle or equipment element is In or Out of Service. In Service elements are under computer control. Out of Service elements are not under computer control but may be operated in manual or maintenance modes. All system elements are normally left In Service. Setting elements Out of Service is done prior to performing maintenance to enable existing missions to complete while preventing new ones from being initiated. A screen should be available to enable mission completions related to SRMs, aisles, stations, locations, and destinations to be monitored so maintenance or operating personnel know when carrier and vehicle moves have been completed. Once completed, manual activities can be initiated. Current missions are typically limited to 1 to 3 per SRM. When the final mission is complete, system activity halts for the element which was set Out of Service. The normal maintenance shutdown and lockout procedures are then followed to ensure that equipment will not operate under automatic control while maintenance is being performed.

An *aisle* may be taken Out of Service to perform maintenance or to prevent any stores or retrievals in a particular aisle. In a system with one SRM per aisle, the SRM will either return to its "home" position at the end of the aisle or stop where the final mission completed. Reasons for taking an aisle Out of Service include performing maintenance on the SRM or aisle hardware, housekeeping, inspections, or fixing an anomaly condition such as a jammed load.

Inbound or outbound *stations* may be taken Out of Service to perform maintenance or to exclude a certain station from automatic processing. All current inbound loads will be moved to the SRM and stored, and all current outbound loads will be moved to the station where they can be removed from the system. Where there are multiple outbound stations in a system (for example, with a double-ended system), outbound carriers will be automatically rerouted to an In Service station if their designated station is set Out of Service. Stations may be taken Out of Service to enable size/scan/weigh sensors to be adjusted, drive motors to be replaced, or to accommodate lower manning levels during off shifts. Taking all but one station Out of Service will force all carriers to a particular station.

Individual storage locations may be taken Out of Service to prevent their use during automatic storage selection processing or to prevent a carrier in the location from being retrieved as part of automatic order processing. Any current mission will complete. Note that taking too many locations Out of Service within a particular zone will prevent additional materials for that zone from being stored. Empty storage locations may be taken Out of Service to clear out an area for maintenance purposes, to keep materials from being stored in an area being redesignated as a new zone, to provide access to adjacent carriers for inspection purposes, and to provide access to overhead lighting. Full storage locations may be taken Out of Service to prevent automatic retrieval of the materials in the location.

Taking an SRM Out of Service allows current missions to complete and stops the SRM in position where the last load was dropped or stored or in the 'home' position. The Storage Retrieval Machine is normally set Out of Service to perform maintenance, adjustments, repairs, and inspections.

Logical destinations relate to physical areas within the facility. These may include shipping, quality control, production lines, cycle count, R&D, scrap, error correction, and so on. Retrieval orders are associated with these logical destinations. The destination may be used to identify the proper charge account for materials and/or to identify the proper type of transaction as required to interface with the host system. For example, it is not necessary to differentiate between a shipping and assembly issue as far as a retrieval from the AS/RS is concerned. However, such issues require different cost accounting charges to reflect finished goods versus Work in Process issues. The destination provides the cost accounting relationship. Where there are multiple outbound stations as may occur with a dual-ended system (production vs. shipping), a system with multiple sideports (workstations fed directly from the AS/RS) or a system accessing multiple levels (different floors), the "logical" destination is associated to the "physical" station closest to the department.

Some logical destinations may be treated differently than others. The difference is related to whether the AS/RS maintains logical control of the material or whether logical control is at the host system level. Materials retrieved for cycle counting remain under logical control of the AS/RS, for example, even though they have been physically removed from the rack system. The AS/RS storage location (a logical destination) should indicate cycle count, to reflect the fact that a transfer transaction has occurred. Materials in the cycle count location are not available for automatic order processing until the cycle count process is completed and the materials are returned to regular storage.

This same logic may apply to carriers which have been automatically rejected due to overheight, overwidth, overdepth, underwidth, and overweight conditions. These loads will be moved to a logical Error Correction Station (ECS) and only stored after the error condition is resolved. Other examples include carriers retrieved for inspection or test purposes which will be returned to storage. It is unnecessary to add a new expected receipt to return material to storage when it remains under logical control since the AS/RS computer system already expects the material to be transferred from the particular logical destination to storage. This also maintains the original storage date/time stamp for FIFO purposes, which is lost if the product is stored as if it is new material.

Storage

An AS/RS storage process differs significantly from that used in a conventional storage operation. Both types of storage typically coexist in an operation, with actual bar code identification labels being the same. However, the two primary areas of difference include mode of operation and physical checks.

With conventional storage, an operator stores the material in what would be considered manual mode in an AS/RS. This means that an operator initiates the storage process and selects the storage location. Once the material is stored, the computer system is updated. This may be via RF terminal or via some type of paperwork. With an AS/RS, automated storage processing is initiated once the carrier is placed on the inbound station and released. This requires all of the checks normally performed by an operator in conventional storage such as size and weight checks and location selection to be performed automatically. Loads must pass these checks, or the load is rejected for manual resolution. Refer to Table 11.9 for a general comparison of automatic versus conventional storage processes.

Normal storage mode is automatic. After an operator places a carrier on the inbound station and releases it, all further conveying, checking, storage location selection, and location update processes are automated. The first check is to verify the carrier ID at the point of induction. If the ID is invalid, the system has no record (via the expected receipt) of which materials are contained on the carrier and, therefore, no storage location selection can be selected.

Once the carrier ID is validated, the size is checked. If the load is oversize, it may jam on the conveyor or in the storage location. If the width (in the down-aisle direction) is undersize, the load may miss one of the supporting load arms and partially fall into the lower location, making automated retrieval impossible. If the depth (into the rack) is too long, the load may stick out into the aisle too far and hit another being transported by the SRM. There are only 2 to 3 inches of clearance between a load on the SRM and a load in each storage location to either side in the aisle.

Table 11.9   AS/RS vs. Conventional Storage Comparison

AREA OF COMPARISON	AS/RS	CONVENTIONAL
Primary Mode	Automatic (Host Communicating)	Manual
Backup Mode	Semiautomatic (Host Not Communicating)	Not Applicable
Emergency Mode	Manual (AS/RS Computer Not Communicating)	Not Applicable
Carrier Identification	Carrier ID Bar Code Labels on Carrier	Not Applicable or the Same
Material Identification	Material ID Bar Code Labels on Load	Same
Visible Location Numbers	Not Applicable	Location ID or Bar Code Labels on Rack Structure
Size Check	Automatic Checks via Photoeyes or Scanners: Overheight – Overwidth (for storage opening) – Underwidth (for rack load arms spacing) – Overlength	Operator Visually Checks
Weight Check	Overweight (Go/No Go) via Scale or Load Cell	Operator Responsibility
Zone Identification	Fast Mover (front of system, low levels) Slow Mover (rear of system, high levels) Type of Material (separate bases from acids, drum storage low, heaviest weights low, and so on)	Operator Selection
Storage Location Selection	Closest Height Location within Zone Any Greater Height Location within Zone	Operator Selection

In systems which accommodate several different location heights, the size check is used to determine which loads must be stored in which height storage locations. In a conventional storage system, these are the types of checks which are visually made by the operator. In an AS/RS, they are made by photoeyes or scanners which provide a go/no go indication. Photoeyes are beams of light against a reflector. Breaking or not breaking the beam provides the size indication. For example, an overheight photoeye placed at a 4′ 1/8″ height will be broken by any loads which exceed 4 feet, the 1/8 inch being the allowable overheight tolerance.

The weight check may be a go/no go check or provide an actual readout. The scale is mounted underneath one of the inbound conveyor queue positions. If the check fails, the carrier is rejected and some of the material must be removed and transferred to another carrier. The proper carrier inventory updates must be made to reflect the change.

Once all checks have passed successfully, the carrier is conveyed to the SRM pick position. The SRM picks the load, transports it to the selected storage location, and checks for a load in the location. If no load is detected, the carrier is stored and the database location is updated. If a load is detected, a full bin error occurs. The AS/RS or host computer system selects another storage location and the load onboard the SRM is stored. An internal retrieve mission is then created to pick the carrier in the original storage location and move it to the error correction station (if it is available). This load must be reidentified by the operator and then restored. Full bin errors can occur if a load is stored in manual mode and the location is not updated or if the host determines the storage location and timing discrepancies exist.

Retrieval

All retrievals are via orders. Host-generated orders are typically specified in terms of a SKU or SKU/Lot and quantity. This enables the AS/RS computer system to optimize actual retrievals based on specific aisle and carrier selection within a generally FIFO sequence. Strict FIFO sequence based on storage or receipt date/time stamp is not required for most operations, as long as generally FIFO sequence is maintained. Order priority varies based on the type of order and may be increased by an authorized individual to sequence an "emergency" order ahead of the others.

When there are multiple orders to be retrieved, sequencing is a function of order priority and system and material availability. Emergency retrievals are the highest priority. They will be retrieved as soon as the in-process missions are completed.

Demand orders refer to retrievals "on demand." These are usually entered by the operator via an AS/RS terminal on an as-required basis. Demand priority is second only to emergency priority. The general thinking is that orders which are initiated by an operator should be satisfied prior to those initiated via some type of automatic host computer processing logic. Demand priority is often used by the QC inspector and to pick materials to support a "window service" type of demand.

Each type of order has a priority relative to each other type of order. This may vary from one company to another. Orders for QC or QA are typically higher than production or shipping orders. These orders are initiated by inspectors and testers via AS/RS terminals. If assigned a lower priority, there could be a long wait before materials are retrieved if they are slotted in FIFO sequence into the order list after all existing active orders. Orders which have been specifically requested by someone should be capable of being assigned a higher priority than those initiated by normal host computer processing. Systems normally provide a selection list of priorities so the operator can set an "other than default priority" when the actual order is entered.

Cycle count orders are typically a lower priority than other orders. This ensures that orders for production or shipping are retrieved prior to nonproduction orders. Note that there is often less cycle counting with a unit load AS/RS as compared to conventional storage, since loads are often received and issued without any partial picks. Another consideration is the security and limited access provided by the AS/RS.

It may be important for certain types of orders to be retrieved at certain times.

Shipping orders may need to be retrieved to support truck loading and shipment schedules. Cycle count orders may need to be retrieved at the beginning or end of a shift. In order to override order priorities in time-constrained situations, order logical destinations may be set Out of Service to permit lower priority orders to be retrieved. Note that this affects all but emergency priority orders which will be retrieved at any time as long as the proper set of In Service conditions exist.

For all types of orders, the various system elements must be In Service, the order must not be on hold, and any order criteria must be satisfied. This may require that the full quantity is available, as opposed to a partial pull, and that full quantities of all other parts on each order line item are available. The AS/RS computer system will reassess order sequence whenever an Out of Service condition is changed to In Service.

QA/QC

An AS/RS can provide the capability to obtain and issue sample quantities and modify quarantine status by lot or individual carrier inventory. Companies which perform inspection or testing on incoming materials, Work in Process, or finished goods may need to exercise control by SKU, SKU/Lot, serial number, carrier, location, order, or supplier.

When sample quantities are removed, it is necessary to identify the quantity per carrier so the carrier quantity can be updated. A transfer to a QC location or issue to a QC charge account maintains the proper inventory and accounting balances. If no materials are rejected, destroyed, or contaminated by the inspection or testing process, the materials may be returned to the proper carrier for storage. If material is returned to a different carrier, a transfer transaction increases the carrier quantity and removes the inventory from QC.

If the inspection or testing process determines that the SKU/Lot should be rejected, the lot is placed on QC hold. With mixed loads, other materials on the carrier may still be retrieved for orders, but the AS/RS computer system will reject any attempt to issue the on hold materials to a production or shipping order. Automatic order processing will not consider on hold materials as available. Company procedures vary but generally any rejected materials are kept in a "defective material" location (possibly locked) to prevent unauthorized use before a disposition has been determined.

If QA makes a decision to dispose of the materials, any carriers in storage must be retrieved and the inventory issued to a scrap or a return-to-vendor charge number. The QC hold will not prevent QA from retrieving the carriers using a retrieve by carrier ID dialogue or a retrieve by SKU/Lot dialogue. The sample quantities in the QC location must also be scrapped.

Cycle Counting

Cycle counting operations may require transactions in both the host and AS/RS computer systems. The host system provides all of the planning-level functions related to establishing cycles, selecting parts to cycle count, control group identification, and problem identification and resolution. The AS/RS computer system provides the control-level functions related to actual selection of carriers and inventory records for counting and entry of the actual cycle count quantities. The reason for having a balance between the two systems is that the host may only contain the aggregate inventory balances, while the AS/RS computer system maintains the actual inventory balances by carrier and location.

When the official inventory is maintained at the host level, details are maintained at the carrier level by the AS/RS computer system. Refer to Figure 11.14.

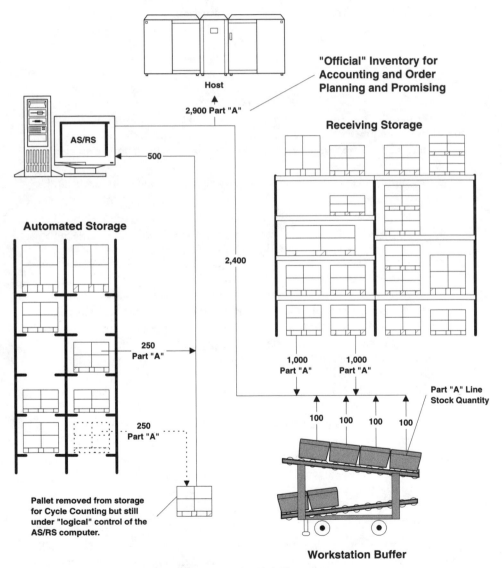

Figure 11.14   "Official" Inventory

Actual counts are uploaded to the host, and adjustment authorization is downloaded to the AS/RS computer system. The count at the carrier level is maintained in a separate Carrier Cycle Count Quantity field, but no change occurs to the carrier inventory quantity until the host downloads the proper authorization. This can be a problem if the host system does not have a real-time interface or if the inventory planner does not respond to the discrepancy in a timely manner.

Cycle count orders are in essence retrieval orders with multiple line items (one for each carrier inventory record) for the entire inventory balance by SKU or SKU/Lot. As the carriers are retrieved, operators count the materials and enter the actual count quantity on an AS/RS screen. If the count matches the carrier inventory balance, the carrier inventory Date of Last Cycle Count is updated and the carrier is returned to storage. If all carrier inventory records match the actual count, a confirmation transaction is uploaded to the host to update the Host Date of Last Cycle Count for the SKU or SKU/Lot. This reinitializes the cycle.

If there is a mismatch, the carrier should be placed in a secure area until all of the carriers have been counted. If the net shortages exactly offset the overages (i.e., the total carrier inventory is correct but individual carrier balances were incorrect), the individual carrier inventory balances can be updated accordingly. A confirmation transaction is uploaded to the host to update the Host Date of Last Cycle Count for the SKU or SKU/Lot. This reinitializes the cycle.

If the total counted quantity does not match, there is a net mismatch. The counted quantity is automatically accepted if the total magnitude of the change across all carriers is within policy guidelines (based on quantity or dollars). The net change quantity per carrier updates each carrier quantity. The total net change quantity directly updates the host as a plus or minus to the existing quantity, but only if the two systems match in the beginning. Otherwise, the problem illustrated in Table 11.10 occurs. If the two systems are not in sync to begin with, an absolute adjustment (e.g., 80 in the table) can be used to force a match. The magnitude of the change must be processed by cost accounting to update the inventory value.

If the magnitude of the change is outside policy guidelines, a manual override (via dialogue authorization) is required to accept the change and initiate the ad-

Table 11.10 Problem of Net Change Adjustment When Host and AS/RS Quantities Are Not in Sync

SCENARIO	AS/RS	HOST	NET CHANGE RESULT
Initial Condition	100	110	Host Discrepancy = +10
Actual Count = 80	(20)	(20)	Net Change = (20)
Final Condition	80	90	Host Discrepancy = +10

The Net Change process simply continued the mismatch between the computer balance (90) and the actual balance (80). An absolute adjustment of 80 is required in order to correct the Host.

justment process. This may be performed automatically by the host via download transactions for the specific carriers or require an operator to manually accept the adjustments.

If there is a mismatch and the carrier is returned to storage without setting a cycle count hold, the system may include the carrier inventory in the automatic order processing. Both the Carrier Inventory Quantity and the Cycle Count Quantity fields in the carrier record will be maintained synchronously as inventory is received or issued. The restriction is that neither balance is allowed to go negative.

Note that the carrier SKU inventory record is normally deleted when the carrier inventory balance equals zero. In cases where the Carrier SKU Cycle Count field is not also zero, the carrier record cannot be deleted. Resolution of the discrepancy must be resolved by the planner through the host or via an AS/RS computer dialogue.

Due to the risk of creating a count discrepancy as a result of trying to correct a discrepancy, carriers should not be returned to storage if there is a known discrepancy.

STORAGE RETRIEVAL MACHINE (SRM)

Storage Retrieval Machines come in a variety of standard capacities and heights. The material handling company then modifies the standard machines as required for nonstandard applications. Machines fall into two general categories of miniloads and unit loads. Miniloads handle the smaller, lighter loads such as totes, trays, and bins. Unit loads handle the larger, heavier loads such as pallets, rolls, and racks.

Standard weight capacities for a miniload are 110 lb. and 330 lb. with a fork shuttle. A fork shuttle mechanism picks up the load from underneath (as opposed to a fork truck where the forks pick up a pallet under the top boards). This is used for standard size totes and boxes.

An extractor mechanism which pushes and pulls loads via a handle on the load or slave pallet allows miniloads to handle up to 750 lb. loads. This technique can be used for auto seat sets buffered prior to shipping to the assembly operation in In Line Vehicle Sequence (ILVS), for example. The seat pallet is automatically placed into a captive pan when buffered in the AS/RS, and the pan is dropped out from under the shipping pallet when the seats are removed from the AS/RS.

Other types of shuttles which are gaining in popular use grip the carton or tote from the side in order to store them on regular shelving. This reduces the cost of a fabricated rack system and accommodates boxes of varying widths. This technique can be used with meat packed in cartons, clothing in cartons, and so on. Five to ten meter heights are common for miniloads, with greater heights possible.

Unit loads commonly handle 2,200 lb., 2,500 lb., 3,000 lb., 4,000 lb., and greater weight capacities. Machines can handle heights well over 100 feet, though less than 100 feet are most common. Storage can be single- or double-deep with a shuttle mechanism. Note that while double-deep systems improve storage density, a larger fork allowance between vertical pallets (approximately 12″ versus 6″) is required to allow for the larger shuttle mechanism.

In addition to the rack and fire protection systems, a storage system includes the SRM, aisle mechanical, and aisle electrical hardware. The mechanical elements consist of the floor rail, the upper guide rail, and the shock absorbers at both ends of the floor rail which prevent overtravel. The electrical elements consist of the power rail for the SRM which runs the length of the aisle, an E-Stop pull cord which runs the length of the aisle, as applicable, the End-of-Aisle panel which contains the controls devices and the infrared or other communications from the SRM to the computer system.

Figure 11.15 illustrates a typical unitload SRM. Such machines operate in automatic mode under host computer control, in semiautomatic mode under operator control from an AS/RS computer terminal, and maintenance mode from either onboard, pendant, or other controls in slow speed. Machines can also be fitted with operator cabs. These are used to perform picking and putaway operations in systems where computers direct the operators who ride the machines (like a turret truck, only faster) and to provide a backup mode of operation in automatic systems.

SRMs essentially balance on the floor rail on two wheel block assemblies. One or both wheels may be driven, with the more common application being one. Idler wheels lock the SRM to the bottom rail. The top guide rail keeps it balanced and accurately aligned down the length of the aisle. Positioning is absolute via encoders or is confirmed by targets located at each bin (mounted on the floor) and tier height (on the mast).

Loads coming onboard are checked for overweight via a load cell. Overheight loads are checked via a photoeye as the load is brought onboard by the shuttle mechanism. Either type of fault causes the load to be transferred to the outbound drop station.

The SRM accelerates to speed and then decelerates as it approaches the storage location. For a store, the lift carriage assembly stops in position slightly above the load arms (bin high). The load is stroked into the location by the fork mechanism, and then the entire lift carriage assembly lowers, leaving the load on the load arms. To perform a pick, the lift carriage stops in the bin low position so the fork shuttle can stroke in under the load. The lift carriage has sensors which detect load overhang and fork shuttle centered.

Selection of the proper model SRM is dependent on the load characteristics, system height, system throughput, and level of automation. Costs vary widely, with the most specialized SRMs carrying the heaviest loads in the $400,000 to $500,000 range. As a comparison, the smallest single-aisle buffer systems for light loads may be in the $300,000 to $400,000 range. The greater the number of aisles, the more the fixed project costs related to project management, engineering, and the computer system can be spread.

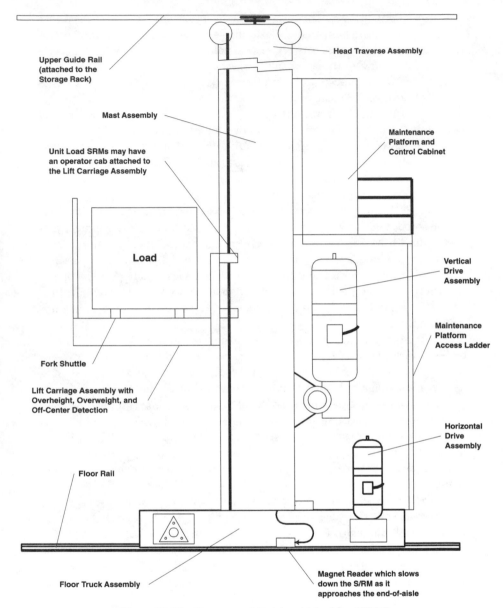

Figure 11.15   Storage and Retrieval Machine (SRM)

SUMMARY

Projects have elements which are essentially the same, regardless of the area of application. Within an integral strategy, implementation of an AS/RS is very representative of the type of project which benefits from a design/build approach and an integration methodology. Also, like any project, there are customer prerequisites which help to ensure success.

1. Support the material handling company in developing the required integral and design specifications and related documentation early in the project. Proactively identify and resolve issues. Work together as a team. Set targets and keep management informed of the progress.

2. Assign personnel to manage or support the teams who have an understanding of projects and the various system elements for which they are responsible. Delays, misunderstandings, obstructions, inefficiencies, or deviations from the contract delay the project and end up costing everyone money. Give qualified people the level of authority to match the breadth of their responsibilities.

3. Develop a formal communications forum. Set time limits within which to make decisions. Establish a hierarchy where the team can appeal decisions which are being bottlenecked at lower levels within the organization. Keep the project on schedule.

4. Establish boundaries of responsibility. The material handling company is responsible for providing the specified system. Scope or other changes must be documented and approved via the project change notice process.

Companies need to be realistic about integral projects. They cannot be managed and controlled as if they are an equipment purchase. They involve a long duration and a number of changes within the company's infrastructure. The systems will work as specified if provided by a reputable company. It is up to all parties to ensure that the experience is a win-win situation for all involved. However, it is really the customer who sets the tone of the business and working relationships.

Perhaps the biggest single problem experienced with integral system projects is that customer personnel get more knowledgeable over time. While this is actually a desirable outcome, it does lead to scope changes and delays. Scope changes occur because the customer discovers that areas important to the success of the project have been overlooked or improperly assigned. Delays occur because the company initially takes on more responsibility than it has resources for and gets behind schedule. Team members usually have business as well as project responsibilities; the business comes first, but not always without a cost to the project.

These problems are significantly greater with a bid spec as compared to a design/build approach. With bid specs, the company must accept full responsibility for project scope—it is their bid spec. With a design/build approach, the company shares its knowledge with a partner for the purpose of making scope and design a joint responsibility.

Chapter 12

Market-Based Production System

Transfer lines are used to produce parts where the volume and types of operations justify the investment in dedicated equipment. While most commonly dedicated to a single part, some designs enable a family of very similar parts to be produced. High volume automotive machined parts such as cam shafts or cylinder heads may justify the use of transfer lines.

The less variability there is between operations, the more manufacturing tends to appear as a transfer line. As variability and the number of operations increases, manufacturing tends to become more of a batch or job shop environment. The choice to implement a market-based production system can have significant cost and operating benefits in manufacturing environments where order shipments, incoming materials, and manufacturing operations conform to a rate-based schedule.

Markets act as barriers to prevent waste at upstream operations from affecting downstream operations (refer to Figure 12.1). The receiving market buffers supplier materials prior to usage. Production markets buffer manufactured parts and assemblies prior to the consuming (downstream) operation and empties being returned to the producing (upstream) operation. The shipping market buffers finished goods for shipment to customers and returned empty shipping racks or containers. Markets are limited in capacity and hours or days supply by design. Material has dedicated locations, while visible indicators identify normal and emergency float levels. Emergency float is the level at which inventory must be replenished in order to prevent a production line stoppage.

Like inventory, buffers exist because of factors related to the operation itself and sources of supply. Their existence and effectiveness are indicators of the ability of the organization to reduce variability and achieve level production and replenishment rates.

Market-based production systems encompass some portion of all of the as-

438

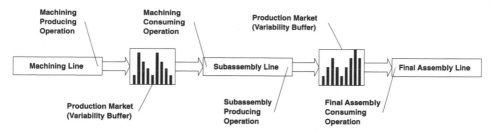

Figure 12.1   Markets Buffer Producing and Consuming
Operations from Each Other's Variability

pects discussed in previous chapters. The emphasis to now has been on understanding how to apply the various principles in an integral strategy to the specific
company operating environment. This chapter covers the specific principles and
design characteristics required to implement markets in a repetitive manufacturing environment.[1]

- A Market-based production system is closed loop by design. It is engineered
  based on principles of eliminating waste, a place for everything and everything in its place, simple number schemes, shift cancel, line-of-sight, ergonomics, visualizations, and zero-tolerance to deviations from targets. It
  relies on organizational, facilities, equipment, systems, and technologies improvements to provide the necessary infrastructure.

- Market-based production systems place design of the process infrastructure
  into the hands of the various production and engineering teams. The teams
  then incorporate visual operational controls into the design itself so feedback to supervisors and production team members regarding inventory level
  and availability is obvious.

Markets are a recognition within certain environments that a given inventory
hours supply is required to ensure uninterrupted service between producing and
consuming operations. In the end, markets exist because the risk of not having
them is unacceptable from an operational and responsiveness perspective.

MARKET TYPES MEET THE "CUSTOMER/SUPPLIER" NEEDS

Markets are sized for the days or hours supply required to support production.
This includes a factor for emergency float. Markets contain both full and empty
containers or carts where returnable dunnage is used. Materials may be floor
stacked, in pallet or flow racks or in an automated system. Flow is generally (not
strictly) FIFO. Additional space is required for those parts with complexity. This
refers to products which offer options such as different gear ratios, colors, and so
on, which must be buffered at the same time to accommodate mixed model sched-

---

1. The basis of this chapter came from work with Ford and Mazda.

uling or frequent line changeovers. The three types of markets are shown in Figure 12.2. They provide buffers between *suppliers* (actual suppliers, producing stations, or lines) and *consumers* (consuming stations or lines).

Partial quantities should never be returned to the market. Since materials are replenished on a demand-pull[2] basis, material leaving a market frees up space for new material. Once that new material is received, there is no longer any room for returned material. Partial returns defeat the visual controls which rely on counting the number of (full) totes, cartons, bins, baskets, racks, or carts to determine the inventory level.

Receiving (Dock) Market

The receiving market encompasses receiving, incoming inspection, repack, and storage or staging processes. The intent is to receive as much material directly to point-of-use (production market) or point-of-fit (workstation) locations as possible, with as few intermediate processes as possible. The receiving market buffers the remainder. Replenishment routes are then run as required to replenish workstations from the receiving market. Returnable dunnage is picked up for shipment back to the suppliers. Receiving markets primarily exist because the company has elected to purchase more inventory in terms of volume or days supply than can be buffered at the line or workstation. This is due to a combination of financial decisions based on freight and inventory costs and on the hours supply targeted for the product.

The receiving market is equivalent to a centralized storage area in a more traditional environment. The primary difference is in the operation. Some or all of the materials may be retrieved directly by the production teams without relying on a separate material handling department for deliveries. This means that storage height is restricted or that automation makes it equally easy to store and retrieve materials. Computerization may or may not be required.

Receiving Processes

Receiving processes confirm that the correct type and quantity of material has been received, that there is no visible damage, and that any special routing or material identification processes are performed. Any materials not moved directly to the point-of-use or point-of-fit are moved to the market or possibly to incoming inspection. Otherwise, materials are normally buffered in their designated floor or rack storage location. If the supplier bar code label is not usable, an in-plant label may need to be applied to the material. This identifies part number, quantity, and market and workstation ID for automatic and manual handling purposes. This initiates the *logical* tracking process.

---

2. "Demand-pull" refers to an operation where material is "pulled" from the producing operation to the market and then "pulled" from the market by the consuming team to the consuming operation. The producing team cannot push materials directly to the consuming team.

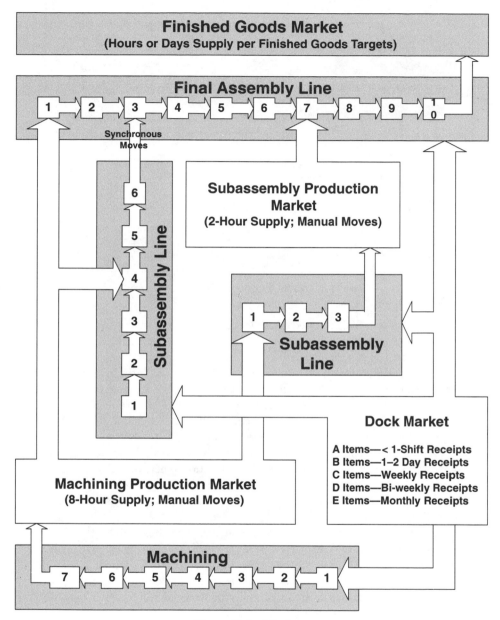

Figure 12.2   Markets

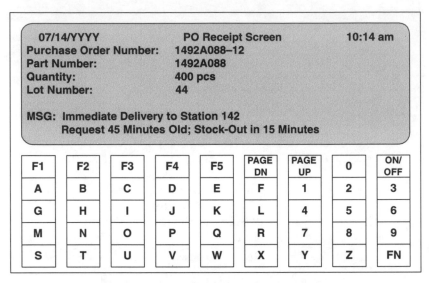

Figure 12.3   Radio Frequency PO Receipt Screen

With a RF terminal mounted on the forklift, the Receipt screen may appear as shown in Figure 12.3. The team member scans the bar code label to enter the required fields. The system then displays the proper disposition. This process initiates a receipt transaction against the purchase order and adds the material to raw material inventory if the disposition is inspection, test, or the receiving market. A disposition to move the material directly to a point-of-use production market or a point-of-fit workstation initiates a combination raw material inventory receipt[3] and then an issue transaction to Work in Process.

Moving material directly to production may be the normal disposition for the part or may be necessary due to a stock-out situation. There may also be a pending issue in queue for the part which has not been serviced yet. In this case, it may be faster and more efficient to deliver it directly from receiving than to obtain material from the receiving market.

Once the team member is instructed to deliver the material to Station 142 as shown in Figure 12.3, the message is acknowledged by pressing the F1 function key (for example). This assigns the delivery to the particular team member performing the receipt and prevents anyone else from servicing the request. When the material is actually delivered, scanning the material and location bar codes completes the transfer process.

---

3. If the days supply is low enough overall, the receiving market may be considered as Work in Process rather than Raw material. This implies that material pickups will *not* require an issue transaction and that inventory is relieved via some type of backflush transaction after product completion.

Issuing Processes

Retrieving and issuing material from the receiving market is accomplished in a similar fashion as just discussed. A running list of requested materials is maintained by the system. Team members may request a current listing by age, priority, station, line, market, and so on. Selecting "age" lists requests in FIFO sequence. In cases where line team members request replacement on a container-by-container basis but where routes are run based on delivering multiple containers, the system will queue the requests until the proper total is received. For example, if four containers are normally delivered every four hours, individual requests at the line as each new container is opened are buffered by the system until the fourth container is requested. At that time, a request for four containers is added to the receiving market queue.

Priority is normally FIFO in order of delivery requests. There needs to be a capability to request an emergency priority which will move the request to the top of the list. This may be due to a stock-out condition or possibly an unplanned line changeover. Requests for inventory which is not available will not show on the team member's screen until the inventory has been received. This prevents the team member from having to scroll down the list to bypass the requests which cannot be serviced. When material is received, these items will have the highest priority since they will be the oldest requests in the system.

Every effort should be made to minimize the amount of key entry, scrolling, and paging that is required. This applies to any type of computer system but to RF systems in particular. Response times with RF terminals are generally not as fast as terminals networked directly to the computer. In fact, several seconds or longer can be experienced on a random basis with just about any type of RF transaction. Delays can be caused by traffic on the network and by location in the facility. With a delay, for example, the operator may see that the cursor is on a particular line of the display. Pressing the F1 key at this point initiates the action. If the cursor is really supposed to be on the next line and just has not gotten there yet due to the delay, the computer system will execute the action on the next line. The operator thinks one thing is occurring, and the computer does another.

Providing sorts by station, line, drop zone area, and so on enables the receiving market team member to process issues which can be delivered together via tow train, tugger AGV (with trailers), or by production team members servicing designated routes. Otherwise, a large laydown area may be required to queue materials across a wide variety of workstations or drop zones.

Production Market

Production markets service machining, subassembly, and final assembly. These markets buffer parts for the downstream (consuming) operation and empties for return to the upstream (producing) operation. Like receiving markets, each production market is sized for the target hours supply to support the customer service and inventory turns targets, plus emergency float. For parts with complexity, additional space is required. Unlike receiving markets, no issue transactions are required; materials are already in Work in Process.

Specialty Carts

Consider a market for specialty carts containing machined parts for subassembly. A specialty cart (refer to Figure 12.4 for one type) is one which is designed specifically for the particular part and is, therefore, dedicated. Such carts provide part protection during handling and movement and transfer an exact simple number quantity. They may be designed to enable parts to roll or slide to the team member to minimize reaching. They may contain trays of parts which can be fed to the operator via a conveyor. Oily parts may incorporate a drip pan and removable reservoir. Turntables may be incorporated into the design to improve ergonomics. Parts may be skewered to assist loading into automatic machines.

Specialty carts typically range in price from $2,000 to $10,000 each, with capacities of 500 to 1,500 lb. or more. Price will vary based on number of carts required, necessity to produce prototypes first, and difficulty of protecting and handling the part. Use of stainless steel, plating, or other means to prevent rust increases the cost. Dust covers may be used to protect the parts during the time they are in the market.

Carts should be designed to be towed by a tugger or AGV for long distance moves and to be pushed by an operator for short distance moves and positioning. Long distance is relative but may be any move over 100 feet. A 100 foot move for an operator requires a 200 foot round-trip walking distance. At a walking speed

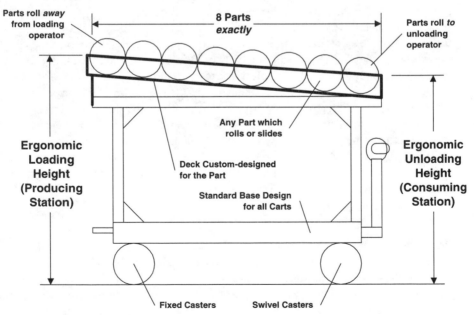

Figure 12.4   Specialty Cart Design for Parts Which Roll

of 2 mi./hr., 200 feet requires 1.14 min./move (60 min./hr./2 mi./hr./5,280 ft./mi. × 200 ft./move). Adding normal handling time to drop off a full cart and pick up an empty can push the move time to two minutes. At some distance and frequency, it becomes inefficient for an operator to perform individual cart moves and more efficient for a tow operator or AGV to tow 3 to 5 carts at a time. This is all a function of size of the facility, ability of an operator to leave the production line for short periods, and divisions of responsibility between production and material handling.

Market Rules and Exceptions

Market rules apply equally to both the producing and consuming teams. The producing team is allowed to produce only as much inventory as the market is sized to buffer. Production *must* stop once that level is reached. This is regulated by physically restricting the total number of containers, carts, bins, racks, and so on, in the pipeline. The consuming team can return only as many empties to the market for which there is space. The total of all fulls and empties in the pipeline must equal the market plus producing workstation plus consuming workstation capacity, with allowances for complexity and empty spaces to segregate materials for FIFO control, as applicable. For example, if hours supply is eight hours and each cart has a 2-hour capacity, there can be any mix of full and empty containers, carts, and so on, in the market as long as there are never more than four fulls. If the number of empties begins to exceed the number of fulls, that is an indication that the producing team is falling behind. Refer to Figure 12.5 for a specialty cart market for a part with a complexity of "2."

From a practical perspective, there may be cases where an extra full cart ends up in the production market. This can occur when the producing station fills a cart and moves it to the market, only to find that there is no empty cart to exchange. This indicates a problem at the consuming station. In the previous example, the producing station can operate for a maximum of two more hours, at which time the final cart will be filled. Filling all carts results in an on-hand inventory of two days: two hours at the producing station, ten hours in the market, and four hours at the consuming station. This is four hours greater than the target, assuming an average of one full and one empty at the producing and consuming stations and four fulls in the market. Other considerations must be accounted for when lines operate at significant rate differentials. Heat treat may operate 24 hours per day, seven days per week to keep pace with two 10-hour per day production shifts (20 hours total), six days per week. The 4-hour difference means that a gradual buildup in the market feeding heat treat will occur over the course of the day and week. This buildup becomes significantly higher than four hours if the production lines do not operate on Saturday or Sunday. This is just one example of a situation where the hours supply target must be modified to accommodate capacity constraints. Heat treat is a very expensive area in which to increase capacity.

If the consuming team has a partial quantity remaining in the cart when a line

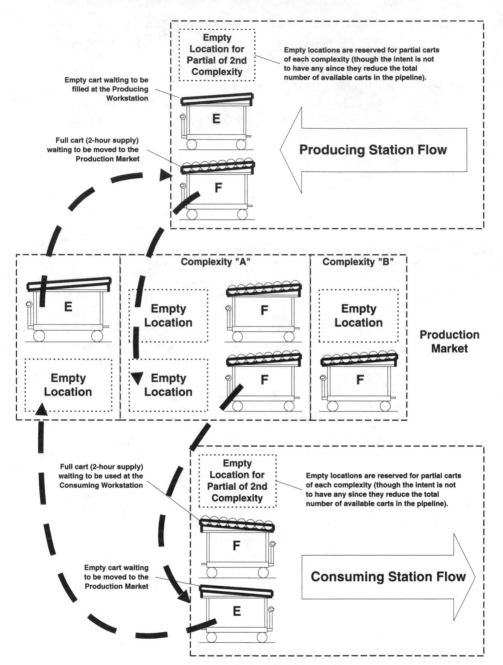

Figure 12.5   Specialty Cart Production Market with Complexity of 2

changeover occurs, the partial *cannot* be returned to the market. The exception to this rule is that the partial can be returned directly to the producing station in order to have the cart refilled to capacity. Production runs may not always result in exact simple number multiples. Consolidating partials at both the producing and consuming stations after switching over to a new complexity may free up one additional container or cart which can be used for current production. This is an exception situation which the theory does not permit but which must be accommodated for practical purposes.

Shipping Market

The shipping market services final assembly and the customers. It operates in the same manner as the other markets.

MARKET VISION

Market-based production systems provide a highly visible means of monitoring a company's ability to operate within established inventory targets. The market inventory level targets themselves are established based on the quantity of inventory required to support production. This quantity varies over time as the effect of waste in other areas of the business on inventory levels is reduced. The simpler and more consistent production operations become, the easier it is to manage and control the flow of inventory. Relying less on overhead (clerical, managerial, and indirect[4]) personnel, reducing the need for extra floor space for overshipments, not tying up equipment for storing and handling excess inventory, and reducing expediting to manage shortage conditions leaves more time to focus on making the system work effectively. The market vision translates the company's integral strategy into very visible controls at the factory level. Personnel can see with their own eyes whether and how the system is working.

Each area of integration must first be defined via a simple matrix format for vision purposes as shown in Figure 12.6. The reason for simplicity is to facilitate understanding within the organization, since the actual implementation may be fairly complex in terms of its range of change within the operational and infrastructural areas of integration. The Vision Chart covers the to-be concept, the as-is baseline, areas of change via initiatives, projects, and programs, and significant open issues or obstacles to improvement.

Extensions of the vision chart are then developed for each machining and subassembly area and the final assembly line. A display board is created showing a CAD layout of the line, with all of the parts and their point-of-fit. This includes the receiving market layout and capacity for those parts used on the line, any production market layouts and cart or container sketches, timing charts for material

---

4. Some companies refer to hourly personnel who directly produce a product as *direct* personnel and to hourly material handling and other personnel who provide support as *indirect* personnel.

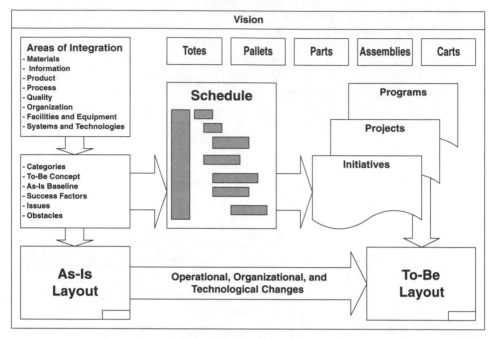

Figure 12.6   Vision Chart

moves, process flow descriptions, exploded drawings for assemblies, and so on. The emphasis is on providing a graphic overview of the entire operation in a single visualization in a manner which will make the application of the market principles easier to understand to those who will be operating the line.

Table 12.1 provides an overview of the types of elements which must be considered when locating and sizing markets. The assessment begins with an understanding of the operating pattern and basic material handling and buffering requirements and progresses through basic methodologies, inventory requirements, containerization and dunnage, and operator considerations. Once the generalities are identified, they can be further defined in terms of the areas of integration, initiatives, projects, programs, and performance measures.

MARKET PRINCIPLES

"Principles" are the guidelines by which the market-based production system is designed and operated. Adherence to the principles ensures consistency with the vision established for the integral system. Deviation from a principle is allowed only for business reasons which cannot be addressed at that particular time or if another principle takes precedence. For example, if it is not cost effective to receive an expensive part on a daily basis due to freight costs or geographic location of the supplier (e.g., overseas), the principle of receiving expensive parts on a daily basis is overridden by the business need to minimize total costs. If a par-

Table 12.1 Market Vision Considerations

AREA	AS-IS (PROBLEMS BEING ADDRESSED)	TO-BE (TARGETS)	VISION
Operating Pattern (hours and sequence of operation)	- Production mix, quantity, and schedule changes daily - Too much overtime - Machining and subassembly operations not in sync with final assembly - Actual inventory levels vary widely over time	- Fix schedule for 1 to 2 weeks - Set schedule based on demonstrated capacity while allowing some flexibility - Synchronize production and related material handling - Synchronize inventory to production level	- Mixed model production - Small batches in Simple Number quantities - Shift cancel - Reserve capacity for short lead time orders - Synchronized delivery of 3 to 7 subassemblies direct to final assembly - Buffer 8 hours of inventory between machining and subassembly - Buffer 2 hours of inventory between subassembly and final assembly
Inventory	- 16 Days Supply - No control over FIFO - Most parts in central storage	- 7 Days Supply - (Generally) FIFO - Self-manufactured parts and assemblies in Production Markets - Purchased parts in Receiving Market and at Point-of-Use and Point-of-Fit locations	- Stratify inventory by Days Supply based on cost and geographic proximity - Force in-line or round-robin activity - Markets for all production areas - Receiving Market at each dock - Centralized storage for ≥ 1 Days Supply inventory - Point-of-Use storage for < 1 Days Supply - Point-of-Fit storage for < 2 to 4 hours supply

Table 12.1 *Continued*

AREA	AS-IS (PROBLEMS BEING ADDRESSED)	TO-BE (TARGETS)	VISION
Methodologies	- Push material to next operation whether they need it or not	- Use pull system based on Receiving, Production, and Shipping Markets	- Dock Market managed by Inventory Control - Production Markets managed by production teams
	- Production personnel are restricted from performing material handling	- Teams perform all work within their area	- Teams push/pull materials to/from their Production Markets - Materials Team delivers purchased items via routes
	- Very little container standardization	- Standard containers, quantities, and identification	- Standard bins, pallets, and totes for internal handling - Formed returnable dunnage for supplier materials
	- Forklifts required due to weight of containers	- Set weight limits and reduce weights where operators will perform their own handling	- Carts with turntables for pallets - Eliminate stands requiring forklift loading/unloading at stations
	- Material is handled multiple times	- Receive at point-of-use or buffer in Markets	- A-items stored at point-of-fit - B-items stored at point-of-use - C-items stored as close to the line as possible, subject to their size
	- Material availability must be visually verified	- Make inventory availability visual	- Place for everything; everything in its place
Containerization	- Large containers with many days supply of inventory	- Small containers which meet ergonomic requirements for each distance and weights	- Standardize on a small number of plastic totes which fit the standard size pallet footprint - Deliver totes to operator via roller conveyor with separate take-away
	- Cardboard cartons create contamination	- Plastic or metal returnable dunnage	- Standard totes for loose parts - Formed dunnage for parts requiring part separation and protection
	- Containers (even when the same size) do not always contain the same quantity	- Separators to ensure same quantity and orientation per layer	- Simple Number scheme for container quantities
	- Operators lose time opening cartons and removing dunnage	- Use easy-to-open containers and nesting dunnage	- Open containers when delivered - Spring-load shelves on racks so they tilt up when empty
	- Operators cannot move loads and must wait for a forklift operator	- Use rollers to move materials to operator and carts for heavy containers	- Pallets on carts - Turntables which buffer an extra container

Table 12.1 *Continued*

AREA	AS-IS (PROBLEMS BEING ADDRESSED)	TO-BE (TARGETS)	VISION
Operator	- Production personnel are restricted from performing material handling - Material handlers assigned to a department are underutilized - Production personnel must wait for loads to be moved to and from the station	- Integrate all required functions into job classification - Spread work among all team personnel - Provide team with equipment necessary to maintain production rates	- Rebalance work to include production, material handling, and inspection tasks - Cross-train personnel and assign long distance moves to a material handling team - Decouple production operator from materials-related efforts through ergonomics and workstation layout and design

ticular part is an odd size and too heavy to adhere to the simple number scheme, a nonsimple number quantity per load will be permitted as an exception condition. The intent is to minimize the number of exception conditions, realizing that a few exceptions will not seriously impair overall performance or achievement of performance targets.

The market principles illustrated in Figure 12.7 are cross-referenced to the areas of integration in Table 12.2. With respect to order of precedence, a principle such as a "simple number" which affects suppliers and customers as well as the company is less likely to be subject to dynamic change than principles which apply internally. Once a simple number scheme has been established, for example, the supplier will modify dunnage and shipping quantities to match. The company will modify ordering policies and shipping requirements to match. Market layouts and equipment will be sized to match, and delivery routes of fulls carriers to

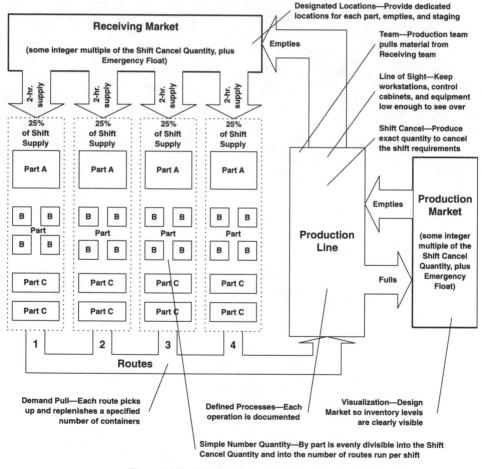

Figure 12.7   Market Principles Visualization

Table 12.2   Market Principles in Terms of the Areas of Integration

AREAS OF INTEGRATION	MARKET PRINCIPLES	AREAS OF APPLICATION
Materials Management	Float Quantities	Market and workstation sizing
Information Management	Shift Cancel	Production scheduling
Product Management	Simple Numbers	Containerization and identification
Process Management	Defined Processes	Team member instructions
Quality Management	Designated Locations	Market and workstation layout
Organization	Visualizations	Consensus and consistency
Facilities and Equipment	Line of Sight	Equipment sizing and layout
Systems and Technologies	Demand-Pull	Material replenishment and routes

production and pickups of empties from production will be scheduled to match. This involves a considerable amount of time, effort, and expense. While the company may change the scheduled shift production rate from time to time, the simple number quantity will not change. In this case, the simple number is an external integration factor while the daily production rate is an internal factor. If possible, any changes to the shift production quantity should still be evenly divisible by at least a subset of the simple numbers used.

The global principle is to eliminate waste in all of its forms, which all of the market principles address. This applies to any business but is certainly easier to see and explain in a repetitive manufacturing environment. The following subsections provide a discussion of the various principles and their areas of application, with "eliminating waste" being the foundation principle behind a market-based production system.

Eliminate Waste

Waste exists as a hierarchy. How waste is dealt with depends on its position in the hierarchy and on how it is impacted by other operational or infrastructure conditions (refer to Figure 12.8). The design of a Market-based Production System addresses as many elements of time, storage, and handling-related waste as possible. As such, it is very consistent with Short Cycle/Lean/Agile Manufacturing and Just in Time philosophies.

Fixed Waste

The lowest level of waste is based on fixed conditions or constraints. This level is either permanent or only addressable by changing infrastructural elements related to the facility, equipment, systems, or technologies. Improvements will be either impossible to achieve or possible only in the long-term and then only at significant cost. For example, the waste in terms of labor and equipment of receiving material at one end of the facility and transporting it to the other end may be significantly reduced if a point-of-use dock is installed at the other end. However, there may be access restrictions based on the position of the building on the site

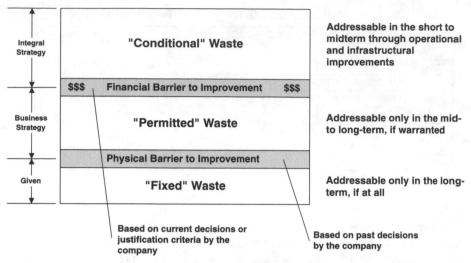

Figure 12.8   "Waste" Hierarchy

which prevents this from occurring. In this case, the waste associated with material handling is permanent as long as manufacturing remains on this site.

"Fixed" waste is, therefore, based on company conditions related to the infrastructure areas of facility, equipment, systems, and possibly geographic location. These areas of waste are addressed by the 5 to 10-year integral vision, if at all. From an inventory management perspective, fixed waste which results in physical barriers to improvement is not going to change in the foreseeable future. Barriers to smooth or shortened material flows within the facility will not be eliminated, aisles will not be widened to permit automated delivery of materials, new docks will not be installed at the point-of-use, production operations will not be consolidated from multifloor to a single floor, and so on.

Permitted Waste

The middle level of waste is permitted to exist because the cost of correction cannot be financially justified in the short-term based on the company's financial hurdle rate. The company may make improvements in the future but is not currently targeting any engineering or other effort to address the waste areas. A conscious decision has been made to live with the consequences of such waste. For example, it is desirable to receive all materials on a daily basis and eliminate centralized storage requirements. However, there may be a point where considerations of total cost and risk of stock-out force a company to store material. Lower order quantities and shorter receipt frequencies may be addressed over time as conditions warrant. In the meantime, storage is a requirement and must be addressed in a cost-effective manner. The middle level of waste is, therefore, based on business conditions related to product designs and part availability and manufacturing processes which are essentially fixed in the short-term. These areas may be addressed by the 2 to 5-year portion of the integral strategy.

From an inventory perspective, these permitted waste areas are visible to company personnel and are probably sources of ongoing irritation. Personnel will not understand why the company is not implementing the required changes as part of the current initiatives or projects. An explanation will be in order to explain the company's position.

Conditional Waste

The highest level of waste is conditional on other factors. Once these internal and external integration factors are changed, the resulting waste can be addressed. These items are the ones targeted by engineering improvement initiatives, projects, and programs as part of an integral strategy. As barriers to improvement are eliminated, step-function increases in performance are achieved. These improvements are measured in terms of inventory turns, customer service level, cycle time, quality, accuracy, flexibility, reliability, maintainability, serviceability, responsiveness, and so on.

At the conditional level, Mazda refers to three types of waste. MUDA is waste related to time or materials. This includes waiting (standing doing nothing), inefficiencies (walking around looking for materials, tools, instructions, and so on), double-handling (repack a pallet load to individual totes, moving tools from a cabinet to the workstation, and so on), inventory (in excess of target level), inferior goods (poor quality which the customer discovers, scrap, rework, and so on), processing inefficiencies (due to poor workstation design or process flow), and overproduction (using available time to produce more than what is scheduled). MURA is waste associated with an irregular or inconsistent use of a person or machine in such a way as to cause inconsistent results. Temporary assignments, random quality checks, changing suppliers, and using different machines with varying capabilities may all lead to inconsistent results. MURI is waste associated with working a person or machine beyond a reasonable capacity or limit. This may damage the equipment, result in poor quality products, or cause injury. The result can be unplanned downtime and related costs associated with repairs, replacements, and retraining.

Float (Inventory) Quantities

Once the integral strategy inventory days and hours supply targets are established in terms of dollars and related quantities, float levels can be defined for each individual part or assembly. Float quantities essentially distribute the total allowable inventory quantities to the various areas of operation where the inventory is stored/staged/buffered and used. This includes each of the markets, as well as the various workstations and lines. For any part, adding the inventory waiting on the dock apron in trucks for unloading, the receiving and production markets, and the workstations and production lines provide a 4-wall inventory which cannot exceed the target.

Maximum Float Quantity

The maximum float quantity at any market or workstation is the design and operating maximum set by management. This quantity cannot be exceeded without authorization by management.

For a *receiving market,* maximum float is normally defined in hours or days supply for expensive items and weeks or months supply for less expensive items. The maximum float is a function of order quantity and that residual quantity which is expected to be in the market or workstation when the replenishment occurs. For a part where delivery is controlled with precision, the order or transfer quantities may be low and the part near or at stock-out condition as each new replenishment occurs. This is the same as reorder point logic. For an expensive part received daily as part of a scheduled route, management may establish an 8-hour order quantity and a 4-hour minimum float level. When the daily receipt occurs, there should be four hours of inventory still in the market. This provides a small safety factor for variability in delivery timing and will vary by part based on distance and conditions. Management may also lengthen the minimum during winter months where delivery may be subject to weather-related interruptions. Receiving market average inventory level is equal to the minimum float level plus one-half of the order quantity assuming a steady usage rate.

$$\text{Receiving Market Maximum Float Level} = \text{Receiving Market Minimum Float Level} + \text{Order Quantity}$$

For a *production market,* maximum float is normally defined in hours or days supply, with 1-hour, 2-hour, 4-hour, 1-shift, or 1-day maximums being common. Float levels are regulated by the number of carts or containers available and by physical layout. Unlike a receiving market where each receipt brings the float level back up to or near the maximum, each replenishment in a production market may be only an incremental (simple number) portion of the maximum. Average inventory level tends to remain near the maximum float level as long as the producing station keeps up with the demand-pull requirements of the consuming station.

For a *workstation,* the maximum float is normally defined in terms of hours supply (including less than one hour). Like production markets, float levels are regulated by the number of carts or containers available and by physical layout. Average inventory is more like a receiving than a production market, where half of the carts or containers are full and the other half are empty on average.

Minimum Float Quantity

The minimum float quantity is the level of inventory which is normally on-hand when the next replenishment occurs. In the receiving market, this is the safety stock level when comparing to a reorder point, for example. However, it differs from traditional replenishment logic in that the float level is not expected to fall below this point during half of the replenishment cycles. Falling below this level is a signal that the replenishment timing should be confirmed with the supplier. Under normal conditions, however, there should be no immediate cause for alarm.

For the receiving market, the minimum float quantity is essentially that quantity which provides a level of comfort that no unplanned stock-out condition will occur. This is based on experience with the supplier and weather or other conditions. Therefore, it is most similar to a safety lead time. Falling below this level is an indication that manual intervention to determine where the material is may be required. This quantity essentially becomes the time period safety stock for the part and should be consistent for all parts across a particular product.

Minimum float in a production market is set in a manner similar to that for the receiving market. It is based on normal operating conditions and variability between the producing and consuming operations. Falling below the minimum indicates that the producing operation is falling behind and that there may be a risk of shutting down the consuming operation if replenishment does not occur in the near term. Someone should verify that the producing operation is not having production problems. In general, though, the production markets should not be operating near the minimum float level but at some average between the maximum and minimum float levels. The intent of a production market is not to drive inventory levels down but to ensure a given hours supply of operation in case the producing team experiences a line stoppage.

Minimum float in a workstation is set in a manner similar to that for the receiving market. Falling below the minimum indicates that the workstation may be in risk of shutting down if not replenished. Someone should verify that the producing operation is not having a production problem, that the receiving market is not stocked-out, or that the replenishment route is in process.

Emergency Float Quantity

The emergency float quantity indicates that production is subject to an unplanned shutdown before materials can be replenished unless the situation is resolved immediately. In the case of a receiving market, delivery by air counter-to-counter services, express ground transportation, taxi, or other means may be required. With a production market, materials may need to be moved directly from the producing to consuming operation in less than full cart or container quantities to maintain production. With a workstation, emergency float is restricted to a small quantity kept only for the purpose of replacing a defective or dropped part.

Consider the effect of removing the final full cart from a production market. If the cart capacity is one hour, the consuming station has sufficient material to maintain production rates for one hour. The producing team then has the same one hour (if no parts are currently in process) to obtain needed components from the receiving and related production markets, set up the line, produce the parts, and move the parts to the consuming station. For complex assemblies with many production steps, this may not be sufficient time. In this case, the emergency float quantity may be two or more carts.

Shift Cancel

With any continuous, line, or batch manufacturing process, each shift is scheduled to produce a given mix and quantity. Ideally, the same product mix and quantity are produced every shift. Realistically, the same quantity is targeted for production, and the mix will vary. When customer demand changes, manufacturing will produce less than the production capacity by working fewer hours or produce more by working overtime. Once manufacturing has produced the required quantity, the shift requirement has been "canceled." Producing fewer products than scheduled places a burden on the next shift to overproduce, while producing more consumes inventory and labor beyond what is planned. The shift cancel quantity is, therefore, the target production quantity, with zero-deviation allowed.

The established shift quantity must be based on a demonstrated and achievable production rate. The intent is not to spur the organization on to ever greater heights but to commit to a production level which can be used for order promising and scheduling. It must also be evenly divisible by one of the possible simple numbers established for the product. This allows the company to vary the actual quantity produced, without having a significant impact on replenishment quantities. This is the same philosophy as is used with a firm plan order horizon in MRP. The intent is to minimize nervousness at upstream processes (including suppliers) of schedule changes at the final assembly point.

Simple Number Scheme

With respect to inventory, the greatest contributions to variability reduction from production's perspective relate to the container and quantity per container. Once a standard container is adopted, workstations can be designed to ensure that sufficient capacity is available and that materials are presented to the team member in an ergonomic and expeditious manner. To the extent that this same type of container is used across multiple stations and lines, handling and buffer storage or staging can also be standardized. With a standard quantity, team members know how much inventory is at the station at any time in terms of quantity and hours supply. This visual control identifies how much has been produced, how much remains to be produced, and possibly when a changeover will occur.

Determining the type of container and quantity is a function of material handling and storage standards established for the operation, ergonomics in terms of container size and weight capacity, and production rate. The more repetitive the environment and the higher the production volume, the more the company can justify the use of returnable dunnage. Container size, weight, and rate all act as qualifiers to the simple number scheme.

A "simple number" is developed based on the following five characteristics.

Note that a part, product, workstation, or line may have multiple valid simple numbers.

1. It is evenly divisible into the shift or daily production rate (e.g., 100 percent, 50 percent, 25 percent, 10 percent).

2. It can be easily added, subtracted, multiplied, and divided in one's head relative to the shift production rate (answers range from 1 to 10; e.g., 800 units per shift with a simple number of 100 units per container equals eight containers, one per hour).

3. It relates to the hours per shift or day (e.g., 60, not 47, minutes of supply).

4. It conforms to weight and handling ergonomics.

5. It is consistent among parts at the workstation or line (e.g., one part may have one container per hour, another part may have one container per two hours, another part may have one container per each half hour, and so on).

The intent of the simple number is to eliminate having to count individual parts. Once the number of containers required to support production for a shift is known, counting becomes easier and much more visible. For example, if the production rate is 1,000 per shift as illustrated in Figure 12.9 and each container of a particular part contains 100 units, exactly 10 containers are required to cancel the shift demand. If the workstation is designed to hold exactly 10 containers, management has procedurally enforced a 1-day supply. If material is replenished

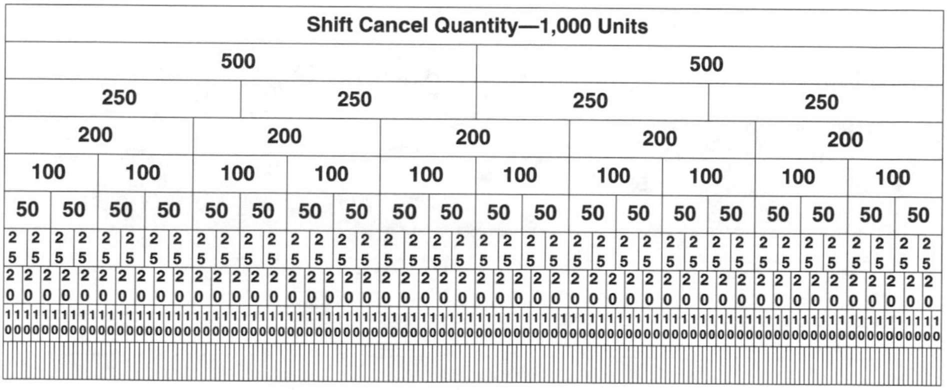

1. All of the preceding Simple Numbers are evenly divisible into the Shift Production (Shift Cancel) Rate
except
2. Only 1,000, 500, 250, and 100 Simple Numbers are simple to calculate (1 to 10 range)
and
3. Only 1,000 (8 hours), 500 (4 hours), and 250 (2 hours) relate to the hours per shift for an 8-hour shift.

Other considerations then include:
4. The weight of the parts for 1,000, 500, and 250 container quantities, and
5. Relationship of the Simple Number for this part to the Simple Numbers selected for other parts at the workstation or line based on their weights.

Figure 12.9   Simple Number Characteristics

twice per shift, five empty containers are replaced every half-shift with five full containers.

There will be some exceptions when implementing a simple number scheme. Some suppliers will not be willing or able to ship a simple number due to the size or weight of the part or due to the increased cost to accommodate a single customer. The existing package design may be a standard for other customers and products. Robotic handling may result in an odd number of parts due to the stacking pattern or end-of-arm tooling. While these situations will occur, the company should still attempt to enforce quantity, weight, and sizing standards for storage, handling, and identification which meet the needs of the business. Exceptions can then be dealt with over time as it becomes cost justifiable to do so.

Simple Numbers Based on the Shift Cancel Production Rate

Table 12.3 identifies the simple number scheme for a 1,000-unit per shift production rate. Note that while numbers such as 50, 25, 10, 5, and 2 are all evenly divisible into 1,000, they are not necessarily appropriate simple numbers as they are not easy to use for calculating. In general, calculating with a simple number should result in answers from 1 to 10.

The simple number for the shift cancel production rate must also be a simple number for the production shift hours. This relates number of containers to hours of supply. This is compared in Table 12.3 in terms of an 8-hour shift and a 10-hour shift. Note that the smaller quantities which are evenly divisible into the shift rate but which do not pass all of the simple number requirements may still be used for demand-pull operations from one workstation to another on the production line. Very small transfer quantities from one workstation to another

Table 12.3 Simple Number Scheme Based on Shift Production Rate

PRODUCTION RATE SIMPLE NUMBER	EVENLY DIVISIBLE INTO 1,000	EASY TO CALCULATE (i.e., 1 to 10)	RELATE TO 8-HOUR SHIFT "SIMPLE NUMBERS"	RELATE TO 10-HOUR SHIFT "SIMPLE NUMBERS"
1,000	1	Yes	1-Shift = 8 Hours	1-Shift = 10 Hours
500	2	Yes	1/2-Shift = 4 Hours	1/2-Shift = 5 Hours
250	4	Yes	1/4-Shift = 2 Hours	
200	5	Yes		1/5-Shift = 2 Hours
100	10	Yes		1/10-Shift = 1 Hour
50	20	No		1/20-Shift = 1/2 Hour
25	40	No		1/40-Shift = 1/4 Hour
20	50	No		
10	100	No		
5	200	No		
2	500	No		

Note: The numbers are for a bill of material quantity of one for the part. If quantities are for two or more of a particular bill of material item, extend the table quantities by the bill of material quantity.

which do not pass the simple number requirements should still attempt to be at least a multiple of the shift quantity. Simple numbers relate more to materials which must be moved in larger batches. For the 8-hour shift, only three simple numbers meet the "even number" and "under 10" criteria. For the 10-hour shift, four simple numbers meet the criteria.

Simple Numbers Fine-Tuned for Load Size and Weight

Once the simple numbers are determined, a load size and weight check is made. For small containers which must be handled by a person, a 35 to 45 lb. ergonomic maximum may be set. For unit loads to be pushed or pulled on dollies or carts, a 1,500 to 2,000 lb. maximum may be set (including the dolly). For loads to be moved by forklift, a 3,000 to 5,000 lb. maximum may be set. Any loads which deviate from these maximums must be reviewed on an individual basis. These weights are also subject to the allowable Length × Width × Height (L × W × H) load dimensions.

Table 12.4 calculates the container weights for the simple number scheme in Table 12.3. With a 45 lb. maximum, any container quantity of 200 or less is acceptable. Above that point, some type of lift assist may be required. Given the calculated weights and an 8-hour shift, the 250-unit quantity meets the simple number requirements. However, the 54 lb. container is outside the ergonomic limit and so requires a lift assist. Note that this may fall into an exception category if the lifting is infrequent and if the majority of containers are within ergonomic limits. Otherwise, the simple number quantity must be 200, 100, or 50, which potentially require an odd number of replenishment routes per shift, depending on the workstation hours supply.

For the 10-hour shift, the 200-unit and 100-unit containers meet the simple number criteria for at least a one hour supply and weight criteria of 45 maximum pounds. The larger containers may lend themselves to unit load handling.

Table 12.4 Simple Number Scheme Based on Ergonomics

SIMPLE NUMBER	CONTAINERS PER SHIFT	WEIGHT PER CONTAINER (0.2 LB./UNIT)	ERGONOMICS
1,000	1	4 + 0.2 × 1,000 = 204 lb.	Above ergonomic range for 1-person lifting
500	2	4 + 0.2 × 500 = 104 lb.	Above ergonomic range for 1-person lifting
250	4	4 + 0.2 × 250 = 54 lb.	Above ergonomic range for 1-person lifting
200	5	4 + 0.2 × 200 = 44 lb.	OK (45 lb. or less)
100	10	4 + 0.2 × 100 = 24 lb.	OK (45 lb. or less)
50	20	4 + 0.2 × 50 = 14 lb.	OK (45 lb. or less)

Note: Weight per container is based on a 4 lb. tote and 0.2 lb. part in this table

Simple Number Consistency with Other Parts

The final step in evaluating simple numbers is to compare them to other parts at the workstation, production line, and route from the market. If possible, the numbers should be consistent with each other. If each container of Part A at a workstation contains a 2-hour supply, it is advantageous if containers of Parts B and C at the workstation also contain a 2-hour supply. Failing that, each container should be a multiple of each other such as 8-hours, 4-hours, or 1-hour. In this way, a consistent route can be established for replenishing the workstation.

In any event, visual indicators should be established for each part to indicate the hours supply at the workstation. This is often an actual mark on a flow rack or table to indicate the hours supply for a given number of containers. Another alternative is to use a simple graphic which associates number of containers to hours supply as shown in Figure 12.10. The emergency float level is the point at which there is just sufficient time to obtain more materials before stocking-out at the workstation. If materials are replenished twice per shift, the route includes two As and five Bs. The graphic indicates that the route will typically replenish materials before the workstation inventory level reaches the 2-hour mark. The timing of the route will be such that two empty A containers and five empty B containers can be picked up in exchange for an equal number of full containers.

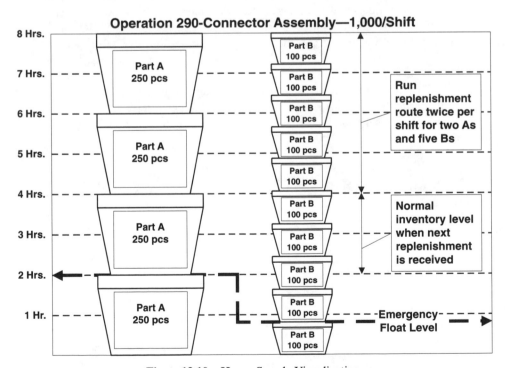

Figure 12.10   Hours Supply Visualization

Simple Number Analysis

A simple number analysis can be done with a spreadsheet or database. The general process is as follows:

1. Develop a list of containers for reference.

   - Container ID and tare weight (totes, baskets, bins, and so on)
   - Container capacity in terms of cubic inches and weight

2. Develop a list of parts.

   - Part number, description, product, and workstation
   - Part size (determined as units per cubic inch; e.g., 100 units in a $10'' \times 10'' \times 10''$ carton is equivalent to 0.1 units per cubic inch)
   - Part weight (determined as 100 units per 20 lb. carton; e.g., 20 lb./100 units = 0.2 lb./unit)
   - Part quantity per product (from bill of material)
   - Extended part quantity for the shift volume (e.g., at 1,000 products per shift, a bill of material requiring one of Part A and two of Part B will require 1,000 As and 2,000 Bs)

3. Perform a calculation to determine the maximum number of parts which can be contained in each type of container, subject to the ergonomic weight limits. Containers will either reach the maximum on weight or volume. For parts in totes, it makes sense to assess four to five different sizes of totes. Extend the number of totes to determine how many totes can be shipped on a unit load subject to weight (2,000 to 4,000 lb.) and size ($4' \times 4' \times 4'$) limits.

4. Determine the acceptable simple numbers for the production rate and shift hours and reduce the maximum quantities in each container to each applicable simple number. If a container can hold 200 units and be full and 100 units and be one-half full, include both alternatives in the analysis. Identify the percent of fill for each scenario.

5. Identify the preferred tote or container for each part and calculate the number required to support the logistics pipeline. This will include totes at the supplier, full totes en route to the company, full totes in the markets and at workstations, empty totes waiting return, and empty totes en route to the supplier, as applicable.

6. Sum the totals by tote across all products and calculate the cost. If totes are used, transportation pallets with covers may also be required. Other loads may include returnable dunnage molded specifically for the parts, or bins, baskets, or racks.

7. Identify the parts which do not meet simple number or ergonomic criteria and perform another iteration to determine if they can be brought into line with the targets.

Defined Processes

Consistency of results can only be achieved when all personnel and equipment perform in a consistent and capable manner, using materials which conform to requirements. Once a process has been developed and proven, documentation must be developed to ensure that each iteration is repeatable by properly trained personnel.

Process definition ensures that standard operating procedures are developed for all functions performed by the various team members. This encompasses normal as well as exception (infrequent) and anomaly (fault) conditions. Providing a step-by-step process ensures that informal procedures do not develop and that training and results measurement is consistent over time.

Process documentation varies by the type of process being described. Instructions for operating equipment via control cabinets are different from those for assembling a product. However, the format in Figure 12.11 illustrates the basic concept. The key is to provide a step-by-step procedure which any trained individual can follow. The process should define what actions to take and how to confirm that the proper results were achieved. If additional information is available such as manuals, specifications, and so on, they should be listed as well. Cross-referencing each step to an area in a figure is especially helpful.

There are three basic techniques which are commonly used to define processes. Any or all may be used depending on the particular application.

1. Functional flows provide a sequence of the various steps, conditions, and branching points. These are used when a process may have more than one outcome, depending on certain conditions. Functional flows are used in functional specifications or any documentation involving decision points.

2. Task charts use graphics to reinforce and supplement the specific steps required to complete an action. These are used by operators to compare what they are actually doing or seeing to a hard copy or computer screen displaying a pictorial view of the process. Task charts are used in assembly, inspection, and test instructions.

3. A step-by-step write-up applies to any situation requiring a number of sequential steps. This is the form typically used to computerize process steps such as those included within the production activity control/manufacturing execution subsystem for routing and manufacturing instructions. Step-by-step write-ups are used in computer system and equipment operation and maintenance manuals.

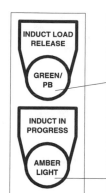

Press to initiate the induction process.

A flashing light indicates that the Conveyor Control PLC is waiting for a response from the AS/RS Computer System that the Pallet ID has a valid Expected Receipt associated with it.

No light at all indicates that the operator may not have fully pressed the button.

The light is turned OFF when:
1. The AS/RS Computer System commands the Conveyor Control System to move the load, or
2. If there is a problem reading the bar code, or
3. If there is no Expected Receipt on file.

In the case of a fault, the INDUCT IN PROGRESS light will not turn ON. Check the OIT for a bar code scanning fault or the Expected Receipts Screen for a missing Expected Receipt.

Turned ON when the AS/RS Computer System commands the Conveyor Control System to move the load.

Turned OFF when the load is completely out of the forklift interface position.

PROCESS DESCRIPTION	Inbound Conveyor Release Controls
SAFETY CONSIDERATIONS	Load is subject to automatic movement
INITIAL CONDITION(S)	Pallet ID must be within scanner distance of bar code scanner (approximately 6 to 12 inches)

STEP	ACTION	RESULT AND MEASURE	COMMENTS	ADD'L. INFO.
1	INDUCT LOAD RELEASE (Green Illuminated Push Button) Press to initiate the physical induction process	- Flashing light indicates that message has been sent to the AS/RS Computer. - No light indicates that AS/RS Computer has accepted the load (INDUCT IN PROGRESS light turns ON) or that the load has been rejected (INDUCT IN PROGRESS LIGHT REMAINS off).	Refer to the OIT on the Conveyor Cabinet for the fault condition (invalid bar code or no Expected Receipt) if the light turns OFF and the INDUCT IN PROGRESS light does not turn ON).	Operator Interface Terminal (OIT) Manual
2	INDUCT IN PROGRESS Amber Light	Indicates that induction has been accepted by the AS/RS Computer and that the load is subject to move automatically when the scale position is open.	Once inducted, this light only goes OUT if: 1. Load has transferred completely to the scale position. 2. Load is removed from the forklift position. 3. The PLC program is reloaded. 4. Loss of system power (main disconnect is turned OFF or loss of facility power).	

Figure 12.11 Process Definition

Designated Locations

With a market concept, everything has a designated location. This refers to materials in the market, empty containers or carts in the market, tools and materials at a workstation, empties at a workstation, parking areas for forklifts, drop zones for AGVs, and so on. Each location is identified with an ID, paint, or other designation. All related equipment is sized for a particular quantity such as the length of a flow lane relative to the length of the containers required for a given hours supply. An allowable exception to designated locations for material is where automated storage is used. In this case, visual controls are replaced with computer controls.

The principle of designated locations affects market and workstation layouts. Sizing is based on hours or days supply, given the quantity per container or cart and shift cancel quantity. Sizing includes the physical area in square footage as well as any equipment required to buffer or transport materials.

With material, designated locations identify the maximum quantity allowable, the emergency float quantity below which there is a risk of stock-out, and the minimum quantity range within which a replenishment is normally expected to occur. If the location is full, no more material can be delivered. As the location empties, replenishment materials are delivered via scheduled routes. An empty position acts as a demand-pull signal to replenish the specific quantity removed.

Designated locations also ensure that the team member always knows where to find whatever is required in terms of tools, equipment, and maintenance, repair, or operating supplies. Tools or other durable items need to be returned to the proper place when the team member is finished. Consumables need to be replenished when they reach a certain level.

Ergonomics may be an issue with any designated location. The team member should not have to bend or reach unduly, especially for frequent moves associated with progressive assembly lines. Items should be positioned where they are easy to see or where the team member knows where they are without looking.

Visualizations

Market-based production systems are engineered solutions to operating needs and, therefore, encompass a significant amount of detail. This detail takes the form of functional and detailed specifications, analyses, simulation, CAD layouts, manuals, training instructions, and related documentation. The purpose of visualizations is to translate the detail into a form which is easy for everyone to understand.

Figure 12.12 illustrates a greatly simplified visualization for a subassembly production team. This can be posted in the area and updated over time as improvements are implemented. A CAD layout which uses multiple colors is an effective visualization tool. Black indicates that the various principles in terms of containerization, simple numbers, workstation layout, and so on, have been satisfied. Blue indicates areas still undergoing change (the visualization should include target dates where applicable). Red indicates areas which do not meet the market principles and which are not being addressed at this time. Containerization which is dictated by the supplier and which does not conform to simple number requirements is a common "red" example. Red indicates that extra work (waste) exists for the teams.

The visualization should include all elements of interest to the team. This en-

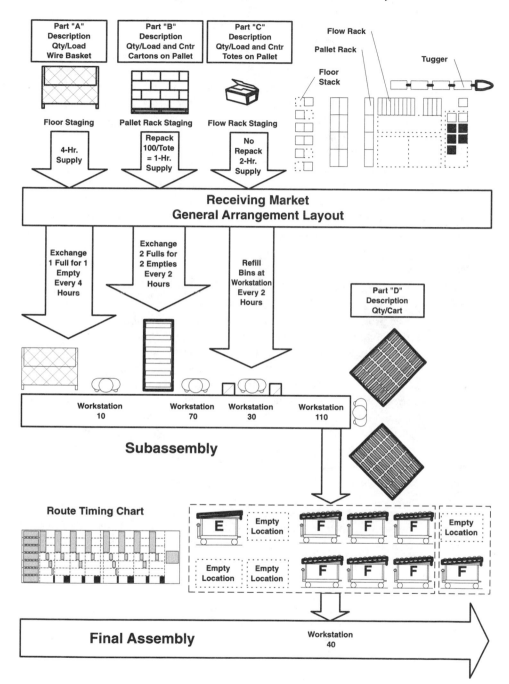

Figure 12.12 Production Team Visualization

compasses an actual CAD layout of the line equipment, every part used in the subassembly, all market and workstation equipment, all layouts, all containers or carts, all quantities, all routes and timing, and any schedule information related to the implementation. Additional information may include container weights, ergonomic guidelines, examples of material ID labels, rack faces showing actual part storage locations, and so on. These can all be added as callouts surrounding the subassembly line.

Visualizations may be composites of actual CAD layouts and equipment designs as long as such detail does not make the operation too complex and cluttered to understand. It may be that a certain amount of detail can be removed from the original by excluding certain CAD layers in the visualization. This permits a properly dimensioned top view of the production line to be included, for example, without any of the detail associated with comments, electrical wiring, air and hydraulic piping, pits, and so on.

Line of Sight

The ability to effectively communicate and determine production status by looking at material levels on a production line and in the markets is a key requisite of a market-based production system. The line of sight principle affects layouts and equipment design and selection. The target is to ensure that anyone standing at one end of the production line can see to the end. In this way, operators can directly communicate to those around them. Any anomaly condition signaled by activating a red light or other indicator can be seen from any point on the line.

From a layout perspective, an in-line design has several advantages. Operators can be positioned on one side of the production line with control cabinets and other equipment on the other. Material replenishment is then (typically) from the operator side. Note that control cabinets are often higher than a person, so specifications must dictate a maximum height for new installations. This will likely result in cabinets requiring more doors and floor space in order to trade-off height with width.

The disadvantage of a long in-line layout is that it is impossible to see the end. This is encountered in automotive assembly facilities. Looping the line back on itself is a common tactic to return fixtures or product back to the beginning point. Therefore, the process itself will create some restrictions.

Pallet racks on the aisle for point-of-use storage may block line of sight. These are one of the first targets for removal. To do this, material levels must be reduced and replenishment routes must be implemented. On the other hand, point-of-use buffers are desirable for eliminating centralized stores and positioning materials near where they are required. Some balance must be found between these requirements.

Inventory "Ownership" in a Demand-Pull Environment

In a market-based production system, material moves only if there is a demand for it. Supplier shipments move only to the receiving market when ordered. Machined parts or subassemblies move only to production markets when there is space available. Finished goods move only to the shipping market when previous goods have been shipped. No material is "pushed" past a market to the next operation. The need is in the form of a hole into which the material moves.

This raises the question of inventory ownership, which varies by company. One scenario is where inventory management shares ownership of materials in the receiving market with production, who sets the build schedule, and with marketing who forecasts the demand over the planned horizon. The producing and consuming operations own any materials at their point-of-fit workstations and in their downstream production markets. The consuming operations own any materials at the workstations. Material does not flow backwards. Finished goods are owned by sales and marketing.

Layout Considerations

Market-based production systems integrate the location and design of receiving, production, and shipping markets with workstation layouts. Decisions must consider location within the facility, future automation such as AGVs for material delivery, planned relocation of equipment or production lines, maintenance access to equipment, safe operating distances, aisle widths, staging or other height restrictions due to line of sight requirements, and equipment or facilities such as rest rooms which may not be able to be moved in the short-term to midterm. All of these considerations must reflect the production rate and hours of supply targets for each part and area of the facility.

Market Layout Considerations

Receiving, production, and shipping markets all have their own peculiarities since each has a slightly different purpose. As such, layout rules may differ slightly within a plant and among companies. Figure 12.13 illustrates representative considerations for a receiving market supporting a production line which has a combination of container and cart types.

Figure 12.13 illustrates the following layout principles:

- *Separation of vehicle traffic from manual operations*—Vehicle and personnel traffic and operating areas should be segregated to the greatest extent possible. In the normal course of business, team members working in an assigned area should not have to worry about potentially unsafe conditions such as someone walking into a vehicle aisle or a vehicle operating in a manned area. In the figure, vehicle aisles and work areas are provided to the left and top, while manned areas are provided at the right. Normal care is then exercised when crossing the boundaries. For operations which regularly require both forklift and personnel access to the storage rack, the design allows for team member access to the right pallet rack from the right side and forklift access from the middle aisle.

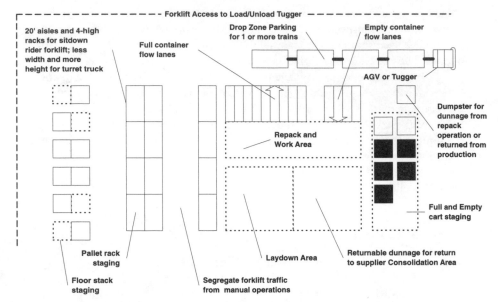

Figure 12.13   Market Layout and Sizing Considerations

- *Separation of full from empty containers*—Visual controls require a clear indication of the quantity of parts available for every part number. Full carts or full containers in the floor stack, pallet rack, and flow racks indicate the hours supply available, knowing the hours supply per container. Since it is impossible to differentiate full from empty containers in some cases, a separate marshaling area is required for empty containers. In this way, empty locations are left for incoming materials, while containers to be returned to suppliers can be staged in designated locations.

- *Size equipment for the hours supply target*—The market contains only as much equipment as is required for the parts to be buffered based on the quantity per container and replenishment cycle. Sizing must accommodate the hours supply target plus emergency float plus additional quantity which might be in the market when the next shipment is received. Where the parts are subject to some degree of shipping variability in terms of quantity or timing, additional space or racks must be provided and designated as overflow. In this way, the team members can clearly differentiate between the target and excess quantities.

- *Standardize equipment*—In the case of pallet or flow racks, whole rack increments are installed. If two positions of an eight-position rack are all that is required, all eight are installed. Flow racks will come in modules as well. Adjustable lanes enable a variety of totes or containers to be used. With respect to rack opening dimensions, there is no need to use a maximum size if there is good control over quantities and load dimensions. With respect to rack capacity, it makes sense to standardize on equipment which meets the maximum load weight requirements, regardless of the actual loads to be buffered. This rack can then be reused anywhere in the facility as needs change over time.

- *Floor stacking* Floor stacking is used for containers, racks, or bins which have been designed for stacking. Stacks of $4' \times 4' \times 4'$ containers 4-high require 16 square feet of space, plus clearance around the sides and back. For layout purposes, considerations include FIFO and the number of loads which will be present in the market when the next shipment arrives. Consider a part with a daily receipt frequency of four unit loads, each containing a 2-hour supply. With 4-high stacking, this is a single stack. However, if there is an emergency float of a 2-hour supply (one load), there will be a container in the market when the new receipt arrives. In this case, the market requirements for the part are for two floor locations. Alternating usage ensures FIFO control. A built-in safety factor of three load's capacity is available, if needed.

- *Double-deep or deeper floor stacks (not shown)*—With unit loads or racks of parts which are received or shipped by truckload or railcar, multideep floor stacking is commonly used. The number of stacks may simply maximize use of available space or be dimensioned in shipping load quantities. If access to the loads is available from either end, FIFO can be maintained by alternating ends for staging and shipping. If the stacking is against a wall, the company will have to ensure that the stacks against the wall are used on a regular basis.

Workstation Layout Considerations

Production team member efficiency is a function of workstation layout. Materials should be easy to reach, easy to replenish, and easy to identify. Layout considerations must accommodate all parts for all tasks performed at the station, material handling equipment, drop zone area, maintenance access to equipment, safety perimeters around equipment, and general work space. Figure 12.14 illustrates some of the basic layout considerations.

- *Small parts* can be positioned in front of the team member in bins. When one bin is empty, it can be removed for replenishment in the market, and the second bin can be used. Four or eight hours supply should be considered to minimize the replenishment labor, consistent with the low value and small size of the parts. Other alternatives include movable carts which are designed to present the parts from the back of the line or at either side of the team member. Positioning considerations include whether the team member is sitting, standing, or moving, whether a tool is used in one hand or the other, and whether parts are similar and so should be separated so as not to mix up one with the other.

- *Totes, cartons, trays, bins, containers, or unit loads* can be positioned on flow lanes, turntables, lift tables, and so on. In Figure 12.14 full totes are replenished and placed on the conveyor twice per shift (two totes per route as indicated by the route pickup point). Placards can be clamped to the conveyor at maximum, emergency float, and route pickup levels as visual indicators

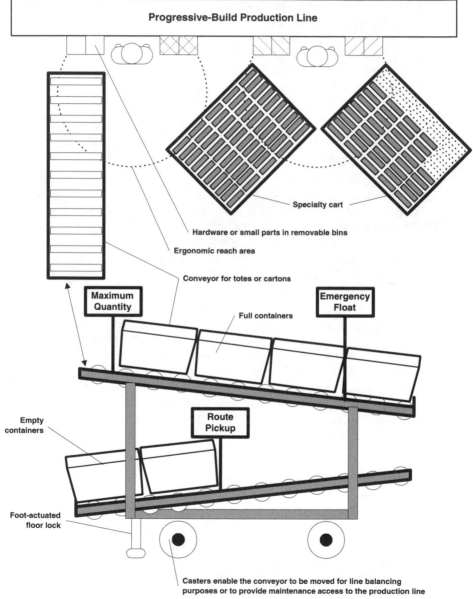

Figure 12.14   Workstation Layout Considerations

for team members. Information includes part number, product (as applicable), quantity per container, hours supply per container, type of container, workstation ID, description, and quantity per assembly.

- *Specialty parts* (typically those produced in-house) can be positioned at ergonomic heights and reach distances in carts designed specifically for the parts. This ensures that the simple number scheme is maintained (50/cart in Figure 12.14) and that each team member has some flexibility with regard to part positioning. With round parts which roll, each part which is removed enables another part to roll into its place; the reach is always at the face of the cart.

- *Parts with complexity* must either be fed to the line in the exact sequence required or will require some additional floor or air space for additional flow lanes, carts, and so on. With complexity, containers or carts must remain at the line once they have had any parts removed. If a changeover occurs and the container is still partially full, the new part is moved into position by the team member and the partial must be buffered nearby. With carts, an extra parking space is provided near the aisle for a partial of each complexity beyond one. The intent is not to use these spaces, but the reality is that production quantities do not always match the cart quantity exactly. Therefore, for a gear with a complexity of four, two positions are provided at the line and three more are reserved at the aisle. With containers, this might be a flow lane at the lower level and space for three containers on an overhead shelf.

ERGONOMICS

From a market perspective, ergonomics establishes constraints on load weights and load/unload heights. This affects cart and container quantities and sizes and designs related to moving, presenting, and protecting materials.

Consideration is given to how frequently an action is performed, and the constraint gets tighter as frequency increases. For example, a container target maximum weight may be set at 40 lb. as a design guideline. One part may require a 55 lb. container in order to meet the simple number and hours supply principles. If the container is lifted infrequently, the 55 lb. capacity may be acceptable as an exception condition. If the weight is associated with a small container capacity requiring many lifts and moves per hour, either a lift assist or workstation conveyor can be provided. Another alternative is that the quantity may have to be lowered below the simple number target to meet the 40 lb. target.

Weight and ease of handling the container should be considered as an upper constraint when determining simple numbers for a particular part. The analysis can set one limit for the maximum target weight considering manual lifting and a second limit considering the use of a lift assist.

With respect to unit loads (e.g., material on pallets or in wire baskets or tubs), maximum weights are determined based on whether the load will be moved manually on a cart or dolly or whether all handling will be via automation or forklift.

With mechanization, load weight limits are a function of the capacity of the storage and handling systems and vehicles. A 3,000 to 4,000 lb. range is common. With loads which must be pushed or pulled by team members, load weights are a function of the force required to start and stop the load, since less force is required once a load is moving. This is also affected by the type of caster and bearings used. One evaluation technique is to position the movable casters at a 90° angle to the direction of travel and use a spring scale to determine the force required to get the load moving. Anything less than 50 lb. of force, for example, may be acceptable.

Load and unload heights are a function of the design of the producing and consuming stations and the comfortable work heights of the team members. Anything in the 2 to 4 feet high range provides a reasonable load and unload height, with heights to 5 feet or 6 feet for unit loads on a dolly (dolly height plus 4 feet). Any height which requires only a minimal bending in the 20 to 30° range is preferable to that which requires fully bending at the waist. For bins or baskets, having a drop-down door on one or both sides of the container improves access to the parts. As shown in the specialty cart example in Figure 12.3, any transfers at a height which requires little bending or reaching is desirable. If the parts do not roll or slide to the team member as shown in Figure 12.3, use of turntables or lift tables improves access.

Ergonomic Considerations

General ergonomic considerations for workstations include the following:

- *Work Height*—Work height of the part or assembly should place a minimal lifting and bending stress on the operator. Fine work and that requiring visual inspection should position the unit at a comfortable distance from the operator, typically above the elbow several inches. Assembly tasks should be below the elbow 2 to 4 inches, with lifting minimized. Keeping work at or below the level of the heart helps to reduce fatigue.

- *Reach*—Parts should be within half the distance of the individual's reach if possible, such that the individual is able to maintain a comfortable arm position. Motions which require body rotation or wrist twisting should be minimized, especially with respect to part weight. If parts are harder to reach, it may be advantageous to provide a shelf where the operator can place multiple parts in a convenient orientation to minimize the number of individual moves.

- *Field of Vision*—Operators should be able to perform a majority of their work with a minimum of eye movement. Containers should be equally accessible. Parts should slide to the same pick position if possible so the operator does not have to search to find a part. Station layout should be consistent such that the operator knows where parts and tools are without having to reverify for each operation.

Other considerations involve lighting, adjustability of equipment to accommodate individual preferences and sizes, and proximity of one station with respect to another to enable work to be balanced based on product mix.

Ergonomics is definitely an area where an investment in prototypes pays for itself in reduced total system costs. Nothing is better than actually handling totes, pushing carts, and reaching for parts before making a significant investment.

DELIVERY ROUTES

Once the production line is setup, workstation design for each progressive manufacturing step determines the floor space required for the team members, materials, and workstation equipment. This may require some type of work balancing to ensure that team members can perform the required tasks in the cycle times allowed. This is especially important for progressive assembly lines where products index to the next position at a given rate. The build sequence and workstation in turn identify where the specific materials are required to support the line. The hours supply and emergency float quantities determine the maximum and minimum quantities which the station must buffer. The production rate, quantity per operation, and container capacity (or transfer quantity for carts, racks, and so on) then determine the frequency with which materials must be replenished.

A "route" is a scheduled delivery and pickup operation. Materials are delivered to the workstation from the receiving or production market, and empties (as applicable) are returned to the market. The first and simplest type of route is run at the same time every shift. The same quantity of the same materials are delivered. This type of route may lend itself to automation via Automated Guided Vehicle, Automated Electrified Monorail, conveyor, overhead power and free (carriers pulled through a route by a chain), or other delivery systems. A minor variation of this type of route is when complexity at a workstation changes the particular part number delivered (but not the quantity or container).

The second type of route is one which is run to the same set of workstations but where the actual materials vary over time. This is typically the result of different capacity containers having different hours supply. If the simple number scheme has been successfully applied based on the shift production rate, these routes will repeat at least once per shift.

The third type of route is one which varies based on demand. This is usually the result of changes in product mix changing required materials, container quantities not being in simple number increments, or in the environment being more of batch or job shop oriented and less a line or continuous flow.

Route Timing

Route timing is based on a predefined schedule, elapsed time since the last route, rate of production, or on demand. A scheduled route is executed at the same time each shift. A rate-based route accommodates changes in production rate and matches replenishment to consumption rates. Note that from a market perspective, this is not desirable since nervousness in line rates is directly translated back into the route schedules, making it difficult to plan the routes. Synchronizing deliveries with the rate of production is a demand-pull technique which lends itself to computerized signals and either manual or automated delivery of materials from producing to consuming stations. Downstream operations regulate upstream operations. Routes run on demand are more typical of an environment which has not implemented a simple number program and is, therefore, subject to random replenishment requirements as material is used. The lower the hours supply at a workstation, the greater the benefit of radio frequency or other electronic means to signal the need for replenishment.

Note that routes are the result of not being able to buffer all of the in-plant quantities of materials directly at the workstations. Once the need for a route is established, it is often uneconomical to deliver materials in lots of one, lots of one container, or even in hours supply less than one hour. Therefore, routes have a cost in personnel and equipment. Routes must be developed to minimize these costs while satisfying the vision and principles established for the operation. Routes may be as simple as a production team member taking an empty cart or container to a production market and returning with a full one. Receiving markets tend to be more complex and may require dedicated material handling team members to execute the routes, especially when forklifts or tow vehicles are required.

Routes and related workloads must be balanced according to the support required by each of the production lines. A team member may appear to have sufficient time in a day to perform four 1-hour routes for one department and four 1-hour routes for another. However, if any of the route timing overlaps, a single team member cannot perform the work.

A timing chart, illustrated in Figure 12.15, shows the actual duration of the routes assigned to a particular individual. This ensures that routes are not assigned which overlap in time with each other. Without a timing chart, the individual appears to have approximately 16 minutes ([480 minutes/day – 348 minutes assigned]/8 hours/day) available per hour for additional work. In fact, it is only six minutes during some periods since all deliveries do not conform to the average. The chart can be used among individuals to determine if there is a better way to balance the work, in the same manner in which work is balanced on the production line.[5]

Types of Routes

Scheduled Routes run at specified times each shift are the easiest to execute. The same material (or generally the same based on complexity) is picked up in the

---

5. Note that team members cannot be 100 percent utilized over the course of the day. In this example, an assumption is made that the hours used are at "engineering standard," which already allows for a utilization factor. Therefore, 10 minutes of assigned work at an 80 percent factor is actually eight minutes of actual work. This allows for breaks, cleaning up, normal inefficiencies, and so on.

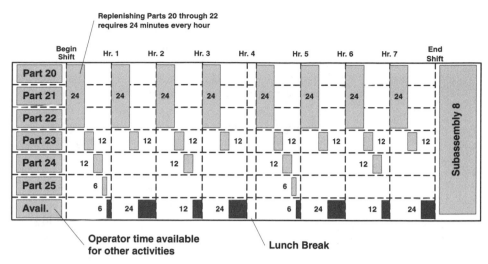

Figure 12.15   Route Timing Chart

market and delivered to one or more workstations. As much material is carried, moved, or towed as is required to support the workstations on the specific route at the scheduled time. In this way, the team member delivering the material knows what is required ahead of time, makes a pass through the market to obtain the materials, delivers the materials, picks up an equal number of empties for return to the market, and then goes on to the next route. As long as the production rate is being maintained, a scheduled route can somewhat dissociate the timing of the route from actual production.

There are several considerations for setting up a scheduled route:

- The timing of the route should provide some flexibility for the team member. Replenishing hardware at a workstation where a container holds a 4 to 8-hour supply provides a 4 to 8-hour window in which to execute the route. Scheduling the route enables the team member to level-load their work schedule.

- The route is based on an inference that material needs to be replenished. No electronic signal or empty container acts as the demand-pull mechanism. The risk is that the material in one or more containers is not actually required and will have to be returned to the market. An RF system identifying replenishments is useful in dynamic environments.

- Production rates must be uniform. Scheduled routes are based on replenishing at a rate equal to the consumption rate. Unplanned downtime or slowdowns can impact a scheduled route if there is little time flexibility with regard to when they are run. With routes scheduled to be run every two, four, or eight hours, some degree of downtime can be absorbed without affecting the timing.

Rate-Based Routes base the route timing on the production rate. As the rate varies, the elapsed time since the last route varies as well. In this way, a trigger can be set to execute the route after a given number of units have been produced. This is more indicative of a production process where product mix results in a variation in process times and, therefore, output rate. It is not appropriate to use this technique to accommodate unplanned variation in normal production rates due to quality or equipment problems, since these are off-standard conditions (i.e., not planned for within the industrial standards established for the process).

Synchronized Routes are executed in direct response to demand-pull signals from the consuming workstation to the producing workstation. This may encompass return of an empty container for a full container or return of an empty cart for a full cart. In this case, the production market is probably in close proximity to both the producing and consuming workstations. As long as the number of containers, carts, and so on, are kept small, the producing station production rate is generally synchronized with that of the consuming station. Where automation is used to move full and empty carts directly between the workstations, the automation essentially becomes the market, and the capacity becomes the market capacity. Once the conveyor, monorail, and so on, are full, the producing station is constrained to producing in lockstep with the rate at which the consuming station is operating.

Demand Routes are executed on an as-required basis. For example, empty dolly trains are parked in dedicated drop zones near the receiving dock, receiving market, warehouse, AS/RS, or central stores. As signals to replenish the materials are received, team members or automation retrieve the materials to the drop zone area. Here they are loaded on the dollies by forklift, by hand, or by some type of automation. The signals may be manual based on visually identifying which materials have been used, electronic signals from a bar code scanner indicating that a new container has been opened, a RF transaction indicating that additional material is required, and so on. Material for the same drop zone (dedicated areas where dolly trains are parked or dropped off for unloading by other personnel) is pulled from central stores and loaded to a dolly train. When the train is full, it is towed by AGV or tow operator to the designated drop zone.

Milk Runs refer to routes between the company and one or more suppliers. The same concepts of schedules, return of empties for fulls, shift cancel, simple numbers, and so on, applies as for in-house routes. The value of a milk run is that smaller quantities can be picked up from multiple suppliers in a geographic area, resulting in more frequent receipts and lower average inventory levels. In Line Vehicle Sequence (ILVS) deliveries of seat sets, engines, and so on, are examples of milk runs in an automotive environment.

12.7 SUMMARY

A market-based production system is a total commitment to synchronized manufacturing. Such a system regulates all aspects of a company's inventory flow. Implementation and operation of such a system requires an integral strategy and a long-term commitment to supplier partnering. Adherence to market principles visibly transforms a company's layouts and operations. When the physical space available matches the target inventory level, any excess or out-of-tolerance condition becomes very visible to the organization.

Markets buffer that portion of the target inventory level which is in excess of that allowed at the workstations. As target inventory levels change over time, so will the market layout and capacity. As compared to other types of environments, the receiving market is a combination of receiving and central stores. If a facility has multiple dock locations, each will have its own receiving market. The production markets are replacements for Work in Process buffer storage, and the shipping market is a replacement for shipping and warehousing.

Note that of the three types, shipping tends to change the least when adopting a market approach since the next operation (transportation and customer delivery) tends to remain the same. The greatest change is usually with the use of the production markets, though the greatest visible change may be with the receiving market since that is where the majority of material is located.

Abbreviations and Terminology

For a comprehensive dictionary of terms, refer to the APICS Dictionary, APICS, 500 West Annandale Road, Falls Church, VA 22046-4274.

AEM Automated Electrified Monorail System

AGV Automated Guided Vehicle

AGVS Automated Guided Vehicle System

AS/RS Automated Storage and Retrieval System

BOM Bill of Material

Carrier General term for a pallet, bin, rack, pan, load, and so on, stored in a location

Cntr Container

Drop Location in which an SRM or AGV or Monorail Carrier "drops" (delivers) a "carrier/load"

EOQ Economic Order Quantity

ERP Enterprise Resource Planning System (next generation MRPII System)

FAS Final Assembly Schedule

FG Finished Goods

FIFO First In/First Out

FM Factory Mutual

LT Lead Time

MES Manufacturing Execution System

MPS/MS Master Production Schedule or more generally Master Schedule

MRO Maintenance, Repair, and Operating supplies

MRP/MP Material Requirements Planning or more generally Material Planning

NFPA   National Fire Protection Association

OQ   Order Quantity

P&D   Pick & Drop (Stand or Position)

PC   Personal Computer

Pick   Location from which an SRM or AGV or Monorail Carrier "picks" up a "carrier/load"

PLC   Programmable Logic Controller

Plt   Pallet

Process-Oriented   Company which produces a broad range of parts or products based on the flexibility of their equipment. They are generally a supplier of product-oriented companies. Note that this definition corrects some of the older APICS references which have the definitions of product and process focus switched.

Product-Oriented   Company which produces a given family of products by dedicating their equipment, even though their equipment may be capable of producing other parts or assemblies. Note that this definition corrects some of the older APICS references which have the definitions of product and process focus switched.

QA   Quality Assurance

QC   Quality Control

Retrieve   Term which refers to the SRM retrieving a carrier from a location and dropping it on an outbound drop stand

ROP   Reorder Point

Shift Cancel   Term used to refer to the quantity required to exactly meet the scheduled demand for a shift

Simple Number   Number which is evenly divisible into the Shift Cancel quantity.

SRM   Storage and Retrieval Machine; machine in an automated storage and retrieve system which stores and retrieves pallets or other types of carriers automatically in storage racks.

SS   Safety Stock

Store   Term which refers to the SRM picking a carrier from the Pick stand and storing it in a storage/bin location.

T-Car   A Transfer Car is used to transfer a SRM from one aisle to another in a system which has fewer SRMs than the number of aisles.

TPOP   Time Phase Order Point

U/M   Unit of Measure

WCS   Warehouse Control System; usually restricted to inventory control within an automated storage and retrieval system (AS/RS) but possibly also including conventional storage as well

W/H   Warehouse

WIP   Work in Process

WMS   Warehouse Management System; usually including order management, wave picking, inventory control, shipping, yard management, and so on

Bibliography and References

Much of this book was written based on manufacturing and project experience, which explains why this list is so short. However, it is impossible after twenty plus years not to have internalized the many books, articles, and papers read over that time. By rights, the list should be much longer. However, the best compliment I can give to those many authors before me is that I no longer need to retain hard copies of their work to jog my memory.

Chapter 1 Having the Integral Strategy Choice

1. Crosby, Philip. *Quality Education System.* Florida: Philip Crosby Associates, Inc., 1988.

2. Garwood, Dave and Michael Bane. *Shifting Paradigms.* Marietta, GA: Dogwood Publishing Co., 1990.

3. Harry, Mikel J., "The Nature of Six Sigma Quality." In *Second Annual Best Manufacturing Practices Workshop Proceedings.* Office of the Assistant Secretary of the Navy, September 27–28, 1988.

4. Hayes, Robert H., Steven C. Wheelwright and Kim B. Clark. *Dynamic Manufacturing.* New York: The Free Press, 1988.

5. Hill, Terry. *Manufacturing Strategy Text and Cases,* 2nd ed. Burr Ridge, Illinois: Irwin, 1994.

6. Schonberger, Richard J. *World Class Manufacturing.* New York: The Free Press, 1986.

Chapter 2 Establish a Business Case for Changing the Status Quo

1. Hayes, Robert H., Steven C. Wheelwright, and Kim B. Clark. *Dynamic Manufacturing.* New York: The Free Press, 1988.

2. Hayes, Robert H. and Steven C. Wheelwright. *Restoring Our Competitive Edge.* New York: John Wiley & Sons, Inc., 1984.

3. Hill, Terry. *Manufacturing Strategy Text and Cases,* 2nd ed. Burr Ridge, Illinois: Irwin, 1994.

4. Kulwiec, Raymond A. *Advanced Material Handling.* Pittsburgh, PA: The Material Handling Institute, Inc.

Chapter 3 Integral Strategy Development Methodology

1. Davies, John R. "Defining the Responsibilities of the Project Manager." *Plant Engineering Magazine* 48:9 (July 1994): 82–84.

2. Davies, John R. "Using Work Breakdown Structure in Project Planning." *Plant Engineering Magazine* 49:14 (November 6, 1995): 54–56.

3. Fogarty, Donald W., John H. Blackstone, Jr., and Thomas R. Hoffman. *Production and Inventory Management,* 2nd ed. Cincinnati: South-Western Publishing Co., 1991.

Chapter 4   Project Management

1. Fogarty, Donald W., John H. Blackstone, Jr., and Thomas R. Hoffman. *Production and Inventory Management,* 2nd ed. Cincinnati: South-Western Publishing Co., 1991.

2. Hayes, Robert H., Steven C. Wheelwright, and Kim B. Clark. *Dynamic Manufacturing.* New York: The Free Press, 1988.

3. Katzel, Jeanine, ed. "Management Side of Engineering—Focus on Benchmarking: Achieving World-Class Maintenance and Superior Competitive Performance." *Plant Engineering Magazine* 49:7 (June 5, 1995): 120–118.

Chapter 5 Inventory System

1. Fraser, Julie. "Synchronized Success, the Next Generation of Manufacturing Management Systems." *Manufacturing Systems Magazine* 13:10 (October 1995): 70–76.

2. McIlvane, Bill. "Manufacturing Is a Software World after All." *Manufacturing Automation Magazine* 11:1 (January 1996): 30–31.

3. Supplement. "A Handbook for Selecting Enterprise Applications Software." *Manufacturing Systems Magazine* 13:10 October 1995.

4. Vollman, Thomas E., William L. Berry, and D. Clay Whybark. *Manufacturing Planning and Control Systems.* McGraw-Hill, 4th ed., 1997.

5. Womeldorff, Tom. "What is an Interactive Planning System?" *Manufacturing Systems Magazine* 13:10 (October 1995): 78–80.

Chapter 6 Zero-Tolerance Inventory Count Accuracy

1. APICS Magazines, Journals, and Conference Proceedings; over 40 articles and papers since 1980, including several by author.

2. Fogarty, Donald W., John H. Blackstone, Jr., and Thomas R. Hoffman. *Production and Inventory Management,* 2nd ed. Cincinnati: South-Western Publishing Co., 1991.

Chapter 7 Reorder Triggers

1. Fogarty, Donald W., John H. Blackstone, Jr., and Thomas R. Hoffman. *Production and Inventory Management,* 2nd ed. Cincinnati: South-Western Publishing Co., 1991.

2. Plossl, George W. *Production and Inventory Control, Principles and Techniques.* Englewood Cliffs, New Jersey: Prentice-Hall, Inc., 1985.

3. Vollman, Thomas E., William L. Berry, and D. Clay Whybark. *Manufacturing Planning and Control Systems.* McGraw-Hill, 4th ed., 1997.

Chapter 8 Forecasting

1. Fogarty, Donald W., John H. Blackstone, Jr., and Thomas R. Hoffman. *Production and Inventory Management,* 2nd ed. Cincinnati: South-Western Publishing Co., 1991.

2. Miller, Irwin and John E. Freund. *Probability and Statistics for Engineers.* Englewood Cliffs, New Jersey: Prentice-Hall, Inc., 1965.

3. Plossl, George W. *Production and Inventory Control, Principles and Techniques.* Englewood Cliffs, New Jersey: Prentice-Hall, Inc., 1985.

4. Vollman, Thomas E., William L. Berry, and D. Clay Whybark. *Manufacturing Planning and Control Systems.* McGraw-Hill, 4th ed., 1997.

Chapter 9 Order Quantities

1. Fogarty, Donald W., John H. Blackstone, Jr., and Thomas R. Hoffman. *Production and Inventory Management,* 2nd ed. Cincinnati: South-Western Publishing Co., 1991.

2. Plossl, George W. *Production and Inventory Control, Principles and Techniques.* Englewood Cliffs, New Jersey: Prentice-Hall, Inc., 1985.

3. Vollman, Thomas E., William L. Berry, and D. Clay Whybark. *Manufacturing Planning and Control Systems.* McGraw-Hill, 4th ed., 1997.

Chapter 10 Safety Stock

1. Fogarty, Donald W., John H. Blackstone, Jr., and Thomas R. Hoffman. *Production and Inventory Management,* 2nd ed. Cincinnati: South-Western Publishing Co., 1991.

2. Harry, Mikel J., "The Nature of Six Sigma Quality." In *Second Annual Best*

Manufacturing Practices Workshop Proceedings. Office of the Assistant Secretary of the Navy, September 27–28, 1988.

3. Miller, Irwin and John E. Fruend. *Probability and Statistics for Engineers.* Englewood Cliffs: New Jersey: Prentice-Hall, Inc., 1965.

4. Plossl, George W. *Production and Inventory Control, Principles and Techniques.* Englewood Cliffs: New Jersey: Prentice-Hall, Inc., 1985.

5. Vollman, Thomas E., William L. Berry, and D. Clay Whybark. *Manufacturing Planning and Control Systems.* McGraw-Hill, 4th ed., 1997.

Chapter 11   AS/RS Project

1. Bernard, Paul A. "Do Integral Systems Require an Integral Specification?" *Industrial Management* 39, (March/April 1997): 11–15.

2. FEM Series Lifting Equipment, Determining the reliability and availability of SRMs, October 1981.

3. Frazier Industrial Company Sentinel Series Structural Steel Storage Racks brochure, Long Valley, New Jersey 07853.

Chapter 12   Market-Based Production System

1. Bernard, Paul A. "Manufacturing Buffer Management." *APICS—The Performance Advantage* 3:7 (July 1993): 46–48.

2. Graphic. "Why a JIT System Needs a Buffer." *Modern Materials Handling Magazine* 50:6 (May 1995): 38.

3. Schonberger, Richard J. *World Class Manufacturing.* New York: The Free Press, 1986.

4. Soni, Avi. "Eight Steps to a JIT-Focused Factory." *Manufacturing Systems Magazine* 10:2 (February 1992): 46–55.

5. Valder, Jeff. "Seven Steps to Ergonomic Workstations." *Assembly Magazine* 39:8 (September 1996): 18.

6. Wantuck, Kenneth A. *Just in Time for America.* Milwaukee, WI: The Forum Ltd., 1989.

7. Wiebe, Alvin F., David Johnson, Glen A. Harcey, and Marti Teter. "The Task-Training Guideline: A Powerful Format for How-To Instructional Training Materials." *Technical Communication* 40:1 (First Quarter 1993): 49–61.

General Note:

Each of the APICS Certification testing areas has a listing of primary and secondary references. These need to be complemented and supplemented by current magazine and journal articles. The following is a representative listing of sources of current articles and papers which cover most of the eight areas of integration:

1. *APICS International Seminar Proceedings,* APICS, included with membership but must be requested via form included in *APICS—The Performance Advantage* or by telephone.

2. *APICS—The Performance Advantage,* monthly magazine, (703) 237-8344, included with membership.

3. *Industrial Engineering Solutions,* monthly magazine, Institute of Industrial Engineers (770) 449-0461, included with Institute of Industrial Engineering membership.

4. *Managing Automation,* monthly magazine, Thomas Publishing Company, (212) 629-1551.

5. *Manufacturing Systems,* monthly magazine, (847) 842-1750 (Midwest Office).

6. *Modern Materials Handling,* monthly and semimonthly (in some months) magazine, Cahners Publishing Co., (617) 964-3030.

7. *Plant Engineering,* monthly magazine and semimonthly in June, Cahners Publishing Co., (847) 635-8800.

8. *Production and Inventory Management Journal,* quarterly journal, APICS, included with membership.

Index